The New
Cambridge Bibliography
of English Literature

in five volumes
Volume 5

The New Cambridge Bibliography of English Literature

Volume 5
Index

Compiled by
J. D. PICKLES

CAMBRIDGE
AT THE UNIVERSITY PRESS
1977

Published by the Syndics of the Cambridge University Press
The Pitt Building, Trumpington Street, Cambridge CB2 IRP
Bentley House, 200 Euston Road, London NW1 2DB
32 East 57th Street, New York, NY 10022, USA
296 Beaconsfield Parade, Middle Park, Melbourne 3206, Australia

First published 1977

Library of Congress Catalog Card Number: 69–10199

ISBN 0 521 21310 x

Printed in Great Britain at the
University Press, Cambridge

The New Cambridge Bibliography of English Literature
>
> Volume 1: 600–1660
> Volume 2: 1660–1800
> Volume 3: 1800–1900
> Edited by GEORGE WATSON
>
> Volume 4: 1900–1950
> Edited by I. R. WILLISON
>
> Volume 5: Index
> Compiled by J. D. PICKLES

CONTENTS

EDITOR'S PREFACE

The *New Cambridge Bibliography of English Literature* began to appear in 1969, with volume 3; and since then three more volumes have appeared, to complete a bibliography of the literature of the British Isles in English from its Anglo-Saxon beginnings down to authors established by 1950.

The present volume, which is the fifth, completes *New CBEL*. It is a general index to all four volumes, listing primary authors and major anonymous works, as well as certain headings from the Bibliography as a whole. Each of the earlier volumes already includes a brief provisional index; but this General Index, which is the work of Dr J. D. Pickles, is based directly on the Bibliography itself, and represents his patient work for more than three years.

Its scope is wider than that of the existing indexes. Along with authors and headings, it includes titles of periodicals from sections devoted to Newspapers and Magazines, as well as the names of their editors and proprietors; and the names of certain minor authors listed under such sections as Travel and Sport, with an emphasis on literature rather than mere publication. It also lists foreign writers from the comparative sections on Literary Relations.

The conventions of the index are intended, so far as possible, to be self-explanatory. Italic signifies a title, e.g. *Beowulf*; an initial lower-case signifies a subject or heading, e.g. 'science'. Pseudonyms are in inverted commas, e.g. 'Orwell, George', and dates are sometimes used to distinguish authors and titles of similar name.

Our thanks are due to Mr Ian Willison, editor of volume 4, for help with the proofs; to Mr Terence W. Moore for arranging the general entries; and to Mr Peter Burbidge of the University Press for seeing the Bibliography to a conclusion over a period of more than twenty years.

GEORGE WATSON

St John's College, Cambridge
March 1976

LIST OF CONTRIBUTORS
TO VOLUMES 1-4

B.W.A.	Brian W. Alderson	J.C.C.	J. C. Corson
M.A.	Miriam Allott	J.C.	James Craigie (vol. 1)
R.C.A.	R.C. Alston	J.E.C.	J. E. Cross
J.F.A.	J. F. Arnott	S.J.C.	S. J. Curtis
E.L.A.	Emmett L. Avery	R.T.D.	R. T. Davies
G.A.	Geoffrey Axworthy	P.D.	Peter Davison
N.J.B.	Nicolas J. Barker	R.A.D.	Robert A. Day
J.B.	John Barnard	V.A.D.	Vinton A. Dearing
C.B.L.B.	C. B. L. Barr	E.D.	Eric Domville
M.C.B.	Martin C. Battestin	H.W.D.	H. W. Donner
P.J.B.	Priscilla J. Bawcutt	T.S.D.	T. S. Dorsch
G.B.	Gillian Beer	R.P.D.	R. P. Draper
T.B.	Terry Belanger	R.D.D.	R. D. Dunn
J.A.W.B.	J. A. W. Bennett	N.E.	Norman Endicott
G. E. B.	G. E. Bentley jr	G.S.F.	George S. Fayen
N.F.B.	Norman F. Blake	O.W.F.	Oliver W. Ferguson
D.S.B.	D. S. Bland	W.E.F.	W. E. Fredeman
A.J.B.	A. J. Bliss	A.F.	Arthur Friedman
E.B.	Edmund Blunden	J.F.	John Fuller
R.R.B.	R. R. Bolgar	J.G.	Janet Garrod
D.F.B.	Donald F. Bond	R.M.G.	Richard M. Gollin
B.A.B.	Bradford A. Booth	R.L.G.	Roger Lancelyn Green
W.W.S.B.	W. W. S. Breem	D. H. G.	David H. Greene
R.L.B.	R. L. Brett	S.B.G.	Stanley B. Greenfield
T.J.B.	T. J. Brown	D.G.	David Greer
P.G.B.	Peter G. Burbidge	R.H.	Robert Halsband
A.B.	Anthony Burton	A.C.H.	A. C. Hamilton
M.S.B.	Marilyn S. Butler	H.H.	Henry Hargreaves
A.C.	Alistair Campbell	J.B.H.	J. B. Harmer
C.C.	Christophe Campos (vol. 2)	B.H.	Bernard Harris
G.D.C.	Geoffrey D. Carnall	J.H.	John Harrison (vol. 2)
J.C.	John Carroll (vol. 2)	W.J.H.	W. J. Harvey
J.A.V.C.	John A. V. Chapple	A.T.H.	Allen T. Hazen
G.C.	Gloria Cigman	P.H.	Peter Heyworth
C.C.	Cecily Clark (vol. 1)	G.R.H.	G. R. Hibbard
P.C.	Peter Clemoes (vol. 1)	T.F.H.	T. F. Hoad
R.C.	Robert Cockcroft	J.H.	John Horden (vol. 1)
P.A.W.C.	Philip A. W. Collins	A.P.H.	A. P. Howse
R.L.C.	Rowland L. Collins	C.H.	Cyrus Hoy
C.E.C.	Christina E. Colvin	P.H.-B.	Peter Hunter-Blair
P.C.	Pat Conoley (vol. 4)	N.H.	Nancy Hyde
C.P.C.	C. P. Corney	A.J.	Arthur Johnson

LIST OF CONTRIBUTORS

H.W.J.	H. W. Jones	J.M.P.	Jill M. Perry
J.E.J.	John E. Jordan	H.P.	Henry Pettit
E.J.K.	E. J. Kenney	C.H.E.P.	C. H. E. Philipin
L.M.K.	Lewis M. Knapp	A.P.	Arthur Pollard (vol. 3)
D.K.	David Knott	H.G.P.	H. G. Pollard
G.J.K.	Gwin J. Kolb	H.C.P.	H. C. Porter
F.K.	Franz Kuna	F.A.P.	Frederick A. Pottle
C.Y.L.	Cecil Y. Lang	B.R.	Barbara Raw
R.L.	Robert Latham	W.A.R.	William A. Ringler
D.H.L.	Dan H. Laurence	R.J.R.	R. J. Roberts
R.H.L.	Roger H. Lonsdale	J.W.R.	John W. Robinson
J.L.	Joyce Lorimer	J.M.R.	John M. Robson
D.A.L.	Donald A. Low (also D.L.)	P.R.	Patrick Rogers
J.K.M.	J. K. McConica	H.M.R.	Henry M. Rosenberg
J.R.M.	J. R. MacGillivray	S.K.R.	Sheila K. Rosenberg
D.J.M.	D. J. McKitterick	G.R.R.	G. Ross Roy
R.E.M.	R. E. Maddison	N.H.R.	Norma H. Russell
A.H.M.	Alfred H. Marks	J.R.-S.	Joy Russell-Smith
G.M.M.	G. M. Matthews	C.R.S.	Charles Richard Saunders
W.M.	William Matthews	V.J.S.	V. J. Scattergood
O.M.	Oscar Maurer	N.J.S.	Nigel J. Seeley
E.M.	Edward Mendelson	R.S.	Roger Sharrock
J.H.M.	John H. Middendorf	A.S.	Arthur Sherbo
A.D.M.	A. David Mills	I.S.	Irène Simon
J.M.	James Mosley	J.S.	Joan Simon (vol. 1)
A.M.	Arnold Muirhead	A.H.S.	Albert H. Smith
E.L.N.	Eleanor L. Nichols	B.C.S.	Brian C. Southam
J.N.-S.	J. Norton-Smith	J.S.	John Sparrow (vol. 3)
M.E.N.	Maximillian E. Novak	P.G.S.	Paul G. Stanwood
J.C.T.O.	J. C. T. Oates	M.S.	Michael Statham
P. and I.O.	Peter and Iona Opie	L.S.	Lionel Stevenson
L.O.	Leonee Ormond	G.S.	Graham Storey
W.J.B.O.	W. J. B. Owen	C.J.S.	Carl J. Stratman
W.D.P.	W. D. Paden	R.H.S.	R. H. Super
R.I.P.	R. I. Page	D.S.T.	Donald S. Taylor
R.P.	Roy Park	S.S.B.T.	Samuel S. B. Taylor
G.B.P.	George B. Parks	M.T.	Marjorie Thompson
A.P.	André Parreaux (vol. 2)	W.B.T.	W. B. Todd
C.A.P.	C. A. Patrides	F.G.T.	F. G. Townsend
M.L.P.	M. L. Pearl	J.T.	James Trainer
D.A.P.	Derek A. Pearsall	E. de W.	E. de Waal
R.B.P.	Robert B. Pearsall	K.W.	Keith Walker
M.P.	Morse Peckham (vol. 3)	J.W.	Joanna Watson (vol. 1)
E.D.P.	Eric D. Pendry	C.W.	Charles Webster (vol. 1)
M.P.	Michael Perkin (vol. 4)	G.Wh.	George Whalley

LIST OF CONTRIBUTORS

W.W.	William White	K.J.W.	Katherine J. Worth
J.S.W.	John S. Wilders (vol. 2)	J.W.Y.	John W. Yolton
	(also J.W.)	T.Y.	Theodore Yonge
R.M.W.	R. M. Wiles	C.A.Z.	Curt A. Zimansky
C.W.	Cecil Woolf (vol. 3)		

ABBREVIATIONS

Acad	Academy	HLQ	Huntington Library Quarterly
addn	addition	illustr	illustrated by
Amer	American	Inst	Institute
anon	anonymous	introd	introduction
Archiv	Archiv für das Studium der neueren Sprachen	JEGP	Journal of English and Germanic Philology
AS	Anglo-Saxon	JHI	Journal of History of Ideas
Assoc	Association	Jnl	Journal
b.	born	Lang	Language
Bibl	Bibliographical	Lib	Library
bk	book	Lit	Literature
BM	British Museum	MÆ	Medium Ævum
Br	British	Mag	Magazine
Bull	Bulletin	ME	Middle English
BNYPL	Bulletin of New York Public Library	ML	Muses' Library
		MLN	Modern Language Notes
c.	circa	MLQ	Modern Language Quarterly
ch	chapter	MLR	Modern Language Review
CHEL	Cambridge History of English Literature	MP	Modern Philology
		ms	manuscript
Chron	Chronicle	Nat	National
col	column	nd	no date
CQ	Critical Quarterly	no	number
d.	died	N & Q	Notes and Queries
DNB	Dictionary of National Biography	OE	Old English
		OHEL	Oxford History of English Literature
ed	edited by		
edn	edition	OSA	Oxford Standard Authors
E & S	Essays and Studies	p.	page
et al	and others	pbd	published
EC	Essays in Criticism	pbn	publication
EETS	Early English Text Society	PBSA	Papers of the Bibliographical Society of America
EHR	English Historical Review		
EL	Everyman's Library	PMLA	Publications of the Modern Language Association of America
ELH	Journal of English Literary History		
EML	English Men of Letters	PQ	Philological Quarterly
Eng	English	priv	privately
E Studien	Englische Studien	Proc	Proceedings
E Studies	English Studies	prop	proprietor
facs	facsimile	pt	part
fl.	floruit	ptd	printed
GM	Gentleman's Magazine	Quart	Quarterly

ABBREVIATIONS

REL	Review of English Literature	SP	Studies in Philology
rev	revised by	STS	Scottish Text Society
Rev	Review	Stud	Studies
RES	Review of English Studies	suppl	supplement
rptd	reprinted	TLS	Times Literary Supplement
SB	Studies in Bibliography (University of Virginia)	tr	translated by
		trn	translation
SE	Studies in English (University of Texas)	Univ	University
		unpbd	unpublished
ser	series	UTQ	University of Toronto Quarterly
Sh Jb	Shakespeare Jahrbuch	vol	volume
Soc	Society	WC	World's Classics

Abrahams, Israel, 3. 1611, 1858
Abreu de Galindo, Juan de, 2. 1450
'Abricht, Johann' (Jonathan Birch), 1. 1329
Absalon, 1. 1777
Abse, Dannie, 4. 1378
Abstract and brief chronicle of the time, 2. 1336
Abstract of a sermon, An, 2. 352
Abstract of the remarkable passages in the life of a private gentleman, An, 2. 985
Abu Bakr Ibn Al-Tufail, 2. 978
Academiae cantabrigiensis luctus in obitum Frederici Walliae principis, 2. 375
Academiae cantabrigiensis luctus in obitum Georgii II, 2. 381
Academic (1792), 2. 1289
Academic (1877), 3. 1869
Academica, 3. 1865
Academical contributions of original and translated poetry, 2. 420
Academician, 2. 1289
'Academicus', 2. 1287
Academy, 3. 1821–2, 1837; 4. 1351
Academy of complements, 1. 1010; 2. 329
Academy of play, 2. 1567
Accomplish'd courtier, 2. 395
Account from Scotland and London-derry, 2. 1319
Account of a tour in Scotland 1677, An, 2. 1397
Account of Frobisher's first voyage, An, 1. 2149
Account of Hawkins' third slaving voyage, An, 1. 2149
Account of Jamaica, An, 2. 1459
Account of some remarkable passages in the life of a private gentleman, An, 2. 985
Account of the character and manners of the French, An, 2. 1421
Account of the chief occurrences of Ireland, An, 2. 1381
Account of the colony of Sierra Leone, An, 2. 1452
Account of the present state of Virginia, An, 2. 1457
Account of the proceedings of the meeting of the Estates in Scotland, An, 2. 1319
Account of the publick transactions in Christendom An, 2. 1319
Account of the several late voyages, An, 2. 1391
Account of the southern maritime provinces of France, An, 2. 1420
Account of the Spanish settlements in America, An, 2. 1466
Accountant, 3. 1828
Accurate description of . . .Sicily, An, 2. 1426
Ace magazine, 4. 1385
Achard of Bridlington or S. Victor, 1. 759
Achelley, Thomas, 1. 1079
Achilles Tatius, 1. 2165

Achillini, Claudio, 2. 194
Ackerley, Joe Randolph, 4. 905, 1406
Ackermann, Rudolph, 3. 77, 1843, 1873
Ackermann's juvenile forget me not, 3. 1877
Ackers, Charles, 2. 263
Ackland, Rodney, 4. 905–6
Acland, Arthur H. D., 3. 1730
Acontius, Jacobus, 1. 843
Acorn, 4. 1357
Acosta, Jose de, 1. 2162
Action stories, 4. 1389
Activity, 4. 82
Acton, Harold Mario Mitchell, 4. 229, 1397
Acton, John, 2. 1561
Acton, John Emerich Edward Dalberg, 1st Baron, 3. 1476–8, 1848, 1856, 1857, 1858
Acton, William, 2. 1413
Actor (1780), 2. 1286
Actor (1789), 2. 1288
Actor (1793), 2. 1289
Actor for player and public, 4. 866, 873
Actor illustrated, 4. 824, 866
actors
    Renaissance to Restoration, 1. 1387–91
    Restoration and eighteenth century, 2. 733–40,
    nineteenth century, 3. 1117–22
    twentieth century, 4. 863–8
Actors' Association yearbook, 4. 866, 873
actresses, Restoration and eighteenth century, 2. 733–40
Actresses' Franchise League, 4. 866, 873
Acunha, Christoval de, 2. 1453
Ad astra, 4. 58
adages, 1. 2029–32
Adair, James, 2. 1469
Adair, John, 2. 1399
Adam, Edward O., 3. 1820
Adam, Robert, 2. 1420
Adam, 4. 1375
Adam Bell, 1. 1080
Adam Davy's five dreams, 1. 473
Adam du Petit Pont (or de Balsham), Bishop of St Asaph, 1. 759
Adam of Buckfield (or Bockfeld), 1. 768–9
Adam of Dryburgh, 1. 769
Adam of Eynsham, 1. 759
Adam of Godham, 1. 785
Adam of Woodham, 1. 785
Adamnan of Iona, 1. 342–3
Adams, Abigail, 2. 1405
Adams, Charles F., 3. 1846
Adams, George, 2. 1901
Adams, John (alias Alexander Smith, 1760?–1829), 2. 1481
Adams, John (fl. 1772), traveller, 2. 1468

Adams, John (fl. 1788), traveller, 2. 1393
Adams, John (fl. 1799), horseman, 2. 1555; 3. 1704
Adams, Sir John (1857–1934), 3. 1730
Adams, Sarah Fuller, 3. 499–500
Adams, Thomas, 1. 1970, 2046
Adams, W. A., 3. 1713
Adams, W. E., 3. 1761
Adams, William, 1. 2146
Adams, William Davenport, 3. 1369–71
Adams, William Henry Davenport, 3. 1105, 1814
Adams's weekly courant, 2. 1347, 1355–6
Adamson, Henry, 1. 2431
Adamson, John, 1. 2431–2, 2453
Adamson, Robert, 3. 1512
Adanson, Michel, 2. 1450
Adcock, Marion St John, 4. 794
Addison, H. R., 3. 1879
Addison, Joseph, 2. 1098–1112, 41, 103, 117, 125, 161, 176, 188, 191, 211, 233–4, 1269, 1272, 1274, 1276, 1321, 1369, 1377, 1415
Addison, Lancelot, 2. 1445
Additions to the works of Pope, 2. 396
Address to Dissenters, An, 3. 1732
Address to friends and foes, An, 2. 1385
Adelard of Bath, 1. 751
Adelphi (1923), 4. 1366
Adelphi magazine, 4. 1365
Adelung, Johann Christoph, 2. 68
Adis, Henry, 1. 2036
Admirable deliverance of 266 Christians, 1. 2122
Admiral Vernon's weekly journal, 2. 1331
Admiralty and Horse Guards' gazette, 3. 1826
Adolphus, John, 2. 1799
Adrian and Ritheus, 1. 336
Adrichom, Christian van, 1. 2138
Adrift and astern, 4. 1393
Adshead, Mary, 4. 808
Advent lyrics, see *Christ*, 1. 269
Adventure, 4. 819
adventure stories, twentieth century, 4. 129–30
Adventurer (Eton), 3. 1870
Adventurer or London University magazine, 3. 1867
Adventurer (1752), 2. 1280–1
Adventurer (1791), 2. 1288
Adventures in an easy chair, 2. 1286
Adventures of a hackney coach, 2. 1006
Adventures of a jesuit, 2. 1003
Adventures of a valet, 2. 997
Adventures of a whipping-top, 2. 1026
Adventures of an author, 2. 1001
Adventures of Catullus, 2. 344
Adventures of Charles Careless, 2. 1001
Adventures of Jack Wander, 2. 1001

Adventures of Lindamira, 2. 984
Adventures of Master Headstrong and Miss Patient, 2. 1023
Adventures of Oxymel Classic, 2. 1002
Adventures of Sylvia Hughes, 2. 1000
Adventures of the Helvetian hero, 2. 983
Adventures of the little girl in the wood, 3. 1107
Advertiser's aid, 4. 1342
Advertiser's annual, 4. 1342
Advertiser's daily magazine, 3. 1790
Advertiser's journal, 3. 1758
Advertiser's review, 3. 1758; 4. 1342
Advertisers' ABC, 3. 1758; 4. 1342
Advertisers' guardian, 3. 1758; 4. 1342
Advertisers' monthly circular, 3. 1758
Advertisers' weekly, 4. 1342
advertising
    nineteenth century, 3. 1755–8
    twentieth century, 4. 1341–4
Advertising (1891), 3. 1758; 4. 1342
Advertising (1931), 4. 1343
Advertising ABC, 4. 1342
Advertising art annual, 4. 1344
Advertising display, 4. 1343
Advertising manager, 4. 1344
Advertising, marketing, packaging, print, 4. 1344
Advertising monthly, 4. 1343
Advertising news (1904), 3. 1758; 4. 1342
Advertising news (1928), 4. 1343
Advertising notes, 3. 1758; 4. 1342
Advertising register, 3. 1758
Advertising review, 4. 1343
Advertising world, 4. 1342
Advertising year book, 4. 1342
Advice from Parnassus (1681), 2. 1340
Advice from Parnassus (1727), 2. 1294
Advice from the scandal club, 2. 1269
Advice to a sister, 2. 1285
Adviser: a new periodical paper, 2. 1372
Advocate (1720), 2. 1277
Advocate (1725), 2. 1277
Advocates' Library, Edinburgh, 2. 305–6
Adyar theosophist, 4. 1352
'A.E.' or 'AE' (George William Russell), 3. 1912–16
Aelfric, 1. 317–21
Aelian, 1. 2165; 2. 1487
Aelred of Rievaulx, 1. 759–61
Æneas Silvius, Pope Pius II, 1. 850, 857, 2064, 2191; 2. 1548
Aengus, 4. 1364
Aerostatic spy, 2. 1007
Aerssen, Francois van, 2. 1410
Aeschines, 2. 1487
Aeschylus, 2. 1487

Aesop, 1. 2165; 2. 1487-8, 34
'Aesop, Abraham' (John Newbery?), 2. 1020
Aesop in select fables, 2. 340
Aethelwald, 1. 344-5
Aethelwulf, 1. 349-50
Af n-Éire, 4. 1362
Affaires du temps, 2. 1307
Affection's gift, 3. 1874
Affection's keepsake, 3. 1875
Affection's offering, 3. 1874
Affinity love stories, 4. 1391
Aflalo, Frederick G., 3. 1690
Africa, travel and literary relations,
    Renaissance to Restoration, 1. 2141-50
    Restoration and eighteenth century, 2. 1445-54
    nineteenth century, 3. 1669-72
    Shakespeare, 1. 1631
African Association, publications of travel, 2. 1445
Africanus, Johannes Leo, 1. 2148
Agarde, Arthur, 1. 997
Agate, James Evershed, 4. 997-8
Agatharchides, 1. 2148
Age (and argus), 3. 1810
Agenda, 4. 1393
Aglionby, William, 2. 1410
Agnostic journal, 3. 1823
Agreeable companion, An (1742), 2. 369
Agreeable companion (1745), 2. 371
Agreeable companion (1783), 2. 403
Agreeable medley, 2. 372
Agreeable miscellany, 2. 1350
Agreeable variety, 2. 350
Agricola, Rudolphus, 1. 843
Agricultural gazette, 3. 1824
agriculture
    Renaissance to Restoration, 1. 2277-8
    nineteenth century, 3. 1823-4, 1837
Agrippa, (Henricus) Cornelius, 1. 2179, 843
Agrippa von Nettesheim, 2. 1537
Ahiman rezon, 2. 378
Aikin, Anna Laetitia, 2. 639-40, 1004, 1023
Aikin, Arthur, 2. 1407
Aikin, John, 2. 1800, 1023, 1311, 1805; 3. 1841
Aikin, Lucy, 3. 1099
Aileran the Wise (d. 664) 1. 343
Aimé, Jean Jacques, 2. 1476
Ainger, Alfred, 3. 1417
Ainsworth, Henry, 1. 1842, 1908, 2295
Ainsworth, Robert, 2. 1823
Ainsworth, Ruth Gallard, 4. 810
Ainsworth, William Francis, 3. 1814, 1843, 1844
Ainsworth, William Harrison, 3. 911-14, 1843, 1844, 1846, 1847, 1874

Ainsworth's magazine, 3. 1847
Air force poetry, 4. 1376
Air news, 4. 1386
Air stories, 4. 1390
'Aircastle, Plume', 2. 1290
Aird, Andrew, 3. 1762
Aird, Thomas, 3. 500-1
Airy, George B., 3. 1747
Aistrop, Jack, 4. 1375, 1378
Aitken, George Atherton, 3. 1635
À Kempis, Thomas, 1. 848
Akenside, Mark, 2. 637-8, 41, 168, 193, 1298, 1901
Akerman, John Yonge, 3. 1689
Aksakov, Sergey Timofeyevich, 3. 151
Al., G., 1. 1776
Alabaster, William, 1. 1080, 1295, 1763
Alamode musician, 2. 340
Alan of Melsa, 1. 769
Alan of Tewkesbury, 1. 769
Alane, Alexander, 1. 2437-8
Alarum, 4. 1382
Alba, 4. 1379
Alba nuadh, 4. 1371
Albanis de Beaumont, Jean François, 2. 1428
Albannach, 4. 1373
Albany magazine, 4. 1357
Albany review, 4. 1356
Albemarle, 3. 1853
Alberic of London, 1. 761
Alberti, Leon Battista, 1. 843, 2179; 2. 1541
Albery, James, 3. 1191
Albery, Peter, 4. 1375
Albin, T., 3. 1875
Albion and evening advertiser (1799), 2. 1338; 3. 1792
Albion (1830), 3. 1793
Albion (c. 1950), 4. 1376
Albizzi, Bartolomeo, 1. 843
Album, 3. 1855
Album of Streatham, 2. 409
Album wreath and bijou littéraire, 3. 1875
Album wreath of music and literature, 3. 1876
Albyon knight, 1. 1406
Alcafarado, Francisco, 2. 1446
Alcantara, San Pedro de, 1. 908
alchemy, 1. 2361-4
Alciphron, 2. 1488
Alcock, A., 3. 1711
Alcock, Charles William, 3. 1882
Alcock, John, 1. 801, 1935
Alcoforado, Marianna, 2. 140, 202
Alcoran of Mahomet...newly englished, 1. 2140
Alcuin, 1. 350-1, 328
Alderson, Amelia, 3. 753-4

Amsterdam slip, 2. 1320
Amulet, 3. 1873
Amurath, Tragedy of, 1. 1777
Amusement for the ladies, 2. 400
Amusement workers news, 4. 873
Amusement world, 4. 860
Amusements serious and comical, 2. 1018
Amusing instructor, 2. 1023
Anacreon, 1. 2165; 2. 1488–9
Anacreon done into English, 2. 334
Anacreontic magazine, 2. 415
Anacreontic song, 2. 407
Anacreontic songs, 2. 405
Analytical review, 2. 1308
anatomy, Renaissance to Restoration, 1. 2369–74
Anburey, Thomas, 2. 1472
Anburey's weekly journal, 2. 1384
'ancestral' romances, 1. 447–50
Ancient and modern Scots songs, 2. 389
Ancient and present state of Poland, 2. 1414
Ancient and present state of Portugal, 2. 1416
Ancient ballads, songs and poems, 2. 422
Ancient Scottish poems (1786), 2. 407
Ancient Scottish poems (1770), 2. 390
Ancient songs, 2. 412
Ancients and Moderns controversy, 2. 25–6
Ancrene riwle, 1. 498–500
Ancrene wisse, 1. 498–500
Andersen, Hans-Christian, 3. 146, 1109
Anderson,— (fl. 1795), 3. 1789
Anderson, Adam, 2. 1896
Anderson, Aeneas, 2. 1442
Anderson, Alexander, 3. 607
Anderson, E. G. 3. 1748
Anderson, G. 3. 1714
Anderson, George (d. 1756), 2. 2039
Anderson, George (1802–78), 3. 1682
Anderson, George William, 2. 1476, 1480
Anderson, James (1662–1728), 2. 1706–7
Anderson, James (1739–1808), 2. 2059–60, 1312, 1371, 1372
Anderson, Jean, 4. 1380
Anderson, John, 3. 1855
Anderson, Margaret Caroline, 4. 1362
Anderson, Patrick (d. 1624) jesuit, 1. 2453
Anderson, Patrick (fl. 1618–35), 1. 2469
Anderson, Robert (1750–1830) editor, 2. 1803
Anderson, Robert (1770–1833) poet, 3. 361–2
Anderson, T., 3. 1707
Anderson, Wilhelmina Johnstone, 4. 679–80
Anderson, William Wemyss, 2. 1455
André, John, 2. 1470
Andreae, Johann Valentin, 1. 843
Andreas, 1. 237–9
Andreini, Giovanni Battista, 2. 1541

Andrew Brice's old Exeter journal, 2. 1358
Andrewes, John, 1. 1296
Andrewes, Lancelot, 1. 1918–22
Andrewes, Margaret, 3. 1106
Andrews, Alexander, 3. 1762
Andrews, Cicily Isabel, 4. 770–1
Andrews, Eliza, 2. 1027
Andrews, J., 4. 828
Andrews, Miles Peter, 2. 823
Andrews, S. A., 4. 1386
Andrews, William Eusebius, 3. 1822
Andro, 2. 1567
Andromana, 1. 1758
Andronicus, 1. 1777
Aneau, Barthélmi, 1. 872, 2059
Anecdotes and adventures of fifteen gentlemen, 3. 1108
Anecdotes of a little family, 2. 1026
Anecdotes on the origin and antiquity of horse-racing, 3. 1704
Angel, Moses, 3. 1822
Angell, Sir Norman, 4. 1136–7; 3. 1791
Angelo, Domenico, 2. 1563
Angelo, H. C. W., 3. 1701
Angelo, Michael, 2. 1447
'Angelo, Master Michael' (Richard Johnson), 2. 1021
Angerianus, Hieronymus, 1. 855
Anghiera, Pietro Martire, 1. 2111
Angler's complete assistant, 2. 1560
Anglerius, Petrus Martyr, 1. 843
Angles, Johannes, 1. 843
Angliae Ruina, 1. 2098
Anglicanism, 1. 19
angling
    Restoration and eighteenth century, 2. 1555–61
    nineteenth century, 3. 1687–91
Anglo-Irish, nineteenth century, 3. 1885–1948
    anthologies, 3. 1899–1900
    biographies, 3. 1897–8
    drama, 3. 1939–48
    Gaelic, 3. 1885–96
    literary history, 3. 1895–8
    poetry, 3. 1899–1916
    Yeats and Synge, 3. 1915–38
    see also Irish
Anglo-Norman
    drama, 1. 725–8
    Latin, 1. 751–60
    see also Middle English
Anglo-Saxon
    Old English, 1. 187–336
        anthologies, 1. 189–92
        general background, 1. 187–98
        Germanic background, 1. 197–206

Archdale, John, 2. 1459
Archenholtz, Johann Wilhelm von, 2. 1537, 1406
Archer, 2. 1285
Archer, James, 2. 161
Archer, William, 3. 1417–18
Archer's Bath chronicle, 2. 1353
Archer's register, 3. 1691, 1882
archery
    Restoration and eighteenth century, 2. 1562–4
    nineteenth century, 3. 1691
Archery: a poem, 2. 1564
Architect, 3. 1828
Architectural magazine, 3. 1846
Architectural review for the artist and craftsman, 3. 1854
architecture, Restoration and eighteenth century, 2. 67–70
Arctic, travel, 2. 1483–6
Arden of Feversham, 1. 1470
Ardizzone, Edward Jeffrey Irving, 4. 806
'Ardmes', 2. 1289
Arena (1937), 4. 1372
Arena (1949), 4. 1379
Aretino, Pietro, 1. 845, 890, 895, 2182
Arfeuille, Nicolas de Nicolay, Seigneur d', 1. 2122
'Argences, — d', 2. 980
Argens, Jean Baptiste de Boyer, Marquis d', 2. 1502–3, 90, 138, 994, 995, 997
Argentine, John, 1. 997
'Argonaut' (E. D. Brickwood), 3. 1711
Argonaut, 3. 1851
Argosy (1865), 3. 1850; 4. 1351
Argosy (1926), 4. 1367
Argosy of complete stories, 4. 1367
Argus (1789), 2. 1337
Argus (1792), 2. 1289
Argus (1795), 2. 1310
Argus (1828), 3. 1793
Argus (1839), 3. 1813
Argus (1880), 3. 1801
Argus (1925), 4. 874, 1367
Argus, Arabella, 3. 1100
Argyll, George Douglas Campbell, 8th Duke of, 3. 513, 1512–13, 1605
Arias, Francisco, 1. 908
Ariel: the BBC staff magazine, 4. 864
Arioso, Lodovico, 1. 2180, 890, 894, 896; 2. 1541, 191–2
Aris's Birmingham gazette, 2. 1353; 3. 1797
Aristocrat, 4. 1386
Aristophanes, 1. 2166; 2. 1489
Aristophanes: being a classic collection of true Attic wit, 2. 398

Aristotle, 1. 2166; 2. 1489, 34, 63–5
Ark, 4. 1396
Arkwright, John S., 3. 1870, 1871
Arlen, Michael, 4. 514–15
Arliss' pocket magazine, 3. 1844
Armadillo, 4. 1356
Armeno, Christoforo, 2. 989
Armies intelligencer, 1. 2107
Armies modest intelligencer, 1. 2104
Armies painfull-messenger, 1. 2106
Armies post, 1. 2102
Armies scout, 1. 2107
Armies weekly intelligencer, 1. 2104
Armin, Robert, 1. 1729–30, 1082, 2027, 2055
Arminian magazine, 2. 1306; 3. 1840, 1859
Armistead, J. J., 3. 1690
'Armstrong, Anthony' (George Anthony Armstrong Willis), 4. 906–8
Armstrong, Archibald, 1. 2029
Armstrong, Clement, 1. 2039
Armstrong, Sir George C. H. (1836–1907), 3. 1792, 1812
Armstrong, Sir George Elliot (1866–1940), 3. 1792
Armstrong, Henry Edward, 3. 1731
'Armstrong, Humphry', 2. 1274
Armstrong, John, 2. 534–5, 1419, 1559, 1901
Armstrong, Martin Donisthorpe, 4. 796
Armstrong, N. S., 4. 1374
Armstrong, Neville, 4. 1379
Armstrong, R. A., 3. 1858
Armstrong, Richard, 4. 808
Armstrong, Terence Ian Fytton, 4. 279–81, 1359, 1374
Armstrong, Sir Walter, 3. 1418–19
Army and navy gazette, 3. 1826
Army list, 3. 1879
Army, navy and air force gazette, 3. 1826
Arnall, William, 2. 1278, 1328
Arnaud, François Thomas Marie de Baculard d', 2. 1503, 138, 1001, 1004, 1007
Arnell, Charles John, 4. 1366
Arnim, Achim von, 3. 119
Arno miscellany, 2. 404
Arnold, A. F., 4. 1385
Arnold, Arthur, 3. 1793
Arnold, C. H., 4. 1373
Arnold, Cornelius, 2. 535
Arnold, Edward, 3. 1852
Arnold, Sir Edwin, 3. 607–8, 1790
Arnold, F., 3. 1821
Arnold, Mary Augusta, 3. 1081–2, 1616
Arnold, Matthew, 3. 465–83, 92, 110–11, 130, 1605, 1726
Arnold, Richard, 1. 2203, 681

Arnold, Samuel James, 3. 1125, 1088
Arnold, Sidney, 4. 1380
Arnold, Thomas (1795–1842), 3. 1461–3, 1602, 1721, 1733
Arnold, Thomas (1823–1900), 3. 1636–7
Arnold, William Thomas, 3. 1763
Arnott, Neil, 3. 1728
Arraignment of lewd, idle, froward and unconstant women, 2. 343
Arrian, 2. 1489, 1438
Arrom de Ayala, Cecilia, 3. 142
Arrow, 4. 824, 854, 1358
Arrows, 4, 1398
Arrowsmith, Joseph P., 3. 1720
Ars amandi, 2. 374
Arson, 4. 1375
Art and craft of letters, 4. 71
Art and humour, 4. 1356
Art and industry, 4. 1342
Art and letters (1888), 3. 1853
Art and letters (1917), 4. 1363
Art and poetry, 3. 1848
Art-journal, 3. 1846–7, 1862; 4. 1349
Art of courtship (1662), 2. 328
Art of courtship (1686), 2. 336
Art of dress, 2. 350
Art of English poetry, 2. 342
Art of manual defence, 2. 1563
Art of poetry made easy, 2. 371
Art of poetry on a new plan, 2. 383
Art of story-telling, 2. 412
Art-union, 3. 1846
Arth, H., 1. 2277
Arthington, Henry, 1. 1082
Arthour and Merlin, 1. 398
Arthur (15th-century poem), 1. 396
Arthur and Alice, 3. 1107
Arthurian romances, Middle English, 1. 389–416
articles, writing of, twentieth century, 4. 67
Artistes bulletin, 4. 868
Artists and photographers in advertising, 4. 1343
Artists in advertising, 4. 1343
Artists' repository, 2. 1307
Arts, 4. 1377
arts, fine
  Old English, 1. 208–9
  Restoration and eighteenth century, influence, 2. 39–41
Arts and philosophy, 4. 1380
Arts Council (monthly) bulletin, 4. 874, 1374
Arts gazette, 4. 826, 1363
Arts in Britain, 4. 1377
Arts in war time, 4. 1376
Arts news and review, 4. 1408
Arts review, 4. 1408

Arundale, George Sydney, 4. 1352
Arundel, Henry Fitzalan, 12th Earl of, 1. 1000
Arundel, Philip Howard, 1st Earl of, 1. 1118–19
Arundel, Thomas Howard, 2nd Earl of, 1. 1001
Arvieux, Laurent d', 2. 1437
Arville Castle, 2. 1012
Arwaker, Edmund, 2. 468; 1. 1329
Asbjørnsen, Peter Christen, 3. 146, 1109
Ascham, Roger, 1. 1822–3, 2276, 2307
'Asche, Oscar' (John Stanger Heiss), 4. 908
Asgill, John, 2. 161, 1896
Ash, Thomas, 2. 1455
Ashburnham, John, 1. 2251
Ashby, George, 1. 648
Ashe, Simeon, 1. 2100
Ashendene Press, 3. 56; 4. 96
Ashford, Daisy, 4. 794
Ashley, Robert, 1. 2050
Ashley-Cooper, F. S., 3. 1698
Ashmole, Elias, 2. 1695–6, 1901–2; 1. 997
Ashmole Firumbras, 1. 418
Ashmole fragment (ME play), 1. 738
Ashmore, John, 1. 1336
Ashton, Dorothy Violet, 4. 375–6
Ashton, Robert, 3. 1880
Ashton, Winifred, 4. 927–9
Ashurst, W. H., 3. 1819
Ashwell, Arthur Rawson, 3. 1858
Asia, travel
  Renaissance to Restoration, 1. 2141–50
  Restoration and eighteenth century, 2. 1431–46
  nineteenth century, 3. 1673–6
Asiatic annual register, 2. 1314; 3. 1877
Asiatic journal and monthly miscellany, 3. 1844
Asiatic journal and monthly register, 3. 1844
Asiatic quarterly review, 3. 1844
Asiatick miscellany, 2. 405
Aske, James, 1. 1082
Aspland, Robert, 3. 1602, 1843
Assarino, Luca, 1. 898, 2059
Assembly of ladies, 1. 652
Asser, 1. 352
Assistant librarian, 4. 117
Association medical journal 3. 1826
Associator, 2. 1289
assonance, 1. 47–8
Assumption of Mary, 1. 531–2
Astle, John, 3. 1798, 1799
Astley, Philip, 2. 1429, 1554, 1568
Astley, Thomas, 1. 2112; 2. 1392
Aston, John, 1. 2128
Astor, William Waldorf, 1st Viscount, 3. 1793, 1815, 1854
Astrologer's magazine, 2. 1309
Astrological observator, 2. 1343

astrology, 1. 2355–60
astronomy, Renaissance, 1. 2353–6
Astrophel and Stella, 1. 1009
Astry, Sir James, 1. 1329
Asylum, 2. 1374
Asylum for fugitive pieces, An, 2. 405
Asylum for fugitives, An, 2. 396
Atalanta, 3. 1852–3
Athelston, 1. 434
Athenae redivivae, 2. 343
Athenaeum, 3. 1821, 1836; 4. 1349
Athenian catechism, 2. 1344
Athenian gazette, 2. 1342
Athenian library, 2. 1294
Athenian mercury, 2. 1342
Athenian news, 2. 1345
Athenian oracle, 2. 342, 1342
Athenian sport, 2. 344
Athenian spy, 2. 1294
Athenianism, or the new projects of J. Dunton, 2. 346
Atherstone, Edwin, 3. 363
Athletic exercise, 2. 1563
Athletic news, 3. 1691, 1824
athletics, nineteenth century, 3. 1691
Athlone chronicle, 2. 1387
Athlone herald, 2. 1387
Athlone sentinel, 2. 1387
Atkin, Edmund, 2. 1465
Atkins, Frederick Anthony, 3. 1815, 1854
Atkins, Henry Martin, 3. 1679
Atkins, John (d. 1757), 2. 1395, 1448, 1462
Atkins, John (b. 1916), 4. 1376
Atkinson, E., 4. 1381
Atkinson, H., 3. 1695
Atkinson, H. K., 3. 1827
Atkinson, Mary Evelyn, 4. 805
Atkinson, Robert, 3. 1892
Atkinson, Thomas, 1. 1763
Atkyns, Sir Robert, 2. 1714
Atlantis, 3. 1857
Atlas, 3. 1810
Attard, W., 4. 1386
Attempt on the island of Jamaica, An, 1. 2160
Atterbury, Francis, 2. 1620–1, 161
Atterburyana, 2. 356
Attey, John, 1. 1356
Attic miscellany, 2. 410 , 1309
Attick wit, 2. 414
Atwood, Thomas, 2. 1473
Aubignac, François Hédelin, Abbé d', 2. 1515, 115
Aubigné, Françoise d', Marquise de Maintenon, 2. 1520

Aubin, Penelope, 2. 989, 991
Aubonne, J. B. Tavernier, Baron d', 2. 1433
Aubrey, John, 2. 1682–4, 1806
Auckland, William Eden, 1st Baron, 2. 1480
Auction register and law chronicle, 3. 1826
Audelay, John, 1. 683
Auden, Wystan Hugh, 4. 207–20, 1397
Audigier, Vital d', 1. 872, 2059
Auditor (1733), 2. 1278
Auditor (1762), 2. 1283
Audley, Thomas, 1. 2091, 2098, 2101
August annual, 4. 1386
Augustine, St, 1. 2180–1; 2. 1495
Augustine the Irishman (fl. 655), 1. 343
Aulnoy, Marie Catherine le Jumel de Barneville, Baronne d', 2. 1503, 138, 979, 982, 983, 984, 985, 1029–31, 1413
Ault, Norman, 4. 793
Aulus Gellius, 2. 1497
Aunt Judy's magazine, 3. 1851, 1863
'Aunt Mary' (George Mogridge), 3. 1089
'Aunt Newbury' (George Mogridge), 3. 1089
'Aunt Upton' (George Mogridge), 3. 1089
Aurora (1781), 2. 1336
Aurora (1799), 2. 1312
Aurora and British imperial reporter (1807), 3. 1790
Aurora Borealis (1821), 3. 1809
Aurora borealis (1833), 3. 1875
Ausonius, 1. 2166
Austen, James, 2. 1351
Austen, Jane, 3. 692–700
Austen, P. Britten, 4. 1377
Austin, Alfred, 3. 608–9, 1763, 1852
Austin, John (1613–69), 1. 1296
Austin, John (1790–1859), 3. 1513
Austin, Stella, 3. 1103–4
Austin, William, 1. 2049
Australasia, travel
  Restoration and eighteenth century, 2. 1475–84
  nineteenth century, 3. 1675–8
Austyn, John, 1. 2152
Authentic account of Commodore Anson's expedition, An, 2. 1478
Authentic and interesting narrative of the late expedition to Botany Bay, An, 2. 1481
Authentic narrative of the Russian expedition against the Turks, An, 2. 1422
Author (1762), 2. 1283
Author (1890), 3. 1853; 4. 71, 823, 873, 1353
Authorized version of the Bible, 1. 1839–41
Authors and artists, 3. 1851
Author's annual, 4. 73
Authors' playwrights' and composers' handbook, 4. 73, 874

Baers, Jan, 1. 2157–8
Baffin, William, 1. 2156
Bage, Robert, 2. 1006, 1007, 1008, 1010, 1012
Bagehot, Walter, 3. 1368–70, 1763, 1824, 1857
Bagford, John, 2. 311
Bagnold, Enid, 4. 908–9, 799
Bagot, A. G., 3. 1706
Bagshaw, H. R., 3. 1856
Bagster, Samuel, 3. 77
Bagwell, William, 1. 2035
Baikie, William Balfour, 3. 1670
Bailey, Henry Christopher, 4. 515–16
Bailey, James, 4. 1372
Bailey, Philip James, 3. 504–5, 130
Bailey, Samuel, 3. 1513–14
Baillie, Alexander, 1. 2453
Baillie, Joanna, 3. 363–4
Baillie, John, 4. 1243–4
Baillie, Marianne, 3. 1678
Baillie, Robert, 1. 2453–5, 2465
Baillie, Sir William, 1. 2465
Baily, A. H., 3. 1876
Baily, Francis, 2. 1475
Baily's fox-hunting directory, 3. 1883
Baily's hunting directory, 3. 1703, 1883
Baily's monthly magazine, 3. 1684
Baily's turf guide, 3. 1882
Bain, Alexander, 3. 1514–16, 1729
Bain, Andrew Geddes, 3. 1669
Bain, James, 3. 86
Baines, Edward (1774–1848), 3. 1682, 1763, 1796
Baines, Sir Edward (1800–90), 3. 1723, 1796
Baines, Frederick, 3. 1796
Baines, Talbot, 3. 1796
Baines, Thomas (1822–75) traveller, 3. 1671
Baines, Thomas (fl. 1887) journalist, 3. 1796
Baker, Augustin, 1. 1989
Baker, Charles, 3. 1745
Baker, Daniel, 2. 469
Baker, David (Augustin), 1. 1989
Baker, David Erskine, 2. 1802
Baker, Denys Val, 4. 1374, 1376, 1380
Baker, Elizabeth, 4. 909
Baker, Sir George, 2. 1902
Baker, Henry, 2. 536, 1278, 1326, 1902
Baker, John Holland, 3. 1677
Baker, M., 3. 1101
Baker, Margaret, 4. 799
Baker, Margaret Joyce, 4. 814
Baker, Peter, 4. 1377
Baker, Sir Richard, 1. 2244
Baker, Robert, 1. 1083
Baker, Sir Samuel White, 3. 1671, 1675
Baker, Thomas, 2. 783–4, 1271
Baker's news: or the Whitehall journal, 2. 1325

Baker Street journal, 4. 1377
Bakewell, Mrs J., 3. 1847
Bakewell, Robert, 3. 1678
Balbani Niccolò, 1. 886
Balcanquhall, Walter, 1. 2242, 2455
Balchin, Nigel Marlin, 4. 516–17
Baldaeus, Philip, 2. 1436
Balding and Mansell, 4. 80
Baldry, W. Burton, 4. 74, 1359
Baldwin, Cradock and Joy, 3. 1844
Baldwin, Charles, 3. 1763, 1793, 1807, 1808, 1812
'Baldwin, Edward' (William Godwin), 3. 1099
Baldwin, Edward (fl. 1827–57), 3. 1789, 1793
Baldwin, Henry, 3. 1808, 1812
Baldwin, Robert, 3. 1812
Baldwin, Walter, 3. 1763
Baldwin, William, 1. 1083–4, 2029, 2051, 2308, 2329
Baldwin, William Charles, 3. 1713
Baldwin's London (weekly) journal, 2. 1334; 3. 1812
Bale, John, 1. 1403–5, 852, 997, 1084, 1899, 2131
Balfour, Andrew, 2. 2057
Balfour, Arthur James, 1st Earl of Balfour, 3. 1516–17
Balfour, Clara Lucas, 3. 1103
Balfour, John Hutton, 3. 1855
Balfour, Margaret Melville, 4. 811
Balfour, Mary, 3. 712
Balguy, John, 2. 1855
Balguy, Thomas, 2. 161
Ball, Edward, 3. 1125–6
Ball, John, 3. 1709
Ball, W., 3. 1875
Ball room, 4. 826
Ball room annual, 3. 1876
ballads
    Middle English, 1. 697–720
    Renaissance, 1. 953–4, 1007–14, 2041–4
    nineteenth century, 3. 170
    see also song books, miscellanies
Ballads and some other occasional poems, 2. 350
Ballads and songs: Scotish, 2. 426
Ballantyne, Hanson and Co, 3. 57
Ballantyne, Robert Michael, 3. 1092–3
Ballantyne, Thomas, 3. 1795, 1796, 1808, 1810, 1814
Ballard, George, 2. 1806
Ballet annual, 4. 828
Ballin, Rossetta, 2. 1009
Balloon, 2. 1007
Ballot, 3. 1819
Balm of Gilead, 2. 1275
Balnaves, Henry, 1. 2438

Balthorpe, John, 2. 1445–6
Baltimore, Frederick Calvert, 6th Baron, 2. 1421
Balzac, Honoré de, 3. 98–9
Balzac, Jean Louis Guez de, 1. 2181, 862, 867; 2. 1503, 90
Bamber, G., 4. 1387
Bambridge, Thomas, 2. 1553
Bamburgh Castle Library, 2. 305
Bamford, Robert Walker, 3. 1720
Bampfylde, John Codrington, 2. 639
Banba (1904), 4. 1357
Banba (1921), 4. 1365
Banbury, printing, 2. 265
Banchieri, Adriano, 1. 2024
Bancroft, Edward, 2. 1003, 1468
Bancroft, John, 2. 755
Bancroft, Richard, 1. 1922, 1960
Bancroft, Thomas, 1. 1297, 1336
Band, Cuffe and Ruffe, A merrie dialogue betweene, 1. 1777
Bandello, Matteo, 1. 898–9, 2181
Banim, John, 3. 707–9
Banim, Michael, 3. 707–9
Bank holiday budget, 4. 1386
Banker's almanac, 3. 1882
Banker's circular (and monetary times), 3. 1824
Bankes, George Nugent, 3. 1866
Banking almanac, directory and year book, 3. 1882
Banks, John, 2. 755, 176
Banks, Sir Joseph, 2. 1403, 1902
Banks, Kathleen, 4. 1388
Banks's currant intelligence, 2. 1317
Bannatyne, Richard, 1. 2439
Bannatyne Club, 3. 56
Bannerman, Helen, 3. 1098
Bannister, M., 4. 1388
'Bannoc, Adolphus', 2. 999
Banquet of dainties, 1. 1084
Banquet of musick, 2. 336
Banquet of Thalia, 2. 409
Banquet of the Muses, A, 2. 371–2
Bansley, Charles, 1. 2032
Banting, John, 4. 1375
Bantling, 3. 1871
Baptist annual register, 2. 1314
Baptist magazine, 3. 1843
Baptist times and freeman, 3. 1823
Baptist Union magazine, 3. 1842
Baptists
  general, 1. 19–20
  Restoration and eighteenth century, 2. 1665–6, 1669–72
Baratariana, 2. 394
Baratti, Giacomo, 2. 1445
Barbaro, Francesco, 2. 1541

Barbaro, Giosafatte, 1. 2142
Barbauld, Anna Laetitia, 2. 639–40, 1023
'Barbellion, W. N. P.' (Bruce Frederick Cummings), 4. 1137–8
Barber, John, 2. 263
Barber, John Thomas, 3. 1681
Barber, Margaret Fairless, 3. 1050
Barber, Mary, 2. 536
Barbeyrac, Jean, 2. 1503
Barbon, Nicholas, 2. 1896
Barbot, Jean, 2. 1448
Barbour, John, 1. 466–7
Barckley, Sir Richard, 1. 2331, 2027
Barclay, Alexander, 1. 1019–20
Barclay, James, 2. 1470
Barclay, John, 1. 2300–2, 857–8, 2139, 2181; 2. 75
Barclay, Patrick, 2. 1392
Barclay, Robert, 2. 1648, 114, 162
Barclay, Sir Thomas, 3. 1763
Barclay, Vera Charlesworth, 4. 800
Barclay, William (1546–1608), 1. 2465–6, 852
Barclay, William (1570?–1630?), 1. 2455, 2469–70, 2038
Bard, Josef, 4. 1369
Bare aspect, 4. 1370
'Barebone, I.' (J. Ralph), 2. 1281, 1332
Baretti, Giuseppe, 2. 185–6, 38, 68, 189, 1421
Barfield, Arthur Owen, 4. 999
Barge, 4. 1396
Barham, Francis Foster, 3. 1841
Barham, Richard Harris, 3. 365
Baring, Maurice, 4. 517–19
Baring-Gould, Sabine, 3. 1034–6, 1105
Barker, Andrew, 1. 2125
Barker, Cicely Mary, 4. 801
Barker, Sir Ernest, 4. 1138–9
Barker, George Granville, 4. 231
Barker, Jane, 2. 469, 987, 988, 989, 991
Barker, Mary Anne, Lady, 3. 1104
Barking Abbey, library, of, 1. 987
Barksted, William, 1. 1297–8
Barlas, John Evelyn, 3. 609
Barley, William, 1. 959, 2066
Barlow, Antoinette Pratt, 4. 1377
Barlow, Edward, 2. 1393, 1436, 1455, 1902
Barlow, Francis, 2. 1556
Barlow, George, 3. 610
Barlow, Jane, 3. 1908
Barlow, Roger, 1. 2118
Barlow, Thomas, 2. 1604
Barlow, William, 1. 1084
Barmby, J. Goodwin, 3. 1763
Barnard, Lady Anne, 2. 2027; 3. 1669
Barnard, Caroline, 3. 1100
'Barne, Kitty' (Marion Catherine Barne), 4. 796

Barne, Marion Catherine, 4. 796
Barnes,— (fl. 1548), 1. 2026
Barnes, Barnabe, 1. 1085, 1730–1
Barnes, F. G., 4. 1385
Barnes, Joshua, 2. 978
Barnes, Thomas, 3. 1763, 1789
Barnes, William, 3. 505–7
Barnett, H. N., 3. 1792
Barnett, Henry N., 3. 1810
Barnett, J. P., 3. 1843
Barnett, Morris, 3. 1144–5
Barnett, P. A., 3. 1731
Barnfield, Richard, 1. 1085–6, 1335
Barnwell Priory, library of, 1. 987
Baron, Joseph Alexander, 4. 519
Baron, Robert (1539–1639) Scottish theologian, 1. 2455
Baron, Robert (1630–58) poet, 1. 1298, 1731, 2057
Baron, Samuel, 2. 1438
Baron, William, 4. 1361
Baronius, Caesar, 1. 2297
Barr, Robert, 3. 1853; 4. 1353
Barradell-Smith, Walter, 4. 794
Barratt, Alfred, 3. 1517
Barret, Robert, 1. 1298
Barrett, Eaton Stannard, 3. 709
Barrett, Elizabeth, 3. 435–9
Barri, Giacomo, 2. 1411
Barrie, Sir James Matthew, 3. 1188–92, 1098, 1698
Barriers, 1. 1777
Barrin, Jean, 2. 980
Barrington, Daines, 2. 246, 1485–6, 1563, 1797
'Barrington, George' (George Waldron), 2. 1482
Barrington, John Shute, 2. 162
Barron, Richard, 2. 1779
Barrow, Henry, 1. 1935
Barrow, Isaac, 2. 1604–5, 162, 1902; 1. 2303
Barrow, John (fl. 1756), 2. 1392
Barrow, Sir John (1764–1848), 3. 1669, 1673, 1680
Barrow, John (fl. 1886), 3. 1710
Barrow, William, 3. 1717
Barrow evening echo, 3. 1803
'Barrowcliffe, A. J.' (Albert Julius Mott), 3. 914
Barry, Edward, 2. 1563
Barry, Lording (Lodowick), 1. 1731
Barry, Thomas, 2. 1476
Barrymore, William, 3. 1126
Barth, C. G., 3. 1101
Bartholomew of Glanville, 1. 771
Bartlet, John (fl. 1606), 1. 1352
Bartlet, John (fl. 1754), 2. 1553
Bartlett, John, 2. 1482

Bartlett, Roger, 2. 292
Bartoli, Daniello, 2. 1542
Bartolomaeus Anglicus, 1. 771, 2117
Bartolozzi, Francesco, 3. 64
Barton, Bernard, 3. 365–6, 1087, 1099, 1877
Barton, John, 1. 2317
Barton, Lucy, 3. 1099
Barton, Maria, 3. 1089
Barton, R. C., 3. 1101
Barton, William, 1. 1912
Bartram, John, 2. 1464
Bartram, William, 2. 1473
Barwell, Louisa Mary, 3. 1101, 1723
Basia Joannis Secundi, 2. 359
Basia of Bonefonius, 2. 353
Basileon(a), 3. 1867; 4. 1393
Basilisk, 4. 1391
Baskerville, John, 2. 266
Baskerville, Sir Thomas, 1. 2152
Baskerville, Thomas, 2. 1398
Basse, William, 1. 1086, 1298
Basson, Thomas, 1. 959
Bastard, Thomas, 1. 1086, 1335
Bastien typographica, 4. 83
Bastile, 2. 1008
'Bat', 3. 1882
Batchelor, 2. 1284
Batchelor, Margaret, 4. 798
Bate, George, 2. 1902
Bate, Sir Henry, later Dudley, 2. 833, 1335, 1336
Bate, John, 4. 1374, 1377
Bate, Julius, 2. 162
Bateman, Mrs, 3. 1679
Bateman, J. F., 3. 1711
Bateman's tragedy, 2. 984
Bates, Henry Walter, 3. 1674
Bates, Herbert Ernest, 4. 520–1
Bates, Ralph, 4. 521–2
Bates, William, 2. 1605, 162
Bateson, Frederick Noel Wilse, 4. 999–1000, 1397
Bateson, Thomas, 1. 1351
Bath
    Restoration and eighteenth century
        magazines, 2. 1349
        newspapers, 2, 1353
        periodical essays, 2. 1347
Bath advertiser, 2. 1353
Bath and Bristol chronicle, 2. 1353
Bath and Bristol magazine, 2. 1349
Bath and west and southern counties society: letters, 2. 1349
Bath and west of England agricultural society: correspondence, 2. 1349

Bath and Wilts chronicle (and herald), 3. 1800
Bath and Wilts evening chronicle, 3. 1800
Bath argus and West of England advertising register, 3. 1799–1800
Bath argus evening telegram, 3. 1799
Bath, Bristol, Tunbridge and Epsom miscellany, 2. 363
Bath chronicle (1760), 2. 1353
Bath chronicle (1770), 2. 1353
Bath contest, 2. 389
Bath courant, 2. 1353
Bath daily argus, 3. 1800
Bath daily chronicle, 3. 1800
Bath evening chronicle, 3. 1800
Bath gazette, 2. 1353
Bath Harmonic Society: glees, 2. 427
Bath herald, 2. 1353
Bath journal, 2. 1353
Bath miscellany, 2. 368, 1349
Bath register, 2. 1353
Batman, Stephen, 1. 1086
Batsford, B. T., 3. 77
Battersby, H. F. P., 3. 1703
Battersea amateur magazine, 4. 1388
Batteux, Charles, 2. 1503, 65
Battie, William, 2. 1823, 1903
Battle of Brunanburh, 1. 239–40
Battle of Finnsburh, 1. 240–1
Battle of Maldon, 1. 241–3
Battle of the quills, 2. 388
Batty, Beatrice, 3. 1103
Bauchope, C. Robertson, 3. 1883
Bauchope, John, 3. 1883
Baudelaire, Charles, 3. 99
Baudier, Michel, 1. 2148
Bauer, Bettina, 4. 808
Baumann, Arthur A., 4. 1351
Baumgarten, Martin von, 2. 1537, 1436
Bawbee, 3. 1804
'Bawdycoat, Mother', 2. 1345
Bax, Clifford, 4. 910–11, 1358, 1365
Bax, Ernest Belfort, 3. 1852
Baxter, Andrew, 2. 1855–6
Baxter, George, 3. 64
Baxter, Herbert, 4. 1391
Baxter, Langley, 3. 1795
Baxter, Nathaniel, 1. 1086
Baxter, Richard, 1. 1971–3, 1892, 1914; 2. 162
Baxter, William, 2. 1823
Bay psalm book, 1. 1911–12
'Bayard', 4. 859
Bayle, Pierre, 2. 1503–4, 90–1
Bayley, Frederick W. N., 3. 1816
Baylie, Simon, 1. 1731
Bayliss, John, 4. 1376

Bayly, Ada Ellen, 3. 1064, 1097, 1698
Bayly, Lewis, 1. 1936, 866
Bayly, Thomas, 1. 2058
Bayly, Thomas Haynes, 3. 366–7
Bayly, W., 3. 1882
Bayly, William (fl. 1673), 2. 162
Bayly, William (1737–1810), 2. 1480
Bayne, Peter, 3. 1419
Baynes, Thomas Spencer, 3. 1517–18
Bazaar, 4. 1384
Beach, Sylvia, 4. 1367
'Beachcomber' (John Bingham Morton), 4. 1088–9
Beachcroft, Thomas Owen, 4. 522
Beacon (Oxford etc. 1921), 4. 1365, 1397
Beacon (Hull 1932), 4. 1391
Beacon and Christian times, 3. 1823
Beaconsfield, Benjamin Disraeli, Earl of, 3. 771–9, 1814
Beale, Dorothea, 3. 1747
Beale, Robert, 1. 997
Beaman, Sydney George Hulme, 4. 807
Beano (comic), 4. 820
Bear university magazine, 3. 1865
Beard, Charles (1827–88), 3. 1605, 1858
Beard, Charles (fl. 1922), 4. 1365
Beard, John, 3. 1704
Beard, John Relly, 3. 1856
Beardsley, Aubrey Vincent, 3. 610–11, 64–5, 1858
Beare, Philip O' Sullivan, 3. 1887
Beattie, James, 2. 640–1, 41, 104, 239, 1784
Beatty, Charles, 2. 1467–8
Beatty-Kingston, William, 3. 1763
Beau's academy, 2. 340
Beau's miscellany, 2. 359
Beauchamp, Kathleen Mansfield, 4. 653–9
Beauchamp, William Lygon, 7th Earl, 3. 1870
Beauchamps, Pierre François Godart de, 2. 992
Beaumarchais, Pierre Augustin Caron de, 2. 1504, 118
Beaumont,— (fl. 1682), 2. 1291
Beaumont, Augustus, 3. 1818
Beaumont, Cyril William, 4. 1363
Beaumont, Francis, 1. 1709–19, 1763–4; 2. 31
Beaumont, J. L. de, 2. 1300
Beaumont, Sir John, 1. 1298–9, 1087, 2037
Beaumont, Joseph, 1. 1299
Beaumont, Wentworth, 3. 1856
Beaumont Press, 4. 96
Beauties in prose and verse, 2. 403
Beauties of all the magazines selected, 2. 1303
Beauties of ancient poetry, 2. 419
Beauties of England, 2. 1402
Beauties of English poesy, 2. 387
Beauties of fables in verse, 2. 400

Beauties of literature, 2. 414
Beauties of music and poetry, 2. 402
Beauties of poetry, 2. 396
Beauties of poetry display'd, 2. 379
Beauties of the Anti-Jacobin, 2. 426
Beauties of the English drama, 2. 397
Beauties of the English stage, 2. 365
Beauties of the magazines (1775), 2. 1352
Beauties of the magazines (1788), 2. 1372
Beauties of the poets, 2. 394
Beauties of the Spectators, 2. 379
Beauties of thought, 2. 417
Beaver, 4. 1396
Beawes, William, 2. 1439
Beazley, Samuel, 3. 1127
Becanus, Martinus, 1. 843–4
Beccadelli, Lodovico, 2. 1542
Beccaria, Cesare Bonesana, 2. 1542, 188
Beccaria, Giovanni Battista, 2. 1542
Bechstein, Ludwig, 3. 1109
Becker, Lydia Ernestine, 3. 1851
Becket, Andrew, 2. 1787, 1426
Becket, Thomas à, 1. 475, 766, 1148
Beckett, Samuel Barclay, 4. 885–906
Beckford, Peter, 2. 1426, 1560
Beckford, Richard, 2. 1281, 1332
Beckford, William, 2. 973–6, 145, 182, 195, 1334, 1426; 3. 92, 1679
Beckford, William (d. 1799) of Jamaica, 2. 1473
Beckingham, Charles, 2. 785
Beckington, Thomas, 1. 683, 802–3
Becon, Thomas, 1. 1922–3, 1087, 1898
Bedborough, George, 3. 1854
Beddoes, Thomas, 2. 1903
Beddoes, Thomas Lovell, 3. 409–11, 130
Bede, 1. 345–9, 2130, 2181
'Bede, Cuthbert' (Edward Bradley), 3. 914–15, 1684
Bede's death song, 1. 243
Bede's history (OE version), 1. 317–18
Bedell, William, 2. 1694
Bedford, Arthur, 2. 1831
Bedford, Francis Russell, 2nd Earl of, 1. 1003
Bedford, Francis Russell, 5th Duke of, 2. 1426
Bedford, Grosvenor, 2. 1289
Bedford, John of Lancaster, Duke of, 1. 997
Bedford, Thomas, 1. 2075
Bedford College (union) magazine, 4. 1395
Bedford writing, 4. 1395
Bedfordshire, general bibliography, 1. 15
Bedwell, William (Wilhelm), 1. 2134, 2148
Bee (1715), 2. 349
Bee (1733), 2. 1278, 1297, 1327
Bee (1759), 2. 1282, 1302

Bee (1777), 2. 1347
Bee (1790), 2. 1371, 1372–3
Bee (1793), 2. 417
Bee (1910), 4. 1381
Bee-hive (1798), 2. 1350
Bee-hive (1861), 3. 1820, 1836
Bee newly revived, 2. 1300
Beeching, Henry Charles, 3. 611
Beechman, N. A., 4. 1397
Beeckman, Daniel, 2. 1437, 1448
Beedell, Edwin, 3. 1881
Beedome, Thomas, 1. 1299
Beer, Frederick Arthur, 3. 1807
Beer, Mrs F. A., 3. 1810
Beer, Julius, 3. 1807
Beerbohm, Sir Max, 4. 1000–3
Beesly, Edward Spencer, 3. 1518, 1854
Beeton, Samuel Orchart, 3. 1763, 1791, 1816, 1850, 1878
Beeton's annual, 3. 1878
Beeton's boy's own magazine, 3. 1853
Behind the scenes, 4. 827, 1377
Behme, Anthony, 2. 1459
Behn, Aphra, 2. 755–7, 145, 980, 981, 982, 983, 984
Behrens, Georg Henning, 2. 1417
Beith, John Hay, 4. 598–600
Bekynton, Thomas, 1. 683, 802–3, 997
Bel-vedere or the garden of the Muses, 1. 1009
Belany, J. C., 3. 1700
Belcher, J., 3. 1846
Belchier, Daubridgcourt, 1. 1732
Belfast
  Restoration and eighteenth century
    magazines, 2. 1380
    newspapers, 2. 1387
    printing, 2. 273–4
  nineteenth century newspapers, 3. 1805–7, 1833–4
  twentieth century, university journalism, 4. 1392
Belfast courant, 2. 1387
Belfast critic, 4. 1404
Belfast daily Mercury, 3. 1805
Belfast daily times, 3. 1806
Belfast evening post, 2. 1387
Belfast evening star, 3. 1806
Belfast evening telegraph, 3. 1806; 4. 1402
Belfast mercury (1783), 2. 1387
Belfast Mercury (1851), 3. 1805
Belfast monthly magazine, 3. 1843
Belfast morning news, 3. 1806
Belfast news-letter, 2. 1387; 3. 1806
Belfast telegraph, 3. 1806; 4. 1402
Belfast times, 3. 1806

Belgian, literary relations
  Shakespeare, 1. 1631
  Restoration and eighteenth century, 2. 217
Belgravia, 3. 1850
Beling, Richard, 1. 2056
Bell, A. W., 3. 1811
Bell, Adrian Hanbury, 4. 522-3
Bell, Andrew, 3. 1717
Bell, Arthur Clive Heward, 4. 1003-4
Bell, Charles Dent, 3. 507
Bell, Charles William, 3. 1870
Bell, Clive, 4. 1003-4
Bell, George, 3. 77, 1763
Bell, Gertrude Margaret Lowthian, 4. 1311
Bell, Henry Thomas Mackenzie, 3. 612
Bell, John (1691-1780), 2. 1439
Bell, John (1745-1831), 2. 263; 3. 57, 1763,
  1789, 1793, 1808, 1842
Bell, John (1763-1820) 2. 1903
Bell, John Browne, 3. 1763, 1808, 1809, 1810,
  1811, 1823, 1844
Bell, John William, 3. 1811
Bell, Julian Heward, 4. 231-2
'Bell, Neil' (Stephen Southwold), 4. 523-4
Bell, Priscilla, 2. 1027
Bell, Robert (1800-67) journalist, 3. 1810, 1846
Bell, Robert (fl. 1801-20) journalist, 3. 1808,
  1809, 1810
Bell, Thomas (fl. 1596), 1. 2276
Bell, Thomas (fl. 1665), 2. 2032
Bell, Walter John, 3. 1811
Bell, 4. 1374
Bell's classical arrangement of fugitive poetry, 2.
  410
Bell's life in London and sporting chronicle, 3.
  1683, 1809
Bell's new weekly messenger, 3. 1810
Bell's news, 3. 1811
Bell's penny dispatch and penny Sunday chronicle,
  3. 1811
Bell's penny life in London, 3. 1791
Bell's Sunday dispatch, 3. 1809
Bell's weekly messenger, 2. 1338; 3. 1808
Bellamy, Daniel, the elder, 2. 536-7, 1567
Bellamy, Henry, 1. 1764
Bellamy, John, 1. 959
Bellamy's picturesque magazine, 2. 1310
Bellarmino, Roberto Francesco, 1. 844
Bellefond, Nicolas Villaut, Sieur de, 2. 1445
Belleforest, François de, 1. 2060
Bellenden, John, 1. 2421, 2439
Bellers, John, 2. 1649, 1896
Bellicard, Jérôme Charles, 2. 1506, 1419
Bellings, Sir Richard, 1. 2245
Belloc, Hilaire, 4. 1004-10, 1406; 3. 1100

Belloc, Marie Adelaide, 4. 639-40
Bellon, Peter, 2. 982
Beloe, William, 3. 1637, 1841; 2. 1027, 1309
Belsham, Thomas, 3. 1602
Belshis, A., 2. 1372
Belson, Mary, 3. 1089
Beltaine, 3. 1858; 4. 823, 854, 1355
Bembo, Pietro, 1. 890
Bemrose and Co., 3. 57; 4. 80
Ben, John, 1. 2130
Ben Johnson's jests, 2. 375
Ben Johnson's last legacy, 2. 378
Bendyshe, T., 3. 1821
Benedict, 3. 1867; 4. 1393
Benedicta, 2. 1009
Benedicti, Jean, 1. 865
Benedictine office (OE), 1. 328
Benedictine rule (OE), 1. 327
Benefactor, 2. 1275
Benese, R., 1. 2277
Benezet, Anthony, 2. 1450
Benisch, Abraham, 3. 1822
Benlowes, Edward, 1. 1300
Benn, William, 2. 162
Bennet, Benjamin, 2. 1673
Bennet, James, 2. 1781
Bennet, John (fl. 1599), 1. 1350
Bennet, John (fl. 1774), 2. 641
Bennet, Thomas, 2. 279
Bennett, Anna Maria, 3. 710; 2. 1007, 1011, 1012
Bennett, Arnold, 4. 429-36; 3. 111, 1828
Bennett, Enoch Arnold, 4. 429-36; 3. 111, 1828
Bennett, Edward, 1. 2038
Bennett, G. J., 3. 1682
Bennett, Henry Stanley, 4. 1011
Bennett, Joseph, 3. 1419-20, 1692
Bennett, Samuel, 3. 1820
Bennett, William Cox, 3. 507-8
Bennie, Archibald, 3. 1843
Benson, Arthur, 4. 1354
Benson, Arthur Christopher, 3. 1420-1, 1870
Benson, Edward Frederic, 3. 1854; 4. 790
Benson, Edward White, 3. 1101
Benson, Eleanor Theodora Roby, 4. 524
Benson, G., 1. 2276
Benson, George, 2. 1673, 162
Benson, Joseph, 3. 1840
Benson, Maria, 3. 1718
Benson, Stella, 4. 524-5
Benson, Thomas, 2. 1796
Bensusan, Samuel Levy, 3. 1854
Bent, James Theodore, 3. 1672
Bent, Robert, 3. 81
Bent, William, 3. 81
Bent's literary advertiser, 3. 81

Bentham, George, 3. 1518
Bentham, Jeremy, 2. 1882–4, 104; 3. 1602, 1717, 1855
Bentivoglio, Guido, 1. 2141; 2. 1542
Bentley, Edmund Clerihew, 4. 525
Bentley, George, 3. 1846, 1849, 1850
Bentley, H., 3. 1696
Bentley, Phyllis Eleanor, 4. 525–6
Bentley, Richard (1662–1742), 2. 1819–22, 41, 104, 1769, 1856, 1903
Bentley, Richard, the younger (1708–82), 2. 824
Bentley, Richard (1794–1871), 3. 77, 1763, 1846, 1849, 1857
Bentley, Richard (1854–1936), 3. 1849
Bentley, Thomas, 1. 1905
Bentley's miscellany, 3. 1846, 1862
Bentley's monthly review, 3. 1849
Bentley's quarterly review, 3. 1857
Benyowsky, Móricz August, Count, 2. 1443, 1451
Beowulf, 1. 244–67
Beowulf manuscript, 1. 227–9
Berenger, Richard, 2. 1553
Beresford, Benjamin, 2. 167
Beresford, John Davys, 4. 526–8
Beresford, William, 2. 1481
Berger, Walter, 4. 1375
Berington, Simon, 2. 994
'Berkeley, Anthony' (Anthony Berkeley Cox), 4. 528
Berkeley, G. C. G. F., 3. 1705
Berkeley, George, 2. 1851–4, 41, 104, 158, 1903
Berkeley, John, 1st Baron, 1. 2251
Berkeley, Reginald Cheyne, 4. 911–12
Berkeley, Sir William, 1. 1732; 2. 1454
Berkeley Hall, 2. 1012
Berkenhead, Sir John, 1. 2091, 2097, 2103
Berkenhout, John, 2. 1802
Berkshire
  general bibliography, 1. 15
  nineteenth century newspapers, 3. 1831
Berkshire chronicle (1771), 2. 1368; 3. 1831
Berkshire chronicle (1798), 2. 1350
Berkshire repository, 2. 423, 1351
Berlin, Sir Isaiah, 4. 1140
Berlin liar, 4. 1408
Bermondsey book, 4. 1366
Bermondsey Priory, library of, 1. 987
Bernal, John Desmond, 4. 1244
Bernard, Catherine, 2. 979
Bernard, Edward, 2. 1767
Bernard, J. B., 3. 1811
Bernard, Richard, 1. 2056, 2127
Bernard, Samuel, 1. 1764
Bernard, Sir Thomas, 3. 1718
Bernard, Thomas Dehaney, 3. 1621

Bernard, William Bayle, 3. 1145
Bernard, Sayings of, 1. 509
Bernardin de Saint-Pierre, Jacques Henri, 2. 1531, 91, 1008, 1450
Berners, Gerald Hugh Tyrwhitt-Wilson, 14th Baron, 4. 529
Berners, John Bourchier, 2nd Baron, 1. 678–80, 2065
Berners, Juliana, 1. 689
Bernier, François, 2. 1432
Berquin, Arnaud, 2. 1032, 1006, 1009
Berrow's Worcester journal, 2. 1368; 3. 1831
Berry, Francis, 4. 232
Berthelet, Thomas, 1. 959
Berthold, Arthur B., 4. 1368
Bertin, Joseph, 2. 1567
Bertius, Petrus, 1. 2120
Bertram, James Glass, 3. 1707, 1763, 1804
Berwick, printing, 2. 271
Berwick museum, 2. 1373
Besant, Annie, 3. 1763, 1819, 1820, 1853; 4. 1352
Besant, Sir Walter, 3. 1036–8, 1763, 1853; 4. 71
Besier, Rudolf, 4. 912–13
Besogne, Nicolas, 2. 1410
Best, George, 1. 2149–50
Best, Oswald Herbert, 4. 801
Best, Thomas (1570?–1638?), 1. 2145
Best, Thomas (fl. 1787), 2. 1561
Best and compleatest academy of compliments, 2. 374
Best and most perfect intelligencer, 1. 2107
Best books, 4. 1362
Best detective stories of the year, 4. 1389
Best of the year, 4. 1365
Best poems of 1922 [–43], 4. 1365
Best poems of 1955 [etc], 4. 1380
best-sellers, 4. 123–4
Best short stories, 4. 1365
Bestiary, 1. 513–14
Betagh, William, 2. 1478
Betham-Edwards, Matilda Barbara, 3. 1102
Bethell, Augusta, 3. 1103
Bethune, Alexander, 3. 508
Betjeman, Sir John, 4. 233–4
Betson, Thomas, 1. 689, 1936
'*Better times*', 4. 1362–3
Betterton, Thomas, 2. 758
Bettesworth, W. A., 3. 1698
Bettie, W., 1. 2056
'Bettina' (Bettina Ehrlich), 4. 808
Betts, D. R., 4. 1383
Beunans Meriasek, 1. 728
Beuvius, Adam, 2. 1537
Bevan, Favell Lee, 3. 1090
Beveridge, William, 2. 1605, 162, 1831

Beveridge, William Henry, 1st Baron, 4. 1140–1
Beverley, John, 3. 1880
Beverley, Peter, 1. 1087
Beverley, Robert, 2. 1459
Beverus, Johannes, 1. 788
Bevis of Hampton, 1. 433
Bewick, Thomas, 2. 294; 3. 65
Bexley and Erith bulletin, 4. 850
Beyle, Marie-Henri, 3. 108
Bèze, Théodore de (Beza), 1. 844, 865, 867, 2181
Bhat, K. S., 4. 1369
Bianco, Margery Winifred, 4. 793–4
Bibby, Joseph, 4. 1358
Bibby's annual, 4. 1358
Biber, George E., 3. 1721
Bible
  Old English
    Latin, 1. 350
    translations, 1. 323–4
  Middle English
    Latin exegesis, 1. 752
    versions, 1. 477–82
  Renaissance to Restoration, 1. 1825–88
    anthologies, 1. 1829–30
    Authorized Version, 1. 1839–41
    Bishops', 1. 1836–7
    commentaries, 1. 1853–88
    concordances, 1. 1827–30
    epitomes and extracts, 1. 1843
    Geneva, 1. 1835–6
    Great, 1. 1834–5
    harmonies, 1. 1844–5
    prayer books, 1. 1887–96
    psalms, 1. 1895–1914
    reconciliations, 1. 1845–6
    Rheims-Douai, 1. 1837–9
    scholarship, 1. 2295–6
    Soldiers' Pocket, 1. 1842
    studies, 1. 1845–54
  Restoration and eighteenth century, 2. 1811–12
  see also religion, theology
Bible summary (ME), 1. 482
bibliographies
  general, 1. 1–22
    English studies, 1. 5–6
    journals, scholarly, 1. 1–4
    library catalogues, 1. 7–10
    manuscripts, 1. 9–12
    new books, 1. 3–6
    periods, 1. 11–16
    reference works, 1. 5–8
    religious bodies 1. 19–22
    universities, 1. 15–20
  Old English, 1. 187–8
  Middle English, 1. 357–8

Renaissance to Restoration, 1. 807–12
  Scottish, 1. 2419–20
Restoration and eighteenth century, 2. 1–4
  Scottish, 2. 1955–6
nineteenth century, 3. 1–4
  Anglo-Irish, 3. 1885–6, 1895–6
twentieth century, 4. 1–4
Bibliophile, 4. 110, 1358
Bibliotheca annua, 2. 1343
Bibliotheca literaria, 2. 1294
Bibliotheca topographica Britannica, 2. 1306
Bibliotheca universalis, 2. 1371
bibliotherapy, 4. 121–2
'Bickerdyke, J.' (Charles Henry Cook), 3. 1690
Bickers, Sheridan, 4. 826, 860
'Bickerstaff, Isaac', 2. 1278
'Bickerstaff, William', 2. 1281
Bickerstaffe, Isaac, 2. 825–6, 145
Bickersteth, Edward, 3. 1619
Bickersteth, Edward Henry, 3. 508–9
Bickford, James, 3. 1674, 1676
Bickham's musical entertainer, 2. 366
Bicknell, Alexander, 2. 1005
Bicycle annual, 3. 1882
Bicycling times, 3. 1824
Biddel, John, 1. 959
Biddulph, William, 1. 2125
Bidpai, 1. 2181–2
Bielfeld, Jakob Friedrich, Baron von, 2. 65, 1402
Bieston, Roger, 1. 1087
Bifur, 4. 1368
Big Ben, 3. 1815
Bigg, John Stanyan, 3. 509
Bigge, Thomas, 2. 1351
Bigges, Walter, 1. 2077, 852
Biggs, C. A., 3. 1851
Biggs, W., 3. 1724
Bigham, Charles Clive, 3. 1871
Bignon, Jean Paul, 2. 992
Bijou, 3. 1874
Bilberg, John, 2. 1414
Bill-o'-Jack's summer annual, 4. 1361
Billiard review, 3. 1692
billiards, 3. 1691–2
Billinge's Liverpool advertiser, 2. 1360
Billingsley, Nicholas, 2. 469
Billington, 2. 412
Billy, Jacques de, 1. 869
Bilson, Thomas, 1. 1936, 2297
Bindley, Charles, 3. 1705, 1713
Bindon, David, 2. 1896
Binfield, Julia, 4. 1385, 1386
Bingham, John, 1. 2146
Bingham, Joseph, 2. 1621
Bingley, Thomas, 3. 1101

Bingley, William (1774–1823), miscellaneous writer, 3. 1099; 2. 1408
Bingley, William (d. 1799), bookseller, 2. 279, 1283, 1334
Bingley's journal, 2. 1334
Bingley's London journal, 2. 1334
Binney, Thomas, 3. 1724
Binning, Hugh, 1. 2455
Binns, Henry Bryan, 4. 1359
Binns, J. A., 4. 1384
Binyon, Helen, 4. 811
Binyon, Margaret, 4. 811
Binyon, Robert Laurence, 3. 612–13
Biograph and review, 3. 1852
Biographical and imperial magazine, 2. 1308
Biographical magazine (1776), 2. 1305
Biographical magazine (1794), 2. 1310
Biographical magazine (1852), 3. 1879
Biographist and (British) review, 4. 1356
biography
    Renaissance to Restoration, 1. 2247–52, 2267–74
    Restoration and eighteenth century, 2. 5–6
    nineteenth century
        Irish, 3. 1897–8
        journalists and publishers, 3. 1761–78
        year books, 3. 1878–9
    twentieth century
        actors, 4. 863–5
        journalists, 4. 1335–8
    see also history, prose
Bion, 1. 2167; 2. 1489
Biondi (Bjundevié), Giovanni Francesco, 1. 886, 899, 2060
Birbeck, C. H., 3. 1801
Birch, A. N., 3. 1880
Birch, Jonathan, 1. 1329
Birch, Thomas, 2. 1702–4, 1749–50, 1797–8
Birch, Timothy, 2. 1327
Birch, 2. 1364
Birchall, Charles, 3. 1796
Birchensha, Ralph, 1. 1087
Birckbek, Simon, 1. 2297
Bird, Henry Edward, 3. 1694
Bird, John, 2. 1011
Bird, Kenneth, 4. 1400
'Bird, Richard' (Walter Barradell-Smith), 4. 794
Bird, 2. 400
Birkbeck, J. A., 4. 84, 1384
Birket, James, 2. 1464
Birks, Thomas Rawson, 3. 1619
Birley, W., 3. 1724
'Birmingham, George A.' (James Owen Hannay), 4. 529–30

Birmingham
    Restoration and eighteenth century
        libraries, 2. 305
        magazines, 2. 1349
        newspapers, 2. 1353–4
        periodical essays, 2. 1347
        printing and bookselling, 2. 265–6
    nineteenth century
        newspapers, 3. 1794–1803, 1830–1
        university, 3. 1733
    twentieth century
        theatre, 4. 845
        university journalism, 4. 1392
Birmingham and Wolverhampton chronicle, 2. 1353
Birmingham chronicle and Warwickshire journal, 2. 1353
Birmingham daily gazette, 3. 1796–7; 4. 1399
Birmingham daily mail, 3. 1798; 4. 1402
Birmingham daily mercury, 3. 1795
Birmingham daily post, 3. 1795; 4. 1401
Birmingham daily press, 3. 1794
Birmingham daily times, 3. 1802
Birmingham evening despatch, 4. 1404
Birmingham evening mail and despatch, 3. 1798; 4. 1402
Birmingham evening news, 3. 1800
Birmingham gazette (1741), 2. 1353
Birmingham gazette (and express) (1904), 3. 1797, 1831; 4. 1399
Birmingham journal, 2. 1347, 1353
Birmingham magazine, 2. 1349
Birmingham mail, 3. 1798; 4. 1402
Birmingham morning news, 3. 1798
Birmingham post, 3. 1795, 1830; 4. 1401
Birmingham programme of amusements, 4. 848
Birmingham register, 2. 1349, 1353
Birmingham Repertory Theatre news-letter, 4. 850
Birmingham Sunday mail, 4. 1404
Birr weekly journal, 2. 1387
Birrel, Robert, 1. 2439
Birrell, Augustine, 3. 1421–2
Birth-day present, A, 2. 1026
Birthe of Hercules, 1. 1420, 1777
Bisaccioni, Hieronimo, 1. 894
Bisani, Alessandro, 2. 1396
Bishop, A. A., 4. 1383
Bishop, Charles, 2. 1483
Bishop, George Walter, 4. 877
Bishop, Isabella Bird, 3. 1673, 1676
Bishop, Jack, 4. 828
Bishop, James, 3. 1102
Bishop, Nicholas, 1. 689
Bishop, Samuel, 2. 641–2

Bishopric garland, 2. 404
Bishops' Bible, 1. 1836–7
Bispham, Thomas, 1. 2130
Bissenden, F. G., 4. 1384, 1385, 1388
Bisset, James, 2. 1030
Bisset, John, 2. 1374
Bisset, Robert, 2. 1308, 1311, 1312
Bitton, W., 3. 1688
Bitzius, Albert, 3. 123
Bjørnson, Bjørnstjerne, 3. 146
Blachford, Mary, 3. 405
Black, Adam, 3. 77
Black, John (fl. 1798), 2. 1475
Black, John (1783–1855) 3. 1789
Black, Joseph, 2. 1903
Black, Robert, 3. 1707
Black, William, 3. 1038–9, 1763, 1814
Black and white, 3. 1817; 4. 1403
Black cat, 4. 1354
Black dwarf, 3. 1817
Black hat, 4. 1369
Black Sun Press, 4. 96
Blackamore, Arthur, 2. 988, 989
Blackbird (1764), 2. 385
Blackbird (1777), 2. 397
Blackbird (1790), 2. 412
Blackbourn, Richard, 2. 981
Blackbourne, John, 2. 1773
Blackburn, Helen, 3. 1851
Blackburn, J., 3. 1880
Blackburn evening express, 3. 1802
Blackburn mail, 2. 1354
Blackburn times, 3. 1831
Blackburne, Francis, 2. 1778
Blackcountryman, 4. 1387
'Blackford, Martha' (Isabella Stoddart), 3. 1101
Blackguardiana, 2. 418
Blackie, John, 3. 77
Blackie, John Stuart, 3. 509–10
Blacklock, Thomas, 2. 2020–1
Blackmore, Sir Richard, 2. 469–70, 237, 1275, 1903
Blackmore, Richard Doddridge, 3. 915–16
Blackpool gazette, 3. 1831
Blackwall, Anthony, 2. 1823–4
Blackwell, Eardley J., 3. 1680
Blackwell, Henry, 2. 1562
Blackwell, Isaac, 2. 1458
Blackwell, Thomas, the elder (1660?–1728), 2. 2039–40
Blackwell, Thomas, the younger (1701–57), 2. 2051, 41
Blackwood, Adam, 1. 2439, 2470
Blackwood, Alexander, 3. 1844
Blackwood, Algernon Henry, 4. 530–1, 791

Blackwood, John, 3. 1844
Blackwood, Robert, 3. 1844
Blackwood, William (1776–1834), 3. 77, 1844
Blackwood, William, the third (1836–1912), 3. 1844
Blackwood's Edinburgh magazine, 3. 1844, 1860–1; 4. 1349, 1345
Blackwood's lady's magazine, 3. 1846
Blackwood's magazine, 3. 1844; 4. 1349, 1345
Blacman, John, 1. 803
Blades, William, 3. 1637–8
Blaeu, Willem Janszoon, 1. 2139
Blagdon, Francis William, 3. 1817, 1873
Blage, Thomas, 1. 2029
Blagrave, Joseph, 2. 1556
Blaikie, Thomas, 2. 1423
Blaikie, William Garden, 3. 1823, 1857
Blaine, Delabere Pritchett, 2. 1555
Blainville, — de, 2. 1418
Blair, Eric Arthur, 4. 690–6
Blair, Hugh, 2. 2061–2, 41, 117, 235–6, 1780
Blair, Robert (1593–1666), 1. 2248
Blair, Robert (1700–46), 2. 537
Blair, William, 2. 1312
Blair-Fish, Wallace Wilfrid, 4. 1370
Blake, Charles W., 3. 1791
Blake, George, 4. 531–2
Blake, Robert, 1. 2130
Blake, William (fl. 1656), 1. 2034
Blake, William (1757–1827), 2. 615–36, 41, 104; 3. 65
Blakesley, J. W., 3. 1731
Blakeston, Oswell, 4. 1367, 1370, 1371
Blakey, Robert, 3. 1689
Blakiston, John, 3. 1669
Blamire, Susanna, 2. 642
Blanchard, Edward Litt Leman (Laman), 3. 1145–6, 1763, 1813
Blanchard, Samuel Laman, 3. 510–11, 1764, 1790, 1792, 1793
Blanco, José Maria, 3. 1604
Bland, Captain —, 2. 987
Bland, Alan, 4. 849, 850
Bland, Edith, 3. 641–2, 1097; 4. 1358
Bland, Edward, 1. 2160
Blane, William, 2. 1560
Blankart, H. E., 4. 1382
Blankett, John, 2. 1421
Blast, 4. 1362
Blatchford, Montagu, 3. 1821
Blatchford, Robert, 3. 1764, 1821
Blau, Zena, 4. 1388
Blavatsky, Helena Petrovna, 3. 1853
Blayds, Charles Stuart, 3. 617
Bleackley, E. O., 3. 1798, 1803, 1812, 1824

Blencowe, John, 1. 1764
Blenerhasset, Thomas, 1. 1087–8
Blessington, Marguerite, Countess of, 3. 710–11, 1874, 1875
Blewitt, George, 2. 1896
Blickling homilies, 1. 324–5
Bligh, William, 2. 1481
Blighty, 4. 1406
'Blinkhoolie', 3. 1706
Bliss, Elam, 3. 1874
Bliss, Philip, 3. 1881
Blith, Walter, 1. 2278
Blitz blotz, 4. 1387
Blitz budget, 4. 1387
Blom, Eric, 4. 1364
Blomberg, Carl Johann, Baron von, 2. 1414
Blome, Richard, 2. 1446, 1455, 1557
Blomefield, Francis, 2. 1719–20
Blond, Anthony, 4. 1379, 1398
Blondel, François, 2. 65
Bloodie banquet, 1. 1758
Bloomfield, Robert, 3. 367, 1101
Blossoms at Christmas, 3. 1873
Blount, Charles, 2. 1844
Blount, Edward, 1. 959
Blount, Henry, 1. 2128
Blount, John, 1. 689
Blount, Thomas, 1. 2320
Blount, Sir Thomas Pope, 2. 1768, 1800
Blower, Elizabeth, 2. 1007, 1008
Blower, R., 1. 959
Blowitz, Henri Stephan de, 3. 1764
Bloxam, John Francis, 3. 1868
Bludder, Sir Thomas, 1. 997
Blue bell magazine, 4. 1383
Blue book, 4. 1397
Blue dwarf, 3. 1818
Blue review, 4. 825, 1361, 1345
Blue'un, 3. 1866
bluestockings, 2. 1595–1600
Bluett, George, 2. 1896
Bluett, Thomas, 2. 1448
Blumenfeld, Ralph David, 3. 1764
Blund, John, 1. 773
Blunden, Edmund Charles, 4. 234–8
Blunderbuss, 4. 1393
Blundeville, Thomas, 1. 1088
Blunt, Anne Isabella, Lady, 3. 1676
Blunt, Anthony, 4. 1368, 1394
Blunt, Henry, 3. 1619, 1822
Blunt, John, 2. 1554
Blunt, John James, 3. 1619
Blunt, Walter, 3. 1870
Blunt, Wilfrid Scawen, 3. 613–15
Blyton, Enid Mary, 4. 805

Boaden, James, 3. 1127, 1789; 2. 1337
Boase, J. J., 3. 1684
Boate, Gerard, 1. 2135
boating, 3. 1711–12
Boaz, Herman, 2. 1561
Boccaccio, Giovanni, 1. 844, 899–901, 2182; 2. 1542, 38, 194; 3. 136
Boccaccio's. . .*Guiscardo*, 1. 683–4
Boccalini, Trajano, 1. 2182, 890; 2. 1542–3, 38, 194, 985
'Boccalini, Trojano' (M. Earbery), 2. 1294
Boddely's Bath journal, 2. 1353
Boden, Samuel Standige, 3. 1694
Bodenham, John, 1. 2313, 2030
Bodin, Jean, 1. 845, 862, 2275
Bodkin, Matthias M'Donnell, 3. 1764
Bodkin, Maud, 4. 1011
Bodleian Library, 2. 305–6
Bodley Head, 3. 79
Bodley homilies, 1. 484
Bodley NT verse passages, 1. 481
Bodley Wycliffite sermons, 1. 487
Bodmer, Johann Jakob, 2. 1537, 167
Body and the soul, 1. 511–13
Boece (Boethius), Hector, 1. 2440, 853, 2130
Boehme, Jacob, 2. 1658–62, 38, 160–1, 1. 877
Boemus, Joannes, 1. 2118–19
Boethius, 2. 1495
Boethius, 1. 313, 2182
Boethius, Hector, 1. 2440, 853, 2130
Bogue, David, 3. 1816
Bohemian, 3. 1854
Bohn, Henry George, 3. 86
Bohun, Edmond, 2. 1797
Boiardo, Matteo Maria, 1. 896–7, 2182
Boig, Adam, 2. 1375
Boileau-Despréaux, Nicolas, 2. 1504, 36, 65, 115, 130, 131
Bois, John, 1. 2295
Boisrobert, François de, 1. 872, 2061
Boissy, Louis de, 2. 1504
Boke of balettes, 1. 1007
Boke of Cupide, 1. 511
Bokenham, Osbern, 1. 649–50
Boland, Bridget, 4. 913
Bolas, Thomas, 3. 1820, 1878
Bold, Henry, 2. 470
Bold, Samuel, 2. 1844
Bolero, 4. 1398
Boletarium, 2. 407
Bolg an tsolair, 2. 1380
Bolger, John, 3. 1826
Bolingbroke, Henry St John, 1st Viscount, 2. 1119–22, 104, 188–9, 1278
Bolland, William, 3. 1696

Bolton, Edmund, 1. 2239, 2316
Bolton, F. R. H., 4. 850
Bolton, Robert, 1. 1989
Bolton, printing 2. 266
Bolton daily chronicle, 3. 1798
Bolton evening chronicle, 3. 1798
Bolton evening guardian, 3. 1799
Bolton evening news, 3. 1797
Bolton morning news, 3. 1798
Bolts, William, 2. 1440
Bolzius, John Martin, 2. 1462
Bon, Ottavio, 1. 2139
Bon-ton magazine, 2. 1309
Bonar, Horatius, 3. 511, 1619
Bonavelli della Rovere, Guido Ubaldo, 1. 894
Bonaventure, 4. 1373
Bond, John, 1. 2095
Bond, William, 2. 1275
Bond of peace, 4. 1374
Bone, D. D., 3. 1698
Bone, Sir David William, 4. 532
Bone, Stephen, 4. 808
Bone to pick for somebody, A, 2. 1385
Bonhote, Elizabeth, 2. 1003, 1013
Boniface, 1. 349
Bonington, Richard Parkes, 3. 65
Bonnecorse, Balthasar de, 2. 981
Bonner and Middleton's Bristol journal, 2. 1354
Bonnet, Charles, 2. 1504, 91
Bonnet, Theodore, 4. 1362
Book and map of all Europe, A, 1. 2141
Book and news trade gazette, 3. 84; 4. 100
Book-auction records, 4. 106
book auctions
    nineteenth century, 3. 85
    twentieth century, 4. 105–6
book binding
    Renaissance to Restoration, 1. 935–40
    Restoration and eighteenth century, 2. 289–92
    nineteenth century, 3. 67–70
    twentieth century, 4. 79
Book circular, 3. 82
Book collector, 4. 110
Book-collector's quarterly, 4. 110
book collectors,
    Renaissance to Restoration, 1. 995–1006
    Restoration and eighteenth century, 2. 309–12
    nineteenth century, 3. 85–8
    twentieth century, 4. 107–10
Book craftsman, 4. 83
Book-dealers' weekly, 4. 108
book design, twentieth century, 4. 83–90
Book exchange (1863), 3. 85
Book exchange (1909), 4. 110
Book exchange (1948), 4. 108

Book finder, 4. 110, 117
Book for the train, 4. 1377
Book guild, 4. 118
Book handbook, 4. 110
Book hour, 4. 118
book illustration
    Renaissance to Restoration, 1. 939–42
    Restoration and eighteenth century, 2, 291–4
    nineteenth century, 3. 61–8
    twentieth century, 4. 88–90
Book index, 4. 117
book jackets, 4. 90
Book list, 4. 118
Book lover, 4, 110
Book-lover's magazine, 4. 108
Book monthly, 4. 117
Book of a ghostly father, 1. 1088
Book of beauty, 3. 1875
Book of book-plates, 4. 108
Book of common order, 1. 2440
Book of common prayer, 1. 1887–96
Book of fun, 2. 380
Book of oddities, 2. 412
Book of poems by the Poet's fellowship, A, 4. 1364
Book of the craft of dying, 1. 504–5
Book of the names of all parishes. . .in England and Wales, A, 1. 2134
Book of the Poet's Club, 4. 1360
Book of trades, 3. 1107
book plates
    Restoration and eighteenth century, 2. 309–10
    twentieth century, 4. 108
Book-prices current, 4. 106
book production and distribution
    Renaissance, 1. 925–1006
        authorship and copyright, 1. 975–8
        bibliography, 1. 925–8
        book binding, 1. 935–40
        book collecting, 1. 995–1006
        book illustration, 1. 939–42
        book trade, 1. 971–6
        libraries, 1. 985–96
        lists and catalogues, 1. 977–86
        manuscript books, 1. 929–36
        paper, 1. 927–30
        printers and booksellers
            general, 1. 955–60
            Irish, 1. 969–70
            London, 1. 959–66
            provinces, 1. 965–8
            Scottish, 1. 967–70
            Welsh, 1. 969–70
        printing abroad, 1. 969–72
        printing, history, 1. 941–50
        publication and distribution, 1. 951–2

Bourrit, Marc Théodore, 2. 1423
Boursault, Edmé, 2. 989
Bousfield, Henry Brougham, 3. 1672
Bouvet, Joachim, 2. 1435
Bouyer, R. G. A., 3. 1718
Bow bells (1862), 3. 1814–15, 1835
Bow bells (1919), 4. 1364
Bowater papers, 4. 78
Bowden, Charles Topham, 2. 1406
Bowden, John William, 3. 1626
Bowden, Samuel, 2. 642
Bowdler, Thomas, 2. 1427
Bowen, Edward E., 3. 1697, 1727
Bowen, Elizabeth Dorothea Cole, 4. 534–5
'Bowen, Marjorie' (Gabrielle M. V. Campbell), 4. 535–8, 799
Bower, Archibald, 2. 1711, 1294
Bowers, Georgina, 3. 1706
Bowes, James S., 3. 1791
Bowes-Lyon, Lilian Helen, 4. 241
Bowker, W., 4. 1384
Bowle, John, 2. 1782
Bowles, Caroline Anne, 3. 368–9
Bowles, Edward, 1. 2091, 2100
Bowles, John, 3. 1718
Bowles, Thomas Gibson, 3. 1764, 1815, 1817; 4. 1362
Bowles, William Lisle, 2. 642–4
Bowlker, Richard, 2. 1559
Bowman, Anne, 3. 1102
Bown, Maud, 3. 1828
Bownas, Samuel, 2. 1465
Bowra, Sir Maurice, 4. 1011–12
Bowrey, Thomas, 2. 1414, 1433
Bowring, Sir John, 3. 369–70, 1675, 1677, 1678, 1764, 1855
Bowring, Lewin Bentham, 3. 1675
Bowtell, John, 2. 292
Bowyear, William, 2. 162
Bowyer, William, 2. 263
Box, Charles, 3. 1696, 1697
Boxall, T., 3. 1695
boxing
    Restoration and eighteenth century, 2. 1562–4
    nineteenth century 3. 1692–3
Boy's own magazine, 3. 1849
Boyars, Arthur, 4. 1376, 1397
Boyce, Samuel, 2. 644
Boyd, Andrew Kennedy Hutchinson, 3. 1371
Boyd, Archibald, 3. 916
Boyd, Elizabeth, 2. 993
Boyd, Frank M., 3. 1764, 1815
Boyd, Henry, 3. 370
Boyd, Hugh, 2. 1286, 1444
Boyd, John, 4. 1377

Boyd, Mark Alexander, 1. 2422
Boyd, Percy, 3. 1846
Boyd, Robert, 1. 2455
Boyd, Zachary, 1. 2456, 1912
Boydell, John, 2. 279
Boyer, Abel, 2. 1707, 1294, 1313, 1322, 1323
Boyer, Jean Baptiste de, Marquis d'Argens, 2. 1502–3, 90, 138, 994, 995, 997
Boyle, Eleanor Vere, 3. 1102
Boyle, Frederick, 3. 1764
Boyle, John, 5th Earl of Cork and Orrery, 2. 1422
Boyle, Robert, 1. 2340; 2. 1903
Boyle, Robert Whelan, 3. 1791
Boyle, Roger, 1st Earl of Orrery, 2. 769–70, 977, 978, 981, 1. 2058
Boyle, William, 3. 1939
Boyle's court guide, 3. 1879
Boyle's paper, 2. 1376
Boys, John, 1. 1936
Boys, Thomas Shotter, 3. 65
Boys friend, 4. 819
Boys of England, 3. 1825
Boys of our Empire, 3. 1825
Boys of the Empire, 3. 1825
Boys' chronicle, 4. 1384
Boys' comic journal, 3. 1826
Boys' illustrated news, 3. 1826
Boys' newspaper, 3. 1825
Boys' own paper, 3. 1825
Boys' standard, 3. 1825
Boys' world, 3. 1825
Boyse, Samuel, 2. 537–8
Bozon, Nicole, 1. 794
Braam Houckgeest, A. E. van, 2. 1444
Brabourne, Edward Hugessen Knatchbull-Hugessen, 1st Baron, 3. 1103
Bracciolini, Francesco, 1. 897
Bracciolini, Poggio, 1. 857
Brace, W. R., 4. 84
Brack, A., 4. 1388
Bracken, Henry, 2. 1553, 1903
Brackley, Elizabeth, Lady, 1. 1732
Brackley, Thomas Egerton, 1st Viscount, 1. 999
Bracton, Henry of, 1. 772–3
Bradbrook, Muriel Clara, 4. 1012–13
Bradbury, J., 3. 1680
Bradbury and Evans, 3. 1790, 1816, 1821, 1825, 1827, 1839, 1848
Bradby, Anne Barbara, 4. 331–2
Braddon, Mary Elizabeth, 3. 1039–40, 1850
Bradford, John (d. 1555), 1. 1936–7
Bradford, John (1750–1805), 2. 1787
Bradford, William, 1. 2157, 2159, 2277
Bradford, library, 2. 305
Bradford chronicle, 3. 1799

Bradford daily argus, 3. 1803; 4. 1404
Bradford daily chronicle and mail, 3. 1799
Bradford daily telegraph, 3. 1797, 4. 1402
Bradford daily times, 3. 1798
Bradford evening mail, 3. 1799
Bradford observer, 3. 1798, 1831
Bradford telegraph and argus, 3. 1797; 4. 1402, 1404
Bradlaugh, Charles, 3. 1764, 1819
Bradley, A., 4. 1385
Bradley, Andrew Cecil, 4. 1013
Bradley, Cuthbert, 3. 1707
Bradley, Edward, 3. 914–15, 1684
Bradley, Francis Herbert, 3. 1522–5
Bradley, Harold F., 4. 1377
Bradley, Henry, 3. 1639
Bradley, James, 2. 1903
Bradley, Katherine Harris, 3. 626–7
Bradley, Margaret Louisa, 3. 1083
Bradley, Richard, 2. 1558, 1294
Bradley, Thomas, 2. 1312
Bradshaw and Co., George, 3. 57; 4. 80
Bradshaw, Henry (d. 1513), 1. 649, 1088
Bradshaw, Henry (1831–86), 3. 1639–40
Bradshaw's journal, 3. 1847
Bradshaw's Manchester journal, 3. 1847
Bradshaw's monthly . . . guide, 3. 1881
Bradshaw's railway companion, 3. 1881
Bradshaw's railway gazette, 3. 1827
Bradshaw's railway guide, 3. 1881
Bradshaw's railway time tables, 3. 1881
Bradstreet, Anne, 1. 1300–1
Bradstreet, John, 2. 1466
Bradwardine, Thomas, 1. 797
Brady, Cheyne, 3. 1845, 1846
Bragg, Sir William Henry, 4. 1244–5
Brailovsky, Alexander, 4. 1369
Brailsford, Henry Noel, 4. 1141–2
Brain: a journal of neurology, 3. 1858
Brainerd, David, 2. 1463
Braithwaite, John, 2. 1448
'Bramah, Ernest' (Ernest Bramah Smith), 4. 538–9
Bramhall, John, 1. 2337
Brampton, Thomas, 1. 684
Brampton's penitential psalms, 1. 480
Bramston, James, 2. 538
Brand, Adam, 2. 1435
Brand, Barbarina, Baroness Dacre, 3. 370–1
Brand, Hannah, 2. 826
Brand, John (1668?–1738), 2. 1399
Brand, John (1744–1806), 2. 1731–2
'Brandane, John' (John MacIntyre), 4. 913–14
Brandes, Johann Christian, 2. 1537
Brandon, Samuel, 1. 1461

Brandon-Cox, Hugh, 4. 1378
Bransby, John, 2. 1350
Brant, Sebastian, 1. 879–80
Brass halo, 3. 1867
Brassey, Anne, Baroness, 3. 1670
Brassey, Thomas, 1st Earl, 3. 1880
Brassey, Thomas Allnutt, 2nd Earl, 3. 1880
Brathwait, Richard, 1. 2020–2, 1336, 1911, 2038, 2044, 2048, 2057, 2316
Braun, B., 4. 57
Braver-Mann, Barnet, 4. 1369
Bray, Anna Eliza, 3. 711–12
Bray, Charles, 3. 1605
Bray, William, 2. 1404
Braybrooke, Neville, 4. 1375, 1377
Brayley, Edward William, 3. 1843
Brazen nose, 4. 1397
Brazen trumpet, 2. 1338
Brazil, Angela, 4. 790
Breakfast for the freeman, A, 2. 1385
Breed, R. A., 4. 1379, 1382, 1383
Breefe notes of the river Amazones, 1. 2163
Breif description of the people [of Virginia], A, 1. 2153
Bremer, Fredrika, 3. 146–7
Bremner, Christina S., 3. 1748
Bremner, Robert, 3. 1679
Brémond, Gabriel de, 2. 1505, 978, 979
Brenan, Edward Fitzgerald, 4. 1014
Brenan, Gerald, 4. 1014
'Brenda' (Mrs G. Castle Smith), 3. 1104
Brent, 2. 386
Brent-Dyer, Elinor, 4. 801
Brentano, Clemens, 3. 1109
Brereton, Austin, 3. 1124
Brereton, Frederick Sadleir, 4. 791
Brereton, Henry, 1. 2079
Brereton, J., 1. 2276
Brereton, Owen Salusbury, 2. 1404
Brereton, Thomas, 2. 1276, 1294
Brereton, Sir William, 1. 2128
Brerewood, Edward, 1. 865, 2120
Brerewood, Thomas, 2. 538
Bresslau, Marcus, 3. 1822
Bretnor, T., 1. 2038
Breton, Nicholas, 1. 1027–9, 1335, 2027, 2030, 2044, 2048, 2054
Breton lays, 1. 435–42
Brett, Edwin John, 3. 1825, 1826; 4. 1352
Brett, Peter, 2. 1378, 1379
Brett, Samuel, 1. 2129
Brett, Thomas, 2. 1621–2
Brett's miscellany, 2. 1378, 1379
Breval, John Durant, 2. 538–9, 1417
Brewer, Anthony, 1. 1732

Bristol oracle (1745), 2. 1354
Bristol playgoer, 4. 849
Bristol Poets Fellowship quarterly, 4. 1367
Bristol post-boy, 2. 1354
Bristol presentments: exports for the year, 2. 1355
Bristol presentments: imports for the year, 2. 1355
Bristol spectator (1777), 2. 1347
Bristol spectator (1800), 2. 1347
Bristol times, 3. 1797
Bristol University College gazette, 4. 1392
Bristol weekly intelligencer, 2. 1354
Bristol weekly mercury (1715?), 2. 1354
Bristol weekly mercury (1878), 4. 1399
Bristow, James, 2. 1443
Britain, 2. 1274
Britain's genius: or the weekly correspondent, 2. 1324
Britains remembrancer, 1. 2100
Britanicus Vapulans, 1. 2099
Britannia (1839), 3. 1813
Britannia (1896), 4. 1404
Britannia (and Eve) (1928), 4. 1406
Britannia (1950), 4. 1408
Britannia abroad, 4. 1406
Britannia curiosa, 2. 1404
Britannia quarterly, 4. 1363
Britannia rediviva, 2. 327
Britannia's delight, 2. 427
Britannic magazine, 2. 1310
British Actors' Equity. . .annual report, 4. 867, 874
British album, 2. 412
British almanac of the Society for the Diffusion of Useful Knowledge, 3. 1877
British amateur (journalist), 4. 1379–80
British amateur journalism, 4. 1384
British and American intelligencer, 3. 1810
British and colonial printer, 3. 32, 61; 4. 81
British and foreign medical review, 3. 1856
British and foreign review, 3. 1856, 1865
British annual and epitome of the progress of science, 3. 1877
British annual of literature, 4. 118, 1373
British antidote to Caledonian poison, 2. 383
British Apollo (1708), 2. 1321, 1344
British Apollo (1711), 2. 347
British Apollo (1792), 2. 416
British architect, 3. 1851
British art printer, 3. 62
British book news, 4. 118
British book trade directory, 4. 100
British books, 4. 100
British books to come, 4. 118
British booksellers, 4. 107
British censor, 2. 1279

British champion, 2. 1330
British chess magazine, 3. 1694
British chronicle (Kelso 1784), 2. 1378
British chronicle: or Pugh's Hereford journal, 2. 1358
British commonwealthsman, 2. 1283
British critic: a new review (1793), 2. 1309; 3. 1840–1
British critic, quarterly theological review, 3. 1841, 1855, 1865
British editorial, 4. 1408
British Empire paper, stationery and printing trades journal, 3. 82
British Empire review, 3. 1854
British film industry year book, 4. 58
British Film Institute, its journals, 4. 57
British film journal, 4. 57
British Film Producers' Association, its annual report, 4. 58
British film review, 4. 58
British film-studio mirror, 4. 57
British film yearbook, 4. 58
British films, 4. 57
British freeholder and Saturday evening journal, 3. 1813
British gazette, 4. 1406
British gazette and public advertiser (1776), 2. 1335
British gazette and Sunday monitor (1780), 2. 1336
British guardian and Protestant advocate, 3. 1813
British Harlequin, 2. 1277
British imperial calendar, 3. 1880
British intelligencer (1706), 2. 1293
British intelligencer (1743), 2. 1331
British journal, 2. 1325
British kinema chronicle, 4. 56
British Kinematograph Society, its journals, 4. 57
British kinematography, 4. 57
British librarian, 2. 1298
British library year book, 4. 117
British lithographer, 3. 62
British luminary, 3. 1809
British lyre, 2. 418
British magazine (1746), 2. 1298
British magazine (1747), 2. 1371
British magazine (1760), 2. 1302
British magazine (1772), 2. 1305
British magazine (1800), 2. 1312
British magazine (1830), 3. 1845
British magazine and review, 2. 1307
British medical journal, 3. 1826
British melody, 2. 367
British merchant (1713), 2. 1345
British merchant (1719), 2. 1325

British Mercury (1643), 1. 2099
British mercury (1710), 2. 1322
British mercury (1787), 2. 1336
British mercury (1798), 2. 1312, 1338
British mercury: or weekly pacquet (1733), 2. 1327
British mercury and evening advertiser (1780), 2. 1336
British military library, 2. 1312
British miner and general newsman, 3. 1820
British miscellany (1762), 2. 383
British miscellany (1765?), 2. 386
British miscellany (1779), 2. 1306
British monitor, 3. 1809
British mothers' family magazine, 3. 1847
British mothers' journal, 3. 1847
British mothers' magazine, 3. 1847
British motion picture news, 4. 57
British Muse (1738), 2. 366
British Muse (1775), 2. 395
British Muse (1800?), 2. 427
British Museum
    library catalogues, 1. 7
    manuscripts, 1. 9
    Renaissance to Restoration, 1. 985
    Restoration and eighteenth century, 2. 303
    nineteenth century, 3. 87
British museum, 2. 1349
British Museum quarterly, 4. 117
British musical miscellany, 2. 363
British Neptune, 3. 1808
British Nestor, 2. 1278
British observator, 2. 1327
British Orpheus, 2. 368
British palladium, 2. 1313
British paper, 4. 78
British Parnassus, 2. 348
British phoenix, 2. 383
British physician, 2. 1345
British poetical miscellany, 2. 427, 1350
British postal guide, 3. 1881
British press, 3. 1789
British printer, 3. 61; 4. 81
British public characters, 2. 1314
British Puppet and Model Theatre Guild: junior news, 4. 880
British Puppet and Model Theatre Guild: wartime bulletin, 4. 860, 880
British puppet theatre, 4. 861, 880
British quarterly review, 3. 1857, 1866
British queen and statesman, 3. 1810
British review (1902), 4. 1356
British review (1913), 4. 1361
British review and London critical journal, 3. 1843, 1860
British songs, 2. 378

British songster (1788), 2. 409
British songster (1791), 2. 414
British songster: or Dibdin's delight (1793), 2. 418
British songwriter and poet, 4. 74, 1374
British spouter, 2. 394
British spy (1725), 2. 1326
British spy (Derby 1727), 2. 1357
British spy (1752), 2. 1332
British stage and literary cabinet, 3. 1123
British statesman (1819), 3. 1790
British statesman (1842), 3. 1819
British tariff, 3. 1881
British telescope, 2. 1313
British television year book, 4. 60, 864
British theatre, 4. 828, 868
British traveller, 3. 1792
British weekly, 3. 1815
British weekly mercury, 2. 1322
British worker, 4. 1406
British year book, 3. 1878
Briton (1723), 2. 1277
Briton, A. (1757?), 2. 1333
Briton (1762), 2. 1283, 1334
Briton (1793), 2. 1351
Briton abroad, A, 3. 1681
Brittons bowre of delights, 1. 1009
Brittain, Vera Mary, 4. 1397
Broad, Charlie Dunbar, 4. 1245
Broad, 4. 1396
Broad arrow, 3. 1826
Broad views, 4. 1405
'Broadbottom, Jeffrey' (W. Guthrie), 2. 1331
'Broadcast', 4. 878
Broadcast listeners' year book, 4. 60, 864
Broadcaster, 4. 60
broadcasting, 4. 58–60
Broadhurst, F., 3. 1745
Broadhurst, Thomas, 3. 1745
Broadsheet, A. (1902), 4. 1356
Broadsheet (1942), 4. 1375
Broadside, A, 4. 1358
broadside ballads, 1. 2041–4
Broadway (annual), 3. 1851
Brobdigranta, 4. 1394
Brodie, Alexander, 2. 2047
Brodrick, George Charles, 3. 1764
Brodrick, William, 3. 1701
Brogan, Sir Denis William, 4. 1142
Broke, Arthur, 1. 1088–9
Broke, Thomas, 1. 1089
Bromby, C. H., 3. 1848
Brome, Alexander, 1. 1301–2
Brome, James, 2. 1398, 1416
Brome, Richard, 1. 1733–4, 2040
Brome Abraham (ME), 1. 737–8

Bromley, Eliza Nugent, 2. 1007
Bromley, Thomas, 2. 1655
Bromley, William, 2. 1413
Bronder, G., 3. 1810
Bronder, H., 3. 1810
Bronowski, Jacob, 4. 1368, 1394
Brontë, Anne, 3. 867
Brontë, Charlotte, 3. 865-6
Brontë, Emily Jane, 3. 866-7
Brontës, The, 3. 864-73
Bronterre's national reformer, 3. 1818
Bronx, 4. 1386
Brooke, Charlotte, 2. 248; 3. 1889
Brooke, Frances, 2. 1000, 1002, 1005, 1282
Brooke, Fulke Greville, 1st Baron, 1. 1057-9, 2314
Brooke, Henry, 2. 785-6, 125, 176, 1001, 1004, 1561
Brooke, J. W., 2. 1283
Brooke, Sir James, 3. 1676
Brooke, Leonard Leslie, 4. 789
Brooke, N., 2. 1430
Brooke, Robert Greville, 2nd Baron, 1. 2333
Brooke, Rupert Chawner, 4. 241-3
Brooke, Samuel, 1. 1765
Brooke, Stopford Augustus, 3. 1422-3, 1611
Brookes, Richard, 2. 1558-9
Brooks, Charles William Shirley, 3. 1147, 1764, 1821, 1825
Brooks, Francis, 2. 1446
Brooks, Sydney, 4. 1351
'Brooksby' (Edward Pennell Elmhirst), 3. 1706
Broom, 4. 1365
Brooman, R. A. 3. 1827
Broome, Mary Anne, Lady, 3. 1104
Broome, William, 2. 539
Brophy, John, 4. 539-40
Brother's gift, 2. 1021
Brotherhood, 3. 1820
Brotherly love, 2. 1290
Brothers: or treachery punish'd, 2. 992
Brough, Robert Barnabas, 3. 1147-8, 1814
Brougham, Henry Peter, 1st Baron Brougham and Vaux, 3. 1484-6, 1719
Broughton, Hugh, 1. 1937
Broughton, John, 2. 1844
Broughton, John Cam Hobhouse, Baron, 3. 1677
Broughton, Rhoda, 3. 1041
Broughton, Thomas, 2. 1777
Brown and Son, John, 3. 57
Brown, Andrew, 2. 2057
Brown, Colin Rae, 3. 1876
Brown, D., 3. 1695
Brown, Edward, 2. 1449
Brown, Ford Madox, 3. 65

Brown, George Douglas, 3. 1046
Brown, George Henry, 3. 1880
Brown, Ivor John Carnegie, 4. 1014-15
Brown, John (1610?-79), 2. 2033
Brown, John (1715-66), 2. 826-7, 41, 176, 1402
Brown, John (1722-87), 2. 2041
Brown, John (fl. 1819), 3. 1682
Brown, John (1810-82), 3. 1372
Brown, John Hoskins, 3. 1880
Brown, John Paton, 3. 1850
'Brown, Maggie' (Margaret Hamer), 3. 1106
Brown, Oliver Madox, 3. 1041
Brown, Pamela, 4. 814
Brown, Peter, 3. 1819
Brown, R. (fl. 1729), 2. 1565
Brown, Sir Ridyard, 3. 1714
Brown, Robert (1757-1831), 2. 1373
Brown, Samuel Sneade, 3. 1674
Brown, Slater, 4. 1365
Brown, Thomas (1663-1704), 2. 1044-6, 984, 1342
Brown, Thomas (1778-1820), 3. 1525-6
Brown, Thomas (1822-82) 3. 1702
Brown, Thomas (fl. 1830), sportsman, 3. 1704
Brown, Thomas Edward, 3. 512-13
Brown, W. (fl. 1793), 2. 1374
Brown, William (fl. 1796), 2. 1372, 1376
Brown book (1864), 3. 1882
Brown book (1906), 4. 1396
Browne, Edward, 2. 1397, 1409
Browne, Edward Granville, 3. 1676
Browne, Felicia Dorothea, 3. 383-4
Browne, Frances, 3. 917, 1091
Browne, George Forrest, 3. 1709
Browne, Gordon Frederick, 3. 1106
Browne, Hablot Knight, 3. 65
Browne, Humphry, 1. 2045
Browne, Isaac Hawkins, 2. 539-40
Browne, J., 1. 2278
Browne, James, 3. 1803
Browne, Sir John, 2. 1896
Browne, Moses, 2. 540, 1558, 1777
Browne, Patrick, 2. 1465
Browne, Peter, 2. 1856
Browne, Robert, 1. 1937-8
Browne, Samuel, 1. 959
Browne, Simon, 2. 1673-4, 1276
Browne, T. B., 3. 1758
Browne, Sir Thomas, 1. 2228-33; 2. 104-5, 158, 189, 207, 233, 1557, 1794
Browne, William, of Tavistock (1590?-1645?), 1. 1195, 1765
Browne, William George, 2. 1452
Browne, Wynyard Barry, 4. 919-20
Browning, Elizabeth Barrett, 3. 435-9, 111, 138

Browning, Robert, 3. 439–61, 111, 130, 138
Brownlee, W. M., 3. 1715
Brownrig(g), Ralph, 1. 1989
Bruce, Carlton, 3. 1101
Bruce, Dorita Fairlie, 4. 799–800
Bruce, George Windham Hamilton Knight, 3. 1672
Bruce, Henry Austin, 1st Baron Aberdare, 3. 1727
Bruce, James, 2. 1451
Bruce, Michael, 2. 2021–2, 239
Bruce, Peter Henry, 2. 1396, 1471
Bruce, Robert, 1. 1938, 2440
Bruce, W. D., 3. 1803
Brudenell, Thomas, 1. 959
Bruin, Cornelis de, 2. 1435–6
Brunanburh, Battle of, 1. 239–40
Brunel, Antoine de, 2. 1410
Bruni, Leonardo (Aretinus), 1. 845, 2182
Brunner, John, 3. 1815
Brunner, Thomas, 3. 1677
Bruno, Giordano, 1. 886, 894
Bruno, Guido, 4. 1362
Bruno chap books, 4. 1362
Brunswick, or true blue, 3. 1809
'Brunt, Samuel', 2. 991
Brunton, Mary, 3. 712
Brunton, Thomas, 1. 797, 1937
Brusoni, Girolamo, 2. 1543, 975
Brussels cross, 1. 267
Brut, 1. 465
Bruto, Giammichele, 1. 886
Bruton, William, 1. 2080, 2147
Bry, Theodore de, 1. 2112
Bryan, Joseph, 1. 1907
Bryant, Sir Arthur Wynne Morgan, 4. 1143
Bryant, John Frederick, 2. 644
Bryant, Sophie, 3. 1730, 1748
Bryce, James, 1st Viscount, 3. 1486–7, 1672, 1676, 1681
Brydges, Grey, 5th Baron Chandos, 1. 2048
Brydges, Sir Samuel Egerton, 3. 1269–71; 2. 1013, 1309
Brydone, Patrick, 2. 1422
Brygon, William, 1. 997
'Bryher, W.' (A. W. Ellerman), 4. 1367
Bubble, 3. 1866
Buc, Sir George, 1. 2240
Bucer, Martin, 1. 845, 877
Buchan, Alexander, 2. 1400
Buchan, John, 1st Baron Tweedsmuir, 4. 540–4; 3. 1100, 1690
Buchanan, David (d. 1652), 1. 2135
Buchanan, David (d. 1848), 3. 1803, 1804
Buchanan, Francis, 3. 1673

Buchanan, George, 1. 2440–3, 853, 855, 856, 1902–3, 2119, 2132, 2275
Buchanan, James, 2. 1783
Buchanan, John, 2. 1406
Buchanan, John P., 3. 1692
Buchanan, Nathaniel, 3. 1671
Buchanan, Robert, 3. 1819
Buchanan, Robert Williams, 3. 615–17
Buchanan, William, 3. 1764, 1804
Buck, Sir George, 1. 2240
Buck below stairs, 2. 1286
Buck's bottle companion, 2. 395, 1560
Buck's delight (1746), 2. 372
Bucks delight (1764), 2. 385
Buck's delight (1783), 2. 403
Buck's delight (1798), 2. 425
Buck's delight: or merry fellow's companion (1799), 2. 426
Buck's merry companion, 2. 385
Buck's pocket companion, 2. 423
Bucke, Charles, 3. 1271–2
Buckeridge, Anthony Malcolm, 4. 812
Buckingham, George Villiers, 2nd Duke of, 2. 758–9
Buckingham, James Silk, 3. 1670, 1679, 1764, 1792, 1793, 1810, 1813, 1821, 1845
Buckingham, John Sheffield, Duke of, 2. 478–9
Buckinghamshire, general bibliography, 1. 15
Buckland, G., 3. 1856
Buckle, George E., 3. 1789
Buckle, Henry Thomas, 3. 1471–2
Buckler, Edward, 1. 1302
Buckley, — (fl. 1703), 2. 1293
Buckley, Samuel, 2. 263, 1321
Buckley, William, 3. 1677
Bucknill, Sir John Charles, 3. 1858
Buckstone, John Baldwin, 3. 1148
Budd, Thomas (fl. 1648), 1. 2104
Budd, Thomas (fl. 1685). 2. 1456
Budden, John, 4. 797
Budge, Lena, 4. 1385
Budgell, Eustace, 2. 1711–12, 1278, 1297, 1327
Budget (1779), 2. 1351
Budget (1782), 2. 1287
Budget (1799), 2. 1029
Budget (1911), 4. 1397
Budget exchange, 4. 82
Buds of genius, 3. 1107
Budworth, Joseph, 2. 1406
Buenting, Heinrich, 1. 2127
Buffier, Claude, 2. 1505
Buffon, George Louis Leclerc, Comte de, 2. 1505–6, 91
Bugbears, 1. 1418
Bugle blast, 4. 1375

Buik of King Alexander, 1. 424
Builder, 3. 1828, 1838
Builder's magazine, 2. 1305
Builder's reporter and engineering times, 3. 1828
Builder's weekly reporter, 3. 1828
Building news, 3. 1828
Bulgarin, Faddey Venediktovich, 3. 151
Bulkeley, John, 2. 1478
Bull, George, 2. 1605–6
Bull, Henry, 1. 1938
Bull, Margaret, 4. 1385, 1386
Bull-finch, 2. 372
Bull's eye (1898), 4. 1355
Bull's eye (1912), 4. 1383
Bulldog, 3. 1868
Bullein, William, 1. 2026
Bullen, Arthur Henry, 3. 1640
Bulletin of the Leeds Science Fiction League, 4. 1390
Bullett, Gerald William, 4. 544–5, 801
Bullinger, Henricus, 1. 845, 877
Bullionist, 3. 1824
Bulloch, John, 3. 1852
Bullock, Christopher, 2. 786
Bullock, W. J., 3. 1695
Bullock, William, 1. 2164
Bullough, Edward, 4. 1015
Bullring, 4. 1388
Bulmer, William, 2. 263–4; 3. 57
Bülow, M., Baroness von, 3. 1746
Bulteel, John, 2. 976
Bulwer-Lytton, Edward George Earle Lytton, 1st Baron Lytton, 3. 917–21, 113, 132, 139, 1844, 1846
Bulwer-Lytton, Rosina Wheeler, Lady, 3. 921–2
Bump, 3. 1868; 4. 1396
Bumps, 4. 1397
Bunbury, Henry William, 2. 1554–5
Bunbury, Henry William St Pierre, 3. 1676
Bunbury, Selina, 3. 1102
Bunce, John Thackray, 3. 1795, 1797
Bungiana, 2. 378
Bunn, Alfred, 3. 1128
Bunting, Basil, 4. 243–4
Bunting, Edward, 3. 1889
Bunting, Jabez, 3. 1840
Bunting, Sir Percy William, 3. 1850
Bunyan, John, 2. 875–80, 114, 162, 182, 195, 199, 207, 1018; 1. 1329
'Bunyano, Don Stephano', 2. 1023
Burbage's Nottingham chronicle, 2. 1364
Burbury, John, 2. 1410
Burchell, William John, 3. 1669
Burchett, Josiah, 2. 1458
urckhardt, John Lewis, 3. 1669, 1673–4

Burden, Mrs, 3. 1102
Burder, George, 2. 1787; 3. 1840
Burder, Henry F., 3. 1840
Burdett, Osbert Henry, 4. 1016
Burdon, William, 2. 1553
Burel, John, 1. 2422–3
Bürger, Gottfried August, 2. 1537, 166, 1561
Burges, Sir James Bland, 2. 644–5
Burgess, Anthony, 1. 2296
Burgess, Henry, 3. 1794
Burgess, Joseph, 3. 1820
Burgh, Benedict, 1. 648
Burgh, James, 2. 1284
Burghley, William Cecil, 1st Baron; 1. 865, 890, 920, 998
Burgon, John William, 3. 1626
Burgoyne, John, 2. 827, 176, 1470–1
Burke, Adela, 2. 1008
Burke, Anne, 2. 1012
Burke, Edmund, 2. 1184–91, 41–2, 105, 117, 158, 189, 1313, 1378, 1453, 1465
Burke, John, 3. 1879
Burke, Sir John Bernard, 3. 1879
Burke, Robert O'Hara, 3. 1677
Burke, Thomas, 4. 545–6
Burke, William, 2. 1465
Burke's genealogical and heraldic dictionary, 3. 1879
Burkhardt, C. B., 3. 1108
Burkhead, Henry, 1. 1734
Burkitt, William, 2. 162
Burlamaqui, Jean Jacques, 2. 1506, 91
burlesque
    Renaissance to Restoration, 1. 2025–30
    Restoration and eighteenth century, 2. 59–60, 317, 489–90
Burlettas, duets, interludes, 2. 405
Burley, Simon, 1. 997
Burley, Walter, 1. 798–9
Burnaby, Andrew, 2. 1469
Burnaby, Mrs. E. A. F., 3. 1709–10
Burnaby, Frederick Gustavius, 3. 1676
Burnaby, William, 2. 786
Burnand, Sir Francis Cowley, 3. 1690, 1764, 1793, 1825; 4. 1400
Burnby, John, 2. 1565
Burne, Nicol, 1. 2443
Burne-Jones, Sir Edward, 3. 65
Burnell, Henry, 1. 1734
Burnell, John, 2. 1437
Burnes, Sir Alexander, 3. 1674
Burnet, Gilbert, 2. 1685–90, 105, 114, 162–3, 1412
Burnet, Thomas (1635?–1715), 2. 1844, 1903
Burnet, Sir Thomas (1694–1753), 2. 1275

Byron, Henry James, 3. 1191–2, 1825
Byron, John, 2. 1478, 1479
Byron, Robert, 4. 1312–13
Bysset, Habakkuk, 1. 2471
By-stander (1789), 2. 1288
Bystander (1903), 4. 1404

C., E. (fl. 1595), 1. 1089
CEMA bulletin, 4. 874, 1374
C., G. (fl. 1576), 1. 1905
C., H. (fl. 1579), 1. 1089
C., H. (Harry Crouch), 4. 1372
C., J. (fl. 1579), 1. 1089
C., J. (fl. 1595), 1. 1089
C., J. (fl. 1603), 1. 1089
C., M. (fl. 1621), 1. 2157
C., R. (fl. 1614), 1. 1336
C., R. (fl. 1652), 1. 2067
C., Ro. (fl. 1609), 1. 2139
C., S. (fl. 1640), 1. 2057
C., T. gent. (fl. 1565–9), 1. 1089–90
C., T. (fl. 1623), 1. 2162
C., T. (Thomas Cooper), 1. 1960
C., T. (fl. 1698), 2. 1395, 1414, 1435
C., W. (fl. 1578–1602) pamphleteer, 1. 2076, 2078
C., W. (fl. 1585), 1. 2053
C., W. (fl. 1618), 1. 2056
C., W. (fl. 1774), 2. 1469
'Caballero, Fernán' (Cecilia Arrom de Ayala), 3. 142
Cabinet (1792), 2. 1337
Cabinet (1795), 2. 420, 1348, 1352
Cabinet (1807), 3. 1843
Cabinet annual register, 3. 1874
Cabinet for wit, 2. 375, 1280
Cabinet magazine, 2. 1311
Cabinet of choice jewels, A, 2. 336
Cabinet of curiosities, 2. 396
Cabinet of fancy, 2. 414
Cabinet of genius, 2. 408
Cabinet of love, 2. 416
Cabinet of modern art, 3. 1873
Cabinet of Momus, 2. 407
Cabinet of wit, 2. 423
Cabinet open'd, 2. 982
Cadell and Davies, 2. 279; 3. 77
Cadett, Herbert, 3. 1764
Cadman, Henry, 3. 1690
'Cadwallader, George' (James Ralph), 2. 1279
Cædmon, 1. 267–8
Cædmon's hymn, 1. 268–9
Caesar, Caius Julius, 1. 2130, 2167; 2. 1495
Caesar's revenge, 1. 1777
Caetani, Marguerite, 4. 1379
Caffyn, William, 3. 1698

Caian, 3. 1867; 4. 1393
Caiaphas' speech, 1. 740
Caine, Sir (Thomas Henry) Hall, 3. 1042
Caird, Edward, 3. 1526–7, 1611
Caird, John, 3. 1527, 1611, 1732
Caius, John, 1. 1821–2, 2182, 2366
Calais, chronicle of, 1. 2206
Calamy, Edmund (1600–66) 1. 1990
Calamy, Edmund (1671–1732), 2. 1671, 1399, 1804
Caldecott, John, 3. 1797
Caldecott, Ralph, 3. 65
Calder, Robert, 2. 2041–2
Calder-Marshall, Arthur, 4. 546–7, 1371
Calderon, George Leslie, 4. 920
Calderón de la Barca, Pedro, 2. 201; 3. 142
Calderwood, David, 1. 2456–7, 1909–10, 2241
Calderwood, Henry, 3. 1527
Calderwood, Margaret, 2. 1419
Caldwell, Anne, 3. 948
Caledonia, 4. 1385
Caledoniad, 2. 395
Caledonian bee, 2. 420
Caledonian chronicle, 2. 1376
Caledonian gazetteer, 2. 1375
Caledonian magazine (1783), 2. 1374
Caledonian magazine (1786), 2. 1373
Caledonian magazine (1788), 2. 1373
Caledonian mercury, 2. 1375; 3. 1803
Caledonian miscellany, 2. 367
Caledonian Muse, 2. 405
Caledonian weekly magazine, 2. 1372
Calendar (of modern letters), 4. 1366, 1345
Calendar of shepherds, 1. 1090
'Calico, Catherine', 3. 1107
Caligula-Jesus poems (ME), 1. 514
Caliope, 2. 410
Call, Wathen Mark Wilks, 3. 513, 1865
Call board, 4. 867
Call boy, 4. 878
Call sheet, 4. 867, 874
Call to the races at Newmarket, 2. 1552
Callanan, Jeremiah J., 3. 1899
Callander, John, 2. 1784, 2062, 1475; 1. 2112
Callcott, Maria, 3. 1089
Callières, François de, 2. 66
Callimachus, 2. 1490
Calliope (1739), 2. 367
Calliope (1777), 2. 397
Calliope (1788), 2. 409
Callipaedia (1710), 2. 346
Callipaedia (1712), 2. 347
Calsabigi, Ranieri de, 2. 1543
Calverley, Charles Stuart, 3. 617
Calvert, Edward, 3. 65

Campbell, George Douglas, 8th Duke of Argyll, 3. 513, 1512–13, 1605
Campbell, Sir Gilbert Edward, 3. 1853
Campbell, H., 3. 1728
Campbell, Ignatius Roy Dunnachie, 4. 244–6, 1379
Campbell, James, 2. 1560
Campbell, John, 2. 1714, 992, 1392, 1401, 1419, 1453, 1805
Campbell, John McLeod, 3. 1605
Campbell, Lawrence Dundas, 3. 1877
Campbell, Patrick, 2. 1474
Campbell, Reginald John, 3. 1611
Campbell, Roy, 4. 244–6, 1379
Campbell, Seamus, 4. 110
Campbell, Thomas (1733–95), 2. 1404
Campbell, Thomas (fl. 1767), traveller in America, 2. 1467
Campbell, Thomas (1777–1844), 3. 261–3, 1765, 1843, 1845, 1875
Campbell, W., 2. 1294
Campe, Joachim Heinrich, 2. 1537, 1032
Campion, Edmund, 1. 2134, 853
Campion, Samuel Smith, 3. 1801
Campion, Thomas, 1. 1069–71, 2074, 2314
Campion, William, 3. 1844
Campion, William Magan, 3. 1732
Camus, Jean Pierre, 1. 865–6, 873, 2061; 2. 978
Canary bird, 2. 371
Cancer: comoedia, 1. 1777
Candid, 4. 1362
Candid disquisition, A, 2. 389
Candid friend, 4. 1356
Candid inquiry into the. . .bucks, 2. 390
Candid review and literary repository, 2. 1304
'Candidus, Agricola', 2. 1332
Candle, 4. 1373
Candlish, Robert Smith, 3. 1619
'Candour', 2. 1567
Cannan, Charles, 3. 1868
'Cannan, Denis' (Dennis Pullein-Thompson), 4. 920–1
Cannan, Gilbert, 4. 547–8
Cannan, Joanna Maxwell, 4. 804
Canne, John, 1. 2106, 2109; 2. 1313
Canning, George, the elder (1770–1827), 2. 645–6, 1350, 1352; 3. 1870
Canning, George, the younger (1801–20), 3. 1870
Canning's farthing post, 2. 1332
canoeing, 3. 1711–12
Canon, John, 1. 788
Cant, Andrew, 1. 2457
Cantab (1873), 3. 1866
Cantab (1898), 3. 1866
'Cantabrigiensis, Chimaericus', 2. 1348

Cantemir, Demetrius, 2. 1417
Canterbury
    Renaissance to Restoration
        libraries, 1. 989–90
        printing and bookselling, 1. 966
    Restoration and eighteenth century
        libraries, 2. 306
        magazines, 2. 1349
        newspapers, 2. 1355
        periodical essays, 2. 1347
        printing and bookselling, 2. 267
Canterbury Cathedral Library, 2. 306
Canterbury cricket week, 3. 1697
Canterbury journal, 2. 1355
Canterbury tales of Chaucer (1737), 2. 365
Canterbury tales of Chaucer (1741), 2. 368
Cantillon, Richard, 2. 1896
Canting academy, 2. 331
Canton, William, 3. 618, 1110
Cantus: songs and fancies, 2. 328
Caorsin, Gulielmus, 1. 2136, 2075
Cap and gown, 4. 1398
Cap of liberty, 3. 1818
Capell, Edward, 2. 1752–3
Capes, Bernard E. J., 3. 1852
Capes, Frederick, 3. 1848
Capes, J. B., 3. 1789
Capes, John Moore, 3. 1848
Capgrave, John, 1. 663–5
Capitalist, 3. 1824
Capper, Benjamin Pitts, 3. 1880
Capper, James, 2. 1441
Capper, R., 3. 1880
Capper, Samuel James, 3. 1681
Capriata, Pietro Giovanni, 2. 1543
Caps well fit, 2. 406
Captaine Thomas Stukeley, 1. 1472
Capture of the five boroughs, see *Poems of the Anglo-Saxon Chronicle*, 1, 295
Capuchin annual, 4. 1368
Caraccioli, Charles, 2. 999
Caraman, Philip, 4. 1351
Caravel, 4. 1371
Cardano, Girolamo, 1. 845, 2183; 2. 1543
Cardiff times, 3. 1831; 4. 1401
Cardinal's hat, 4. 1397
Cardonne, Denis Dominique de, 2. 1506
cards
    Restoration and eighteenth century, 2. 1566–8
    nineteenth century, 3. 1693
Carducci, Giosuè, 3. 136
Cardus, Sir Neville, 4. 1313
Care, Henry, 2. 1318, 1339, 1341
Careri, John F. C., 2. 1400, 1417, 1477
Carew, Bampfylde-Moore, 2. 1401

Carew, George, Baron Carew and Earl of Totnes (1555–1629), 1. 2240
Carew, Sir George (d. 1612?), 1. 2237, 2139
Carew, Richard, 1. 1090, 2133, 2211–12, 2312
Carew, Thomas, 1. 1207–8, 1336, 1908–9
Carey, David, 3. 1792
Carey, George Savile, 2. 828
Carey, Henry, 2. 782–4, 1293
Carey, John, 3. 1100
Carey, Patrick, 1. 1302
Carey, Robert, 1st Earl of Monmouth, 1. 2247
Carey's general evening post, 2. 1387
Carey's Waterford packet, 2. 1390
Caribbean corners, 4. 1387
Caribbeana, 2. 368
Caritat, M. J. A. N. de, Marquis de Condorcet 2. 1507, 91–2
Carleill, Christopher, 1. 2151
Carlell, Lodowick, 1. 1735
Carleton, George, 1. 2240–1
Carleton, John William, 3. 1713, 1847
Carleton, Rowland, 2. 979
Carleton, William, 3. 713–15
Carli, Denis de, 2. 1447
Carlile, Mrs—, 3. 1818
Carlile, Christopher, 1. 1905
Carlile, Richard, 3. 1272, 77, 1765, 1817, 1818
Carlisle, libraries, 1. 990; 2. 306
Carlisle journal, 2. 1355
Carlisle museum, 2. 1349
Carlow journal, 2. 1387
Carlscroon, Jean du Mont, Baron de, 2. 1414
Carlton, Richard, 1. 1350
Carlton house magazine, 2. 1309
Carlyle, Alexander, 2. 2063
Carlyle, Alexander James, 3. 1868
Carlyle, Thomas, 3. 1248–70, 112, 130–1
Carmeni, Francesco, 1. 901, 2061
Carmichael, Elizabeth C., 4. 1357
Carmichael, John, 2. 1440
Carmichaell, James, 1. 2471
Carmina, 4. 1369
Carmina ad nobilissimum Thomam Holles, 2. 378
Carnan, Thomas, 2. 279
Carnaval, 4. 1377
Carnegie, Andrew, 3. 1793
Carnegie, David Wynford, 3. 1672, 1678
Carnegie, G. F., 3. 1702
Carnegie, James, 9th Earl of Southesk, 3. 1673
Carnell, E. J., 4. 1387
Carnie, William, 3. 1765
Carolina described, 2. 1456
Caroline de Montmorenci, 2. 1011
Caron, Frans, 2. 1431
Carpenter, Alexander, 1. 803

Carpenter, Edward, 3. 1423–4
Carpenter, J. W., 4. 1384, 1385
Carpenter, Joseph Estlin, 3. 1612
Carpenter, Lant, 3. 1719
Carpenter, Nathanael, 1. 2332, 2120
Carpenter, Stephen C., 2. 1444
Carpenter, William, 3. 1793, 1810, 1811, 1813, 1818, 1826
Carpenter, William Benjamin, 3. 1528
Carr, Alfred, 3. 1681
Carr, Comyns, 3. 1868
Carr, Edward Hallett, 4. 1145–6
Carr, Sir Emsley, 3. 1765, 1811
Carr, Joseph Williams Comyns, 3. 1852
Carr, Lascelles, 3. 1798, 1811
Carr, William, 2. 1409
Carrick recorder, 2. 1387
Carritt, Edgar Frederick, 4. 1246
'Carroll, Lewis' (Charles Lutwidge Dodgson), 3. 977–80, 1094, 1530, 1694
Carroll, Paul Vincent, 4. 921–2
Carroll, Susanna, 2. 781–2
Carroll, William, 2. 1845
Carruthers, Robert, 3. 1272–3
Carson, Lionel, 4. 825, 859
Carson, Oliver, 4. 1379, 1398
Carswell, Catherine Roxburgh, 4. 548
Carte, Thomas, 2. 1712
Carter, Elizabeth, 2. 1595–6
Carter, Francis, 2. 1423–4
Carter, Lionel, 4. 828
Carter, Matthew, 1. 2254
Carter, R., 3. 1868
Carteret, Sir George, 1. 2128
Carteret, Philip, 2. 1479
Cartier, Jacques, 1. 2150
Cartigny, Jean de, 1. 2061
Cartoon, 4. 1362
Cartwright, Elizabeth, 3. 1089
Cartwright, George (fl. 1650), 1. 1735
Cartwright, George (fl. 1792), 2. 1473
Cartwright, Mrs H., 2. 1007
Cartwright, John, 1. 2145
Cartwright, T., 1. 1962
Cartwright, W., 3. 1689
Cartwright, William, 1. 1765, 1302, 1990
Carve, Thomas, 1. 2128–9
Carver, Jonathan, 2. 1470
Cary, Amelia, Viscountess Falkland, 3. 1675
Cary, Arthur Joyce Lunel, 4. 548–51
Cary, Elizabeth, Viscountess Falkland, 1. 1735
Cary, Henry, 3rd Viscount Falkland, 1. 1736
Cary, Henry Francis, 3. 371–2
Cary, John, 2. 1896
Cary, Joyce, 4. 548–51

Cary, Patrick, 1. 1302
Cary, Walter, 1. 2026
Carye, Christopher, 1. 998
Carye, William, 1. 998
Caryll, John, 2. 759
Casanova de Seingalt, Giacomo, 2. 194, 1402
Casaubon, Isaac, 1. 2297, 2303
Casaubon, Meric, 1. 2303–4, 2297, 2333
Case, John, 1. 2330
Case of Mainwaring, Hawes, Payne, 1. 2159
Cashel Cathedral Library, 1. 990; 2. 306
Casimir, Matthias (Sarbiewski), 1. 855
Casino: a mock-heroic poem, 2. 1568
Casket: or hesperian magazine, 2. 1380
Casley, David, 2. 1775
Caslon, William, 2. 256
Cassandra, 2. 1293
Cassell, John, 3. 77–8, 1765, 1816, 1819, 1850
Cassell and Co, 3. 57, 1765, 1825, 1826, 1828,
   1850, 1851, 1852
Cassell's family magazine, 3. 1851
Cassell's illustrated family paper, 3, 1816
Cassell's magazine, 3. 1816, 1851; 4. 1350
Cassell's popular magazine, 4. 1355
Cassell's Saturday journal, 3. 1815; 4. 1403
Cassell's weekly, 4. 1366
Cassels, Walter Richard, 3. 1605
'Castalio', 2. 1287
Castañiza, Juan de, 1. 908
Caste, 4. 848
Castel of love, 1. 506
Castelden, G., 3. 1696
Castell, William, 1. 2164
Castell of Perseverance, 1. 1403
Castellain, Lois, 4. 809
Castelvetro, Giacopo, 1. 960
Casti, Giovanni Battista, 2. 1543; 3. 136
Castiglione, Baldassare, 1. 2183, 886–7; 2. 1543
Castillo, John, 3. 372
Castillo Solórzano, Alonso, 2. 202, 976
Castle, Egerton, 3. 1701
Castle courant, 2. 1383, 1384
Castle of labour, 1. 1090
Castlean, 4. 1384
Castleford, Thomas, 1. 464, 681
Castlemaine, Roger Palmer, Earl of, 2. 1410
Casual letters, 4. 1367
Casual observator, 2. 1344
Casuist, 2. 1346
Caswall, Edward, 3. 514, 1627
Cat, 4. 1381
Catacomb, 4. 1379
Catalogue of books continued, A, 2. 1339
Cataneo, Girolamo, 1. 2183
Catch club or merry companions (1705), 2. 343

Catch club (1787?), 2. 408
Catch that catch can or a new collection of catches
   (1663), 2. 329
Catch that catch can: or the musical companion
   (1667), 2. 329–30
Caterer, 2. 1350
Cates, Thomas, 1. 2151
Catesby, Mark, 2. 1461
Cathedral magazine, 2. 1305
Cather, Thomas, 3. 1672
Catherine the Great, 2. 216
Catholic directory, 3. 1880
Catholic journal, 3. 1822
Catholic keepsake, 3. 1876
Catholic standard, 3. 1823
Catholic University gazette, 3. 1869
Catholic vindicator, 3. 1822
Catholick intelligence, 2. 1317
Catholics, general literary bibliography, 1. 20
Catley, 2. 392
Catling, Thomas, 3. 1765, 1811
Catnach, James, 3. 78
Catnach Press, 3. 57
Cato, 1. 2167
Caton, William, 2. 1650
Cattermole, Richard, 3. 1875
Cattermole's historical annual, 3. 1875
Catullus, 2. 1495–6, 35
Cauche, François, 2. 1447
'Caudwell, Christopher' (Christopher St John
   Sprigg), 4. 1016–17
Caulfield, James, 2. 1808
Caumont, A. M. de, 2. 292
Caumont, Jean de, 1. 866
Caunter, Hobart, 3. 1875
Causerie, 4. 1374
Caussin, Nicholas, 1. 866
Causton, Bernard, 4. 1370
Cautionary lyrics (ME), 1. 515
Cave, Edward, 2. 264, 1295; 3. 1839
Cave, Richard, 3. 1839
'Caveat Emptor' (Sir George Stephen), 3. 1704
Cavell, Humphrey, 1. 1090
'Cavendish' (Henry Jones), 3. 1693, 1715
Cavendish, Francis William Henry, 3. 1880
Cavendish, George, 1. 1090, 2205–6
Cavendish, Harrie, 1. 2123
Cavendish, Henry, 2. 1903–4
Cavendish, Lady Jane, 1. 1732
Cavendish, Margaret, Duchess of Newcastle, 1.
   1303, 1736, 2058, 2252; 2. 976, 977, 1904
Cavendish, Michael, 1. 1349
Cavendish, William, 1st Duke of Newcastle, 1.
   1303, 1736–7; 2. 1552
Cavyl, — master, 1. 1090

Cawdrey, Robert, 1. 2030
Cawthorn, James, 2. 646
Cawthorne, G. J., 3. 1708
Caxton, William, 1. 667-74, 960-1
Caxton magazine, 4. 81
Caxtonian quarterly, 3. 62; 4. 81
Cay, Armistead, 3. 84
Cayley, Cornelius, 2. 1424
Cayley, George John, 3. 1680
Caylus, A. C. P. de Tubières Grimoard de Pestels de Levis, Comte de, 2. 1506
Cazotte, Jacques, 2. 1506
Cebes, 1. 2167
'Cecil' (Cornelius Tongue), 3. 1705
Cecil, Lord David, 4. 1017-18
Cecil, Edward, Viscount Wimbledon, 1. 2127
Cecil, Lord Edward Christian David Gascoyne, 4. 1017-18
Cecil, Richard, 3. 1616
Cecil, Robert A. T. G., 3rd Marquis of Salisbury, 3. 1857
Cecil, Sabina, 3. 1100
Cecil, William, 1st Baron Burghley, 1. 865, 890, 920, 998
Celebrated Mrs Pilkington's jests, 2. 385
Celebrities of the day, 3. 1852, 1879
Celenia, 2. 994
Celestina, 1. 910, 2183
Cell, 4. 1393
Cellini, Benvenuto, 2. 1543
'Celt' (fl. 1900), 3. 1854
Celtic literature
  early writers, 1. 337-42
  loan words, 1. 164-5
Celtic magazine, 3. 1851
Celtic monthly, 4. 1353
Celtic review, 4. 1357
Celtic story, 4. 1377
Cely papers, 1. 683
'Censor, Dr', 2. 1346
Censor (1715), 2. 1275
Censor (1726), 2. 1326
Censor (Dublin 1749), 2. 1379, 1385
Censor (Dublin 1753), 2. 1385
Censor (Oxford 1769), 2. 1348
Censor (1774), 2. 1285
Censor (1775), 2. 1286
Censor (1783), 2. 1347
Censor (1789), 2. 1288
Censor (1796), 2. 1290
Censor extraordinary, 2. 1385
censorship
  Renaissance to Restoration, 1. 1383-4
  twentieth century, 4. 101-2, 875-6
Censura temporum, 2. 1293

Centinel, 2. 1282
Centlivre, Susanna, 2. 781-2, 125, 211
Central Library for Students, its *annual report*, 4. 117
Central literary magazine, 4. 1351
Century, 4. 1351
Century guild hobby horse, 3. 1858
Cerebralist, 4. 1361
Ceriziers, René de, 1. 873, 2061
Cerri, Urbano, 2. 1543
Certain elegies done by. . .wits, 1. 1010
Certain epigrams in laud and praise of the gentlemen of the Dunciad, 2. 361
Certain inducements to well minded people, 1. 2163
Certain passages of every dayes intelligence, 1. 2108
Certain sermons appointed. . .to be declared (Tudor), 1. 1935
Certain speciall and remarkable passages, 1. 2097
Certain verses written [for] Gondibert, 1. 1010
Certaine informations, 1. 2098
Certaine speciall and remarkable passages, 1. 2096
Certayne chapters of the proverbes, 1. 1007
Certayne worthye manuscript poems, 1. 1009
Cervantes, Miguel de, 1. 913-15, 2183; 2. 202-4, 977, 981; 3. 142
Cespedes y Meneses, Gonzalo de, 1. 915, 2061; 2. 980
Chad, St, 1. 326
Chadwick, Hector Munro, 4. 1018
Chaigneau, William, 2. 997
Chain, 4. 1396
Chalkhill, John, 1. 1303-4
Chalkley, Thomas, 2. 1463
Challes, Robert, 2. 1506, 138
Challoner, Richard, 2. 1804
Chalmeriana, 2. 427
Chalmers, Alexander, 2. 1333, 1334, 1336; 3. 1641, 1789
Chalmers, David (d. 1592), 1. 2443
Chalmers, David (d. 1650?), 1. 2457
Chalmers, George, 2. 1732-3, 1785
Chalmers, James (fl. 1748), 2. 1376
Chalmers, James (1782-1853), 2. 1372, 1376
Chalmers, James (1841-1901), 3. 1678
Chalmers, Thomas, 3. 1602-3, 1616
Chaloner, —, 1. 2142
Chaloner, Sir Thomas, 1. 1091
Chamberlain, Hugh, 2. 1896
Chamberlain, Robert, 1. 1304, 1336, 1737, 2028
Chamberlayne, E., 1. 2040
Chamberlayne, Sir James, 2. 471
Chamberlayne, William, 1. 1304
Chamberlen, Hugh, 2. 1896
Chamberlen, Paul, 2. 989

Chamberlen, Peter, 1. 2277
Chamberlin, R. D., 4. 1386
'Chambers, C.' (T. Smith), 3. 1696
Chambers, Charles Edward Stuart, 3. 1813
Chambers, David, 1. 861
Chambers, Sir Edmund Kerchever, 4. 1019
Chambers, Ephraim, 2. 105, 1297, 1904
Chambers, H. and H., 3. 1813
Chambers, Raymond Wilson, 4. 1019–20
Chambers, Robert (d. 1624?), 1. 2066
Chambers, Robert (1802–71), 3. 1372–4, 78, 1107, 1605, 1765, 1813, 1845
Chambers, Robert, the younger (1832–88), 3. 1702, 1813
Chambers, William, 3. 78, 1679, 1765, 1813, 1845
Chambers's Edinburgh journal, 3. 1813
Chambers's historical newspaper, 3. 1845
Chambers's journal, 3. 1813, 1835; 4. 1349
Chambers's London journal of history, 3. 1813
Chambers's papers for the people, 3. 1814
Chambers's pocket miscellany, 3. 1848
Chambers's repository of instructive and amusing tracts, 3. 1849
Chameleon (1894), 3. 1868
Chamelion (1777), 2. 1286
Chamier, Frederick, 3. 715–16
Chamisso, Adelbert von, 3. 1109
Champion, Henry Hyde, 3. 1820
Champion (1739), 2. 1279, 1330
Champion (1763), 2. 1283
Champion (1814), 3. 1809, 1834
Champion (1836), 3. 1811
Champion (1922), 4. 820
Chancel, A. Doriack; 2. 1399, 1416
Chandler, Edward, 2. 1622
Chandler, Mary, 2. 540
Chandler, Richard, 2. 1824, 1423, 1440
Chandler, Samuel, 2. 1671, 163, 1278
Chandos, Grey Brydges, 5th Baron, 1. 2048
Change, 4. 1363
Changing world, 4. 1378
Channel Isles
 eighteenth-century newspapers, 2. 1389–90
Channing-Renton, Ernest M., 4. 1370, 1374
Chanter, 2. 376
Chanticleer (1885), 3. 1867; 4. 1392
Chanticleer (N.Y. 1934), 4. 1371
Chanticlere, 3. 1867; 4. 1392
Chantreau, P. N., 2. 1429
Chap book, 4. 1371
Chapbook, 4. 1364
chapbooks, 2. 281–2
Chapelain, Jean, 1. 867
Chaperon, 4. 1397

Chapin, Harold, 4. 922–3
Chaplet (1738), 2. 366
Chaplet (c. 1762), 2. 383
Chaplet (1937), 4. 1386
Chaplet of chearfulness, 2. 384
Chaplin, —, 4. 1383
Chapman, Amelia, 4. 1386, 1387
Chapman, George (1559?–1634), 1. 1637–46, 868, 880, 1091, 1765–6, 1908, 2074, 2312–13
Chapman, George (fl. 1861), 3. 1701
Chapman, John (fl. 1597), 1. 2073
Chapman, John (d. 1894), 3. 1765, 1855
Chapman, Mrs. John, 3. 1855; 4. 1349
Chapman, John W. 3. 78
Chapman, Livewell, 1. 961
Chapman, Robert William, 4. 1020–1
Chapman, T. K., 3. 1810
Chapman and Hall, 3. 78, 1850
Chapman's magazine, 4. 1354
Chapone, Hester, 2. 1598
Chappe d'Auteroche, Jean, 2. 1440, 1470
Chappell, Bartholomew, 1. 1091
Chappell, William, 3. 1374
Chapple, A., 4. 1386
character-books, 1. 2043–8
Character of France, A, 1. 2142
Character of Italy, 1. 2142
Character of Spain, 1. 2142
Characters (1776), 2. 1286
Characters (1797), 2. 1290
Charant, Antoine, 2. 1446
Chard, Thomas, 1. 961
Chardin, Sir John, 2. 1433
'Charfy, Guiniad' (James Saunders), 2. 1558
Charges and regulations of the Free and Accepted Masons, 2. 407
Charing-Cross medley, 2. 361
Charington, —, Lord, 2. 1425
Charitable mercury, 2. 1276, 1323
Chariton, 2. 1490
Charlemagne (Elizabethan play), 1. 1759
Charlemagne romances, 1. 415–22
Charles I, 1. 998, 2275
Charles, Duke of Orleans, 1. 684–6
Charles, Elizabeth, 3. 514–15
Charles, Robert H. (b. 1882), 4. 796
Charles, Robert Henry (1855–1931), 3. 1612
Charles the Grete, 1. 418
Charlesworth, Edward, 3. 1845
Charlesworth, Maria Louisa, 3. 1091
Charleton, T. W., 3. 1687
Charleton, Walter, 1. 2058; 2. 1899, 1904
Charlevoix, Pierre F. X. de, 2. 1466
Charlewood, John, 1. 961
Charlin, Louise, 1. 870

Charlton, Mary, 3. 716; 2. 1014
Charlton, Thomas Broughton, 3. 1870
Charlton, Warwick, 4. 1377
Charlton, Yvonne Moyra Graham, 4. 814
Charm, 3. 1849
Charmer (1744), 2. 370
Charmer (1749), 2. 373
Charmer (1764), 2. 385
Charmer (Philadelphia 1790), 2. 412
Charms of chearfulness (1778), 2. 398
Charms of chearfulness (1783), 2. 403
Charms of chearfulness (1791), 2. 414
Charms of liberty, 2. 345
Charms of melody (1776), 2. 396
Charms of melody (1796), 2. 422
Charnock, John, 2. 1733, 1805
Charnock, Stephen, 2. 163
Charrière, Isabelle Agnès Élisabeth, Madame de,
  2. 1506
Charron, Pierre, 1. 862; 2. 66
Charter, 3. 1811
Charter of the Abbey of the Holy Ghost, 1. 505–6
charters, Old English, 1. 70–1, 331–2
Charters of Christ, 1. 505
Chartier, Alain, 1. 2184
Chartist, 3. 1819
Chartist circular, 3. 1819
Chasles, Robert, 2. 991
Chastellux, François Jean de, 2. 1506, 85,
  1472
Chastising of God's children, 1. 517
Chateaubriand, François René de, 3. 99–100
Chater, John, 2. 1004
Chatfield, E. W., 4. 1384
Chats with writers (1944), 4. 73
Chats with writers (St Helens 1946), 4. 1388
'Chatter, Charley', 2. 1023
Chatterton, Thomas, 2. 605–9
Chatto, William Andrew, 3. 1688, 1693
Chatto and Windus, 3. 78, 1765, 1839
Chaucer, Geoffrey, 1. 557–628; 2. 31, 131–2
Chaucer's whims, 2. 341
Chaucerians
  English, 1. 639–52
  Scottish, 1. 651–64
Chaudon, Louis Maïeul, 2. 1506
Chaumont, Alexandre de, 2. 1433
Chaundler, Christine, 4. 798
Chaundler, Thomas, 1. 998
Chavigny de la Bretonnière, François, 2. 1506
Cheadle, Walter Butler, 3. 1673
Chear, Abraham, 2. 1017
Chearful companion (Edinburgh 1766), 2. 387
Chearful companion (1770), 2. 390
Chearful companion (1780), 2. 400

Chearful companion (Glasgow 1786), 2. 407
Chearful companion (Bury 1792), 2. 416
Chearful linnet, 2. 392
Cheerful companion (1768), 2. 388
Cheerful companion (1797), 2. 423
Cheerfull ayres or ballads, 2. 327
'*Cheerio!*', 4. 1370
Cheever, George Barrell, 3. 1680
Cheife heads of each dayes proceedings, 1. 2100
Cheiliad, 3. 1869
Cheke, Henry, 1. 1423
Cheke, Sir John, 1. 1813–14, 1842
Chekov, Anton Pavlovich, 3. 151
Chelmsford and Colchester chronicle, 2. 1355
Chelmsford chronicle, 2. 1355
Chelsea, 4. 1378
Chelsea review, 4. 1368
Cheltenham College magazine, 3. 1871
Cheltenham literary annual, 3. 1876
Cheltonian, 3. 1871
chemistry, Renaissance to Restoration, 1. 2361–4
Chenery, Thomas, 3. 1789
Cheney and Sons, John, 3. 58
Chénier André, 2. 131
Chenier, Louis de, 2. 1451
Chepman, Walter, 1. 2443
Cherub: or vocal miscellany, 2. 425
Cherwell, 4. 1397
Cheshire
  general bibliography, 1. 16
  printing and bookselling, 2. 267
Cheshire daily echo, 3. 1801
Cheshire echo, 3. 1801
Cheshire evening echo, 3. 1801
chess
  Restoration and eighteenth century, 2. 1566–8
  nineteenth century, 3. 1693–5
Chess-monthly, 3. 1694
Chess-player's chronicle, 3. 1694
Chesson, F. W., 3. 1793
Chesson, Nora, 3. 1916
Chester
  Middle English drama, 1. 732–3
  Renaissance to Restoration printing, 1. 966
  Restoration and eighteenth century
    magazines, 2. 1350
    newspapers, 2. 1355–6
    periodical essays, 2. 1347
    printing and bookselling, 2. 267
  nineteenth century press, 3. 1831
Chester, Sir Robert, 1. 1091, 1304
Chester chronicle, 2. 1356
Chester courant, 2. 1356; 3. 1831
Chester miscellany, 2. 374
Chester plays (ME), 1. 732–3

Chester weekly journal, 2. 1347, 1355
Chester weekly tatler, 2. 1356
Chesterfield, Philip Dormer Stanhope, 4th Earl
    of, 2. 1585–8, 85, 136, 1279
Chesterman, Hugh, 4. 797
Chesterton, Gilbert Keith, 4. 1021–8, 1406
Chetham, James, 2. 1557
Chetham's Library, 2. 308
Chettle, Henry, 1. 1461–2, 880, 2054, 2073
Chetwind, Philip, 1. 961
Chetwood, William Rufus, 2. 1779, 989, 991,
    995, 1378, 1460, 1801
Chetwynd, Sir George, 3. 1707
Chetwynd, Mrs H., 3. 1876
Chevalere Assigne, 1. 428
Chevalier, Pierre, 2. 1410
Chevreau, Urbain, 2. 1506
Cheyne, George, 2. 1656
Cheyne, Thomas Kelly, 3. 1612
Cheynell, Francis, 1. 1990
Chichele, Henry, 1. 998
Chicken, George, 2. 1461
Chicks own, 4. 819
Chifney, Samuel, 2. 1555; 3. 1704
Child, Sir Josiah, 2. 1845
Child's new play-thing, 2. 1019
Child's New-Years gift, 2. 1020
Child's own annual, 3. 1878
Child's recreation, 2. 1018
Childe, Vere Gordon, 4. 1147
Childe, Wilfred Rowland Mary, 4. 246, 1397
Childe of Bristowe, 1. 460
Childers, Robert Erskine, 4. 551
Childhood of Christ, 1. 532
Children of the mobility, 3. 1876
Children's annual, 3. 1878
Children's book news, 4. 790
children's books
    Renaissance to Restoration, 1. 953
        dictionaries, 1. 2399
    Restoration and eighteenth century, 2. 282–3,
        1013–34
    nineteenth century, 3. 1085–110
    twentieth century, 4. 783–820
Children's encyclopaedia, 4. 819
Children's literature in education, 4. 790
Children's magazine (1799), 2. 1030, 1312
Children's magazine (1911), 4. 819
Children's miscellany, 2. 412
Children's newspaper, 4. 819
Childrey, Joshua, 1. 2136
Chillingworth, William, 1. 1973–4, 2297
Chilmead, Edmund, 1. 2121, 2304
Chilton, William, 3. 1819
China amateur journalist, 4. 1381

Chinese, literary relations
    Shakespeare, 1. 1631
    twentieth century, 4. 33
Chinese letters, 2. 1282
Ching-Ching's own, 3. 1826
Chirbury, chained library at, 1. 990
Chirm, Sylvanus, 2. 292
Chisholm, Hugh, 3. 1794
Chisholm, William, 1. 2443
Chit-chat (1716), 2. 1276
Chit chat (1754), 2. 997
Chivers, Cedric, 3. 84
Chloe or the musical magazine, 2. 381
Chloe surpriz'd, 2. 361
Choice, 2. 358
Choice ayres, songs and dialogues, 2. 332
Choice collection of ancient and modern Scots songs,
    A, 2. 420
Choice collection of comic and serious Scots poems,
    A, 2. 344
Choice collection of favorite hunting songs, A, 2.
    390
Choice collection of hymns and moral songs, A, 2.
    402
Choice collection of Masons songs, A, 2. 378
Choice collection of new songs, A, 2. 406
Choice collection of 180 loyal songs, A, 2. 335
Choice collection of 120 loyal songs, A, 2. 335
Choice collection of poetry, A. 2. 366
Choice collection of Scotch and English songs, A,
    2. 385
Choice collection of Scots poems, A, 2. 387
Choice collection of songs, A (Dublin 1785), 2.
    406
Choice collection of songs, compos'd by Purcell,
    Blow, Handell, A, 2. 387
Choice compendium, A, 2. 334
Choice emblems (1721), 2. 353
Choice emblems (1732) 2. 361
Choice of the best poetical pieces, 2. 403
Choice selection of favourite new songs, A, 2.
    423
Choice songs and ayres, 2. 332
Choice spirit's chaplet, 2. 392
Choice spirit's delight, 2. 392
Choice spirit's pocket companion, 2. 393
Choice stories for quiet hours, 4. 1356
Choice story magazine, 4. 1366
Choice tales, 2. 1029
Choir of Anacreon, 2. 412
Cholmley, Sir Hugh, 1. 2251
Cholmondeley, Mary, 3. 1042
Chorley, Henry Fothergill, 3. 1374–5
Chorley, W. B., 3. 1874
Chorus poetarum, 2. 339

Choyce drollery, 1. 1010
Choyce poems, 2. 328
Christ, 1. 269–70
Christ and Satan, 1. 270–1
Christ's burial and resurrection, 1. 739
Christ's College magazine, 3. 1867; 4. 1392
Christian, Edmund Brown Vincy, 3. 1698
Christian, 3. 1823
Christian advocate, 3. 1822
Christian commonwealth, 3. 1823
Christian drama, 4. 828, 878
Christian keepsake (1833), 3. 1875
Christian keepsake (1850), 3. 1876
Christian lady's magazine, 3. 1846
Christian magazine, 2. 1373
Christian miscellany, 2. 1309
Christian monthly history, 2. 1371
Christian novels, 4. 1358
Christian observer, 3. 1842
Christian philosophy, 2. 1289
Christian poet (1728), 2. 357
Christian poet (1735), 2. 363
Christian priest, 2. 1346
Christian remembrancer, 3. 1844
Christian reporter, 3. 1813
Christian Socialist, 3. 1819
Christian souvenir, 3. 1876
Christian teacher, 3. 1856
Christian times, 3. 1823
Christian world, 3. 1823, 1837
Christian year book, 3. 1880
Christian's amusement, 2. 1330, 1346
Christian's gazette (1709), 2. 1345
Christian's gazette (1713), 2. 1274, 1345
Christian's magazine (1760), 2. 1303
Christian's magazine (1790), 2. 1309
Christie, Agatha Mary Clarissa, 4. 552–4
Christie, Thomas, 2. 1308
Christie, William Dougal, 3. 1731
Christina, Queen of Sweden, 2. 214
Christmas, Henry, 3. 1821
Christmas annual, 4. 1386
Christmas box, 3. 1877
Christmas-box for masters and misses, A, 2. 1020
Christmas carolles, 1. 1007
Christmas library, 3. 1876
Christmas pie, 4. 1376
Christmas prince, 1. 1777
Christmas treat, 2. 387
Christoforo, Armeno, 2. 1543
Christopher, St, 1. 326
Christopherson, John, 1. 1766
Chromolithograph, 3. 60
Chronicle (OE), 1. 329–32, poems in, 1. 295
Chronicle and echo, 3. 1801

chronicle play, Renaissance to Restoration, 1. 1371
chronicles, Middle English
  pre-1400, 1. 459–68
  fifteenth century, 1. 681–2
Chubb, Thomas, 2. 1858
Chudleigh, Mary, Lady, 2. 471
Chums, 3. 1826
Church, Alfred John, 3. 1093, 1108
Church, Archibald, 4. 1368
Church, Ralph, 2. 1783–4
Church, Richard Thomas, 4. 246–8, 800
Church, Richard William, 3. 1627
Church and household, 3. 1842
Church Langton Library, 2. 306
Church-man (1718), 2. 1324
Church-man (1720), 2. 1325
Church-monitor, 2. 1385
Church of England newspaper, 3. 1822
Church of England quarterly review, 3. 1856
Church quarterly review, 3. 1858
Church times, 3. 1823; 4. 1401
Churchill, Awnsham, 1. 2112; 2. 1391
Churchill, Charles, 2. 593–5, 1563
Churchill, John, 1. 2112; 2. 1391
Churchill, Lady Randolph Spencer, 3. 1858; 4. 1355
Churchill, Sir Winston Leonard Spencer, 4. 1147–50, 1406
Churchman's last shift, 2. 1325
Churchman's year book, 3. 1880
Churchyard, Thomas, 1. 1091–4, 2047, 2071, 2072, 2076, 2124, 2132, 2150
'Churne, William' (Francis Edward Paget), 3. 1090
Churton, Annette, 3. 1731
Chute, Anthony, 1. 1094, 2037
Cibber, Colley, 2. 777–9, 125, 176, 986, 1343
Cibber, Theophilus, 2. 787, 1328, 1801
Cibber and Sheridan, 2. 370
Cicero, 1. 2167–8; 2. 1496–7, 35
Cicero, the tragedy of, 1. 1758
Cieza de Léon, Pedro de, 2. 1459
Cinegoer, 4. 57
Cinegram, 4. 58
Cinegram preview, 4. 58
Cinegram review, 4. 58
Cinema, 4. 58
Cinema and theatre, 4. 57
Cinema and theatre annual review. . .of Ireland, 4. 854
Cinema and theatre construction, 4. 57
Cinema construction, 4. 57
Cinema express, 4. 57

Cinema quarterly, 4. 57, 1370
Cinema studio, 4. 58
Cinema theatre and allied (general) construction, 4. 57
Cinema world illustrated, 4. 57
Cinematograph exhibitor's mail, 4. 56
Cinematograph Exhibitors' Association, its journals, 4. 57
Cinematograph monthly, 4. 56
Cinematograph times, 4. 57
Cinthio, Giovanni Battista Giraldi, 1. 2185, 887, 894, 902; 2. 1545
Circle (17th century), 2. 332
Circle (1874), 3. 1791
Circle (1905), 4. 824, 1358
Circle (1921), 4. 1396
Circles' choice, 4. 1388
Circular to bankers, 3. 1824
Circulations, 4. 1342
Circus, 4. 1380
Cirencester, printing, 2. 267
Cirencester flying-post, 2. 1356
Cirencester post, 2. 1356
Citizen (1716), 2. 1276
Citizen (1727), 2. 1278
Citizen (1739), 2. 1330
Citizen (1756), 2. 1333
Citizen (1764), 2. 1375
Citizen (1776), 2. 1335
Citizen (1788), 2. 1288
Citizen (1878), 3. 1815
Cities weekly post, 1. 2101
City (Letchworth 1909), 4. 1359
City and countrey mercury, 2. 1316
City-hermit, 2. 368
City intelligencer, 2. 1322
City mercury (1667), 2. 1316
City mercury (1675), 2. 1316
City mercury (March 1680), 2. 1317
City mercury (November 1680), 2. 1317
City mercury (1692), 2. 1319
City press, 3. 1808, 1834
City scout, 1. 2101
City sportsmen, 2. 1561
City watchman, 2. 1385
Civic entertainment, 4. 852
Civil Service gazette, 3. 1826
Clacton visitors' guide, 4. 849
Clancy, Michael, 2. 1419
Clapham, Henoch, 1. 1094
Clapham, John, 1. 2209
Clapham, Sir John Harold, 4. 1151
Clapperton, Hugh, 3. 1669
Clapwell, Richard, 1. 776
Clare, John, 3. 356–8

Clare journal, 2. 1388
Clarendon, Edward Hyde, 1st Earl of, 2. 1678–82; 1. 1001, 2342
Clarendon, John Charles Villiers, 3rd Earl of, 2. 1428
Claret de Fleurieu, Charles Pierre, 2. 1482
Clariodus, 1. 448
Clarion (1844), 4. 1400
Clarion (1891), 3. 1821
Clarion (1930), 4. 1369
Clarion (1946), 4. 1398
Clark, Audrey, 4. 814
Clark, Emily, 3. 1101
Clark, Francis, 3. 1880
Clark, Sir George Norman, 4. 1151–2
Clark, James (d. 1724), 2. 2033
Clark, James (fl. 1770–1806), 2. 1554
Clark, John Willis, 3. 1850, 1880
Clark, Kenneth Mackenzie, Baron, 4. 1028–9
Clark, Mabel Margaret, 4. 982
Clark, Robert (fl. 1806), 3. 1792
Clark, Robert (1825–94), 3. 1702
Clark, Samuel, 3. 1090
Clark, T. and T., 3. 78, 1856
Clark, W. M., 3. 1811
Clark, William (fl. 1663–85), 2. 1963
Clark, William (1770–1838), 3. 1671
Clark, William George, 3. 1680
Clarke, Andrew, 3. 1679
Clarke, Austin, 4. 248–9
Clarke, C., 4. 850
Clarke, Charles, 3. 922, 1705
Clarke, Charles Cowden, 3. 1273
Clarke, Charlotte, 2. 998
Clarke, Edward, 2. 1420
Clarke, Edward Daniel, 2. 1406; 3. 1669
Clarke, Edward Hammond, 3. 1729
Clarke, Frances Elizabeth, 3. 1054–5
Clarke, George (fl. 1703), 2. 1458
Clarke, George (fl. 1899), 4. 1355
Clarke, Mrs J. S., 3. 1705
Clarke, James (fl. 1787), 2. 1405
Clarke, James (1824–88), 3. 1823
Clarke, James Greville, 3. 1823
Clarke, James Stanier, 2. 1312
Clarke, John (fl. 1639), 1. 2031
Clarke, John (1682–1757), philosopher, 2. 1858–9
Clarke, John (1687–1734), philosopher, 2. 1858
Clarke, Joseph, 2. 1859
Clarke, Mary, 4. 828
Clarke, Mary Victoria Cowden, 3. 1375–6, 1102
Clarke, Richard Frederick, 3. 1850
Clarke, Samuel (1599–1683), 1. 2121–2, 2150, 2297–8; 2. 1692–3, 1409, 1455, 1803

Clarke, Samuel (1675–1729), 2. 1859–60, 105, 163, 1622, 1824–5, 1904
Clarke, T., 4. 1385
Clarke, William, 3. 1765
Clarke's new law list, 3. 1881
Clarkson, — (fl. 1828), 3. 1810
Clarkson, Thomas, 3. 1487–8; 2. 105, 1451
Classical magazine, 2. 1305
classical studies, Restoration and eighteenth century, 2. 1819–30; *see also* individual authors
Clater, Francis, 2. 1554
Claude, Isaac, 2. 981
Claudian, 1. 2168; 2. 1497
Claudius Tiberius Nero, 1. 1759
Clavell, John, 1. 1737, 2035
Clavell, Robert, 2. 1339
Clavigero, Francesco Saverio, 2. 1472
Clay, T., 3. 1714
Clayton, John. 2. 1457, 1459
Clayton, Robert, 2. 163
Cleanness, 1. 553–4
Cleave, John, 3. 1811
Cleave's London satirist, 3. 1811
Cleave's penny gazette of variety, 3. 1811
Cleaver, Hylton Reginald, 4. 800
Clegg's international directory, 4. 106
Cleghorn, George, 2. 1419
Cleghorn, Hugh, 2. 1444
Cleghorn, James, 3. 1839, 1844
Cleland, John, 2. 145, 182, 996, 1001
Cleland, William, 2. 1963
Clemens Scottus, 1. 353
Clement, John, 1. 998
Clement, Simon, 2. 1896
Clement, William Charles, 3. 1809
Clement, William Innell, 3. 1789, 1807, 1808, 1809
Clements, Arthur, 3. 1825; 4. 1352
Clements, Lewis, 3. 1713
Clenche, John, 2. 1411
Clergy directory and parish guide, 3. 1880
Clergy list, 3. 1880
Clerical directory, 3. 1880
'Clericus' (W. Cartwright), 3. 1689
Clerk, Sir John, 2. 2052
Clerk, William, 2. 1562
Clerk who would see the Virgin, 1. 458
Clerkenwell news, 3. 1791
Cleveland, John, 1. 1304–5, 2040, 2045, 2089, 2091, 2102, 2105; 2. 31
Cliffe, John Henry, 3. 1689
Clifford, Frederick, 3. 1794
Clifford, Henry, 5th Earl of Cumberland, 1. 1912
Clifford, John, 3. 1842
Clifford, Lucy, 3. 1097

'Clifford, Martin' (C. H. St J. Hamilton), 4. 792
Clifton's Oxford post, 2. 1325
Cliftonian, 3. 1871
Clinkard, Mildred, 4. 1374, 1398
Clio and Euterpe, 2. 380
Clio and Strephon, 2. 361
Clipperton, John, 2. 1478
Clique, 3. 85; 4. 106
Clive, Caroline, 3. 922–3
Clive, Catherine, 2. 828
Clock tower, 4. 1397
Clogie (Clogy), Alexander, 2. 1694
Clonmel gazette, 2. 1387
Close, Francis, 3. 1619, 1724
Close-up, 4. 57, 1367
Cloud of unknowing and associated works, 1. 520–1
Clough, Arthur Hugh, 3. 461–5, 1605, 1871
Clowes and Sons, William, 3. 58; 4. 80
Clown, 2. 1288
Club law, 1. 1777
Clubbe, William, 2. 1430
Clue, 4. 118
Cluny, Alexander, 2. 1468
Clutterbuck, Henry, 2. 1310
Clutton-Brock, Arthur, 4. 1029–30; 3. 1870
Cluverius, Philippus, 1. 2122
Clyomon and Clamydes, 1. 1418
Clytophon, 1. 1777
Cnitthon, Henry, 1. 787
Coad, J., 3. 1688
Coal-hole of cupid, 2. 388
Coates, John, 2. 1568
Coates, Thomas, 3. 1745
Coats, Alice Margaret, 4. 808
Coats, William, 2. 1484
Cobb, James, 2. 828
Cobb, James Francis, 3. 1103
Cobb, Samuel, 2. 541, 238
Cobbe, Frances Power, 3. 1376–7, 1746, 1765
Cobbett, James Paul, 3. 1679
Cobbett, Richard, 3. 1811
Cobbett, William (1763–1835), 3. 1199–1210, 1682, 1765, 1789, 1792, 1817, 1845; 2. 1339
Cobbett, William, the younger (d. 1878), 3. 1817
Cobbett's evening post, 3. 1792
Cobbett's political register, 3. 1817, 1836
Cobbett's twopenny trash, 3. 1845
Cobbin, J., 3. 1877
Cobbler, stick to your last, 3. 1106
Cobbold, Richard, 3. 717
Cobley, F., 3. 1698
Cobweb, 4. 1382
Cobweb nest, 4. 1383
Cochin, Charles Nicolas, 2. 1506, 1419

Cochrane, Alfred J. H., 3. 1698
Cochrane, John, 3. 1694
Cochrane, John George, 3. 1803, 1856
Cock, Christopher, 2. 300
cock-fighting, 3. 1695
Cock Lorrel's boat, 1. 1095
Cockburn, Catharine, 2. 802, 1860
Cockburn, James Pattison, 3. 1678
Cockburn, John (1652–1729), 2. 2047, 1371, 1562
Cockburn, John (fl. 1735), 2. 1462
Cockburn, Patrick, 1. 2443, 853
Cockell, Teesdale, 3. 1881
Cockes, John, 1. 1904
Cocking, Matthew, 2. 1469
Cockis, John, 1. 1904
Cockle, Mary, 3. 1088, 1100
Cocks, Richard, 1. 2146
Cockton, Henry, 3. 923
Cocoon, 4. 1393
Codlin, Ellen M, 4. 880
Coe, Katherine Hunter, 4. 1370, 1374
Coetlogon, Charles Edward de, 2. 1307
Coffee house, 2. 1286
Coffee-house evening post, 2. 1327
Coffee-house mercury, 2. 1319
Coffee-house morning post, 2. 1327
Coffey, Charles, 2. 787
Coffin, Paul, 2. 1468
Coffin, Richard, 2. 311
Cogan, Thomas, 2. 1005, 1429
Coghill, Ethel Charlotte, 3. 1105
Coghill, Nevil, 4. 1397
Cohen, Lionel, 3. 1822
Cohn, N. R., 4. 1371
Coignet, Matthieu, 1. 2184, 862
Coit, Stanton, 3. 1528
Cokayne, Sir Aston, 1. 1737–8
Coke, Desmond Francis Talbot, 4. 793
Coke, Sir Edward, 1. 998
Coke, Roger, 2. 1896
Coke, Thomas, 2. 1472
Colburn, Henry, 3. 1810, 1813, 1821, 1843, 1845
Colburn, Zerah, 3. 1827
Colburn's united service magazine, 3. 1845
Colchester journal, 2. 1356
Colchester spie, 1. 2104
Colclough, George, 1. 1095
Colden, Cadwallader, 2. 1461
Coldwell, S. D., 4. 1393
Cole, Alfred W., 3. 1848
Cole, Benjamin, 2. 1563
Cole, George Douglas Howard, 4. 1152–4, 1397
Cole, Sir Henry, 3. 1107
Cole, Ralph, 2. 1561
Cole, Thomas, 1. 1938

Cole, William (fl. 1659), 1. 2036
Cole, William (1714–82), 2. 1402, 1420
Coleman, Edmund Thomas, 3. 1680
Coleman, Edward, 2. 1555
Colenso, John William, 3. 1606
Coleridge, Christabel Rose, 3. 1104, 1848
Coleridge, Hartley, 3. 372–3
Coleridge, Henry J., 3. 1850
Coleridge, Henry Nelson, 3. 1273–4
Coleridge, John Duke, 3. 1870
Coleridge, Sir John Taylor, 3. 1855
Coleridge, Mary Elizabeth, 3. 618–19
Coleridge, Samuel Taylor, 3. 211–54, 131–2, 1603, 1765; 2. 117, 1347, 1430
Coleridge, Sara, 3. 515, 1101
Coles, Vincent S., 3. 1870
Colet, John, 1. 1790–2, 2275
Colgan, John, 3. 1887
Colin Blowbols testament, 1. 1095
Collas, Clare, 4. 813
Collectanea chemica, 2. 1904
Collected poems (Ilfracombe 1947), 4. 1378
Collecting juvenile literature, 4. 1388
Collection and selection of English prologues and epilogues, A, 2. 399
Collection for improvement of husbandry and trade, A, 2. 1342
Collection from the Spectator, A, 2. 376
Collection of all the material news, A, 2. 1366
Collection of all the new songs sung this season, A, 2. 380
Collection of Bacchanalian songs, A (1729), 2. 358
Collection of Bacchanalian songs, A (1763), 2. 384
Collection of ballads, A, 2. 356
Collection of catches and glees, A, 2. 406
Collection of catches by Arne, A, 2. 385
Collection of catches, canons and glees, A, 2. 384
Collection of catches, canons, glees, A, 2. 400
Collection of catches, glees, A, 2. 392
Collection of choice pieces composed on different persons, A, 2. 404
Collection of comic songs, by H— R—, A, 2. 379
Collection of constitutional songs, A, 2. 426
Collection of diverting songs, A, 2. 366
Collection of divine hymns and poems, A, 2. 345
Collection of 86 loyal poems, A, 2. 335
Collection of English prose and verse, A, 2. 402
Collection of English songs, A, 2. 422
Collection of epigrams, A, 2. 356
Collection of favorite glees, A, 2. 427
Collection of favourite English, Scotch, Irish and French songs, A, 2. 398
Collection of favourite songs sung at the Beef Steak Club, A, 2. 414
Collection of hymns and poems, A, 2. 347

Collection of interesting anecdotes, A, 2. 418

Collection of letters and essays publish'd in the Dublin Journal, A, 2. 358

Collection of letters and poems. . .to the late Duke and Dutchess of Newcastle, A, 2. 333

Collection of letters for the improvement of husbandry, A, 2. 1291

Collection of loyal songs, A (1731), 1. 1011; 2. 359

Collection of loyal songs (1744), 2. 370

Collection of loyal songs, A (1750), 2. 374

Collection of loyal songs, as sung at all the Orange Lodges, A (1798), 2. 425

Collection of loyal songs for. . .the Revolution Club, A. (1749), 2. 373

Collection of many wonderful prophesies, A, 2. 338

Collection of Masonic songs, 2. 420

Collection of merry poems, A, 2. 364

Collection of miscellany poems, A, 2. 365

Collection of miscellany poems, letters, A, 2. 341

Collection of modern fables, A, 2. 392

Collection of modern poems, by several hands, A, 2. 383

Collection of moral and sacred poems, A, 2. 370

Collection of more than eight hundred prologues, A, 2. 399

Collection of new songs, A (17th century), 2. 339

Collection of new songs adapted to the times, A (1712), 2. 347

Collection of new songs compos'd by Morgan, A, 2. 340

Collection of new songs, compos'd by several masters, A, 2. 349

Collection of new songs set to musick by Wm. Morley and John Isum, A, 2. 346

Collection of new songs sett to musick by Gillier, A, 2. 340

Collection of new state songs, A, 2. 361

Collection of odes. . .against the Whigs, A, 2. 412

Collection of old ballads, A, 2. 354

Collection of one hundred and eighty loyal songs, A, 2. 339

Collection of one hundred and fifty Scots songs, A, 2. 388

Collection of original miscellaneous poems, A (1770), 2. 390

Collection of original poems, A (1724), 2. 355

Collection of original poems and translations, A (1745), 2. 371

Collection of original poems by Scotch gentlemen, A, 2. 381

Collection of original poems, translations and imitations, A, 2. 348

Collection of original Scotch songs, A (1732?), 2. 361

Collection of original Scots songs, poems, A (1772), 2. 393

Collection of papers, A, 2. 427–8

Collection of pieces. . .publish'd on occasion of the Dunciad, A, 2. 361

Collection of poems, A (1732), 2. 361

Collection of poems [by Pope and others], A (1777), 2. 397

Collection of poems by several hands, A (1744), 2. 370

Collection of poems by several hands, A [Dodsley's miscellany] (1748), 2. 372–3

Collection of poems by several hands, A (1779), 2. 399

Collection of poems, by the author of a poem on the Cambridge ladies, A, 2. 362

Collection of poems, essays and epistles, A, 2. 392

Collection of poems for and against Dr Sacheverell, A, 2. 346

Collection of poems from the best authors, A, 2. 385

Collection of poems in two volumes, A, 2. 388

Collection of poems, mostly original, by several hands, A, 2. 411

Collection of poems on affairs of state, A, 2. 337

Collection of poems on divine and moral subjects, A, 2. 395

Collection of poems on religious and moral subjects, A, 2. 423

Collection of poems on several occasions, A (1731), 2. 359

Collection of poems on several occasions written in the last century, A (1747), 2. 372

Collection of poems on state-affairs, A, 2. 347

Collection of poems on various subjects, A, 2. 416

Collection of poems, the productions of Ireland, A, 2. 394

Collection of poems upon the victories of Blenheim, A, 2. 345

Collection of poems written upon several occasions by several persons, A, 2. 331

Collection of political and humorous letters, A, 2. 373

Collection of pretty poems, A (1757), 2. 379

Collection of pretty poems, A (1777), 2. 397

Collection of right merrie garlands, for North Country anglers, A, 3. 1688

Collection of scarce, curious and valuable pieces, A, 2. 394

Collection of Scots poems, A, 2. 378

Collection of Scots songs, A, 2. 402

Collection of sea songs, A, 2. 355

Collection of select epigrams, A, 2. 379

Collection of select original poems, A, 2. 363

Collection of several pamphlets. . .relative to . . .Byng, A, 2. 378

Collection of songs, A (1762), 2. 383

Collection of songs by Richard Leveridge, A 2. 356

Collection of songs, chiefly such as are eminent for poetical merit, A 2. 402

Collection of songs, compos'd by John Eccles, A, 2. 343

Collection of songs, compos'd by John Sheeles, A, 2. 355

Collection of songs for two and three voices, A, 2. 381

Collection of songs for two or three voices, A, 2. 371

Collection of songs on various subjects, A, 2. 353

Collection of songs, selected from the works of Dibdin, A, 2. 426

Collection of songs set. . .by Mr Pixell, A, 2. 380

Collection of songs set to musick by Henry Purcell and John Eccles, A, 2. 339

Collection of songs set to musick by James Graves, A, 2. 350

Collection of speciall passages, A, 1. 2097

Collection of spiritual songs, A, 2. 414

Collection of state songs, A, 2. 350

Collection of the best English poetry, A, 2. 350

Collection of the best modern poems, A, 2. 392

Collection of the best old Scotch and English songs, A, 2. 383

Collection of the choicest songs and dialogues, A, 2. 343

Collection of the choycest and newest songs, A, 2. 336

Collection of the most celebrated prologues, A, 2. 357

Collection of the most celebrated songs and dialogues. . .by. . .Purcell, A, 2. 343

Collection of the most celebrated songs set. . . adapted for the guittar, A, 2. 384

Collection of the most esteemed pieces, A, 2. 387

Collection of the most favorite new songs, A, 2. 421

Collection of the most favourite Scots, songs, A, 2. 398

Collection of the newest and most ingenious poems against Popery, A, 2. 337

Collection of twenty-four songs, A, 2. 335

Collection of vocal harmony, A, 2. 395

Collection of voyages, A (1729), 2. 1391–2

Collection of voyages, A (1741), 2. 1392

Collection of Welsh tours, A, 2. 1407

Collection revival and refining, A, 2. 374

Collector, 2. 1289

Collector's monthly, 4. 1383

College, 4. 1395

College album, 3. 1869

College clarion, 4. 1398

College echoes, 3. 1869; 4. 1398

College magazine, 3. 1870

College rhymes, 3. 1868

Collegian, 3. 1869

Colles, Ramsay, 3. 1766

Colley Cibber's jests, 2. 382

Collier, Arthur, 2. 1860

Collier, Jeremy, 2. 721–4, 129, 1566, 1705–6, 1797

'Collier, Joel' (George Veal), 2. 1403

Collier, John Henry Noyes, 4. 554–5

Collier, John Payne, 3. 1641–2

Colliery guardian, 3. 1827

Collingridge, William Hill, 3. 1808

Collings, Ernest, 4. 1364

Collings, Richard, 1. 2097, 2098, 2107, 2110

Collingwood, Robin George, 4. 1247–8

Collins, A., 4. 850

Collins, Anne, 1. 1305

Collins, Anthony, 2. 1860–1, 105–6

Collins, Arthur, 2. 1712–13

Collins, Charles Alston, 3. 923

Collins, Charles James, 3. 1825

Collins, Clifford, 4. 1378

Collins, David, 2. 1482

Collins, John 2. 647

Collins, John Churton, 3. 1424–5

Collins, Joseph, 3. 1851

Collins, L., 3. 1758; 4. 1342

Collins, Mabel, 3. 1853

Collins, Mortimer, 3. 923–4

Collins, Norman Richard, 4. 809

'Collins, Ruth', 2. 1297

Collins, Samuel, 2. 1410

Collins, Thomas, 1. 1305

Collins, William, 2. 585–9, 42

Collins, William Wilkie, 3. 924–8, 1683

Collins, Sons and Co, William, 3. 78

Collins for boys and girls, 4. 820

Collins, the magazine for boys and girls, 4. 820

Collinson, John, 2. 1733

Collis, Maurice Stewart, 4. 1314

Collison, Robert Lewis, 4. 118

'Collodi, C.' (Carlo Lorenzini), 3. 1109

Collop, John, 1. 1305–6, 2320

Collyer, Mary, 2. 995

Collyns, C. P., 3. 1705

Colman, George, the elder (1732–94), 2. 812–14, 176, 1281, 1283, 1284, 1783

Colman, George, the younger (1762–1836), 2. 828–30

Colmenero de Ledesma, Antonio, 1. 2163

Colnett, James, 2. 1473

Colom, Jacob, 1. 2140

Colonial and Asiatic review, 3. 1847

Colonial magazine (1840), 3. 1847

Colonial magazine (1849), 3. 1847
Colonial Office list, 3. 1880
colonies, Renaissance tracts, 1. 2276–7
Colonist and commercial weekly advertiser, 3. 1810
Colonist and weekly courier, 3. 1810
Colonna, Francesco, 1. 887, 2061
Colonne, Guido delle, 1. 2184, 857, 2061
Colophon, 4. 84, 120
Colosseum, 4. 1371
Coloured fun, 4. 1381
Coloured journal, 4. 1381
Coloured news, 3. 1816
Colquhoun, Patrick A., 3. 1718
Colse, Peter, 1. 1095
Colt, Sir Henry, 1. 2158
Colt-Hoare, Richard, 3. 1681
Colum, Padraic, 3. 1942–3; 4. 1360
Columba, 1. 341–2
Columbanus, 1. 342
Columbian Muse, 2. 419
Columbian songster, 2. 426
Colvil, Samuel, 2. 1963
Colvill, Robert, 2. 2022
Colville, Elizabeth, Lady, 1. 2428
Colville, John, 1. 2444
Colvin, Sir Sidney, 3. 1425–6
Colwell, Thomas, 1. 961
Comazzi, Giovanni Battista, 2. 1543
Combe, George, 3. 1528–9, 1721
Combe, Thomas, 1. 1095, 1329
Combe, William, 2. 647–9, 145–6, 1006, 1009;
    3. 1789
Comedian (1732), 2. 1297
Comedian (1910), 4. 1382
Comedian's tales, 2. 358
comedy
    Renaissance to Restoration
        early Tudor, 1. 1411–20
        Shakespearean, 1. 1612–13
        special studies, 1. 1371
    Restoration and eighteenth century
        manners, 2. 707–9
        sentimental, 2. 709
Comenius, John Amos, 1. 845
Comer, John, 2. 1461
Comes amoris, 2. 336
Comet (1790), 2. 1337
Comet (1910), 4. 1382
Comfort, Alexander, 4. 249–50, 1375, 1376
Comfort, Bessie, 3. 1105–6
Comic adventures of Old Mother Hubbard, 3. 1106
Comic album, 3. 1876
Comic annual, 3. 1874
Comic bits, 4. 1381
Comic conviviality, 2. 423

Comic cuts, 3. 1826; 4. 819
Comic miscellany (1756), 2. 378
Comic miscellany (1845), 3. 1876
Comic Muse, 2. 393
Comic news, 3. 1825
Comic offering, 3. 1874
Comic pictorial nuggets, 3. 1826
Comic songster, 2. 411
Comical circle, 4. 1381
Comick magazine, 2. 422, 1311
comics, 4. 123–5, 819–20
Comines, Philippe de, 1. 2184, 862
Comitia Westmonasteriensium, 2. 357
Commelin, Isaak, 2. 1391
Commendatory verses on the author of the two
    Arthurs, 2. 341
Comment, 4. 1371
Commentary (Picture Hire Club), 4. 1375
Commentary, art, drama, literature, 4. 1375
Commentary on psalms 90–1, 1. 479
Commentator, 2. 1277
commerce
    Renaissance to Restoration, 1. 2278
    nineteenth century, 3. 1824, 1837
Commercial and agricultural magazine, 2. 1312
Commercial art, 4. 1342
Commercial film, 4. 58
Commercial film review, 4. 58
Commercial world, 3. 1824
Commodore Roggewein's expedition, 2. 1478–9
Common condicions, 1. 1418
Common sense (February 1737), 2. 1279, 1329
Common sense (November 1737), 2. 1279, 1329
Common sense (1824), 3. 1810
Commonweal, 3. 1820
Commonwealth, 3. 1820
Common-Wealths great ship, 1. 2129
Companion (1790), 2. 412
Companion (1828), 3. 1821
Companion (1925), 4. 1384
Companion for a leisure hour, A, 2. 389
Companion for the fire-side, A, 2. 393
Companion in a post-chaise, A, 2. 394
Companion to the [British] almanac, 3. 1877
Companion to the gentleman's diary, A, 2. 1314
Companion to the newspaper, 3. 1846
Companion to the watering and bathing places, A,
    2. 1408
Company keeper's assistant, 2. 390
Compass, 4. 1377
Compendio mercuriale, 2. 1319
Compendious library, 2. 1379
Compendium of the most approved modern travels,
    A, 2. 1392
Competitor, 4. 1382

Constable, Henry, 1. 1095–6
'Constance' legends, 1. 441–4
Constantia, 2. 996
Constitution (1757), 2. 1282
Constitution (1799), 2. 1387
Constitution (1812), 3. 1809
Constitutional and public ledger, 3. 1789
Constitutional chronicle, 2. 1355
Constitutional guardian, 2. 1334
Constitutional letters, 2. 1376
Constitutional magazine (1768), 2. 1304
Constitutional magazine (1793), 2. 1310
Constitutional songs, 2. 426
Constitutional year book and politician's guide, 3. 1878
Constitutionalist, 2. 1284
Constitutions and charges of Freemasons, 2. 375
Constitutions of the Free-Masons, 2. 354
Contact, 4. 1377
Contarini, Gaspero, 1. 845, 2138, 2184
Contemplations of the dread and loue of God, 1. 516
Contemplative philosopher, 2. 1287
contemplative writings, Middle English, 1. 516–24
Contemplator, 2. 1287
Contemporaries (and makers), 4. 1370, 1394
Contemporary issues, 4. 1379
Contemporary poetry (and song), 4. 1366
Contemporary poetry and prose, 4. 1372, 1345
Contemporary poetry and prose editions, 4. 1372
Contemporary review, 3. 1850, 1863; 4. 1351
Contention betwixt. . . Yorke and Lancaster, 1. 1470
Contest (1734), 2. 363
Con-test (1756), 2. 1282
Contest (1768), 2. 388
Contest (Durham 1800), 2. 428
Conti, Antonio, 2. 38
Conti, Lotario (Innocent III), 1. 845–6
Continental annual, 3. 1875
Continental landscape annual, 3. 1875
Continental times, 3. 1791
Continuation of a journall of passages, A, 1. 2101
Continuation of certaine speciall. . . passages, A, 1. 2096, 2097, 2100, 2101, 2102
Continuation of our weekly intelligence from his Majesties army, A, 1. 2097
Continuation of papers sent from the Scots quarters, A, 1. 2101
Continuation of the most remarkable passages, 1. 2097
Continuation of the narrative. . . in the tryal of the King, A, 1. 2104

Continuation of the proceedings of the convention of the Estates in Scotland, A, 2. 1319
Continuation of the true diurnall, A, 1. 2094, 2095, 2096
Continuation of the weekly occurrences, A, 1. 2095
Continuation of true and special passages, A, 1. 2097
Continuation of true intelligence from the Earl of Manchester's army, A, 1. 2100
Continued heads of perfect passages, 1. 2105
'Contour, Charles', 2. 1285
Contrast, 2. 1284
Contributor's journal, 4. 1369
Controller, 2. 1275
Conuertimi, 1. 688
Conventicle-courant, 2. 1318
Convivial companion, 2, 423
Convivial harmony, 2. 428
Convivial jester, 2. 412
Convivial magazine, 2. 1305
Convivial songster, 2. 402
Convoy, 4. 1376
Conway, Edward, 2nd Viscount, 1. 998
Conway, F. W. 3. 1806
'Conway, Hugh' (Frederick John Fargus), 3. 1043
'Conway, James' (J. C. Walter), 3. 1689
Conway, Sir Martin, 3. 1676
Conway, Roger, 1. 796
Conway, William Martin, Baron, 3. 1710, 1857
Conybeare, John, 1. 2032
Conybeare, William John, 3. 1619
Cook, Charles Henry, 3. 1690
Cook, Ebenezer, 2. 1459
Cook, Edward Dutton, 3. 1849
Cook, Sir Edward Tyas, 3. 1766, 1790, 1793, 1794
Cook, Eliza, 3. 516
Cook, James, 2. 1468, 1479, 1480, 1904
Cook, John, MD (fl. 1770), 2. 1440
Cook, John (fl. 1826), 3. 1704
Cook, John Douglas, 3. 1789, 1814, 1857
Cook, Keningale, 3. 1846
Cook, Sir Theodore Andrea, 3. 1714
Cook, Thomas, 3. 1881
Cook, William, 3. 1692
Cook's continental time tables, 3. 1881
Cook's excursionist and international tourist advertiser, 3. 1881
Cooke, Alexander, 1. 866
Cooke, Sir Clement Kinloch, 3. 1793, 1807, 1852
Cooke, Edward, 2. 1477
Cooke, John (fl. 1577) sailor, 1. 2150
Cooke, John (fl. 1612), dramatist, 1. 1738, 1335
Cooke, Nathaniel, 3. 1816

Cooke, Thomas, 2. 542–3, 1297, 1776, 1825
Cooke, William, 2. 1335
Cookson, Christopher, 3. 1731
Cookson, J. C. F., 3. 1713
Coolidge, William Augustus Brevoort, 3. 1680, 1710, 1857
Coomber, R., 4. 1388
Cooney, James Peter, 4. 1373
'Cooper, Rev Mr' (Richard Johnson), 2. 1022
Cooper, Alfred Duff, 1st Viscount Norwich, 4. 1154–5
Cooper, Anthony Ashley, 3rd Earl of Shaftesbury, 2. 1865–7, 44, 111, 159, 189
Cooper, Anthony Ashley, 7th Earl of Shaftesbury, 3. 1728
Cooper, Charles Alfred, 3. 1766, 1804
Cooper, Dawtrey, 1. 2127
Cooper, E., 4. 1380
Cooper, Edith Emma, 3. 626–7
Cooper, Elizabeth, 2. 1801
Cooper, Frederick Fox, 3. 1766
Cooper, George, 2. 1408
Cooper, H. F., 3. 1809
Cooper, J. W., 3. 1695
Cooper, John, 1. 1352
Cooper, Maria Susannah, 2. 1002, 1005
Cooper, Thomas (d. 1594), 1. 1960
Cooper, Thomas (1805–92), 3. 516–17, 1724, 1766, 1819
Cooper, Thompson, 3. 1879
Cooper's journal, 3. 1819
Co-operative Printing Society, 3. 58; 4. 80
Co-operator, 3. 1819–20
Co-optimists, 4. 1385
Coote, Edmund, 1. 2276
Coote, Robert, 2. 1559
Cope's tobacco plant, 3. 1851, 1863
Copeland, Patrick, 1. 2277
Copie of a letter from Virginia, 1. 2153
Copland, Robert, 1. 690, 961, 1096–7, 2031, 2034, 2038, 2065
Copland, William, 1. 2026, 2065
Copleston, Edward, 3. 1274
Copleston, Reginald Stephen, 3. 1868
Coplestone, —, 3. 1794
Copley, Anthony, 1. 1097, 2027
Copley, Esther, 3. 1101
Coppard, Alfred Edgar, 4. 556–7, 793
Copper plate magazine (1774), 2. 1305
Copper plate magazine (1792), 2. 1309
Coppinger, Matthew, 2. 471
Coprario, John, 1. 1352
Copy of a carete, 1. 2136
copyright
  Renaissance to Restoration, 1. 975–8

  Restoration and eighteenth century, 2. 283–90
  nineteenth century, 3. 71–6
  twentieth century, 4. 100–1
  see also book production and distribution
Coranto from beyond the sea, A, 1. 2098
Corbet, H., 3. 1705
Corbet, John, 1. 2458
Corbett, Edward, 3. 1700
Corbett, James Edward, 4. 792
Corbett, Richard, 1. 1306
Corbett, Thomas, 2. 1417
'Corcoran, Peter' (John Hamilton Reynolds), 3. 1692
Cordiner, Charles, 2. 1404
Corelli, Marie, 3. 1043–4
'Coriat Junior' (Samuel Paterson), 2. 1421
Cork
  Renaissance printing, 1. 969–70
  Restoration and eighteenth century
    magazines, 2. 1380
    newspapers, 2. 1387–8
    periodical essays, 2. 1380
    printing, 2. 274
Cork and Orrery, John Boyle, 5th Earl of, 2. 1422
Cork advertiser, 2. 1388
Cork chronicle (1765), 2. 1388
Cork chronicle (1768), 2. 1388
Cork constitution, 3. 1806
Cork courier, 2. 1388
Cork daily advertiser, 3. 1805
Cork daily herald, 3. 1806
Cork evening post, 2. 1388
Cork examiner, 3. 1806
Cork gazette, 2. 1388
Cork general advertiser, 2. 1388
Cork herald (1798), 2. 1388
Cork herald (1856), 3. 1806
Cork intelligence, 2. 1388
Cork journal (1746), 2. 1388
Cork journal (1778), 2. 1388
Cork news-letter, 2. 1388
Cork packet, 2. 1388
Cork surgeon's antidote, 2. 1385
Cork weekly journal, 2. 1388
Corkery, Daniel, 4. 923–4
Corkine, William, 1. 1354
Corkran, Alice, 3. 1096–7
Corlett, John, 3. 1824
Corlett, Joyce, 4. 1387
Cormack, Sir John Rose, 3. 1826
Corn-cutter's journal, 2. 1327
Corn trade circular, 3. 1823
Cornaro, Ludovico, 1. 887
Corneille, Pierre, 1. 867, 2184; 2. 1507, 36, 115, 118–19, 861

Corneille, Thomas, 1. 867; 2. 1507, 119
Corner, Julia, 3. 1090
Corner magazine, 4. 1365
Cornerstone, 4. 83
Corney, Bolton, 3. 1839
Cornfield, L., 4. 1382
Cornford, Frances Crofts, 4. 251
Cornford, Francis Macdonald, 4. 1031
Cornford, Rupert John, 4. 251
Cornhill magazine, 3. 1849, 1862; 4. 1351
Cornish, Charles John, 3. 1714
Cornish, Hubert Warre, 3. 1866
Cornish ordinalia, 1. 727–8
Cornish review, 4. 1380
Cornishman, 4. 1402
Cornwall
   general bibliography, 1. 16
   medieval drama, 1. 727–8
   printing 1740–1850, 2. 267
'Cornwall, Barry' (Bryan Waller Procter), 3. 396–7
Cornwall, Henry, 2. 1437
Cornwallis, Caroline Frances, 3. 1529
Cornwallis, Sir William, 1. 2047
Coronal, 3. 1876
Coronation of Edgar, see *Poems of the Anglo-Saxon Chronicle*, 1. 295
Coronelli, P. M., 2. 1412
Corpus Christi College, Cambridge, library, 2. 306
Corraro, Angelo, 2. 1544, 1409
Correspondence française, 2. 1338
Correspondent, 2. 1384
Correspondents: an original novel, 2. 1004
Corro, Antonio del, 1. 846
Corrozet, Gilles, 1. 2027, 2055
Corte, Claudio, 1. 2184
Cortés, Martín, 1. 2184
Corvinus Press, 4. 97
'Corvo, Baron' (F. W. S. A. L. M. Rolfe), 4. 724–5
Cory, William (formerly Johnson), 3. 528–9, 1727, 1870
Coryat, George, 1. 2133
Coryat, Thomas, 1. 2125, 2145
Cosin, John, 1. 1974–5, 2296
Cosmopolitan, 2. 1308
Cosmopolite, 3. 1818
Cosowarth, Michael, 1. 1906
Costanso, Miguel, 2. 1473
Costeker, John Littleton, 2. 992
Costello, Louisa Stuart, 3. 374
Costigan, Arthur William, 2. 1426
Costlie whore, 1. 1759
Cosworth, Michael, 1. 1906

Cosy corner, 4. 1357
Cosyn, John, 1. 1901
Coterie, 4. 1363
Cotes, Roger, 2. 1904
Cotes's weekly journal, 2. 1327–8
Cotgrave, John, 1. 2100
'Cotswold, Isys' (R. H. Glover), 3. 1690
Cottager, 2. 1283
Cottin, Sophie, 3. 1109
Cottle, Amos Simon, 2. 248
Cottle, Joseph, 3. 374
Cotton, Charles, 2. 437–9, 1556
Cotton, Charles William Egerton, 3. 1871
Cotton, J. A. H., 3. 1702
Cotton, James Sutherland, 3. 1822
Cotton, Nathaniel, 2. 543, 1020
Cotton, Reynell, 2. 1565
Cotton, Sir Robert Bruce, 1. 998, 2040, 2050
Cotton, Roger, 1. 1097
Cotton Vespasian homilies, 1. 487
Couch, A. C., 3. 62
Cougal, S., 2. 163
Couling, S., 3. 1724
Coulson, Walter, 3. 1792
Coulter, W. M., 4. 851
Coulton, David T., 3. 1813, 1814
Coulton, George Gordon, 4. 1155–6
Council of dogs, 3. 1088
Councils' journal, 4. 1404
Counsellor on secular, co-operative and political questions, 3. 1819
Count Piper's packet, 2. 361
Counterpoint, 4. 1377
Countrey foot-post, 1. 2101
Countrey messenger (Sept 1644), 1. 2100
Countrey messenger (Oct 1644), 1. 2101
Country, 2. 1287
Country advertiser, 2. 1354
Country common sense, 2. 1348
Country correspondent, 2. 1330
Country curate, 2. 1287
Country gentleman (London 1726), 2. 1277
Country gentleman (Dublin 1726), 2. 1377, 1383
Country gentleman (1880), 3. 1684, 1824; 4. 1362
Country gentleman's courant, 2. 1321
Country gentleman's vade-mecum, 2. 1569–70
Country heart, 4. 1360, 1364
Country in full cry after poachers, 2. 1559
Country journal (1727), 2. 1326
Country journal (Dublin 1735), 2. 1385
Country life, 3. 1684, 1817, 1835; 4. 1354, 1345, 1404
Country magazine (1736), 2. 1298
Country magazine (1739), 2. 1298, 1330
Country magazine (1763), 2. 1303

Cowan, T. C., 4. 1386
Coward, Sir Noël Pierce, 4. 924–7
Cowdroy's Manchester gazette, 2. 1362
Cowell, John, 1. 2275
Cowell, S. H., 3. 58
Cowell, W. S., 3. 58; 4. 80
Cowen, Joseph, 3. 1766, 1795
Cowen-Hoven, H. D., 4. 1382
Cowley, Abraham, 1. 1219–21, 1913, 2320;
   2. 31
Cowley, Ambrose, 2. 1477
Cowley, Hannah, 2. 830–1, 176
Cowley, Malcolm, 4. 1365
Cowley's history of plants, 2. 421
Cowper, F., 3. 1716
Cowper, William (1568–1619), 1. 1939
Cowper, William (1731–1800), 2. 595–603
Cowton, Robert, 1. 796
Cox, Anthony Berkeley, 4. 528
Cox, Edward William, 3. 1816, 1826
Cox, Sir George, 3. 1108
Cox, H., 2. 982
Cox, John Edmund, 3. 1808
Cox, Leonard, 1. 2307
Cox, Nicholas, 2. 1556
Cox, Nigel, 4. 1378
Cox, Percy Stuart, 3. 1816
Cox, Robert, 1. 1738, 2028
Cox, Samuel, 3. 1606
Cox, Thomas, 2. 1717, 1400
Cox, William Herbert, 4. 1358
Coxcomb, 4. 1392
Coxe, Daniel, 2. 1460
Coxe, John, 1. 1904
Coxe, Tench, 2. 1474
Coxe, William, 2. 1424–5, 1441, 1480, 1483
Coxeter, Thomas, 2. 1774
Coyer, Gabriel François, 2. 997, 1467, 1478
Coyne, Joseph Stirling, 3. 1148–9
Coyote, 4. 1383
Cozens, Zechariah, 2. 1406
Cozens-Hardy, Archibald, 3. 1798
Crab-tree, 2. 1282
Crabb, G., 3. 1717
Crabbe, George, 2. 609–15
Crackanthorpe, Hubert Montague, 3. 1044, 1853
'Crackenthorpe, Mrs' (Thomas Baker), 2. 1271
Cracroft, Sophia, 3. 1677
Cradock, Mrs Henry Cowper, 4. 794
Cradock, Joseph, 2. 831, 1004, 1402
Crafford, John, 2. 1456
Craft of deyng, 1. 2444
Craftsman (1726), 2. 1277, 1326
Craftsman (Dublin 1739), 2. 1385
Craftsman (1752), 2. 1332

Craftsman (1758), 3. 1812
Craftsman (1778), 2. 1335
Craftsman (Egham c. 1900), 4. 1380
Craftsman extraordinary, 2. 1326
Craggs, Robert, Earl Nugent, 2. 559
Craig, Alexander, 1. 2433
Craig, (Edward Henry) Gordon, 4. 1031–3, 1354,
   1359, 1363
Craig, John, 1. 2444, 1903
Craig, Sir Thomas, 1. 2467
Craig, William, 2. 163
'Craigie, David' (Dorothy Craigie), 4. 814
Craigie, Dorothy, 4. 814
Craigie, Pearl Mary Teresa, 3. 1058
Craigie, Sir William Alexander, 4. 1033–4
Craik, Dinah Maria, 3. 951–2, 1093, 1108
Craik, George Lillie, 3. 1274–5
Craik, Sir Henry, 3. 1426, 1729
Crakanthorp, Richard, 1. 2332, 2276, 2297, 2298,
   2332
Crake, Augustine David, 3. 1104
Cramer, Karl Gottlob, 2. 1537
Crampton's magazine, 4. 1354
Crane, Ralph, 1. 1306
Crane, Walter, 3. 65
Crank, 4. 1357
Cranley, Thomas, 1. 1306
Cranmer, Thomas, 1. 1815–17, 999
Cranston, Maurice, 4. 1378
Crantz, David, 2. 1484
Crashaw, Cynthia, 4. 1374
Crashaw, Richard, 1. 1214–17, 1913; 2. 31
Crashaw, W., 1. 2276
Crashawe, William, 1. 999
Crathorn, — (fl. 1330), 1. 785
Crauford, Quintin, 2. 1443
Craufurd, Thomas, 1. 2467
'Craven' (J. W. Carleton), 3. 1713, 1847
Craven, Elizabeth, Baroness, Margravine of
   Anspach, 2. 831–2, 1427
'Craven, Henry Thornton' (Henry Thornton),
   3. 1149
Craven, William George, 3. 1706
Crawford, H., 3. 1714
Crawford, John, 3. 1674
Crawford, Lillian, 4. 1384
Crawfurd, David, 2. 2047–8, 984
Crawfurd, George, 2. 1707–8, 1805
Crawfurd, Oswald J. F., 3. 1817, 1858; 4. 1354
Crawhall, Joseph, 3. 1689
'Crawley, Captain' (G. F. Pardon), 3. 1694
Crealock, H. H., 3. 1714
Creation (Norwich grocers' play), 1. 737
Creation of the world, 1. 728
Creative drama, 4. 880

Crébillon, Prosper Jolyot de (Crébillon père 1674–1762), 2. 1508, 119
Crébillon, Claude Prosper Jolyot de (Crébillon fils 1707–77), 2. 1507–8, 138–9, 993, 995
Crecerelle, B., 3. 1876
Creech, Thomas, 2. 1825
Creed (OE), 1. 271
Creep shadow, 4. 1387
Creighton, Mandell, 3. 1480–1, 1858
Cremer, John, 2. 1395
Cremlin, A. G., 4. 1388
Crespel, Emanuel, 2. 1475
Cresswell, Nicholas, 2. 1470
Cressy, Hugh Paulin, 1. 1990
Creswell, Harry Bulkeley, 4. 791
Creswell and Burbage's Nottingham journal, 2. 1364
Creswell's Nottingham journal, 2. 1364
Crèvecoeur, Michel Guillaume Jean de, 2. 1884–5, 1471
Crew of kind London gossips, A, 2. 329
Crewdson, Jane, 3. 1102
Crewe, Thomas, 1. 2029
Cribbes, G. O., 4. 852
Crichton, A., 3. 1101
Crichton-Browne, Sir James, 3. 1858
cricket
    eighteenth century, 2. 1564–5
    nineteenth century, 3. 1695–9
Cricket, 3. 1695
Cricket chronicle for the season 1863, 3. 1882
Cricketer's almanack, 3. 1695, 1882
Cricketer's handbook for 1865, 3. 1882
Cricketer's manual for 1849, 3. 1882
Crier, 2. 1347
Crier of London, 4. 1388
Cries of London, as they are daily exhibited in the streets, 2. 1022
Cries of London: or child's moral instructor, 2. 1021
Crime book magazine, 4. 1392
Crime club bulletin, 4. 1389
crime fiction, 4. 125–6, 1389–92
Crisis (1775), 2. 1285
Crisis (1792), 2. 1289
Crisis (1832), 3. 1818
Crisis extraordinary, 2. 1285
Crisp, Samuel, 2. 176
Crisp, Stephen, 2. 1457
Crispin, Gilbert, 1. 756
Critchett, Sir George Anderson, 3. 1865
Criterion, 4. 1365, 1345
Criterion miscellany, 4. 1365
Critic (1769), 2. 1284
Critic (1783), 2. 1287

Critic (1793), 2. 1289
Critic (1914), 4. 1362
Critic (1929), 4. 1368
Critic (Bournemouth 1931), 4. 1369
Critic (Mistley 1947), 4. 1378
Critic (1947), amateur journal, 4. 1388
Critical memoirs of the times, 2. 1304, 1334
Critical review: or annals of literature, 2. 1301; 3. 1839, 1859
Criticisms on the Rolliad, 2. 404
Critick, 2. 1276, 1294
Critique, 4. 823, 1404
Croal, David, 3. 1766
Crockett, Samuel Rutherford, 3. 1044–5, 1098
Crockford's clerical directory, 3. 1880
Crockford's scholastic directory for 1861, 3. 1881
Croft, Herbert (1603–91), 2. 1607
Croft, Sir Herbert (1751–1816), 2. 1006, 1286
Croghan, George, 2. 1467
Crokatt, J., 2. 1298
Croke, Sir John, 1. 1899
Croker, John Wilson, 3. 1275–6
Croker, Richard, 2. 1431
Croker, Thomas Crofton, 3. 1107, 1877
Crole, Robert, 1. 1899
Crollius, Oswaldus, 1. 846
Croly, George, 3. 375, 1766
Cromarty, George Mackenzie, 1st Earl of, 2. 1689–90
Cromer, John, 4. 1375
Crompton, Frances Eliza, 3. 1098
Crompton, Hugh, 1. 1306
Crompton, Richmal, 4. 799
Crompton, Sarah, 3. 1102
Crompton, Thomas Bonsor, 3. 1789
Cromwell, Thomas Kitson, 3. 1682
Cronin, Archibald Joseph, 4. 557
Crook, William Montgomery, 3. 1793
Crooke, Andrew, 1. 961
Crooked billet, 4. 1383
Crookes, Sir William, 3. 1858
Crooks, William, 3. 1828
Crookshank, William, 2. 2042
Croone, William, 2. 1904
croquet, 3. 1699–1700
Crosby, Harry, 4. 1367
Crosby's modern songster, 2. 419
Crosland, Thomas William Hodgson, 3. 619, 1766; 4. 1356, 1358, 1361, 1366
Cross, John C., 3. 1128
Cross, John Keir, 4. 813
Cross, Mary Ann, 3. 899–912, 132, 156
Cross, Thomas, 3. 1700
Cross channel, 4. 1374
Crossman, Richard, 4. 1398

Current, A. 1. 2096
Current intelligence (1666), 2. 1316
Current literature of the month, 4. 117
Currie, J., 3. 1726
Currie, Dr James, 2. 1348
Currie, Mary Montgomerie Lamb, Baroness, 3. 625–6
Curry-comb, 2. 1385
Cursor mundi, 1. 500–1
Curtis, George Byron, 3. 1790
Curtis, Samuel, 3. 1840
Curtis, William, 2. 1308; 3. 1840
Curtis's botanical magazine, 3. 1840
Curwen, Samuel, 2. 1404
Curwen Press, 4. 97
Curzon, George Nathaniel, Marquis, 3. 1870
'Curzon, L. H.' (J. G. Bertram), 3. 1707
Curzon, Robert, 3. 1674
Cust, Henry J. C., 3. 1793
Custance, Henry, 3. 1707
Cutts, H. W., 3. 1817
Cutts, John, 1st Baron, 2. 471
'Cutwode, Thomas' (Tailboys Dymoke), 1. 1101
Cycle and motor trades review, 3. 1824–5
Cycle trader and review, 3. 1825
cycling, 3. 1700
Cycling, 3. 1825
Cycling annual, 3. 1882
Cycling times, 3. 1824
Cyclist (trade review), 3. 1824
'Cyclos' (G. Anderson), 3. 1714
Cyder: a poem, 2. 345
Cynegetica, 2. 1558
Cynewulf, 1. 271–2
Cynthia, 2. 981
Cyprian cabinet, 2. 362
Cyprian conqueror, 1. 1759
Cyrano de Bergerac, Hercule Savinien de, 1. 2184, 873; 2. 1508, 139, 981
Cythereia, 2. 354

D., B. (fl. 1648–51), 1. 2103, 2107
D., J. (fl. 1632), 1. 2163
D., John (fl. 1562), 1. 2071
D., T. (fl. 1587), pamphleteer, 1. 2077
D., T. (fl. 1598), poet, 1. 1098
Dabbler, 2. 1287
Dabbs, George Henry Roque, 4. 1358
Daborne, Robert, 1. 1738–9
Daça, Antonio, 1. 908
Dacier, André, 2. 1508, 66
Dackomb, Thomas, 1. 999
Dacre, Barbarina Brand, Baroness, 3. 370–1
Dacre, Charlotte, 3. 718

Daft, Richard, 3. 1698
Daiches, David, 4. 1037
Daily advertiser (1730), 2. 1327
Daily advertiser (1802), 3. 1789
Daily argus (Birmingham), 3. 1802; 4. 1403
Daily argus (Dundee), 3. 1804
Daily benefactor, 2. 1275
Daily Bristol times and mirror, 3. 1797, 1831
Daily bulletin, 3. 1804
Daily bullionist, 3. 1824
Daily chronicle (1858), 3. 1795
Daily chronicle (1872). 3. 1791; 4. 1401
Daily chronicle and argus (1900) 3. 1800
Daily courant (1702), 2. 1269, 1321
Daily courant (Dublin 1716), 2. 1383
Daily courant (Edinburgh 1860), 3. 1804
Daily courier, 3. 1792
Daily courier (Liverpool), 3. 1797; 4. 1399
Daily echo, 3. 1801
Daily examiner, 3. 1806
Daily express (Dublin 1851), 3. 1805; 4. 1401
Daily express (Edinburgh 1855), 3. 1803
Daily express (Glasgow 1870), 3. 1804
Daily express (1877), 3. 1791
Daily express (1900), 3. 1792; 4. 1404
Daily Express fiction library, 4. 1372
Daily Express library of famous books, 4. 1372
Daily film renter, 4. 57
Daily financial mail, 4. 1406
Daily free press, 3. 1805
Daily gazette for Middlesbrough, 3. 1798
Daily gazetteer, 2. 1279, 1328
Daily graphic (1890), 3. 1791, 1817, 1835; 4. 1403
Daily graphic (1946), 4. 1405
Daily guardian, 3. 1802
Daily herald, 4. 1405
Daily herald (Ipswich), 3. 1803
Daily illustrated mirror, 4. 1405
Daily independent press, 3. 1802
Daily intelligencer, 1. 2098
Daily journal, 2. 1325
Daily liar, 4. 1405
Daily mail, 3. 1792, 1828; 4. 1404, 1343
Daily mail (Glasgow), 3. 1803
Daily mail (Hull), 3. 1802
Daily mail sixpenny novels, 4. 1358
Daily messenger, 3. 1791
Daily midland echo, 3. 1800
Daily mirror, 4. 1405, 1343
Daily nation, 3. 1807
Daily news, 3. 1790, 1828; 4. 1400
Daily news (Hull), 3. 1802
Daily oracle (1715), 2. 1323, 1345
Daily oracle (1889), 3. 1791

Daily packet, 2. 1325
Daily paper, 4. 1405
Daily politician, 3. 1790
Daily post (1719), 2. 1324
Daily post (1855), 3. 1795
Daily post boy, 2. 1319
Daily proceedings, 1. 2108
Daily record, 3. 1805; 4. 1404
Daily recorder (of commerce), 3. 1793
Daily review, 3. 1804
Daily Scotsman, 3. 1803
Daily sketch, 4. 1405, 1343
Daily telegram (Wisbech), 3. 1800
Daily telegraph, 3. 1790, 1828; 4. 1401, 1344
Daily telegraph (Manchester), 3. 1794
Daily times, 3. 1794
Daily universal register, 2. 1336; 3. 1789
Daily war telegraph, 3. 1794
Daily western mercury, 3. 1796
Daily worker, 4. 1407
Dainty novels, 4. 1354
Dairymaid, 2. 404
Dalbiac, William W., 3. 1881
Dalby, John Watson, 3. 1821
Dalby, W., 3. 1732
Dale, B., 3. 1697
'Dale, Felix', 3. 1194
Dale, Robert William, 3. 1606
Dale, Sir Thomas (d. 1619), 1. 2155
Dale, Thomas (fl. 1831), 3. 1874
Dale, Thomas F., 3. 1711
Dale's collection of sixty favourite Scotch songs, 2.
    419
Dalgairns, John Dobrée [Bernard], 3. 1627–8
Dalkin, A. E., 4. 1384
Dallam, Thomas, 1. 2124
Dallas, Eneas Sweetland, 3. 1377, 1821
Dallas, H., 4. 1358
Dallas, Robert Charles, 3. 719
Dallaway, James, 2. 1430
Dallaway, R. C., 3. 1719
Dallington, Sir Robert, 1. 2138
Dalrymple, Alexander, 2. 1785, 1440, 1450, 1454,
    1475; 1. 2112
Dalrymple, Sir David, Lord Hailes, 2. 2052–3,
    245, 1733–4, 1782–3
Dalrymple, Sir James, 1st Viscount Stair (1619–
    95), 2. 2057–8
Dalrymple, Sir James (c. 1650–1720), 2. 2048
Dalrymple, Sir John, 2. 1734
Dalrymple, William, 2. 1424
Dalton, John, 2. 1904
Dalton, Regina Maria, 3. 760
Dalton, Richard, 2. 1439, 1449
Dalton's Dublin impartial news letter, 2. 1384

Daly, John, 3. 1890
Daly, Robert, 3. 1720
Dalzel, Archibald, 2. 1452
Dalziel, Charles, 3. 1825
Dalziel, Edward, 3. 66, 1766, 1825
Dalziel, George, 3. 66, 1766, 1825
Dalziel, James Henry, 3. 1805
Daman, William, 1. 1901
Damato, Juan Bautista, 2. 1416
Dame and her donkeys five, 3. 1108
Dame Partlet's farm, 3. 1106
Dame Siriz, 1. 455
Dame Trot and her comical cat, 3. 1106
Dame Wiggins of Lee, 3. 1108
Damon, William, 1. 1901
Dampier, William, 2. 1447, 1477
Dan Jon Gaytryge's sermon, 1. 490
Dana, 4. 1357, 1394
Dance, Charles, 3. 1129
Dance and dancers, 4. 828, 862
Dancer, 4. 826
Dancer and cabaret, 4. 860
Dancing and film news, 4. 860
dancing, Restoration and eighteenth century, 2.
    1565–6
Dancing-master, a satyr, 2. 1565
Dancourt, Florent Carton, 2. 1508, 119
Dandini, Girolamo, 2. 1435
Dando, John, 1. 2024
Dandy (comic), 4. 820
'Dane, Clemence' (Winifred Ashton), 4. 927–9
Dangerfield, Edmund, 3. 1766, 1825
Dangerfield, Fred, 4. 824, 859
Dangler, 2. 1290
Danican, F. A., 2. 1567
Daniel of Morley, 1. 761
Daniel, Charles William, 4. 1357
Daniel, Florence, 4. 1357
Daniel, Gabriel, 2. 982
Daniel, George (d. 1657), 1. 1307
Daniel, George (1789–1864), 3. 1276–7
Daniel, Peter Augustin, 3. 1643
Daniel, Samuel, 1. 1061–5, 1462, 2073, 2235–7,
    2242, 2313–14
Daniel, Walter, 1. 767
Daniel, William, 2. 1435
Daniel, 1. 272–3
Daniel Press, 3. 56; 4. 97
Daniell, J., 1. 2160
Daniell, Samuel, 3. 1669
Daniell, Thomas, 3. 1673
Daniell, William, 3. 1673, 1682
Danielson, Henry, 4. 1365
Dante Alighieri, 1. 897; 2. 1544, 192; 3. 136–7
Danter, John, 1. 961

'D'Anvers, Caleb' (Nicholas Amhurst), 2. 533–4
Danvers, Robert William, 3. 1675
Danyel, John, 1. 1352
Daphnis: or a pastoral elegy, 2. 345
Dapper, Olfert, 2. 1445
D'Arblay, Frances, 2. 970–3, 85, 145
Darby, Charles, 2. 471
D'Arcy, Martin Cyril, 4. 1248–9
Darell, John, 1. 2150
Dares Phrygius, 1. 2168
Darien scheme, 2. 2080–2
Daring detective, 4. 1391
Dark, Sidney, 4. 824
Dark blue (1867), 3. 1868
Dark blue (1871), 3. 1868
Darker side, 4. 1386
Darkin, Walter, 3. 1823
Darley, George, 3. 376–7
Darling, Sir Frank Fraser, 4. 1249
Darlington, William Aubrey Cecil, 4. 929
Darlington mercury, 2. 1356
Darlington pamphlet, 2. 1356
Darmesteter, Agnes Mary Frances, 3. 646–7
Darrell, John, 1. 2073
Dart, John, 2. 544
Darton, William, 2. 1026
Darts, 4. 1398
Darwin, Bernard Richard Meirion, 4. 1314–15, 792
Darwin, Charles Robert, 3. 1364–8, 1670
Darwin, Elinor Mary, 4. 792
Darwin, Erasmus, 2. 650–1, 42, 1904
Darwin, Frances Crofts, 4. 251
Das Tor, 4. 1398
Daston, John, 1. 788
Daudet, Alphonse, 3. 101
D'Aulnoy, Marie Catherine la Motte, Countess, 2. 1399; 3. 1109
Daunce, Edward, 1. 2047, 2137
Dauncey, John, 2. 975
Davenant, Charles, 2. 1897
Davenant, Sir William 1. 1208–10, 1766, 2319
Davenport, John, 4. 1379, 1380
Davenport, Robert, 1. 1739
Davenport, Selina, 3. 719
David, Gustave, 3. 86
David, 4. 1370
David Allen, 4. 80
Davidson, Andrew Bruce, 3. 1612
Davidson, John (d. 1604), 1. 2423
Davidson, John (1797–1836), 3. 1670
Davidson, John (1857–1909), 3. 619–21, 132
Davidson, Samuel, 3. 1606
Davidson, Thomas, 3. 1529–30
Davie, Ian, 4. 1397

Davie, Sampson, 1. 2071
Davies, B. 4. 1388
Davies, D., 3. 1842
Davies, David Ivor, 4. 970
Davies, Emily, 3. 1746
Davies, George Christopher, 3. 1690
Davies, Gerald Stanley, 3. 1866
Davies, Hubert Henry, 4. 929–30
Davies, Hugh Sykes, 4. 1368, 1394
Davies, J. Sanger, 3. 1710
Davies, James, 1. 2154
Davies, John, of Hereford (1565–1618), 1. 1098–9, 1336, 1908
Davies, Sir John (1569–1626), 1. 1071–4, 1333, 1909, 2237, 2275, 2331
Davies, John (O Fallwyd), fl. 1710, 2. 241
Davies, John (1679–1732), 2. 1825
Davies, John Llewelyn, 3. 1612
Davies, Myles, 2. 1769
Davies, Rhys, 4. 558
Davies, Richard, 2. 1399, 1650
Davies, Rowland, 2. 1398
Davies, Samuel, 2. 1401
Davies, Sneyd, 2. 574
Davies, Thomas, 2. 1779
Davies, William (fl. 1614), 1. 2125
Davies, William (1830–96), 3. 517
Davies, William Henry, 4. 251–3, 1363
D'Avigdor, E. H., 3. 1706
Davila, Enrico Caterino, 2. 1544
'Daviot, Gordon' (Elizabeth Mackintosh), 4. 930–1
Davis, Alexander, 3. 1700
Davis, E., 3. 1876
Davis, Emily Jane, 3. 546
Davis, Israel, 3. 1822
Davis, John, 1. 2161
Davis, Nathaniel, 2. 1458
Davis, Thomas Osborne, 3. 1902–3
Davis, William, 2. 1314
Davison, Christopher, 1. 1907
Davison, Francis, 1. 1907
Davison, J., 4. 1380, 1381
Davison, James William, 3. 1377
Davison, John, 3. 1603
Davison, Peter, 4. 1375
Davitt, Michael, 3. 1820
Davy, Sir Humphry, 2. 1904; 3. 1688
Davy, John, 3. 1679, 1689
Davy's five dreams, 1. 473
Davys, Mary, 2. 985, 990, 991
Dawes, Richard (1708–68), 2. 1825
Dawes, Richard (1793–1867), 3. 1724
Dawkins, Horace C., 3. 1870
Dawks, Ichabod, 2. 264, 1320

Dawks's news-letter, 2. 1320
'Dawlish, Peter' (James Lennox Kerr), 4. 805
Dawn (Ilkeston 1902), 4. 1404
Dawn (Swansea 1925), 4. 1398
Dawson, Alec John, 4. 791
Dawson, Christopher Henry, 4. 1157–8
Dawson, George, 3. 1619, 1794, 1798
Dawson, Oswald R., 4. 1391
Day, Angel, 1. 1099, 2311
Day, F. R., 4. 1381
Day, Isaac, 3. 1100
Day, James, 1. 1307
Day, James Wentworth, 4. 1351
Day, John (1522–84), 1. 961–2
Day, John (c. 1574–1640), 1. 1462–3
Day, R., 4. 1387, 1388
Day, Richard, 1. 1939
Day, Thomas, 2. 1025, 146, 1006
Day, William, 3. 1707
Day (1809), 3. 1790
Day (1867), 3. 1791
Day (Glasgow), 3. 1803
Day and new times, 3. 1790
Day-Lewis, Cecil, 4. 253–6, 808, 1377, 1397
Daylight (1878), 3. 1820
Daylight (1941), 4. 1375
Days off, 4. 1377
De passione secundum Ricardum, 1. 516
Deacon, John, 1. 2038
Deacon, Thomas, 2. 1622–3
Deacon, William Frederick, 3. 1792
Dean, Basil, 4. 931
Dean, John, 2. 471
Dean, W., 3. 1849
D[ea]n Sw[if]ts intelligencer, 2. 1384
Dean Swift's medley, 2. 361
Deane, Anthony, 4. 1356
Dear variety, 2. 403
Death and liffe, 1. 546
Death of Alfred; see Poems of the Anglo-Saxon Chronicle, 1. 295
Death of Arthur, 1. 399–400
Death of Edgar; see Poems of the Anglo-Saxon Chronicle, 1. 295
Death repealed by a thankfull memoriall, 1. 1010
Debate, 4. 1386
Debate between nurture and kynd, 1. 515
De Beck, A. M., 3. 1853
Debenham, Mary H., 3. 1106
Debes, Luces Jacobson, 2. 1411
Deborah Dent and her donkey, 3. 1108
Debrett, John, 3. 1880
Debrett's illustrated baronetage and knightage, 3. 1879
Debrett's illustrated peerage, 3. 1879

Decalves, Alonso, 2. 1475
December annual, 4. 1386
Dechachord, 4. 1366
De Chatelain, Clara, 3. 1102
Decker, Sir Matthew, 2. 1897
Deckmann, G., 4. 861
Declaration collected out of the journals, A, 1. 2104
Declaratioun, Ane (1582), 1. 2438
De Clifford, —, Lady, 3. 1677
De Courcy, Beatrice, 3. 1845
De Courcy, Margaret, 3. 1845
Dedekind, Friedrich, 1. 2184, 855; 2. 1537, 75
Dee, John, 1. 999, 2278
Deeping, George Warwick, 4. 559–60
Deevy, Teresa, 4. 931–2
Defoe, Daniel, 2. 880–917, 146, 182–3, 195, 205, 208, 211, 214, 216, 1269, 1277, 1294, 1320, 1322, 1324, 1325, 1343, 1345, 1375, 1400, 1667
'De Graham, Sir John', 2. 1375
Dehn, Olive, 4. 813
Deist: or moral philosopher, 3. 1817
Dekker, Eduard Douwes, 3. 94
Dekker, Thomas, 1. 1673–82, 868, 2025, 2027, 2055, 2073
De Kock, Charles Paul, 3. 103
De Lacy Towle, —, 3. 1823
'Delafield, E. M.' (E. E. M. de la Pasture), 4. 560–1
De la Mare, Walter John, 4. 256–62, 791–2
Delane, John Thaddeus, 3. 1766, 1789
Delany, Mary, 2. 1598
Delany, Patrick, 2. 1378
Delap, John, 2. 832
De la Pasture, Edmée Elizabeth Monica, 4. 560–1
De la Ramée, Marie Louise, 3. 1070–1, 1095
De la Rue and Co, Thomas, 3. 58; 4. 80
De la Warr, Thomas West, 12th Baron, 1. 2155
Delderfield, Ronald Frederick, 4. 932–3
Delicate jester, 2. 401
Delicate objection, 2. 1005
Delicate songster (1767), 2. 388
Delicate songster (1795?), 2. 421
Deliciae musicae, 2. 339
Deliciae poeticae, 2. 344
Delight and pastime, 2. 340
Delightful new academy of compliments, 2. 386
Delightful vocal companion, 2. 395
Delights for the ingenious (1684), 2. 335
Delights for the ingenious (1711), 2. 347, 1294
Delights of the Muses, 2. 366
Delille, Jacques, 2. 131
Delineator, 2. 1286
Dell, H. G., 4. 1384
Dell, William, 1. 1991
Della Casa, Giovanni, 1. 2183, 886; 2. 1543

Della Cruscans, the, 2. 698
Della Valle, Pietro, 2. 1550, 1431
Dellon, Charles, 2. 1447
Dellon, Gabriel, 2. 1435
De Lolme, Jean Louis, 2. 1734-5
Deloney, Thomas, 1. 1099, 2054-5, 2077, 2271
Delphic review, 4. 1379
Delphick oracle, 2. 1294
Del Renzio, Toni, 4. 1375
Delta, 4. 1372
D'Emden, H., 3. 1874
Democrat, 3. 1820
Democratic recorder and reformer's guide, 3. 1818
Democratic review, 3. 1848
'Democritus' (George Bedborough), 3. 1854; 4. 1391
Democritus or the laughing philosopher, 2. 392
Democritus ridens, 2. 1340
'Democritus Secundus' (H. Edmundson?), 1. 2031-2
'Democritus Secundus', 2. 1329
De Morgan, Augustus, 3. 1530
De Morgan, Mary, 3. 1096
De Morgan, William Frend, 4. 561-2
Demosthenes, 1. 2168; 2. 1490
Dench, E. A., 4. 1381, 1382
Denham, Dixon, 3. 1669
Denham, Henry, 1. 962
Denham, Sir John, 1. 1217-18, 2318; 2. 31
Denholm, James, 3. 1681
Denina, Carlo Giovanni Maria, 2. 1544, 68
Denison, George A., 3. 1725
Denison, John, 3. 1845
Denison, W., 3. 1696
Denney, Diana, 4. 810-11
Denney, James, 3. 1612
Dennis, Alexander, 3. 1682
Dennis, G. P., 4. 1397
Dennis, John (1657-1734), 2. 1041-4, 42
Dennis, John (fl. 1863), 3. 1821
Dennis, Nigel Forbes, 4. 562
Dennison, John, 1. 1939
Denny, Sir William, 1. 1740
Dent, Arthur, 1. 1939-40
Dent, Clinton T., 3. 1710
Dent, Joseph Malaby, 3. 78
Dent and Sons, J. M., 3. 58; 4. 80
Denton, Daniel, 2. 1455
Deor, 1. 273-4
Dependent Whig, 2. 1277
Depictor, 2. 1288
De Quincey, Thomas, 3. 1238-47, 112, 133, 1720, 1766
Derby and Burton (evening) gazette, 3. 1801
Derby daily express, 3. 1802; 4. 140'

Derby daily telegraph, 3. 1801; 4. 1402
Derby evening gazette, 3. 1801
Derby evening telegraph, 3. 1801; 4. 1402
Derby express, 3. 1802; 4. 1403
Derby herald, 2. 1357
Derby mercury, 2. 1357; 3. 1831
Derby morning post, 3. 1802
Derby post-man, 2. 1357
Derbyshire
    general bibliography, 1. 16
    Restoration and eighteenth century
        newspapers, 2. 1357
        printing and bookselling, 2. 267
    nineteenth century press, 3. 1831
Derbyshire journal, 2. 1329
Derham, William, 2. 1861, 163, 1904
Dering, Edward (1540?-76), 1. 1940
Dering, Sir Edward (d. 1644), 1. 999
Dermody, Thomas, 3. 377
Dernyll, J. (or W. W.), 1. 2026
Derrick, Samuel, 2. 651, 1392, 1402, 1782
Derrick's jests, 2. 389
Derricke, John, 1. 2132
Derricourt, Stanley, 4. 1378
Desaguliers, Jean Théophile, 2. 1904
Descartes, René, 1. 862-3, 2184; 2. 1508, 36, 92
Descent into Hell (OE), 1. 274-5
Deschamps, François Michel Chrétien, 2. 1509, 119
Description and plat of the sea-coasts of England, A, 1. 2141
Description of a voyage made ... into the East Indies, 1. 2143
Description of all the seats of the present wars, A, 2. 1416
Description of Candia, A, 2. 1410
Description of certaine pairts of the highlands, Ane, 1. 2134
Description of Georgia, A, 2. 1462
Description of Holland, A (1691), 2. 1413
Description of Holland, A. (1743), 2. 1418
Description of love, A, 1. 1010
Description of Muscovy, A, 2. 1418
Description of New England, A, 2. 1455
Description of the Golden Islands, A, 2. 1460
Description of the holy places of Jerusalem, A, 2. 1442
Description of the now discovered ... country of Virginia, 1. 2153
Description of the seven United Provinces, A, 2. 1410
Description of the Windward Passage and Gulf of Florida, A, 2. 1462
Descriptive account of the Devil's Bridge, A, 2. 1407

De Sélincourt, Aubrey, 4. 801
De Sélincourt, Ernest, 4. 1038
De Sélincourt, Hugh, 4. 562–3
Desfontaines, Guyot, 1. 867
Desfontaines, Pierre François Guyot, 2. 1509, 992
Desiderata, 4. 118
Desiderata curiosa, 2. 361
Design for industry, 4. 1342
Desjardins, Marie Catherine, Mme de Villedieu, 2. 977, 979
Desmaizeaux, Pierre, 2. 1770–1, 85
Desmarets de Saint-Sorlin, Jean, 1. 873, 2061
Des Périers, Jean Bonaventure, 1. 873, 2026, 2062; 2. 1509
Desportes, Philippe, 1. 2184, 869
Dessy, Mario, 4. 1364
Destouches, Philippe Néricault, 2. 1509, 85, 119–20
Destruction of Jerusalem, 1. 453
Destructive and poor man's conservative, 3. 1818
Desvoeux, V., 2. 1379
De Tabley, John Byrne Leicester Warren, 3rd Baron, 3. 652–3
Detective album, 4. 1391
Detective and murder mysteries, 4. 1390
detective fiction, 4. 66, 125–6, 1389–92
Detective magazine, 4. 1389
Detective weekly, 4. 1390
Detective yarns, 4. 1390
Detector (1786), 2. 1352
Detector (1800), 2. 1387
Detrosier, Rowland, 3. 1818
D'Evelyn, Rose, 4. 824, 1358
De Vere, Sir Aubrey (formerly Hunt), 3. 377
De Vere, Aubrey Thomas, 3. 1628
De Vere, Edward, 17th Earl of Oxford, 1. 1153–4
Deverell, Robert, 2. 1352
Devereux, Robert, 2nd Earl of Essex, 1. 1099
Devereux, Robert, 3rd Earl of Essex, 1. 999
Devereux, Robert Charles, 3. 1870
Devil (1755), 2. 1281
Devil (1786), 2. 1287
Devil upon crutches in England, 2. 998, 1281
Devil's pocket-book, 2. 1287
Devon and Exeter gazette, 2. 1358
Devon evening express, 3. 1797
Devonshire
  general bibliography, 1. 16
  Renaissance to Restoration printing, 1. 966
  Restoration and eighteenth-century printing, 2. 267
devotional writings
  Middle English, 1. 516–24

Renaissance to Restoration
  English, 1. 1915–48
  Scottish, 1. 2445
Dewar, George Albemarle Bertie, 3. 1690; 4. 1351
De Watteville, A., 3. 1858
D'Ewes, Sir Simonds, 1. 2247–8, 999
Dewsbury, William, 2. 1650
Dexter, Gregory, 1. 962
Dexter, Robert, 1. 962
Deyverdun, Georges, 2. 1314
Diabolus' speech (ME), 1. 738
Diadochus, Proclus, 1. 2117
Dial (1860), 3. 1814
Dial (Chicago 1880), 4. 1352, 1345
Dial (1907), 4. 1393
Dial monthly, 4. 1361
dialects
  Old English, 1. 65–6
  Middle English, 1. 78–9
  Modern English, 1. 103–8
Dialogue between master Truth and master Honesty, A, 2. 1343
Dialogue between two friends concerning the present revolution, 2. 1341
Dialogue containing a compendious discourse [about the West Indies], A, 1. 2160
Diamond, 4. 1383
Diamond magazine, 3. 1845
Diana (Spanish drama), 1. 912
Diaper, William, 2. 544
Diarian miscellany, 2. 395
Diarie, or an exact journall, A, 1. 2102
diaries
  Renaissance to Restoration, 1. 2259–64
  Restoration and eighteenth century, 2. 1569–1600
  see also autobiography, biography, letters, memoirs
Diary: or an exact journal, A, 1. 2100, 2107
Diary: or Woodfall's register, 2. 1337
Diary kept in an excursion to Littlehampton, A, 2. 1404
Diary of the royal tour in 1789, A, 2. 411
Diatribe against backbiting, 1. 514
Dibdin, Charles (1745–1814), 2. 832–3, 1287, 1290, 1406, 1561, 1786; 3. 1704
Dibdin, Charles, the younger (1768–1833), 3. 1129, 1694
Dibdin, Thomas Frognall, 3. 1643–4, 1821; 2. 1290
Dibdin, Thomas John, 3. 1129–30
Dibdin or Irish nosegay, 2. 421
Dibdin's charms of melody, 2. 423
Dicey, Albert Venn, 3. 1488

Dicey, Edward, 3. 1790, 1807
Dicey, Mrs T. E., 3. 1801
Dick, Sir Alexander, 2. 1417
Dick, Robert, 2. 1372
Dick of Devonshire, 1. 1759
Dickens, Charles (1812–70), 3. 779–850, 112,
    132, 144, 156, 1091, 1672, 1725, 1766–7, 1790,
    1821, 1846, 1848
Dickens, Charles, the younger (1837–96), 3.
    1821, 1881
Dickens, John, 3. 1767
Dickens's continental ABC railway guide, 3. 1881
*Dickens's dictionary of continental railways,
    steamboats, diligences*, 3. 1881
Dickenson, John, 1. 1099–1100, 2054
Dickes, William, 3. 66
Dickinson, Goldsworthy Lowes, 4. 1158–9
Dickinson, James, 2. 1463
Dickinson, Jonathan, 2. 1458
Dickinson, Patric Thomas, 4. 262
Dickinson, William Croft, 4. 803
Dicks, John, 3. 1767, 1815
Dickson, David, 1. 2458
Dickson, Lovat, 4. 1370
Dickson's (the Dublin) news letter, 2. 1384
Dictator, 2. 1383
dictionaries
    general
        Old English, 1. 54
        Middle English, 1. 56
        Modern English, 1. 53–4
    Old English poetry, 1. 225–6
    Renaissance to Restoration
        general, 1. 2291–4
        children's, 1. 2399
        drama, 1. 1361–2
        French, 1. 860–1
        Italian, 1. 884–5
        Latin, 1. 842–3
        polylingual, 1. 839–40
        printers and booksellers, 1. 955–8
        song ballads, 1. 1339–40
        Spanish, 1. 905–6
    Restoration and eighteenth century
        general, 2. 1807–16
        biographical, 2. 1797–1808
        drama, 2. 703–8
        French, 2. 77–8
        Scottish, 2. 1955–6
Dictionary of love, 2. 428
Dicts and sayings of the philosophers, 1. 690
Dicuil, 1. 353
didactic legends, Middle English, 1. 449–52
Diderot, Denis, 2. 1509, 92–3, 115–16, 120, 139,
    996, 1013

Digby, Everard, 1. 2330
Digby, George, 2nd Earl of Bristol, 2. 758
Digby, Sir Kenelm, 1. 2250–1, 999, 2127, 2317,
    2337
Digby plays, 1. 738
Digges, Dudley, 1. 2047, 2162
Digges, Thomas, 1. 2047
Dilke, Ashton Wentworth, 3. 1808
Dilke, Charles Wentworth (1789–1864), 3. 1277,
    1767, 1821
Dilke, Sir Charles Wentworth (1810–69), 3. 1821
Dilke, Sir Charles Wentworth (1843–1911), 3.
    1821
Dilke, Thomas, 2. 760
Dillingham, John, 1. 2091, 2098, 2101, 2105,
    2108
Dillon, Sir John Talbot, 2. 1425
Dillon, Peter, 3. 1675
Dillon, Wentworth, 4th Earl of Roscommon, 2.
    483
Dilly, E. and C., 2. 279
Dilucidator, 2. 1341
Dimmock, Nathaniel, 3. 1622
Dimond, William, 3. 1130
Dineley, Thomas, 2. 1398
Dio Cassius, 2. 1490
Diodati, Giovanni, 1. 2296
Diodorus Siculus, 1. 2168, 2121; 2. 1490
Diogenes Laertius, 2. 1490
Dionysius of Halicarnassus, 2. 1490
Dionysius Periegetes, 1. 2168
Diplomatic review, 3. 1849
Direction for the English traviller, A, 1. 2134
Directions for breeding game cocks, 2. 1570
Director (1720), 2. 1277
Director (1807), 3. 1821
Directory for public worship (1644), 1. 1891
Directory of directors, 3. 1882
Directory of paper makers, 4. 77
Directory of second-hand booksellers, 4. 106
Dirom, Alexander, 2. 1443
Dirty dogs for dirty puddings, 2. 361
Discommendatory verses, 2. 341
*Discourse and description of the voyage [Drake and
    Frobisher]*, 1. 2151
Discourse of Ireland c. 1599, A, 1. 2133
Discourse of the Dukedom of Modena, A, 2. 1411
Discoveries of the French in 1768–9, 2. 1477
Discovery, 4. 1357
Discovery of houses under ground, A, 2. 980
Disguise: a dramatic novel, 2. 1003
Disloyal favourite, 1. 1759
Dismal lamentations of a monopolist of game, 2.
    1560
Disney, T., 3. 1698

Disraeli, Benjamin, Earl of Beaconsfield, 3. 771–9, 1814
D'Israeli, Isaac, 3. 1277–9; 2. 1768, 1013
Diss, Walter, 1. 803
Dissenting gentleman's magazine, 2. 1300
'Distaff, Mrs Jenny', 2. 1271
Distichs of Cato, OE, 1. 336; ME, 1. 508
Distillers (universal) magazine, 2. 1298
Ditters von Dittersdorf, Carl, 2. 1537
Ditton, Humphrey, 2. 163
Diurnal occurrances, 1. 2093
Diurnal occurrances, 1. 2094
Diurnal of remarkable occurrents, 1. 2445
Diurnall, 1. 2093
Diurnall and particular of. . .occurrents, 1. 2096
Diurnall occurrances, 1. 2093, 2094
Diurnall occurrances, 1. 2093
Diurnall occurrences in Parliament, 1. 2095
Diutinus Britanicus, 1. 2101
Diver, Katherine Helen Maud Marshall, 4. 563
Diverting muse, 2. 344, 1293
Diverting post (1704), 2. 343, 1293, 1344
Diverting post (1709), 2. 1382
Diverting post (1725), 2. 1383
Dives and pauper, 1. 690
Divine hymns and poems (1704), 2. 343
Divine hymns and poems (1708), 2. 345
Divine, moral and historical miscellanies, 2. 382
Dixon, Charles, 3. 1714
Dixon, Ella Hepworth, 3. 1854
Dixie, Florence Caroline, Lady, 3. 1674
Dixon, George, 2. 1481
Dixon, Henry Hall, 3. 1705
Dixon, Richard Watson, 3. 621–2
Dixon, Thomas (fl. 1744), 2. 1569
Dixon, Thomas (fl. 1900), 3. 1758; 4. 1342
Dixon, W. Willmott, 3. 1693, 1707, 1767
Dixon, William Hepworth, 3. 1675, 1681, 1821
Dixon, William Scarth, 3. 1708
Dobbs, Arthur, 2. 1462–3
Dobell, Bertram, 3. 86
Dobell, C. E., 3. 1822
Dobell, Sydney Thompson, 3. 517–18
Dobie, John Shedden, 3. 1671
Dobrée, Bonamy, 4. 1038–40
Dobson, Henry Austin, 3. 1427–8
Dobson, William, 3. 1712
Dobson's theatre year book, 4. 828
Dock leaves, 4. 1379
Docking, Thomas, 1. 782
Doctor, 2. 1276
Dr Williams's Library, 2. 304
Doctor's miscellany, 2. 360
Doctrinal of sapience, 1. 497
Docultree, Amos, 2. 1567

Documentary film news, 4. 58
Documentary news letter, 4. 58
Documents relating to Anson's voyage, 2. 1478
Dod, Charles Roger, 3. 1878, 1880
Dod, Henry, 1. 1907
Dod, Robert Phipps, 3. 1880
Dod's parliamentary pocket companion, 3. 1880
Dodd, Charles Harold, 4. 1249–50
Dodd, James William, 3. 1691
Dodd, William, 2. 651–3, 998, 1303, 1783
Doddridge, Philip, 2. 1667–8, 163
Dodge, O. G., 4. 1396
Dodgson, Charles Lutwidge, 3. 977–80, 1094, 1530, 1694
Dodridge, Sir John, 1. 2134
Dods, Marcus, 3. 1843
Dodsley, Robert, 2. 788–9, 177, 279, 1332, 1401, 1776
Dodsley's miscellany, 2. 372
Dodwell, E. S., 3. 1849
Dodwell, Henry, the elder (1641–1711), 2. 1607, 1825
Dodwell, Henry, the younger (d. 1784), 2. 1861
Dog of knowledge, 2. 1030
Doggett, Thomas, 2. 760
Doherty, Hugh, 3. 1819
Doherty, J., 3. 1818
Dolben, Digby Mackworth, 3. 622, 1628
Dolce, Lodovico, 1. 894; 2. 1544
Dolden, G., 4. 1383
Dolman, John, 1. 1100
'Dolphin' (J. T. Latey), 3. 1715
Dome, 3. 1858, 1866; 4. 1354
Domestick intelligence (1679), 2. 1316
Domestick intelligence (1681), 2. 1318
Domestick intelligence (1683), 2. 1318
Domestick intelligencer, 2. 1316
Domett, Alfred, 3. 518, 1672
Domiduca oxoniensis, 2. 329
'Domina' (Barbara Hofland ?), 3. 1745
Dominic of Evesham, 1. 754
Dominions Office and Colonial Office list, 3. 1880
Don Tomazo, 2. 979
Donaghue, Bernard, 4. 1397
Donaldson, Alec, 4. 1376
Donaldson, James, 2. 2058, 1374
Donaldson, William, 2. 1002
Doncaster flying-post, 2. 1357
Doncaster gazette, 3. 1831
Doncaster journal, 2. 1357
Doncaster, Nottingham and Lincoln gazette, 2. 1357
Doncaster, Retford and Gainsborough gazette, 2. 1357
Doni, Antonio Francesco, 1. 887, 902

Donne, J. B., 4. 1397

Donne, John, 1. 1169–86, 1333, 1910, 2049, 2305; 2. 31–2

Donnelly, Ned, 3. 1692

Donovan, Edward, 3. 1682

Doolittle, Hilda, 4. 1362

Doolittle, Thomas, 2. 163

Doorly, Victoria Eleanor Louise, 4. 793

Dope, 4. 1370

Doran, George H., 3. 78

Doran, John, 3. 1378, 1821

Dorat, Claude Joseph, 2. 1509

Dorchester and Sherborne journal, 2. 1366

Doré, Gustave, 3. 66

Dorman, Sean, 4. 1375

[Dormer's] country tatler, 2. 1329

Dorrington, C. W., 3. 60, 1762

Dorrington, Theophilus, 2. 1414

Dorset
  general bibliography, 1. 16
  early libraries, 1. 990
  Restoration and eighteenth century printing, 2. 267

Dorset, Catherine Ann, 3. 1087

Dorset, Charles Sackville, 6th Earl of, 2. 472

Dorset, Thomas Sackville, 1st Earl of, 1. 1141–2

Dossie, Robert, 2. 1904

Dostoyevsky, Fyodor Mikhaylovich, 3. 151–2

Douai Bible, 1. 1837–9

Double-action detective, 4. 1390

Double-action western, 4. 1390

Double captive, 2. 988

Doubleday, Thomas, 3. 378, 1689

Douce, Francis, 2. 1788; 3. 1644

Dougall, James D., 3. 1713

Doughty, Charles Montagu, 3. 622–3, 1676

Douglas, Lord Alfred, 3. 623–4, 1868; 4. 1361

Douglas, David, 3. 1857

Douglas, Francis, 2. 1974, 1376, 1405

Douglas, Gavin, 1. 662–4

'Douglas, George' (George Douglas Brown), 3. 1046

Douglas, George Norman, 4. 563–5

Douglas, J. P., 3. 1684

Douglas, John, 2. 1885, 1418

Douglas, Keith Castellain, 4. 262–3

Douglas, Niel, 2. 1408

Douglas, Norman, 4. 563–5

Douglas, Sylvester, Baron Glenbervie, 2. 2064

Douglas, Thomas, 5th Earl of Selkirk, 3. 1671

Douglas, William, 1. 2458, 2471

Douglas-Home, William, 4. 933–4

Douglas Jerrold's shilling magazine, 3. 1847

Douglas Jerrold's weekly news and financial economist, 3. 1814

Douglas Jerrold's weekly newspaper, 3. 1814

Douglass, Norman, 4. 563–5

Douglass, William, 2. 1463

D'Ouvilly, George Gerbier, 1. 1740

'Dove, Walter' (M. Whitelaw), 3. 1714

Dover, library of the Priory, 1. 990

Doves Press, 3. 57–8; 4. 97

Dovey, Frank G., 3. 1789

Dow, Alexander, 2. 833

Dowden, Edward, 3. 1428–9

Dowel, John, 1. 2342

Dowland, John, 1. 1348, 893

Dowland, Robert, 1. 1354

Dowling, Frank Lewis, 3. 1692, 1810

Dowling, Vincent George, 3. 1810

Down west, 4. 1366

Downame, George, 1. 1991

Downes, Andrew, 1. 2305

Downes, George, 3. 1678

Downes, John, 2. 1769

Downes, W. A., 4. 1384, 1385

Downey, Edmund, 3. 1767

Downing, Arthur, 3. 1811

Downing, Clement, 2. 1438, 1449

Downing, S., 3. 1791

Downman, Hugh, 2. 653, 246

Downside review, 3. 1858; 4. 1352

Downton, Nicholas, 1. 2145

Dowrich, Anne, 1. 1100

Dowsing, William, 3. 1680

Dowson, Ernest Christopher, 3. 624–5

Doxat, Lewis, 3. 1807

Doyle, Andrew, 3. 1789

Doyle, Sir Arthur Conan, 3. 1046–9, 1693

Doyle, Sir Francis Hastings Charles, 3. 518–19, 1870

Doyley, Edward, 1. 2160

Dozens, 4. 1387

Dragon (1877), 4. 1398

Dragon (1952), 4. 1397

Drakard's paper, 3. 1809

Drake, Edward Cavendish, 2. 1393

Drake, Sir Francis, 1. 2158, 865, 876

Drake, Frank, 2. 1559

Drake, James, 2. 1269, 1321

Drake, Nathan, 3. 1279; 2. 1288

drama
  general
    anthologies, 1. 32
    history of, 1. 29–30, 1367–80
  Middle English, 1. 719–42
    anthologies and histories, 1. 719–22
    Anglo-Norman, 1. 725–8
    Cornish, 1. 727–8
    folk, 1. 741–2

Dublin literary gazette, 3. 1845
Dublin literary journal, 2. 1379
Dublin literary magazine, 2. 1379
Dublin magazine (1733), 2. 362, 1379
Dublin magazine (1762), 2. 1379
Dublin magazine (1788), 2. 1379
Dublin magazine (1798), 2. 1380
Dublin magazine (1923), 4. 1366
Dublin mercury (1705), 2. 1381
Dublin mercury (1722), 2. 1383
Dublin mercury (Jan 1726), 2. 1383
Dublin mercury (April 1726), 2. 1383
Dublin mercury (1742), 2. 1385
Dublin mercury (1766), 2. 1386
Dublin news-letter (1715), 2. 1382
Dublin news-letter (1736), 2. 1385
Dublin news-letter (1737), 2. 1385
Dublin 19 April 1708, 2. 1381
Dublin, November the 21st 1715 [etc], 2. 1382
Dublin, Octob 29 1714 [etc], 2. 1382
Dublin opinion, 4. 1365
Dublin packet (1730), 2. 1384
Dublin packet (1788), 2. 1386
Dublin post (1702), 2. 1381
Dublin-post (1714), 2. 1382
Dublin-post (1719), 2. 1383
Dublin post boy (1725), 2. 1383
Dublin post-boy (Jan. 1729), 2. 1384
Dublin post boy (March 1729), 2. 1384
Dublin post-boy (1730), 2. 1383
Dublin post-boy (1732), 2. 1384
Dublin post-man (1714), 2. 1382
Dublin post-man (1715), 2. 1382
Dublin post-man (1726), 2. 1383
Dublin postman (1726), 2. 1384
Dublin quarterly maske, 2. 357
Dublin review, 3. 1856, 1865; 4. 1349
Dublin Society's weekly observations, 2. 1385
Dublin songster, 2. 395
Dublin spectator, 2. 1386
Dublin sporting news, 3. 1806
Dublin spy (1710), 2. 1382
Dublin spy (1753), 2. 1379
Dublin typographer, 4. 82
Dublin University magazine, 3. 1845–6, 1862, 1869
Dublin University review (1833), 3. 1869
Dublin University review (1885), 3. 1870
Dublin weekly intelligence, 2. 1382
Dublin weekly journal, 2. 1383
Dublin weekly magazine, 2. 1379
Dublin weekly mercury, 2. 1382
Du Boccage, Marie Anne Fiquet, 2. 1402, 1421
Dubois-Fontenelle, Jean Gaspard, 2. 1003
Du Bos, Jean Baptiste, 2. 1509, 36, 66, 116

Ducarel, Andrew Coltee, 2. 1735, 1419
Du Castel, Christine, 1. 2061
Duchal, James, 2. 1672
Du Chesne, André, 1. 862
Duchess novelette, 4. 1353
Duck, Stephen, 2. 545
Duckett, George, 2. 1277
Duckworth and Co, Gerald, 3. 78
Duclaux, Agnes Mary Frances, 3. 646–7
Duclos, Charles Pinot, 2. 1510, 93
Ducray-Duminil, François Guillaume, 2. 1012, 1033–4
Du Deffand, Marie de Vichy de Chamrond, Marquise, 2. 136
Dudley, Edmund, 1. 2275
Dudley, Sir Henry Bate, formerly Bate, 2. 833, 1335, 1336; 3. 1789
Dudley, Thomas, 1. 2158
duelling, 2. 1562–4
Duff, James, 2nd Earl of Fife, 2. 2064
Duff, Walter, 4. 1358
Duff, William, 2. 2064, 1004
Duffett, Thomas, 2. 761
Duffy, Sir Charles Gavan, 3. 1807
Duffy's Hibernian (sixpenny) magazine, 3. 1850
Du Fresnoy, Charles Alphonse, 2. 1510, 36, 76
Dufton, J., 3. 1724
Dugard, William, 1. 962, 2091, 2106
Dugdale, Gilbert, 1. 2073
Dugdale, Sir William, 1. 999, 2135, 2278; 2. 1675–8
Du Guay-Trouin, René, 2. 1461
Du Halde, Jean Baptiste, 2. 1438
Du Jon, François, 1. 2294, 2317; 2. 1791
Duke, Richard, 2. 472
Duke Rowlande and Sir Ottuell, 1. 419–20
Dukes, Ashley, 4. 934–5, 1354
Dukes, Nicholas, 2. 1566
Dulwich, manuscripts of, 1. 990
Dumas, Alexandre, *père* (1803–70), 3. 101
Dumas, Alexandre, *fils* (1824–95), 3. 101–2
Du Mats de Montmartin, Esau, 1. 2080
Du Maurier, Daphne, 4. 565–6
Du Maurier, George Louis Palmella Busson, 3. 1049, 66
Du Maurier, Gerald, 4. 866
Dumesnil-Morin, Anne Louise, 2. 1510
Dumfries, printing, 2. 271
Dumfries mercury, 2. 1376
Dumfries weekly journal, 2. 1376
Dumfries weekly magazine, 2. 1372, 1374, 1376
Du Mont, Jean, Baron de Carlscroon, 2. 1414
Dun Emer Press, 4. 97
Dunbar, printing, 2. 271
Dunbar, William, 1. 660–2, 742

Dunblane, its library, 2. 307
Duncan, Jonathan, 3. 1813
Duncan, Ronald Frederick Henry, 4. 935–6, 1373
Duncan, William, 3. 1795
Duncan, William Wallace, 3. 1882
Duncan's manual of British and foreign brewery companies, 3. 1882
Dunckley, Henry, 3. 1795
Duncombe, John, 2. 653–4, 1565
Dundass, Maria, 3. 1089
Dundee advertiser (and courier), 3. 1804, 1833
Dundee courier, 3. 1804, 1833
Dundee herald, 3. 1819
Dundee magazine (1757), 2. 1374
Dundee magazine (1775), 2. 1374
Dundee magazine (1799), 2. 1374
Dundee mail, 2. 1376
Dundee repository, 2. 1374
Dundee weekly courier, 3. 1804
Dundee weekly intelligencer, 2. 1376
Dundee weekly magazine, 2. 1374
Dundee weekly news, 4. 1401
Dunedin, Jean Murray, Viscountess, 4. 1361
Dungal, 1. 351–2
Dungannon weekly magazine, 2. 1380
Dunkerley, William Arthur, 4. 696–7
Dunlop, Agnes Mary Robertson, 4. 811
Dunlop, Andrew, 3. 1767
Dunlop, Durham, 3. 1846
Dunlop, John Colin, 3. 1279
Dunmore, Charles Adolphus Murray, 7th Earl of, 3. 1676
Dunn, Henry, 3. 1722
Dunn, J. S., 4. 1385
Dunn, James N., 3. 1789
Dunne, John William, 4. 1250–1, 792
Dunniad, 2. 388
Dunning, R., 3. 1725
Du Noyer, Anne Marguerite Petit, 2. 987
Dunraven, Windham Thomas Wyndham Quin, 4th Earl of, 3. 1673
Duns, John, 3. 1856
Duns Scotus, John, 1. 785–7
Dunsany, Edward John Moreton Drax Plunkett, 18th Baron, 3. 1945–8
Dunsford, Martin, 2. 1408
Dunster, Charles, 2. 1787
Dunton, John (1628–76), religious writer, 2. 980
Dunton, John (fl. 1637), 1. 2128
Dunton, John (1659–1733), bookseller, 2. 279, 982, 1274, 1275, 1292, 1293, 1294, 1319, 1341, 1342, 1343, 1344, 1345, 1399, 1459
Dunton's ghost, 2. 1275, 1345
Dunton's whipping-post, 2. 344
Du Pan, James Mallet, 2. 1312, 1338

Du Perier, —, 2. 1453
Dupin, Aurore, 3. 106–7
Dupont de Nemours, Pierre Samuel, 2. 1510
Duport, James, 1. 2305
Duppa, Baldwin Francis, 3. 1721–2, 1745
Duppa, Brian, 1. 1991
Duppa, Richard, 3. 1678
Duquesne, Abraham, 2. 1434
Durand de Villegagnon, Nicolas, 1. 2121
Durant, Gilles, 1. 870
D'Urfey, Thomas, 2. 761–4, 1562
Durham
  general bibliography, 1. 16
  Middle English drama, 1. 738
  medieval library, 1. 990
  Restoration and eighteenth century
    libraries, 2. 307
    magazines, 2. 1357
    printing and bookselling, 2. 267
  nineteenth century university, 3. 1735
  twentieth century university journalism, 4. 1395
Durham, James, 1. 2458–9
Durham (OE poem), 1. 276
Durham county advertiser, 4. 1400
Durham courant, 2. 1357
Durham prologue (ME play), 1. 738
Durham proverbs, 1. 276
Durham university journal, 4. 1395
Durnford, Richard, 3. 1691
Durrell, Lawrence George, 4. 266–71, 1372, 1375
Dury, Giles, 1. 2110; 2. 1315
Dusart, George C., 4. 1354
Dutch, literary relations
  loan-words, 1. 165
  Renaissance to Restoration, 1. 917–20
    Shakespeare, 1. 1632
    travel, 1. 918–19
  Restoration and eighteenth century, 2. 205–10
  nineteenth century, 3. 93–4
Dutch intelligencer, 1. 2108
Dutch prophet, 2. 1343
Dutch rogue, 2. 980
Dutch spy, 1. 2107
Dutens, Louis, 2. 1424
Dutton, Thomas, 2. 1312, 1338–9
Du Vair, Guillaume, 1. 863
Du Verdier, Gilbert Saulnier, Sieur, 1. 874, 2064
Dux Moraud, 1. 738
Dwarf, 4. 1382
Dwarf's part of the play, 1. 742
Dyce, Alexander, 3. 1644–5
Dyer, Sir Edward, 1. 1101
Dyer, George, 3. 378–9
Dyer, John, 2. 545–6

Elliott, Mary, 3. 1089
Elliott, Ruth, 4. 1369, 1385
Elliott, Thomas, 3. 1793
Ellis (booksellers), 3. 86
Ellis, Albert William, 4. 1378
Ellis, Alexander John, 3. 1645-6, 1870
Ellis, Arthur, 3. 1824
Ellis, B., 4. 860
Ellis, Clement, 1. 2047
Ellis, George, 2. 654, 238, 1443, 1788
Ellis, Henry, 2. 1484
Ellis, Henry Havelock, 3. 1429-31
Ellis, John, 2. 1440, 1904
Ellis, M., Lady, 3. 1745
Ellis, Robert, 3. 1881
Ellis, Robert Leslie, 3. 1531
Ellis, Sarah, 3. 928-9, 1875, 1877
Ellis, T. Mullett, 4. 1355
Ellis, Thomas, 1. 2150
Ellis, William (d. 1758) agriculturalist, 2. 1298,
    1554
Ellis, William (fl. 1782) ship's surgeon, 2. 1480
Ellis, William (1794-1872) of *Christian Keepsake*,
    3. 1875
Ellis, William (1800-81), educationalist, 3. 1745
Ellis-Fermor, Una Mary, 4. 1040-1
Ellison, Cary, 4. 868
Ellison, Henry, 3. 520
Ellwood, Thomas, 2. 473, 1649
Ellyot, George, 1. 2072
Elmhirst, Edward Pennell, 3. 1706
Elmley, William Lygon, Viscount, 3. 1870
Eloisa to Abelard, 2. 353
Elsmie, George Robert, 3. 1675
Elstob, Elizabeth, 2. 1793-4, 234
Elstob, William, 2. 1793, 1771
Elstree radio news, 4. 60
Elton, Oliver, 4. 1041
Elviden, Edmund, 1. 1102
Elwin, Malcolm, 4. 1378
Elwin, Whitwell, 3. 1379, 1767, 1855
Ely, George Herbert, 4. 794
Elyot, Sir Thomas, 1. 1818-19, 2031, 2276, 2307
Elys, Edmund, 1. 1307
Elysium, 4. 1393
Elzivir miscellany, 2. 349
Emare, 1. 441
emblem books, 1. 1327-34
*Emblems for the entertainment and improvement
    of youth*, 2. 1019
Emerald, 4. 1382
Emerson, William, 2. 1904
Emery, T., 3. 1724
Emery, William, 3. 1732
Emett, Mary, 4. 809

Emett, Rowland, 4. 809
'Emiliane, Gabriel d',' (Antonio Gavin), 2. 1413
Emily: or the history of a natural daughter, 2. 998
Emin, Joseph, 2. 1443
Emlyn, Thomas, 2. 1674
Emma: or the child of sorrow, 2. 1005
Emmanuel College magazine, 3. 1867; 4. 1393
Emmett, W. L., 3. 1825
Emotionism, 4. 1368
Empire (news), 3. 1812; 4. 1403
Empire frontier, 4. 1389
Empire news, 3. 1812
Empress dainty novels, 4. 1354
Empress novelette, 4. 1354
Empson, William (1790?-1852), 3. 1854
Empson, William (b. 1906), 4. 272-4, 1368, 1394
Encore (1892), 4. 1353
Encore (1946), 4. 1377
Encyclopédie, its influence, 2. 36, 93
Enemy, 4. 1367, 1345
Enfant sage, L', 1. 513
Enfield, William, 2. 1290
Engineer, 3. 1827
Engineering, 3. 1827
England, 3. 1815
England calling, 4. 1387
England displayed, 2. 1402
England's genius, or wit triumphant, 2. 363
England's glory, 2. 383
Englands Helicon, 1. 1009
Englands memorable accidents, 1. 2096
England's merry jester, 2. 338
England's moderate messenger, 1. 2105
England's monitor, 2. 1341
Englands Parnassus, 1. 1009
Englands Remarques, 2. 1397
England's remembrancer of London's integritie, 1.
    2102
England's witty and ingenious jester, 2. 349
Engle, Paul, 4. 1398
Englefield, Cicely, 4. 800
English, Harriet, 2. 1029
English, John, 2. 1402
English (1919), 4. 1363
English (1936), English Association, 4. 1372
English and French (news) journal, 2. 1325
English archer, 2. 399
English catalogue of books, 3. 84
English Chartist circular, 3. 1819
English chronicle, 2. 1335; 3. 1808
English churchman, 3. 1822
English courant, 2. 1320
English currant (1679), 2. 1316
English currant (1688), 2. 1318
English dance and song, 4. 878

English digest (1938), 4. 1408
English digest (1939), 4. 1374
English Folk Dance and Song Society bulletin, 4. 878
English Folk-Dance Society's journal, 4. 878
English freeholder, 2. 1288
English gazette, 2. 1317
English gentleman, 3. 1810
English gratitude, 2. 347
English Guzman, 2. 1341
English historical review, 3. 1858
English illustrated magazine, 3. 1852; 4. 1352
English independent, 3. 1808, 1822
English intelligencer, 2. 1316
English journal of education, 3. 1847
English labourers' chronicle, 3. 1820
English life and language, 4. 1377
English Lucian, 2. 1342
English lyceum, 2. 408, 1308
English lyricks, 2. 423
English magazine, 4. 1368
English magazine and commercial repertory, 2. 1311
English Marmontel, 2. 1285
English Martial, 2. 1343
English miscellanies, 2. 365
English miscellany, 4. 1380
English nobleman: or peasant of quality, 2. 993
English Orpheus, 2. 370
English Parnassus, 1. 1010; 2. 333
English poems. . .on the death of Frederick Prince of Wales, 2. 375
English post, 2. 1320
English review (1783), 2. 1307
English review (1844), 3. 1856
English review (1908), 4. 1359, 1346
English review magazine, 4. 1376
English Roscius, 2. 389
English-speaking world, 4. 1363
English spy, 2. 1320
English story, 4. 1375
English treasury of wit and language, 1. 1010
English typographia, 3. 61
Englishman (1713), 2. 1275
Englishman (Dublin 1715), 2. 1382
Englishman (1733), 2. 1327
Englishman (1738), 2. 1329
Englishman (1768), 2. 1284
Englishman (1779), 2. 1286, 1335
Englishman (1803), 3. 1808
Englishman's evening post, 2. 1330
Englishman's fortnight in Paris, 2. 1424
Englishman's journal, 2. 1325
Englishman's miscellany, 2. 369
Englishwoman (1895), 3. 1854

Englishwoman (1909), 4. 1360
Englishwoman's domestic magazine, 3. 1849
Englishwoman's journal, 3. 1849
Englishwoman's review (1857), 3. 1849
Englishwoman's review: a journal of woman's work (1866), 3. 1850
Englishwoman's review of social and industrial questions, 3. 1850
Englishwoman's year book, 3. 1878
Enniss chronicle, 2. 1388
Enquirer, 2. 1290
Enquiry, 4. 1378
Ensor, George, 3. 1718
Ensor, Sir Robert Charles Kirkwood, 4. 1159–60
Ent, Sir George, 2. 1904
Enterprise, 4. 1383
Entertainer (1717), 2. 1276
Entertainer (1746), 2. 372
Entertainer (1754), 2. 1281
Entertainer (1765), 2. 386
Entertainer (1766), 2. 387
Entertainer (1913), 4. 849
Entertaining companion, 2. 387
Entertaining correspondent, 2. 1298
Entertaining extracts, 2. 421
Entertaining fables for. . .children, 2. 1021
Entertaining history of William Watling, 2. 411
Entertaining magazine: or repository of general knowledge, 3. 1843
Entertaining medley, 2. 388
Entertainment of. . .Charles II, 2. 329
Entick, John, 2. 1776, 1281, 1332
Entire new collection of humourous songs, An, 2. 374
Entire set of the monitors, An (1713), 2. 347
Entire set of the monitors, An (c. 1730), 2. 358
Entr'acte, 3. 1124, 1826; 4. 823, 848, 858
Entr'acte almanack, 4. 859
Envoy, 4. 1380
'Ephelia', 2. 473
Ephemeral, 3. 1868
Ephemeris, 2. 1313
epic poetry
    Renaissance to Restoration, Italian, 1. 896–8
    Restoration and eighteenth century, 2. 53–9, 315
    nineteenth century, 3. 170
Epicedia academiae oxoniensis in obitum Mariae principis Arausionensis, 2. 328
Epicedia cantabrigiensa in obitum principis Annae, 2. 330
Epicedia oxoniensa in obitum Frederici principis Walliae, 2. 375
Epictetus, 1. 2168; 2. 1490
Epicurus, 2. 1490, 34

epigrams, Renaissance to Restoration, 1. 1333–8
Epilogue, 4. 1371
Epinay, Louise Florence Pétronille, Marquise d', 2. 1510
Epistle of Othea, 1. 690–1
epistolary novel, 2. 870
Epithalamia oxoniensa (1734), 2. 363
Epithalamia oxoniensa (1762), 2. 382
Epithalamium in desideratissimis nuptiis principum Guilielmi-Henrici Arausii & Mariae, 2. 333
Epitome of the weekly news, 2. 1318
epitomes, Biblical, Renaissance to Restoration, 1. 1843
Equator, 4. 1376
Equiano, Olaudah, 2. 1396
Equinox, 4. 1359
Equity letter, 4. 874
Era, 3. 1123, 1826; 4. 823, 858
Era almanack, 3. 1124, 1878; 4. 823, 858
Era annual, 3. 1124
Eragny Press, 3. 56; 4. 97
Erasmus, Desiderius, 1. 1785–90, 846–8; 2. 76
Ercilla y Zúñiga, Alonso de, 1. 2185, 911, 2153
Erdeswicke, Sampson, 1. 2212, 2131
Erdington amateur, 4. 1384
Eremyte and the outlaw, 1. 460
Erigena, Johannes Scotus, 1. 354–6
Erimus, 4. 1387
Erinna, 4. 1396
Erith, Belvedere and district free press, 4. 850
Erkenwald, 1. 554
Ermina, 2. 1003
Erndtel, Christian Heinrich, 2. 1537, 1399
Ernle, Rowland Edmund Prothero, Baron, 3. 1855
Eromena, 2. 980
Erskine, Ebenezer, 2. 2043
Erskine, Ralph, 2. 2043–4
Erskine, Ruaraidh, 4. 1352
Erskine, Mrs Steuart, 4. 1356
Erskine, Thomas, 1st Baron (1750–1823), 3. 1280–1
Erskine, Thomas (1788–1870), 3. 1603
Ervine, St John, 3. 1945; 4. 1354
Escalante, Bernardino de, 1. 2142
Escott, Thomas Hay Sweet, 3. 1767, 1793, 1850
Esdaile, Arundell James Kennedy, 3. 90
Esdall's news-letter, 2. 1385
Esmerica, 4. 1385
'Esmond, Henry Vernon' (Henry Vernon Jack), 3. 1192
Espagne, Jean d', 1. 863
Espejo, Antonio de, 1. 2151
Espinasse, Francis, 3. 1767, 1804
Espinosa, Louisa Kay, 4. 826

Esprit des gazettes, 2. 1306
Esquemeling, John, 2. 1456
Esquillus, Publius, 1. 2075
Essay on friendship, 2. 1286
Essay on gaming, An, 2. 1567
Essay on poetry written by the Marquis of Normanby, An, 2. 340
Essayist (1782), 2. 1287
Essayist (1786), 2. 1287
Essayist (1795), 2. 1289
essays and essayists
  Renaissance to Restoration, 1. 2043–50
  Restoration and eighteenth century, 2. 6, 1035–1256
  nineteenth century, 3. 1197–1458
  twentieth century, 4. 993–1134
Essays (1751), in *Student*, 2. 1348
Essays (1794), 2. 1289
Essays after the manner of Goldsmith, 2. 1290
Essays and poems (Cork 1770), 2. 391
Essays by A. Murphy, 2. 1280
Essays, by a society of gentlemen at Exeter, 2. 422
Essays by 'Gentleman', 2. 1286
Essays by 'Hortensia', 2. 1285
Essays by 'R. Freeman', 2. 1278
Essays by 'Regulus', 2. 1285
Essays for the month, 2. 1276, 1294
Essays from the Batchelor, 2. 394
Essays historical, political and moral, 2. 401
Essays in prose and verse, 2. 428
Essays in the Lady's magazine 2. 1280
Essays on several subjects, 2. 1285
Essays on song-writing, 2. 393
Essays on the Game Laws, 2. 1560
Essays on the vices and follies of the times, 2. 1277
Essays on various subjects (1775), 2. 1286
Essays on various subjects (1778), 2. 1286
Essays serious and comical, 2. 344
Essence of theatrical wit, 2. 388
Essex
  general bibliography, 1. 17
  Restoration and eighteenth century, printing, 2. 267
Essex, James, 2. 1423
Essex, John, 2. 1565
Essex, Robert Devereux, 2nd Earl of, 1. 1099
Essex, Robert Devereux, 3rd Earl of, 1. 999
Essex harmony, 2. 376
Essex herald, 2. 1355
Essex House Press, 3. 56–7
Essex mercury, 2. 1356
Estcourt, Richard, 2. 789
Este, Charles, 2. 1429
Este, Michael, 1. 1351
Estella, Diego de, 1. 908

Estienne, Henri, 1. 2185, 2062, 863
Etherege, Sir George, 2. 741–2
Etherington's York chronicle, 2. 1369
Ethic tales and fables, 2. 395
Eton, William, 2. 1431
Eton bureau, 3. 1870
Eton College
   Renaissance to Restoration, library, 1. 990–1
   Restoration and eighteenth century
     library, 2. 307
      newspapers, 2. 1357
      printing and bookselling, 2. 267
   nineteenth century journalism, 3. 1870–1, 1874
Eton College chronicle, 3. 1870
Eton College magazine, 3. 1870
Eton fortnightly, 3. 1870
Eton idler, 3. 1871
Eton journal, 2. 1357
Eton miscellany, 3. 1870
Eton observer (1860), 3. 1870
Eton observer (1887), 3. 1870
Eton rambler, 3. 1870
Eton review (1867), 3. 1870
Eton review (1886), 3. 1870
Eton review (1889), 3. 1870
Eton School magazine, 3. 1870
Eton scrap book, 3. 1870
Eton spectator, 3. 1871
Etonensia, 3. 1870
Etonian (1820), 3. 1870
Etonian (1875), 3. 1870
Etonian (1883), 3. 1870
Ettingsall, T., 3. 1688
Euclid, 1. 2168
Eudes de Mézeray, François, 2. 1510
Eunapius Sardianus, 1. 2169
Euphrasy, 2. 1284
'Euphrosine', 2. 1282
Eureka, 4. 1354
Euripides, 1. 2169; 2. 1490
Europae modernae speculum, 2. 1410
Europe, travels in
   Renaissance to Restoration, 1. 2121–42
   Restoration and eighteenth century, 2. 1409–32
   nineteenth century, 3. 1677–84
European magazine and London review, 2. 1306;
   3. 1840
European mercury, 1. 2140
European quarterly, 4. 1371
Eusden, Laurence, 2. 547
Eusebius, 1. 345
'Eustace' legends, 1. 441–4
Eustace, John Chetwode, 3. 1677
Eutropius, 1. 2169
Evangelical magazine (1780), 2. 1351

Evangelical magazine (1793), 2. 1310; 3. 1840
Evangelicalism, nineteenth century, 3. 1615–22
Evans, Abel, 2. 547–8
Evans, Anne, 3. 520
Evans, Arthur Henry, 3. 1824
Evans, Caradoc, 4. 566
Evans, Charles S., 4. 1363
Evans, David Caradoc, 4. 566
Evans, David Morier, 3. 1791, 1824, 1882
Evans, Edward Radcliffe Garth Russell, 4. 794
Evans, Evan, 2. 245
Evans, F., 3. 1683
Evans, H. R., 3. 1762
Evans, Howard, 3. 1793
Evans, J., 4. 852
Evans, James, 3. 1822
Evans, John (1767–1827), 2. 1027
Evans, Rev. John (fl. 1804), 3. 1681
Evans, John Randell, 4. 1369
Evans, Lewis (fl. 1561), 1. 2032
Evans, Lewis (d. 1756), 2. 1465
'Evans, Margiad' (Peggy E. A. Williams), 4. 567
Evans, Mary Ann, 3. 899–912, 132, 156
Evans, Myfanwy, 4. 1371
Evans, Patrick, 4. 1372
Evans, Sebastian, 3. 520, 1797, 1812
Evans, Thomas, 3. 1681
Evans, William, 1. 1102
Evans and Co., W., 3. 1798
Evans and Ruffy's farmer's journal, 3. 1823
Evans's edition: old ballads, 2. 397
Evans-Pritchard, Edward Evan, 4. 1160
Eve, H. W., 3. 1729
Eve, 4. 1406
Eve's journal, 4. 1373
Eve's own (*stories*), 4. 1366
Evelegh, B. C., 3. 1883
Evelin, Robert, 1. 2163
Evelyn, John (1620–1706), diarist, 2. 1580–2,
   309–10, 1391; 1. 1000, 2129, 2136, 2141, 2296
Evelyn, John (1655–99), 2. 1582
Evelyn, Mary, 2. 1582
Evening advertiser, 2. 1332
Evening argus (Bath), 3. 1799
Evening argus (Brighton), 3. 1801
Evening chronicle (Dublin 1784), 2. 1386
Evening chronicle (1824), 3. 1792
Evening chronicle (1835), 3. 1807
Evening chronicle (Oldham 1880), 3. 1801
Evening chronicle (Newcastle 1885), 3. 1802
Evening chronicle (Manchester 1914), 3. 1803;
   4. 1404
Evening citizen, 3. 1804; 4. 1400
Evening courant, 2. 1322
Evening despatch (Birmingham 1907), 4. 1404

Evening dispatch (Edinburgh 1921), 3. 1805; 4. 1403

Evening echo (1868), 3. 1793

Evening echo (Cork 1893), 3. 1806

Evening entertainment, 2. 1326

Evening express (Liverpool 1870), 3. 1798; 4. 1402

Evening express (Wolverhampton 1876), 3. 1799

Evening express (Edinburgh 1880), 3. 1805

Evening express (Cardiff 1887), 4. 1403

Evening express (Aberdeen 1899), 3. 1805

Evening express and standard (Blackburn 1888), 3. 1802

Evening express of the Devon weekly times, 3. 1797

Evening express telegram, 3. 1799

Evening freeman, 3. 1806

Evening gazette (Aberdeen), 3. 1805

Evening gazette (Middlesbrough), 3. 1798

Evening general post, 2. 1323

Evening herald (1786), 2. 1386

Evening herald (1857), 3. 1793

Evening herald (Northampton 1880), 3. 1801

Evening herald (Dublin 1891), 3. 1806

Evening herald (Ipswich 1897), 3. 1803

Evening Irish times, 3. 1806

Evening journal (1727), 2. 1326

Evening journal (Glasgow 1869), 3. 1804

Evening mail (1789), 2. 1337; 3. 1807

Evening mail (Portsmouth 1884), 3. 1801

Evening mail (1896), 3. 1794

Evening mail (Dublin 1928), 3. 1806; 4. 1400

Evening news (Greenock 1866), 3. 1804

Evening news (Hull 1870), 3. 1798

Evening news (Dundee 1876), 3. 1805

Evening news (Portsmouth 1877), 3. 1800

Evening news (1881), 3. 1794; 4. 1402

Evening news (Norwich 1882), 3. 1801

Evening news (Waterford 1898), 3. 1807

Evening news (Glasgow 1915), 3. 1804; 4. 1402

Evening news (Nottingham 1948), 3. 1802

Evening news and star (Glasgow 1875), 3. 1804

Evening news and star (1960), 4. 1402

Evening news and times (Worcester 1937), 3. 1801

Evening post (1706), 2. 1321

Evening post (1709), 2. 1322

Evening post (Edinburgh 1710), 2. 1375

Evening post (Dublin 1712), 2. 1382

Evening post (Worcester 1877), 3. 1800

Evening post (Warrington 1878), 3. 1800

Evening post (Exeter 1885), 3. 1802

Evening post (1887), 3. 1794

Evening post (Dundee 1900), 3. 1805

Evening post and news (Nottingham 1963), 3. 1801

Evening press (Belfast), 3. 1806

Evening press (York), 3. 1801

Evening report: the public ledger, 3. 1789

Evening sentinel, 3. 1799

Evening standard, 3. 1793; 4. 1400

Evening Standard book of best short stories, 4. 1370

Evening Standard book of strange stories, 4. 1390

Evening Standard detective book, 4. 1392

Evening star (1788), 2. 1337

Evening star (1842), 3. 1793

Evening star (1856), 3. 1793

Evening star (Glasgow 1872), 3. 1804

Evening star (Wolverhampton 1880), 3. 1801

Evening star of Gwent, 3. 1800

Evening telegram (Newport), 3. 1798

Evening telegram and express (Cheltenham), 3. 1799

Evening telegraph (Dublin 1861), 3. 1806; 4. 1402

Evening telegraph (Dundee 1877), 3. 1805, 1833

Evening telegraph (Blackburn 1956), 3. 1802; 4. 1403

Evening telegraph and star (Sheffield), 3. 1802

Evening times (1825), 3. 1793

Evening times (Liverpool), 3. 1801

Evening times and echo, 4. 1405

Evening weekly packet, 2. 1323

Evening world, 4. 1407

Evens, George Bramwell, 4. 797

Events in Bristol (and Cardiff), 4. 852

Events in the west, 4. 852

Ever green, 2. 355

Everard, John, 1. 2305

Everard, Robert, 2. 1448

Everett-Green, Evelyn, 3. 1105

Evers, Samuel, 2. 1442

Every day book, 3. 1873

Every lady's own Valentine writer, 2. 419

Every man's journal, 2. 1386

Every man's magazine, 2. 1304

Every woman in her humor, 1. 1759

Every writer's herald, 4. 73

Everybody's, 4. 1406

Everybody's journal, 3. 1814, 1835

Everybody's story magazine, 4. 1359

Everyman (morality play), 1. 1406–7

Everyman (literary journal), 4. 1360–1, 1405–6

Everyone's (story magazine), 4. 1359

Everywoman (1911), 4. 1405

Everywoman (1940), 4. 1407

Everywoman's (weekly) (1915), 4. 1405

Everywoman's (1934), 4. 1407

Evill, William, 3. 1681

'Evoe' (E. V. Knox), 4. 295

Ewing, Alexander, 3. 1606

Ewing, Greville, 2. 1373

Ewing, Juliana Horatia, 3. 1049–50, 1095, 1767, 1851

Fairfax, Thomas, 3rd Baron, 2. 1693–4; 1. 1913
Fairies: an opera, 2. 378
'Fairlegh, Frank' (Francis Edward Smedley), 3. 1848
'Fairless, Michael' (Margaret Fairless Barber), 3. 1050
Fairlie, Louisa, 3. 1876
Fairthorne, R., 4. 57
Fairy, 4. 1382
Fairy knight, 1. 1759
fairy tales, nineteenth century, 3. 1107–10
Fairy tatler, 2. 1277
Faithful friends, 1. 1759
Faithful memoirs of the Grubstreet society, 2. 361
Faithful post, 1. 2108; 2. 1315
Faithful scout, 1. 2110; 2. 1313
Faithfull, Emily, 3. 1850
Faithfull intelligencer from the Parliaments army in Scotland, 2. 1373
Faithfull mercury, 2. 1316
Faithfull post, 1. 2108
Faithfull relation of the . . .Scotish army, A, 1. 2100
Faithfull scout, 1. 2107
Falconbridge, Alexander, 2. 1451
Falconbridge, Anna Maria, 2. 1452
Falconer, David, 2. 1439
'Falconer, Lanoe' (Mary Elizabeth Hawker), 3. 1051
Falconer, William, 2. 654–5
falconry, nineteenth century, 3. 1700–1
Falkirk herald, 3. 1831
Falkland, Amelia Cary, Viscountess, 3. 1675
Falkland, Henry Cary, 3rd Viscount, 1. 1736
Falkner, George, 3. 1847
Falkner, John Meade, 3. 1051
Falkner, Thomas, 2. 1469
Fall of Britain, 2. 1335
Fallam, Robert, 2. 1455
Falstaff's annual, 3. 1875
'Falstaffe, Sir John', 2. 1277
Fame's palladium, 2. 1313
Familiar hints on sea-bathing, 3. 1715
Familiar letters of love, 2. 351
Familiar letters written by. . .Rochester, 2. 340
Family friend, 3. 1814; 4. 1350
Family herald, 3. 1813; 4. 1350
Family jewel, A, 2. 1557
Family journal, 4. 1359
Family magazine (1788), 2. 1308
Family magazine (1834), 3. 1846
Family magazine (1910), 4. 1360
Family novelist, 4. 1352
Family pictorial, 4. 1406
Family times, 3. 1811
Famous ballad of Badsworth hunt, 2. 1558

Famous detective cases, 4. 1390
Famous Tommy Thumb's little story-book, 2. 1021
Famous victories of Henry the Fifth, 1. 1471
Fancy, or true sportsman's guide, 3. 1692
Fane, Elizabeth, Lady, 1. 1901
Fane, Sir Francis, 2. 764
Fane, Julian Henry Charles, 3. 521
Fane, Mildmay, 2nd Earl of Westmorland, 1. 1740–1
'Fane, Violet' (Mary M. Singleton), 3. 625–6
Fanfare, 4. 1365
Fanfreluche, 4. 1394
Fanfrolico Press, 4. 97
Fannie Eden's penny stories, 4. 1358
Fanshaw, Sir Richard, 2. 1415
Fanshawe, Althea, 2. 1028
Fanshawe, Catherine Maria, 3. 380
Fanshawe, Sir Richard, 1. 1741, 2147
Fantasia, 4. 1388
Fantasma, 4. 1388
Fantasma Readers' and Writers' Club journal, 4. 1388
Fantasma story collection, 4. 1388
Fantasy (1938), 4. 1390
Fantasy (1946), 4. 1392
Fantasy poets, 4. 1398
Far and wide, 4. 1408
Farewell, Christopher, 1. 2146
Fargus, Frederick John, 3. 1043
Faria y Sousa, Manuel de, 2. 1434
Farish, William, 2. 1904
Farjeon, Benjamin Leopold, 3. 1051–2
Farjeon, Eleanor, 4. 794–5
Farjeon, Herbert, 4. 937–8, 826
Farley, Robert, 1. 1307, 1329
Farley's Bath journal, 2. 1353
Farley's Bristol advertiser, 2. 1354
Farley's Bristol journal (1741), 2. 1354
Farley's Bristol journal (1748), 2. 1354
Farley's Bristol news-paper, 2. 1354
Farley's Exeter journal, 2. 1358
Farley's Exeter weekly journal, 2. 1358
Farlie, Robert, 1. 1307, 1329
Farm and country, 3. 1817; 4. 823, 1402
Farmer, Hugh, 2. 163
Farmer, John, 1. 1350
Farmer, Richard, 2. 1757
Farmer, William, 1. 2238
Farmer, 3. 1823–4
Farmer's express, 3. 1823
Farmer's journal (1807), 3. 1823
Farmer's journal (1839), 3. 1823
Farmer's magazine (1776), 2. 1305
Farmer's magazine (1800), 2. 1373
Farnaby, Giles, 1. 1349

Farnaby, Thomas, 1. 2316, 2305
Farnborough, Sir Thomas Erskine May, Baron, 3. 1492–3
Farnie, H. B., 3. 1702
Faro and Rouge et Noir, 2. 1568
Faro table, 3. 1693
Farquhar, George, 2. 753–6, 177, 984
Farrago (1792), 2. 1289
Farrago (1816), 3. 1867
Farrago (1930), 4. 1398
Farrar, Frederic William, 3. 1052, 1094, 1606, 1727, 1729
Farrer, Richard Ridley, 3. 1681
Farrier's and horseman's dictionary, 2. 1553
farriery, Restoration and eighteenth century, 2. 1551–5
Farrow, George Edward, 3. 1106
Farther hue and cry, A, 2. 348
'Fashion, Francis', 2. 1282
Fashionable magazine, 2. 1307
Fashions of London and Paris, 2. 1310
Fatal amour, 2. 988
Fatal effects of arbitrary power, 2. 987
Fatal maryage, 1. 1759
Fates of the apostles, 1. 279–80
Fatum Vortigerni, 1. 1777
Faujas de Saint Fond, Barthélemi, 2. 1408
Faulkner's Dublin post boy, 2. 1383
Faust, 1. 878–9; 2. 1537–8
Faux, D. P., 4. 1388
Favart, Charles Simon, 2. 1510, 120
Favorite new glees, 2. 416
Favourite, 4. 1358
Favourite collection of songs sung at the Spa Gardens, A, 2. 408
Favourite collection of the most admir'd glees, A, 2. 398
Favourite magazine, 4. 1354
Fawcett, Benjamin, 3. 66
Fawcett, Henry, 3. 1728
Fawcett, Millicent G., 3. 1728, 1748
Fawconer, Thomas, 2. 1314
Fawkes, Francis, 2. 655, 1304, 1559, 1780
Fay, Edward Francis, 3. 1821
Fayre mayde of the exchange, 1. 1759
Fearon, Daniel Robert, 3. 1729
Feast of Apollo, 2. 409
Featley, Daniel, 1. 2089, 2099, 2297
Fedden, H. Romilly, 4. 1368, 1394
Fedele and Fortunio, 1. 1469
Federici, Cesare, 1. 2143; 2. 1544
Feelings of the heart, 2. 1003
Feeney, John, 3. 1795, 1798
Feeney, John F., 3. 1795
Feijóo y Montenegro, Benito, 2. 198–9, 68

Feilden, Henry St Clair, 3. 1870
Feiling, Sir Keith Grahame, 4. 1160–1
Felbermann, Heinrich, 3. 1767, 1815
Felden, Robin, 4. 1375
Felippe, Bartolomé, 1. 907
Felissa, 3. 1107
Felix of Croyland, 1. 345
'Felix, N.' (Nicholas Wanostrocht), 3. 1696
Felix Farley's Bristol journal, 2. 1354
Fell, John, 2. 1608, 1825
Fellow, 3. 1865
Fellowes, Robert, 3. 1809
Felltham, Owen, 1. 1308, 2048, 2140
Feltham, John, 2. 1407
Felton, Samuel, 2. 1787
Female American, 2. 1001
Female duellist, 2. 1564
Female inconstancy display'd, 2. 361
Female jester, 2. 398
Female monitor, 2. 1288
Female poems on several occasions, 2. 334
Female rambler, 2. 1287
Female reader, 2. 411
Female rebellion, 1. 1759
Female reformer, 2. 1286
Female spectator, 2. 1298
Female spy, 2. 1426
Female student, 2. 1348
Female tatler (July 1709), 2. 1271
Female tatler (August 1709), 2. 1271
fencing
    Restoration and eighteenth century, 2. 1562–4
    nineteenth century, 3. 1701
Fénelon, François de Salignac de la Mothe, 2. 1510–12, 66, 85, 93, 114, 116, 139–40, 984
Fenn, Eleanor Frere, Lady, 2. 1024–5
Fenn, George Manville, 3. 1094, 1816, 1821
Fenn, J., 3. 1723
Fenne, Thomas, 1. 1103
Fennell, James, 2. 1337
Fenner, Dudley, 1. 1959
Fennor, William, 1. 2028, 2035
Fenton, Edward, 1. 2143
Fenton, Elijah, 2. 548, 1773
Fenton, Mrs Michael, 3. 1674, 1675
Fenton, Richard, 3. 1681
Fenton, Roger, 1. 2276
Fenwick, Eliza, 3. 1099
Fenwick, John, 3. 1792
Fenwick, Thomas J., 3. 82
Ferber, J. J., 2. 1423
Ferguson, Adam, 2. 2064–5, 106, 158, 1885
Ferguson, Peter, 4. 1397
Ferguson, Sir Samuel, 3. 1901–2
Fergusson, David, 1. 2445, 2031

Fergusson, F., 3. 1875
Fergusson, Hary, 2. 1563
Fergusson, James, 1. 2459
Fergusson, John Duncan, 4. 1360, 1376
Fergusson, Robert, 2. 2022–4
Feriae poeticae, 2. 387
Fermin, Philippe, 2. 1471
Fernandez (Lisboa), Diogo, 1. 913
Fernandez, Jeronimo, 1. 915
Fernandez de Enciso, Martin, 1. 2161
Fernandez de Quiros, Pedro, 1. 2156
Ferrabosco, Alfonso, 1. 1353
Ferrar, John, 2. 1407
Ferrar, Nicholas, 1. 1975–6, 2296
Ferreira, António, 2. 201
Ferrers, George, 1. 1103
Ferrier, J. W., 3. 1869
Ferrier, James Frederick, 3. 1531
Ferrier, Richard, 2. 1412
Ferrier, Susan Edmonstone, 3. 720–1
Ferris, Richard, 1. 2026–7, 2123
Festial, 1. 488
Festival-Gate review, 4. 826, 852
Festival news, 4. 852
Festival of Anacreon (1788), 2. 409
Festival of Anacreon (1789), 2. 411
Festival of humour, 2. 428
Festival of love, 2. 411
Festival of mirth, 2. 428
Festival of Momus, 2. 407
Festival of wit, 2. 403
Festival review, 4. 826, 852
Festival Theatre programme, 4. 826, 852
Festival Theatre review, 4. 826, 852
Festoon, 2. 387
Festum voluptatis, 1. 1010
Feuerbach, Ludwig, 3. 120
Fevrier, D., 3. 1858
Fewtrell, Thomas, 2. 1563
Feylde, Thomas, 1. 1104
Feynes de Montfart, Henri de, 1. 2145
Fialetti, Odoardo, 2. 1544
Fichte, Johann Gottlieb, 3. 120
Ficino, Marsiglio, 1. 848
fiction, prose
    general, 1. 27
    Renaissance to Restoration, 1. 2049–68
        French, 1. 857–8
        German, 1. 882
        Italian, 1. 898–904
        Latin, 1. 857–8
        Spanish, 1. 912–18
    Restoration and eighteenth century, 2. 865–
        1034
        children's books, 2. 1013–34

French, 2. 137–52
German, 2. 180–6
Italian, 2. 194–6
Spanish, 2. 202–6
studies, 2. 29–30
nineteenth century, 3. 657–1084
    children's books, 3. 1085–110
    history, 3. 657–66
twentieth century, 4. 381–820
    children's books, 4. 783–820
    history, 4. 381–96
    individual novelists, 4. 395–784
    popular, 4. 123–30
fiction, manuals on writing, twentieth century,
    4. 66
'Fiction, Francis', 2. 1286
Fiction, 4. 1357
Fiction for library readers, 4. 118
'Fidelio', 2. 1288
Fidge, George, 1. 2036, 2058
'Fidler, Kathleen' (Kathleen Annie Goldie), 4.
    813
Fidler, Peter, 2. 1473
Field, 3. 1683, 1816, 1835; 4. 1346
Field, Mrs E. M., 3. 1105
Field, Louise Frances, 3. 1105
'Field, Michael' (Katherine Harris Bradley and
    Edith Emma Cooper), 3. 626–7
Field, Nathan, 1. 1741–3
Field, Richard, 1. 1940, 962, 2298
Field lawn tennis calendar, 3. 1883
Fieldhouse, H., 3. 1803
Fielding, Anna Maria, 3. 932–3, 1090
Fielding, Henry, 2. 925–48, 42, 126, 146–7, 177,
    183, 195, 205, 208, 211–12, 216–17, 1279, 1280,
    1330, 1331, 1332, 1419
Fielding, Sarah, 2. 147, 995, 996, 1020, 999
Fiennes, Celia, 2. 1398
Fiest, Henry, 3. 1791
Fieux, Charles de, Chevalier de Mouhy, 2. 995
Fife, its libraries, 1. 991; 2. 307
Fife, James Duff, 2nd Earl of, 2. 2064
Fifteen joys of marriage, 1. 1104
Fig tree, 4. 1372
Figaro, 3. 1815
Figaro in London, 3. 1825
Fight against superstition, 4. 1371
Fight of Sayerius and Heenanus, 3. 1692
Filangieri, Gaetano, 2. 1544
Filberd, 2. 412
Fildes, Sir Luke, 3. 66
Filial duty, 2. 1023
film
    general, 4. 54–8
    writing for, 4. 67–8

Film, 4. 57
Film and theatre today, 4. 828
Film art, 4. 57
Film Book Club news (-letter), 4. 58
Film censor, 4. 56
Film fiction, 4. 57
Film fun, 4. 819
Film pictorial, 4. 57
Film picture stories, 4. 57
Film quarterly (1935), 4. 58
Film quarterly (1946), 4. 58
Film renter, 4. 56
Film report, 4. 57
Film review, 4. 58
Film to-day books, 4. 58
Film truth, 4. 57
Filmer, Sir Robert, 1. 2338, 2275, 2276
Films and fiction, 4. 57
Filson, John, 2. 1471
Financial and mining news, 3. 1791
Financial chronicle, 3. 1824
Financial news, 3. 1791, 1828
financial newspapers, nineteenth century, 3. 1824, 1837
Financial times, 3. 1791; 4. 1403
Financial world, 3. 1824
Financier, 3. 1791
Finch, Anne, Countess of Winchilsea, 2. 576–7
Finch, Heneage, 2nd Earl of Winchilsea, 2. 1410
Finch, Sir John, 2. 1411
Finchale Priory, library of, 1. 991
Findens' tableaux, 3. 1875
Findlay, John Ritchie, 3. 1804
Findlay, Joseph John, 3. 1730
Fine arts quarterly review, 3. 1857
Finished rake, 2. 993
Finlason, William Francis, 3. 1881
Finlay, — (fl. 1861), 3. 1795
Finlay, Francis D., 3. 1806
Finlay, George, 3. 1488–9, 1767
Finlay, Hugh, 2. 1469
Finlay, J. W., 3. 1803
Finn's Leinster journal, 2. 1388
Finnemore, John, 4. 789
Finnsburh, Battle of, 1. 240–1
Firbank, A. A. Ronald, 4. 567–9
Firefly (1911), 4. 1382
Firefly (1914), 4. 1362
First edition and book collector, 4. 110
First editions and their values, 4. 110
First flights, 4. 1367
First words, 4. 1398
Firth, Sir Charles Harding, 4. 1161–2
Firumbras, romances of, 1. 417–18

Firumbras (Ashmole and Fillingham versions), 1. 418
Fish, Simon, 1. 1817, 876, 2277
Fishacre, Richard, 1. 776–7
Fisher, Anne, 2. 1021
Fisher, C. H., 3. 1701
Fisher, Daniel, 2. 1465
Fisher, Herbert Albert Laurens, 4. 1162–3
Fisher, Jasper, 1. 1767
Fisher, John, Bishop of Rochester (1469–1535), 1. 1923–6, 853
Fisher, John, student in Oxford (fl. 1558), 1. 1104
Fisher, Jonathan, 2. 1406, 1407
Fisher, P., 3. 1814
'Fisher, P.' (William Andrew Chatto), 3. 1688
Fisher, Samuel, 2. 1650
Fisher, William James, 3. 1791
Fisher's drawing-room scrap book, 3. 1875, 1878
Fisher's juvenile scrapbook, 3. 1877
fisheries, Renaissance to Restoration, 1. 2277–8
Fishing and hunting, 2. 1558
Fishing gazette (1865), 3. 1687
Fishing gazette (1877), 3. 1824
Fiston, W., 1. 2026
Fitch, Sir Joshua, 3. 1726, 1732, 1746
Fitch, Tobias, 2. 1461
Fitt, J. N., 3. 1706
'Fitz-Adam, Adam' (E. Moore), 2. 1281
Fitzalan, Henry, 12th Earl of Arundel, 1. 1000
Fitzball, Edward, 3. 1125–6
Fitzer, William, 1. 962
Fitzgeffrey, Charles, 1. 1104, 1308
Fitzgeffrey, Henry, 1. 1308, 1336
Fitzgerald, — (fl. 1815), 3. 1792
Fitzgerald, Lord Edward, 2. 1472
FitzGerald, Edward, 3. 483–6, 1865
Fitzgerald, Edward Arthur, 3. 1674, 1678, 1710
Fitzgerald, Francis, 2. 1307
Fitzgerald, George, 3. 1842
Fitzgerald, Gerald, 2. 1560
Fitzgerald, Percy Hetherington, 3. 1053–4
Fitzgerald, R. A., 3. 1697
Fitzgerald, Shafto Justin Adair, 4. 824
Fitzgerald, Thomas, 2. 548
Fitzgerald, W., 3. 1854
Fitzgibbon, Constantine, 4. 1374
Fitzherbert, John, 1. 2277
Fitzjames, Richard, 1. 1941
Fitzmaurice, George, 3. 1941–2
Fitzneal, Richard, 1. 765
Fitznigel, Richard, 1. 765
Fitzpatrick, Sir James Percy, 4. 789
Fitzpatrick, R. H., 4. 1356
Fitzralph, Richard, 1. 795

Fitzroy, Caroline Blanche Elizabeth, Lady Lindsay, 3. 1105
Fitzwilliam Hall magazine, 4. 1393
Fitzwyram, J., 3. 1746
Five love-letters from a nun to a cavalier, 2. 978
Five love-letters written by a cavalier, 2. 980
Five o'clock, 4. 1357
Flagel, 2. 1002
Flagellant, 2. 1289
Flame, 4. 1390
'Flammenberg, Lorenz' (K. F. Kahlert), 2. 1538, 1011
Flamsteed, John, 2. 1904
Flanders delineated, 2. 1418
Flanders new garland, 2. 345
Flapper, 2. 1380
Flatman, Thomas, 2. 473–4, 975
Flaubert, Gustave, 3. 102
Flavel, John, 1. 2333
Fleay, Frederick Gard, 3. 1646
Flecker, James Elroy, 4. 274–6
Flecknoe, Richard, 2. 764; 1. 2046, 2129
Fleet Street gazette, 3. 61, 1762
Fleet Street gleaner, 4. 1340
Fleetwood, Edward, 1. 2034
Fleming, Abraham, 1. 1104, 2071
Fleming, Caleb, 2. 1674
Fleming, G. A., 3. 1818
Fleming, John, 4. 1394
Fleming, Robert Peter, 4. 1315–16
Fleming, William, 2. 1471
Fleming's British farmer's chronicle, 3. 1823
Fleming's weekly express, 3. 1823
Flemmyng, Robert, 1. 803, 1000
Fletcher, Alfred Ewen, 3. 1791, 1815
Fletcher, Alfred H., 3. 1799
Fletcher, Anthony, 1. 2030
Fletcher, Francis, 1. 2150
Fletcher, Giles, the elder (d. 1611), 1. 1104–5, 2137–8, 2312
Fletcher, Giles, the younger (d. 1623), 1. 1190–1; 2. 32
Fletcher, J., 3. 1842
Fletcher, John, 1. 1709–19, 868, 920, 2315; 2. 31
Fletcher, John William, 2. 1623
Fletcher, Joseph, 1. 1308
Fletcher, Phineas, 1. 1187–8, 1767, 1910; 2. 32
Fletcher, R., 1. 1308
Fletcher, Thomas, 2. 474
Flete, William, 1. 515, 799
Fleur-de-lys, 3. 1867
Fleuriot, Jean-Marie-Jérôme, Marquis de Langle, 2. 1426
Fleuron, 4. 82
Fleury, Claude, 2. 1512, 66

Flinders, Matthew, 2. 1482; 3. 1675
Flint, Frank Stewart, 4. 276
Flint, George, 2. 1323
Flint, Robert, 3. 1531–2
'Flint, Violet' (J. E. Thomson), 3. 1703
Flloyd, Thomas, 2. 1798
Flodden field, 1. 1105
Flora's fair garland, 2. 336
Flora's gala, 3. 1088
Floreamus!, 4. 1398
Florence of Worcester, 1. 755
'Florence' legends, 1. 441–4
Florence miscellany, 2. 406
Flores, Juan de, 1. 915, 2062
Florian, Jean Pierre Claris de, 2. 1512, 1010
Florimene, Argument of the pastorall of, 1. 1759
Florio, John, 1. 2029, 2137, 2150
Floris, Peter, 1. 2145
Floris and Blaunchefleur, 1. 451–2
Florus, 1. 2169
Floure and the leaf, 1. 652
Flower, Benjamin, 3. 1843
Flower, Desmond, 4. 110
Flower, Newman, 4. 1366
Flower, Sarah Fuller, 3. 499–500
Flower's political review, 3. 1843
Flower-piece (1731), 2. 360
Flower-piece (1780), 2. 401
Flowers of harmony, 2. 424
Flowers of literature, 3. 1873
Flowers of loveliness, 3. 1875
Flowers of Parnassus, 2. 364
Fludd, Robert, 1. 2332
Flying eagle, 1. 2108
Flying horse, 4. 1366
Flying post (1644), 1. 2100
Flying post (Dublin 1699), 2. 1381
Flying post (Dublin April 1704), 2. 1381
Flying post (Dublin August 1704), 2. 1381
Flying post (Dublin March 1705), 2. 1381
Flying post (Dublin July 1705), 2. 1381
Flying-post (Dublin 1707), 2. 1381
Flying post (Dublin 1708), 2. 1381
Flying post (Dublin 1710), 2. 1382
Flying-post (1714), 2. 1322
Flying-post (Dublin 1715), 2. 1382
Flying post (Dublin 1719), 2. 1381
Flying post (Dublin 1720), 2. 1383
Flying-post (Dublin 1723), 2. 1382
Flying-post (December 1727), 2. 1326
Flying-post (Dublin 1727), 2. 1384
Flying-post (October 1728), 2. 1326
Flying post (Dublin April 1729), 2. 1384
Flying post (Dublin May 1729), 2. 1384
Flying post (Dublin 1744), 2. 1385

Frankz, Thomas, 2. 1417
Fraser, Alexander Campbell, 3. 1532, 1856
Fraser, Sir Arthur Ronald, 4. 579
Fraser, George Sutherland, 4. 276–7
Fraser, James, 3. 1728
Fraser, James Baillie, 3. 721, 1674
Fraser, John, 3. 1851
Fraser, John Foster, 3. 1854
Fraser, Lydia Falconer, 3. 1102
Fraser, P. Galloway, 3. 1815
Fraser, Ronald, 4. 579
Fraser, W. (fl. 1828), 3. 1874
Fraser, William, 3. 1726
Fraser-Lovat, Arnold, 4. 1356
Fraser's magazine for town and country, 3. 1845, 1861–2
'Frater', 2. 1285
Fraternity of drinkers, 1. 688
Fraud detected, 2. 355
Frauds of Romish monks and priests, 2. 982
Fraunce, Abraham, 1. 1106, 1905, 2053, 2311
Fraus Pia, 1. 1777
Frazer, Sir James George, 3. 1482–4
Frederick II, King of Prussia, 2. 1538
Frederick, Col— (fl. 1795), 2. 1429
Free, John, 1. 804, 1000
Free Briton (1727), 2. 1278, 1326
Free Briton (1729), 2. 1278
Free critic, 4. 1368
Free-enquirer, 2. 1283
Free expression, 4. 1374
Free-holder (1715), 2. 1276
Free-holder (Dublin 1715), 2. 1382
Free-holder (Cork 1716), 2. 1387
Free lance, 4. 1385
Free Lance Literary and Book Club news letter, 4. 1387
Free-lance's own, 4. 1385
Free-lance weekly (1926), 4. 72
Free-lance weekly (1936), 4. 73
Free-lance writer and photographer, 4. 74
Free lancer, 4. 1388
Free-mason's magazine (1793), 2. 1309
Free Mason's pocket companion (1736), 2. 364–5
Free-Mason's pocket companion (1752), 2. 376
Free Masons songs, 2. 381
Free Masonry for the ladies, 2. 415
Free notes, 4. 1381
Free Oxford, 4. 1397
Free press, 3. 1849
Free review, 3. 1854; 4. 1391
Free-thinker (1711), 2. 1274
Free-thinker (1718), 2. 1276
Free-thinker extraordinary (1718), 2. 1276
Free-thinker extraordinary (1719), 2. 1277

Free unions, 4. 1377
free verse, studies of, 1. 48
Freehold land times and building news, 3. 1828
Freeholder (1716), 2. 1375
Freeholder (1784), 2. 1336
Freeholder extraordinary, 2. 1276
Freeholder's journal, 2. 1277, 1325
Freeholder's magazine, 2. 1304
Freelance (1900), 4. 71
Freelance (1925), 4. 72
Freelance market news, 4. 74
Freelance register (1931), 4. 73
Freelance register (1936), 4. 73
Freeman, Edward Augustus, 3. 1473–5
Freeman, Gage Earle, 3. 1701
Freeman, George, 4. 1351
Freeman, James, 3. 1794
Freeman, John, 4. 277–8
Freeman, Sir Ralph, 1. 1743
Freeman, Thomas, 1. 1336
Freeman, 3. 1823
Freeman's journal (1781), 2. 1336
Freeman's journal (before 1820), 3. 1805
Freemason, 2. 1289
Freemason's journal, 2. 1387
Freemason's monthly magazine, 3. 1856
Freemasonry stripped naked, 2. 386
Freemasons' magazine, 3. 1856
Freemasons' quarterly (magazine and) review, 3. 1856
Freemens' magazine, 2. 1351
Freethinker, 3. 1820
Freiligrath, Ferdinand, 3. 120
Freind, John, 2. 1416, 1905
Frejus, Roland, 2. 1446
Fremantle, Henry E. S., 3. 1871
French, literary relations
  loan-words, 1. 165–7
  Renaissance to Restoration, 1. 859–76
    allegory, 1. 871–2
    dictionaries, 1. 860–1
    drama, 1. 867–9
    philosophy, 1. 862–5
    satire, 1. 871–2
    Shakespeare, 1. 1619–26
    theology, 1. 865–7
    translations, 1. 2179–94
    travel, 1. 861
  Restoration and eighteenth century, 2. 77–152
    criticism, 2. 65–8, 115–18
    dictionaries, 2. 77–8
    drama, 2. 118–30
    literary theory, 2. 35–8
    letters, 2. 136
    periodicals, 2. 86–90

French, literary relations (*cont.*)
    philosophy, 2. 90–113
    prose fiction, 2. 137–52
    theology, 2. 114–15
    translations, 2. 1501–38
    travel, 2. 84–5
  nineteenth century, 3. 93–116
  twentieth century, 4. 25–6
French, Sydney, 3. 1808
French convert, 2. 983
French intelligencer, 1. 2107
French occurrences, 1. 2107
French rogue, 2. 977
Frend, William, 2. 1288; 3. 1721
Frere, Eleanor, Lady Fenn, 2. 1024–5
Frere, John Hookham, 2. 656; 3. 1870
Freshfield, Douglas William, 3. 1675, 1681, 1709, 1857
Freshman, 3. 1865
Freund, John Christian, 3. 1868
Freytag, Gustav, 3. 120
Frezier, Amédée François, 2. 1460
Friday fun, 4. 1381
Fridegodus, 1. 352
Friend (1755), 2. 1281
Friend (1788), 2. 1288
Friend (1796), 2. 1290
Friend of the people (1783), 2. 1287
Friend of the people (1850), 3. 1819
Friend of the people (1860), 3. 1819
Friend to the fair sex, A, 2. 1285
Friendly couriere, 2. 1345
Friendly debate upon the next elections, A, 2. 1341
Friendly intelligence, 2. 1316
Friendly writer, 2. 1297
Friends, Society of, bibliography, 1. 20
Friends: or the history of Billy Freeman and Tommy Truelove, 2. 1024
Friends' quarterly (examiner), 3. 1858
Friendship, 4. 827
Friendship's offering, 3. 1873
Frisky songster (1770), 2. 391
Frisky songster (1800?) 2. 428
Frithegode, 1. 352
Fritillary, 3. 1868; 4. 1396
Frobisher's new select collection of epitaphs, 2. 412
Froebel, Friedrich W. A., 3. 1729
Froger, François, 2. 1447, 1457
Froissart, Jean, 1. 2185, 862
From the (mercury) office, 2. 1318
Front page detective, 4. 1391
Front page review, 4. 1408
Frontier (stories), 4. 1389
Frontinus, 1. 2169
Frost, John (fl. 1816), 3. 1714

Frost, John (d. 1877) chartist, 3. 1767
Frost, Thomas, 3. 1767
Frost, Walter, 1. 2091, 2106
Frostiana: or a history of the river Thames in a frozen state, 3. 1714
Froude, James Anthony, 3. 1468–71, 1690, 1768, 1845
Froude, Richard Hurrell, 3. 1628
Frowde, Philip, 2. 789
Fruitless repentance, 2. 1002
Frulovisi, Tito Livio, 1. 804
Fry, Caroline, 3. 1618
Fry, Charles Burgess, 3. 1698
Fry, Christopher, 4. 938–41
Fry, Elizabeth, 3. 1679
Fry, Herbert, 3. 1882
Fry, Roger, 3. 1866
Fry, Roger Eliot, 4. 1042–4
Fryer, C. E., 3. 1690
Fryer, John, 2. 1435
Fryke, Christopher, 2. 1435, 1447
Fudge, William Kingston, 4. 1370
Fugitive miscellany, 2. 394
Fugitive pieces, 2. 424
Fulford, William, 3. 1868
Fulke, William, 1. 1825–6, 1959, 2357
Full collection of all poems upon Charles, Prince of Wales, A, 2. 371
Fullarton, William, 2. 1442
Fuller, — (fl. 1800), 3. 1840
Fuller, Anne, 2. 1009
Fuller, Nicholas, 1. 2296
Fuller, Roy Broadbent, 4. 278, 812
Fuller, Thomas, 1. 2233–5, 2045, 2049, 2140; 2. 1797
Fullerton, Lady Georgina Charlotte, 3. 929
Fullonius, Gulielmus, 1. 854
Fulwell, Ulpian, 1. 1106, 1407
Fun, 3. 1825; 4. 1351
Fun and fiction, 4. 1360
Fund, 2. 1349
Funerall elegies upon. . .John Stanhope, 1. 1010
Funnell, William, 2. 1477
Funny wonder, 4. 819
Furetière, Antoine, 2. 1513, 977
Furius (Furio), Frederico Ceriol, 1. 2185, 907
Furly, Benjamin, 2. 1650
Furniss, Harry, 3. 66, 1698, 1768
Furnivall, Frederick James, 3. 1647–9
Furst, Herbert, 4. 1364
Furst, Robert, 4. 82
Future (1907), 4. 1358
Future (1916), 4. 1363
Future (1947), 4. 119, 1378
Future books, 4. 119, 1377

Futurian, 4. 1390
Futurian war digest, 4. 1390
Fyfe, H. Hamilton, 3. 1768
Fyge, Sarah, 2. 472–3
Fyleman, Rose, 4. 793
Fyvie, Isabella, 3. 1104

G., C., gent (fl. 1600), 1. 1106
G., C. (fl. 1705), 2. 1557
G., D. (fl. 1683), 2. 980
G., H. (Sir Henry Goodere?), 1. 1329
G., J. (fl. 1694), 2. 1018
G. K.'s weekly, 4. 1406
G. K. C., 4. 1367
G-men detective, 4. 1391
G., R. (fl. 1600), 1. 2055
G., T. (fl. 1640), 1. 2067
Gaboriau, Emile, 3. 102
Gadfly, 3. 1866
Gaelic literature, nineteenth century, 3. 1885–96
  anthologies, 3. 1893–6
  folklore, 3. 1895–6
  history and scholarship, 3. 1885–94
  journals, 3. 1893–4
Gage, Thomas, 1. 2159
Gager, William 1. 1767
Gaiety, 4. 1365
Gailhard, Jean, 2. 1410
Gainsford, Thomas, 1. 2048, 2056, 2074, 2134
Galaup de la Pérouse, Jean François, 2. 1482
Galbraith, Angus, 3. 1799
Gale, Dunstan, 1. 1106
Gale, Fred, 3. 1696, 1697
Gale, John, 2. 1669
Gale, Norman Rowland, 3. 627, 1697
Gale, Samuel, 2. 1897
Gale, Theophilus, 1. 2341
Galen, 1. 2169
Galignani's messenger, 3. 1791
Galileo, 2. 1544, 188
Gall, John, 1. 2445
Gall, Richard, 2. 2024
Galland, Antoine, 2. 985
Gallenga, Antonio, 3. 1768
Gallery of fashion, 2. 1310
Gallery of poets, 2. 412–13
Gallimaufry, 2. 422
Gallini, Giovanni Andrea, 2. 1566
Galloway, Robert, 3. 1746
Gally, Henry, 2. 1826
Galpin, Sidney, 3. 1852
Galsworthy, John, 4. 579–86, 1363
Galt, John, 3. 721–4, 1792
Galton, Sir Francis, 3. 1381, 1670, 1709, 1728
Galvam, Antonio, 1. 2111

Galvanist, 3. 1865
Galway chronicle, 2. 1388
Galway evening post, 2. 1388
Gamage, William, 1. 1336
'Gambado, Geoffrey' (Henry William Bunbury), 2. 1554–5
Gamble, F., 4. 1384
Gamble, John, 1. 1358–9
Gamble, W., 3. 62
Gambolier, 4. 1395
Game, 4. 1363
Game cock, 3. 1695
Game of quadrille, 2. 1567
Gamelyn, 1. 434–5
Gamester, 2. 1568
Gamesters garland, 2. 1567
Gamiad, 2. 1567
Gammer Gurton's garland, 2. 428
Gangrel, 4. 1376
Gant, Roland, 4. 1377
Garbett, Edward, 3. 1822
Garcia, Carlos, 1. 915, 2062
Garcie, Pierre, 1. 2136
Garcilaso de la Vega, 1. 911; 2. 1456
Garden, Alexander, 1. 2433
Garden, Francis, Lord Gardenstone (d. 1793), 2. 1428
Garden, Francis (d. 1884), 3. 1844
Garden of the Muses, 1. 1009
Gardener, John, 1. 686
Gardener, Lion, 1. 2164
Gardener's chronicle, 3. 1827
Gardener's gazette, 3. 1827
Gardener's magazine, 3. 1845
Gardenstone, Francis Garden, Lord, 2. 1428
Gardiner, Alfred George, 4. 1163
Gardiner, Edmund, 1. 2038
Gardiner, John Smallman, 2. 1559
Gardiner, Richard, 2. 1466, 1559
Gardiner, Rolf, 4. 1393
Gardiner, S. J., 2. 1566
Gardiner, Samuel Rawson, 3. 1475–6, 1858
Gardiner, Stephen, 1. 1811–12
Gardiner, William Nelson, 2. 279
Gardiner, Wrey, 4. 1374, 1376
Gardner, Percy, 3. 1613
Gardnor, John, 2. 1427
Gardyne, Alexander, 1. 2433
Gardyner, George, 1. 2164
Garfield, John, 2. 1339
Garfit, Arthur, 3. 1727
'Garioch, Robert' (Robert Garioch Sutherland), 4. 278
Garland of good will, 1. 1010
Garlick, Raymond, 4. 1379

Garman, Douglas, 4. 1366
Garner, W., 3. 1693
Garnered grain, 4. 1360
Garnett, David, 4. 586
Garnett, Eve, 4. 811
Garnett, Jeremiah, 3. 1795
Garnett, Richard, 3. 1431
Garnett, Thomas, 2. 1408
Garnier, Robert, 1. 867
Garrett, Edmund, 3. 1768
'Garrett, Edward' (Isabella Fyvie), 3. 1104
Garrick, David, 2. 801–9, 42, 85–6, 117, 126, 1419
Garrick magazine, 4. 851
Garrick's jests, 2. 413
Garrod, Heathcote William, 4. 1044–5
Garroway's directory, 4. 860
Garshin, Vsevolod Mikhaylovich, 3. 152
Garter, Bernard, 1. 1106–7, 1076, 2071
Garter, Thomas, 1. 1407–8
Garth, Sir Samuel, 2. 474
Garvie, Alfred Ernest, 3. 1613
Garvin, James Louis, 3. 1768
Gas alert, 4. 1387
Gascoigne, George, 1. 1025–7, 1333, 1419, 1424, 1768, 1905, 2051, 2076, 2309
Gascoigne, Thomas, 1. 804
Gascoyne, David Emery, 4. 279
Gaskell, Elizabeth Cleghorn, 3. 873–8, 156
Gaskell, Frank, 3. 58
Gaspey, Thomas, 3. 724–5, 1810
Gasquet, Francis Aidan, Cardinal, 3. 1858
Gassendi, Pierre, 2. 1513
Gast of Gy, 1. 458
Gataker, Thomas, 1. 2305
Gate (1930), 4. 1369
Gate (Oxford 1947), 4. 1398
Gateshead and Tyneside echo, 3. 1801
Gateway (1912), 4. 1360
Gateway (Lampeter College 1947), 4. 1395
Gatonbe, John, 1. 2155–6
Gatty, Mrs Alfred (Margaret), 3. 930, 1090, 1851
Gatty, Horatia Katharine Frances, 3. 1851
Gatty, Juliana Horatia, 3. 1049–50, 1095
Gatty, Margaret (Mrs Alfred), 3. 930, 1090, 1851
Gau, John, 1. 2445
Gauden, John, 1. 1976–7, 865
Gaunt, L., 4. 1388
Gauntlet, 3. 1818
Gauthier de Metz, 1. 2117
Gautier, Théophile, 3. 102
Gaver, James, 1. 959
Gavin, Antonio, 2. 1413
Gawain, romances of, 1. 400–9
Gawain and the Green Knight, 1. 401–6

'Gawsworth, John' (T. I. F. Armstrong), 4. 279–81, 1359, 1374, 1375
Gay, John, 2. 497–500, 126, 132, 193, 1558
Gay cornet, 4. 1387
Gaylard, Dr. —, 2. 1325
Gayton, Edmund, 1. 2028, 2036, 2047
Gaytryge, Jon, 1. 490
Gazette-a-la-mode, 2. 1345
Gazette de Guernsey, 2. 1390
Gazette de l'Ile de Jersey, 2. 1389
Gazette of current literature, 4. 117
Gazetteer and London daily advertiser, 2. 1281, 1328
Gazetteer and new daily advertiser, 2. 1284, 1328
Geach, E. F. A., 4. 1397
Ged, William, 2. 264
Geddes, Michael, 2. 1447
Geddes, William, 2. 2034
Gee, Joshua, 2. 1897
Gee's weekly, 4. 1356
Geer, E. E., 4. 1384
Geering, T., 3. 1697
'Gêlert', 3. 1705
Gellert, Christian Fürchtegott, 2. 1538, 180, 997
Gelli, Giovanni Battista, 1. 2185, 902; 2. 1544
Gem: a literary annual (1829), 3. 1874
Gem (1929), 4. 819
Gem library, 4. 819
Gem of loveliness, 3. 1876
Gemini (Manchester 1943), 4. 1387
Gemini (Derby 1949), 4. 1379
Gemmingen–Hornberg, Otto von, 2. 1538
Gems of beauty, 3. 1875
Gen, 4. 851
General account, 1. 2101
General advertiser (Dublin 1737), 2. 1385
General advertiser (1744), 2. 1328
General advertiser (Liverpool 1765), 2. 1360
General advertiser (1776), 2. 1335
General and heraldic dictionary, A, 3. 1879
General Baptist magazine (1798), 2. 1312
General Baptist magazine (1860), 3. 1842
General Baptist repository, 3. 1842
General Baptist year book, 3. 1880
General correspondent, 2. 1385
General dictionary, A (Bayle), 2. 363
General election, 2. 1005
General evening post (1733), 2. 1327; 3. 1807
General evening post (1771), 2. 1334
General evening post (Dublin 1781), 2. 1386
General history of the principal discoveries, A, 2. 1294
General history of the stage, A, 2. 373
General history of the Turks, Moguls and Tatars, 2. 1438

George Faulkner's Dublin journal, 2. 1383
George Swiney's Corke journal, 2. 1388
Georgi, Johann Gottlieb, 2. 1425
Georgian poetry, 4. 1361
Georgian stories, 4. 1365
georgic, Restoration and eighteenth century, 2. 317
Georgievitz, Bartholomaeus, 1. 2137
Georgirenes, Archbishop of Samos, 2. 1411
Gerald of Barry, 1. 771–2
Gerald of Wales, 1. 771–2
Gerard, Alexander, 2. 2065, 42
Gerard, John (d. 1637), 1. 2247
Gerard, John (1840–1912), 3. 1850
Gerbier, Sir Balthazar, 1. 2165
Gerbier, Charles, 1. 2034
Geree, John, 1. 2046
Gerfalk, Axel, 4. 1363
Gerhard, Johann, 1. 848
Gerhardie, William Alexander, 4. 587–8
Geritszoon, Cornelius, 1. 2143
Germ, 3. 1848
German, literary relations with
    Old English, Germanic background, 1. 197–206
    Renaissance to Restoration, 1. 875–82
        drama, 1. 880–2
        legends, 1. 878–9
        novel, 1. 882
        satire, 1. 879–80
        Shakespeare, 1. 1625–32
        theology, 1. 877–8
        translations, 1. 2179–94
        travel, 1. 876
    Restoration and eighteenth century, 2. 151–86
        criticism, 2. 68
        drama, 2. 172–80
        literary theory, 2. 38–9
        philosophy, 2. 156–60
        poetry, 2. 166–71
        prose fiction, 2. 180–6
        satire, 2. 171–2
        theology, 2. 160–5
        translations, 2. 1537–42
    nineteenth century, 3. 115–34
    twentieth century, 4. 26–7
German Atalantis, 2. 987
German museum, 2. 1312
German rogue, 2. 988
Germinal (1903), 4. 1357, 1405
Germinal (1923), 4. 1366
Gervaise, Isaac, 2. 1897
Gervase de Saltu Lacteo, 1. 771
Gervase of Melkey, 1. 771
Gervase of Tilbury, 1. 761

Gesner, Conrad, 1. 2185
Gessner, Salomon, 2. 1538, 166, 168
Gest historiale of the destruction of Troy, 1. 426
Gesta romanorum, 1. 691
Ghiselin de Busbecq, Ogier, 1. 2130
Ghismonda, 1. 1759
Ghost, 2. 1372
Ghost, or the woman wears the breeches, 1. 1759
ghost stories, twentieth century, 4. 129–30
ghosting, twentieth century, 4. 68
Giannone, Pietro, 2. 1544, 188
Gibbes, Phebe, 2. 1001, 1002
Gibbings, Robert John, 4. 1317, 799
Gibbon, Edward, 2. 1721–9, 106, 117, 158, 189, 312, 1314, 1420
'Gibbon, Lewis Grassic' (James Leslie Mitchell), 4. 588–9
Gibbons, Alfred, 3. 1817
Gibbons, Orlando, 1. 1354
Gibbons, Stella Dorothea, 4. 589, 807
Gibbons, W. F., 4. 1386
Gibbs, Henry Hucks, 1st Baron Aldenham, 3. 1794
Gibbs, Sir Philip Hamilton, 4. 1164–6
Giberne, Agnes, 3. 1103
Giblet pye, 2. 428
Gibson, Edmund, 2. 1623–4, 241, 1715–16, 1770, 1795
Gibson, W., 2. 1406
Gibson, Wilfrid Wilson, 4. 281–2
Gibson, William, 2. 1553
Gielgud, Val Henry, 4. 941–2
Giffard, Stanley Lees, 3. 1768, 1789, 1793, 1808
Giffen, G., 3. 1698
Giffen, Robert, 3. 1824
Gifford, Humfrey, 1. 1107, 2052
'Gifford, John' (John Richards Green), 3. 1841
Gifford, William, 2. 656–7, 1290, 1338; 3. 1768, 1855
Gifts of men (OE), 1. 284
Gil, Alexander, 1. 2316
Gil Polo, Gaspar, 1. 912
Gilbert of the Haye, 1. 2447
Gilbert the 'Universal', Bishop of London, 1. 757
Gilbert, Ann, 3. 1087
Gilbert, Sir Humphrey, 1. 2076, 2161
Gilbert, Thomas (d. 1747), 2. 549
Gilbert, Thomas (fl. 1788), 2. 1481
Gilbert, Sir Thomas (1829–98), 3. 1891
Gilbert, William (fl. 1676), 2. 1556
Gilbert, William (1760?–1825?), 3. 381
Gilbert, William (1804–90), 3. 1103
Gilbert, Sir William Schwenck, 3. 1159–64
Gildas, 1. 337–9, 393–6
Gildon, Charles, 2. 1047–50, 42, 982, 986, 988, 989, 1769

Gleam, 4. 1385
Gleaner (1793), 2. 1379
Gleaner (Edinburgh 1795), 2. 1373
Gleaner (1798), 2. 1290
Gleaner (Edinburgh 1798), 2. 1372
Gleason, George Scott, 4. 1368
Gleig, George Robert, 3. 725–6
Glen, James, 2. 1466
Glen, William, 3. 381
Glenbervie, Sylvester Douglas, Baron, 2. 2064
Glenesk, Algernon Borthwick, Baron, 3. 1764
Glenny, George, 3. 1809, 1827
Glisson, Francis, 2. 1846, 1905
Globe, 3. 1792, 1829
Gloria I (OE), 1. 284
Gloria II (OE), 1. 284
glossaries
    Old English, 1. 74
    Middle English, 1. 85
    Renaissance to Restoration
      Shakespeare, 1. 1475
    Restoration and eighteenth century, 2. 1807–16
Gloucester(shire)
    general bibliography, 1. 17
    medieval libraries, 1. 991
    Middle English sermons, 1. 487
    Restoration and eighteenth century
      newspapers, 2. 1358
      periodical essays, 2. 1348
      printing and bookselling, 2. 267
    nineteenth century newspaper, 3. 1831
Gloucester, Humphrey, Duke of, 1. 1000
Gloucester gazette, 2. 1358
Gloucester journal, 2. 1358; 3. 1831
Gloucester sermons, 1. 487
Glover, Richard, 2. 549, 168, 177
Glover, Richard H., 3. 1690
Glover, Thomas, 2. 1455
Glover, W., 3. 1697
Glover, William (d. 1870), 3. 1789
Glow-worm (1865), 3. 1793
Glow worm (1928), 4. 1385
Gluckstein, S., 4. 1356
Glyn, Elinor Sutherland, 4. 589–90
Gmelin, Johann Georg, 2. 1439
Gnaphaeus, Gulielmus, 1. 854
Gnat, 3. 1871
Goad of loue, 1. 516
Goadby, Edwin, 3. 1796, 1799
Goadby, Joseph, 3. 1842
Goadby, Joseph Jackson, 3. 1842
Goblio, 4. 1398
God, John, 1. 1107
Godard, John, 1. 773
Godard, John G., 3. 1746

Goddard, Edward, 2. 1461
Goddard, William, 1. 1335
Godden, Margaret Rumer, 4. 590–1, 809
Godefroy of Boloyne, 1. 430
Godfrey of Bouillon, cycle of, 1. 427–30
Godfrey of Cambrai, 1. 757
Godfrey, David Williams, 3. 1822
Godfrey, John, 2. 1563
Godfrey, Thomas, 1. 962
Godley, Alfred Denis, 3. 1868
Godly Queene Hester, 1. 1407
Godolphin, Sidney, 1. 1309
Godric, St., 1. 709
Godwin, Francis, 1. 2239–40, 853, 874, 2057
Godwin, George, 3. 1828
Godwin, Mary Wollstonecraft (Mrs Shelley),
    3. 761–4
Godwin, Paul, 1. 2066
Godwin, William, 2. 1249–54, 106, 183, 1007,
    1011, 1014; 3. 78, 1099
Godwin, Mrs William (Mary Wollstonecraft),
    2. 1254–6, 112, 183, 1008, 1013, 1026, 1430
Godwyn, Thomas, 1. 2139
Goes, Damianus de, 1. 2142
Goethe, Johann Wolfgang von, 3. 120–3; 2. 38,
    167, 172–3, 180, 863, 1006
Goffe, Thomas, 1. 1744–5
Gogarty, Oliver St John, 4. 283–4
Goggin's Ulster magazine, 2. 1380
Gogol, Nikolay Vasil'yevich, 3. 152
Golagrus and Gawain, 1. 407
Goldborne, Sophia, 2. 1009
Golden annual, 3. 1876
Golden book magazine, 4. 1367
Golden bowl, 4. 1385
Golden coast: or a description of Guinney, 2. 1445
Golden Cockerel Press, 4. 97
Golden garland of princely delight, 1. 1010; 2.
    337
'Golden Gorse' (Mrs M. A. Wace), 4. 807
Golden hind, 4. 1365
Golden hours, 4. 1354
'*Golden Hynde*', 4. 1361
Golden legend, 1. 531
Golden magazine, 4. 1386
Golden star, 4. 1373
Golden stories, 4. 1354
Goldfinch, 2. 373
Goldie, Kathleen Annie, 4. 813
Golding, Arthur, 1. 1107–8, 2071, 2119, 2130
Golding, Louis, 4. 591–2
Goldingham, William, 1. 1768
Goldoni, Carlo, 2. 1545, 190; 3. 137
Goldring, Douglas, 4. 1360
Goldschmidt, Meïr Aron, 3. 147

Goldsmid-Montefiore, Claude Joseph, 3. 1614, 1858
Goldsmith, Francis, 1. 1745
Goldsmith, Lewis, 3. 1809
Goldsmith, Oliver, 2. 1191–210, 42, 106, 126, 132, 147, 177, 183, 208, 212, 1282, 1302, 1905
Goldson, William, 2. 1486
Goldston, W., 4. 860
Goldwel, Henry, 1. 2072
Goldwell, James, 1. 1000
Goldwin, William, 2. 1564
golf, 3. 1702–3
Golf, 3. 1702
Golf illustrated, 3. 1702
Golfing, 3. 1702
Golfing and cycling (illustrated), 3. 1702
Golfing annual, 3. 1702, 1883
Gollancz, Sir Israel, 3. 1649
Golsworthy, Arnold, 3. 1853; 4. 1353
Gombauld, Jean Ogier de, 1. 873, 2062
Gomberville, Marin Leroy de, 1. 873, 2062
Gomersall, Robert, 1. 1309
Gomez, Madeleine Angelique Poisson de, 2. 990, 993
Gomme, Sir George Laurence, 3. 1858
Goncharov, Ivan Aleksandrovich, 3. 152
Gondi, J. F. P. de, Cardinal de Retz, 2. 1528
Gong (Nottingham University 1884), 4. 1396
Gong (1921), 4. 849
Gongora, Luis de, 1. 911
Gongster, 4. 1396
Gonsalvius Montanus, Reginaldus, 1. 2185
Gonzales Carranza, Domingo, 2. 1462
Gonzalez, Manoel, 2. 1401
Gonzalez de Mendoza, Juan, 1. 2143
Gooch, George Peabody, 4. 1166–7
Gooch, Thomas, 2. 1555
Good, Thomas, 1. 782
Good, William, 1. 2100
Good and true. . .Christmas carols, 1. 1010
Good cheer, 4. 1386
'Good copy', 4. 77
Good housekeeping (1885), 4. 1352
Good housekeeping (1922), 4. 1365
Good lesson of nine vertewis, A, 1. 515
Good luck, 4. 1364
Good luck magazine, 4. 1358
Good man and the devil, 1. 513
Good news from New England, 1. 2164
Good order, 1. 1407
Good speech, 4. 1368
Good stories library, 4. 1360
Good times, 4. 1403
Good words, 3. 1849
Goodal, Walter, 2. 1735

Goodall, Charles, 2. 475
Goodall, Walter, 2. 1735
Goodall, William, 2. 997
Goodcole, Henry, 1. 2074
Goode, William, 3. 1620
Goodere, Sir Henry, 1. 1329
Goodhall, Walter, 2. 1560
Goodlake, Thomas, 3. 1695
Goodland, John, 4. 1373
Goodman, Albert, 3. 1714
Goodman, Christopher, 1. 2275
Goodman, Godfrey, 1. 1992, 2245–6
Goodman, Neville, 3. 1714
Goodman, Nicholas, 1. 2057
Goodman, Richard, 4. 1397
'Goodwill, Jasper', 2. 1299
Goodwin, Charles Wycliffe, 3. 1821
Goodwin, Thomas, 2. 163
Goodwine, Thomas Pope, 1. 2066
Goodwyn, Christopher, 1. 1108
Goodyear, Robert Arthur Hanson, 4. 793
Googe, Barnabe, 1. 1108
Gookin, Daniel, 2. 1455
'Goose, Mother', 2. 1023
Gordon, Lord Adam, 2. 1467
Gordon, Alexander, 2. 1400
Gordon, Daniel M., 3. 1671
Gordon, Harry, 2. 1467
Gordon, James, 1. 2467, 2135
Gordon, John, 1. 2471
Gordon, Patrick (fl. 1614–50), 1. 2433
Gordon, Patrick (1635–99), general, 1. 2471
Gordon, Patrick (fl. 1693), geographer, 2. 1457
Gordon, Peter, 3. 1673
Gordon, Sir Robert, 1. 2162
Gordon, Thomas, 2. 106, 1277
Gordon, William, 2. 2053
Gordon's merry chronicle, 2. 1389
Gore, Catherine Grace Frances, 3. 726–8, 1875
Gore, Charles, 4. 1252–3
Gore's general advertiser, 2. 1360
Gore's Liverpool general advertiser, 2. 1360
Gorell, Ronald Gorell Barnes, 3rd Baron, 4. 1351
Gorer, Geoffrey Edgar Solomon, 4. 1167
Gorges, Sir Arthur, 1. 1108–9
Gorges, Sir Ferdinando, 1. 2160
Gorgious gallery of gallant inventions, A, 1. 1008
Gorgon, 3. 1817
Gori, Antonio Francisco, 2. 1419
Goring, Agnes Venetia, 3. 1106
Gorrell, F. S., 4. 1382
Gorrell, James, 2. 1467
Gorst, Sir John, 3. 1790, 1793
Goscelin of Canterbury, 1. 757
Gospel magazine (1766), 2. 1304

Gospel magazine (1774), 2. 1305
Gospel magazine (1779), 2. 1306
Gospel magazine (1796), 2. 1311; 3. 1841
Gospel of Nicodemus, OE, 1. 326–7; ME, 1. 482
Goss, J., 4. 1382
Goss, J. L., 4. 1382
Gosse, Sir Edmund William, 3. 1432–5, 1681
Gossip, G. H. D., 3. 1694
Gossip (1902), 4. 1356
Gossip (Newcastle 1910), 4. 1382
Gossip for the garden, 3. 1849
Gossips braule, 1. 1759
Gosson, Stephen, 1. 2310, 2023–4, 2052
Gosynhyll, Edward, 1. 1109, 2031–2
gothic novel, 2. 870–1
Gott, Samuel, 1. 2318
'Gotthelf, Jeremias' (Albert Bitzius), 3. 123
Goudge, Elizabeth, 4. 806
Gouge, Thomas, 2. 1609
Gouge, William, 1. 1941
Gough, H. F., 3. 61
Gough, John, 1. 1745
Gough, Richard, 2. 1735–6, 1404, 1442
Goulart, Simon, 1. 862, 2062
Gould, Gerald, 4. 284–5, 1371
Gould, J., 3. 1694
Gould, Robert, 2. 475
Goulden, W. E., 3. 82, 85
Goulston, Theodore, 1. 2305
Governess, 2. 1290
Governor, a tragicomedy, 1. 1759
Gow, Ronald, 4. 943–4
Gower, Charles, 2. 1288, 1308
Gower, John, 1. 553–6, 804
Gownsman (1829), 3. 1865
Gownsman (1933), 4. 1394
Goyder, David George, 3. 1720
Grabbe, Christian Dietrich, 3. 123
Grace, Edward Mills, 3. 1697
Grace, William Gilbert, 3. 1697
Graces, 3. 1873
Gracián Dantisco, Lucas, 1. 907, 915
Gracián y Morales, Baltasar, 1. 907; 2. 199, 979
Graffanio-Mastix, 2. 358
Graffigny, Françoise d'Issembourg d'Happon-court de, 2. 1514, 996
graffiti, 4. 123–5
Grafton, Richard, 1. 2209, 962
Graham, Catherine, 2. 1738
Graham, Dougal, 2. 2025
Graham, Eleanor, 4. 803
Graham, Harry, 4. 792
Graham, James, 1st Marquis of Montrose (1612–50), 1. 2436
Graham, James (fl. 1795), 2. 1373

Graham, Robert Bontine Cunninghame, 4. 1318–19
Graham, Stephen, 4. 1319–20
Graham, Thomas, 3. 1799
Graham, William, 3. 1532–3
Graham, William Sydney, 4. 285
Grahame, James, 2. 2025–6
Grahame, Kenneth, 4. 593; 3. 1097–8
Grahame, Simion, 1. 2433
Grail, romances of the, 1. 411–14
Grainger, James, 2. 657
grammar, textbooks and teaching
    Renaissance to Restoration, 1. 2397–9
    Restoration and eighteenth century, 2. 1815–20
Grammar and rhetorick, 2. 397
Grammatical drollery, 2. 334
Grammont, Antoine Hamilton, Comte de, 2. 1515, 136, 140, 987
gramophone, its relation to literature, 4. 53–4
Gramophone, 4. 54
Gramophone record, 4. 54
Granada, Luis de, 1. 908–9, 2188
'Grand, Sarah' (Frances Elizabeth McFall), 3. 1054–5
Grand diurnall, A, 1. 2097
Grand guignol annual review, 4. 860
Grand magazine of magazines (1750), 2. 1300
Grand magazine of magazines (1759), 2. 1302
Grand magazine of universal intelligence, 2. 1302
Grand politique post, 1. 2108
Grandage, Esther, 4. 802
'Grandfather Gregory' (George Mogridge), 3. 1089
'Grandmamma Gilbert' (George Mogridge), 3. 1089
Grange, John, 1. 1109, 2052
Granger, James, 2. 1736–7, 1799
Granger, Timothy, 1. 2071
Grangewood magazine, 4. 1370
Grant, A. R., 3. 1727
Grant, Albert, 3. 1791, 1793
Grant, Anne, 2. 2026
Grant, J. P., 4. 1386
Grant, James (fl. 1736–45), 2. 1375
Grant, James (1802–79), newspaper editor, 3. 1680, 1789, 1841, 1845
Grant, James (1822–87), novelist, 3. 930–1
Grant, James Augustus, 3. 1671
Grant, Joan Marshall, 4. 810
Grant, Johnson, 2. 1407
Grant, Patrick, 3. 1792, 1793, 1809
Grant, Philip, 3. 1727
Grant, Sir Robert, 3. 381
Granta, 3. 1866, 1872; 4. 1392
Grantham, library of, 1. 991

Grantham, Sir Thomas, 2. 1460
Grantham journal, 3. 1831
Granville, George, Baron Lansdowne, 2. 790
Granville, Mary, 2. 1598
Granville, Sir Richard, 1. 2127
Granville-Barker, Harley, 4. 944–6
Graph herald, 4. 1383
Graphic, 3. 1817; 4. 1402
graphic processes
   nineteenth century, 3. 45–54
   twentieth century, 4. 88–90
   see also printing, typography
Graphis, 4. 83
Gratalorus, Gulielmus, 1. 848
Grattan, Henry, 3. 1805
Grattan, Thomas Colley, 3. 728–9
Gratton, John, 2. 1400, 1650
Gratulatio academiae cantabrigiensis de reditu Georgii II, 2. 373
Gratulatio academiae cantabrigiensis Frederici . . .et Augustae. . .nuptias celebrantis, 2. 365
Gratulatio academiae cantabrigiensis Georgii III et Charlottae nuptias celebrantis, 2. 382
Gratulatio academiae cantabrigiensis Gulielmi . . .et Annae. . .nuptias celebrantis, 2. 362
Gratulatio academiae cantabrigiensis in pacem, 2. 384
Gratulatio academiae cantabrigiensis natales Georgii Walliae principis. . .celebrantis, 2. 2. 383
Gratulatio academiae oxoniensis in nuptias Frederici et Augustae, 2. 365
Gratulatio solennis universitatis oxoniensis ob Georgium. . .natum, 2. 383
Gratulationes juventutis academiae dubliniensis, 2. 382
Graunt, John, 2. 1897, 1905
Graves, Alfred Percival, 3. 1907–8
Graves, John, 2. 1459
Graves, Richard, 2. 1174–6, 1004, 1006, 1007, 1009
Graves, Robert von Ranke, 4. 201–7, 801–2, 1364, 1371, 1397
Gray, A., 4. 864
'Gray, Alan' (George Mogridge), 3. 1089
Gray, Andrew, 1. 2460–1
Gray, David, 3. 628
Gray, Edmund Dwyer, 3. 1805, 1806
Gray, Gilbert, 1. 2471
Gray, J. H., 3. 1732
Gray, John (17th century) book collector, 2. 311
Gray, Sir John (1816–75), editor, 3. 1805
Gray, John (1866–1934), poet, 3. 628
Gray, Joshua, 3. 1722

Gray, Robert (fl. 1609), 1. 2276
Gray, Robert (fl. 1662), 2. 1454
Gray, Robert (1762–1834), 2. 1429
Gray, Stephen, 2. 1905
Gray, Thomas, 2. 577–85, 42, 132, 193, 200, 1403, 1418, 1780
Gray, W., 1. 2135
Gray, William (d. 1478), 1. 1000
Gray, William (d. 1557), 1. 1109
Gray's Inn, plays at, 1. 1768
Gray's inn journal, 2. 1281, 1332
Grazzini, Antonio Francesco, 1. 894
Greacen, Robert, 4. 1375, 1378
Great and wonderful victory [by Pen and Venables], *A*, 1. 2160
Great assises holden in Parnassus, 1. 2318
Great Bible, 1. 1834–5
Great Britaines paine-full messenger, 1. 2106
Great Britain's rules of health, 2. 1345
Great Britain's weekly pacquet, 2. 1323
Great Brittain's post, 1. 2108
Great Tom, 3. 1868
Great thoughts and great reading, 4. 1352
Great thoughts from master minds, 4. 1352
Great victory. . .given unto eight Holland shippes, 1. 2145
Greater western action novels magazine, 4. 1390
Greatheed, — (fl. 1823), 3. 1840
Greatheed, Bertie, 2. 177; 3. 1677
Greatheed, S., 3. 1842
Greatrex, Charles Butler, 3. 1705
Greaves, John, 1. 2148–9, 2305; 2. 1435
Greaves, Thomas, 1. 1351
Greek, literary relations with
  Renaissance to Restoration
    education, 1. 2404–5
    scholarship, 1. 2303–6
    Shakespeare, 1. 1631
    translations of classics, 1. 2165–80
  Restoration and eighteenth century
    criticism, 2. 63–5
    literary relations, 2. 218–19
    literary theory, 2. 34–5
    translations of classics, 2. 1487–96
  nineteenth century, 3. 157–8
Greek anthology, 1. 2169
Greek drama (amateur players) broadsheet, 4. 878
Green, Frederick Lawrence, 4. 593–4
Green, George Smith, 2. 1778
'Green, Henry' (Henry Vincent Yorke), 4. 594–5
Green, John, 2. 1438
Green, John Richard, 3. 1478–9, 1681
Green, John Richards, 2. 1311, 1339; 3. 1841
Green, L. Dunton, 4. 826
Green, Matthew, 2. 550, 1558, 1905

Green, Russell, 4. 1363
Green, Sarah, 3. 729
Green, Thomas, 2. 1284
Green, Thomas Hill, 3. 1533-4, 1606
Green and gold, 4. 1364
Green leaf, 4. 1388
Green magazine, 4. 1365
Green quarterly, 4. 1366
Green register, 4. 860, 868
Green room, 2. 1283
Green room book, 4. 824, 859
Green room mirror, 4. 851
Green room songster, 2. 421
Green sheaf, 4. 1357
Greenaway, Catherine ('Kate'), 3. 1096, 66
'Greendrake, Gregory' (J. Coad), 3. 1688
Greene, Carleton, 3. 1865
Greene, Graham, 4. 503-12, 808, 1374
Greene, Hon. Mrs Richard, 3. 1103
Greene, Robert, 1. 1437-43, 874, 2034, 2052-3
Greener, W. W., 3. 1713
Greenham, Richard, 1. 1941, 2047
Greenock advertiser, 2. 1378
Greenock daily press, 3. 1804
Greenock news, 3. 1804
Greenock telegraph, 3. 1804
Greenwell, Dora, 3. 522
Greenwood, Arthur, 4. 1349
Greenwood, E., 4. 1398
Greenwood, Frederick, 3. 1768, 1793, 1794, 1849
Greenwood, James, 3. 1103
Greenwood, John, 1. 1941-2
Greenwood, Walter, 4. 947
Greenwood, William, 2. 1561
Greenwood's library year book, 4. 117
Greepe, Thomas, 1. 1109, 2151
Greg, Sir Walter Wilson, 4. 1048-50
Greg, William Rathbone, 3. 1607
Gregg, Josiah, 3. 1673
Gregg, T. H., 3. 1850
Gregory I, Pope, 1. 2185
Gregory the Englishman, 1. 772
Gregory, Barnard, 3. 1810, 1813
Gregory, Benjamin, 3. 1840
Gregory, David, 2. 1905
Gregory, George, 3. 1839, 1841
Gregory, Isabella Augusta, Lady, 3. 1939-41
Gregory, James, 2. 1905
Gregory, Robert, 3. 1730
Gregory, William (fl. 1765), 2. 1467
Gregory, William (fl. 1799), 2. 1475
Gregory's dialogues (OE translation), 1. 315
Gregynog Press, 4. 97
Grein, James Thomas, 3. 1854; 4. 825, 826, 849
Grenadine, Sebastian, 2. 979

Grene Knight, 1. 406
Grenfell, Julian Henry Francis, 4. 285
Grenside, Dorothy, 4. 1364
Gresham, T., 1. 2278
Gresley, William, 3. 1102
Gresset, Jean Baptiste Louis, 2. 1514, 130
Greville, Fulke, 1st Baron Brooke, 1. 1057-9, 2314
Greville, Robert, 2nd Baron Brooke, 1. 2333
Greville, Robert Kaye, 3. 1875
Grévin, Jacques, 1. 867
Grew, Nehemiah, 2. 1905
Grey, Maria Georgina, 3. 1724, 1729, 1748
'Grey, Mrs Martha', 2. 1285
Grey, Mrs W., 3. 1745, 1748
Grey, Zachary, 2. 1743-5
Grey Friars of London, their chronicle, 1. 2206
'Greydrake, Geoffrey' (T. Ettingsall), 3. 1688
Gribble, F. H., 3. 1710
Griboyedov, Aleksandr Sergeyevich, 3. 152
Grierson, Constantia, 2. 550
Grierson, Sir Herbert John Clifford, 4. 1050-1
Grieve, Christopher Murray, 4. 299-302
'Griff, Alan' (W. D. Suddaby), 4. 806
Griffin, Bartholomew, 1. 1109-10
Griffin, Benjamin, 2. 790
Griffin, Elizabeth, 2. 1028
Griffin, Gerald, 3. 931-2
Griffin and Co, Charles, 3. 78
Griffin, 4. 1393
Griffith, Elizabeth, 2. 835, 999, 1002, 1003, 1005
Griffith, John, 2. 1470
Griffith, Richard, 2. 999, 1001, 1002
Griffith's iron trade exchange, 3. 1827
Griffiths, George Edward, 3. 1839
Griffiths, John, 3. 1732
Griffiths, Ralph, 2. 279, 1299; 3. 1839
Griffiths, Roger, 2. 1559
Griffiths, William, 2. 1554
Grigson, Geoffrey Edward Harvey, 4. 1052-3, 1370, 1371, 1377
Grillparzer, Franz, 3. 123-4
Grimald, Nicholas, 1. 1110
Grimalkin: or the rebel cat, 2. 979
Grimble, Augustus, 3. 1690, 1713
Grimeston, Edward, 1. 2305
Grimm, Jakob Ludwig, 3. 124, 1109
Grimm, Wilhelm Karl, 3. 124, 1109
Grimsby daily telegraph, 3. 1803
Grimsby evening telegraph, 3. 1803
Grimsby express, 3. 1800
Grimston, Edward, 1. 2305
Grimston, James, Earl of Verulam, 2. 1402
Grimstoun (Grymeston), Elizabeth, 1. 1110, 1907, 2047
Grindal, Edmund, 1. 1942

Grindea, Miron, 4. 1375
Gringoire, Pierre (Vaudemont), 1. 2186, 871
Grisone, Federico, 1. 2186
Grobiana's nuptialls, 1. 1777
Grocer, 3. 1828
Grocin, William, 1. 1000
Groome, Francis Hindes, 3. 1435
Grosart, Alexander Balloch, 3. 1650
Grose, Francis, 2. 1737
Grose, John Henry, 2. 1439
Groser, Albert, 3. 1796
Groser, William, 3. 1843
Grosier, Jean B. G. A., 2. 1443
Grosley, Pierre Jean, 2. 1403, 1421
Grosse, Karl, 2. 1538, 181, 1012
Grosseteste, Robert, 1. 777–9, 1001
Grote, George, 3. 1460–1
Grote, John, 3. 1535, 1727
Grotius, Hugo, 1. 848, 854, 2140; 2. 76
Grouler, 2. 1272
Grove, Archibald, 3. 1853
Grove, Sir George, 3. 1384–5, 1849
Grove, J., 3. 1727
Grove, Joseph, 2. 1779
Grove, Matthew, 1. 1110
Grove, 2. 354
Growing point, 4. 790
Grub-street journal, 2. 1278, 1327
Grub-Street miscellany, 2. 360
Grubiana, 2. 361
Grueber, Johann, 2. 1433
Grumbler (1715), 2. 1275
Grumbler (1791), 2. 1289
Grundy, Sydney, 3. 1193
Grymeston, Elizabeth, 1. 1110, 1907, 2047
Gryphius, Andreas, 1. 881
Gryphon, 4. 1395
Gualdo-Priorato, Galeazzo, 2. 1545
Guardian (1713), 2. 1274–5
Guardian (1819), 3. 1809
Guardian (1846), 3. 1823
Guardian (Manchester 1959), 3. 1795; 4. 1400,
  1344
Guardian angel, 2. 1288
Guardian journal, 3. 1796
Guarini, Giovanni Battista, 1. 894, 1111, 2186;
  2. 1545, 190
Guazzo, Stefano, 1. 2186, 887
Guedalla, Philip, 4. 1167–8
Guénée, Antoine, 2. 1514
Gueulette, Thomas Simon, 2. 990, 993, 994
Guevara, Antonio de, 1. 2186, 907–8, 908
Guicciardini, Francesco, 1. 2186, 887
Guicciardini, Lodovico, 1. 2187, 887, 2138; 2.
  1545

Guide, 4. 820
Guide for malt-worms, A, 2. 352
Guide to cricketers, 3. 1882
Guide to selecting plays, 4. 825
Guide to the turf, 3. 1882
Guild, William, 1. 2461–2
Guild news, 4. 1392
Guilleragues, G. J. de Lavergne de, 2. 1514, 140
Guillet de Saint-George, Georges, 2. 1411
Guilpin, Edward, 1. 1111, 1334
'Gulliver, Lilliputius' (Richard Johnson), 2.
  1021
Gulliveriana, 2. 358
Gunn, Neil Miller, 4. 595
Gunning, Peter, 1. 1992
Gunning, Susannah Minifie, 2. 1001, 1002, 1010
Gunthorpe, John, 1. 804, 1001
Guppy, Henry, 3. 90
Gurney, Edmund, 3. 1435
Gurney, Mary, 3. 1748
Gutch, J. M., 3. 1790
Guthlac (OE poems), 1. 284–5
Guthlac, St (OE prose), 1. 326
Guthrie, — (fl. 1760), 3. 1839
Guthrie, James (d. 1661), 1. 2462
Guthrie, James (b. 1874), 4. 83, 1355, 1361
Guthrie, Thomas, 3. 1620, 1823
Guthrie, Thomas Anstey, 3. 1034, 1097
Guthrie, Sir Tyrone, 4. 947–8
Guthrie, Walter Murray, 3. 1866
Guthrie, William (1620–65), 2. 2034
Guthrie, William (1708–70), 2. 1737, 998, 1326,
  1331
Guthrie, Sir William Tyrone, 4. 947–8
Guthry, Henry, 1. 2245
Guy of Amiens, 1. 757
Guy, Thomas, 2. 279–80
Guy, Earl of Warwick (Caroline play), 1. 1759–60
Guy of Warwick (ME romance), 1. 432–3
Guylforde, Sir Richard, 1. 2121
Guyon, Claude Marie, 2. 1439
Guyon, Jeanne Marie Bouvier de la Mothe, 2.
  1514–15, 114
Guys, Pierre Augustin, 2. 1422
Gwreans an bys, 1. 728
Gwynn, Edward, 1. 1001
Gwynne, Matthew, 1. 1769
Gyles, John, 2. 1462
Gyllius, Petrus, 2. 1417
Gypsy, 4. 1362

H., G. (fl. 1642), 1. 2097
H., I. (fl. 1642), 1. 2033
H., J. (John Hall), 1. 1329–30
H., J. (fl. 1602), 1. 2037

H., J. (fl. 1657), 1. 2050
H., L. (fl. 1628), 1. 2028
H., M. (fl. 1818), 3. 1107
H., S. (fl. 1610), 1. 2305
'H., S. T.', 4. 826, 860
H., T. (fl. 1560), 1. 1111
H., T. (fl. 1594), 1. 1111
H., T. (fl. 1638), 1. 2467
H., T. (fl. 1647–60), 1. 2039, 2040
H., T. (fl. 1723), 2. 1018
Haak, Theodore, 1. 1841
Habesci, Elias, 2. 1426
Habington, Thomas, 1. 2253
Habington, William, 1. 1208, 2047
Hack, David, 4. 1378
Hack, Maria, 3. 1089
Hacke, William, 2. 1391
Hacket, John, 1. 1769
Hackett, Walter, 4. 948–9
Hackluyt, John, 1. 2089, 2091, 2102, 2104, 2105
Hackney and Kingsland gazette, 3. 1807
Hackney gazette and north London advertiser, 3. 1807
Hadath, John Edward Gunby, 4. 794
Haddan, Thomas Henry, 3. 1823
Hadden, R., 3. 1797
Haddington, printing, 2. 272
Haddon, Walter, 1. 853
Haden, Sir Frank Seymour, 3. 66
Hadfield, Alan, 4. 1374
Hadfield, John, 4. 1375
Hadfield, Joseph, 2. 1472
Hadow, James, 2. 2044
Hadow, Sir William Henry, 3. 1435–6
Haeckel, Ernst, 3. 124
Haerlem courant (1679), 2. 1317
Haerlem courant (1682), 2. 1318
Haermai, 4. 1383
Hager, Dr —, 2. 1431
Haggard, Sir Henry Rider, 3. 1055–6, 1097
Hagthorpe, John, 1. 1309, 2162
Hailes, Sir David Dalrymple, Lord, 2. 2052–3, 245, 1733–4, 1782–3
Haileyburyian, 3. 1871
Hailing's circular, 3. 61
Haines, E. M., 4. 1386
Haines, John Thomas, 3. 1130–1
Haiton of Armenia, 1. 2147
Hake, Edward, 1. 1111, 2023
Hake, Thomas Gordon, 3. 523
Hakewill, George, 1. 1993, 2317, 2333
Hakluyt, Richard, 1. 2111, 2151, 2161, 2276
Hal's looking glass, 2. 404
Haldane, John Burdon Sanderson, 4. 1253–4, 800
Haldane, John Scott, 4. 1255

Haldane, Naomi M. M., 4. 673–4, 803
Haldane, Robert, 2. 1407
Haldenstone, James, 1. 804
Hale, Kathleen, 4. 804
Hale, Sir Matthew, 2. 1901
Hales, John, 1. 1993
Hales, John Wesley, 3. 1650, 1727
Hales, Stephen, 2. 1905
Haley, Nelson Cole, 3. 1670
Half-holiday, 4. 1403
Half-penny London journal (Nov 1724), 2. 1326
Half-penny London journal (Dec 1724), 2. 1326
Halfpenny, John, 2. 1552–3
Halfpenny journal, 3. 1816
Halfpenny London spy, 2. 1329
Hali meidenhad, 1. 524
Halifax
    parish library, 1. 991
    printing, 2. 268
Halifax, Charles Montagu, 1st Earl of, 2. 476
Halifax, George Savile, 1st Marquis of, 2. 1040–1
Halifax, William, 2. 1435
Halifax daily courier and guardian, 3. 1803
Halifax evening courier, 3. 1803
Halkett, Anne, Lady, 1. 2252
Hall, Alice, 4. 802
Hall, Anna Maria, 3. 932–3, 1090
Hall, Anthony, 2. 1400
Hall, Arthur, 1. 1111–12
Hall, Basil, 3. 1282, 1672, 1673, 1674
Hall, Mrs Basil, 3. 1672
Hall, Donald, 4. 1397
Hall, Edward, 1. 2203
Hall, F. Ayrer, 2. 1461
Hall, Herbert Byng, 3. 1705
Hall, James, 1. 2153
Hall, John (1529?–66?), 1. 1112, 1344, 1901
Hall, John (1627–56), 1. 1309–10, 1329–30, 2049, 2091, 2103, 2106, 2305, 2334
Hall, Joseph, 1. 1112–13, 858, 866, 878, 920, 1333, 1907, 1977–80, 2043, 2047–8, 2062, 2249, 2298, 2331; 2. 163–4
Hall, Marguerite Radclyffe, 4. 596
Hall, Robert, 2. 1885–6; 3. 1616
Hall, Samuel Carter, 3. 1768, 1843, 1844, 1847, 1873
Hall, Mrs Samuel Carter (Anna Maria), 3. 1848, 1850, 1875, 1877
Hall, Thomas, 1. 1993, 2026
Hall, W., 4. 1383
Hall, William Cornwallis, 2. 1471
Hallam, Arthur Henry, 3. 1385–6
Hallam, Henry, 3. 1459
Hallam, Isaac, 2. 1569
Haller, Albrecht von, 2. 1538, 168, 181

Hallett, Joseph, 2. 1675
Halley, Edmund, 2. 1905
Halliwell [-Phillipps], James Orchard, 3. 1650–2, 1108, 1684
Halton Library, 2. 307
Hamber, Thomas, 3. 1789, 1790, 1791, 1793
Hamel, Henry, 2. 1436
Hamer, Margaret, 3. 1106
Hamerton, Philip Gilbert, 3. 1436, 66, 1851; 4. 1351
Hamilton, A., 2. 1304
Hamilton, Alexander (fl. 1688–1723), 2. 1437, 1448
Hamilton, Alexander, M. D. (fl. 1744), 2. 1463
Hamilton, Andrew, 3. 1822
Hamilton, Anthony Walter Patrick, 4. 949–50
Hamilton, Antoine, Comte de Grammont, 2. 1515, 136, 140, 987
Hamilton, Archibald, 1. 2445
Hamilton, Charles Harold St John, 4. 792
Hamilton, Elizabeth, 3. 729–30, 1717; 2. 1012, 1014
Hamilton, Lord Frederic, 3. 1854
Hamilton, George, 2. 1482
Hamilton, Sir George Rostrevor, 4. 286
Hamilton, Janet, 3. 382
Hamilton, John, Archbishop (d. 1571), 1. 2446
Hamilton, John (d. 1610?), 1. 2446
Hamilton, Lady Mary, 2. 1005
Hamilton, Patrick (d. 1528), 1. 2446
Hamilton, Patrick (1904–62), 4. 949–50
Hamilton, Richard Winter, 3. 1723
Hamilton, Samuel, 3. 1839
Hamilton, Thomas, 3. 730
Hamilton, W. (fl. 1784), journalist, 2. 1307
Hamilton, William (1665?–1751) of Gilbertfield, 2. 1975
Hamilton, William (1704–54) of Bangour, 2. 1975
Hamilton, Sir William (1730–1803), 2. 1422
Hamilton, Sir William (1788–1856), 3. 1535–6, 1731, 1732
Hamlain, 2. 1029
Hämmerlein, Thomas (à Kempis), 1. 848
Hammerton, Sir John Alexander, 3. 1768
Hammond, Anthony, 2. 1325
Hammond, Barbara, 4. 1169
Hammond, Henry, 1. 1980–1
Hammond, James, 2. 550
Hammond, John, 1. 2164
Hammond, John Lawrence le Breton, 4. 1168–9
Hammond, Lawrence, 2. 1457
Hammond, Lucy Barbara, 4. 1169
'Hammond, Ralph' (Hammond Innes), 4. 812
Hammond, William, 1. 1310
Hamond, Thomas, 1. 2073

Hamond, Walter, 1. 2148
Hamor, Ralph, 1. 2156, 2277
Hampden, Renn Dickson, 3. 1607
Hampshire
   general bibliography, 1. 17
   Restoration and eighteenth century, printing, 2. 268
   nineteenth century newspapers, 3. 1832
Hampshire advertiser, 3. 1832
Hampshire chronicle (1772), 2. 1366, 1367–8
Hampshire chronicle (1778), 2. 1364, 1366
Hampshire journal and county register, 2. 1368
'Hampson, John' (John F. N. H. Simpson), 4. 596
Hampton, Benjamin, 2. 1846
Hamyarde, 4. 1365
Hanbury-Williams, Charles, 4. 1355
Hanchet, Daniel, 2. 1276
Handefull of pleasant delites, A, 1. 1008
Handlo, Robert, 1. 796
Handlyng synne, 1. 503–4
handwriting
   after 1500, 1. 220
   Renaissance to Restoration, 1. 933–6
Hane, Joachim, 1. 2129
Hankey, Donald William Alers, 4. 1255–6
Hankey, Montagu, 3. 1870
Hankin, St John Emile Clavering, 4. 950–1
Hanley, James, 4. 596–7
Hanmer, Sir John, Baron Hanmer, 3. 523
Hanmer, Sir Thomas, 2. 1772
Hann, Dorothy, 4. 800
Hanna, William, 3. 1856
Hannay, James, 3. 1386–7, 1768, 1804
Hannay, James Owen, 4. 529–30
Hannay, Patrick, 1. 1310, 2433
Hannington, James, 3. 1676
Hanno the Carthaginian, 2. 1452
Hanover tales, 2. 987
Hansard, firm of, 2. 264
Hansard, George Agar, 3. 1688, 1691
Hansard, Luke, 3. 58
Hansom, Joseph A., 3. 1828
Hanson, C. H., 3. 1805
Hanson, Sir Richard Davies, 3. 1792
Hanway, Jonas, 2. 1402, 1419, 1439
Hanway, Mary Anne, 2. 1011, 1404
Happy family, 2. 1026
Happy hours, 3. 1815
Happy magazine, 4. 1367
Harangues or speeches of quack doctors, 2. 383
Harbert, William, 1. 1310
Harbinger (Chatham 1933), 4. 1385
Harbinger (West Bromwich 1941), 4. 1387
Harcourt, Robert, 1. 2155

Hardcastle, Ephraim, 3. 1821
Hardenberg, Friedrich Leopold, Freiherr von, 3. 126–7
Hardey's universal theatrical directory, 4. 850, 867
Hardiman, James, 3. 1889
Harding, Denys Wyatt, 4. 1370
Harding, Samuel, 1. 1745
Harding, Silvester, 2. 1799
Harding's (Dublin) impartial news letter, 2. 1383
Harding's weekly impartial news letter, 2. 1383
Hardman, Sir William, 3. 1768, 1789
Hardouin, Jean, 2. 1515, 66
Hardwicke, Albert E. P. H. Yorke, 6th Earl of, 3. 1814
Hardwicke, Philip Yorke, 2nd Earl of, 2. 1742
Hardwicke's annual biography, 3. 1879
Hardy, Godfrey Harold, 4. 1256
Hardy, John, 2. 1455
Hardy, Nathaniel, 1. 1993–4
Hardy, P. D., 3. 1845, 1873
Hardy, Thomas (d. 1832), 2. 1311
Hardy, Thomas (1840–1928), 3. 980–92, 112, 132, 1095
Hardyng, John, 1. 682
Hare, Augustus John Cuthbert, 3. 1436–7
Hare, Augustus William, 3. 1604
Hare, John, 2. 1770
Hare, Julius Charles, 3. 1282–3, 1604, 1724
Hare, Robert, 1. 1001
Hare: or hunting incompatible with humanity, 2. 1561
Harflete, Henry, 1. 2050
Hargrove, Ely, 2. 1563
Hargrove, W. Wallace, 3. 1799
Hargrove, William, 3. 1799
Harington, Henry, 2. 1788
Harington, Sir John (1560–1612) poet, 1. 1113–14, 1336, 1906, 2010–11, 2133, 2312
Harington, John (d. 1582) of Stepney, 1. 1113
Harington, John (1627–1700), 2. 476
Hariot, Thomas, 1. 2161, 865
Harker, P. N., 4. 1378
Harland, Henry, 3. 1858
Harland, John, 3. 1768
Harleian miscellany, 1. 2112; 2. 370, 1720
Harleian voyages, 1. 2112
Harlem currant, 2. 1319
Harlem's courant, 2. 1320
Harlequin (1733), 2. 1285
Harlequin (1949), 4. 1379, 1398
Harley, Edward, 2nd Earl of Oxford, 2. 311–12, 1400
Harley, Mrs M., 2. 1007
Harling, Robert, 4. 83
Harllum currant, 2. 1319

Harman, Thomas, 1. 2034, 2277
Harmar, John, 1. 2297
Harmer, Barry, 4. 1397
Harmer, James, 3. 1808
Harmon, Daniel Williams, 3. 1671
Harmonia anglicana, 2. 381
Harmonia sacra, 2. 336
Harmony of the Muses, 1. 1010
Harmsworth, Alfred Charles William, Viscount Northcliffe, 3. 1773, 1792, 1794, 1815, 1825, 1826, 1828
Harmsworth London magazine, 3. 1854; 4. 1355
Harmsworth magazine, 3. 1854; 4. 1354
Harmsworth monthly pictorial magazine, 3. 1854; 4. 1354
Harnett, Cynthia Mary, 4. 800–1
Harney, George Julian, 3. 1818, 1819, 1848
Harp (1730), 2. 358
Harp (1750), 2. 374
Harp of Erin, 2. 1388
Harper (publishers), 3. 78
Harper, Edith Alice Mary, 4. 377
Harper, F., 3. 1850
Harper, Thomas, 1. 1910
Harper, Thomas Norton, 3. 1536
Harpsfield, John, 1. 1942
Harpsfield, Nicholas, 1. 2205
Harraden, Beatrice, 3. 1056–7
'Harriet' (Lydia Falconer Miller), 3. 1102
Harrington, —, 4. 1383
Harrington, James, 1. 2339, 2058
Harrington, M., 4. 1389
Harrington, Richard, 1. 2072
Harris, A., 1. 2035
Harris, Arthur, 4. 1379, 1380, 1381
Harris, Benjamin, 2. 1018
Harris, Edward, 3. 1673
Harris, Elizabeth Furlong Shipton, 3. 1629
Harris, Frank, 4. 1054–5, 1356; 3. 1768, 1794, 1814, 1850
Harris, Irene, 4. 1380, 1387
Harris, James (1709–80), 2. 1886, 42
Harris, James (fl. 1841), 3. 1819
Harris, James Edward, 2nd Earl of Malmesbury, 3. 1714
Harris, James Thomas Frank; *see* Frank Harris
Harris, John (fl. 1648), 1. 2089, 2092, 2101, 2103, 2104, 2105
Harris, John (1667?–1719), 2. 1275, 1321, 1391, 1905; 1. 2112
Harris, Joseph (d.c. 1715), 2. 765
Harris, Joseph (1702–64), 2. 1897
Harris, Kenneth, 4. 1374, 1398
Harris, Mary Kathleen, 4. 808–9
Harris, Moses, 2. 1905

Harris, S. S., 4. 73
Harris, Stanley, 3. 1700
Harris, W. A., 4. 1393
Harris, Walter, 2. 1414
Harris, Walter Burton, 3. 1672, 1676, 1768
Harris, William (1675–1740), 2. 1675–6
Harris, William (fl. 1855), newspaper owner, 3. 1794
Harris, Sir William Cornwallis, 3. 1712
Harrison, A. P., 3. 1691
Harrison, Austin, 4. 1359
Harrison, Cecil, 3. 79
Harrison, Charles, 4. 1352
Harrison, Frederic, 3. 1437–8, 1536–7, 1729
Harrison, G., 3. 1717–18
Harrison, George Bagshawe, 4. 1055–7
Harrison, Jane Ellen, 4. 1057–8
Harrison, John (fl. 1619), 1. 2079
Harrison, John (1693–1776), 2. 1905
Harrison, Mary St Leger, 3. 1066
Harrison, Robert, 1. 1942
Harrison, W., 3. 1798
Harrison, William (1534–93), 1. 2131, 2275
Harrison, William (1685–1713), 2. 551
Harrison, William Henry, 3. 1826, 1873, 1874
Harrison's Derby (and Nottingham) journal, 2. 1357
Harrison and Sons, printers, 3. 58; 4. 80
Harrisson, Tom, 4. 1408
Harrop's Manchester mercury, 2. 1361
Harrovian (1828), 3. 1871
Harrovian (1869), 3. 1871
Harrovian (1878), 3. 1871
Harrovian (1888), 3. 1871
Harrow notes, 3. 1871
Harrow School, magazines, 3. 1871
Harrower, John, 2. 1470
Harrowing of Hell, OE, 1. 274–5; ME, 1. 482
Harry, Blind, 1. 657
Hart, Miss —, 3. 1674
Hart, Alexander, 1. 2066
Hart, Sir Basil Henry Liddell, 4. 1187–8
Hart, Elizabeth Anna, 3. 1092
Hart, Ernest A., 3. 1826–7
Hart, H. C., 3. 1710
Hart, Henry George, 3. 1879
Hart, Mollie Moncrieff, 4. 827
Hart, William, 1. 2472
Harte, Walter, 2. 551
Hartford mercury, 2. 1358
Harting, James Edmund, 3. 1701
Hartley, David, 2. 1886, 42
Hartley, Leslie Poles, 4. 597–8
Hartlib, Samuel, 1. 2334, 2276
Hartson, Hall, 2. 835

Hartwell, Abraham, 1. 2147
Hartwell, Henry, 2. 1461
Hartwell, Robert, 3. 1820
Harvey, Alexander, 2. 1469
Harvey, Christopher, 1. 1310–11, 1330
Harvey, Daniel W., 3. 1768, 1793, 1810
Harvey, Gabriel, 1. 2008–9, 1001, 1962, 2309
Harvey, John, 2. 1975–6
Harvey, Philip Whitfield, 3. 1805
Harvey, Richard, 1. 1961
Harwood, Edward, 2. 1826
Harwood, Harold Marsh, 4. 951–2
Harwood, J. A., 3. 1714
Harwood, Philip, 3. 1768, 1814
Hary, Blind, 1. 657
Haskell, Arnold Lionel David, 4. 808, 826, 828, 860
Hasleton, Richard, 1. 2124
Haslewood, Joseph, 3. 1652–3
Haslop, Henry, 1. 2077, 2122
Hassall, Christopher Vernon, 4. 952–3
Hassell, John. 2. 1406; 3. 1682
Hasselquist, Frederick, 2. 1440
Hasted, Edward, 2. 1737
Hastings, Beatrice, 4. 1373
Hastings, James, 3. 1613, 1853; 4. 1352
Hastings, Thomas, 3. 1691
Hastings, Warren, 2. 1441
Hasty sketch of a tour through part of the Austrian Netherlands, A, 2. 1427
Hatch, Edwin, 3. 1607
Hatch, Richard Warren, 4. 804
Hatchard and Co. 3. 79
Hatt, Ella Mary, 4. 810
Hatton, Sir Christopher, 1. 1776, 1001
Hatton, Joseph, 3. 1057–8, 1810, 1811, 1817, 1839
Hatton, Joshua, 3. 1852
Hau Kiou Choaan, 2. 1000
Hauboys, John, 1. 804
Haughton, William, 1. 1463–4
Hauksbee, Francis, 2. 1905
Haultain, Charles, 3. 1880
Hauptmann, Gerhart, 3. 124
Hauser, Jacob, 4. 1371
Hausted, Peter, 1. 1769
'Hauteville, — de' (Gaspard de Tende), 2. 1414
Harvard, William, 2. 790–1
Have at you all, 2. 1280, 1332
Havelok, 1. 431–2
Haverfield, Eleanor Louisa, 3. 1106
Havergal, Frances Ridley, 3. 628–9, 1103, 1681
Haviland, Matthew, 1. 1311
Haweis, Hugh Reginald, 3. 1816, 1865
Haweis, Thomas, 3. 1840
Hawes, Stephen, 1. 650–1, 1114–15

Hawick, printing, 2. 268
Hawk, 4. 1382
Hawke, Martin Bladen Edward, 2. 1347; 3. 1704
Hawker, G., 3. 1842
Hawker, Mary Elizabeth, 3. 1051
Hawker, Peter, 3. 1712
Hawker, Robert Stephen, 3. 524
Hawkes, D., 4. 880
Hawkes, John, 3. 1704
Hawkesworth, John, 2. 835–6, 1000, 1280, 1475, 1479
Hawkesworth, Walter, 1. 1769
Hawkey, John, 2. 1777
hawking
    Restoration and eighteenth century, 2. 1555–61
    nineteenth century, 3. 1700–1
Hawking moralised, 2. 1560
Hawkins, A. Desmond, 4. 1368
Hawkins, Sir Anthony Hope, 3. 1058–9
Hawkins, Henry, 1. 1329
Hawkins, Sir John (1532–95), 1. 2149
Hawkins, Sir John (1719–89), 2. 1753–4
Hawkins, Sir Richard (d. 1622), 1. 2152
Hawkins, Richard (fl. 1658), 1. 2136
Hawkins, Sir Thomas (d. 1640), 1. 2066, 2120
Hawkins, Thomas (d. 1772), 2. 1783
Hawkins, William (fl. 1583), 1. 2143
Hawkins, William (1602–37), 1. 1745
Hawkins, William (1722–1801), 2. 836
Hawkshaw, Ann, 3. 1091
Hawkshaw, Benjamin, 2. 476
Haworth, Martin E., 3. 1700
Hawtrey, M., 3. 1730
Hawtrey, Stephen Thomas, 3. 1726
Hay, George, 1. 2446
Hay, Gilbert, 1. 424
'Hay, Ian' (John Hay Beith), 4. 598–600
Hay, John (1546–1607), 1. 2447
Hay, John (fl. 1617), 1. 2074
Hay, Peter, 1. 2472
Haydn, Joseph Timothy, 3. 1806
Haydock, Roger, 2. 1399
Haydon, Benjamin Robert, 3. 1283–4
Hayek, Friedrich August von, 4. 1169–70
Hayes, Alfred, 3. 629; 4. 1363
Hayes, M. H., 3. 1706
Hayes, Samuel, 2. 1563
Hayes, W. C., 4. 1388
Haygarth, Arthur, 3. 1697
Hayley, William, 2. 657–9, 1009, 1786
Hayman, Robert, 1. 1336, 2163
Haynes, James, 3. 1131
Haynes, Robert, 3. 1673
Haynie, Henry, 3. 1768
Hays, Mary, 2. 1012, 1014

Hayward, Abraham, 3. 1387–8, 1679, 1768
Hayward, Sir John, 1. 2237–8
Hayward, John Davy, 4. 1058
Hayward, Thomas, 2. 1779
Haywood, Eliza, 2. 791, 147, 988, 989, 990, 991, 992, 994, 995, 996, 997, 998, 1277, 1278, 1279, 1298, 1332
Hazell, Watson and Viney, 3. 58; 4. 80
Hazlitt, William, 3. 1230–8, 112, 1678, 1692, 1715, 1768
Hazlitt, William Carew, 3. 1653–4
Head, Sir Francis Bond, 3. 1674, 1705
Head, Sir George, 3. 1682
Head, Richard, 2. 976, 977, 978
Headlam, S. D., 4. 826
Headley, Henry, 2. 659–60, 1790
Headley, J. T., 3. 1680
Heads of a diarie, 1. 2104
Heads of all the proceedings in. . .Parliament, 1. 2095
Heads of chiefe passages in Parliament, 1. 2103
Heads of severall proceedings in. . .Parliament, 1. 2093
Heads of some notes of the citie scout, 1. 2101
Healey, John, 1. 2297, 2305
Healey, T. P., 3. 1826
Healy, Christopher, 3. 1769
Heap, Jane, 4. 1362
Heard, — (fl. 1778), 2. 1404
Heard, Gerald, 4. 1256–7, 1368
Heard, Henry Fitzgerald, 4. 1256–7, 1368
Hearne, Mary, 2. 988
Hearne, Samuel, 2. 1474, 1486
Hearne, Thomas, 2. 1699–1701, 241, 311, 1773, 1793
Heart, Jonathan, 2. 1472
Hearth and home, 4. 1353
Heartsease library of high class fiction, 4. 1354
Heath, Benjamin, 2. 1777
Heath, Charles, 2. 1408; 3. 1681
Heath, Frederick, 4. 1366
Heath, John, 1. 1335, 2046
Heath, Robert, 1. 1311, 1336, 2050
Heath's book of beauty, 3. 1875
Heath's picturesque annual, 3. 1875
Heath-Stubbs, John Francis Alexander, 4. 287
Heaton review, 4. 1367
Hebbel, Friedrich, 3. 124
Heber, Reginald (fl. 1752), 2. 1313
Heber, Reginald (1783–1826), 3. 382–3, 1604
Heberden, William, 3. 1720
Hebrew, study of
    Renaissance to Restoration, 1. 2405
    Restoration and eighteenth century, 2. 284
    see also scholarship

Hectors, 1. 1759
Hedderwick, Edwin C., 3. 1804
Hedderwick, James, 3. 1769, 1804
Hédelin, François, Abbé d'Aubignac, 2. 1515, 115
Hedge, Mary Ann, 3. 1101
Hedgeland, Isabella, 3. 739–40; 2. 1011
Hedges, Sir William, 2. 1434
Hedley, J. C., 3. 1856
Hegel, Georg Wilhelm Friedrich, 3. 124
Hegge plays (ME), 1. 733–4
Heiberg, Peter Andreas, 2. 212
Heine, Heinrich, 3. 124–5
Heinemann, William, 3. 79
Heinse, Johann Jacob Wilhelm, 2. 181
Heinsius, Daniel, 1. 849
Heiss, John Stanger, 4. 908
Heliodorus, 1. 2169; 2. 1491, 981
Heliogenes del Epy, 2. 1434
Helm, William Henry, 3. 1769
Helme, Elizabeth, the elder (d. 1813), 3. 730–1; 2. 1008, 1012, 1029
Helme, Elizabeth, the younger, 2. 1029
Help to discourse, A, 2. 329
Help to history, A, 2. 1293
Helps, Sir Arthur, 3. 1388–9
Helps, Thomas W., 3. 1870
Helsham, Richard, 2. 1905
Helvetic liberty, 2. 1563
Helvétius, Claude Adrien, 2. 1515, 66, 94, 1004
Helyas, 1. 428–9
Hemans, Felicia Dorothea, 3. 383–4
Heminges, William, 1. 1745–6
Hénault, Charles Jean François, 2. 1515
Henchman, William, 2. 1317
Henderson, Alexander, 1. 2462–3
Henderson, Alexander John, 4. 1370
Henderson, J. D., 4. 1344
Henderson, Sir James (1848–1914), newspaper editor, 3. 1806
Henderson, James (fl. 1871–97), editor of children's paper, 3. 1825
Henderson, James Alexander, 3. 1806
Henderson, John Scott, 3. 1804, 1824
Henderson, R., 3. 1706
Henderson, W., 4. 848
Henderson, William, 3. 1690
Henderson-Smith, Flora, 4. 1359
Hendred, William, 1. 1115
Hendry, James Findlay, 4. 287–8, 1373
Hendyng, Proverbs of, 1. 507–8
Henley, John, 2. 1796, 1278, 1299
Henley, William Ernest, 3. 629–31, 1769, 1815, 1852, 1853
Hennell, Charles Christian, 3. 1607

Hennepin, Louis, 2. 1457
Henniker, L., 4. 1404
Henniker, S., 4. 1404
Henning, F. W. J., 3. 1693
Henry VIII, 1. 1115, 853
Henry of Avranches, 1. 772
Henry of Bracton, 1. 772–3
Henry of Harclay, 1. 787
Henry of Huntingdon, 1. 761
Henry of Silgrave, 1. 773
Henry, David, 2. 1476; 3. 1839
Henry, Leigh, 4. 1365
Henry, Matthew, 2. 1672
Henry, Michael, 3. 1822
Henry, Robert, 2. 1737, 1796, 106
Henry, William, 2. 1905
Henry's Reading journal, 2. 1365
Henry's Winchester journal, 2. 1365, 1367
Henry of Northumberland, 2. 1014
Henryson, Robert, 1. 658–60
Henshall, Samuel, 2. 1798
Henshaw, Joseph, 1. 2049
Henson, Herbert Hensley, 4. 1257–8
Henty, George Alfred, 3. 1094, 1769, 1825, 1853
Hepburn, Edith Alice Mary, 4. 377
Hepburn, George, 3. 1673
Hepburn, Robert, 2. 1369, 1562
Hepburn, Thomas, 2. 1402
Hepworth, T. C., 3. 1878
Heraclitus and Democritus, 1. 1115
Heraclitus ridens (1681), 2. 1340, 347
Heraclitus ridens (1703), 2. 1343
Heraclitus ridens (1718), 2. 1345–6
Herald, Kathleen Wendy, 4. 816
Herald: or patriot proclaimer (1757), 2. 1333
Herald (Clonmel 1800), 2. 1387
Herald (1914), 4. 1405
Herald of progress, 3. 1819
Herald of revolt, 4. 1405
Heraud, John Abraham, 3. 384, 1841, 1845
Herb o' grace, 4. 1355
Herbart, Johann Friedrich, 3. 1730
Herbert de Losinga, Bishop of Norwich, 1. 757
Herbert, Sir Alan Patrick, 4. 288–90
Herbert, Auberon Edward William, 3. 1438
Herbert, Edward, 1st Baron, 1. 1311–12, 853, 2129, 2249–50, 2333
Herbert, George, 1. 1201–6, 1910, 2031, 2047; 2. 32
Herbert, Henry, 10th Earl of Pembroke, 2. 1554
Herbert, Mary, Countess of Pembroke, 1. 1115–16, 1468–9, 1906
Herbert, Sir Percy, 1. 2041, 2050
Herbert, Sydney, 3. 1789
Herbert, Sir Thomas, 1. 2251, 2146–7

Herbert, William, 3. 385
Herd, David, 2. 245
Herd, Harold, 4. 1407
Herder, Johann Gottfried von, 2. 156
Herdman, E., 4. 1381, 1382, 1383, 1384, 1386
Herdman, E. F., 4. 1379
Herdman, R., 4. 1381, 1382
Herdman's miscellany, 4. 1379
Here and now, 4. 1375
Here prophecy, 1. 473
Here today, 4. 1376
Herebert, William, 1. 710–12
Hereford, libraries of, 1. 991; 2. 307
Hereford journal, 2. 1358
Hereford times, 3. 1832
Herefordshire, printing, 2. 268
Heresbach, Conrad, 1. 2278, 849
Herford, Charles Harold, 3. 1439
Herford, William Henry, 3. 1730
Heriot, John, 2. 1009, 1338; 3. 1789, 1792
Hermathena, 3. 1870; 4. 1394
Ἑρμῆς (1892), 4. 1395
Hermes (1907), 4. 1358, 1394
Hermes Straticus, 1. 2104
Hermit (1711), 2. 1274
Hermit (1752), 2. 1348
Hermit in town, 2. 1284
Hernandez de San Pedro, Diego, 1. 2187, 916
Herod, R. S., 3. 1708
Herodian, 1. 2169; 2. 1491
Herodotus, 1. 2169, 2137; 2. 1491
Heron, Haly, 1. 2047
Heron, Robert, 2. 1372, 1406; 3. 1789, 1792, 1807, 1808
Herrera, Antonio de, 2. 1453
Herrick, Robert, 1. 1196–8, 1336; 2. 32
Herring, Robert, 4. 1368
Herring, Thomas, 2. 1624, 1403
Herringman, Henry, 2. 280
Herschel, Sir John Frederick William, 3. 1537
Herschel, Sir William, 2. 1905
Hertslet, Sir Edward, 3. 1880
Hervey, C. W., 4. 1372
Hervey, Christopher, 2. 1426
Hervey, Elizabeth, 2. 1008, 1013
Hervey, Lord Francis, 3. 1870
Hervey, James, 2. 1861–2, 147
Hervey, John, 2nd Baron, 2. 1713, 1278
Hervey, Thomas Kibble, 3. 1821, 1873, 1876
Herzen, Aleksandr Ivanovich, 3. 152, 1769
Heseltine, Nigel, 4. 1373
Hesiod, 1. 2170; 2. 1491
Hessey, James, 3. 1844
Heteroclite, 2. 1288
Hetherington, Henry, 3. 1769, 1811, 1818

Hetherington, J., 4. 1384
Hetherington's twopenny dispatch and people's police register, 3. 1818
Heward, Constance, 4. 797
Hewat, Peter, 1. 2463
Hewatt, Alexander, 2. 1470
Hewitt, Grailey, 4. 1358
Hewlett, Esther, 3. 1101
Hewlett, Henry G., 3. 1769
Hewlett, Maurice Henry, 4. 600–2
Hexham, Henry, 1. 2080
Heylyn, Peter, 1. 2242–3, 2097, 2120, 2142
Heyman, John, 2. 1439
Heyrick, Thomas, 2. 476, 1557
Heytesbury, William, 1. 799
Heywood, Jasper, 1. 1116, 1421
Heywood, John, 1. 1413–14, 1116, 1333, 2029, 2032
Heywood, Thomas, 1. 1682–9, 2043, 2058, 2075, 2315; 2. 32
Hibbert, H. G., 3. 1769
Hibernian chronicle, 2. 1388
Hibernian gazette, 2. 1387
Hibernian journal, 2. 1386
Hibernian magazine (1771), 2. 1379; 3. 1840
Hibernian magazine (1864), 3. 1850
Hibernian morning post, 2. 1388
Hibernian patriot, 2. 358
Hibernian telegraph, 2. 1387
'Hibernicus' (J. Arbuckle), 2. 1377
Hibernicus's letters, 2. 363
Hichecoke, W., 1. 686
Hichens, Robert Smythe, 4. 602–3
Hickeringill, Edward, 2. 1454
Hickes, George, 2. 1791–2, 241, 1609
Hickey, Emily Henrietta, 3. 631
Hickey, Theodosia Frances Wynne, 4. 811
Hicklin, John, 3. 1683
Hickman, C. D., 4. 859
Hickox, S. A., 4. 1381
Hicks, George Dawes, 4. 1258–9
Hickson, William Edward, 3. 1855
Hidalgo, Gaspar Lucas, 1. 908
Hidden, N. F., 4. 1371
'Hieover, Harry' (C. Bindley), 3. 1705, 1713
Hiffernan, Paul, 2. 1378
Higden, Henry, 2. 476
Higden, Ranulf, 1. 794, 2117, 2130
Higgin, Anthony, 1. 1001
Higgins, Bertram, 4. 1366
Higgins, Bryan, 2. 1905
Higgins, Francis, 3. 1805
Higgins, Frederick Robert, 4. 290, 1358
Higgins, John, 1. 1117
Higgins, Matthew James, 3. 1769

Higgins, William, 2. 1905
Higginson, Francis, 1. 2158
Higginson, Nesta, 3. 1910
Higgons, Bevil, 2. 551
Higgs, Henry, 2. 1002
Higgs, Marjorie, 4. 1385, 1387
High-German doctor, 2. 1275
High hatter, 4. 1372
High House Press, 4. 97
Highbury (Players') bulletin, 4. 851
Highet, Gilbert, 4. 1398
Highland gentleman's magazine, 2. 1371
Highway, 4. 1405
Hilaria, 2. 425
Hilarie, Hugh, 1. 1117
'Hilario', 2. 1280
Hilary the Englishman, 1. 757
Hildersham, Arthur, 1. 1994, 2296
Hildyard, Edward Digby, 3. 1870
Hiler, Hilaire, 4. 1372
Hill, Aaron, 2. 791–3, 1277, 1278, 1321, 1344, 1416, 1437
Hill, Abraham, 2. 1906
Hill, Alexander, 3. 1725
Hill, Brian, 2. 1428
Hill, Florence Davenport, 3. 1728, 1747
Hill, Frank Harrison, 3. 1790
Hill, Geoffrey, 4. 1397
Hill, George, 4. 1365
Hill, George Birkbeck Norman, 3. 1654
Hill, J. W. F., 4. 1393
Hill, 'Sir' John, 2. 996–7, 1279, 1280, 1298, 1332
Hill, Matthew Davenport, 3. 1720
Hill, Rowland, 3. 1617; 2. 1408
Hill, S., 3. 1881
Hill, Thomas (16th century), 1. 2023
Hill, Thomas (fl. 1799), 2. 1475
Hill, Thomas Ford, 2. 247
Hill, William, 3. 1818
Hillary, Richard Hope, 4. 1170
Hillmn, 4. 1364
Hills, Henry, 2. 265
Hilton, Arthur Clement, 3. 1866
Hilton, James, 4. 604
Hilton, John (1599–1657) 1. 1356
Hilton, John (fl. 1682), 2. 1318
Hilton, John (fl. 1919), 4. 1363
Hilton, Walter, 1. 521–2
Hilton, William, 2. 1454
Him, George, 4. 810
Hinchcliff, Thomas Woodbine, 3. 1680
Hind, Charles Lewis, 3. 1815, 1822
Hind, Henry Youle, 3. 1673
Hind, James, 1. 2306
Hind, John, 1. 2055

Hinderer, Anna, 3. 1671
Hindmarsh, Robert, 2. 1309
Hinkson, Katharine, 3. 1910–11
'Hint, Tobias', 2. 1289
Hinton, James, 3. 1537, 1607
Hinton, John Howard, 3. 1723, 1725
Hippocrates, 1. 2170; 2. 1491
Hippocrates ridens, 2. 1341
Hippodrome, 4. 859
Hippodrome tatler, 4. 851
Hirst, — (fl. 1880), 3. 1801
Hispanus, Petrus, Pope John XXI, 1. 2187
Hispanus, 1. 1777
Hisperica famina, 1. 340–2
Historia Britonum, 1. 339–40
Historia litteraria, 2. 1294
Historian, 2. 1274
Historic times, 3. 1816
Historical account of Russia, An, 2. 1414
Historical account of the publick transactions, An, 2. 1319
Historical and poetical medley, 2. 366
Historical and political mercury, 2. 1302
Historical, biographical, literary and scientific magazine, 2. 1312
Historical chronicle, 2. 1307
Historical description of the Kingdom of Macassar, An, 2. 1435
Historical detail of the most remarkable public occurrences, An, 2. 1338
Historical journal, An (1697), 2. 1320
Historical journal (1732), 2. 1327
Historical list of horse matches, An, (1752), 2. 1313
Historical list of horse matches, An (1770), 2. 1314
Historical list of horse races, An (1729), 2. 1313, 1346
Historical magazine, 2. 1308
Historical narrative of the discovery of New Holland, An, 2. 1480
Historical recorder, 4. 1388
Historical register (1716), 2. 1294
Historical register (1772), 2. 1335
Historical register (1791), 2. 1373
Historical relation of the island of Ceylon, An, 2. 1438
Historicall and true discourse of a voyage made by . . .Mateleif, An, 1. 2144
Historie and life of King James the Sext, 1. 2447
history
    Old English period, modern studies of, 1. 205–10
    Middle English period, source-material, 1. 357–68
    Renaissance writers, 1. 2201–54, 2465–70

Hodges, Cyril Walter, 4. 810
Hodges, William, 2. 1442
Hodges, William Henry, 4. 1361
Hodgkin, Thomas, 3. 1790
Hodgkinson, — (fl. 1794), 2. 1474
Hodgson, Frances, 3. 1096
Hodgson, Ralph, 4. 291
Hodgson, Shadworth Holloway, 3. 1537-8
Hodgson, Thomas, 3. 81
Hodgson, William Ballantyne, 3. 1728, 1746
Hodgson, William Earl, 3. 1792
Hodson, J., 2. 1287
Hody, Humphrey, 2. 1609
Hoey, Cashel, 3. 1856
Hoffman, Francis, 2. 1274
Hoffmann, Ernst Theodor Amadeus, 3. 125, 1109-10
Hoffmann, Heinrich, 3. 1110
Hofland, Barbara, 3. 733-5, 1088
Hofland, Thomas Christopher, 3. 1688
Hofmannstahl, Hugo von, 3. 125
Hog, James, 2. 2044
Hog's wash, 2. 1310
Hogan, —, 3. 1790
Hogarde, Miles, 1. 1117, 1903
Hogarth, David George, 3. 1676, 1868
Hogarth, George, 3. 1807, 1875
Hogarth, Paul, 4. 1380
Hogarth, William, 2. 42
Hogarth Press, 4. 97
Hogben, Lancelot Thomas, 4. 1259-60
Hogg, Capt. —, 2. 1477
Hogg, Garry Lester, 4. 807
Hogg, James (1770-1835), 3. 267-70, 1769
Hogg, James (fl. 1895), 3. 1693
Hogg, W. T. M., 3. 1702
Hogg's (weekly) instructor 3. 1847
Hohenheim, T. B. von (Paracelsus), 1. 850
Höhler, Mrs Edwin, 3. 1106
Holbach, Paul Henri Dietrich, Baron d', 2. 1515, 94
Holberg, Ludwig, 2. 212, 995
Holborn, John Bernard, 3. 1858
Holborn-Drollery, 2. 332
Holborn monthly magazine, 4. 1356
Holborne, Antony, 1. 1348
Holcombe, J., 2. 1282
Holcot, Robert, 1. 796
Holcroft, Thomas, 2. 837-40, 147, 177, 183, 208, 212, 1006, 1010, 1011, 1286, 1287, 1307, 1309
Holder, William, 2. 1906
Hölderlin, Friedrich, 3. 125
Holdsworth, Sir William Searle, 4. 1173-4
Hole, James, 3. 1745
Hole, Philippa, 4. 1366

Hole, Richard, 2. 239
Holes, Andrew, 1. 1001
'Holding, Ephraim' (George Mogridge), 3. 1089
Holiday entertainment, 2. 1026
Holinshed, Raphael, 1. 2208-9
Holland, — (fl. 1836), newspaper editor, 3, 1841
Holland, C. F., 4. 1365
Holland, H. W., 3. 1728
Holland, Henry Fox, 1st Baron, 2. 1282, 1284
Holland, Hugh, 1. 1118
Holland, John, 3. 1682, 1769
Holland, Philemon, 1. 2119
Holland, Richard, 1. 657
Holland, Robert, 1. 1118
Holland, Samuel, 1. 2058
Holland, W., 2. 1288
Holland pacquet-boat, 2. 1319
Holles, Lord Denzil, 2. 1693
Holliday, Francis, 2. 1346
Hollingshead, John, 3. 1769
Hollingsworth, Nathaniel John, 3. 1718
Hollingsworth, S., 2. 1451, 1472
Hollins, R., 4. 1388
Hollis, Thomas, 2. 312
Holloway, B., 4. 1381
Holloway, Mark, 4. 1394
Holly branch, 3. 1876
Holman, Henry, 3. 1731
Holman, James, 3. 1669, 1678
Holman, Joseph George, 2. 840
Holme, Benjamin, 2. 1395, 1464
Holme, Charles, 3. 1853
Holme, Charles Geoffrey, 3. 1853
Holme, Constance, 4. 604
Holme, Stamford, 4. 850
Holme, Thea, 4. 850
Holme, Wilfrid, 1. 1118
Holmes, Mrs Dalkeith, 3. 1679
Holmes, Edmond Gore Alexander, 3. 631
Holmes, George, 2. 1407
Holmes, James, 3. 1821
Holmes, R. S., 3. 1698
Holmes, Samuel, 2. 1442
Holt, Gresham's School library at, 2. 307
Holt, Francis Ludlow, 3. 1808
Holt, John, 2. 1778
Holt, Thomas, 3. 1810
Holt, Thomas Littleton, 3. 1789, 1790, 1811, 1825
Holtby, Winifred, 4. 605
Holthan-Hobson, E. S., 4. 1385
Holwell, John Zephaniah, 2. 1440
Holworthy, S. M., 3. 1681
Holy Grail, romances of the, 1. 411-14
Holyday, Barten, 1. 1769, 1994

Holyoake, George Jacob, 3. 1769, 1819, 1823
Holywood, John, 1. 773
Homage aux dames, 3. 1873
Home, Anne, 2. 2026–7
Home, Henry, Lord Kames, 2. 2065–6, 43, 158, 1887
Home, John, 2. 840–1
Home, 3. 1828
Home and empire, 4. 1376
Home and foreign review, 3. 1848, 1857–8
Home chat, 3. 1828
Home journal, 4. 1367
Home magazine, 4. 1355
Home magazine of fiction, 4. 1355
Home mirror (*novels*), 4. 1364
Home novels, 4. 1369
Home stories (1896), 4. 1354
Home stories (1923), 4. 1360
Home weekly, 4. 1358
Homer, 1. 2170; 2. 1491, 34
Homes, Nathaniel, 1. 2041
Homiletic fragments (OE), 1. 285
homilies, Old English, 1. 324–6
Hone, J. P., 3. 1707
Hone, William, 3. 1284–6, 79, 1769, 1817, 1873, 1874, 1875
Honest amusements, 2. 350
Honest fellow (1763), 2. 384
Honest fellow or buck's necessary companion (1794), 2. 419
Honest gentleman, 2. 1276
Honest lawyer, 1. 1760
Honest true Briton, 2. 1326
Honey-Moon, 2. 356
Honey-suckle (1734), 2. 363
'Honeycombe, Charles' (Robert Lloyd), 2. 1302
Honeysuckle (1731), 2. 360
Honyman, Andrew, 2. 2034
Hood, Edwin Paxton, 3. 1842, 1851
Hood, Thomas (1799–1845), 3. 359–62, 1704, 1769, 1844, 1847, 1874
Hood, Thomas ('Tom') (1835–74), 3. 1094, 1825
Hood's magazine, 3. 1847
Hook, F., 4. 880
Hook, James, 3. 731
Hook, Theodore Edward, 3. 731–3, 1769, 1809, 1844
Hook, Walter Farquhar, 3. 1629, 1723
Hooke, Daniel Burford, 3. 1840
Hooke, Nathaniel, 2. 1713–14
Hooke, Robert, 2. 1291, 1906
Hooke, S. H., 4. 1391
Hooker, A. O., 4. 1382
Hooker, John, 1. 2131
Hooker, Sir Joseph Dalton, 3. 1672, 1675, 1840

Hooker, Richard, 1. 1949–58, 2275
'Hooker, Richard' (William Webster), 2. 1327, 1331
Hooker, Sir William Jackson, 3. 1840
Hookes, Nicholas, 1. 1312
Hookham, Thomas, 3. 1677
Hoole, Barbara, 3. 733–5, 1088
Hoole, Charles, 1. 2276
Hoole, John, 2. 841–2
Hooper, John, 1. 1926–7
Hooper, William, 2. 1568
Hope, Alexander James Beresford, 3. 1814
'Hope, Anthony' (Sir Anthony Hope Hawkins), 3. 1058–9
'Hope, Ascott' (R. Hope-Moncrieff), 3. 1096
Hope, F. E., 4. 1385
Hope, John, 2. 1285
Hope, John Harold, 3. 1870
Hope, P. Beresford, 3. 1814
Hope, Sir Thomas, 1. 1908
Hope, Thomas, 3. 735
Hope, Sir William, 2. 1553, 1562
Hope-Moncrieff, Robert, 3. 1096
Hopeman, Thomas, 1. 797
Hopkins, Charles, 2. 765
Hopkins, F. P., 3. 1690
Hopkins, Gerard Manley, 3. 581–93, 132
Hopkins, John (d. 1570), 1. 1899–1900
Hopkins, John (b. 1675), 2. 477
Hopkins, John Baker, 3. 1810
Hopkins, Mary, 2. 1014, 1028
Hopper, Nora, 3. 1916
Hoppus, John, 3. 1722
Hopton, Ralph, 1st Baron, 1. 2250
Horace, 1. 2170–1, 2. 1497–8, 35, 65
Horae Beatae Mariae, 1. 1935
Hore, Annie, 3. 1672
Horizon, 4. 1374, 1346
Horlick's magazine, 4. 1357
Horlock, K. W., 3. 1705
Horn Book magazine, 4. 790
Horn Childe, 1. 430
'Hornbook, Adam' (Thomas Cooper), 3. 516–17
Horne, Herbert P., 3. 1858
Horne, Nathaniel Freebody, 2. 1284
Horne, Richard Henry (or Hengist), 3. 524, 1843
Horne, Thomas Hartwell, 3. 1617, 1682
Horneck, Anthony, 2. 1610
Horneck, Philip, 2. 1275
Horner, Leonard, 3. 1722
Hornibrook, John L., 4. 1365
Horrebov, Niels, 2. 1420
Horrox, Reginald, 4. 110
Horse and hound, 3. 1703, 1825
Horse's levée, 3. 1088

Horse-manship of England, 2. 1553
Horse-race: or the pleasures of the course, 2. 1555
horsemanship, Restoration and eighteenth century, 2. 1551–5
Horsey, Sir Jerome, 1. 2123
Horsley, John, 2. 1717–18
Horsley, Samuel, 2. 1886, 1906
Hort, Fenton John Anthony, 3. 1607, 1726
Horton, A., 4. 1385, 1386, 1388
Hortop, Job, 1. 2152
Hoskin, K., 4. 1386
Hoskyns, John, 1. 2314
Hotham, Durant, 1. 2100
Hothby, John, 1. 804
Hotman, François, 1. 2076
Hotspur, 4. 820
Houghton, Arthur Boyd, 3. 66
Houghton, John, 2. 1291, 1342
Houghton, Richard Monckton Milnes, 1st Baron, 3. 539, 1727
Houghton, William Stanley, 4. 954
Houlding, Henry, 3. 1684
Hoult, Norah, 4. 605–6
Hour, 3. 1791
Hour glass, 4. 1383
Hours Press, 4. 97
House, Arthur Humphry, 4. 1059
House, J., 4. 852
Household, Geoffrey Edward West, 4. 606, 806
Household narrative of current events, 3. 1848
Household words, 3. 1821, 1836–7
Housman, Alfred Edward, 3. 601–6
Housman, John, 2. 1408
Housman, Laurence, 3. 632, 1098; 4. 1357
Houston, A., 1. 2467
Houston, Fanny Lucy, Lady, 4. 1351
Houston, James, 2. 1395, 1464
Houston, T., 3. 1695
Houstoun, John, 2. 1448
Houtman, Frederik de, 1. 2148
Houy, George, 3. 1804
Hovell, William Hilton, 3. 1675
Hovell-Thurlow, Edward, 2nd Baron Thurlow, 3. 404
How, John, 2. 280
How, William Walsham, 3. 526
How do you do? 2. 1290
How the psalter of Our Lady was made, 1. 456
Howard, Birkin, 4. 1375
Howard, Edward (1624–c. 1700), 2. 765
Howard, Edward (1792?–1841), 3. 735–6, 1090
Howard, Henry, Earl of Surrey, 1. 1023–4
Howard, James, 2. 766
Howard, John, 2. 1424
Howard, Philip, 1st Earl of Arundel, 1. 1118–19

Howard, Sir Robert (1626–98), 2. 766
Howard, Robert (d.c. 1676), Franciscan, 1. 1312
Howard, Thomas, 2nd Earl of Arundel (1586–1646), 1. 1001
Howard, Thomas (fl. 1633), 2. 976
Howard, Lord William, 1. 1001
Howe, John, 2. 1610
Howel, Thomas, 2. 1443
Howell, James, 1. 2225–8, 2032, 2040, 2049, 2057, 2089, 2135, 2140, 2318; 2. 1409
Howell, Thomas, 1. 1119
Howes, Frank, 4. 878
Howgill, Francis, 2. 1650
Howgrave's Stamford mercury, 2. 1367
Howie, John, 2. 2045, 1805
Howitt, Mary, 3. 1286, 1090, 1769, 1814, 1875, 1876
Howitt, Samuel, 3. 1687
Howitt, William, 3. 1286–8, 1089, 1769, 1814, 1875
Howitt's journal of literature and popular progress, 3. 1814
Howlett, Robert, 2. 1557, 1569
Howson, John Saul, 3. 1619
Hoyland, Francis, 2. 660
Hoyle, Edmond, 2. 1567
Hozyusz, Stanislaw, 1. 849
Huarte Navarro, Juan de Dios, 1. 2187, 908
Hubbard, Louisa Maria, 3. 1878
Hubberthorn, Richard, 2. 1651
Huber, Marie, 2. 1515, 94
Huber, Victor A., 3. 1731
Hubert, Sir Francis, 1. 1312
Huby, William, 1. 2107
Huck, Joseph, 2. 1407
Huddersfield daily chronicle, 3. 1798
Huddersfield daily examiner, 3. 1798, 1831
Huddersfield examiner, 3. 1832
Huddesford, George, 2. 660
Hudson, Charles, 3. 1709
Hudson, Edward, 3. 1817
Hudson, J. W., 3. 1745
Hudson, John, 2. 1826
'Hudson, Stephen' (Sydney Schiff), 4. 606–7
Hudson, Thomas, 1. 1119
Hudson, William Henry, 3. 1059–60, 1674; 4. 789
Hue and cry (1755), 2. 1386
Hue and cry (1791?); 2. 1337
Hueffer, Ford Madox (later Ford), 4. 569–75, 1359, 1366, 1367; 3. 1105
Hueffer, Francis, 3. 1858
Huet, Pierre Daniel, 2. 1515, 66, 94, 116, 140
Huffumbourghausen, 'Baron', 2. 1538
Huggarde, Miles, 1. 1117, 1903
Hugh of Leicester, 1. 1119

Hugh of Newcastle, 1. 787-8
Hugh the Cantor, 1. 761
Hughes, Charles, 2. 1554
Hughes, Griffith, 2. 1464
Hughes, Gwilym Fielden, 4. 814
Hughes, Jabez, 2. 552
Hughes, John (1677-1720), 2. 552-3, 1275, 1772-3
Hughes, John (fl. 1798), 3. 1881
Hughes, Lewis, 1. 2156
Hughes, Mary, 3. 1089
Hughes, Richard Arthur Warren, 4. 607, 806, 1397
Hughes, Robert Edgar, 3. 1716
Hughes, T., 3. 1715
Hughes, Thomas (fl. 1587), 1. 1770
Hughes, Thomas (fl. 1778-89), soldier, 2. 1473
Hughes, Thomas (1822-96), 3. 933-4, 1092, 1701
Hughlings-Jackson, John, 3. 1858
Hugo de Novo Castro, 1. 787-8
Hugo, Victor-Marie, 3. 102-3
Huguenots, general bibliography, 1. 21
Huie, Richard, 3. 1875
Huish, Marcus, 3. 1847, 1878
Hull
    Restoration and eighteenth century
        newspapers, 2. 1359
        printing and bookselling, 2. 268
    twentieth century, university magazine, 4. 1395
Hull, J., 3. 1722
Hull, Katharine, 4. 814
Hull, Thomas, 2. 842, 1003, 1424
Hull advertiser, 2. 1359
Hull courant (1739), 2. 1359
Hull courant (1755), 2. 1359
Hull daily mail, 3. 1802
Hull daily news, 3. 1802
Hull evening news, 3. 1802
Hull express, 3. 1798
Hull journal, 2. 1359
Hull morning telegraph, 3. 1795
Hull news, 3. 1802
Hull packet, 2. 1359
Hulme, Thomas Ernest, 4. 1059-61
Hulsius, Levinus, 1. 2112
Hulton, Sir Edward (1869-1925), 3. 1791, 1798, 1803, 1809, 1812, 1824
Hulton, Sir Edward (b. 1906), 4. 1379, 1408
Hulton, Henry, 2. 1469
Humanism, Renaissance, 1. 1781-826
Humanist (1757), 2. 1282
Humanist (1956), 4. 1352
Humanitas, 4. 1396
Humanity, 3. 1854
Humber amateur, 4. 1383

Humble, A., 4. 1384
Hume, Alexander (d. 1609), poet, 1. 2424
Hume, Alexander (d.c. 1630), scholar, 1. 2472
Hume, Anna, 1. 2434
Hume, David (d. 1630), 1. 2434, 2468
Hume, David (1711-76), 2. 1873-80, 42-3, 107-8, 117, 158-9, 189, 1778
Hume, Sir Patrick (d. 1609), 1. 2424
Hume, Patrick (fl. 1695), 2. 1767
Hume, Tobias, 1. 1351
Humfrey, Laurence, 1. 854
Humming bird, 2. 396-7
humorous papers, nineteenth century, 3. 1825, 1837-8
humour writing, manuals on, 4. 66
Humourist, 2. 1351
Humourist's magazine (1787), 2. 1307
Humourist's magazine (1788), 2. 1308
humourists, twentieth century, 4. 993-1134
Humours of a coffee house, 2. 1344
Humours of a country election, 2. 363
Humours of cycling, 3. 1700
Humours of London, 2. 391
Humours of new Tunbridge Wells, 2. 363
Humours of the age, 2. 1329
Humours of the times, 2. 392
Humours of whist, 2. 1567
Humphrey, R., 1. 2297
Humphreys, Cecil Frances, 3. 527
Humphreys: a monthly review, 4. 1408
Humphries, R., 3. 1692
Humphries, Richard, 2. 1563
Hungarian, literary relations with
    Renaissance to Restoration
        general, 1. 923-4
        Shakespeare, 1. 1632-3
    Restoration and eighteenth century, 2. 219
Hunnis, William, 1. 1119, 1902
Hunt, Frederick Knight, 3. 1790, 1816, 1826
Hunt, Henry George Bonavia, 3. 1850, 1851
Hunt, Isobel Violet, 4. 607-8
Hunt, John, 3. 1792, 1808, 1809, 1817
Hunt, Leigh, 3. 1216-23, 139, 1770, 1790, 1809, 1814, 1821, 1843, 1855
Hunt, Robert, 1. 2149
Hunt, Thornton, 3. 1770, 1790, 1813, 1814
Hunt, Violet, 4. 607-8
Hunt, William, 3. 1770, 1797
Hunt, William Holman, 3. 66
Hunt's universal yacht list, 3. 1716
Hunt's yachting magazine, 3. 1716
Hunter, Anne, 2. 2026-7
Hunter, David, 3. 60
Hunter, James, 2. 1555
Hunter, John (1728-93), surgeon, 2. 1906

Hunter, John (1738–1821), admiral, 2. 1472, 1482
Hunter, Joseph, 3. 1654–5
Hunter, Norman, 4. 805–6
Hunter, Norman Charles, 4. 955
Hunter, Robert, 2. 1472
Hunter, Samuel, 3. 1804
Hunter, Stella, 4. 1386
Hunter, William (1718–83), anatomist, 2. 1906
Hunter, William (1755–1812), orientalist, 2. 1442
Hunter, William (fl. 1792), traveller, 2. 1430
Hunter, William Alexander, 3. 1808
Hunter's annual, 3. 1876
Hunter's garland, 2. 1560
hunting
    Restoration and eighteenth century, 2. 1555–61
    nineteenth century, 3. 1703–8
Hunting of the Cheviot, 1. 1120
Hunting of the hare's garland, 2. 1560
Huntingdonshire, general bibliography, 1. 17
Huon of Burdeux, 1. 422, 2187
Hurault, Jaques, 1. 2187, 863
Hurd, Richard, 2. 1780–1, 43, 235, 1625
Hurdis, James, 2. 660–1
Hurlock, Joseph, 2. 1906
'Hurlothrumbo, Doctor', 2. 1023
Hurry, Mrs Ives, 2. 1027; 3. 1099
Hurtado de Mendoza, Antonio, 2. 201
Husbandman's jewel, 2. 1557
Husband's message, 1. 285–6
Husbands, John, 2. 235
Hush, 4. 1369
Hutcheon, William, 3. 1770
Hutcheson, Charles, 2. 1405
Hutcheson, Francis, 2. 1862–3, 43, 108, 117
Hutchings, Monica, 4. 1387
Hutchings, Reginald, 4. 1372
Hutchins, John, 2. 1738
Hutchins, Thomas, 2. 1470
Hutchinson, Arthur Stuart Menteth, 4. 608
Hutchinson, Benjamin, 2. 1806
Hutchinson, G. A., 3. 1825
Hutchinson, Horace G., 3. 1697, 1702–3
Hutchinson, John, 3. 1682
Hutchinson, Lucy, 2. 1694–5
Hutchinson, Ray Coryton, 4. 609
Hutchinson, Roger, 1. 1942
Hutchinson, Thomas, 2. 1403
Hutchinson, William, 2. 1738, 1010, 1403
Hutchinson's adventure and mystery story magazine, 4. 1389
Hutchinson's adventure-story magazine, 4. 1389
Hutchinson's best story magazine, 4. 1367
Hutchinson's mystery-story magazine, 4. 1389
Hutchinson's Punch anthologies, 4. 1377

Hutchinson's story magazine, 4. 1364
Hutten, Leonard, 1. 1770
Hutton, Catherine, 3. 1288
Hutton, Charles, 2. 1906
Hutton, Clarke, 4. 804
Hutton, Henry, 1. 1336
Hutton, James, 2. 1906
Hutton, John (d. 1806), 2. 1404
Hutton, John (fl. 1847), 3. 1811
Hutton, Luke, 1. 2034
Hutton, Richard Holt, 3. 1389, 1607, 1770, 1813, 1857
Hutton, William, 2. 1405; 3. 1681
Huxley, Aldous Leonard, 4. 609–17, 801, 1397
Huxley, Sir Julian Sorell, 4. 1260–1
Huxley, Leonard, 4. 1351
Huxley, Thomas Henry, 3. 1538–40, 1730, 1857
Huysmans, Joris Karl, 3. 103
Hwætberht, 1. 345
Hyckescorner, 1. 1407
Hyde, Douglas, 3. 1909–10
Hyde, Edward, 1st Earl of Clarendon, 2. 1678–82; 1. 1001, 2342
Hyde, Thomas, 2. 1831
Hymenaeus cantabrigiensis, 2. 334
Hymeneus, 1. 1777
Hynd, John, 1. 2047
Hyndman, Henry Mayers, 3. 1820
Hyndman, R., 4. 1382
Hyne, Charles John Cutliffe Wright, 3. 1105
Hyp-doctor, 2. 1278
Hypochondriack, 2. 1286
Hypocrite unmasked, 2. 1336
Hyslop, James, 3. 385

I., N. (fl. 1616), 1. 2074
I spy, 4. 1374
Ibis, 3. 1857
Ibn Haukal, 2. 1444
Ibsen, Henrik, 3. 147–8
Icarus, 4. 1395
Idea and form, 4. 1373
Idea of Christian love, 2. 336
Ideal, 4. 1357
Ideal kinema, 4. 57
Ides, Everard Ysbrants, 2. 1436
Idler (1714), 2. 1275
Idler (Cork 1715), 2. 1387
Idler (1758), 2. 1282
Idler (1896), 4. 1353
Idler magazine, 3. 1853; 4. 1353
Idley, Peter, 1. 504, 686
Idyls of the rink, 3. 1714
Iffland, August Wilhelm, 2. 1539, 173
Ihesu for Thy holy name, 1. 515

Il mercurio britannico, 2. 1312, 1338
Il mercurio italico, 2. 1308
Il pastor fido, 1. 1472
Il vagabondo, 3. 1867
'Iles, Francis' (Anthony Berkeley Cox), 4. 528
Iliffe, William, 3. 1825
Illegal lovers, 2. 991
Illuminated magazine, 3. 1847
Illustrated, 4. 1407
Illustrated British film aspirant, 4. 57
Illustrated chips, 4. 819
Illustrated family novelist, 4. 1352
Illustrated historic times, 3. 1816
Illustrated household journal, 3. 1849
Illustrated London life, 3. 1816
Illustrated London magazine, 3. 1849
Illustrated London news, 3. 1816, 1835; 4. 1400
Illustrated mail, 3. 1817; 4. 1404
Illustrated Midland news, 3. 1817
Illustrated news of the world, 3. 1816
Illustrated newspaper, 3. 1817
illustrated papers, nineteenth century, 3. 1816–17, 1835
Illustrated shooting times, 3. 1712
Illustrated sporting and dramatic news (1874), 3. 1684, 1817; 4. 823, 1402
Illustrated sporting (and theatrical) news (1864), 3. 1816
Illustrated sporting mail, 4. 848
Illustrated times, 3. 1816
Illustrated weekly news, 3. 1816
Illustrated weekly times, 3. 1816
Illustrations of Masonry, 2. 393
Illustrious history of women, 2. 336
Illustrissimi principis ducis Cornubiae et comitis Palatini, Genethliacon, 2. 336
Image, Selwyn, 3. 632–3
Image, 4. 83
Image of hypocrisy, 1. 1120
Imitation of Christ (15th century translation), 1. 517
Imlay, Gilbert, 2. 1010, 1474
'Immerito' (Moses Browne), 2. 1558
Imp, 4. 1358
Impacyent poverte, 1. 1407
Impartial account of the Grand Fleet, An, 2. 1415
Impartial examiner, 2. 1385
Impartial history of the life of John Barber, An, 2. 368
Impartial London intelligence, 2. 1317
Impartial occurrences, 2. 1381
Impartial Protestant mercury, 2. 1318
Impartial report of the debates, 2. 1338
Impartial reporter, 3. 1832
Impartial review, 2. 1302

Impartial scout, 1. 2106
Impartialist, 2. 1286
Impartiall intelligencer, 1. 2105
Imperial and colonial magazine, 3. 1854
Imperial magazine, 2. 1302
Imperial review or London (Edinburgh) and Dublin literary journal, 3. 1842
Imperial weekly gazette and Westminster journal, 3. 1812
Impression, 4. 83
Imprint (1913), 4. 82
Imprint (1949), 4. 1394
Impromptu, 4. 84
Inchbald, Elizabeth, 2. 842–4, 1010, 1012
Inchbold, John William, 3. 527
incunabula, 1. 369–76
Independent (and nonconformist) (1890), 3. 1822
Independent (1939), 4. 1387
Independent chronicle (1769), 2. 1334
Independent chronicle and universal advertiser (Dublin 1777), 2. 1386
Independent chronicle and universal evening post (1773), 2. 1335
Independent Irishman, 2. 1386
Independent London journal(ist), 2. 1328
Independent observer, 3. 1810
Independent review, 4. 1356
Independent theatre goer, 4. 825, 849
Independent theatrical observer, 3. 1123
Independent Whig (1720), 2. 1277
Independent Whig (1806), 3. 1809
Index, 2. 1288
Index to current literature, 3. 81
India list, civil and military, 3. 1880
India Office list and Indian Army list, 3. 1880
Indian, literary relations with
    Shakespeare, 1. 1633
    twentieth century, 4. 34
Indian Army and Civil Service List, 3. 1880
Indian writing, 4. 1374
Indicator, 3. 1821
Individual, 3. 1865
Industrial review, 3. 1820
industrialism, its relation to nineteenth century poetry, 3. 174
Industrious bee (Chester 1733), 2. 1356
Industrious bee (Plymouth 1758), 2. 1352
Infallible astrologer, 2. 1343
Infant annual, 3. 1877
Infernal congress, 2. 986
Informacio Alredi, 1. 516
Informacion for pylgrymes, 1. 2121
Informational film year book, 4. 58
Informator Rusticus, 1. 2099
Informed reading, 4. 1378

Inge, William Ralph, 4. 1261–2; 3. 1613
Ingelend, Thomas, 1. 1416–17, 1419
Ingelo, Nathaniel, 1. 1994; 2. 975
Ingelow, Jean, 3. 547, 1091
Ingleby, Clement Mansfield, 3. 1655
Inglefield, John Nicholson, 2. 1480
Ingler, William, 1. 2098
Inglis, Henry David, 3. 1679, 1873
Inglis, Sir Robert Harry (1786–1855), 3. 1724
Inglis-Palgrave, Sir Robert Harry (1827–1919), 3. 1824, 1882
Ingram, David, 1. 2151
Ingram, Herbert, 3. 1790, 1814, 1816
Ingram, John Kells, 3. 1904–5, 1870
Ingram, Robert A., 3. 1718
Ingram, Sir William, 3. 1816, 1817, 1825, 1852
Inisfáil, 4. 1357
ink, printing
    nineteenth century, 3. 31–2
    twentieth century, 4. 78
Ink, 4. 1375
Inkdrops, 4. 1385
Inky way annual, 4. 84
Inky ways, 4. 1386
Inman, Philip, 4. 1380
Inner Temple, revels at, 1. 1770
Innerpeffray Library, 2. 307
Innes, Anne, 3. 1879
Innes, Arthur, 3. 1848
Innes, Eliza, 3. 1879
Innes, Hammond, 4. 812
Innes, Maria, 3. 1879
'Innes, Michael' (John Innes Mackintosh Stewart), 4. 617–18
Innes, Thomas, 2. 2054
Innocent III, Pope, 1. 845–6
Innocent epicure, 2. 1557
Innocui sales, 2. 339
Inns of Court
    history and place in education, 1. 637–8, 2415
    Renaissance libraries, 2. 303
Inquisitor (1711), 2. 1274
Inquisitor (1724), 2. 1277
Inquisitor (1808), 3. 1808
Inscriptions upon the tombs, 2. 351
Inside detective, 4. 1390
Inspector, 2. 1280
Institoris, Henricus, 1. 851
Institute of journalists' journal, 4. 1340
Institute register and handbook of reference, 3. 1881
Institutes of Freemasonry, 2. 409
Instructions for Christians, 1. 286
Instructions how to play at billiards, 2. 1566
Instructions to parish priests, 1. 497
Instructor, 2. 1277

Insurance record, 3. 1824
Intelligence domestick and foreign, 2. 1319
Intelligence from the Scottish army, 1. 2100
Intelligence from the south borders of Scotland (1644), 1. 2100
Intelligence from the south borders of Scotland (1664), 2. 1315
Intelligencer (1663), 2. 1315
Intelligencer (Dublin 1728), 2. 1377, 1384
Intelligencer for publishers and booksellers, 3. 81
Interesting account of the early voyages, An, 2. 1394
Interesting and affecting history of Prince Lee Boo, 2. 1026
Interesting anecdotes, 2. 419
Interesting items, 4. 1380
Interesting tales, 2. 1012
Interesting walks of Henry and his tutor, 3. 1108
Interim, 4. 1387
Interim drama, 4. 827
Interludium de clerico et puella, 1. 742
International amateur (Folkestone 1911), 4. 1382
International amateur (Brighouse 1943), 4. 1385
International bibliographer, 4. 110
International book finder, 4. 110
International detective cases, 4. 1391
International directory of second-hand booksellers, 4. 106
International entertainer, 4. 859
International favourite, 4. 1386
International herald, 3. 1820
International literature, 4. 1369
International mercantile directory, 3. 1882
International P.E.N., its *bulletin of selected books*, 4. 110
International press review, 4. 1344
International printing, 4. 84
International publisher and stationer, 4. 100
International short stories, 4. 1376
International studio, 4. 1353
International theatre, 4. 824
International writers' digest, 4. 73
Interval, 4. 1356
Interviews in the realm of death, 2. 1277
Intimate, 4. 1387
Intimate theatre group news letter, 4. 852
Intrepid magazine, 2. 1307
Introduction to singing, An, 2. 371
Introduction to the history of poetry in Scotland, An, 2. 425
Introduction to the London mercury, 2. 1342
Introduction to the skill of musick, An, 2. 327
Investigated press circulations, 4. 1344
Investigator (1762), 2. 1283
Investigator (1822), 3. 1809
Investor, 3. 1824

Isherwood, Christopher William Bradshaw, 4. 619–20
Isis: a London weekly (1832), 3. 1818
Isis (Oxford 1892), 3. 1868, 1873; 4. 1396
Isla y Rojo, José Francisco de, 2. 204
Island, 4. 1369
Isle of Man
  general bibliography, 1. 18
  Restoration and eighteenth century printing and bookselling, 2. 268
  nineteenth century newspaper, 3. 1832
Isle of Man daily times, 3. 1803
Isle of Man times, 3. 1832
Isocrates, 1. 2171; 2. 1491–2
'Isys, Cotswold' (R. H. Glover), 3. 1690
Italian, literary relations with
  Renaissance to Restoration, 1. 883–904
    allegory, 1. 890
    drama, 1. 894–6
    epic, 1. 896–8
    lyric, 1. 890–3
    madrigals, 1. 893–4
    philosophy, 1. 886–90
    prose fiction, 1. 898–904
    satire, 1. 890
    Shakespeare, 1. 1633
    translations, 1. 2179–94
    travel, 1. 885–6
  Restoration and eighteenth century, 2. 185–96
    criticism, 2. 68
    drama, 2. 189–91
    literary theory, 2. 38
    philosophy, 2. 188
    poetry, 2. 191–4
    prose, 2. 194–6
    translations, 2. 1541–50
  nineteenth century, 3. 133–40
  twentieth century, 4. 27
Italian magazine, 2. 1310
Italian tracts, 2. 1310
Items of news, 4. 1382
Iter Carolinum, 1. 2130
Ives, Chester, 3. 1791
Ives, Edward, 2. 1441

JCR, 3. 1868
J. C. Walls authors' quarterly, 4. 74
J. Cleaveland revived, 1. 1011; 2. 328
J. Lillywhite's cricketer's annual, 3. 1882
J. Lillywhite's cricketer's companion, 3. 1882
'J., R.' (Richard Johnson), 2. 1022
J., S. (Stephen Jones?), 2. 1025
J., W. (William Jole), 2. 1017
Jabberwock, 4. 1395
Jachin and Boaz, 2. 388

Jack, Henry Vernon, 3. 1192
Jack, William, 3. 1804
Jack-daw, 4. 1393
Jack Sprit-Sail's frolic, 2. 411
Jack Upland, 1. 546, 687–8
Jacke Jugeler, 1. 1420
Jacke Straw, 1. 1470
Jacks, Lawrence Pearsall, 3. 1613
Jackson, Catherine Hannah Charlotte, Lady, 3. 1681
Jackson, D., 3. 1703
Jackson, F. E., 4. 82, 1358
Jackson, Holbrook, 4. 1061–3, 1353, 1354, 1356
Jackson, J. L., 2. 1554
Jackson, John (1686–1763), 2. 1863
Jackson, John (d. 1807), 2. 1444
Jackson, N. L., 3. 1702
Jackson, Robert, 2. 1376
Jackson, Thomas (d. 1640), 1. 1994
Jackson, Thomas (d. 1873), 3. 1840
Jackson, William, 1. 2159
Jackson's Oxford journal, 2. 1364
Jacky Dandy's delight, 2. 1024
Jacob, Edward, 2. 1778
Jacob, Giles, 2. 1801, 1558
Jacob, Hildebrand, 2. 553
Jacob, M., 2. 1305
Jacob (Tudor poem), 1. 1120
Jacob and Esau (Tudor play), 1. 1420
Jacob and Josep (ME poem), 1. 479
Jacobi, Johann Christian, 2. 161
Jacobite literature, 2. 2069–80
Jacobite's journal, 2. 1279, 1332
Jacobs, Joseph, 3. 1109–10
Jacobs, Lewis, 4. 1369
Jacobs, William Wymark, 4. 620–1
Jacques, Francis, 1. 1746
Jaffray, Alexander, 2. 2048
Jaffray, John, 3. 1795, 1798
Jaggard, William, 1. 962
Jago, Richard, 2. 661
Jamaica: a poem, 2. 1470
James I of Scotland, 1. 654–6
James I of England (VI of Scotland), 1. 2425, 865, 922, 1002, 1905, 2037–8, 2047, 2050, 2275, 2311, 2447, 2472
James, David Gwilym, 4. 1063
James, E., 4. 1380
James, Edwin Oliver, 4. 1262–3
James, George, 2. 1321
James, George Payne Rainsford, 3. 736–9, 1102
James, Grace, 4. 798
James, Henry, 3. 992–1000, 112–13, 139, 156
James, Montague Rhodes, 4. 621–2, 789
James, Robert, 2. 108, 1906

James, Silas, 2. 1444
James, Thomas (d. 1635?), 1. 2159
James, Thomas (fl. 1771), 2. 1422
James, William, 3. 1730
James Lillywhite's cricketers' annual, 3. 1697
Jameson, Anna Brownell, 3. 1288–9
Jameson, Laurence, 3. 1855
Jameson, Margaret Storm, 4. 622–3
Jameson, Robert, 2. 1407; 3. 1855
Jameson, William 2. 2034
Jamieson, John, 3. 1656
Jamieson, Nina, 4. 1385, 1386
Jamieson, Peter, 4. 1378
Jamieson, Robert, 3. 1877
Jamnes and Mambres, 1. 327
Janeway, James, 2. 1017
Janin, Jules, 3. 1875
Januaries account, 1. 2101
Janus (1826), 3. 1873
Janus (1936), 4. 1372
Japanese, literary relations with
   Shakespeare, 1. 1633
   twentieth century, 4. 33–4
Jardine, Alexander, 2. 1396, 1427
Jardine, Alfred, 3. 1690
Jardine, George, 3. 1720
Jardine, Sir William, 3. 1855
Jarrold and Sons, 3. 58, 79; 4. 80
Jazz forum, 4. 1377
Je-ne-scai-quoy, 2. 363
Jeaffreson, Christopher, 2. 1456
Jeanette, G. K., 4. 828
Jeannie Maitland's stories, 4. 1360
Jeannie Maitland's weekly, 4. 1360
Jeans, Alexander G., 3. 1801
Jeans, Sir James Hopwood, 4. 1263–4
Jeans, James Stephen, 3. 1804
Jeans, Thomas, 3. 1713
Jeaste of Syr Gawayne, 1. 408, 1107
Jebb, Samuel, 2. 1294
Jefferies, Richard, 3. 1060–2, 1096, 1713
Jefferson R. L. 3. 1700
Jefferson, Thomas, 2. 1471
Jeffery, Peter, 1. 2143
Jefferys, Thomas, 2. 1420, 1466
Jeffrey, Francis, Lord, 3. 1289–90, 1770, 1854
Jeffreys, George, 2. 553
Jeffries, John, 2. 1405
Jeffs, Harry, 3. 1770, 1801
Jellinek, Frank, 4. 1375
Jemmat, Catherine, 2. 661
Jemmy Carson's collections, 2. 370
Jemmy Twitcher's jests, 2. 391
Jenkins, Charles, 2. 1453
Jenks, Edward, 4. 1356

Jenkyn(s), Pathericke, 1. 1312
Jennens, Charles, 2. 1776
Jenner, Charles, 2. 1002, 1003
Jenner, Edward, 2. 1906
Jenner, Matthew, 2. 1443
Jenner, Thomas, 1. 1330
Jennings, Gertrude Eleanor, 4. 956–7
Jennings, H. J., 3. 1770, 1798
Jennings, J. Clayton, 3. 1809
Jennings, John, 2. 1467
Jennings, Louis John, 3. 1815
Jennings, Theodore, 1. 2041, 2104
Jennings' landscape annual, 3. 1874
Jenny, Thomas, 1. 1120
Jenynges, Edward, 1. 1120
Jenyns, Soame, 2. 554, 1566
Jephson, John Mounteney, 3. 1821
Jephson, Robert, 2. 844
Jerdan, William, 3. 1770, 1790, 1792, 1821
Jerningham, Edward, 2. 661–2, 237
Jerome, Jerome Klapka, 3. 1062, 1700, 1711,
   1770, 1815, 1853; 4. 1353
Jeronimo, 1. 1472
Jerram, Jane Elizabeth, 3. 1090
Jerrold, Douglas Francis, 4. 1174, 1359, 1376
Jerrold, Douglas William, 3. 1149–50, 1770,
   1811, 1847, 1865
Jerrold, William Blanchard, 3. 1811
Jervis, John, 3. 1826
Jesse, Edward, 3. 1102, 1688
Jesse, Fryniwyd Marsh Tennyson, 4. 623–4
Jessey, Henry, 2. 1017
jest-books, Renaissance to Restoration, 1. 2025–
   30
Jester (1901), 4. 1356
Jester (Oxford 1902), 4. 1396
Jester (1910), amateur journal, 4. 1382
Jester (1912), comic, 4. 819
Jester and wonder, 4. 819
Jester's magazine, 2. 1304
Jesting astrologer, 2. 1343
Jesuit, 2. 1287
Jesuite, 2. 1324
Jesus College, Oxford, library, 2. 306
Jesus College magazine, 4. 1397
Jeu d'Adam, 1. 725–6
Jevons, John W., 3. 1796
Jevons, Mary Anne, 3. 1874
Jevons, William Stanley, 3. 1540
Jewel, John, 1. 1927, 854
Jewish chronicle, 3. 1822, 1837; 4. 1400, 1346
Jewish literary annual, 4. 1357
Jewish quarterly review, 3. 1858
Jewish review, 4. 1370
Jewsbury, Geraldine Ensor, 3. 935

Jeyes, Samuel Henry, 3. 1770
jigs, Renaissance to Restoration, 1. 2043–4
Jilted bridegroom, 2. 985
Jinarajadasa, C., 4. 1352
Jingles, 4. 820
'*Jo*, 4. 1404
Joachim, Harold Henry, 4. 1264
Joad, Cyril Edwin Mitchinson, 4. 1264–6
Joanereidos, 2. 332
Joannes de Mediolano, 1. 2187
Job, Life of (M.E.), 1. 688
Jobbing printer, 4. 84
Jobson, Richard, 1. 2146
Jockey, 3. 1825
Jockies intelligencer, 2. 1318
Jodelle, Etienne, 1. 868
Joe Miller's jests, 2. 369
Johan the evangelyst, 1. 1408
Johannes de Irlandia, 1. 2447
Johannes de Sicca Villa, 1. 775
Johannes Scotus Erigena, 1. 354–6
John XXI, Pope (Petrus Hispanus), 1. 2187
John de Hanville (Hauteville), 1. 762
John de Sacro Bosco, 1. 773
John of Basingstoke, 1. 1002
John of Bordeaux, 1. 1474
John of Bromyard, 1. 788
John of Capistrano, 1. 1121
John of Cornwall, 1. 762
John of Garland, 1. 773–4
John of Hoveden (Howden), 1. 774
John of London, 1. 788
John of Mirfield, 1. 788
John of Reading (OFM, fl. 1320), 1. 789
John of Reading (Benedictine, late 14th century),
   1. 789
John of Rodington, 1. 789
John of St Giles, 1. 774
John of Salisbury, 1. 762–3
John of Sheppey, 1. 789
John of Wales, 1. 774
John of Wallingford, 1. 774
John of Walsham, 1. 789
'John, Little', 2. 1027
John and Robert Baldwin's volunteer journal, 2.
   1388
John Baldwin's volunteer journal, 2. 1388
John Bull (1820), 3. 1809
John Bull (1906), 4. 1358, 1346, 1405
John Bull's British journal, 3. 1809
John Lillywhite's cricketers' companion, 3. 1697
John O' London's weekly, 4. 1364
'John the-Giant-Killer' (John Newbery?), 2.
   1019
John Waddington's annual, 4. 848

John Wisden's cricketer's almanack, 3. 1695, 1882
Johnian, 4. 1395
Johns, Thomas, 2. 1338
Johns, William, 3. 1856
Johns, William Earl, 4. 801
Johnson, — (fl. 1858), 3. 1814
Johnson, Anna Maria, 2. 1568
Johnson, C. W., 3. 1870
Johnson, Charles (1679–1748), dramatist, 2.
   793–4
'Johnson, Capt. Charles' (fl. 1724), 2. 990
Johnson, Edward, 1. 2160
Johnson, Frank C., 4. 1366
Johnson, James, 2. 248
Johnson, John (fl. 1641), 1. 2057
Johnson, John (1662–1725), 2. 1626
Johnson, Lionel Pigot, 3. 633–4
Johnson, Pamela Hansford, 4. 624–5
Johnson, R. W., 3. 1817
Johnson, Reginald Brimley, 4. 1063–4
Johnson, Richard (1573–1659?), 1. 1121, 2025,
   2027, 2053–4
Johnson, Richard (1733?–93), 2. 1021–2
Johnson, Robert, 1. 2047, 2155, 2276
Johnson, Samuel (1649–1703), 2. 1846–7
Johnson, Samuel (1709–84), 2. 1122–74, 43, 86,
   108, 117, 148, 183, 195, 205, 217, 1403, 1423,
   1279, 1282, 1371, 1751–2, 1796, 1802
Johnson, Thomas Burgeland, 3. 1704, 1712
Johnson, William (d. 1614), 1. 1770
Johnson, William (later Cory), 3. 528–9, 1727,
   1870
Johnson, William Ernest, 4. 1266
Johnson's lottery song book, 2. 391
Johnson's Sunday monitor and British gazette, 3.
   1807
Johnston, Archibald, Lord Warriston, 1. 2463
Johnston, Arnrid, 4. 802
Johnston, Arthur, 1. 2434, 1910
Johnston, Denis William, 4. 957–8
Johnston, Edward, 4. 82
Johnston, George, 2. 1374
Johnston, George Milligen, 2. 1468
Johnston, Sir Harry Hamilton, 3. 1672
Johnston, Robert, 1. 2468
Johnston, William, 2. 1376
Johnston, W. and A. K., 3. 79
Johnstone, Charles, 2. 999, 1000, 1004, 1005,
   1006, 1007
Johnstone, Christian Isobel, 3. 739, 1845
Johnstone, Edward, 3. 1824
Johnstone, James (d. 1798), 2. 246
Johnstone, James (d. 1865), 3. 1789, 1790, 1793,
   1808
Johnstone, W. S., 3. 1794

Joke upon joke, 2. 428
Joker, 4. 820
Jolas, Eugene, 4. 1367
Jole, William, 2. 1017
Jolly, William, 3. 1730
Jolly companion, 2. 411
Jolly jester, 4. 819
Jolly Roger, 4. 1382
Jones, A. (fl. 1773), 2. 1570
Jones, David (fl. 1750–80) Welsh poet, 2. 245
Jones, David (fl. 1774) traveller, 2. 1469
Jones, David Michael, 4. 292
Jones, E., 3. 1878
Jones, Ebenezer, 3. 529
Jones, Edward, 2. 247
Jones, Ergo, 4. 1377
Jones, Ernest, 4. 1266–7
Jones, Ernest Charles, 3. 529–30, 1819, 1848
Jones, Frederick M., 3. 1799
Jones, George W., 3. 58
Jones, Griffiths, 2. 1333
Jones, Gwyn, 4. 1373
Jones, H., 4. 1381, 1382
Jones, Harold, 4. 808
Jones, Henry (1721–70), 2. 662–3
Jones, Henry (1831–99), writer on games, 3. 1693, 1715
Jones, Sir Henry (1852–1922), philosopher, 3. 1540–1
Jones, Henry Arthur, 3. 1164–6
Jones, Henry Bence, 3. 1746
Jones, Herbert, 4. 1370
Jones, Hugh (fl. 1724), 2. 1461
Jones, Hugh, Bardd Llangwm (fl. 1759), 2. 245
Jones, Jeremiah, 2. 1668
Jones, John (fl. 1635), dramatist, 1. 1746
Jones, John (fl. 1651), lawyer, 1. 2036
Jones, John Gale, 2. 1407
Jones, Kennedy, 3. 1770, 1794
Jones, Owen, 2. 248
Jones, Owen Glynne, 3. 1710
Jones, Robert (b.c. 1577), 1. 1350, 2033
Jones, Robert (fl. 1772), 2. 1570
Jones, Stephen, 2. 1799, 1025, 1309, 1312, 1332; 3. 1807
Jones, T., 3. 1695
Jones, William (fl. 1607), 1. 962, 2074
Jones, William (fl. 1777), traveller, 2. 1424
Jones, William (1726–1800), scientist, 2. 1906
Jones, Sir William (1746–94), orientalist, 2. 663–5, 1568
Jones, William (fl. 1852), 3. 1814
Jones's Coventry and Warwick ledger, 2. 1356
Jones's Coventry, Warwick and Birmingham magazine, 2. 1350

Jones's evening news letter, 2. 1323
Jonghe, Ellert de, 1. 2144
Jongleur, 4. 1368
Jonson, Ben, 1. 1655–73, 1002, 1336, 2049, 2315; 2. 32
Jonsone, John, 1. 2447
Jonsonus virbius, 1. 1010
Jopson's Coventry and Northampton mercury, 2. 1356, 1363
Jopson's Coventry and Warwick mercury, 2. 1356
Jopson's Coventry mercury, 2. 1356
Jordan, Denham, 3. 1439–40
Jordan, John, 2. 1786
Jordan, Thomas, 1. 1746–7, 2040, 2045, 2087
Jordan's elixir of life, 2. 411
Jordan's parliamentary journal, 2. 1337
Jortin, John, 2. 1748, 164, 1295
Jos. Bliss's Exeter post-boy, 2. 1357
Joseph of Exeter, 1. 763
Joseph, Horace William Brindley, 4. 1267
Joseph, S., 4. 1356
Joseph of Arimathie (ME), 1. 413–14
Joseph of Armathia (1520), 1. 1121
Josephson, Matthew, 4. 1365, 1367
Josephus, 1. 2171, 2138; 2. 1492
Josephus Scottus, 1. 351
Josselyn, John, 2. 1455
Joubert, Joseph, 3. 103
Joubert, Laurent, 1. 863
Jourdain, John, 1. 2146
Jourdain, Silvester, 1. 2155
Jourdan, B. A., 3. 1728
Journal (1886), 3. 1791
Journal (Working Men's College 1933), 3. 1871; 4. 1395
Journal (Newcastle 1958), 3. 1796; 4. 1400
Journal de France et d'Angleterre, 2. 1338
Journal de l'Europe, 2. 1337
Journal de Middlesex, 2. 1337
Journal du voyageur neutre, 2. 1430
Journal étranger de littérature, 2. 1306
Journal from New York to Canada 1767, 2. 1467
Journal of a tour in France (1821), 3. 1678
Journal of a tour to Scarborough, 2. 1407
Journal of a voyage for making discoveries towards the North Pole, 2. 1485
Journal of a voyage from Grand Cairo to Mount Sinai, 2. 1449
Journal of a voyage round the world in the Endeavour, A, 2. 1479
Journal of an English medical officer, 2. 1401
Journal of commerce, 3. 1796
Journal of first thoughts. . .in a journey to Scarborough, A, 2. 1404
Journal of librarianship, 4. 118

Journal of natural philosophy, 2. 1311; 3. 1841

Journal of printing and kindred trades, 3. 62

Journal of science, 3. 1858

Journal of the English Folk Dance and Song Society, 4. 878

Journal of the English Folk Dance Society, 4. 878

Journal of the late motions. . .against the French, A, 2. 1412

Journal of the Leeds College of Music, 4. 879

Journal of the march. . .from Carlisle to Boston, A, 2. 1469

Journal of the Poetry Recital Society, 4. 1359

Journal of the typographic arts, 3. 60

Journal of the Venetian campaigne, A, 2. 1412

Journal or narrative of the Boscawen's voyage, 2. 1439

Journal politique et littéraire d'Angleterre, 2. 1336

journalism
  nineteenth century
    general, 3. 1759–88
    school and university, 3. 1865–74
  twentieth century, 4. 1337–44

Journalism, 3. 1762

Journalist (1879), 3. 1762

Journalist (1886), 3. 1762; 4. 1340

Journall or dayly register. . .of the voyage, 1. 2144

Journey from London to Scarborough, A, 2. 1400

Journey of the Queen's ambassadors unto Rome, 1. 2121

Journey through part of England and Scotland, A, 2. 1401

Journey to Jerusalem, A, 2. 1432

Journey to Llandrindod Wells, A, 2. 1400

Journey to Scotland, A, 2. 1399

Jousts of May and June, 1. 1121

Joutel, Henri, 2. 1460

Jovellanos, Gaspar Melchor de, 2. 204

Jovial companion (1755?), 2. 378

Jovial companion (1800?), 2. 428

Jovial companions, or merry club, 2. 346

Jovial garland, A, 2. 330

Jovial mercury, 2. 1342

Jovial sailor's chearful companion, 2. 428

Jovis et Junonis nuptiae, 1. 1777

Jovius, Paulus, 1. 849, 887, 2136

Jowett, Benjamin, 3. 1607

Joy, George, 1. 1832, 1897

Joy street, 4. 820

Joy street poems, 4. 1366

Joyce, Heath, 3. 1817

Joyce, James Augustine Aloysius, 4. 444–72, 796

Joyce, Patrick Weston, 3. 1891

Joyce, Robert Dwyer, 3. 1905

Joyful cuckoldom, 2. 339

Joyfull newes from sea, 1. 2129

Juan, Jorge, 2. 1465

Judgment Day I, 1. 286

Judgment Day II, 1. 286–7

Judith, 1. 287

Judy: or the London serio-comic journal, 3. 1825, 1838; 4. 1351

Jugge, Richard, 1. 962

Jukes, Andrew John, 3. 1620

Julian of Norwich, 1. 522–3

Juliana, OE, 1. 288; ME, 1. 525

July annual, 4. 1386

June annual, 4. 1386

Junior, 4. 1381

Junior bookshelf, 4. 790

Junior review, 4. 1382

Junior staff journal, 4. 106

'Junius' (Sir Philip Francis), 2. 1178–83

Junius, Franciscus, 1. 2294, 2317; 2. 1791

Junius, Patricius (P. Young), 1. 2298, 2300

Junius manuscript, 1. 229–30

Jurieu, Pierre, 2. 1515–16

Jurist, 3. 1826

Just a line, 4. 1384

Justa Edouardo King naufrago, 1. 1010

Justel, Henri, 2. 86

Justice, Elizabeth, 2. 1418

Justice, 3. 1820

Justus, Johann, 1. 849

Juvenal, 1. 2171; 2. 1498, 35

Juvenile adventures of Miss Kitty F——r, 2. 999

Juvenile chatter, 4. 1381

Juvenile forget me not, 3. 1877

Juvenile instructress, 2. 1288

Juvenile keepsake, 3. 1877

Juvenile library, 2. 1312

Juvenile magazine, 2. 1029, 1308

Juvenile missionary keepsake, 3. 1878

Juvenile offering, 3. 1878

Juvenile olio, 2. 1311

juvenile papers
  eighteenth century, 2. 1029–30
  nineteenth century, 3. 1825–6, 1838
  see also comics

Juvenile speaker, 2. 408

'K., E.' (fl. 1579), 1. 2310

'K., E.A.' (E. A. Kendall), 2. 1029

K-H news-letter (*service*), 4. 1407

'K., J.A.C.', 3. 1703

'*K.P.*' illustrated, 3. 1866

K.P. magazine, 4. 1394

K., T. (fl. 1767), 2. 1399

Kaempfer, Engelbert, 2. 1438

Kaestlin, John, 4. 1370, 1394
Kahlert, K. F., 2. 1538
Kahn, Derek, 4. 1398
Kaleidoscope, 3. 1870
Kalm, Pehr, 2. 1401, 1468
Kames, Henry Home, Lord, 2. 2065–6, 43, 158, 1887
Kane, Sir Robert John, 3. 1842
Kant, Immanuel, 2. 38, 156–7; 3. 125–6
Kantemir, Antiokh Dmitriyevich, 2. 216
Kapélion, 2. 374, 1300
Karamzin, Nikolay Mikhaylovich, 2. 216
Karslake, Frank, 4. 106
Katherine, St (ME), 1. 525
Katherine group, saints' lives, 1. 523–6
Katterns, D., 3. 1843
Kavanagh, Julia, 3. 935
Kavanagh, Patrick, 4. 292–3
Kay, David, 3. 1729
Kay, Joseph, 3. 1723
Kay-Shuttleworth, Sir James, 3. 1722–3
Kaye, Thomas, 3. 1797
Kaye-Smith, Sheila, 4. 625–6
Keach, Benjamin, 2. 477, 980, 1017, 1669–70
Kearton, Richard, 3. 1106
Keary, Annie, 3. 1093, 1108
Keary, Eliza, 3. 1093, 1108
Keary, Peter, 3. 1854
Keate, George, 2. 665–6, 132, 193, 1006, 1404, 1420, 1481
Keating, Joseph, 4. 1351
Keating's Stratford and Warwick mercury, 2. 1367
Keats, John, 3. 344–56, 132
Keble, John, 3. 1629–30
Keble, Thomas, 3. 1630
Keddie, Henrietta, 3. 1103
Keegan, Barry, 4. 1377
Keene, Charles, 3. 66–7, 1770
Keene, Dennis, 4. 1397
Keepsake, 3. 1874
Keepsake Press, 4. 98
Keighley, Gladys, 4. 1377
Keightley, Thomas, 3. 1107
Keill, James, 2. 1558
Keill, John, 2. 1847
Keir, Susanna Harvey, 2. 1008
Keith, Sir Arthur, 4. 1267–8
Keith, Charles, 2. 2027
Keith, George, 2. 2035, 1459
Keith, William (d. 1608?), 1. 1122, 1903
Keith, Sir William (1680–1749), 2. 2054
Kelleher, D. L., 4. 1364
Keller, Gottfried, 3. 126
Kelly, — (fl. 1845), 3. 1856
Kelly, Harold, 4. 1369

Kelly, Hugh, 2. 845, 177–8, 1001, 1283, 1303, 1304
Kelly, Isabella, 3. 739–40
Kelly, John, 2. 794, 995
Kelly, Samuel, 2. 1396, 1474
Kelly, Thomas, 3. 79
Kelly, W. K., 3. 1795
Kelly's handbook to the titled, landed and official classes, 3. 1879
Kelly's handbook of the upper ten thousand, 3. 1879
Kelly and Co, The Post Office London directory, 3. 1881
Kelmscott Press, 3. 56
Kelsey, Henry, 2. 1457
Kelso, printing, 2. 272
Kelso chronicle, 2. 1378
Kelso mail, 2. 1378
Keltie, Sir John Scott, 3. 1878
Kelton, Arthur, 1. 1121
Kelty, Mary Ann, 3. 1101–2
Kelvin, William Thomson, Baron, 3. 1842
Kemble, Charles, 3. 1131
Kemble, Frances Anne, 3. 530
Kemble, John Mitchell, 3. 1770, 1856
Kemble, John Philip, 2. 845–6
Kemmel times, 4. 1362
Kemmish's annual-harmonist, 2. 418
Kemmish's new weekly miscellany, 2. 1308
Kemp, Dixon, 3. 1716, 1883
Kemp, T. L., 3. 1878
Kemp, William, 1. 2027, 2124
Kempe, Anna Eliza, 3. 711–12
Kempe, Margery, 1. 524
Kempe, William, 1. 2276
Ken, Thomas, 2. 1611
Kendal weekly courant, 2. 1359, 1348
Kendal weekly mercury, 2. 1359
Kendall, Abram, 1. 2152
Kendall, Edward Augustus, 2. 1029
Kendall, Henry E., 3. 1724
Kendall, Timothy, 1. 1121–2, 1333
Kendall, William, 2. 666
Kendon, Frank Samuel Herbert, 4. 293
Kendricke, John, 1. 2075
Kennard, Coleridge, 3. 1794
Kennard, Mary E., 3. 1690, 1703, 1706–7
Kennedy, Charles Rann, 3. 531
Kennedy, Edward Shirley, 3. 1709
Kennedy, Hugh, 4. 1394
Kennedy, Hugh A., 3. 1694
Kennedy, John (fl. 1620–30), 1. 2435
Kennedy, John (1813–1900), 3. 1840
Kennedy, Margaret Moore, 4. 626–7
Kennedy, Quintin, 1. 2447–8
Kennedy, Walter, 1. 662

Kennedy, William 3. 1875
Kennett, Basil, 2. 1414
Kennett, White, 2. 1626, 1706
Kenney, James, 3. 1131–2
Kennington, A. C., 4. 1385, 1387
Kenny, James, 2. 1466
Kenny, William Stopford, 3. 1694
Kenrick, W. S., 2. 1305, 1561
Kenrick, William, 2. 846–7, 1300, 1303, 1304, 1305
Kensington: a magazine, 4. 1355–6
Kent
  general bibliography, 1. 17
  Old English texts, 1. 73, 288
  Middle English sermons, 1. 486–7
  nineteenth century newspapers, 3. 1832
Kent, Charles, 3. 1792
Kent, George, 3. 1808
Kent, John, 3. 1707
Kent's weekly dispatch and sporting mercury, 3. 1824
Kentfield, Edwin, 3. 1692
Kentish chronicle, 2. 1355
Kentish express and Ashford news, 3. 1832
Kentish gazette, 2. 1355; 3. 1832
Kentish herald, 2. 1355
Kentish hymn (OE), 1. 288
Kentish post (1717), 2. 1355
Kentish post (1769), 2. 1355
Kentish register, 2. 1349
Kentish repository, 2. 1347
Kentish sermons (ME), 1. 486–7
Kentish songster, 2. 395
Kentish spectator, 2. 1347
Kentish weekly post, 2. 1355
Kenyon, John, 3. 387
Ker, David, 3. 1095
Ker, John, 2. 1708
Ker, Peter or Patrick, 2. 477
Ker, William Paton, 3. 1440
Kerr, James Lennox, 4. 805
Kerr, John, 3. 1714
Kerr, Robert, 1. 2113
Kerry evening post, 2. 1390
Kersey, Richard, 4. 1369
Kethe, William, 1. 1122, 1903
Kettlewell, John, 2. 1611
Key of knowledg, 2. 334
Key poets, 4. 1380
Keyes, Sidney Arthur Kilworth, 4. 294
Keymis, Lawrence, 1. 2153
Keynes, Sir Geoffrey Langdon, 4. 1064–5
Keynes, John Maynard, Baron, 4. 1175–7
Keynes, John Neville, 3. 1541
Keysler, Johann Georg, 2. 1539, 1419

'*Khaki*', 4. 1362
Khaki and blue, 4. 1377
Khojah Effendi, 1. 2141
Kiddell-Monroe, Joan, 4. 810
Kidgell, John, 2. 998
Kielland, Alexander, 3. 148
Kielmannsegge, Friedrich, Graf von, 2. 1402
Kilburne, Richard, 1. 2136
Kilham, Alexander, 2. 1350
Kilkenny, printing, 2. 274
Killigrew, Anne, 2. 478
Killigrew, Henry, 1. 1747
Killigrew, Thomas (1612–83), dramatist, 1. 1747–8
Killigrew, Thomas (1657–1719), author of *Chit-chat*, 2. 794
Killigrew, Sir William, 2. 766–7
Killigrew's jests, 2. 380
Killmister, A. K., 3. 1712
Kilner, Dorothy, 2. 1024
Kilner, Mary Ann, 2. 1024
Kilwardby, Robert, 1. 779–80
Kimber, Edward, 2. 996, 998, 999, 1332, 1463
Kimber, Isaac, 2. 1294
Kindersley, Jemima, 2. 1450
Kinematograph monthly record, 4. 56
Kinematograph weekly, 4. 56
Kinematograph Weekly monthly alphabetical film record, 4. 56
King, Adam, 1. 2448
King, Charles, 2. 1345
King, Elizabeth, 4. 1377
King, Gregory, 2. 1898
King, Harriet Eleanor Hamilton, 3. 634
King, Henry, 1. 1199, 1913, 1981
King, J. E., 3. 1868
King, J. W., 3. 1684
King, James, 2. 1480
King, John (1559?–1621), 1. 1942–3
King, John (1696–1728), 2. 1826
King, John Glen, 2. 1424
King, Maud Egerton, 4. 1360
King, Peter, 2. 1673
King, Philip, 1. 2050
King, Samuel William, 3. 1680
King, Thomas, 2. 847–8
King, V. 4. 1381, 1382, 1383
King, William (1650–1729) philosopher, 2. 1847
King, William (1662–1712), miscellaneous writer, 2. 1046–7, 1271, 1293, 1398
King, William (1685–1763) poet, 2. 554–5
King and Queenes entertainment at Richmond, 1. 1760
King Charles I, Tragedie of, 1. 1758
King Daryus, 1. 1410

King Edward the Fourth, 1. 1471
King Horn, 1. 429–30
King Leir, 1. 1472
King of Tars, 1. 444
King Ponthus and the fair Sidone, 1. 430–1
King Satan or the hunting of the senator, 2. 1558
King's amateur newspaper, 4. 1382
King's College literary and scientific magazine, 3. 1867
King's College magazine (1842), 3. 1867
King's College magazine (1850), 3. 1867
King's College magazine (1877), 3. 1867
King's College magazine (ladies' dept.), 3. 1867; 4. 1395
King's College miscellany, 3. 1869
King's College review, 4. 1395
King's courier, 4. 1396
King's fool, 2. 1284
King's Lynn, church libraries, 1. 991
King's Norton Library, 1. 991; 2. 307
King's own, 3. 1853
King's Printing Office, Edinburgh, 3. 58
King-Hall, Magdalen, 4. 808
King-Hall, William Stephen Richard, Baron, 4. 958–9, 1372, 1407
King-Hall news-letter, 4. 1407
Kingdom come, 4. 1374, 1398
Kingdom's weekly post, 1. 2103
Kingdomes faithfull scout, 1. 2105
Kingdomes intelligencer, 1. 2110; 2. 1315
Kingdomes scout, 1. 2101
Kingdomes weekly intelligencer, 1. 2097
Kingdomes weekly post, 1. 2099, 2101
Kingdoms intelligencer (1659?), 2. 1315
Kingdoms intelligencer (Edinburgh 1661), 2. 1373
Kingdoms intelligencer (1662), 2. 1315
Kingdoms weekly account, 1. 2103
Kinglake, Alexander William, 3. 1489–90
Kingsley, Charles, 3. 935–9, 132, 1091, 1108, 1608, 1674, 1690, 1729
Kingsley, G., 2. 1313
Kingsley, Henry, 3. 939–40, 1093–4, 1770, 1804
Kingsley, Mary Henrietta, 3. 1672
Kingsley, Mary St Leger, 3. 1066
'Kingsmill, Hugh' (Hugh Kingsmill Lunn), 4. 1065–6
Kingston, J. S., 3. 1880
Kingston, William Henry Giles, 3. 940–1, 1091, 1770, 1825, 1847
Kinloss, library of, 1. 991
Kinwelmershe, Francis, 1. 1424, 1768
Kipling, Rudyard, 3. 1019–32, 1098, 1711
Kippis, Andrew, 2. 1303, 1314, 1480
Kirby, Sarah, 2. 1023
Kirbye, George, 1. 1348

Kirchmeyer, Thomas, 1. 849, 854
Kirk, Robert, 2. 2058–9
Kirk, Thomas, 2. 1398
Kirkcaldy, Sir William, 1. 2425
Kirke, John, 1. 1748
Kirkham, R., 1. 1748
Kirkman, Francis, 2. 280, 976, 978; 1. 962
Kirkton, James, 2. 2049
Kirkup, James Falconer, 4. 294–5
Kirwan, Richard, 2. 1906
Kitcat (bookbinders), 2. 292
Kitchell, S. G., 4. 1384
Kitchin, Clifford Henry Benn, 4. 627, 1397
Kitto, John, 3. 1620
Kittowe, Robert, 1. 2055
Klein, Herman, 4. 825, 849
Kleist, Heinrich von, 3. 126
Klickmann, Flora, 4. 1359
Klingender, Martin, 4. 1355
Klinger, Friedrich Maximilian von, 2. 1539, 173, 181
Klopper, Harry, 4. 1378
Klopstock, Friedrich Gottlieb, 2. 1539, 168, 173
Knacke to know an honest man, A, 1. 1471
Knacke to knowe a knave, A, 1. 1470
Knapman, J., 4. 1377
Knapwell, Richard, 1. 776
Knatchbull-Hugessen, Edward Hugessen, 1st Baron Brabourne, 3. 1103
Knave in graine, 1. 1760
Knell, Thomas, 1. 1122, 2071
Knevet, Ralph, 1. 1313, 1748
Kniáznin, Franciszek Dionizy, 2. 216
Knigge, Adolf Franz Friedrich 2. 1539, 181
Knight, Charles, 3. 1656–7, 79, 1770–1, 1809, 1813, 1844, 1846, 1855, 1873, 1877
Knight, Edward Frederick, 3. 1716
Knight, Ellis Cornelia, 2. 1009
Knight, Francis, 1. 2129
Knight, Henry G., 3. 1870
Knight, George Wilson, 4. 1066–7
Knight, James, 2. 1460
Knight, Joseph, 3. 1390, 1771, 1810, 1821, 1839
Knight, Philippina, 2. 1423
Knight, Richard Payne, 2. 1826
Knight, Sarah K., 2. 1458
Knight's official advertiser, 4. 1401
Knight's quarterly magazine, 3. 1855, 1864
Knight-errant (1729), 2. 1278
Knight-errant (1782), 2. 1287
Knight of Curtesy and the fair lady of Faguell, 1. 450
Knighton, Henry, 1. 787
Knights, Lionel Charles, 4. 1067–8, 1370

Knipe, J. W., 4. 1391
Knoblock or Knoblauch, Edward, 4. 959–60
Knock-out comic, 4. 820
Knolles, Richard, 1. 2138
Knollys, Francis, 1. 1914
Knowles, David, 4. 1177–8
Knowles, Sir James, 3. 1108
Knowles, James Sheridan, 3. 1132–3, 1865
Knowles, James Thomas, 3. 1771, 1850
Knowles, Michael Clive, 4. 1177–8
Knowles, Richard Brinsley, 3. 1849
Knox, Alexander, 3. 1630
Knox, Arthur Edward, 3. 1690, 1713
Knox, Edmund George Valpy, 4. 295, 1400
Knox, John (1505–72), 1. 1928–30, 1902, 2032, 2448–9
Knox, John (1720–90), Scottish philanthropist, 2. 1405
Knox, John (fl. 1765–7), compiler of travel books, 2. 1392
Knox, John (fl. 1769), captain in Canada, 2. 1468
Knox, Robert (1641?–1720), 2. 1691–2, 1433
Knox, Robert (d. 1859), 3. 1789, 1793
Knox, Ronald Arbuthnott, 4. 1268–71, 1389
Knox, Vicesimus, 3. 1720
Knyghthode and bataile, 1. 688
Knyveton, John, 2. 1464
Knyvett, Thomas, 1st Baron, 1. 1002
Koenigsmarck, Marie Aurora, Countess of, 2. 1539
Koestler, Arthur, 4. 628–9
Kolben, Peter, 2. 1448
Korda, Tibor, 4. 1344
Korean translation of Shakespeare, 1. 1633
Korzeniowski, J. T. K. N., 4. 395–417
Kottabos, 3. 1869, 1874
Kotzebue, August Friedrich Ferdinand, 2. 1539, 38, 166, 173–4, 181, 863–4, 1013; 3. 126
Kozlov, Ivan Ivanovich, 3. 152
Krasheninnikof, Stephen Petrovitch, 2. 1439
Krasinski, Zygmunt, Count, 3. 152
Kratter, Franz, 2. 1539, 174
Kreymborg, Alfred, 4. 1365
Krylov, Ivan Andreyevich, 3. 152
Kurzer Versuch, Ein, 2. 366
Kuyumjian, Dikran, 4. 514–15
Kyd, Thomas, 1. 1427–31, 881
Kykeley, — (14th century), 1. 793
'Kyle, Elizabeth' (Agnes M. R. Dunlop), 4. 811
Kyle, Galloway, 4. 1359, 1364
Kylpont, Robert, 1. 1903
Kynaston, Sir Francis, 1. 1313
Kyng Alisaunder, 1. 422–3
Kynpont, Robert, 1. 1903
Kyrkham, W., 1. 2071

Kyttes, G. 1. 1122
Kyukhel'beker, Vil' gel'm Karlovich, 3. 152

L.A.G., 4. 826
L., E. (fl. 1596), 1. 1122
L., E. (fl. 1841), 3. 1723
L., F. (fl. 1600), 1. 1122
L., G. (fl. 1687), 2. 1553
L., R. gent (fl. 1596), 1. 1122–3
L., S. (fl. 1670), 2. 1445
L., S. (fl. 1730), 2. 992
L., S. P. (fl. 1627), 1. 1909
L., U. (fl. 1552), 1. 1123
L., V. (fl. 1552), 1. 1123
'L., W.' (William Lisle), 1. 1123
L., W. (fl. 1642), 1. 2035
Laban Art of Movement Guild: news sheet, 4. 860
La Barre, François Poulain de, 2. 1526, 96
Labarthe, André, 4. 1374
'Labé, Louise' (Louise Charlin), 1. 870
La belle assemblée, 3. 1842
Labillardière, Jacques Julien Houton de, 2. 1483
La Boétie, Etienne de, 2. 1516
Labouchere, Henry, 3. 1771, 1790, 1815
Labour elector, 3. 1820
Labour leader, 3. 1821
Labour monthly, 4. 1406
Labour world, 3. 1820
Labourer, 3. 1848
La Bruyère, Jean de, 2. 1516, 66, 94
La Calprenède, Gautier de Costes de, 1. 2187, 868, 873; 2. 1516, 140, 976
Lacedemonian mercury, 2. 1342
Lacey, E., 3. 1876
Lacey, Thomas Alexander, 3. 1823
La Chapelle, Jean de, 2. 985
Lachrymae academiae Marischallanae, 1. 2473
Lacrymae cantabrigienses in obitum reginae Mariae, 2. 339
Lachrymae Musarum, 1. 1010
Lackington, James, 2. 280; 3. 1745
'Lackrent, Lancelot' (C. Wyvill?), 2. 1370
Laclos, Pierre Choderlos de, 2. 1516, 140–1, 1007
La Condamine, Charles Marie de, 2. 1516, 1420, 1463
La Crose, Jean Cornand de, 2. 1291, 1292, 1413
Lacy, John, 2. 767
Lacy, Michael Rophino, 3. 1133
Lacy, R., 3. 1713
Ladder of four rungs, A, 1. 516
Ladies amusement, 2. 373
Ladies and gentlemen's musical memorandum, 2. 413
Ladies' cabinet of fashion, music and romance, 3. 1845

255 256

Lancashire
   general bibliography, 1. 17
   Renaissance to Restoration libraries, 1. 991
   Restoration and eighteenth century
      libraries, 2. 307
      printing and bookselling, 2. 268
Lancashire daily express and standard, 3. 1802
Lancashire daily post, 3. 1802
Lancashire evening express and standard, 3. 1802
Lancashire evening post, 3. 1802
Lancashire evening telegraph, 3. 1802; 4. 1403
Lancashire journal, 2. 1329, 1361
Lancashire magazine, 2. 1351
Lancashire stage-land, 4. 849
Lancaster, Charles, 3. 1713
Lancaster, Henry Hill, 3. 1729
Lancaster, Joseph, 3. 1718
Lancaster, Osbert, 4. 1068-9
Lancaster guardian, 3. 1832
Lancelot (prose), 1. 399-400
Lancelot of the Laik, 1. 400
Lancet, 3. 1826, 1838
Land and building news, 3. 1828
Land and water, 3. 1684, 1816; 4. 1362
Land of Canaan, 1. 2141
Land of Cockaygne, 1. 456-7
Landells, Ebenezer, 3. 1102, 1825, 1847
Lander, John, 3. 1669
Lander, Richard Lemon, 3. 1669
Landi, Ortensio, 1. 887
Landmark, 4. 1363
Landon, Joseph, 3. 1730
Landon, Laetitia Elizabeth, 3. 531, 1875, 1878
Landor, Owen, 3. 1105
Landor, Robert Eyres, 3. 387
Landor, Walter Savage, 3. 1210-16, 139
landscape, influence on nineteenth century
   poetry, 3. 171-2
Landscape album, 3. 1875
Landscape annual, 3. 1874
landscape gardening, 2. 67-70
Landscape magazine, 2. 1312
Lane, Edward, 4. 1376
Lane, George, 3. 1789, 1792
Lane, John (fl. 1600-30), 1. 1123, 2025
Lane, John (1854-1925), 3. 79, 1771, 1858
Lane, Lucy, 3. 1097
Lane, R., 4. 1387
Lane, Ralph Norman Angell, 4. 1136-7
Laneham, Robert, 1. 2071
La Neuville, Foy de, 2. 1414
Lanfranc. 1, 757
Lang, Andrew, 3. 1440-4, 1096, 1108-9, 1690,
   1699, 1703, 1771
Langbaine, Gerard, the elder (d. 1658), 1. 2305

Langbaine, Gerard (1656-92), 2. 1743, 1557,
   1800
Lange, Lorenz, 2. 1437
Langford, John A., 3. 1797
Langham, Simon, 1. 1002
Langhorne, John, 2. 666-7, 1000
Langlade, Jean Louis Ignace de la Serre, Sieur de,
   2. 1518
Langland, William, 1. 533-48
'Langle, Marquis de' (J. M. J. Fleuriot), 2. 1426
Langley, Noel, 4. 812
Langley, W. H., 3. 1882
Langman, Christopher, 2. 1459
Langton, Robert, 1. 2121
Langton, Stephen, 1. 782
language
   general, 1. 53-186
      dictionaries, 1. 53-6
      history, 1. 55-6
      loan-words, 1. 163-70
      phonology and morphology, 1. 59-112
         Old English, 1. 59-76
         Middle English, 1. 75-90
         Modern English, 1. 89-112
      place and personal names, 1. 169-86
      syntax, 1. 111-42
         Old English, 1. 117-22
         Middle English, 1. 121-6
         Modern English, 1. 127-42
      vocabulary, 1. 141-64
         Old English, 1. 143-54
         Middle English, 1. 153-6
         Modern English, 1. 157-64
   Renaissance to Restoration, 1. 839-40
Lanket, Thomas, 1. 2205
La Noue, François de, 1. 2187, 863
Lanquet, Thomas, 1. 2205
Lansdowne, George Granville, Baron, 2. 790
Lantern (1799), 2. 1387
Lantern (1915), 4. 1362
Lantern (1946), 4. 828
Lantern of the Cam, 3. 1866
La Pena, Juan Antonio de, 1. 2080
La Peyrere, Isaac de, 2. 1483
La Primaudaye, Pierre de, 1. 2187, 863
La Ramée, Pierre de (Ramus), 1. 851; 2. 37
Lardner, Dionysius, 3. 1846
Lardner, Nathaniel, 2. 1676, 164, 1863-4
Laresol review, 4. 1358
Lark (1740), 2. 367
Lark (1765), 2. 386
Lark (1768), 2. 388
Lark (1770?), 2. 391
Lark (1780?), 2. 401
Larkins, John P., 2. 1443

Lavelle, Patrick, 3. 1805
Laver, James, 4. 1069–70
Lavrin, Janko, 4. 1371
law
   Old English, 1. 331–2
   Renaissance to Restoration, 1. 2277–86
   Restoration and eighteenth century, 2. 299–
      300, 1911–16
Law, Edmund, 2. 1864
Law, James, 3. 1804
Law, John, 2. 1898
Law, Robert, 2. 2049
Law, William, 2. 1653–6, 1864
Law chronicle and estate advertiser, 3. 1826
Law gazette, 3. 1826
Law journal, 3. 1826
Law list, 3. 1881
Law magazine, 3. 1856
Law quarterly review, 3. 1858
Law review, 3. 1857
Law suit or the farmer and the fisherman, 2. 1558
Law times, 3. 1826
Lawath, Geoffrey de, 1. 1002
Lawes, Henry, 1. 1357–8
Lawless, Emily, 3. 1907
Lawn tennis (and croquet and badminton), 3. 1715
Lawn tennis annual, 3. 1882
Lawn tennis handbook, 3. 1715
Lawrence, Arthur, 3. 1853; 4. 1353
Lawrence, David Herbert, 4. 481–503, 1362
Lawrence, George Alfred, 3. 941
Lawrence, Herbert, 2. 1002, 1003
Lawrence, John, 2. 1555; 3. 1704
Lawrence, Leonard, 1. 1313
Lawrence, Thomas Edward, 4. 1181–5
laws (OE), 1. 331
Laws of poetry, 2. 354
Lawson, Edward Levy, 1st Baron Burnham, 3.
   1790
Lawson, George, 1. 2339
Lawson, Henry L. W. L., 1st Viscount Burnham,
   3. 1790
Lawson, John, 2. 1459
Lawson, W. J., 3. 1879
Lawson, W. R., 3. 1804
Lawyer's and magistrate's magazine, 2. 1309, 1379
Lawyer's companion, 3. 1881
Lawyer's magazine (1773), 2. 1305
Lawyers's magazine (1761), 2. 1303
Lay-folks' catechism, 1. 496–7
Lay-folks' mass-book, 1. 496
Lay-monk, 2. 1275
Layamon, 1. 460–3; 2. 32
Layard, Sir Austen Henry, 3. 1675, 1681
lays, Breton, 1. 435–42

Lays of the Belvoir hunt, 3. 1705
Lazarillo de Tormes, 1. 2187–8, 913; 2. 202,
   981
Leach, Edmund, 1. 2036
Leach, John, 2. 1449
Lead, Jane, 2. 1656–7
Leader (1850), 3. 1814
Leader (1900), 4. 1355
Leader (1922), 4. 1406
Leaflet, 3. 1871
Leaflet newspaper, 3. 1820
League, 3. 1819
Leahy, J., 3. 1715
Leahy, Maurice, 4. 1369
Leake, William Martin, 3. 1674, 1679
Lean, Francis, 3. 1880
Leanerd, John, 2. 767
Lear, Edward, 3. 1091, 67, 1680
Leask, Thomas Smith, 3. 1671
Leask, William, 3. 1823
Leatham, James, 4. 1360
Leatham, John, 4. 1375
Leathes, Stanley M., 3. 1870
Leathley, Mary E. S., 3. 1102
Leaven, 4. 1377
Leavis, Frank Raymond, 4. 1070–2, 1370
Leavis, Queenie Dorothy, 4. 1073
Le Blanc, Jean Bernard, 2. 66, 86, 1401
Le Blanc, Vincent, 1. 2147
Le Blond, Mrs E. A. F., 3. 1709–10
Le Blond, Robert, 3. 67
Le Bone Florence of Rome, 1. 444
Le Bossu, Réne, 2. 1518, 66, 116
Le Bouyer de Fontenelle, Bernard, 2. 1512–13,
   66, 93, 116
Le Brun, Corneille, 2. 1435–6
Le Challeux, Nicholas, 1. 2149
Lechford, Thomas, 1. 2163
Leckie, Daniel Robinson, 2. 1444
Lecky, William Edward Hartpole, 3. 1479–80
Leclerc, Jean, 2. 1518, 66, 1416
Leclerc de Buffon, Georges Louis, 2. 1505–6, 91
L'Ecluse, Jean de, 1. 2106
Le Cocq, R., 4. 1383, 1384
Le Cocq's comment, 4. 1384
Lecointe, Jean, 2. 1566
Le compilateur des nouvelles, 2. 1306
Le Comte, Louis Daniel, 2. 1435
LeCouteur, John, 2. 1443
Lectures on education, 3. 1724
Lederer, John, 2. 1455
Ledger, Edward, 3. 1826, 1878; 4. 823
Ledger, Frederic, 3. 1826; 4. 858
Lediard, Thomas, 2. 1711, 994, 1418
Ledwidge, Francis, 4. 295–6

Ledyard, John, 2. 1480
Lee, Francis, 2. 1657
Lee, Harriet, 3. 742; 2. 183, 1008, 1013
Lee, Henry, 2. 1847
'Lee, Holme' (Harriet Parr), 3. 941–2, 1093
Lee, James, 2. 1906
Lee, James N., 3. 1808
Lee, Laurie, 4. 296
Lee, Nathaniel, 2. 746–7
Lee, Samuel, 3. 1732
Lee, Sir Sidney, 3. 1657–8
Lee, Sophia, 3. 742; 2. 178, 1007, 1013
'Lee, Vernon' (Violet Paget), 3. 1444–6
Lee-Hamilton, Eugene Jacob, 3. 635
Lee Priory Press, 3. 55
Leech, Andrew, 1. 2473
Leech, David, 1. 2473
Leech, John (fl. 1594–1616), 1. 2473
Leech, John (1817–64), 3. 67, 1771
Leedes intelligencer, 2. 1359
Leeds
  Restoration and eighteenth century
    libraries, 2. 307
    magazines, 2. 1350
    newspapers, 2. 1359
  nineteenth century
    newspaper, 3. 1831
    university, 3. 1735–6
  twentieth century
    theatre, 4. 846
    university 4. 1395
Leeds and Yorkshire mercury, 3. 1796
Leeds daily news, 3. 1799; 4. 1402
Leeds magazine, 2. 1350
Leeds mercury (1718), 2. 1359
Leeds mercury (1767), 2. 1359
Leeds mercury (1861), 3. 1796, 1831
Leeds playgoer, 4. 850
Leeds triad, 4. 879
Leeds typographical circular, 3. 62
Leeds University poetry, 4. 1395
Leek, 4. 1381
Lees, John, 2. 1468
Le Fanu, Joseph Sheridan, 3. 942–3, 1806, 1845, 1846
Le Feuvre, Amy, 3. 1106
Lefroy, Edward Cracroft, 3. 635–6
Le Froy, Sir John Henry, 3. 1673
Left review, 4. 1371
Le Gallienne, Richard, 3. 1063–4
legends
  Old English, 1. 326–7
  Middle English
    didactic, 1. 449–52
    saints', 1. 523–34

Renaissance to Restoration, German, 1. 878–9
  nineteenth century, 3. 1107–10
Legends of the cross, 1. 327
Legge, Edward, 3. 1815
Legge, Thomas, 1. 1770–1
Legrand, Antoine, 1. 2341
Le Grand, Jacques, 1. 863
Le Grand, Marc Antoine, 2. 1518
Le Grand d'Aussy, Pierre Jean Baptiste, 2. 1518–19
Le Grice, Charles Valentine, 3. 387–8
Leguat, François, 2. 1436, 1447
Lehmann, Beatrix, 4. 1375
Lehmann, Rosamond Nina, 4. 630, 1377
Lehmann, Rudolph Chambers, 3. 1866
Lehmann, Rudolph John Frederick, 4. 297, 1371, 1372, 1375, 1379, 1380
Leibniz, Gottfried Wilhelm von, 2. 157
Leicester(shire)
  general bibliography, 1. 17
  Renaissance to Restoration libraries, 1. 991–2
  Restoration and eighteenth century
    libraries, 2. 307
    magazines, 2. 1350
    newspapers, 2. 1359
    periodical essays, 2. 1348
  twentieth century university magazine, 4. 1395
Leicester and Nottingham journal, 2. 1359
Leicester chronicle, 2. 1359
Leicester daily express, 3. 1803
Leicester daily mail, 3. 1798
Leicester daily post, 3. 1799
Leicester evening news, 3. 1799
Leicester herald, 2. 1359
Leicester journal, 2. 1359
Leicester weekly express, 3. 1798
Leiden riddle, 1. 288–9
Leigh, Edward, 1. 2136, 2296, 2298
Leigh, John, 2. 794
Leigh, Percival, 3. 1390
Leigh, Richard, 2. 478
Leigh, Richard Austen, 3. 1866
Leigh, Sir Samuel Egerton, 2. 1013
Leigh, William, 1. 2074
Leigh Hunt's journal, 3. 1814
Leigh Hunt's London journal (*and printing machine*) 3. 1821, 1836
Leighton, A., 2. 1373
Leighton, Clare Veronica Hope, 4. 806
Leighton, Frederic, Baron, 3. 67
Leighton, Robert (1611–84). 1. 1994–5
Leighton, Robert (1822–69), 3. 532
Leighton, Sir William, 1. 1314, 1355, 1908
Leinster journal, 2. 1388
Leisewitz, Johann Anton, 2. 1540, 174

Leishman, James Blair, 4. 1073
Leisure (1907), 4. 1358
Leisure (1936), 4. 1372
Leisure and sport, 4. 1406
Leisure annual, 4. 1386
Leisure hour, 3. 1848; 4. 1350
Leisure hour improved, 2. 428
Leisure moments, 4. 1385
Leitch, J. H., 3. 1729
Leith, Alicia A., 3. 1852
Leith commercial list, 2. 1338
Leland, John (1506–52), 1. 2204, 2121, 2188
Leland, John (1691–1766), 2. 1673, 1864
Leland, Thomas, 2. 1738, 184, 1000
Le magazin du monde politique, 2. 1306
Le Maire, Jacques Joseph, 2. 1447
Lemaire de Belges, Jean, 1. 871
Lemaistre, J. G., 3. 1677
Le memorial des marchands à Londres, 2. 1318
Le Mercure anglois, 1. 2100
Le mercurie britannique, 2. 1322
Lemierre, Antoine Marin, 2. 1519
Lemoine, Henry, 2. 1563
Lemon, — (fl. 1782), 2. 1560
Lemon, Mark, 3. 1150–1, 1090, 1771, 1813, 1814, 1816, 1821, 1825
Le monde élégant, 3. 1844
Le morte Arthur (stanzaic poem), 1. 400
Lempriere, William, 2. 1451, 1475
Lenanton, Carola Oman, Lady, 4. 688–9, 803
Le navire d'argent, 4. 1367
Lenclos, Anne ('Ninon') de, 2. 1519
Lending library, 4. 118
Le Neve, John, 2. 1804, 1313
L'enfant sage, 1. 513
Leng, Sir John, 3. 1804
Leng, Robert, 1. 2123
Leng, William, 3. 1794
Lennox, Charlotte, 2. 848, 996, 997, 999, 1000, 1009, 1282, 1303, 1781
Lennox, John, 3. 1771
Lennox, Lord William Pitt, 3. 1700
Le Noble de Tenelière, Eustache, 2. 983, 988, 989
Lenormand d'Etioles, J. A. P., Marquise de Pompadour, 2. 1526
Lenthall, William, 1. 2076
Lenton, Francis, 1. 2045
Leochaeus, John, 1. 2473
Leofric (OE), 1. 327
Leonard, Eliza Lucy, 3. 1100–1
Leonard, Lionel Frederick, 4. 961–2
Léonard, Nicolas-Germain, 2. 1008
'Leonardo', 2. 1290
Leonardo y Argensola, Bartolome, 2. 1436

Leonhard, Johann, 2. 1416
Leopardess, 4. 1396
Leopardi, Giacomo, 3. 137–8
Leopold, J. F., 2. 1416
Le Page du Pratz, —, 2. 1467
Le Pays, René, 2. 978
Le Petit, Jean François, 1. 2139
Le petit bijou, 3. 1874
Le Poivre, Pierre, 2. 1396
Le post-man, 2. 1321
Leprecaun, 4. 1405
Le prince d'amour, 1. 1011; 2. 328
Le Prince de Beaumont, Jeanne Marie, 2. 1031
Leptologist, 2. 1290
L'Epy, Heliogenes de, 2. 982
Lermontov, Mikhail Yur'yevich, 3. 152–3
Leroy, Amélie Claire, 3. 1104
LeRoy, Julien David, 2. 1420
Le Roy, Louis, 1. 863
LeRoy, Pierre Louis, 2. 1485
Lesage, Alain René, 2. 1519–20, 120, 141, 986, 988, 994
Les amusemens des Allemands, 2. 1568
Lescarbot, Marc, 1. 2162
Leslie, Charles (1650–1722), 2. 1847, 1293, 1344
Leslie, Charles (fl. 1739), 2. 1462
Leslie, John, 1. 2450, 2132
Leslie, Sir (John Randolph) Shane, 4. 1186–7
Leslie, W. M., 3. 1795
Leslie, William, 1. 2463
Lesseps, Jean B. B., Baron de, 2. 1443
Lesser-known markets guide, 4. 73
Lessing, Gotthold Ephraim, 2. 38–9, 171, 174–5, 863
L'Estrange, C. James, 4. 794
L'Estrange, Sir Hamon, 1. 2245, 2164
L'Estrange, Sir Roger, 2. 1035–8, 1315, 1316, 1340
L'état présent de l'Europe, 2. 1318
Let us to billiards, 3. 1692
Leti, Gregorio, 2. 1545, 1411–12
Letter from a Russian sea-officer, A, 2. 1484
Letter from Italy, A, 2. 345
Letter from Mrs Jane Jones, A, 2. 994
Letter giving a description of the Isthmus of Darien, A, 2. 1458
Letter of Alexander to Aristotle (OE), 1. 335–6
Letter of Peter Winne, 1. 2154–5
Letter-mag, 4. 1374
letters
  fifteenth century, 1. 683–4
  Renaissance to Restoration, 1. 2253–60, 2404, 2407–8
  Restoration and eighteenth century
    French, 2. 136

letters (*cont.*)
    general, 2. 1569–1600
    studies, 2. 7
  nineteenth century, 3. 19–26
  twentieth century, 4. 15–26
Letters (1771), 2. 1284
Letters: a journal (1922), 4. 1365
Letters and observations written in a short tour, 2. 1426
Letters and papers on agriculture, 2. 1306
Letters and poems in honour of Margaret, Dutchess of Newcastle, 2. 333
Letters by 'Attorney general to the Gazetteer', 2. 1285
Letters by 'Cato', 2. 1277
Letters by 'Democritus', 2. 1286
Letters by 'Probus', 2. 1282
Letters concerning the present state of the French nation, 2. 1421
Letters describing the . . . English and French nations, 2. 1417
Letters from a Moor, 2. 994
Letters from an English gentleman during his travels through Denmark, 2. 1423
Letters from Mr Fletcher Christian, 2. 1481
Letters from Paris. . .1791 and 1792, 2. 1429
Letters from Scandinavia, 2. 1430
Letters from several parts of Europe and the east, 2. 1427
Letters from the dead, 2. 1284
Letters from the living to the living, 2. 342
Letters from the Westminster journal, 2. 1331
Letters in defence of religion, 2. 1348
Letters in prose and verse to. . .Polly Peachum, 2. 358
Letters of Abelard and Heloise (1713), 2. 986
Letters of Abelard and Heloise (1781), 2. 402
Letters of 'Junius', 2. 1284
Letters of 'Modestus', 2. 1284
Letters of 'Momus', 2. 1277
Letters of Momus from Margate, 2. 1005
Letters of 'Roderic M'Alpin', 2. 1286
Letters of the critical club, 2. 1370
Letters of wit, politicks and morality, 2. 341
Letters, poems and tales (1718), 2. 352
Letters received by the East India Company, 1. 2146
Letters to a nobleman from a gentleman travelling through Holland, 2. 1416
Lettice, John, 2. 1406
Lettres à Monsieur le Comte de B. 2. 1337
Lettsom, John Coakley, 2. 1568
LeVaillant, François, 2. 1451
Levasseur, Guillaume Beauplan, Sieur de, 2. 1415

Le Vayer de Boutigny, Rolland, 2. 980
Leveller, 2. 1285
Lever, Charles James, 3. 943–4, 1846
Lever, Christopher, 1. 1314
Lever, Ralph, 1. 2329
Lever, Thomas, 1. 1824, 1943
Leverpoole courant, 2. 1360
Leverson, Ada, 4. 630
Levett, Christopher, 1. 2158
Levi, Sinori, 4. 880, 1365
Levitt, William, 1. 2041
Levy, Benn Wolfe, 4. 960–1
Levy, Joseph Moses, 3. 1771, 1790, 1810
Lewes, library, 2. 308
Lewes, George Henry, 3. 1542–4, 1814, 1849, 1850
Lewes and Brighthelmston pacquet, 2. 1360
Lewes newsmen's new year verses, 2. 1360
Lewicke, Edward, 1. 1123–4
Lewis, A., 4. 1382
Lewis, A. C., 4. 1383
Lewis, Alun, 4. 298
Lewis, Clive Staples, 4. 1073–8, 804
Lewis, Dominic Bevan Wyndham, 4. 1078–9
Lewis, Sir George Cornewall, 3. 1771, 1854–5
Lewis, Harold, 3. 1796
Lewis, Hilda, 4. 803
Lewis, John (1675–1747), 2. 1716, 1772
Lewis, John (twentieth century editor), 4. 1377
Lewis, Leopold David, 3. 1151
Lewis, Lorna, 4. 811
Lewis, Matthew Gregory, 3. 742–4; 2. 148, 184, 212, 1011
Lewis, Percy Wyndham, 4. 631–4, 1362, 1365, 1367
Lewis, Robert, 2. 999
Lewis, Thomas, 2. 1276
Lewis, William, 3. 1694
Lewis, William Garrett, 3. 1843
Lewis, Wyndham, 4. 631–4, 1362, 1365, 1367
Lewis and Co, H. K., 3. 79
Lewisham, library of, 1. 992
Lewitt, Jan, 4. 810
Lewkenor, John, 2. 1398
Leybourn, William, 1. 962
Leycester, John, 1. 2031
Leyden, John, 3. 388–9; 2. 1408, 1445, 1452
Lhuyd, Edward, 2. 1906
Libeaus Desconus, 1. 409–10
Libel of English policy, 1. 686
Liberal: verse and prose from the south (1822), 3. 1855, 1864
Liberal (1829), 3. 1810
Liberalitie and prodigalitie, 1. 1410
Libertine, 2. 1280

Lincoln(shire) (*cont.*)
  eighteenth century, newspapers, 2. 1360
  nineteenth century, newspapers, 3. 1832
Lincoln Cathedral library, 1. 992
Lincoln gazette, 2. 1360
Lincoln imp, 4. 1397
Lincoln journal, 2. 1360
Lincoln, Rutland and Stamford mercury, 2. 1367;
  3. 1832
Lind, James, 2. 1906
Lind, John, 2. 1423
Lindanus, Gulielmus, 1. 849
Lindesay, Patrick, 2. 1898
Lindley, John, 3. 1827
Lindsay, Alexander, 1. 2131
Lindsay, Lady Anne, 2. 2027
Lindsay, Caroline Blanche Elizabeth Fitzroy,
  Lady, 3. 1105
Lindsay, Sir David (d. 1555), 1. 2426–7, 1405
Lindsay, David (d. 1641), 1. 2450
Lindsay, David (1876–1945), 4. 634–5
Lindsay, Jack, 4. 635–6, 806, 1366, 1368, 1379
Lindsay, Maurice, 4. 1376
Lindsay, Patrick, 2. 1898
Lindsay, Robert, 1. 2451
Lindsay, Thomas Martin, 3. 1613
Lindsey, John, 2. 1450
Lindt, Willem van der, 1. 849
Ling, Nicholas, 1. 962
Lingard, John, 3. 1490–1
Lingham, John, 1. 2076
Linguet, Simon Nicolas Henri, 2. 1520
Link (1888), 3. 1820
Link (1916), 4. 1363
Link (1924), 4. 880
Link (1930), 4. 118
Link boy, 2. 1287
Linklater, Eric Robert Russell, 4. 636–8, 806
Linkman, 4. 1363
Linnet (1749), 2. 373
Linnet (1783), 2. 404
Linnet (1792), 2. 416
Linnets, 2. 398
Linotype and machinery news, 4. 82
Linotype and printing machine record, 4. 82
Linotype matrix, 4. 83
Linotype notes, 4. 81
Linotype record, 4. 81, 82
Linotype Users' Association, its *monthly circular*,
  4. 81
Linschoten, Jan Huighen van, 1. 2143
Linton, Eliza Lynn, 3. 944–5, 1771
Linton, William James, 3. 533, 66, 1771, 1816,
  1818, 1847
Lintot, Bernard, 2. 280

Lion (1829), 3. 1818
Lion (London University 1916), 4. 1395
Lion hunting (1826), 3. 1678
Lion university magazine, 3. 1865
Lion's parliament, 3. 1088
Lipscomb, George, 2. 1408
Lipsius, Justus, 1. 849
Lisander: or the souldier of fortune, 2. 979
Lisle, William, 1. 1124, 2119
'*Lisp of leaves*', 4. 1379
List of the flag officers of HM Fleet, A, 3.
  1879
List of the general and field officers, A, 3. 1879
*List of the officers of the several regiments and corps
  of militia*, 3. 1879
List of the principal newspapers, A, 4. 1343
Listener, 4. 60, 864, 1406
Listener's pictorial, 4. 1407
Lister, Martin, 2. 1414, 1906
Lister, Thomas, 4th Baron Ribblesdale, 3. 1707
Lister, Thomas Henry, 3. 945
Lister's Sheffield weekly journal, 2. 1365
'*Lit*' magazine, 4. 1384
Lit. news, 4. 1387
Litchfield, Richard B., 3. 1871
Literary adventurer, 4. 1384
literary agents, twentieth century, 4. 69–70
Literary amateur, 4. 1384
Literary and biographical magazine, 2. 1308
Literary and educational year book, 3. 1881
Literary and musical review, 4. 1359
*Literary and Philosophical Society of Newcastle
  reports*, 2. 1351
Literary annals, 2. 1304
Literary aspirant (Leicester 1904), 4. 1380
Literary aspirant (Salford 1931), 4. 1384
Literary chronicle and weekly review, 3. 1821
Literary club magazine, 4. 1384
literary conferences and festivals, 4. 71–2
Literary courier of Grub-street, 2. 1279, 1327
literary criticism
  Renaissance to Restoration, 1. 2307–22
  Restoration and eighteenth century, 2. 23–70
    aesthetic theory, 2. 45–54
    anthologies, 2. 43–4
    art, general, 2. 67–70
    drama, 2. 715–22
    forms, 2. 53–62
    French, 2. 115–18
    individual criticism, 2. 61–4
    studies, 2. 23–44
    translations, 2. 63–8
  nineteenth century, 3. 1115–18
  twentieth century, 4. 993–1134
  see also literary history

London kalendar, 2. 1313
London lampoon'd, 2. 342
London library, 4. 1360, 1405
London life, 3. 1816; 4. 1401
London magazine (1732), 2. 1297
London magazine (1741), 2. 1379
London magazine (1820), 3. 1844, 1861
London magazine (1903), 3. 1854; 4. 1355, 1346
London medical directory, 3. 1881
London medical guide, 3. 1881
London medical journal, 2. 1306
London medical review, 2. 1312
London medley (1731), 2. 360
London medley (1732), 2. 361
London mercantile journal, 3. 1824
London mercury (1669), 2. 1316
London mercury (1682), 2. 1318
London mercury (1688), 2. 1318
London mercury (1692), 2. 1342
London mercury (1695), 2. 1320
London mercury (1696), 2. 1320
London mercury (1719), 2. 1324
London mercury (1721), 2. 1325
London mercury (1780), 2. 1314
London mercury (1781), 2. 402
London mercury (1836), 3. 1811
London mercury (1919), 4. 1364
London miscellany, 2. 359
London morning, 3. 1791
London morning advertiser (May 1742), 2. 1331
London morning advertiser (Dec. 1742), 2. 1328
London morning penny advertiser, 2. 1331
London morning penny post, 2. 1331
London museum, 2. 1304
London musical museum, 2. 426
London mystery magazine, 4. 1392
London news-letter (1696), 2. 1320
London newsletter (1695), 2. 1319
London novels, 4. 1368
London official amusement guide, 4. 826
London opinion, 4. 1356
London 'Owl', 4. 1359
London packet, 2. 1334; 3. 1807
London phalanx, 3. 1819
London pioneer, 3. 1813
London polite songster, 2. 384
London post (1644), 1. 2100, 2101
London post (1697), 2. 1320
London post (1699), 2. 1320
London post (April 1715), 2. 1323
London post (October 1715), 2. 1323
London post (1717), 2. 1324
London post (1722), 2. 1325
London post (1725), 2. 1326
London post boy, 2. 1382

London-postman (Dublin 1707), 2. 1381
London post-man (Dublin 1722), 2. 1383
London post-man (Dublin 1727), 2. 1384
London press journal, 3. 59
London price courent, 2. 1335
London printers' circular, 3. 61
London prodigall, 1. 1760
London program, 4. 825
London, provincial and colonial press news, 3. 60, 1762; 4. 81, 1340
London quarterly (and Holborn) review, 3. 1857, 1866; 4. 1350
London reader, 4. 1351
London record, 4. 824, 1357
London recorder, 2. 1336, 1338; 3. 1807
London register, 2. 1303
London review (1749), 2. 1299
London review (1800), 2. 1312
London review (1809), 3. 1843
London review (1829), 3. 1856
London review (1835), 3. 1856
London review and weekly journal (1860), 3. 1814, 1835
London review of English and foreign literature, 2 1305
London Shakespeare League journal, 4. 825
London slip of news, 2. 1320
London society, 4. 1401
London songster (1767), 2. 388
London songster (1799), 2. 426
London spy (1698), 2. 1342-3
London spy and Read's weekly journal (1761), 2. 1323
London spy revived, 2. 1329
London stage annual, 4. 824
London student, 3. 1867
London students' gazette, 3. 1867
London tatler, 2. 1329
London telegraph, 3. 1790
London terrae filius, 2. 1293
London theatre, 4. 823-4
London University calendar, 3. 1881
London University chronicle, 3. 1867
London University College magazine, 3. 1867
London University inquirer, 3. 1867
London University Journalism Society gazette, 4. 1396
London University magazine (1829), 3. 1867
London University magazine (1842), 3. 1867
London University magazine (1856), 3. 1867
London University magazine (1922), 4. 1396
London weekly chronicle, 2. 1333
London weekly gazette, 3. 1813
London weekly times, 3. 1810
Londons diurnal, 2. 1315

London's intelligencer, 2. 1315
Londonderry journal, 2. 1389
Lone eagle, fighting ace, 4. 1390
Lonericus, Philippus, 1. 2138
Long, Edward, 2. 999, 1469
Long, John, 2. 1473
Long, Robert, 2. 1568
Longchamps, Nigel de, 1. 763–4
Longfield, Edward, 3. 1820
Longinus, 1. 2172; 2. 1492, 34, 65
Longland, John, 1. 1943
Longman, Charles James, 3. 1852
Longman's magazine, 3. 1852, 1863; 4. 1352
Longmans, Green and Co, 2. 280; 3. 79, 1771, 1845, 1852, 1854
Longueville, Peter, 2. 991
Longus, 1. 2172; 2. 1492
Lonnergan, A., 2. 1563
'Lonsdale, Frederick' (Lionel Frederick Leonard), 4. 961–2
Look about you, 1. 1471
Looker-on, 2. 1289, 1349
Looking forward, 4. 1363
Lopes, Duarte, 1. 887
Lopes de Castanheda, Fernao, 1. 2143
Lopez de Gomara, Francisco, 1. 2150
Lopez de Mendoza, Iñigo, 1. 911
Loquela mirabilis, 4. 1372
Lord, E., 3. 1723
Lord, Henry, 1. 2148
Lord's Munster herald, 2. 1387
Lord's Prayer, OE versions, 1. 289; Tudor version, 1. 1125
Lord Chesterfield's witticisms, 2. 394
Lord of Lorn, 1. 1125
Loredano, Giovanni Francesco, 1. 902, 2063; 2. 1546, 979
Lorenzini, Carlo, 3. 1109
Lorimer, James, 3. 1731
Loring, T., 4. 1386
Losa, Francisco de, 1. 908
Loskiel, Georg Heinrich, 2. 1474
Lossius, Caspar Friedrich, 3. 1110
Lotinga's weekly, 4. 825
Lottery magazine, 2. 1306
Loudon, Jane, 3. 1848
Loudon, John Claudius, 3. 1845, 1846
Louis of Nazareth (Robert Howard), 1. 1312
Louise Heilgers magazine, 4. 71
Lounger, 2. 1371
Lounger's miscellany, 2. 1288, 1308
Lovat Dickson's magazine, 4. 1370
Love, Christopher, 1. 1995
Love, David, 2. 1408
Love, James, 2. 1564–5

Love: romantic magazine (1941), 4. 1391
Love and beauty, 2. 389
Love and fortune, 1. 1418
Love and romance, 4. 1392
Love at first sight (1742), 2. 369
Love at first sight (1750), 2. 374
Love feigned and unfeigned, 1. 1410
Love gift, A, 3. 1876
Love in all shapes, 2. 993
Love letters between a certain late nobleman and the famous Mr Wilson, 2. 989
Love letters between Polydorus. . .and Messalina, 2. 982
Love stories, 4. 1389
Love tales and elegies, 2. 395
Love upon tick, 2. 990
Love without artifice, 2. 993
Loves changelings change, 1. 1760
Loves garland, 1. 1010; 2. 332
Love's last shift, 2. 353
Loves martyr, 1. 1009
Loves posie, 2. 981
Love's repository, 2. 428
Loves school, 2. 332
Love's victorie, 1. 1760
'Lovechild, Mrs' (Lady Eleanor Fenn), 2. 1024–5
'Lovechild, Nurse', 2. 1019
Lovecraft, — 4. 1383
Loveday, John, 2. 1401
Lovelace, Richard, 1. 1221–2
Lovelich, Henry, 1. 686–7; Grail, 1. 414; Merlin, 1. 398
Lovell, Daniel, 3. 1792
Lovell, Dorothy Ann, 4. 809
Lovell, George William, 3. 1151
Lovell, John, 3. 61, 1795, 1816
Lovell, Thomas, 1. 1125
Lover, Samuel, 3. 744–6, 1845
Lover, 2. 1275
Lover's best instructor, 2. 391
Lover's cabinet, 2. 378
Lover's instructor, 2. 398
Lover's magazine, 2. 367
Lover's manual, 2. 377
Lovers pacquet, 2. 362
Lover's secretary, 2. 984
Lovers' mass, 1. 688
Loves of Hero and Leander, 1. 1010; 2. 337
Lovett, Richard, 2. 1906
Lovibond, Edward, 2. 669
Low, George, 2. 1403
Low, Sir Hugh, 3. 1676
Low, John Low, 3. 1703
Low, Sampson, 3. 81

Low, Sir Sidney, 3. 1771, 1794
Lowbury, Edward, 4. 1376
Lowde, James, 2. 1847
Lowe, Charles, 3. 1771
Lowe, George S., 3. 1791
Lowe, John, 2. 2027
Lowe, L., 4. 1387
Lowe, Robert, Viscount Sherbrooke, 3. 1727, 1771
Lowe, Robert William, 3. 1658
Lower, Richard, 2. 1906
Lower, Sir William, 1. 1748–9
Lowman, Moses, 2. 1673–4
Lowndes, Joan Selby, 4. 813
Lowndes, Marie Adelaide, 4. 639–40
Lowndes, William, 2. 1847
Lownds and Son, M., 3. 59
Lowry, A. E., 4. 1375
Lowry, Arthur B., 3. 1870
Lowry, (Clarence) Malcolm, 4. 640–2
Lowth, Robert, 2. 1561
Loyal garland, 2. 330
Loyal impartial mercury, 2. 1318
Loyal intelligence, 2. 1317
Loyal intelligencer (1654), 1. 2108
Loyal intelligencer (Stamford 1793), 2. 1367
Loyal London mercury (June 1682), 2. 1318
Loyal London mercury (August 1682), 2. 1318
Loyal messenger (1653), 1. 2108
Loyal messenger (1654), 1. 2109
Loyal mourner, 2. 350
Loyal observator (1704), 2. 1343
Loyal observator (1723), 2. 1325
Loyal observator reviv'd (1722), 2. 1325
Loyal poems and satyrs upon the times, 2. 335
Loyal post, 2. 1321
Loyal Protestant and true domestick intelligence, 2. 1317
Loyal weekly journal, 2. 1324
Loyalist, 2. 1289
Loyall scout (July 1659), 1. 2110; 2. 1313
Loyall scout (Dec. 1659), 1. 2110
Loyola, Ignatius, 1. 908
Lozano, Pedro, 2. 1463
Lubbock, Montagu, 3. 1870
Lubbock, Percy, 4. 1079
Lucan, 1. 2172; 2. 1498
Lucas, C., 2. 1379
Lucas, David, 3. 67
Lucas, Edward Verrall, 4. 1079–82; 3. 1099, 1697, 1867
Lucas, Frank Laurence, 4. 1082–3
Lucas, Frederick, 3. 1771, 1822, 1867
Lucas, Percival, 4. 878
Lucas, Peter G., 4. 1394

Lucas, Richard, 2. 164
Lucas, Samuel (1811–65) of *The morning star*, 3. 1790
Lucas, Samuel (1818–68), newspaper proprietor, 3. 1771, 1814, 1821, 1850
Lucas, Theophilus, 2. 1566
Lucas, William, 2. 1419
Luciad, 4. 1395
Lucian, 1. 2172; 2. 1492, 976, 980
Lucian's dialogues not from the Greek, 2. 1341
Lucifer: a theosophical monthly, 3. 1853
Luckcombe, Philip, 2. 1404
Luckman and Sketchley's Coventry gazette, 2. 1356
Lucky charm, 4. 1373, 1390
Lucretius, 1. 2172; 2. 1498, 35
Luctus britannici, 2. 341
Lucubrator, 2. 1287
Lucy, Sir Henry William, 3. 1771–2, 1790, 1815
Lucy, William, 1. 2340
Ludgate, 3. 1853; 4. 1353
Ludgate illustrated magazine, 3. 1853
Ludgate monthly, 3. 1853; 4. 1353
Ludlam, H., 4. 1387, 1388
Ludlow, Edmund, 2. 1694
Ludlow, J. M., 3. 1819, 1821
Ludlow post-man, 2. 1360
Ludolphus, Hiob, 2. 1446
Ludus Coventriae (ME cycle), 1. 733–4
Ludwig, Otto, 3. 126
Luffman, John, 2. 1473
Lugard, Flora Louise, Lady, 3. 1096
Lukin, Robert, 3. 1715
Lukin, Vladimir Ignat'yevich, 2. 216
Lumisden, Andrew, 2. 1430
Lumisden, Charles, 1. 1906
Lumley, Jane, Lady, 1. 1423
Lumley, John, 1st Baron, 1. 1002
Lunadoro, Girolamo, 1. 2141
Lunardi, Vincent, 2. 1405
Lund, K. 4. 1398
Lunn, Hugh Kingsmill, 4. 1065–6
Lupset, Thomas, 1. 1817
Lupton, Donald, 1. 2045, 2142
Lupton, Thomas, 1. 1408
Lurcott, W., 3. 1877
Lurting, Thomas, 2. 1650–1
Luscious poet: or Venus's miscellany, 2. 361
Lushington, Henrietta, Lady, 3. 1103
Lusignan, S., 2. 1427, 1441–2, 1450
Lussan, Marguerite de, 2. 992
Lusus Westmonasteriensis, 2. 359
Lutel soth sermun, A, 1. 489
Luther, Martin, 1. 849, 877, 2188; 2. 157
Lutterell, John, 1. 788

Luttrell, Henry, 3. 389–90, 1693
Lutyens, F. M., 3. 1707
Luytel sarmoun of good edificacioun, A, 1. 490
Lyall, Sir Alfred Comyns, 3. 636
'Lyall, Edna' (Ada Ellen Bayly), 3. 1064, 1097
Lyall, J. G., 3. 1707
Lyall, William Rowe, 3. 1841
Lycidus: or the lover in fashion, 2. 336
Lycosthenes, Conradus, 1. 849
Lydgate, John, 1. 639–46, 740
Lye, Edward, 2. 1794
Lyell, Sir Charles, 3. 1731
Lyfe of Joseph of Arimathia, 1. 414
Lying intelligencer, 2. 1283
Lyle, Robert, 4. 1379
Lyly, John, 1. 1423–7, 1125, 1961, 2052; 2. 988
Lyly, William, 1. 2069
Lynch, John, 3. 1888
Lynch, Patricia Nora, 4. 804–5
Lynch, Thomas Toke, 3. 535
Lynd, Robert Wilson, 4. 1083–4
Lynn, Eliza, 3. 944–5
Lynn and Wisbech packet, 2. 1360
Lynx, 2. 1290
Lyre, 2. 372
lyric poetry
    Middle English, 1. 697–720
    Renaissance to Restoration, Italian, 1. 890–3
    Restoration and eighteenth century, 2. 53–9,
        315–16
    nineteenth century, 3. 169
    see also ballads, miscellanies, poetry, songs
Lyric repository, 2. 408
Lyschinska, M. J., 3. 1729
Lysias, 2. 1492
Lyster, A. C., 4. 859
Lyte, Henry Francis, 3. 390
Lyte, Sir Henry Maxwell, 3. 1870
Lyttelton, Robert Henry, 3. 1698
Lyttleton, Charles, 2. 1440
Lyttleton, Edward, 3. 1730
Lyttleton, George, 1st Baron, 2. 555–6, 994, 995,
    1402
Lyttleton, George William, 4th Baron, 3. 1870
Lytton, Edward George Earle Lytton Bulwer-
    Lytton, 1st Baron, 3. 917–21, 113, 132, 139,
    1844, 1846
Lytton, Edward Robert Bulwer Lytton, 1st Earl
    of, 3. 636–7

M., A. (fl. 1581), 1. 2072
M., A. (fl. 1621), 1. 2079
M., A. (fl. 1788), 2. 1026
M.A.B.: mainly about books, 4. 117
M., C. (fl. 1596), 1. 2054

M., D. F. R. de (fl. 1589), 1. 2077
M., E. (Edward Manning?), 1. 1330
M., E. (Edward Marsh), 4. 1361
M., J. (Gervase Markham?), 1. 2066
M., Jo. (fl. 1591), 1. 2053
M., R. (fl. 1618), 1. 2156
M., R. (fl. 1629), 1. 2045
M., Mr R. (fl. 1716), 2. 1460
M., R. (fl. 1722), 2. 1461
M., T. (fl. 1599), 1. 1335
M., T. (fl. 1657), 1. 2058
M., W. (fl. 1585), 1. 2077
M., W. (fl. 1609), 1. 2046
Mabbe, James, 1. 1749
Mabbott, Gilbert, 1. 2100, 2101, 2104, 2105
Macalister, J. Y., 3. 90
Macaroni, 2. 1305
Macaroni jester, 2. 385
McArthur, J., 2. 1563
Macartney, George, Earl, 2. 1403, 1421, 1442
Macaskie, Charles, 3. 1799
Macaskie, Frank, 3. 1799
Macaulay, Catherine, 2. 1738
Macaulay, Emilie Rose, 4. 642–3
Macaulay, George Campbell, 3. 1658, 1870
Macaulay, James, 3. 1825, 1848
Macaulay, Rose, 4. 642–3
Macaulay, Thomas Babington, Baron, 3. 1463–8
Macaulay, Zachary, 3. 1617, 1842
Macbain, Alexander, 3. 1851
McBane, Donald, 2. 1562
MacBeth, George, 4. 1398
McCabe, J. I., 4. 1396
MacCaig, Norman, 4. 298–9
McCall, John Erwin, 4. 1354
McCarthy, Albert John, 4. 1377, 1379
MacCarthy, Denis Florence, 3. 1904
MacCarthy, Sir Desmond, 4. 1084–5, 1358, 1368
McCarthy, F. H., 4. 1384
McCarthy, Justin, 3. 1491–2, 1772, 1790
McCarthy, Justin Huntly, 3. 1807
Macclesfield courier and herald, 3. 1832
McClintock, Sir Francis Leopold, 3. 1670
MacCodrum, John, 2. 1976
McColl, G. T., 4. 1383
MacColl, Norman, 3. 1821; 4. 1349
McCombie, William, 3. 1726
McCormick, Robert, 3. 1669
McCosh, James, 3. 1544–6
McCracken, Esther Helen, 4. 962–3
McCreery, John, 2. 265
McCrie, J., 3. 1728
McCrory, Patrick, 4. 1376, 1378
McCulloch, John Ramsay, 3. 1772, 1804
McCullock, W., 2. 1376

MacCunn, John, 3. 1732
M'Dermott, — (fl. 1865), 3. 1807
Macdermott, Norman, 4. 1364
'MacDiarmid, Hugh' (Christopher Murray Grieve), 4. 299–303, 1365, 1366, 1373
MacDiarmid, John, 3. 1808
Macdonagh, Donagh, 4. 963
MacDonagh, Thomas, 4. 302–3
Macdonald, Alec, 4. 1391
Macdonald, Andrew, 2. 1337; 3. 1792
Macdonald, Sir Claude Maxwell, 3. 1672
Macdonald, D., 3. 1678
MacDonald, George, 3. 945–7, 1092
Macdonald, John, 2. 2067, 1396
Macdonald, William Russell, 3. 1809, 1810
MacDonell, Archibald Gordon, 4. 643
Macdonell, James, 3. 1772
Macdonell, John, 2. 1474
Macdonnel, D. E., 2. 1338
M'Donnel's Dublin weekly journal, 2. 1386
MacDonnell, George A., 3. 1694
Macdougall, Roger, 4. 963–4
McDougall, William, 4. 1271–2
McEvoy, Charles Alfred, 4. 964
McEwan, Oliver, 4. 1381
McEwan's amateur journalist, 4. 1381
McFadden, Roy, 4. 1375
McFall, Frances Elizabeth, 3. 1054–5
MacFarlane, Catherine Roxburgh, 4. 548
Macfarlane, John, 3. 1805
McFee, William Morley Punshon, 4. 643–4
MacFirbis, Duald, 3. 1887
M'Gillivray, Duncan, 2. 1474
McGlashan, James, 3. 1846
Macgregor, Alexander, 3. 1851
MacGregor, John, 3. 1670, 1711
McGregor, Reginald James, 4. 807
Machen, Arthur Llewelyn Jones, 4. 644–8
Machiavelli, Niccolò, 1. 887–9, 902, 2063, 2188, 2275; 2. 1546, 38, 188
Machin, Lewis, 1. 881
Machlinia, William de, 1. 962
Machrie, William, 2. 1562, 1569
MacInnes, Angus, 4. 852
MacIntosh, Charles, 3. 1878
MacIntosh, William, 2. 1396, 1441
Macintyre, Donald, 3. 1713
MacIntyre, John, 4. 913–14
Mackail, Denis George, 4. 648–9
Mackail, John William, 4. 1085–6
Mackarness, Matilda Anne, 3. 1093
Mackay, Alexander, 3. 1806
Mackay, Charles, 3. 535, 1683, 1772, 1814, 1816, 1875
McKay, Herbert, 4. 795

Mackay, Robert William, 3. 1608
Mackay, William, 3. 1772
McKeag, E. L., 4. 1383
McKenna, Stephen, 4. 649–50
Mackenzie, Sir Alexander (d. 1820), 2. 1474
Mackenzie, Alexander (fl. 1876–86), 3. 1851
Mackenzie, Anna Maria, 2. 1010
Mackenzie, Sir Compton, 4. 650–2, 796–7, 1396
Mackenzie, Sir Edward Montague Compton, 4. 650–2, 796–7, 1396
McKenzie, G., 4. 1357
Mackenzie, George, 1st Earl of Cromarty (1630–1714) historian, 2. 1689–90
Mackenzie, Sir George (1636–91), lawyer, 2. 1690–1, 975, 2049–50
Mackenzie, George (1669–1725), biographer, 2. 1805, 2055
Mackenzie, Georgina Mary Muir, 3. 1680
Mackenzie, Henry, 2. 148, 184, 1003, 1004, 1005, 1371
Mackenzie, John Campbell, 3. 1791
Mackenzie, Murdoch, 2. 1401
Mackenzie, R. C., 3. 1804
Mackenzie, Roderick, 2. 1443
Mackenzie, Ronald, 4. 964
McKenzie's loyal magazine, 2. 1380
Mackern, L., 3. 1703
McKerrow, Ronald Brunlees, 4. 1086–8
Mackie, S. J., 3. 1849
Mackie, William, 3. 1804
McKiernan, Gerald, 3. 1671
Mackinder, H. J., 3. 1746
MacKinnon, Donald, 4. 1357
Mackintosh, Alexander (fl. 1806), 3. 1687
Mackintosh, Alexander (1858–1948), 3. 1772
Mackintosh, Elizabeth, 4. 930–1
Mackintosh, Sir James, 3. 1492, 1546
Mackintosh, Robert, 3. 1613
Macklin, Charles, 2. 849–50
Macklin's British poets, 2. 410
Mackmurdo, A. H., 3. 1858
MacKnight, Thomas, 3. 1806
Macky, John, 2. 1399, 1417
Maclaren, Archibald, 3. 1728
Maclaren, Charles, 3. 1804
Maclaurin, Colin, 2. 1906
MacLaurin, John, 2. 2045
Maclean, Laetitia Elizabeth, 3. 531
MacLean, Neil, 2. 1472
Macleay, John, 3. 1795
McLennan, Donald, 3. 1795
McLennan, John Ferguson, 3. 1390
M'Leod, Allan, 3. 1792
Macleod, Donald (d.c. 1791), 2. 2055
Macleod, Donald (fl. 1870?), 3. 1849

'MacLeod, Fiona' (William Sharp), 3. 1064–6
Macleod, Mary, 3. 1110
Macleod, Norman, 3. 1620, 1091, 1725, 1849
MacLiammóir, Michéal, 4. 964–5
Maclise, Daniel, 3. 67
Macliver, Peter Stewart, 3. 1796
Macmichael, W. F., 3. 1711
Macmillan, Alexander, 3. 1772
Macmillan, Hugh, 3. 1622
Macmillan's magazine, 3. 1849, 1862; 4. 1351
Macmillan and Co, 3. 79, 1772, 1827, 1849, 1850, 1852, 1858
Macmullan, Charles Kirkpatrick, 4. 969
Macmullen, Richard Turrill, 3. 1716
Macnab, Henry Grey, 3. 1720
MacNab, Roy, 4. 1397
MacNaghten, Sir Malcolm Martin, 3. 1870
Macnair, J., 3. 1714
MacNally, Leonard, 2. 850
'Macnamara, Brinsley' (John Weldon), 4. 965
M'Nayr, James, 2. 1407
MacNeice, Louis, 4. 303–5, 1397
McNeile, Herman Cyril, 4. 729–30
McNeill, A. M., 4. 1385
MacNeill, Hector, 2. 2027–8
MacNevin, William James, 3. 1677
M'Nicoll, Thomas, 3. 1857
Macpherson, Charles, 2. 1396, 1476
Macpherson, Hector C., 3. 1805
Macpherson, Hugh Alexander, 3. 1714
Macpherson, James, 2. 603–5, 132–3, 168–9, 193, 200, 207, 212, 217, 1738
Macpherson, John, 2. 2055
Macpherson, Kenneth, 4. 1367
Macpherson, R., 2. 1570
Macpherson, William, 3. 1855
MacQuarie, Lachlan, 3. 1675
MacRitchie, William, 2. 1407
Macro plays, 1. 1403–4
M'Robert, Patrick, 2. 1470
MacSparran, James, 2. 1464
'MacStaff, Donald' (R. Hepburn), 2. 1369
McTaggart, John McTaggart Ellis, 4. 1272–3
McTear, Robert, 3. 1680
Macvine, John, 3. 1690
McWard, Robert, 2. 2035–6
Madan, Martin, 2. 1286
Madden, Sir Frederic, 3. 1659, 1694
Madden, Samuel, 2. 993
Maddick, George, 3. 1791
Maddison, Sir Ralph, 1. 2041
Maddoks, A. R., 4. 1387
Maddox, George, 3. 1828
Madge, Charles Henry, 4. 305–6, 1408
Madge, W. T., 3. 1812

Madox, Richard, 1. 2143
Madox, Thomas, 2. 1699
madrigals
    general, 1. 1339–60
    Italian, 1. 893–4.
    see also ballads and songs
Maeterlinck, Maurice, 3. 104
Maetzger, R., 3. 1193
Maffei, Francesco Scipione, 2. 1546, 190
Mag-pie, 4. 1384
Magaillans, Gabriel, 2. 1434
Magalhaes, Gabriel, 2. 1434
Magalotti, Lorenzo, 2. 1397
Magazin de l'Ile de Jersey, 2. 1389
Magazin de Londres, 2. 1299
Magazine (Cardiff 1885), 4. 1398
Magazine (Bangor 1915), 4. 1398
Magazine a la mode, 2. 1306
Magazine for the home, 3. 1840
Magazine for the young, 3. 1847
Magazine of ants, 2. 1351
Magazine of art illustrated, 3. 1852; 4. 1352
Magazine of female fashions, 2. 1312
Magazine of fiction, 3. 1852; 4. 1352
Magazine of fine arts, 4. 1358
Magazine of magazines (1750), 2. 1300
Magazine of magazines (1751), 2. 1380
Magazine of magazines (1758), 2. 1302
Magazine of natural history, 3. 1845
Magazine of the beau monde, 3. 1845
Magazine of the Buxton Literary Society, 4. 1364
Magazine of the future, 4. 1377
Magazine of the University College of North Wales, 4. 1398
Magazine of the Wesleyan Methodist Church, 3. 1840
Magazine of today, 4. 1369
Magazine of zoology and botany, 3. 1846
Magazine programme (Grand Theatre Swansea, 1906), 4. 848
Magazine programme (1924), 4. 826
magazines
    Restoration and eighteenth century
        Irish, 2. 1379–80
        London, 2. 1291–1312
        provinces, 2. 1349–52
        Scottish, 2. 1371–4
    nineteenth century, 3. 1839–84
        annuals, 3. 1873–8
        monthly, 3. 1839–54, 1859–63
        quarterly, 3. 1853–8, 1863–6
        school and university, 3. 1865–74
        year books, general, 3. 1877–8
            biography, 3. 1878–9
            commerce, 3. 1881–2

magazines (*cont.*)
        education, 3. 1880–1
        official, 3. 1879–80
        peerage, 3. 1879
        professions, 3. 1881
        religion, 3. 1880
        sport, 3. 1882
  twentieth century, 4. 1329–1408
    general, 4. 1329–32
    advertising, 4. 1341–4
    amateur, 4. 1379–88
    biography, 4. 1335–8
    detective, 4. 1389–92
    journalism, 4. 1337–40
    lists, 4, 1347–50
    literary, 4. 1349–80
    little, 4. 1335–6, 1349–50
    romance, 4. 1389–92
    science fiction, 4. 1389–92
    studies, 4. 1345–8
    university, 4. 1335–6, 1391–8
    see also annuals, newspapers, periodical essays
Magdalen College record, 4. 1397
Magdalen Hall, its library, 2. 306
Magdalene College magazine, 4. 1393
Magee, James, 3. 1806
Magee, John, 3. 1806
Magee, William Kirkpatrick, 4. 1357, 1394
Magee's weekly packet, 2. 1386
Magens, Nicholas, 2. 1898
Maggi, Carlo Maria, 2. 1546
magic
  Old English, 1. 333–4
  Renaissance to Restoration, 1. 2377–80
Magic and conjuring magazine, 2. 1311
Magic comic, 4. 820
Magician, 4. 859
Maginn, William, 3. 1293–4, 1772, 1793, 1845
Magnet (1837), 3. 1823
Magnet (*library*) (1908), 4. 819
Magnet (Bristol University), 4. 1392
Magnus, Olaus, 1. 2142
Magnus, Sir Philip, 3. 1746
Magpie (Belfast 1898), 4. 1404
Magpie (1911), 4. 1360
Magpie (1940), 4. 1393
Mahaffy, Sir John Pentland, 3. 1681, 1870
Mahon, Andrew, 2. 1562
Mahon, Philip Henry Stanhope, Viscount, 3. 1498
Mahony, Francis Sylvester, 3. 1390–1, 1772, 1845
Mahumetane of Turkish historie, 1. 2138
Maid Emlyn, 1. 1102
Maidment, James, 3. 1659–60
Maidstone, Richard, 1. 480

Maidstone and district day by day, 4. 850
Maidstone and district what's on, 4. 850
Maidstone day by day, 4. 850
Maidstone journal (1737), 2. 1360
Maidstone journal (1786), 2. 1361
Maidstone mercury, 2. 1360
Maier, Jakob, 2. 175
Maihows, Dr — (fl. 1763), 2. 1420
Mail (1868), 3. 1807; 4. 1399
Mail (Portsmouth 1895), 3. 1801
Mail and Waterford daily express, 3. 1806
Main, Mrs E. A. F., 3. 1709–10
Maine, Sir Henry James Sumner, 3. 1472–3
Maintenon, Françoise d'Aubigné, Marquise de, 2. 1520
Mainwaringe, M., 1. 2057
Mair, John (fl. 1791), 2. 1473
Mair, John (fl. 1936), 4. 1372
Mair, Robert Henry, 3. 1879
Mairet, Philip, 4. 1368, 1370
Maison Neuve, Etienne de, 1. 873, 2063
Maister Benet's Cristemasse game, 1. 740
Maistre, Joseph Marie de, 3. 104
Maitland, Edward F., 3. 1856
Maitland, Fredegond, 4. 342
Maitland, Frederick William, 3. 1481–2
Maitland, Sir John (d. 1595), 1. 2427
Maitland, John (nineteenth century), 3. 1795
Maitland, Julia Charlotte, 3. 1102
Maitland, Sir Richard, 1. 2427
Maitland, Samuel Roffey, 3. 1855
Maitland, William, 2. 1719
Maittaire, Michael, 2. 1831
Major, John, 1. 2451, 2130
Major, Thomas, 2. 1419
Makgill, James, 1. 2473
Makluire, John, 1. 2474
Makower, Stanley, 3. 1866
Malachy, 1. 793
Malcolm, Ian Zachary, 3. 1870
Malcolm, Sir John, 3. 1674
Maldon, Battle of, 1. 241–3
Male mag, 4. 1378
Malebranche, Nicolas, 2. 1520, 36, 95, 114
Malet, Harold E., 3. 1700
'Malet, Lucas' (Mary St Leger Harrison), 3. 1066
Malinowski, Bronislaw Kaspar, 4. 1190–1
Malkin, A. T., 3. 1857
Malkin, Benjamin Heath, 3. 1681
Mallarmé, Stéphane, 3. 104
Malleson, William Miles, 4. 966–7
Mallet, David, 2. 556–7, 178, 238, 1778
Mallet, Paul Henri, 2. 235
Malloch, David, 2. 556–7, 238, 1778

Mallock, William Hurrell, 3. 1066–7
Mallowan, Agatha Mary Clarissa, 4. 552–4
Malmesbury, James Edward Harris, 2nd Earl of, 3. 1714
Malone, Edmond, 2. 1758–61, 312
Malory, Sir Thomas, 1. 674–8
Malsachanus, 1. 353
Malthus, Thomas Robert, 3. 1294–5; 2. 1906
Malvern Festival, 4. 852
Malvern Theatre's monthly post, 4. 850, 852
Malvernian, 3. 1871
Malynes, Gerard de, 1. 2278
Man (1755), 2. 1281
Man (1915), 4. 1362
Man in the moon (1660), 2. 1315
Man in the moone (1649), 1. 2105
Man of fancy, 2. 1285
Man of pleasure, 2. 1284
Man of pleasure's song book, 2. 410
Man of the town, 2. 1287
Man's treachery to woman, 2. 342
Manager and stage business gazette, 4. 874
Managing printer, 4. 82
Manchester
  Renaissance to Restoration
    libraries, 1. 993
    printing and bookselling, 1. 966
  Restoration and eighteenth century
    libraries, 2. 308
    magazines, 2. 1351
    newspapers, 2. 1361–2
    periodical essays, 2. 1348
    printing and bookselling, 2. 268
  nineteenth century
    newspapers, 3. 1830
    university, 3. 1737
  twentieth century
    theatre, 4. 846
    university journalism, 4. 1396
Manchester and Liverpool museum, 2. 1351
Manchester chronicle (1762), 2. 1361
Manchester chronicle (1781), 2. 1361
Manchester courier, 3. 1796
Manchester daily telegraph, 3. 1794
Manchester daily times, 3. 1794
Manchester dramatic and musical review, 3. 1124
Manchester evening chronicle, 3. 1803; 4. 1404
Manchester evening mail, 3. 1799; 4. 1402
Manchester evening news (and chronicle), 3. 1798; 4. 1402
Manchester examiner, 3. 1795
Manchester express, 3. 1794
Manchester gazette (1730), 2. 1361
Manchester gazette (1795), 2. 1362
Manchester guardian, 3. 1795, 1830; 4. 1400, 1344

Manchester herald, 2. 1361
Manchester journal (1736), 2. 1361
Manchester journal (1754), 2. 1361
Manchester journal (1780), 2. 1361
Manchester literary and philosophical society memoirs, 2. 1351
Manchester magazine, 2. 1361
Manchester mercury, 2. 1361
Manchester news-letter, 2. 1361
Manchester playgoer (1910), 4. 849
Manchester playgoer (1925), 4. 850
Manchester quarterly, 4. 1352
Manchester Repertory Theatre magazine, 4. 851
Manchester songster, 2. 416
Manchester weekly courant, 2. 1361
Manchester weekly journal 2. 1361
Mancini, Dominic, 1. 805, 855
Mandelslo, Johann Albrecht von, 2. 1397, 1431, 1540
Mandeville, Bernard, 2. 1095–8, 109, 172, 207
Mandeville, Sir John, 1. 471–4, 2141
Mandragora, 4. 1393
Mandrake, 4. 1376, 1398
Mangan, James Clarence, 3. 1900–1
Manilius, 2. 1499
Mankind, 1. 1403–4
Mankowitz, Wolf, 4. 1378, 1394
Manley, John Jackson, 3. 1690, 1713
Manley, Mary de la Riviere, 2. 767, 148, 983, 985, 986, 987, 989
Manley, Thomas, 2. 1898
Mann, Horace, 3. 1723
Manner of the crying of a play, 1. 742
Manners, James R., 3. 1803
Manners, John Henry, 5th Duke of Rutland, 3. 1682
Mannheim, Karl, 4. 1191
Manning, Anne, 3. 947–8
Manning, Edward, 1. 1330
Manning, Francis, 2. 795
Manning, Frederic, 4. 652
Manning, Henry Edward, Cardinal, 3. 1631–2, 1823, 1856
Manning, M., 4. 854
Manning, Olivia, 4. 653
Manning, Owen, 2. 1796
Manning, Samuel, 3. 1843
Manning, William Oke, 3. 1733
Manning-Sanders, Ruth, 4. 802
Mannyng, Robert, of Brunne, 1. 465–6, 503–4
Mansel, Henry Longueville, 3. 1546–7, 1608
Mansel, Sir Robert, 1. 2078
'Mansfield, Katherine' (Kathleen Mansfield Beauchamp), 4. 653–9, 1360, 1361, 1362
Mansfield, Robert Blachford, 3. 1711

Manship, Henry, 1. 2134
Manson, James Bolivar, 3. 1804
Mant, Alicia Catherine, 3. 1100
Mant, Richard, 3. 390–1
Mante, Thomas, 2. 1469
Manton, Thomas, 2. 1612
Mantuanus (Baptista Spagnuoli), 1. 856, 2191, 2193; 2. 1549
Mantz, E. S., 3. 59
Mantz's cricket directory, 3. 1882
Manual of British and foreign brewery companies, 3. 1882
Manucci, Niccolao, 2. 1437
Manuche, Cosmo, 1. 1749
Manuel, Niklas, 1. 877
Manuel de péchés (ME version), 1. 504
Manufacturer, 2. 1325
Manuscript, 4. 1375
Manuscript magazine monthly, 4. 1387
manuscripts
   general catalogues, 1. 9–12
   Old English
      general, 1. 214–18
      Irish, 1. 214
      Latin, 1. 212–13
      runes, 1. 220–6
      studies, 1. 227–30
      Welsh, 1. 214
   Middle English
      general, 1. 218–20
      studies, 1. 369–76
   Renaissance to Restoration, 1. 929–34
   twentieth century, preparation of, 4. 66
   see also classical studies, scholarship
Manwaring, George (fl. 1607), 1. 2144
Manwaring, George (fl. 1860), 3. 1855
Manxmaid, 4. 1387
Manzolli, Pietro Angelo (Marcellus Palingenius), 1. 2190, 855
Manzoni, Alessandro, 3. 138
Map, Walter, 1. 783
Maples, John, 2. 1554
Mappa mundi (1536), 1. 2136
maps
   Renaissance to Restoration, 1. 954–5
   Restoration and eighteenth century, 2. 284
Marana, Giovanni Paolo, 2. 1546, 194, 981
Marauder, 3. 1867
Marbeck, John, 1. 1125
Marbres, John, 1. 788
March, J., 3. 1688
March, John, 1. 2036
March annual, 4. 1386
March of time, 4. 58
Marchant, Bessie, 3. 1105–6

Marchant, John, 2. 1021
Marckant, John, 1. 2071
Marcus Aurelius, 1. 2166; 2. 1489
Marcus, David, 4. 1377
Mardeley, John, 1. 1125
Marett, Robert Ranulph, 4. 1192
Margaret, St, 1. 326
Margaret of Scotland, St, 1. 1125
Marguerite de Valois (or d'Angoulême), Queen of Navarre, 1. 870, 873, 2063; 2. 1520, 141
Mariage of witte and science, 1. 1410
Marine intelligencer, 2. 1322
Marini, Giovanni Ambrogio, 2. 1546, 993
Marino, Giovanni Battista, 1. 894, 897; 2. 1546, 192
Marionette, 4. 1363
Marisco, Adam de, 1. 768
Marishall, Jean, 2. 1001
Mariti, Giovanni, 2. 1443
Marivaux, Pierre Carlet de Chamblain de, 2. 1520, 120, 141–2, 994, 996
Mark and Moody, 3. 59
Mark Lane express, 3. 1823, 1837
Markby, Thomas, 3. 1728
Market place, 4. 1388
Markham, Edward, 3. 1676
Markham, Gervase, 1. 2011–13, 1126, 2056, 2124
Markham, William Orlando, 3. 1826
Markland, George, 2. 1558
Markland, Jeremiah, 2. 1827
Marks, Ellen M., 4. 880
Marks, Harry H., 3. 1791
Marks, Terence, 4. 1375
'Markwell, Marmaduke', 3. 1712
Markwell, W. R. S., 3. 1152
Marlborough, vicar's library, 1. 993
Marlborough journal, 2. 1362
Marlburian, 3. 1871
Marlianus, Joannes Bartholomaeus, 1. 2138
Marlow, John, 4. 1368
'Marlow, Louis' (Louis Umfreville Wilkinson), 4. 659
Marlowe, Christopher, 1. 1443–56, 868, 1126, 1333
Marmion, Shakerley, 1. 1750, 1314
Marmontel, Jean François, 2. 1521, 120, 142, 1000, 1002, 1031
Marnau, Fred, 4. 1376
Marnix, Philips van, 1. 919
Marot, Clément, 1. 870
Marprelate controversy, 1. 1957–64
Marra, John, 2. 1479
Marriage broker, 1. 1760
Marriage of wit and wisdom, 1. 1410
Marriott, Charles, 3. 1632

Marriott, Sir John Arthur Ransome, 4. 1192–3
Marrow of complements, 1. 1010; 2. 335
Marryat, — (fl. 1836), 3. 1811
Marryat, Frederick, 3. 704–8, 1089, 1845
Marsden, Dora, 4. 1361
Marsden, Francis, 4. 1363
Marsden, John Buxton, 3. 1842
Marsden, Kate, 3. 1676
Marsden, William, 2. 1442
Marsh, A., 2. 979
Marsh, Adam, 1. 768
Marsh, Anne (later Marsh-Caldwell), 3. 948
Marsh, Edward, 4. 1361
Marsh, Herbert (1757–1839), 3. 1718
Marsh, Herbert (fl. 1895), 3. 1681
Marsh, Richard, 4. 1373
Marsh, T., 3. 1702
Marshall, — (fl. 1788), 2. 1802–3
Marshall, Mrs —, 3. 1101
Marshall, Archibald, 4. 789–90
Marshall, Emma, 3. 1094
Marshall, Francis, 3. 1701
Marshall, George, 1. 1126
Marshall, H. M., 3. 1877
Marshall, John, 2. 1432
Marshall, Joseph, 2. 1422
Marshall, Julian, 3. 1715
Marshall, Stephen, 1. 1995, 2088
Marshall, W., 3. 1877
Marshall, W. R., 4. 1365
Marshall's Christmas box, 3. 1877
Marsham, Sir John, 2. 1831
Marston, Edward, 3. 79, 1690
Marston, John, 1. 1689–94, 1126, 1334
Marston, John Westland, 3. 1152, 1849
Marston, Philip Bourke, 3. 637–8
Marston, Roger, 1. 781
Martel, Peter, 2. 1418
Martelli, C., 3. 1701
Martens, Friedrich, 2. 1483
Martial, 1. 2172; 2. 1499, 35
Martialis epigrammata selecta, 2. 378
Martin of Alnwick, 1. 793
Martin, Monsieur —, 2. 1567
Martin, Ann, 3. 1087
Martin, Benjamin, 2. 1300, 1906
Martin, Emma, 3. 1094
Martin, Frederick, 3. 1878
Martin, John, 3. 67
Martin, Martin, 2. 1398
Martin, N. Barnwall, 4. 1356
Martin, Robert Montgomery, 3. 1847
Martin, Samuel, 2. 669
Martin, Sarah Catherine, 3. 1106
Martin, Stephen, 2. 1395

Martin, Sir Theodore, 3. 537
Martin, Violet, 4. 739–40; 3. 1707
Martin, William, 3. 1089–90, 1878
Martin Burke's Connaught journal, 2. 1388
Martin nonsense his collections, 1. 2104
Martin's Bath chronicle, 2. 1353
Martindale, Cyril Charlie, 4. 1273–5
Martineau, Harriet, 3. 949–50, 1090, 1722, 1772
Martineau, James, 3. 1547–9, 1608, 1772, 1856
Martinelli, Fioravante, 1. 2141
Martinengo, Nestore, 1. 2137
'Martingale' (James White), 3. 1705, 1713
Martini, Martinus, 1. 2150
Martinus Anglicus, 1. 793
Martyn, Benjamin, 2. 795, 1462
Martyn, Edward, 3. 1939
Martyn, Henry, 3. 1617
Martyn, John, 2. 265, 1278, 1327
Martyn, Joseph, 1. 1336
Martyn, Thomas, 2. 1427
Martyrology (OE), 1. 326
Marvell, Andrew, 1. 1222–9; 2. 193
Marx, Enid, 4. 807
Mary Bull, 4. 1405
Mary Magdalene, St, 1. 1126
Mary the Blessed Virgin, 1. 1126
Mascall, Eric Lionel, 4. 1275
Mascardi, Agostino, 2. 1546
Mascot, 4. 1398
Mascot novelettes, 4. 1370
Mascot novels, 4. 1361
Masefield, John Edward, 4. 306–13, 793
Mask, 4. 1359
Maskell, Alfred, 3. 1858
Maskerpiece, 4. 880, 1365
Mason, Alexander Way, 3. 1880
Mason, Alfred Edward Woodley, 4. 660–1
Mason, F., 4. 1382
Mason, Francis, 1. 2298
Mason, G. Finch, 3. 1706
Mason, George (fl. 1618), 1. 1355
Mason, George (1735–1806), 2. 1784
Mason, Harold A., 4. 1370
Mason, J. (fl. 1873), editor of fairy tales, 3. 1108
Mason, J. (fl. 1876), compiler, 3. 1877, 1878
Mason, John (b. 1581), author of 'The Turke', 1. 1750
Mason, John (1586–1635), colonist, 1. 2162
Mason, John (fl. 1647), schoolmaster, 1. 1751
Mason, John (c. 1646–94), writer of hymns, 2. 478, 1018
Mason, John H., 4. 82
Mason, John Monck, 2. 1754
Mason, Philip, 4. 809
Mason, R. C., 4. 1388

Mason, Richard Oswald, 2. 1564
Mason, Sandys, 3. 1868
Mason, William (fl. 1621), 1. 2048
Mason, William (1725–97), 2. 669–71, 239
Mason, William, of Rotherhithe (fl. 1778), 2. 1784
Masonic miscellanies, 2. 424
masque, 1. 1368, 1370–1
Masque (1767), 2. 388
Masque (c. 1780), 2. 401
Masque, a theatre notebook, 4. 828
Masquerade (1798), 2. 1352
Masquerade (1933), 4. 1370
Masquerades, 2. 1006
Massey, Gerald, 3. 538
Massey, William, 2. 1774
Massi, Coustard de, 2. 1563
Massie, James William, 3. 1680
Massie, Joseph, 2. 312, 1898
Massillon, Jean Baptiste, 2. 1521, 95
Massinger, Philip, 1. 1703–9, 868, 869, 920; 2. 32
Massingham, Harold John, 4. 1321–2
Massingham, Henry William, 3. 1772, 1791, 1794
Masson, Charles François Philibert, 2. 1033
Masson, David, 3. 1391–2, 1821, 1849
Masson, Frédéric, 3. 1853
Master, William, 1. 2050
Master detective (1929), 4. 1389
Master detective (1950), 4. 1392
Master printer (1906), 4. 82
Master printer and newspaper owner, 3. 1759; 4. 1343
Master printers' annual, 4. 82
Masterman, Anne, 2. 1003
Masterman, Charles Frederick Gurney, 4. 1193–4; 3. 1866
Masters, Mary, 2. 557
Masters, Maxwell T., 3. 1827
Masters of literature, 4. 1360
'Mastiz, Marmaduke', 2. 1288
Masuccio, Salernitano, 1. 902
Mas'udi, Abul Hasan ibn Ali, 2. 1438
Matelief, Cornelis, 1. 919
Mathematical and philosophical repository, 2. 1310
Mathematical, geometrical and philosophical delights, 2. 1309
Mathematical magazine, 2. 1303
mathematics, Renaissance to Restoration, 1. 2349–54
Mather, Joseph, 2. 671
Mather, Richard, 1. 2159
Mathers, Helen Buckingham, 3. 1068
Matheson, Percy E., 3. 1868
Mathews, Mrs — (fl. 1789), 2. 1009

Mathews, Charles Edward, 3. 1710
Mathews, Charles James, 3. 1152–3
Mathews, T., 3. 1693
Mathewson, T., 3. 1701
Mathias, Roland, 4. 1376, 1379
Mathias, Thomas James, 2. 671–3, 240
Mathieson, Augustus, 3. 1842
Mathison, John, 3. 1880
Mathison, T., 2. 1569
Maton, William George, 2. 1407
Matrimonial magazine, 2. 1305
Matrimonial preceptor, 2. 1286
Matron, 2. 1285
Matson, G. J., 4. 73
Matthew, J. M., 2. 1443
Matthews, Dr — (fl. 1763), traveller, 2. 1420
Matthews, John, 2. 1451
Matthews, R., 4. 1382
Matthews, Walter Robert, 4. 1275–6
Matthison, Friedrich von, 2. 1431
Maturin, Charles Robert, 3. 746–7
Maty, Paul Henry, 2. 1307
Matz, Bertram W., 4. 1359
Maudslay, Athol, 3. 1700
Maudsley, Henry, 3. 1748
Maugham, Robin, 4. 1376
Maugham, William Somerset, 4. 661–8, 1357
Maunder, S., 3. 1696
Maundrell, Henry, 2. 1436
Maunsell, H., 3. 1806
Maupassant, Guy de, 3. 104–5
Maurelle, Francisco Antonio, 2. 1471
Maurice, John Frederick Denison, 3. 1392–3, 1608–9, 1722, 1745–6, 1819, 1821
Maury, Jean Siffrein, 2. 66
Mausoleum, 1. 1009
Maverick, Samuel, 1. 2166; 2. 1454
Mavor, Osborne Henry, 4. 914–17
Mavor, William Fordyce, 2. 1799, 1028, 1311, 1312, 1394, 1397
Mawer, John, 2. 1553
Mawman, Joseph, 3. 1682
'Maw-worm, Richard', 2. 1372
maxims, Renaissance books of, 1. 2029–32
Maxims I & II (OE), 1. 289–90
Maxse, Frederick Augustus, 3. 1728
Maxse, Leopold James, 3. 1852
Maxwell, Mrs — (fl. 1842), 3. 1876
Maxwell, G. M., 3. 1866
Maxwell, Sir Herbert Eustace, 3. 1690
Maxwell, James, 2. 1401
Maxwell, John (1590?–1647), 1. 2463
Maxwell, John (fl. 1708), 2. 1447
Maxwell, John (1824–95), 3. 1814, 1850
Maxwell, Mary Elizabeth, 3. 1039–40

Maxwell, Shaw, 3. 1820
Maxwell, William Babington, 4. 668–9
Maxwell, William Hamilton, 3. 747–8, 1683
May, Charles, 2. 1461
May, Derwent, 4. 1397
May, Phil, 3. 67, 1853
May, Thomas, 1. 1751, 2046, 2058, 2244
May, Sir Thomas Erskine, Baron Farnborough, 3. 1492–3
May annual, 4. 1386
May bee (1884), 3. 1866
May bee (1900), 4. 1396
May bee (1906), 4. 1393
May card, 4. 1394
May-Day, 2. 1026
Maydes metamorphosis, 1. 1471–2
Maydestone's penitential psalms, 1. 480
Mayer, J. W., 4. 1384
Mayer, Mildred, 4. 1387
Mayer, W. F., 4. 1386
Mayeres, Randulph, 1. 2128
Mayfair, 3. 1815
Mayfly, 3. 1871
Mayhew, Augustus Septimus, 3. 950–1, 1102
Mayhew, Henry, 3. 1393–4, 1790
Mayhew, Horace, 3. 1394
Maynard, John, 1. 1354
Maynarde, Thomas, 1. 2152
Mayne, Ethel Colburn, 4. 669
Mayne, Jasper, 1. 1751–2, 1995
Mayne, John, 2. 2028, 1376; 3. 1792
'Mayne, Rutherford' (Samuel Waddell), 3. 1941
Maynwaring, Arthur, 2. 1272, 1322
Maynwaring, Roger, 1. 1996
Mayo, Charles, 3. 1720, 1721
Mayo, Elizabeth, 3. 1721
Mayo, I. I. (John J.), 3. 1880
Mayo, Isabella, 3. 1104, 1772
Mayo, John, 2. 1907
Mayo, John Joseph, 3. 1880
Mayouwe, John, 2. 1907
Mayow, John, 2. 1907
Maze, Mary Ann, 2. 1024
Mazzella, Scipione, 1. 2142
Mazzini, Giuseppe, 3. 138
Mazzoni, Giacomo, 1. 889
Mead, George Robert Stow, 3. 1853; 4. 1352
Mead, Joseph, 1. 2296
Mead, Richard, 2. 1907
Mead, Robert, 1. 1771
Meade, Elizabeth Thomasina, 3. 1097
'Meade, L. T.' (Elizabeth Thomasina Meade), 3. 1097, 1852, 1853
Meades, Anne, 2. 1003

Meadowcourt, Richard, 2. 1775
'Meadows, Lindon' (C. B. Greatrex), 3. 1705
Meanderer, 4. 1385
'Meanwell, Miss Nancy' (Richard Johnson), 2. 1022
Meares, John, 2. 1481–2
Mearne, Samuel, 2. 291
Mease, Peter, 1. 1771
Mechanics' magazine, 3. 1827
Meddler (1744), 2. 1378
Meddler (1760), 2. 1282
Mede, Joseph, 1. 2296
media, mass, their relation to literature, 4. 53–60
Medical and chirurgical review, 2. 1310
Medical and philosophical commentaries, 2. 1372
Medical and physical journal, 2. 1312
Medical annual, 3. 1881
Medical commentaries, 2. 1372
Medical directory for Ireland, 3. 1881
Medical directory for Scotland, 3. 1881
Medical directory of Great Britain and Ireland, 3. 1881
Medical essays and observations, 2. 1371
Medical extracts, 2. 1311
Medical facts and observations, 2. 1306
Medical magazine, 2. 1305
Medical museum, 2. 1303
Medical spectator, 2. 1289
Medical times, 3. 1826
Medicina curiosa, 2. 1291
medicine
    Old English, 1. 333–4
    Renaissance to Restoration, 1. 2365–70
medieval drama, Middle English, 1. 719–42
medieval influences on Restoration and eighteenth century, 2. 231–50
medieval libraries, 1. 369–76
Medina, Pedro de, 1. 2188
Meditatio de passione domini (fourteenth century), 1. 516
Meditations on the supper of Our Lord (ME), 1. 504
Medley (1710), 2. 1272, 1322, 1382
Medley (March 1712), pbd Baker, 2. 1274, 1322
Medley (March 1712), pbd Baldwin, 2. 1274, 1322
Medley (May 1712), 2. 1274
Medley (August 1712), 2. 1274
Medley (1715), 2. 1275
Medley (Cork 1738), 2. 1388
Medley (1766), 2. 1284
Medley (1934), 4. 1371
Medulla poetarum romanorum, 2. 366
Medusa or penny politician, 3. 1818
Medwall, Henry, 1. 1405, 1412

Medwin, Thomas, 3. 1688
Meeke, Mary, 3. 748; 2. 1011
Méhégan, Guillaume Alexandre de, 2. 1521
Meier, Georg Friedrich, 2. 1540
Meikle, Andrew, 3. 1799
Meister, Jakob Heinrich, 2. 1408
Mela, Pomponius, 1. 2119
Melanchthon, Philipp, 1. 2189, 849, 877
Melbancke, Brian, 1. 2053
Meldola, David, 3. 1822
Melia's magazine, 4. 1352
Meliora, 3. 1857
Melissus, Paulus, 1. 856
Mellers, Wilfrid Howard, 4. 1370
Mello, Francisco Manuel de, 2. 200
'Melmoth, Courtney' (Samuel Jackson Pratt),
    2. 677–8, 1005, 1006, 1424
Melodious songster, 2. 408
Melodist or chearful songster, 2. 425
Melody (1931) National Poetry Circle, 4. 1369
Melody (1937), 4. 1386
Melpomene (1678), 2. 333
Melpomene (1753), 2. 377
Melrose's book post, 4. 107
Melusine, 1. 447–9
Melvill, Henry, 3. 1620
Melville, Andrew, 1. 2428, 2435–6
Melville, D., 3. 1727
Melville, Elizabeth, Lady Colville, 1. 2428
Melville, James, of Kilrenny (d. 1614), 1. 2428,
    2451
Melville, Sir James, of Halhill (d. 1617), 1. 2451
Memnon, 1. 2148
Mémoires littéraires, 2. 1314
memoirs
    Restoration and eighteenth century, 2. 1569–
        1600
    nineteenth century
        education, 3. 1751–6
        journalism, 3. 1761–78
        literary, 3. 19–26
    twentieth century
        literary, 4. 15–26
        publishing, 4. 93–5
    see also autobiography, letters
Memoirs for the curious, 2. 1293
Memoirs for the ingenious (1693), 2. 1292
Memoirs for the ingenious (1694), 2. 1292
Memoirs of a coquet, 2. 1001
Memoirs of a demi-rep of fashion, 2. 1005
Memoirs of an Oxford scholar, 2. 998
Memoirs of Charles I, 1. 2252
Memoirs of Charles Townly, 2. 1008
Memoirs of Dick, the little poney, 2. 1030
Memoirs of Lady Woodford, 2. 1003

Memoirs of literature, 2. 1294
Memoirs of love and gallantry, 2. 993
Memoirs of Sir Charles Goodville, 2. 997
Memoirs of the celebrated Miss Fanny M—, 2. 999
Memoirs of the Danby family, 2. 1029
Memoirs of the life and actions of Charles Osborne,
    2. 997
Memoirs of the life and actions of Cromwell, 2. 368
Memoirs of the life and writings of Pope, 2. 371
Memoirs of the life of Theophilus Keene, 2. 352
Memoirs of the Manstein family, 2. 1006
Memoirs of the noted Buckhorse, 2. 998, 1563
Memoirs of the present state of Europe, 2. 1292
Memoirs of the Shakespear's-Head, 2. 998
Memoirs of the society of Grub-street, 2. 366
Memorial des marchands, 2. 1318
Men and women of the time, 3. 1879
Men of the time, 3. 1879
Men only, 4. 1371
Menander, 2. 1492
Mendelssohn, Moses, 2. 1540, 157
Mendes Pinto, Fernao, 1. 2147
Mendez, Moses, 2. 673
Mendoza, Bernardino de, 1. 2189
Mendoza, Daniel, 2. 1563; 3. 1692
Menet, J., 3. 1727
Mennes, John, 1. 2028
Mennons, John, 3. 1804
Menologium, 1. 290
Mental amusement, 2. 424
Mental counsellor, 2. 1287
Mentet, Robert, 1. 2468, 2474
Mentieth de Salmonet, Robert, 1. 862
Mercantile chronicle, 3. 1807
Mercantile gazette, 3. 1794
Mercantile navy list, 3. 1880
Mercator, Gerard, 1. 2120
Mercator: or commerce retrieved, 2. 1345, 1898
Mercenary marriage, 2. 1004
Mercer, Cecil William, 4. 781
Mercer, William, 2. 1397
Merchant Taylors' School library, 2. 304
Merchants news letter, 2. 1321
Merchant's remembrancer, 2. 1316
Mercian texts, Old English, 1. 71
Mercier, Louis Sebastien, 2. 1521, 120, 1004,
    1431
Mercier du Paty, Charles M. J. B., 2. 1427
Mercure britannique, 2. 1338
Mercure de France (1775), 2. 1386
Mercure de France (1800), 2. 1312
Mercure historique, 2. 1300
Mercure scandale, 2. 1269
Mercurii, Scipione, 1. 889
Mercurio Volpone, 1. 2104

Mercurius &c. (1644), 1. 2100
Mercurius Academicus, 1. 2101, 2103
Mercurius Anglicus (1644), 1. 2100, 2104, 2107
Mercurius anglicus (1679), 2. 1317
Mercurius anglicus (1681), 2. 1318
Mercurius Anti-Britannicus, 1. 2101
Mercurius Anti-Melancholicus, 1. 2102
Mercurius Anti-Mercurius, 1. 2103
Mercurius Anti-Pragmaticus, 1. 2102
Mercurius Aquaticus, 1. 2104
Mercurius Aulico-Mastix, 1. 2100
Mercurius Aulicus, 1. 2097–8, 2103, 2104, 2106, 2109; 2. 1315
Mercurius Bellicus, 1. 2103
Mercurius Bellonius, 1. 2107
Mercurius bifrons, 2. 1340
Mercurius Britanicus, 1. 2098–9, 2102, 2103
Mercurius Britannicus (1652), 1. 2107
Mercurius Britannicus (1653), 1. 2108
Mercurius britannicus (Edinburgh 1659), 2. 1373
Mercurius britannicus (1690), 2. 1342
Mercurius britannicus (1692), 2. 1341
Mercurius Britannicus (1718), 2. 1294
Mercurius Brittanicus (1648–9), 1. 2103, 2105
Mercurius Caledonius (1660), 2. 1373
Mercurius Caledonius (1661), 2. 1315
Mercurius Cambro-Britannus, 1. 2099
Mercurius Candidus, 1. 2101, 2102
Mercurius Carolinus, 1. 2105
Mercurius Catholicus, 1. 2104
Mercurius Censorius, 1. 2103
Mercurius Cinicus, 1. 2108
Mercurius Civicus (1643), 1. 2098
Mercurius civicus (1660), 2. 1315
Mercurius civicus (1680), 2. 1317
Mercurius Clericus (24 Sept. 1647), 1. 2102
Mercurius Clericus (25 Sept. 1647), 1. 2102
Mercurius Critticus, 1. 2103
Mercurius Democritus (1652), 1. 2107, 2108, 2109
Mercurius democritus (1661), 2. 1315
Mercurius democritus in querpo, 2. 1315
Mercurius Diutinus, 1. 2101
Mercurius Dogmaticus, 1. 2103
Mercurius Domesticus, 1. 2103
Mercurius Elencticus, 1. 2102, 2105, 2106, 2107
Mercurius eruditorum, 2. 1292
Mercurius Fidelicus, 1. 2104
Mercurius Fumigosus (1654), 1. 2109
Mercurius fumigosus (1660), 2. 1315
Mercurius Gallicus, 1. 2103
Mercurius Heraclitus, 1. 2107
Mercurius hibernicus, 2. 1381
Mercurius Honestus (1648), 1. 2103
Mercurius honestus (1660), 2. 1315
Mercurius Hybernicus, 1. 2106

Mercurius Impartialis, 1. 2104
Mercurius infernus, 2. 1340
Mercurius Insanus Insanissimus, 1. 2103
Mercurius Jocosus, 1. 2109
Mercurius latinus, 2. 1332
Mercurius librarius (1668), 2. 1339
Mercurius librarius (1680), 2. 1291
Mercurius Mastix, 1. 2108
Mercurius Medicus, 1. 2102
Mercurius mediterraneus, 2. 1319
Mercurius Melancholicus, 1. 2102, 2104, 2105
Mercurius Militaris, 1. 2103, 2104, 2105
Mercurius Morbicus, 1. 2102
Mercurius musicus, 2. 341, 1293
Mercurius Nullus, 1. 2109
Mercurius Pacificus, 1. 2104, 2105
Mercurius phanaticus, 2. 1315
Mercurius Philo-Monarchicus, 1. 2105
Mercurius Phreneticus, 1. 2107
Mercurius Poeticus (1648), 1. 2103, 2109
Mercurius poeticus (1660), 2. 1315
Mercurius politicus (1650), 1. 2106; 2. 1313
Mercurius politicus (Edinburgh 1653), 2. 1373
Mercurius politicus (1660), 2. 1315
Mercurius politicus (1705), 2. 1269, 1321
Mercurius politicus (1716), 2. 1294
Mercurius Populus, 1. 2102
Mercurius Pragmaticus, 1. 2102, 2105, 2106, 2107, 2108, 2109, 2110; 2. 1315
Mercurius Psitacus, 1. 2104
Mercurius Publicus (1648), 1. 2103
Mercurius publicus (1660), 2. 1315
Mercurius publicus (Edinburgh 1660), 2. 1373
Mercurius publicus (1680), 2. 1317
Mercurius Republicus, 1. 2105
Mercurius reformatus (1689), 2. 1341
Mercurius reformatus (1690), 2. 1374
Mercurius reformatus (1691), 2. 1342
Mercurius Rhadamanthus, 1. 2108
Mercurius romanus, 2. 1344
Mercurius rusticans, 1. 1777
Mercurius Rusticus, 1. 2098, 2099, 2102
Mercurius Scommaticus, 1. 2107
Mercurius Scoticus, 1. 2104, 2107
Mercurius theologicus, 2. 1293
Mercurius Urbanicus, 1. 2103
Mercurius Urbanus, 1. 2099
Mercurius Vapulans, 1. 2103
Mercurius Verax, 1. 2105
Mercurius Veridicus (1644), 1. 2100, 2101, 2103
Mercurius veridicus (1660), 2. 1315
Mercurius veridicus (1681), 2. 1317
Mercurius Zeteticus, 1. 2107
'Mercury, Charles', 2. 1281
Mercury (1667), 2. 1316

Mercury (1678), 2. 1316
Mercury (1717), 2. 1370
Mercury: a review of the arts in Wessex, 4. 852
Mercury of England, 2. 1321
Mercy and righteousness (fifteenth century), 1. 688
Meredith, George, 3. 889–99, 113, 132–3, 139–40
Meredith, Gladys Mary, 4. 768–9
Meredith, Hal, 3. 1106
'Meredith, Owen' (Edward Robert Bulwer Lytton, 1st Earl of Lytton), 3. 636–7
Meres (printers), 2. 265
Meres, Francis, 1. 2030
Meres, John, 2. 1294
Merigot, J., 2. 1430
Mérimée, Prosper, 3. 105
Merin, John Baptist, 2. 1415
Meriton, Thomas, 1. 1752
Merivale, Charles, 3. 1493–4
Merivale, Herman Charles, 3. 1194
Merivale, John Herman, 3. 391
Merle, Gibbons, 3. 1772, 1791, 1792, 1817
Merlin, 1. 397–9, his *prophecy*, 1. 477
'Merlin the Second', 2. 1297
Merlin (poem by Lovelich), 1. 398
Merlin (prose version), 1. 399
Merlin: the weekly monitor, 2. 1342
Merlinus phanaticus, 2. 1315
Mermaid, 4. 1392
Mermaid or nautical songster, 2. 422
Merolla da Sorrento, Girolamo, 2. 1448
Merret(t), Christopher, 2. 1901, 1907
Merrick, James, 2. 673
Merrick, Leonard, 3. 1068–9
Merrick, Rice, 1. 2132
Merrick, William, 2. 1555
'Merriman, Henry Seton' (Hugh Stowell Scott), 3. 1069
Merriman, Nathaniel James, 3. 1670
'Merritt, Paul' (R. Maetzger), 3. 1193
Merriwell, Mark, 3. 1878
Merry, Robert, 2. 674
Merry and wise, 3. 1850
Merry-Andrew, 2. 1277
Merry companion (1739), 2. 367
Merry companion (1752), 2. 376
Merry companion (1772), 2. 393
Merry companion (1786), 2. 407
Merry devill of Edmonton, 1. 1760
Merry droll, 2. 389
Merry drollery, 2. 328
Merry England, 3. 1852
Merry fellow, 2. 377
Merry-go-round, 4. 820
Merry lad, 2. 377
Merry mag, 4. 1366

Merry man's companion, 2. 374
Merry medley, 2. 370
Merry mercury, 2. 1343
Merry minutes, 4. 1383
Merry mountebank, 2. 361
Merry musician, 2. 350
Merry quack doctor, 2. 399
Merry-thought, 2. 360
Merryn, A., 4. 828
Merseyside home journal, 4. 1367
Merseyside Unity Theatre: membership bulletin, 4. 851
'Merton, Ambrose' (W. J. Thoms), 3. 1108
Merveilles, Blaise François de Pagan, Comte de, 2. 1454
Mesens, E. L. T., 4. 1373
Mesopotamia amateur, 4. 1383
Meston, William, 2. 1976–7
Metamorphoses of the town, 2. 370
'Metaphoricus, A.' (W. Kenrick), 2. 1300
Metastasio, Pietro Antonio Domenico Bonaventura, 2. 1546–7, 190–1
Metcalfe, W. M., 4. 1352
Meteor, 3. 1871
Meteors, 2. 428, 1312
Metham, John, 1. 687
Methinks the poor town has been troubled too long, 2. 332
Methodism, general bibliography, 1. 21
Methodist, 3. 1823
Methodist magazine (1798), 2. 1306; 3. 1840
Methodist magazine (Leeds 1798), 2. 1350
Methodist monitor, 2. 1311, 1350
Methodist monthly, 3. 1846
Methodist recorder, 3. 1823; 4. 1401
Methodist times, 3. 1823
Methodist's journal, 2. 1330
Methuen, Sir Algernon, 3. 79
Metres of Boethius, 1. 290–1
Metrical charms (OE), 1. 291–2
Metrical epilogue to MS 41 CCCC, 1. 292
Metrical epilogue to the pastoral care, 1. 292
Metrical paraphrase of the Old Testament (ME), 1. 477–8
Metrical preface to Gregory's dialogues, 1. 292
Metrical preface to the pastoral care, 1. 292–3
Metro, 4. 1342, 1384
Metropolis, 4. 1388
Metropolitan: a monthly journal, 3. 1845
Metropolitan Conservative journal, 3. 1813
Metropolitan magazine, 3. 1845
Metropolitan nuncio, 1. 2105
Meulen, M., 4. 1378
Meun, Jean de, 1. 871
Mew, Charlotte Mary, 4. 313

Mewe, William, 1. 1771
Mexia, Pedro, 1. 2189, 908, 915–16, 2063
Meyer, Kuno, 3. 1894
Meynell, Alice, 3. 638–9
Meynell, G. T., 4. 82
Meynell, Laurence, 4. 806
Meynell, Viola, 4. 669–70
Meynell, Wilfrid, 3. 1823, 1852
Meyrick, Frederick, 3. 1622
Meyrick, Henry Howard, 3. 1670
Meysey-Wigley, Caroline, 3. 922–3
Miall, Edward, 3. 1772, 1822
Micanzio, Fulgentio, 1. 889; 2. 1547
Michael of Cornwall, 1. 776
Michaelson, John, 1. 2463
Michel of Northgate, Dan, 1. 502
Michelangelo, 1. 894
Michele, C. E., 3. 1789
Michelet, Jules, 3. 105
Michell, E. B., 3. 1701
Michell, John, 2. 1907
Michie, James, 4. 1397
Mickey Mouse weekly, 4. 820
Mickiewicz, Adam Bernard, 3. 153
Mickle, William Julius, 2. 674–5
Microcosm (1757), 2. 1282
Microcosm (1786), 2. 1350, 1352; 3. 1870
Microcosm (Leeds 1915), 4. 1362
Microcosmus, 1. 1777
Microdoc, 4. 118
Microscope: or minute observer, 2. 1380
Mid-day, 4. 1377, 1398
Middle English, 1. 357–806
  anthologies, 1. 381–4, 651–3, 679–82, 721–2, 745–6
  ballads, 1. 711–20
  Bible, 1. 477–82
  bibliography, general, 1. 357–8
  Chaucer, 1. 557–628
  Chaucerians
    English, 1. 639–5
    pseudo, 1. 652
    Scottish, 1. 651–64
  chronicles, 1. 459–68
  drama, 1. 719–42
    general, 1. 719–22
    Anglo-Norman, 1. 725–8
    Cornish and Welsh, 1. 727–8
    folk, 1. 741–2
    liturgical, 1. 721–6
    mystery and miracle, 1. 727–40
    spectacles, 1. 739–42
  education, 1. 627–40
  fifteenth century prose and verse, 1. 663–98
  history, 1. 357–68

  language, 1. 75–90
    dialects, 1. 78–9
    dictionaries, 1. 56
    syntax, 1. 121–6
    vocabulary, 1. 153–6
  Latin, 1. 743–806
    anthologies, 1. 745–6
    Anglo-Norman, 1. 751–60
    fifteenth century, 1. 801–6
    fourteenth century, 1. 785–802
    Plantagenet, 1. 759–68
    thirteenth century, 1. 767–84
  literary history, 1. 375–82
  lyrics and songs, 1. 697–712
  manuscripts, 1. 218–20, 369–76
  prophecies, 1. 473–8
  prosody, 1. 37–8
  religious writings, 1. 495–524
  romances, 1. 383–454
  Scottish poets, 1. 651–64
  sermons, 1. 481–90
  tales, 1. 455–60
  travel, 1. 467–74
Middle Temple, play at, 1. 1771
Middlesex chronicle, 3. 1832
Middlesex journal, 2. 1334
Middleton, Christopher (d. 1628), 1. 1127, 2054
Middleton, Christopher (d. 1770), 2. 1484
Middleton, Conyers, 2. 1711, 1328, 1827
Middleton, E. E., 3. 1716
Middleton, Erasmus, 2. 1805
Middleton, Richard (fl. 1283), 1. 777
Middleton, Richard (fl. 1608), 1. 1335
Middleton, Richard Barham, 4. 670
Middleton, Thomas, 1. 1646–54, 1127, 1335, 1771, 2027, 2035, 2074, 2145
Middleton, Thomas Fanshaw, 2. 1348; 3. 1841
Midget magazine, 4. 1383
Midget mail, 4. 1385
Midland amusements, 4. 848
Midland counties evening express, 3. 1799, 1831
Midland daily telegraph, 3. 1802
Midland echo (Wolverhampton 1879), 3. 1800
Midland echo (Birmingham 1883), 3. 1801
Midland evening news, 3. 1801
Midland express, 4. 1404
Midland mercury, 2. 1362
Midland prose psalter, 1. 479
Midlander, 4. 850, 1406
Midnight oil, 4. 1386
Midsummer holydays, 2. 1026
Midwife, 2. 1279, 1300
Midwinter, John, 1. 687
Miège, Guy, 2. 1410
Mierdman, Stephen, 1. 963

Miers, John, 3. 1674
Mifflin, Benjamin, 2. 1467
Mildmay, Sir William, 2. 1898
Mildred, St, 1. 326
Miles, Hamish, 4. 1368, 1371
Miles, Henry Downes, 3. 1692, 1882
Milford, John, 3. 1677
Military actions of Europe, 1. 2101
Military magazine, 2. 1310
Military obituary, 3. 1879
Military register, 3. 1826
Military scribe, 1. 2100
Milkmaid, 3. 1108
Mill, Humphrey, 1. 1314
Mill, James, 3. 1549–51, 1718–19, 1842
Mill, John, 2. 1864–5
Mill, John Stuart, 3. 1551–76, 113, 1609, 1733, 1747, 1772, 1855, 1856
Millais, Sir John Everett, 3. 67
Millais, John Guille, 3. 1714
Millar, John, 2. 2055
Millar, Ronald, 4. 967
Millar, Vera, 4. 1364
Millard, John, 2. 1421
Millard, Lionel, 4. 826
Miller, A., 3. 1869
Miller, Anne, Lady, 2. 675, 1423
Miller, Edward Darley, 3. 1711
Miller, Henry, 4. 1372
Miller, Hugh, 3. 1395–6, 1609, 1772, 1822
Miller, James, 2. 795–6, 178
Miller, Johann Martin, 2. 1540, 181
Miller, John, 2. 1457
Miller, John Cale, 3. 1725
Miller, Leonard, 3. 1068–9
Miller, Lydia Falconer, 3. 1102
Miller, M. 3. 1846
Miller, Robert Kalley, 3. 1865
Miller, Thomas, 3. 538
Miller, W. H., 3. 1848
Miller, William, 3. 539
Miller of Abington, 1. 1127
Millett, Nigel, 4. 687
Millgate and playgoer, 4. 824, 1357
Millgate monthly, 4. 824, 1357
Milliken, Edwin James, 3. 1698
Milliken, Richard Alfred, 3. 1899, 2. 1380
Million, 4. 1376
Mills, Clifford, 4. 800
Mills, John (d. 1784?), 2. 1554
Mills, John (d.c. 1885), 3. 951
Milman, Henry Hart, 3. 1459–60
Milne, Alan Alexander, 4. 671–3, 796
Milne, Marjorie Bruce, 4. 1377
Milner, Mrs —, 3. 1877

Milner, Henry M., 3. 1133–4
Milner, Isaac, 2. 1907
Milner, John, 2. 1847
Milner, Joseph, 3. 1617
Milnes, Richard Monckton, 1st Baron Houghton, 3. 539, 1727
Milton, Frances, 3. 769–70
Milton, John, 1. 1237–96, 854, 865, 1909, 2092, 2106, 2141, 2275, 2276, 2317–18, 2341–2; 2. 32–3, 109, 127, 133–4, 169–70, 193, 199, 200, 207, 212, 213, 217, 319, 1412
Milton magazine, 3. 1868
Minadoi, Giovanni Tommaso, 1. 2189, 889, 2147
Mind, 3. 1858
Mine, 4. 820
Mine host, 4. 1355
Miner (and workmen's advocate) 3. 1820
Miners' advocate, 3. 1820
Miner's weekly news, 3. 1820
Minerva, 4. 1388
Minerva magazine of knowledge, 2. 1379–80
Miniature, 3. 1870
Miniature news journal, 4. 1381
Mini-cinema, 4. 58
Minifie, Margaret, 2. 1001
Minifie, Susannah, 2. 1001
Mining journal, 3. 1827
Minor poets (1751), 2. 375
Minor's pocket-book, 2. 1029
Minot, Laurence, 1. 710
Minstrel, 2. 1010
Minstrell, 2. 401
minstrelsy, Middle English, 1. 739–42
Mint, 4. 1377
Minto, William, 3. 1446–7, 1809
Mintoft magazine, 4. 1382
Minutes of several conversations between the Methodist Ministers, 3. 1880
Mirabeau, Honoré Gabriel de Riquetti, Comte de, 2. 1521–2, 1405
miracle plays, Middle English, 1. 727–40
Miracles of Mary, 1. 459–60
Miraculum Beatae Mariae, 1. 516
Mirk, John, 1. 488, 497, 687, 692, 804
Mirror (Dublin 1750), 2. 1385
Mirror (1757), 2. 1282
Mirror (Edinburgh 1779), 2. 1371
Mirror for magistrates, A, 1. 1024–5
Mirror of literature, amusement and instruction, 3. 1816
Mirror of simple souls, 1. 516–17
Mirror of the times, 2. 1338; 3. 1812
Mirrour (1719), 2. 1276
Mirrour (1730), 2. 1294
Mirrur, 1. 489

Mirth and glee, 2. 403
Mirth diverts all care, 2. 345
Mirth's magazine, 2. 388
Miscellanea (1694), 2. 339
Miscellanea (1727), 2. 357
Miscellanea aurea, 2. 353
Miscellanea curiosa (journal), 2. 363, 1352
Miscellanea curiosa (travels), 2. 1391
Miscellanea curiosa mathematica, 2. 1346
Miscellanea nova et curiosa, 2. 373
Miscellanea sacra (1696), 2. 339
Miscellanea sacra (1705), 2. 343
Miscellanea sacra (1797), 2. 1350
Miscellaneæ curiosæ, 2. 363, 1352
Miscellaneous and fugitive pieces, 2. 394
Miscellaneous antiquities, 2. 1306
Miscellaneous collection of poems, songs and epigrams, A, 2. 354
Miscellaneous collection of songs, ballads and elegies, A, 2. 422
Miscellaneous collection of the best English and Irish songs, A, 2. 413
Miscellaneous correspondence, 2. 1298
Miscellaneous extracts, chiefly poetical, 2. 416
Miscellaneous letters and essays (1694), 2. 339
Miscellaneous letters giving an account of the works of the learned, 2. 1292
Miscellaneous observations upon authors, 2. 1295
Miscellaneous pieces consisting of select poetry, 2. 376
Miscellaneous pieces in prose and verse, 2. 386
Miscellaneous pieces of poetry, 2. 386
Miscellaneous pieces, original and collected, by a clergyman, 2. 408
Miscellaneous poems (1772), 2. 393
Miscellaneous poems (Manchester c. 1790), 2. 413
Miscellaneous poems and translations (1712), 2. 347
Miscellaneous poems and translations (1726), 2. 356
Miscellaneous poems by several hands (1726), 2. 356
Miscellaneous poems by several hands . . . publish'd by Ralph (1729), 2. 358
Miscellaneous poems on several occasions, by Dawson, 2. 364
Miscellaneous poems on state-affairs, 2. 351
Miscellaneous poems, original and translated, 2. 355
Miscellaneous poetical novels, 2. 343
Miscellaneous tracts, 2. 377
Miscellaneous works (of Prior), 2. 367
Miscellaneous works of Rochester and Roscommon, 2. 344

Miscellaneous works written by. . .Buckingham, 2. 343
miscellanies
    Renaissance to Restoration, 1. 1007–14
    Restoration and eighteenth century periodicals, 2. 1291–1312, 1349–52, 1371–4, 1379–80
    poetry, 2. 327–436
    see also anthologies and bibliographies
Miscellanies by Swift, Arbuthnot, Pope and Gay, 2. 416
Miscellanies in prose and verse (1721), 2. 354
Miscellanies in prose and verse (edited Addison 1725), 2. 355
Miscellanies in prose and verse (1785), 2. 406
Miscellanies in prose and verse (Edinburgh 1791), 2. 415
Miscellanies in prose and verse...by Swift and Pope (1728), 2. 358
Miscellanies, moral and instructive, 2. 408
Miscellanies over claret (1697–8), 2. 340
Miscellanies over claret (1697), edited Pittis, 2. 1292
Miscellanies: the last volume, 2. 357
Miscellanies, written by Jonathan Swift, 2. 354
Miscellany (1685), 2. 335
Miscellany (1711), 2. 1274
Miscellany (1732), 2. 1278, 1327
Miscellany, A. (1753), 2. 377
Miscellany (1768), 2. 1284
Miscellany numbers, 2. 1375
Miscellany of ingenious thoughts, A, 2. 354
Miscellany of lyric poems, A, 2. 368
Miscellany of new poems, A, (1736), 2. 365
Miscellany of original poems, 2. 362
Miscellany of poems by several hands, A, 2. 360
Miscellany poems and translations by Oxford hands, 2. 335
Miscellany poems by Pope, 2. 356
Miscellany poems, by the most eminent hands, 2. 335
Miscellany poems upon several occasions, 2. 338
Miscellany poems; with the cure of love, 2. 340
Misogonus, 1. 1420
Miss Catley and Miss Weiwitzer's new London and Dublin songbook, 2. 391
Missionary magazine, 2. 1373
Missionary register, 3. 1880
Misson, François, 2. 986
Misson, Maximilian, 2. 1413
Misson de Valbourg, Henri, 2. 1399
Missy, César de, 2. 1306
Mist's weekly journal, 2. 1323
Mister, Mary, 3. 1101
Mr Henry Purcell's favourite songs, 2. 355

Mr Mathew's comic annual, 3. 1874
Mr Peters report from the army, 1. 2101
Mr Pope's literary correspondence, 2. 364
Mr Punch's limerick book, 4. 1371
Mr Redhead Yorke's weekly political review, 3. 1817
Mrs Bull, 4. 1405
Mrs Crouch's favourite pocket companion, 2. 411
Mrs Lovechild's golden present, 2. 1021
Mrs Norton's story book, 2. 1026
Mrs Pilkington's jests, 2. 380
Mitchel, John, 3. 1773
Mitchell, — (fl. 1861), 3. 1804
Mitchell, — (Mrs Ives Hurry), 2. 1027; 3. 1099
Mitchell, A. E., 4. 1383
Mitchell, Adrian, 4. 1397
Mitchell, Charles, 3. 1758
Mitchell, James Leslie, 4. 588–9
Mitchell, John, 2. 2067
Mitchell, Joseph (d. 1738), 2. 558
Mitchell, Joseph (fl. 1844–54), 3. 1822
Mitchell, W. (fl. 1734), 2. 1562
Mitchell, William, 3. 1793
Mitchell, William Andrew, 3. 1844
Mitchell's Sunday London gazette, 2. 1337
Mitchison, Naomi Mary Margaret, 4. 673–4, 803
Mitford, John (1781–1859), poet: 3. 391, 1839
Mitford, John (1782–1831) humourist, 3. 1825
Mitford, Mary Russell, 3. 748–50, 1696, 1773, 1875
Mitford, Nancy Freeman, 4. 674
Mitford, William, 2. 1739
Mitre and crown, 2. 1299
Mnemonic poem on usury, 1. 514
Moberly, George, 3. 1732
mock-heroic, Restoration and eighteenth century genre, 2. 317
Mock-press, 2. 1341
Mock songs and joking poems, 2. 332
Mocquet, John, 2. 1395, 1434
Model stage, 4. 860
Modena, Leon, 1. 2141; 2. 1547
Moderate communicating martial affaires, 1. 2104
Moderate informer, 1. 2110
Moderate intelligence, 1. 2105
Moderate intelligencer (1645), 1. 2101, 2105, 2108
Moderate intelligencer (1682), 2. 1318
Moderate Mercury, 1. 2105
Moderate messenger, 1. 2101, 2102, 2105, 2108
Moderate occurrences, 1. 2108
Moderate publisher, 1. 2106, 2108
Moderator (1692), 2. 1342
Moderator (1705), 2. 1344
Moderator (1710), 2. 1271, 1322
Moderator (1719), 2. 1276

Moderator (1721), 2. 1325
Moderator (1757), 2. 1375
Moderator (1763), 2. 1284
Modern advertising, 3. 1758; 4. 1342
Modern authors, 3. 1851
Modern beauties in prose and verse, 2. 418
Modern boy, 4. 820
Modern catch-club, 2. 391
Modern characters illustrated by histories in real life, 2. 997
Modern dance, 4. 827, 860
modern English, linguistic studies
    dictionaries, 1. 53–4
    language, 1. 89–112
    prosody, 1. 39–52
    syntax, 1. 127–42
    vocabulary, 1. 157–64
Modern fine gentleman, 2. 1004
Modern first editions, 4. 110
Modern Freemason's pocket book, 2. 395
Modern gladiator, 4. 1385
Modern history, 2. 1291
Modern husbandman, 2. 1298
Modern intelligencer, 1. 2107
Modern journalist, 4. 1381
Modern literary course, 4. 1367
Modern lithographer, 4. 82
Modern magazine (Liverpool 1909), 4. 1359
Modern magazine (1928), 4. 1385
Modern miscellany, 2. 370
Modern monitor, 2. 1380
Modern musick-master, 2. 359
Modern poems, 2. 397
Modern poets (1892), 3. 1851
Modern poets (1945), 4. 1377
Modern publicity, 4. 1343
Modern quarterly, 4. 1377
Modern reading, 4. 1375
Modern review, 3. 1858
Modern Scot, 4. 1369
Modern songster, 2. 413
Modern story magazine, 4. 1378
Modern syren, 2. 402
Modern thought, 3. 1852
Modern traveller (1776–7), 2. 1393
Modern traveller (1800), 2. 1445
Modern view of such parts of Europe . . . of great transactions, A, 2. 1412
Moderne intelligencer, 1. 2102
modernism, nineteenth century, 3. 177–8
Modest narrative of intelligence, A, 1. 2105
Moe, Joergen, 3. 146, 1109
Moeser, Justus, 2. 1540
Moestissimae ac laetissimae academiae cantabrigiensis affectus, 2. 335

Moffat, D., 3. 1698
Moffat, John Smith, 3. 1671
Moffat, Mary, 3. 1669
Moffat, Robert, 3. 1669
Moffatt, James, 4. 1276–7
Moffet, Thomas, 1. 1127
Mogridge, George, 3. 1089
Mohawk minstrels' annual, 4. 859
Mohawk minstrels' 'nigger' dramas, 4. 859
Moir, David Macbeth, 3. 750–1
Moir, John M., 3. 1816
Moivre, Abraham de, 2. 1904
Molesworth, Mary Louisa, 3. 1094–5, 1110
Molesworth, Robert, 1st Viscount, 2. 1692, 1276, 1413
Molesworth, William, 3. 1855, 1856
Molière, Jean Baptiste Poquelin de, 2. 1522–4, 36–7, 120–3
Molina, Antonio de, 1. 909
'Molina, Tirso de' (G. Téllez), 1. 910
Moll, Herman, 2. 1400
Mollineux, Mary, 2. 478
Molloy, Charles, 2. 796
Molyneux, T. 2. 1399
Molyneux, William, 2. 1847–8
Momerie, Alfred Williams, 3. 1613
Momus (1772), 2. 1285
Momus (Cambridge, 1866), 3. 1865
Momus's cabinet of amusement, 2. 428
Momus ridens, 2. 1342
Monardes, Nicholas, 1. 2161
Monboddo, James Burnett, Lord, 2. 1887
Monckton, Sir Philip, 1. 2252
Monconys, Balthasar de, 2. 1900
Moncrief, — (fl. 1759), 2. 1466
Moncrieff, Ann Scott, 4. 811
Moncrieff, Sir Colin Scott, 3. 1868; 4. 1396
'Moncrieff, William Thomas' (William Thomas Thomas), 3. 1134–5
Moncrif, François Augustin Paradis de, 2. 988
Monetary times and bankers' circular, 3. 1824
Monethly account, 2. 1291
Money market review, 3. 1824
Monget, M., 3. 1099
Monier-Williams, Montagu S. F., 3. 1714
Monier-Williams, Stanley F., 3. 1714
Monings, Edward, 1. 2078
Monipennie, John, 1. 2133
Monitor (1713), 2. 1274
Monitor (1714), 2. 1275
Monitor (1724), 2. 1277
Monitor (1727), 2. 1326
Monitor (1755), 2. 1281, 1332
Monitor (1767), 2. 1284, 1334
Monitor (1790), 2. 1349

Monitor (1800), 2. 1380
Monk, Mary, 2. 558
Monk Bretton Priory library, 1. 993
Monkhouse, Alan Noble, 4. 968
Monkhouse, Patrick, 4. 1397
Monmouth, Robert Carey, 1st Earl of, 1. 2247
Monologue, 4. 1371
Monotype news letter, 4. 82
Monotype recorder, 4. 82
Monro, A., 4. 1361
Monro, Alexander, 2. 2036
Monro, Sir Donald, 1. 2131
Monro, Edward, 3. 1620
Monro, Harold Edward, 4. 313–14, 825, 1359, 1361, 1364
Monro, Robert, 1. 2248, 2128
Monro, Thomas, 2. 1307
Monsarrat, Nicholas John Turney, 4. 674–5
Monsell, Elinor Mary, 4. 792
Monsieur, Adrienne, 4. 1367
Monson, Sir William, 1. 2238–9, 2127
Monstrous droll songs, 2. 422
Monstrous good songs, 2. 418
Monstrous magazine, 2. 1379
Montagu, Charles, 1st Earl of Halifax, 2. 476
Montagu, Edward, 1st Earl of Sandwich, 2. 1409
Montagu, Elizabeth, 2. 1597–8
Montagu, George, 2. 1561
Montagu, John, 4th Earl of Sandwich, 2. 1418, 1431
Montagu, Lady Mary Wortley, 2. 1584–5, 86, 1279, 1329
Montagu, Ralph, 1st Duke of, 2. 1416
Montagu, Richard, 1. 1997, 2297, 2298, 2299
Montagu, Samuel, 3. 1822
Montagu, Walter, 1. 1752, 2050
Montague, Charles Edward, 4. 675–6; 3. 1773
Montaigne, Michel de, 1. 2189, 863–4; 2. 1524, 37, 95
Montalba, Anthony, 3. 1108
Montalvo, Garci Gutierrez de, 1. 912
Montanus, Arnoldus, 2. 1431–2
Montauban, —, Sieur de, 2. 1447
Montchrestien, Antoine de, 1. 868
Montefiore, Claude Joseph Goldsmid, 3. 1614, 1858
Montefiore, Joshua, 2. 1452
Monteith, Lionel, 4. 1379
Monteith, Robert, 1. 2468, 2474
Montemayor, Jorge de, 1. 2189, 912
Montenay, Georgette de, 1. 1329
Montesquieu, Charles de Secondat, Baron de, 2. 1524–5, 37, 67, 86, 95–6, 989
Montfaucon, Bernard de, 2. 1416
Montfaucon de Villars, Nicolas de, 2. 979

Montgomerie, Alexander, 1. 2428–9, 1907
Montgomery, Bertram, 3. 1868
Montgomery, Florence, 3. 1095
Montgomery, James, 3. 392–3, 1720, 1773
Montgomery, Jemima, 3. 968
Montgomery, Robert, 3. 539–40
Month, 3. 1850, 1862; 4. 1351
Month's tour in North Wales, A, 2. 1404
Monthly account, 1. 2101
Monthly account of the land-bank, 2. 1342
Monthly account of the present state of affairs, 2. 1293
Monthly advertiser, 4. 1382
Monthly alphabetical film record, 4. 56
Monthly amusement, 2. 1293
Monthly and critical review, 2. 1301
Monthly army list, 3. 1879
Monthly banquet of Apollo, 2. 422
Monthly beauties, 2. 1309
Monthly catalogue (1714), 2. 1345
Monthly catalogue (1723), 2. 1346
Monthly chapbook, 4. 1364
Monthly chronicle (1728), 2. 1294
Monthly chronicle (1838), 3. 1846
Monthly collection of songs, 2. 356
Monthly collector of elegant anecdotes, 2. 1312
Monthly communications, 2. 1310
Monthly criterion, 4. 1365
Monthly epitome . . . of new publications, 2. 1311, 1346
Monthly extracts, 2. 1309
Monthly film record, 4. 56
Monthly guide, 4. 117
Monthly guide to periodical literature, 4. 1343
Monthly intelligencer, 2. 1315
Monthly intelligencer relating the affairs of . . . Quakers, A, 2. 1315
Monthly journal of the affairs of Europe, 2. 1293
Monthly ledger, 2. 1305
Monthly literary advertiser, 3. 81
Monthly London journal, 2. 1294
Monthly magazine (1796), 2. 1311; 3. 1841, 1860
Monthly magazine (Chelmsford 1800), 2. 1350
Monthly magazine of fiction, 3. 1852; 4. 1352
Monthly masks of vocal musick, 2. 342, 1293
Monthly masque, 2. 379
Monthly melody, 2. 1303
Monthly midget, 4. 1381
Monthly mirror, 2. 1310
Monthly miscellany (1707), 2. 1293
Monthly miscellany (1734), 2. 1350
Monthly miscellany (1774), 2. 1305
Monthly miscellany (Cork 1796), 2. 1380
Monthly museum, 2. 1306
Monthly notes of the Library Association, 3. 90

Monthly packet of advice from Parnassus, 2. 1294
Monthly packet of evening readings, 3. 1848
Monthly part of the English catalogue of books, 3. 84
Monthly preceptor, 2. 1030, 1312
Monthly record of eminent men, 3. 1853
Monthly record of literature, 2. 1304
Monthly recorder of all true occurrences, 2. 1318
Monthly register, 2. 1293
Monthly register of experiments, 2. 1294
Monthly register of literature, 2. 1309
Monthly remembrancer, 2. 1295
Monthly repository, 3. 1843, 1860
Monthly review (1749), 2. 1299; 3. 1839, 1859
Monthly review (1900), 3. 1854; 4. 1355
Monthly visitor, 2. 1311
Monthly weather-paper (1705), 2. 1344
Monthly weather-paper (1711), 2. 1345
Montolieu, Jeanne Isabelle, Baronne de, 2. 1008
Montresor, James, 2. 1466
Montresor, John, 2. 1466
Montreux, Nicolas de, 1. 873, 2063
Montrose, James Graham, 1st Marquis of, 1. 2436
Mont-Sacré, Ollenix (N. de Montreux), 1. 873
Monumenta anglicana, 2. 351
Monumenta Westmonasteriensia, 2. 334
Moody, Catherine Grace Frances, 3. 726–8
Moody, George, 3. 1847
Moon, George Washington, 3. 1879
Moone, Peter, 1. 1127
Moonshine, 3. 1825, 1838; 4. 1352
Moor, Edward, 2. 1444
Moor, James, 2. 2067
Moorcroft, William, 2. 1555
Moore, A. W., 3. 1709
Moore, Alexander Leys, 3. 1789
Moore, Andrew, 1. 2142
Moore, Arthur, 4. 1354
Moore, Edward (1712–57), 2. 558–9, 127, 178, 208, 1281
Moore, Edward (fl. 1793), 2. 1429
Moore, Frances, 2. 1013
Moore, Francis, 2. 1449, 1463
Moore, Frank Frankfort, 3. 1773
Moore, Geoffrey, 4. 1394
Moore, George, 3. 1014–19, 113–14, 133
Moore, George Edward, 4. 1277–8
Moore, H. G., 4. 1385, 1386, 1387
Moore, Henry, 3. 1881
Moore, J. C., 4. 57
Moore, John (d. 1657), 1. 1996, 2277
Moore, John (1729–1802), 2. 148, 1008, 1012, 1014, 1425
Moore, John Hamilton, 2. 1393

Moore, Sir John Henry, 2. 675
Moore, Sir Jonas, 2. 1557
Moore, L. G., 4. 1386, 1387
Moore, Mordaunt, 2. 1396
Moore, Nicholas, 4. 314–15, 1373, 1376, 1394
Moore, Reginald, 4. 1375, 1376
Moore, Sturge, 4. 315–16
Moore, Thomas, 3. 263–7, 113, 156, 1692
Moore, Thomas Sturge, 4. 315–16
Moore, William, 2. 1284, 1285
Moorehead, Alan McCrae, 4. 1194–5
Moorhead, Ethel, 4. 1367
Moraes, Francisco de, 1. 913
Moral amusement, 2. 1028
Moral and entertaining magazine, 2. 1306
Moral and instructive tales for…young ladies, 2. 1026
Moral and political magazine, 2. 1311
Moral instructions of a father, 2. 395
Moral instructor, 2. 421
Moral miscellany, 2. 380, 1021
Moral reflector, 2. 1288
Moral sketches, 2. 1288
Moral tales, 2. 1288
Moral world, 3. 1819
Moraley, William, 2. 1462
Moralist (1746), 2. 1279
Moralist (1772), 2. 1285
Moralist (1790), 2. 1288
Moralist (1792), 2. 1289
moralities, Renaissance to Restoration, 1. 1401–12
Moralizer, 2. 1290
Morand, Paul, 4. 1367
Morant, Philip, 2. 1739
More, Cresacre, 1. 2247
More, Edward, 1. 1128, 2032
More, Gertrude, 1. 1996
More, Hannah, 2. 1598–1600, 109, 178, 1024; 3. 1745
More, Henry, 1. 2334–6; 2. 76, 1901, 1907
More, Humphrey, 1. 2122
More, John, 1. 2142
More, Sir J[onas], 2. 1557
More, Sir Thomas, 1. 1792–1809, 854, 858, 1128, 1841–2, 2050, 2275, 2329; 2. 33, 76, 109, 199, 217
More, Sir William (1520–c. 76), 1. 1002
More (Mure), Sir William (1594–1657), 1. 2436, 1911
More excellent observations [*of Dutch trade*], 1. 2162
More songs from the ship and castle, 4. 1369
Moreau, Simeon, 2. 1405
Morell, John Daniel, 3. 1576

Morell, L. L., 3. 1868
Morell, Thomas, 2. 1777, 242, 1827
Morer, Thomas, 2. 1399
Moréri, Louis, 2. 1525
Moreto y Cabana, Agustín, 2. 201
Moreton, J. B., 2. 1473
Morfitt, John, 2. 1563
Morgan, Charles Langbridge, 4. 676–7
Morgan, John, 2. 1448, 1449
Morgan, John Minter, 3. 1680
Morgan, Mary, 2. 1407
Morgan, Matthew Somerville, 3. 1825
Morgan, Richard Cope, 3. 79
Morgan, Sydney Owenson, Lady, 3. 754–5
Morgan, Thomas, 2. 1676, 1865
Morgan, W. J., 3. 1850
Morganwy, Iolo, 2. 248
Mori, Nicolas, 3. 1875
Morice, James, 1. 1002
Morier, James Justinian, 3. 751–2, 1673
Morison, John, 3. 1840
Morison, Richard, 1. 2039
Morison, Robert, 2. 1781, 1374
Morison, Stanley, 4. 82
Moritz, Karl Philipp, 2. 1540, 166, 1407
Morland, N., 4. 73
Morland, Sir Samuel, 1. 2142; 2. 1907
Morland, Thomas Hornby, 2. 1555; 3. 1704
Morley, George, 1. 1996
Morley, Henry, 3. 1396–7, 1725, 1809 1867
Morley, Henry Parker, 8th Baron, 1. 1132
Morley, John, Viscount, 3. 1447–8, 1728, 1773, 1790, 1793, 1815, 1821, 1849, 1850
Morley, John Royston, 4. 1372
Morley, Samuel, 3. 1790, 1850
Morley, Thomas, 1. 1346–7, 880, 893
Mornay, Philippe de, 1. 2189–90, 866
Morning, 3. 1791
Morning advertiser, 2. 1338; 3. 1789, 1827
Morning bulletin, 3. 1803
Morning chronicle (1769), 2. 1334; 3. 1789, 1827
Morning chronicle (Dublin 1796), 2. 1387
Morning gazette, 3. 1790
Morning herald (1780), 2. 1336; 3. 1789
Morning herald (1899), 3. 1791
Morning journal (1828), 3. 1790
Morning journal (Glasgow 1858), 3. 1804
Morning leader, 3. 1792
Morning mail (1864), 3. 1791
Morning mail (Dublin 1870), 3. 1806
Morning mail (1885), 3. 1791
Morning mail (Newcastle 1901), 3. 1803
Morning news (Sheffield 1855), 3. 1795
Morning news (1856), 3. 1790
Morning news (Dublin 1859), 3. 1806

Morning news (Belfast 1882), 3. 1806
Morning post (1772), 2. 1335; 3. 1789, 1827; 4. 1399, 1344–5
Morning post (1776), 2. 1335
Morning post (Dublin 1788), 2. 1387
Morning star (1789), 2. 1337
Morning star (Dublin 1793), 2. 1387
Morning star (1805), 3. 1790
Morning star (1856), 3. 1790
Morning visitor, 2. 1347
Morning walk, 2. 375
Morosini, Francesco, 2. 1547
morphology, general, 1. 59–112
   Old English, 1. 59–76
   Middle English, 1. 75–90
   Modern English, 1. 89–112
Morpurgo, Jack Eric, 4. 1373
Morrell, William, 1. 2162
Morris, Francis Orpen, 3. 67
Morris, Isaac, 2. 1478
Morris, Lewis (1700–65), 2. 1390
Morris, Sir Lewis (1833–1907), 3. 640
Morris, Mowbray, 3. 1773, 1849
Morris, Ralph, 2. 997
Morris, Richard, 3. 1660
Morris, Thomas, 2. 1473
Morris, William, 3. 563–71, 56, 145–6, 1820
Morris, William O'Connor, 3. 1773
Morrison, Arthur, 3. 1069–70
Morrison, Nancy Agnes Brysson, 4. 677–8
Morrison, Wilson E. W., 3. 1868
Morriss, J. S., 3. 82
Morriss's Trade journal, 3. 82
Morse, Jedediah, 2. 1473
Morselli, Adriano, 2. 1549, 191
Morte Arthur, Le (stanzaic poem), 1. 400
Morte Arthure (alliterative poem), 1. 396–7
Morthland, John, 2. 1376
Mortimer, Cromwell, 2. 1907
Mortimer, Favell Lee, 3. 1090
Mortimer, George, 2. 1482
Mortimer, James, 3. 1793, 1815
Mortimer, John, 2. 1557
Mortimer, Thomas, 2. 1798
Mortoft, Francis, 1. 2130
Morton, Henry Canova Vollam, 4. 1322–3
Morton, John, 2. 1907
Morton, John Bingham, 4. 1088–9, 801
Morton, John Chalmers, 3. 1824
Morton, John Maddison, 3. 1153
Morton, Thomas (1564–1659), divine, 1. 1996–7
Morton, Thomas (fl. 1637), writer on New England, 1. 2163, 2277
Morton, Thomas (fl. 1642), peace pamphleteer, 1. 2041

Morton, Thomas (1764?–1838), 2. 850–1
Moryson, Fynes, 1. 2240, 2125
Moschus, 1. 2173; 2. 1492
Moseley, Benjamin, 2. 1472
Moseley, Humphrey, 1. 963; 2. 280
Moseley, Walter Michael, 2. 1564
Mosely, G. Gordon, 4. 1394
Mosleian, 3. 1870
Moslem in Cambridge, 3. 1866
Moss, W. Keith, 4. 860, 867, 874
Mosse, Miles, 1. 2039
Most agreeable companion, 2. 403
Most execrable and barbarous murder. . .aboard an English ship, A, 1. 2147
Mote, Humphrey, 1. 2077
Motets, madrigals and other pieces, 2. 372
Mother Chit-Chat's curious tales, 2. 1026
Mother Goose's melody (1780?), 2. 1023
Mother Goose's melody (1796?), 2. 422
Mother's gift, 2. 1021
Motherless Mary, 3. 1107
Motherwell, William, 3. 393–4
Motion picture news, 4. 57
Motion picture studio, 4. 57
Motley (Oxford 1930), 4. 1369
Motley (Dublin 1932), 4. 854
Motley (Birkenhead 1948), 4. 1388
Mott, Albert Julius, 3. 914
Motteux, Peter Anthony, 2. 768–9, 1292
Mottley, John, 2. 796, 995
Mottoes of the Spectators, Tatlers and Guardians, 2. 364
Mottram, Ralph Hale, 4. 678–9
Moüette, Germain, 2. 1447
Mouhy, Charles de Fieux, Chevalier de, 2. 995
Moule, Handley Carr Glyn, 3. 1622
Moule, Thomas, 3. 1875
Moult, Thomas, 4. 1364, 1365
Moultrie, John, 3. 394
Moung, Margaret Aye, 4. 1374
Mountague, Richard, bishop (d. 1641), 1. 1997, 2297, 2298, 2299
Mountague, Richard (bookbinder), 2. 292
Mountague, William, 2. 1414
mountaineering, nineteenth century, 3. 1708–11
Mountebank, 2. 1327
Mountfort, Walter, 1. 1752
Mountfort, William, 2. 769
Mouse, 4. 1384
Movement, 4. 861
Movement, anti-persecution gazette and register of progress, 3. 1819
Moving picture offered list, 4. 56
Mowat, Robert Balmain, 4. 1195–6
Moxon, Edward, 3. 540

Moxon, Joseph, 1. 963; 2. 1566, 1907
Moyes, James, 3. 1856
Moysie, David, 1. 2214, 2451
Mozeen, Thomas, 2. 997
Mozley, Charles, 3. 1847
Mozley, Harriet, 3. 1090
Mozley, James Bowling, 3. 1632, 1844
Mozley, John, 3. 1847
Mozley, Thomas, 3. 1632, 1855
Mucedorus, 1. 1471
Muddiman, Henry, 1. 2092, 2110; 2. 1313, 1315, 1316
Mudford, William, 3. 752–3, 1792
Mudford, William Henry, 3. 1790, 1793
Mudie, George, 3. 1773, 1818
Mudie, Robert, 3. 1875
Muggins, William, 1. 1128
Mughouse-Diversion, 2. 351
Muir, A. S., 4. 1385
Muir, Edwin, 4. 316–19, 1371, 1377
Muir, Wilhelmina Johnstone, 4. 679–80
'Muir, Willa' (Wilhelmina Johnstone Muir), 4. 679–80
Muir (Mure), Sir William, 1. 2436, 1911
Muirhead, James, 2. 1375
Muirhead, Lockhart, 2. 1427
Mulcaster, Richard, 1. 1128, 2276
Mulgrave, Constantine John Phipps, 2nd Baron, 2. 1485
Mulgrave, John Sheffield, 3rd Earl of, 2. 478–9
Muller, H. S., 3. 1854
Muller, Robert, 4. 1378
Müller, Samuel (Gerhard Friedrich), 2. 1483
Mullins, Donald, 4. 1378
Mulock, Dinah Maria, 3. 951–2, 1093, 1108
Mulso, Hester, 2. 1598
Mum and the sothsegger, 1. 545
Mumford, Erasmus, 2. 1567
Mumford, John, 2. 1341
mummers' plays, 1. 741–2
Mummery, Albert Frederick, 3. 1681, 1710
Mumming of the seven philosophers, 1. 741
Mun, Thomas, 1. 2278; 2. 1898
Munby, Arthur Joseph, 3. 541
Münchhausen, Karl Friedrich von, 2. 1540
Munday, Anthony, 1. 1464–7, 1128, 2052, 2066, 2072, 2122
Mundy, John, 1. 1347
Mundy, Peter, 1. 2128, 2147; 2. 1397
Municipal corporations companion 3. 1882
Municipal corporations directory, 3. 1881
Municipal player, 4. 850, 866
'Munro, C. K.' (Charles Kirkpatrick Macmullan), 4. 969
Munro, Elsie Smeaton, 4. 802

Munro, Hector Hugh, 4. 727–8
Munro, Innes, 2. 1443
Munster, Sebastian, 1. 879, 2118, 2136–7
Munster journal, 2. 1388
Munster packet, 2. 1390
Muralt, Béat Louis de, 2. 1525, 67, 86, 1400
Muratori, Lodovico Antonio, 2. 1547, 1466
Murav'yov-Apostol, Ivan Matveyevich, 2. 216
Mure, James, 3. 1804
Mure, Sir William, 1. 2436, 1911
Murimuth, Adam, 1. 785
Murison, James William, 3. 1867
Murphy, Anna Brownell, 3. 1288–9
Murphy, Arthur, 2. 851–3, 178, 1280, 1281, 1282, 1283, 1332
Murphy, James Cavanah, 2. 1429–30
Murphy, Joseph John, 3. 541
Murray, — (fl. 1793), 2. 1374
Murray, Alexander Davidson, 3. 1796
Murray, Charles Adolphus, 7th Earl of Dunmore, 3. 1676
Murray, Sir Charles Augustus, 3. 952
Murray, Sir David, 1. 2436, 1908
Murray, David Christie, 3. 1773
Murray, David Leslie, 4. 1405
Murray, Emma, 3. 1670
Murray, Eustace Clare Grenville, 3. 1815
Murray, F. E., 3. 85
Murray, George Gilbert Aimé, 4. 1089–92
Murray, Gilbert, 4. 1089–92
Murray, Henry, 3. 1773
Murray, Hugh, 2. 1445
Murray, James (1732–82), journalist, 2. 1351, 1372, 1403
Murray, Sir James (fl. 1773–80), in America, 2. 1471
Murray, Sir James Augustus Henry, 3. 1660–1
Murray, John (publishers), 2. 280; 3. 79, 1773, 1855
Murray, John (1778–1843), 3. 1773, 1790, 1844
Murray, John (1808–92), 3. 1679, 1821, 1852
Murray, Sir John (1851–1928), 3. 1855
Murray, Patrick, 5th Baron Elibank, 2. 1898
Murray, Robert Fuller, 3. 640
Murray, Sarah, 2. 1408
Murray, Thomas Cornelius, 3. 1944–5
Murray, William Henderson, 3. 1803
Murray's magazine, 3. 1852
Murry, John Middleton, 4. 1092–6, 825, 1349, 1360, 1361, 1362, 1366, 1370
Murtadi ibn Gaphiphus, 2. 1446
Murthadá ibn al Khalif, 2. 1446
Musae Berkhamstedienses, 2. 419
Musae cantabrigiensis, 2. 337
Musae seatonianae, 2. 393

Musaeus, 1. 2173; 2. 1493
Musapaedia, 2. 352
Musarum cantabrigiensium threnodia in obitum Georgii ducis Albemarlae, 2. 330
Musarum deliciae, 1. 1010
Musarum lachrymae, 2. 352
Musäus, Johann Karl August, 2. 1540, 181
Muscovite, 2. 1275
Muse in a moral humour, 2. 379
Muse in good humour, 2. 370
Muse in masquerade, 2. 371
Muses banquet (1752), 2. 376
Muse's banquet (1760), 2. 381
Muses banquet (1790), 2. 413
Muses delight (1754), 2. 377
Muse's delight (1760), 2. 381
Muses farewel to Popery, 2. 337
Muses holiday, 2. 359
Muses library (1737), 2. 366
Muses library (1760?), 2. 381
Muses mercury, 2. 344, 1293
Muse's mirrour, 2. 399
Muse's vagaries, 2. 371
Muses welcome to. . .Prince James, 1. 1010
Muses and Graces on a visit to Grosvenor Square, 2. 395
Muses' choice, 2. 377
Muses' delight, 2. 387
Muses' gazette, 2. 1277
Museum (1746), 2. 1298, 1332
Museum (Leicester 1795), 2. 1350
Museum (Cork 1796), 2. 1380
Museum for young gentlemen, A, 2. 384
Museum of wit, 2. 428
Museum rusticum et commerciale, 2. 1303
Musgrave, Samuel, 2. 1827
Musgrave, Sir W., 2. 1002
music
    Renaissance to Restoration, 1. 953–4, 1393–4
    Restoration and eighteenth century, 2. 67–70, 283–4
Music and dancing, 2. 415
Music and letters, 4. 1364
'*Music and poetry*' '*art and language*' society, 4. 1356
music-hall, 4. 853–62
Music hall and theatre review, 4. 823, 859
Music hall pictorial, 4. 859
Musica oxoniensis, 2. 340
Musicae vocalis deliciae, 2. 413
Musical and poetical relicks of the Welsh bards, 2. 405
Musical banquet of choice songs, 2. 424
Musical banquet or buck's delight, 2. 428
Musical bouquét, 2. 426

Musical charmer, 2. 416
musical comedy, 4. 853–62
Musical companion (1667), 2. 330
Musical companion (1741), 2. 368
Musical companion (1745?), 2. 371
Musical companion (1759), 2. 380
Musical companion (1765?), 2. 386
Musical companion (1768), 2. 1304
Musical companion (1777), 2. 398, 1306
Musical companion (c. 1791), 2. 415
Musical entertainer, 2. 366
Musical gem, 3. 1875
Musical magazine (1760), 2. 1303
Musical magazine (1767), 2. 388
Musical magazine, by Mr Oswald (1761?), 2. 382
Musical Mason, 2. 395
Musical miscellanies, 2. 405
Musical miscellany (1729), 2. 358
Musical miscellany (1760), 2. 381
Musical miscellany (1786), 2. 407
Musical miscellany (1789), 2. 411
Musical miscellany (1790), 2. 413
Musical olio, 2. 428
Musical repository, 2. 426
Musical times (*and singing class circular*), 3. 1847, 1862
Musical world and dramatic observer, 4. 823
Musicall banquet, 1. 1357
Musick's delight on the cithren, 2. 329
Musicks recreation, 1. 1357
Musset, Alfred de, 3. 105
Musset, Paul de, 3. 1110
Musters, George Chaworth, 3. 1674
Musters, John Chaworth, 3. 1706
Mutt's mutterings, 4. 1369
My children's magazine, 4. 819
My garden, 4. 1381
My journal, 4. 1358
My magazine, 4. 819
My own treasury, 3. 1878
'*My queen*' *library*, 4. 1354
My queen magazine, 4. 1362
My queen novels, 4. 1354
My real friend, 3. 1107
My story weekly, 4. 1367
My weekly, 4. 1360
Myers, Asher, 3. 1822
Myers, Ernest James, 3. 640–1
Myers, Frederic, 3. 1609
Myers, Frederic William Henry, 3. 641
Myers, Leopold Hamilton, 4. 680
Myers, Thomas, 3. 1720
Myllar, Andrew, 1. 2443
Mylne, James, 2. 240
Mynshul, Geffray, 1. 2035, 2044, 2048

Myrour of lewed men (ME), 1. 506
Myrrour of the blessed lyf of Jesu Crist (fifteenth century), 1. 516
Myrrour of the chyrche (ME), 1. 516
Myrtle, 2. 378
Myrtle and vine, 2. 429
Mystère d'Adam, 1. 725–6
Mysteries of love and eloquence, 1. 1010; 2. 335
Mystery and detection, 4. 1390
mystery plays, Middle English, 1. 727–40
mystics
    Middle English, 1. 516–24
    Renaissance to Restoration, Spanish, 1. 908–10
    Restoration and eighteenth century, 2. 1651–62
Myvyr, Owain, 2. 248

N., A. (fl. 1586), 1. 1128
N., A. (fl. 1608), 1. 2125
NATE journal, 4. 873
N., D. (fl. 1652), 1. 2031
N.F.R.B quarterly, 4. 1407
N., G. (fl. 1642), 1. 2135
N., N. (fl. 1754), 2. 1464
NODA bulletin, 4. 860
N-town cycle (ME plays), 1. 733–4
Nabbes, Thomas, 1. 1752–3
Nagle, David A., 3. 1806
Nairn, C. W., 3. 1882
Nairn, Thomas, 2. 1459
Nairne, Caroline Oliphant, Baroness, 2. 2029
names
    personal, 1. 181–6
    place, 1. 169–82
Namier, Sir Lewis Bernstein, 4. 1196–7
Nan's novels, 4. 1369
Nani, Giovanni Battista Felice Gasparo, 2. 1547
Nannini, Remigio, 1. 2190, 889
Naogeorgus, 1. 849, 854
Napier, Macvey, 3. 1773, 1854
Napier, Marjorie, 4. 1361
Napier, Sir William Francis Patrick, 3. 1494
Naps upon Parnassus, 1. 1011
Narborough, Sir John, 2. 1457
Narcissus, 1. 1778
Nares, Robert, 3. 1661, 1841; 2. 1286, 1309, 1566
Narrative of a voyage to Maryland, 2. 1459
Narrative of all the robberies. . .of John Sheppard, A., 2. 990
Narrative of the journey of an Irish gentleman, 2. 1401
Narrative of the proceedings at. . .Norwich, 2. 401
Narrative of the successe of the embassy. . .to Turkey, A, 2. 1409
Nash, Rowland, 3. 1792

Nash, Treadway Russell, 2. 1782
Nash's and Pall Mall magazine, 3. 1854; 4. 1353, 1359
Nash's annual, 4. 1377
Nash's magazine, 4. 1359
Nash's–Pall Mall magazine, 4. 1359
Nash's weekly, 4. 1406
Nashe, Thomas, 1. 1456–60, 1128, 1961, 2054, 2311–12
Nat Gould's annual, 4. 1357
Nation (1824), 3. 1793
Nation (1907), 3. 1815; 4. 1352–3
National (1839), 3. 1818
National (1846), 3. 1814
National adviser, 3. 1808
National agricultural labourers' chronicle, 3. 1820
National Amateur Operatic and Dramatic Association directory, 4. 877
National and English review, 4. 1376, 1403; 3. 1852
National Book Council, its publications, 4. 118
National Book League, its publications, 4. 99, 118
National Central Library, its *annual report*, 4. 117
National Covenant, Scottish, 1. 2464
National graphic, 3. 1817; 4. 1402
National journal (1746), 2. 1332
National journal (1792), 2. 1387
National magazine (and Dublin literary gazette) (1830), 3. 1845
National magazine (1856), 3. 1849
National magazine (1909), 4. 1359
National mirror, 2. 1284
National monthly, 4. 1359
National news letter reports, 4. 1407
National newsletter, 4. 1407
National observer, 3. 1815
National Operatic and Dramatic Association. . . directory, 4. 877
National Operatic and Dramatic Association year book, 4. 877
National reformer (1844), 3. 1819
National reformer (1860), 3. 1819
National register, 3. 1809
National review (1855), 3. 1857
National review (1883), 3. 1852, 1863; 4. 1403
National scout, 1. 2110; 2. 1313
National Society for Women's Suffrage journal, 3. 1851
National temperance chronicle, 3. 1847
National Temperance mirror, 3. 1852
Native, 4. 1405
Nativity sermon, A (ME), 1. 490
Natural history review, 3. 1857
Natural son, 2. 1014

Naturalist's miscellany, 2. 1309
Naturalists' pocket magazine, 2. 1312
Nature, 3. 1827
Nature stories, 4. 1379
Naubert, Christiane Benedikte, 2. 1540, 181, 1011
Naunton, Sir Robert, 1. 2241
Naval and military gazette, 3. 1826
Naval annual, 3. 1880
Naval chronicle (1760), 2. 1392
Naval chronicle (1799), 2. 1312
Naval glory, 2. 413
Naval magazine, 2. 1312
Naval songster, 2. 429
Navarette, Domingo Fernandez, 2. 1436
navigation, Renaissance to Restoration, 1. 2359–62
Navy list, 3. 1880
Nayland miscellany, 2. 364
Nayler, James, 2. 1651
Neal, Daniel, 2. 1710, 1460
Neale, Sir John Ernest, 4. 1197
Neale, John Mason, 3. 541
Neale, William Johnson, 3. 953
Neale, Thomas, 1. 1771
Neaves, Charles, Lord, 3. 542
Nebuchadnezzars fierie furnace, 1. 1760
Necker, Anne Louise Germaine, Baronne de Staël-Holstein, 3. 107–8; 2. 1533, 116
Necker, Jacques, 2. 1525
Neckham, Alexander, 1. 770
Ned Ward's jests, 2. 379
Nedham (Needham), Marchamont, 1. 2092, 2098, 2102, 2103, 2105, 2106, 2107, 2109, 2110; 2. 109, 1313
Needham, John Turberville, 2. 1907, 109
Needham, Joseph, 4. 1279
Needham, Marchamont, 1. 2092, 2098, 2102, 2103, 2105, 2106, 2107, 2109, 2110; 2. 109, 1313
Needham, N. J. T. M., 4. 1279
Needham, Violet, 4. 811
Needham's post-man, 2. 1382
Needler, Henry, 2. 559
'Negri, Solomon', 2. 1562
Negri de Bassano, Francesco, 1. 2190, 894
Neill, Charles, 4. 1376
Neill and Co, 3. 59; 4. 81
Neilson, J. F., 3. 1804
Nekrasov, Nikolay Alekseyevich, 3. 153
Nelson, A., 3. 1697
Nelson, Abraham, 1. 2039
Nelson, Francis, 1. 2107
Nelson, William, 3. 79
Nelson and Sons, Thomas, 3. 59; 4. 81
Nennius, 1. 339–40, 393–6

Neolith, 4. 1358
Neri, Antonio, 2. 1547
Nero, Tragedy of, 1. 1760
Nesbit, Edith, 3. 641–2, 1097; 4. 1358
'Nestor', 2. 1288
Netter, Thomas, 1. 805
Nettle (1751), 2. 1385
Nettle (1789), 2. 411
Nettleship, Richard Lewis, 3. 1577
Neuberg, Victor, 4. 1359
Neve, Philip, 2. 237, 1787
Nevile, Henry, 2. 977
Nevill, William, 1. 1129
Neville, Alexander, 1. 1129, 1421
Neville, George, 1. 1002
Neville, Henry, 1. 2033, 2058
Nevinson, Henry Woodd, 4. 1197–8; 3. 1773
Nevyle, Alexander, 1. 1129, 1421
New academy, A, 2. 341
New academy of complements, 2. 330
New account of Italy, A, 2. 1414
New acorn, 4. 1380
New adelphi, 4. 1366
New age, 3. 1815; 4. 1353–4, 1347
New alliance, 4. 1374
New and choice collection of loyal songs, A, 2. 373
New and complete collection of Scots songs, A, 2. 410
New and complete collection of voyages, A, 2. 1392
New and complete English traveller, 2. 1406
New and correct history of New Holland, A, 2. 1482
New annual army list, 3. 1879
New annual register, 2. 1314; 3. 1877
New anti-Roman pacquet, 2. 1339
New at ninepence illustrated thrillers, 4. 1390
New Athenian broadsheet, 4. 1378
New ayres and dialogues, 2. 333
New ballad on the game of bragg, A, 2. 1567
New boghouse miscellany, 2. 382
New bon ton magazine, 3. 1844
New book list for bookbuyers, librarians and booksellers, 3. 84
New book of constitutions of. . .Masons, 2. 366
New booke of tabliture, 1. 1347–8
New books, 4. 790
New Britain, 4. 1370
New British songster, 2. 406
New buck's delight, 2. 387
New Calliope, 2. 370
New canting dictionary, A, 2. 355
New carolls for this merry time, 2. 328
New century review (1897), 3. 1854; 4. 1354
New century review (1900), 4. 1355

New charter, 4. 1406
New children's encyclopaedia, 4. 819
New children's friend, 2. 1034
New Christian uses, 1. 2099
New Christian's magazine, 2. 1307
New Christmas carrols, 2. 330
'New church' times, 4. 1362
New clarion, 3. 1821
New collection of miscellany poems, A, 2. 349
New collection of new songs and poems, A, 2. 332
New collection of original poems, A, 2. 349
New collection of original Scotch songs, A, 2. 359
New collection of poems, A (1701), 2. 341
New collection of poems, A (1721), 2. 354
New collection of poems. . .by Prior and others,
    A (1725), 2. 355
New collection of poems and songs, A, 2. 332
New collection of poems relating to state affairs, A,
    2. 343
New collection of the choicest songs, A (1676), 2.
    333
New collection of the choicest songs, A (1682), 2.
    334
New college, 3. 1869
New comic annual, 3. 1875
New copper plate magazine, 2. 1311
New Cork evening post, 2. 1388
New coterie, 4. 1367
New court-songs and poems, 2. 331
New criterion, 4. 1365
New crown garland of princely pastime and mirth,
    2. 337
New custome (Elizabethan play), 1. 1410
New daily advertiser, 2. 1333
New days, 4. 1362
New decameron, 4. 1367
New description and state of England, 2. 1399
New description of Holland, A, 2. 1415
New description of Spain and Portugal, A, 2. 1415
New dialogue between some body and no body, A,
    2. 1341
New discoveries concerning the world, 2. 1476
New display of the beauties of England, A, 2. 1403
New Dublin mercury, 2. 1383
New Edinburgh gazette, 2. 1375
New Edinburgh musical miscellany, 2. 419
New Edinburgh review, 3. 1844
New election budget, 2. 407
New English review (magazine), 4. 1376
New English weekly, 4. 1369-70
New entertaining frisky songster, 2. 395
New entertaining humorist, 2. 391
New epoch, 4. 1398
New era, 4. 1378
New Etonian, 3. 1871

New European magazine, 3. 1844
New evening post, 2. 1386
New excitement, 3. 1877
New express, 2. 1320
New farmer's journal, 3. 1823
New female spectator, 2. 1281
New forget-me-not, 4. 1368
New foundling hospital for wit, 2. 389
New freewoman, 4. 1361
New frisky songster, 2. 419
New futurian, 4. 1390
New game at cards, A, 2. 1568
New, general and complete weekly magazine, 2.
    1311
New general songster, 2. 429
New generation, 4. 1378
New globe, 3. 1792
New green quarterly, 4. 1366
New half-penny post, 2. 1329
New help to discourse, 2. 330
New Heraclitus ridens, 2. 1341
New history of the empire of China, A, 2. 1434
New hotspur, 4. 820
New hunting song, A, 2. 1558
New idea, 4. 1385
New instructive history of Miss Patty Proud, 2.
    1026
New introduction to Enfield's Speaker, A, 2. 429
New Ireland, 4. 1362
New Ireland review, 4. 1353
New Jerusalem journal, 2. 1309
New Jerusalem magazine, 2. 1309
New journey to France, A, 2. 1416
New juvenile keepsake, 3. 1878
New keepsake, 4. 1369
New lady's magazine, 2. 1307
New lapsus linguae, 3. 1869
New law journal, 3. 1826
New law list, 3. 1881
New leader book, 4. 1366
New leader reprints, 4. 1366
New left review, 4. 1371
New Liverpool songster, 2. 411
New London and country jester, 2. 429
New London and country songster, 2. 401
New London drollery, 2. 336
New London jester, 2. 421
New London journal, 3. 1814; 4. 1350
New London magazine (1785), 2. 1307
New London magazine (1930), 3. 1854; 4. 1355
New London medical journal, 2. 1309
New London price courant, 2. 1336
New London review, 2. 1312
New lyric repository, 2. 416
New magazine (Dublin 1799), 2. 1380

337   338

New magazine (Strabane 1800), 2. 1380
New magazine (1909), 4. 1359
New magazine of knowledge (1760), 2. 1303
New magazine of knowledge (1790), 2. 1309
New man, 4. 1378
New melody, 4. 1369
New memoirs of literature, 2. 1294
New mercury, 2. 1363
New meridian magazine, 4. 1378
New merry companion (1720), 2. 353
New merry companion (c. 1772), 2. 393
New ministry, 2. 369
New miscellaneous poems, 2. 350
New miscellany (1720), 2. 353
New miscellany, A (1726?), 2. 356
New miscellany, A. (1730), 2. 359
New miscellany for the year 1734, A, 2. 363, 1313
New miscellany in prose and verse, A, 2. 369
New miscellany of original poems, A (1701), 2. 341
New miscellany of original poems, A (1720), 2. 353
New miscellany of Scot's sangs, A, 2. 357
New miscellany published for. . .John Maxwell, A, 2. 373
New model for the rebuilding Masonry, A, 2. 359
New monthly, 3. 1843
New monthly magazine, 3. 1843, 1860
New monthly review, 3. 1849
New moral world, 3. 1818
New morning post, 2. 1335
New musical and universal magazine, 2. 395, 1305
New muscial magazine (c. 1780), 2. 1306
New Navy list, 3. 1880
New news, strange news, true news, 1. 2103
New news-book, A, 2. 1317
New northman, 4. 1392
New novelist's magazine, 2. 1307
New numbers, 4. 1362
New observator, A (1704), 2. 1343
New observator on the present times, A (1701), 2. 1343
New observer, 3. 1810
New olio, 2. 421
New olla-podrida, 2. 1289
New Oxford outlook, 4. 1398
New Oxford review, 4. 1397
New paradise of dainty devices, 2. 398
New paths, 4. 1363
New Pearson's and today, 3. 1815; 4. 1403
New Pearson's weekly, 3. 1815; 4. 1403
New penny magazine, 4. 1355
New phineas, 4. 1396
New Phoenix, 2. 1387
New play book for children, A, 2. 1020

New poetry, 4. 1376
New poets series, 4. 1378
New polite instructor, 2. 393
New political state of Great Britain, 2. 1294
New print magazine, 2. 1311
New Punch library, 4. 1358
New quarterly, 4. 1358
New quarterly magazine, 3. 1858
New quarterly review (1844), 3. 1856
New quarterly review (1852), 3. 1857
New rattle, 3. 1868
New red stage, 4. 867, 874
New register book of shipping, 2. 1314
New review, A (1782), 2. 1307
New review (1889), 3. 1853
New road, 4. 1376
New Rolliad, 2. 406
New royal and universal magazine, 2. 1300
New royal magazine, 3. 1854; 4. 1355
New Rugbeian, 3. 1871
New Savoy, 4. 1378
New Saxon pamphlets, 4. 1376
New school of love, 2. 407
New Scotland, 4. 1371
New Scots spy, 2. 1371, 1375
New select collection of epitaphs, A, 2. 395
New Shetlander, 4. 1378
New short stories, 4. 1376
New spectator, 2. 1287
New spiritual magazine, 2. 1307
New sporting magazine, 3. 1683
New spouters companion (1798?), 2. 425
New spouter's companion (1800?), 2. 429
New spur, 4. 1407
New state of Europe (May 1701), 2. 1321
New state of Europe (September 1701), 2. 1321
New statesman, 4. 1361, 1347
New stories, 4. 1371
New story-teller, 2. 403
New syren, 2. 425
New system of castle-building, A, 2. 1348
New tea-table miscellany, A, 2. 375
New Testament, Paues's (ME), 1. 480
New theatre, 4. 827
New theatre of fun, 2. 399
New theatrical songster, 2. 429
New theological repository, 2. 1350
New Thespian oracle, 2. 415
New times, 3. 1790
New Tom Spring's life in London, 3. 1811
New town and country magazine, 2. 1307
New treasury of musick, 2. 339
New Troy, 4. 1395
New universal history of voyages, A, 2. 1392
New universal magazine (1751), 2. 1300

Newnham, William, 3. 1720
Newport and Monmouthshire evening telegraph, 3. 1800
Newry journal, 2. 1389
News (1805), 3. 1808
News (Portsmouth 1959), 3. 1800
news agencies, twentieth century, 4. 1341–2
News and book trade review, 3. 1758
News and times, 3. 1801
News-chronicle, 3. 1790; 4. 1400, 1401
News circular, 4. 1384
News-expositour, 2. 1342
News from abroad, 2. 1361
News from Parnassus, 2. 1340
News from the dead (1715), 2. 1294
News from the dead (1739?) 2. 1329
News from the fairy island, 2. 1346
News from the land of chivalry, 2. 1340
News journal English and French, 2. 1325
News letter (1685), 2. 1381
News letter (1716), 2. 1323
News letter (1962), 3. 1806
News letter of the International Small Printers' Association, 4. 84
News-letter news, 4. 1407
News-letter of the LXIVMOS, 4. 1344
News-letter to members (Verse-speaking Fellowship), 4. 1368
News of the world, 3. 1811, 1834; 4. 1400
News-paper wedding, 2. 1004
News sheet (National Book Council), 4. 118
news sheets, Renaissance to Restoration, 1. 2067–110
Newsagent and advertisers' record, 3. 83, 1758
Newsagent and booksellers' review, 3. 83, 1758
Newsagents', booksellers' review and stationers' gazette, 3. 1758
Newsagents' chronicle, 3. 1759
newsbooks, Renaissance to Restoration, 1. 2067–110
Newsboy, 4. 106
newsletters, Restoration and eighteenth century, 2. 1339–40
Newsman, 3. 1812
Newsman and publication register, 3. 83
Newsmen's weekly chronicle, 3. 1758
Newspaper and poster advertising, 3. 1758
Newspaper owner, 3. 1759; 4. 1343
Newspaper press, 3. 1762
Newspaper press directory, 3. 1758; 4. 1343
Newspaper world, 3. 1760; 4. 1343
newspapers
  Renaissance to Restoration, 1. 953
  Restoration and eighteenth century
    Irish, 2. 1381–90

    London, 2. 1313–40
    provinces, 2. 1353–70
    Scottish, 2. 1373–8
  nineteenth century, 3. 1755–1838
    advertising, 3. 1755–8
    bi- and tri-weekly, 3. 1807–8, 1834
    daily, 3. 1789–1808; Irish, 3. 1805–7; London, 3. 1789–94, 1827–9; provinces, 3. 1794–1803, 1829–31; Scottish, 3. 1803–5, 1833
    history, 3. 1777–84
    journalism, 3. 1759–78
    lists, 3. 1783–8
    management and distribution, 3. 1757–60
    wages and conditions, 3. 1759–60
    weekly, 3. 1807–28
      agricultural, 3. 1823–4, 1837
      financial and commercial, 3. 1824, 1837
      general, 3. 1812–15, 1834–5
      humorous, 3. 1825, 1837–8
      illustrated, 3. 1816–17, 1835
      juvenile, 3. 1825–6, 1838
      provincial, 3. 1831–3
      radical, 3. 1817–21, 1835–6
      religious, 3. 1822–3, 1837
      reviews, 3. 1821–2, 1836–7
      sporting, 3. 1824–5, 1837
      Sunday, 3. 1807–12, 1834
  twentieth century, 4. 1329–1408
    general, 4. 1329–34
    advertising, 4. 1341–4
    amateur, 4. 1379–88
    biography, 4. 1335–8
    journalism, 4. 1337–40
    lists, 4. 1347–9
    literary, 4. 1349–80
    non-literary, 4. 1399–1408
    periodicals, 4. 1343–4
    studies, 4. 1343–6
  see also magazines, newsbooks, news-sheets, periodicals, periodical essays
Newsvendor, 3. 1758
Newte, Thomas, 2. 1406
Newton, Humfrey, 1. 687, 1129
Newton, Sir Isaac, 2. 1907–8, 76, 110
Newton, John, 2. 1626–7, 1783
Newton, Thomas (1542?–1607), 1. 1129, 2024
Newton, Thomas (fl. 1603), 1. 1129
Newton, Thomas (1704–82), 2. 1777
Niccols, Richard, 1. 1315, 1336
Nice wanton, 1. 1408, 1420
Nichol, John, 3. 1868
Nicholas of St Albans, 1. 763
Nicholas, Conan, 4. 1374
Nicholas, Thomas, 1. 2150

Nicholas y Sacharles, Juan, 1. 909
Nicholl, John, 1. 2154
Nicholls, C. E., 4. 1381
Nicholls, Charlotte, 3. 865–6
Nicholls, Sir George, 3. 1725
Nichols, Beverley, 4. 681–2, 806, 1397
Nichols, John, 2. 1729–32, 265, 1762–3; 3. 59, 1839
Nichols, John Beverley, 4. 681–2, 806, 1397
Nichols, John Bowyer, 3. 59, 1839
Nichols, John Gough, 3. 59, 1839
Nichols, P. P. Ross, 4. 1393
Nichols, Robert Malise Bowyer, 4. 319–20
Nichols, Thomas, 1. 2147
Nicholson, Irene, 4. 57
Nicholson, John, 3. 395
Nicholson, Norman Cornthwaite, 4. 320–1
Nicholson, Renton, 3. 1811, 1813, 1816
Nicholson, Samuel, 1. 1130
Nicholson, Thomas, 2. 1464
Nicholson, William (1753–1815), scientist, 2. 1311, 1908; 3. 1841
Nicholson, William (1783–1849), poet, 3. 395
Nicholson, William (1872–1949), 4. 791
Nicholson's weekly register, 3. 1824
Nicker nicked or the cheats of gaming, 2. 1566
Nickisson, George William, 3. 1845
Niclas, Hendrik, 1. 1130, 919
Nicol, Alexander, 2. 1977
Nicolai, Christoph Friedrich, 2. 1540, 181
Nicolas of Fakenham, 1. 805
Nicolas, Sir Nicholas Harris, 3. 1661, 1855
Nicolay, Nicolas de, Seigneur d'Arfeuille, 1. 2122
Nicole, Pierre, 2. 1525
Nicoll, Allardyce, 4. 1097–8
Nicoll, John, 2. 2050
Nicoll, John Ramsay Allardyce, 4. 1097–8
Nicoll, Robert, 3. 543
Nicoll, Sir William Robertson, 3. 1773, 1815, 1853
Nicolson, Sir Harold George, 4. 1198–9
Nicolson, William, 2. 1612, 1795
Niebuhr, Carsten, 2. 1443
Nieremberg, Juan Eusebio, 1. 909
Nietzsche, Friedrich, 3. 126
Nieuhof, Jan, 2. 1431, 1458
Nieuwentydt, Bernard, 2. 207
Nigel de Longchamps (Wireker), 1. 763–4
Niger, Ralph, 1. 776
Night and day, 4. 1372
Night-life, 4. 860
Night post, 2. 1322
Night walker (1696), 2. 1292
Night-walker (1784), 2. 1287

Nightingale, 2. 367
Nightwatchman, 4. 1380
Nijenburg, J. E. van Egmont van der, 2. 1439
Nimble heave, 2. 368
'Nimrod' (fl. 1788), 2. 1561
'Nimrod' (Charles James Apperley), 3. 1704
Nimrod, 3. 1810
Nimrod's songs of the chace, 2. 410
Nin, Anaïs, 4. 1372
Nine, 4. 1380
Nine Muses, 2. 341
Nine Worthies, 1. 741
Nineteenth century (and after), 3. 1852, 1863; 4. 1351–2
nineteenth century literature
  general, 3. 3–20
  Anglo-Irish
    general, 3. 1895–1900
    drama, 3. 1939–48
    Gaelic, 3. 1885–96
    poetry, 3. 1899–1916
    Yeats and Synge, 3. 1915–38
  bibliographies, general, 3. 1–4
  book production and distribution, 3. 25–90
  children's books, 3. 1085–110
  drama, 3. 1111–96
  education, 3. 1717–56
  history, 3. 1457–1510
  letters, 3. 19–26
  literary history, 3. 3–8
  literary relations with the continent, 3. 91–158
    Dutch, 3. 93–4
    French, 3. 93–116
    German, 3. 115–34
    Italian, 3. 133–40
    Portuguese, 3. 141–4
    Scandinavian, 3. 143–50
    Slavonic, 3. 149–56
    Spanish, 3. 141–4
  magazines, 3. 1839–84
  memoirs, 3. 19–26
  newspapers, 3. 1755–1838
  novel, 3. 657–1084
  philosophy, 3. 1509–1600
  poetry, 3. 159–656
  prose, 3. 1197–1458
  religion, 3. 1599–1636
  scholarship, 3. 1635–68
    Gaelic, 3. 1887–94
  sport, 3. 1683–1716
  travel, 3. 1669–84
Nisbet, James, 3. 80
Nisbet, Murdoch, 1. 2452
Nixon, Anthony, 1. 1130, 2027, 2074, 2144
Noah's ark (ME play), 1. 737

Nobbes, Robert, 2. 1557
Noble, Peter, 4. 58, 828, 860
Noble birth and gallant atchievements of Robin Hood, 2. 975
Noble cricketers, 2. 1565
'Nobody, A.' (Gordon Frederick Browne), 3. 1106
No-body and some-body, 1. 1760
Nodder, Richard P., 2. 1309
Nodier, Jean Emmanuel Charles, 3. 105
Noel, Lady Augusta, 3. 1070, 1103
Noel, Baptist Wriothesley, 3. 1620
Noel, Henry, 1. 1776
Nolan, Edward, 3. 1868
Nolan's theatrical observer, 3. 1123
Nollius, Henricus, 1. 849–50
Nonconformist (and independent) 3. 1822
Nonesuch, 4. 1392
Nonesuch Press, 4. 98
Nonpareil, 2. 379
Nonsense of Common-sense, 2. 1279, 1329
Noon gazette and daily spy, 2. 1336
Noonan, Robert, 4. 751
Noorthouck, John, 2. 1799
Noot, Jan Baptista van der, 1. 919–20
Norbury review, 4. 118
Norden, Friderik Ludvig, 2. 1449
Norden, John, 1. 2212, 1130, 1944, 2132–3, 2278
Norfolk
  general bibliography, 1. 18
  Middle English drama, 1. 738
  Restoration and eighteenth century printing, 2. 269
  nineteenth century newspaper, 3. 1832
Norfolk chronicle, 2. 1363
Norfolk daily standard, 3. 1802
Norfolk epilogue (M.E. play), 1. 738
Norfolk evening standard, 3. 1802
Norfolk news, 3. 1832
Norfolk poetical miscellany, 2. 370
Norman, H. F., 4. 1354
Normanby, Constantine Henry Phipps, 1st Marquis of, 3. 756
Normanby, John Sheffield, Marquis of, 2. 478–9
Norris, Isaac, 2. 1463
Norris, John (1657–1711), 2. 479, 1848
Norris, John (fl. 1714), 2. 1460
Norris, John Pilkington, 3. 1728
Norris, Robert, 2. 1451
Norris, William Edward, 4. 682–3
Norris's Taunton-journal, 2. 1367
Norry, Charles, 2. 1452
Norseman, 4. 1376
'North, Christopher' (John Wilson), 3. 1308–10

North, Dudley, 3rd Baron (1581–1666), 1. 2047, 2049
North, Sir Dudley (1641–91), 2. 1848
North, Roger, 2. 1698–9, 1558
North and east London star, 3. 1820
North and South Shields (daily) gazette, 3. 1795
North British advertiser, 3. 1832
North British daily mail, 3. 1803
North British intelligencer, 2. 1372
North British magazine, 2. 1372
North British miscellany, 2. 1374
North British review, 3. 1856, 1865
North Briton, 2. 1283
North country angler, 2. 1561
North country journal, 2. 1362
North eastern daily gazette, 3. 1798
North London press and star, 3. 1820
North mail and Newcastle daily chronicle, 3. 1795; 4. 1401
North of England and Scotland in 1704, 2. 1399
North of England magazine, 3. 1847
North of Scotland gazette, 3. 1805
North tatler, 2. 1369
North-west monthly, 4. 1379
North western daily mail, 3. 1803
North-western evening mail, 3. 1803
Northall, John, 2. 1420
Northampton(shire)
  general bibliography, 1. 18
  Middle English drama, 1. 737
  Restoration and eighteenth century
    magazines, 2. 1351
    newspapers, 2. 1362–3
    printing and bookselling, 2. 269
  nineteenth century newspaper, 3. 1832
  twentieth century theatre, 4. 846
Northampton Abraham (ME play), 1. 737
Northampton daily chronicle, 3. 1801
Northampton daily echo, 3. 1801
Northampton daily reporter, 3. 1801
Northampton journal, 2. 1363
Northampton mercury, 2. 1362–3; 3. 1832
Northampton mercury daily reporter, 3. 1801
Northampton miscellany, 2. 1351
Northamptonshire journal, 2. 1331, 1363
Northbrooke, John, 1. 2023
Northcliffe, Alfred Harmsworth, Viscount, 3. 1773
Northcote, James Spencer, 3. 1848
Northcote, Sir Stafford, 3. 1792
Northern amateur, 4. 1384
Northern counties daily mail, 3. 1799
Northern daily express, 3. 1794
Northern daily mail, 3. 1800
Northern daily telegraph, 3. 1802; 4. 1403

novel (*cont.*)
    German, 1. 882
    Italian, 1. 898–904
    Spanish, 1. 912–18
    Restoration and eighteenth century
      English, 2. 865–1034
      French, 2. 137–52
      German, 2. 180–6
      Italian, 2. 194–6
      Jacobite, 2. 2078–80
      Spanish, 2. 202–6
      theory of, 2. 60
      types of; epistolary, 2. 870; Gothic, 2. 870–1; picaresque, 2. 870; romance, 2. 869
    nineteenth century, 3. 657–1084
    twentieth century, 4. 381–784
      authors' manuals, 4. 66
    see also children's books
Novel magazine, 4. 1357
Novel reader, 2. 1312
Novel review, 3. 1851
Novelist's magazine, 2. 1306
'Novello, Ivor' (David Ivor Davies), 4. 970
Novello, Mary Victoria, 3. 1375–6
Novello, Ewer and Co, 3. 80
Novelty, 4. 1368
November annual, 4. 1387
Noverre, Jean Georges, 2. 1566
Novice (Dorset 1910), 4. 1382
Novice (Dublin 1927), 4. 1385
Now, 4. 1374
Now and then, 4. 1365
Now-days, 4. 1378
Noyes, Alfred, 4. 321–3, 793
Nuce, Thomas, 1. 1130–1, 1422
Nugae antiquae, 2. 390
Nugent, Christopher, 2. 1908
Nugent Maria, 3. 1673
Nugent, Robert, Earl, 2. 559
Nugent, Thomas, 2. 166, 1418
Nuggets, 3. 1826
Nulli secundus, 4. 1384
Nursery morals, 3. 1108
Nursery offering, 3. 1877
Nursery rhymes, 4. 1371
Nut-cracker, 2. 375
Nutbrown maid, 1. 1131
Nutshell, 2. 1287
Nutt (printers), 2. 265
Nuttall, Thomas, 3. 1671
Nyren, John, 3. 1696

'05 Club magazine, 4. 1358
O. P. record, 4. 1381

Oakeley, Frederick, 3. 1632
Oakes, Charles Henry, 3. 1879
Oakholme, 4. 1398
'Oakleigh, Thomas' (A. K. Killmister), 3. 1712
Oasis, 4. 1374
Oastler, Richard, 3. 1773
Oaten pipe, 2. 406
Oban times, 4. 1402
O'Brien, Edward Joseph, 4. 1365, 1371
'O'Brien, Flann' (Brian O' Nolan), 4. 683
O'Brien, James Bronterre, 3. 1811, 1818, 1819
O'Brien, John, 3. 1888
O'Brien, Kate, 4. 683–4
O'Brien, William, 2. 853, 1563
obscenity, 4. 101–2
Observations historical, political and philosophical, 1. 2109
Observations on the weekly bill, 2. 1341
Observations upon the most remarkable occurrences in our weekly news, 2. 1342
Observator (1654), 1. 2109
Observator (1681), 2. 1340
Observator (1702), 2. 1343
Observator (1704), 2. 1344
Observator (1705), 2. 1375
Observator (1715), 2. 1275
Observator (1725), 2. 1326
Observator observ'd, 2. 1341
Observator reformed, 2. 1344
Observator reviv'd, 2. 1344
Observer (1688), 2. 1318
Observer (1773), 2. 1285
Observer (1782), 2. 1347
Observer (Glasgow 1786), 2. 1372
Observer (Edinburgh 1793), 2. 1376
Observer (1791), 2. 1337; 3. 1807, 1834; 4. 1399, 1345
Observer (1792), 2. 1289
Observer of the times (and constitution), 3. 1809
O'Casey, Sean, 4. 879–85
Occasional and miscellaneous critic, 2. 1287
Occasional courant, 2. 1276
Occasional historian, 2. 1295
Occasional letters, 2. 1279
Occasional letters to 'Bob Short', 2. 1286
Occasional magazine, An (1899), 4. 1355
Occasional magazine (1932), 4. 850
Occasional paper (1697), 2. 1293
Occasional paper (1716), 2. 1276
Occasional paper upon the subject of religion, 2. 1279
Occasional papers, 4. 1357
Occasional papers by 'Nestor', 2. 1288
Occasional poems on the late Dutch war, 2. 347
Occasional respondent, 2. 1347

Occasional spectator, 2. 1279
Occasional writer (1727), 2. 1278
Occasional writer (1738), 2. 1279
Occasional writer (1762), 2. 1283
Occasionalist, 2. 1284
Occleve, Thomas, 1. 646-7
Occurrences from foreign parts, 1. 2110; 2. 1314
Occurrences of certain speciall. . .passages, 1. 2100
Ochino, Bernardino, 1. 2190, 850, 889
Ockham, William of, 1. 800-2
Ockley, Simon, 2. 1710-11, 1448
Ocland, Christopher, 1. 1131
O'Clery, Lughaidh, 3. 1887
O'Clery, Michael, 3. 1887
O'Connor, Charles, 3. 1888
O'Connor, Dermod, 3. 1888
O'Connor, Feargus, 3. 1818, 1848
'O'Connor, Frank' (Michael Francis O'Donovan) 4. 684-5
O'Connor, Matthew, 3. 1679
O'Connor, Thomas Power, 3. 1773-4, 1794, 1812; 4. 1356
Octavian, 1. 443
October: a poem, 2. 1558
October annual, 4. 1386
Octopus (1895), 3. 1868
Octopus (1912), 4. 1382
O'Curry, Eugene, 3. 1889-90
Odam, E. D., 4. 1381
O'Day, Edward F., 4. 1362
Odd fellow's song book, 2. 423
Odd volume, 4. 1359
Odell, Thomas, 2. 797
Odes (1800), 2. 429
Odes and satyrs of Horace, 2. 349
Odes, cantatas, songs. . .set to music by Pixell, 2. 396
Odingsells, Gabriel, 2. 797
Odo of Cheriton, 1. 776
O'Donnell, Peadar, 4. 1374
O'Donoghue, Mrs N. P., 3. 1706
O'Donovan, Edmund, 3. 1676
O'Donovan, John, 3. 1890
O'Donovan, Michael Francis, 4. 684-5
Oeconomist (1733), 2. 1327
Oeconomist (1798), 2. 1351
Oedipus: or the post-man remounted, 2. 1320
Oehlenschläger, Adam, 3. 148
O'Faoláin, Seán, 4. 685-6, 1374
Official army list, 3. 1879
Official news, 4. 1382
Official year book of the Church of England, 3. 1880
Offspring of fancy, 2. 419

Offspring of Russell, 2. 1011
Offspring of wit and harmony, 2. 401
O'Fihely, Mauritius, 1. 805
O'Flaherty, Liam, 4. 686-7
O'Flaherty, Roderic, 3. 1888
Ogden, Charles Kay, 4. 1098-9
Ogden, Peter Skene, 3. 1672
Ogilby, John, 2. 1397, 1445, 1455
Ogilvie, John, 2. 239-40
Ogle, Barbarina, Baroness Dacre, 3. 370-1
Ogle, George, 2. 559-60, 238
Ogle, Sir John, 1. 1131
Ogle, Ponsonby, 3. 1792
Oglethorpe, James Edward, 2. 1461
O'Grady, Standish James, 3. 1892-4, 1106; 4. 1355
Ogston, William, 1. 2474
O'Halloran, Sylvester, 3. 1888-9
O'Hara, Kane, 2. 854
O'Hara, Robert Patrick, 3. 1865
'Oke, Richard' (Nigel Millett), 4. 687
O'Keeffe, Adelaide, 3. 1087, 1100
O'Keeffe, John 2. 854-6
Okeley, William, 2. 1446
O'Kelly, Seumas, 4. 687-8
Olcott, Henry Steel, 4. 1352
Old and new interest, 2. 377
Old and young, 3. 1825
Old British spy, 2. 1332
'Old Calabor', 3. 1706
Old college, 3. 1869
Old common sense, 2. 1279, 1329
Old Dublin intelligence, 2. 1381
Old England (1743), 2. 1279, 1331
Old England (1824), 3. 1810
Old England (1832), 3. 1813
Old England's journal, 2. 1331
Old English literature, 1. 187-356
  anthologies, 1. 189-92
  bibliographies, 1. 187-8
  charters, 1. 70-1, 331-2
  Chronicle, 1. 329-32
  folklore, 1. 334-6
  Germanic background, 1. 197-206
  history, 1. 205-10
  language
    general, 1. 59-76
    dialects, 1. 65-6
    dictionaries, 1. 54
    syntax, 1. 117-22
    vocabulary, 1. 143-54
  Latin, 1. 335-56
    Anglo-Saxon, 1. 343-52
    anthologies, 1. 335-6
    British Celtic, 1. 337-42

Operative (1838), 3. 1811
Operative (1851), 3. 1819
Opie, Amelia, 3. 753–4
Opitz, Martin, 1. 880
Oppenheim, E. C., 3. 1710
Oppenheim, Henry, 3. 1790
Oppidan, 3. 1870
Optical lantern, 4. 56
Opus, 4. 1374
Opzoomer, Adèle S. C., 3. 94
Oracle (1715), 2. 1323
Oracle (Bristol 1742), 2. 1354
Oracle (1789), 2. 1328, 1337; 3. 1789
Oracle (Dublin 1797), 2. 1387
Oracle (1798), 2. 1327
Oracle (1933), 4. 1371
Oracle country advertiser, 2. 1354
Oracle of reason, 3. 1819
Oracle of rural life, 3. 1683
Oracles, containing some particulars of the history of Billy and Kitty Wilson, 2. 1027
Orage, Alfred Richard, 4. 1099–1100, 1353, 1370
Orange gazette (1688), 2. 1318
Orange gazette (Edinburgh 1689), 2. 1374
Oratava observer, 4. 1383
oratory, Restoration and eighteenth century, 2. 7.
Oratory magazine, 2. 1299
Orbach, John, 4. 1374
Orcherd of Syon, 1. 517
Ord, John Walker, 3. 544
Order of the world, 1. 293
Ordericus Vitalis, 1. 758
Ordinalia (Cornish), 1. 727–8
Ordish, W. H., 4. 1388
Ordo representacionis Ade, 1. 725–6
O'Reilly, Edward, 3. 1889
Oriel record, 4. 1397
Oriental annual, 3. 1875
Oriental asylum for fugitive pieces, 2. 410
Oriental collections, 2. 1311
Oriental fabulist, 2. 1286
Oriental herald and colonial review, 3. 1845
Oriental literature
　Restoration and eighteenth century studies, 2. 1831–2
　twentieth century relations with, 4. 32–4
Oriental Masonic Muse, 2. 415
Oriental repertory, 2. 1309
Origen, 2. 1499
Origin of Rugby football, 3. 1702
Original and genuine letters, 2. 356
Original half-penny London journal, 2. 1326
Original Ipswich journal, 2. 1359
Original letters from a young American, 2. 1285
Original letters, moral and entertaining, 2. 1287

Original London post (1719), 2. 1324
Original London post (1738), 2. 1329
Original mercury, 2. 1368
Original poems and translations, 2. 348
Original prologues, epilogues and other pieces, 2. 378
Original prologues, epilogues and other theatrical pieces, 2. 387
Original star, 2. 1337
Original weekly journal, 2. 1275, 1322
Original York journal, 2. 1368
'Orinda' (Katherine Philips), 2. 480
Orion, 4. 1377
Orion Adams's Manchester journal, 2. 1361
Orion Adams's weekly journal, 2. 1361
Orme, Robert, 2. 1739, 1439–40
Ormulum, 1. 485–6
Orosius (OE version), 1. 315–16
Orphan, 2. 1323
Orphan reviv'd: or Powell's weekly journal, 2. 1324
Orpheus (1749), 2. 373
Orpheus (1909) theosophist journal, 4. 1358
Orpheus (1923), 4. 1366, 1384
Orpheus (1948), 4. 1379
Orpheus britannicus (1698), 2. 340
Orpheus britannicus (1760), 2. 381
Orpheus caledonius, 2. 356
Orrery, Roger Boyle, 1st Earl of, 2. 769–70, 977, 978, 981; 1. 2058
Ortelius, Abraham, 1. 2120
Ortigue, Pierre d', Sieur de Vaumorière, 2. 1533, 975
Ortiz de Melgarejo, Antonio, 1. 916
Ortulus animae, 1. 1935
Ortúñez de Calahorra, Diego, 1. 2190, 913
'Orwell, George' (Eric Arthur Blair), 4. 690–6
Osbaldeston, George, 3. 1708
Osbaldiston, William Augustus, 2. 1561
Osbeck, Peter, 2. 1440
Osbern of Gloucester, 1. 764
Osbert of Clare, 1. 764
Osborn's penny post, 2. 1327
Osborne, Francis, 1. 2246–8, 2047, 2050, 2142
Osborne, J. H., 3. 1758
Osborne, Thomas, 1. 2112; 2. 1392
Osborne's railway time table, 3. 1881
O'Shaughnessy, Arthur William Edgar, 3. 1906–7
O'Shea, John Augustus, 3. 1774
Osiander, Andreas, 1. 877
Osmer, William, 2. 1554
Osorio da Fonseca, Jeronimo, 1. 850, 2190; 2. 1392
'Ossian'; *see* Macpherson 2. 603–5, 132–3, 168–9, 193, 200, 207, 212, 217, 1738
Ostrovsky, Aleksandr Nikolayevich, 3. 153

Oxford and district morning echo, 3. 1803
Oxford critic and university magazine, 3. 1868
Oxford diurnall, 1. 2097
Oxford drollery, 2. 330
Oxford essays, 3. 1868
Oxford flying weekly journal, 2. 1364
Oxford fortnightly, 4. 1397
Oxford fortnightly review, 4. 1397
Oxford gazette (1665), 2. 1364
Oxford gazette and Reading mercury (1745), 2. 1365
Oxford herald, 4. 1396
Oxford journal: or the tradesman's intelligencer, 2. 1328, 1364
Oxford literary gazette, 3. 1868
Oxford magazine (1736), 2. 1297
Oxford magazine (1737), 2. 1298
Oxford magazine (1768), 2. 1304
Oxford magazine (1845), 3. 1868
Oxford magazine (1883), 3. 1868, 1872; 4. 1396
Oxford mercury, 2. 1364
Oxford miscellany, 3. 1867
Oxford morning echo, 3. 1803
Oxford movement, 3. 1621–36
Oxford outlook, 4. 1397
Oxford packet, 2. 348
Oxford poetry, 4. 1397
Oxford point of view, 4. 1396
Oxford post: or the ladies new tatler, 2. 1324
Oxford quarterly magazine, 3. 1868
Oxford Repertory Company: annual report, 4. 851
Oxford review (1807), 3. 1867
Oxford review (1882), 3. 1868
Oxford review (1885), 3. 1868; 4. 1396
Oxford review (1919), 4. 1397
Oxford sausage, 2. 385
Oxford spectator, 3. 1868
Oxford times, 4. 1402
Oxford to John O'Groats, 3. 1684
Oxford undergraduates journal, 3. 1868; 4. 1396
Oxford University calendar, 3. 1881
Oxford University gazette, 3. 1868
Oxford University magazine (1834), 3. 1868
Oxford University magazine and review (1869), 3. 1868
Oxford University Press, 3. 59; 4. 95
Oxford University review, 4. 1397
Oxford viewpoint, 4. 1398
Oxfordshire, general bibliography, 1. 18
Oxfordshire contest, 2. 377
Oxfordshire in an uproar, 2. 377
Oxley, John Joseph William Molesworth, 3. 1675
Oxonian (1817), 3. 1867, 1873
Oxonian (1847), 3. 1868
Ozanam, Jacques, 2. 1566
Ozell, John, 2. 1293

PAD, 4. 859
P., G. (fl. 1584), 1. 2077
P., H. (H. Punchard), 2. 1017
P.I.P., 3. 1816; 4. 1401
P., L. (fl. 1656), 1. 2058
PL pamphlets, 4. 1373
PLA quarterly, 4. 118
'P., M.' (Dorothy Kilner), 2. 1024
P.M. (Penny magazine), 4. 1355
P., R. (fl. 1642), journalist, 1. 2095
P., R. (fl. 1642), satirist, 1. 2040
P., R. (fl. 1659), writer on geography, 1. 2122
P., Theophilus, 1. 2036
P., W. (fl. 1720), 2. 989
Pace, Richard, 1. 854
Pacifick postscript to the post boy, 2. 1319
Pack, Richardson, 2. 560
Packet of letters from Sir Thomas Fairfax, A, 1. 2101
Packets of letters, 1. 2103
Pacquet-boat from Holland and Flanders, 2. 1319
Pacquet from Parnassus, 2. 342, 1293
Pacquet from Will's, A, 2. 341–2
Pacquet of advice from France, 2. 1342
Pacquet of advice from Rome, A, 2. 1339
Pacquet of advice from Rome restored, 2. 1341
Paddy Whack's bottle companion, 2. 415
Paddy's resource, 2. 425
Paez de Ribera, Ruy, 1. 912
Pagan, Blaise François de, Comte de Merveilles, 2. 1454
Pagan, James, 3. 1804
Pagan prince, 2. 982
Page, Charlotte A., 3. 1670
Page, John, 1. 682
Page, Samuel, 1. 1315
Page, Thomas, 2. 1559, 1563
Page, William, 1. 802
Page, 4. 1354
Pageant post, 4. 1396
Pagès, Pierre-Marie François de, 2. 1473, 1482, 1486
Paget, E., 3. 1730
Paget, Francis Edward, 3. 1633, 1090
Paget, Guy, 3. 1708
Paget, Thomas Catesby, Baron, 2. 561
Paget, Violet, 3. 1444–6
Pagitt, Ephraim, 1. 2120
Paglia, Antonio dalla, 1. 2190
Pagula, William de, 1. 802
Paignton's amusements and visitor's guide, 4. 848
Pain, Barry Eric Odell, 4. 697–9; 3. 1815
Paine, Thomas, 2. 1888–90, 159
Painter, William (d. 1594), 1. 2051
Painter, William (fl. 1623), 1. 2028

Painter, William (fl. 1787), 2. 1568
painting, Restoration and eighteenth century, 2. 67–70
Paish, George, 3. 1824
Paisley daily express, 3. 1805
Palace miscellany, 2. 362
Palacio Valdés, Armando, 3. 142
palaeography, Old and Middle English, 1. 209–26
  see also manuscripts
Palatine review, 4. 1362, 1397
Paley, William, 2. 1890, 159, 164, 1908
Palgrave, Francis Turner, 3. 545, 1092
Palgrave, William Gifford, 3. 1670, 1675
Palingenius, Marcellus (P.A. Manzolli), 1. 2190, 855
Pall Mall budget, 3. 1815
Pall Mall gazette, 3. 1793, 1829; 4. 1347
Pall Mall magazine, 3. 1854; 4. 1353
Pall-Mall miscellany, 2. 362
Palladio, Andrea, 2. 1547
Palladium (1749), 2. 1313
Palladium (1825), 3. 1821
Palladius, 1. 687
Pallavicino, Sforza, 2. 1547
Palliser, John, 3. 1673
Palmer, Cecil, 4. 1365
Palmer, Charlotte, 2. 1006
Palmer, Edward Henry, 3. 1675, 1865
Palmer, F. P., 3. 1108
Palmer, George, 1. 2040
Palmer, George Josiah, 3. 1823
Palmer, Henry John, 3. 1797
Palmer, Herbert, 1. 1997, 2045, 2049
Palmer, Herbert Edward, 4. 326–7
Palmer, Joseph, 2. 1423
Palmer, Roger, Earl of Castlemaine, 2. 1410
Palmer, Samuel, 3. 67
Palmer, T. A., 3. 1194
Palmer, Thomas, 1. 805
Palmer, Sir William (1803–85), 3. 1633
Palmer, William (1811–79), 3. 1633
Palmer, William Stern, 3. 1880
Palmerin romances, 1. 913
Palmerston, Henry Temple, 2nd Viscount, 2. 1428
Palmerston, Henry John Temple, 3rd Viscount, 3. 1298–9, 1733
Pals, 4. 1384
Palsgrave, John, 1. 1419–20
Paltock, Robert, 2. 997
Pam's paper, 4. 1366
Paman, Clement, 1. 1315
pamphlets and pamphleteers
  Renaissance to Restoration, 1. 2007–22, 2069–80

Restoration and eighteenth century, 2. 1035–1256;
  see also essays, magazines, newspapers, prose
Παν (1903), 4. 1396
Pan (1919), 4. 1363
Pancharis, queen of love, 2. 354
Panciroli, Guido, 2. 1548
Pancratia, or a history of pugilism, 3. 1692
Panegyrick on Oliver Cromwell, A, 1. 1011; 2. 345
Paneth, Philip, 4. 1361
Panorama, 4. 1394
Panther (O.E.); see *Physiologus*, 1. 294
pantomime, 4. 853–62
Pantomime and vaudeville favourites, 4. 860
Panton, Edward, 2. 977
Panton magazine, 4. 1367
Pantosfinx, 4. 1395
Paolino da San Bartolomeo, 2. 1444
paper and papermaking
  Renaissance to Restoration, 1. 927–30
  Restoration and eighteenth century, 2. 251–4
  nineteenth century, 3. 27–32
  twentieth century, 4. 76–7;
  see also book production and distribution
Paper and print (1879), 3. 61
Paper and print (1928), 4. 77
Paper and printing bits, 3. 32, 62
Paper and printing trades journal, 3. 32, 61
Paper and pulp, 3. 32
Paper box and bag maker, 3. 32
Paper consumers' circular, 3. 32
Paper exchange news, 3. 32
Paper maker (1891), 3. 32; 4. 77
Paper-maker (1937), 4. 78
Paper Makers' Association, its *reports*, 4. 78
Paper makers' circular and rag price current (1861), 3. 32
Paper makers' circular and rag price current (1874), 3. 32; 4. 77
Paper-making abstracts, 4. 78
Paper market, 3. 32; 4. 77
Paper record, 3. 32
Paper trade news, 3. 32
Paper trade review (1862), 3. 32
Paper trade review (1879), 3. 32; 4. 77
paperbacks, 4. 98–9
Papermakers' monthly journal, 3. 32; 4. 77
Papermaking, 3. 32; 4. 77
Papers for the schoolmaster, 3. 1848
Papers sent from the Scotts quarters, 1. 2101
Paphian doves, 2. 406
Papin, Denis, 2. 1908
Paracelsus, 1. 850
Parachute, 3. 1870
Parade (1915), 4. 1406

Parade (1937), 4. 1373
Paradyse of daynty devises, 1. 1008
Parasol, 4. 1396
Pardoe, Margot Mary, 4. 807
Pardon, George Frederick, 3. 1693, 1694, 1825
Parental monitor, 2. 1290
Parini, Guiseppe, 2. 1548
Paris, John, 2. 1427
Paris, Matthew, 1. 775–6
Paris gazette, 2. 1375
Paris gazette english'd, 2. 1321, 1381
Paris mercury, 2. 1337
Paris pendant l'année, 2. 1310
Paris psalter, 1. 293, 323–4
Parish councils' journal, 4. 1404
Park, Mungo, 2. 1452; 3. 1669
Park, Thomas, 3. 1662
Parke, Ernest, 3. 1794
Parker, Charles Stuart, 3. 1727
Parker, D. (fl. 1805), 3. 1842
Parker, Frederick M. S., 3. 1870
Parker, George (fl. 1719), 2. 1460
Parker, George (1732–1800), 2. 1404
Parker, Henry, 8th Baron Morley (d. 1556); 1. 1132
Parker, Henry (1604–52), 1. 2087–8
Parker, John (1875–1952), 4. 825, 859
Parker, John Henry, 3. 1839
Parker, John William (1792–1870), 3. 1819, 1845
Parker, John William, the younger (1820–60), 3. 1845
Parker, Louis Napoleon, 4. 971–2
Parker, Martin, 1. 2031, 2033, 2080, 2102
Parker, Mary Ann, 2. 1482
Parker, Matthew, 1. 1820–1, 2207–8, 1002, 1132, 1902
Parker, Samuel (1640–88), 1. 2341; 2. 1612–13
Parker, Samuel (1681–1730), 2. 1293
Parker's general advertiser, 2. 1335
Parker's London news, 2. 1324
Parker's penny post, 2. 1324
Parkes, Bessie R., 3. 1746
Parkes, Samuel, 2. 1908
Parkhurst, Anthony, 1. 2161
Parkinson, James, 3. 1100
Parkinson, Sydney, 2. 1479
Parks, Joseph, 4. 1382, 1383, 1384
Parkyns, Mansfield, 3. 1670
Parkyns, Sir Thomas, 2. 1569
Parlement of the thre ages, 1. 547
'Parley, Peter' (Goodrich *et al.*), 3. 1089–90
Parliament-kite, 1. 2103
Parliament porter, 1. 2104
Parliament scout, 1. 2098

Parliaments post, 1. 2101
Parliaments scouts discovery, 1. 2098
Parliaments scriche owle, 1. 2104
Parliaments vulture, 1. 2104
Parliamentary intelligencer, 1. 2110; 2. 1315
Parliamentary pocket companion, 3. 1880
Parliamentary register, 2. 1305
Parliamentary review (and family magazine), 3. 1813
Parliamentary spy (extraordinary), 2. 1284
Parlour window, 2. 1380
Parminter, Jane, 2. 1426
Parnassian, 4. 1366
Parnassian garland, 2. 424
Parnassium, 2. 383
Parnassus, 4. 1385
Parnassus biceps, 1. 1010
Parnassus plays, 1. 1778, 2314
Parnell, James, 2. 1651
Parnell, Thomas, 2. 561
Parr, Catherine, 1. 1938
Parr, Harriet, 3. 941–2, 1093
Parr, Samuel, 2. 1827–8
Parr, Wolstenholme, 2. 1789
Parrot, Henry, 1. 1335, 2044
Parrot (1728), 2. 1278
Parrot (1735), 2. 1328
Parrot (1746), 2. 1279, 1332
Parry, Catherine, 2. 1007
Parry, Sir Charles Hubert Hastings, 3. 1449
Parry, Sir Edward Abbott, 3. 1106
Parry, J. D., 3. 1874
Parry, Robert, 1. 1132, 2054
Parry, William, 1. 2144
Parry, Sir William Edward, 3. 1671–2
Parsley's (fashionable) lyric companion, 2. 408
Parsley's lyric repository, 2. 410
Parson's daughter, 2. 351
Parsons, Benjamin, 3. 1723
Parsons, Clere Trevor James Herbert, 4. 327, 1397
Parsons, Eliza, 3. 755; 2. 1010, 1011, 1012
Parsons, Philip (d. 1653), 1. 1772
Parsons, Philip (d. 1812), 2. 1554
Parsons, Robert, 1. 1930–1, 854, 878, 2275
Partes, Robert, 1. 766
Parthenia, 1. 1778
Parthenon, 3. 1821
Partiall law, 1. 1760
Particular advice from the office of intelligence, A, 1. 2110; 2. 1314
Particular description of the city of Dantzick, A, 2. 1417
Particular relation of the most remarkable occurrences, A, 1. 2100

Payne, J. B., 3. 1697
Payne, John (d. 1787), 2. 280
Payne, John (1842–1916), 3. 643–4
Payne, Joseph, 3. 1728
Payne, Robert, 1. 2132
Payne, Roger, 2. 292
Payne, William, 2. 1567
Payne's universal chronicle, 2. 1333
Payne-Gallwey, Sir R. W. F., 3. 1713
Peach, Louis du Garde, 4. 973–5
Peacham, Henry, the elder, 1. 2309
Peacham, Henry, the younger, 1. 1315–16, 1335, 1330, 2316, 2026, 2049, 2135
Peacock, Lucy, 2. 1007, 1010, 1025, 1029
Peacock, Thomas Love, 3. 700–4, 1100, 1694
Peacock, W., 3. 1711
Peake, Mervyn Laurence, 4. 699, 812
Peake, Richard Brinsley, 3. 1135, 1712
Peake, Thomas, 1. 2164
Peaps, William, 1. 1753
Pearce, P. H., 3. 1715
Pearce, Zachary, 2. 1774, 1828
Pearl, 1. 549–52
Pearl poet, 1. 547–54
Pearse, Andrew, 4. 1377
Pearson, Mrs —, 3. 1108
Pearson, Sir C. Arthur, 3. 1774, 1792, 1815,/1854
Pearson, Charles Henry, 3. 1857
Pearson, Edward Hesketh Gibbons, 4. 1201–2
Pearson, Gabriel, 4. 1397
Pearson, George, 3. 1732
Pearson, Hesketh, 4. 1201–2
Pearson, John, 1. 1997–8, 2295, 2299
Pearson, Karl, 3. 1577
Pearson, Mary, 4. 808
Pearson's magazine, 3. 1854; 4. 1354
Pearson's weekly, 3. 1815; 4. 1403
Peasant, 4. 1405
Pease, Sir Alfred Edward, 3. 1707
Pease, [John?], 2. 2067
Pebody, Charles, 3. 1797
Pecham, John, 1. 774–5
Peck, Francis, 2. 1774
Pecke, Samuel, 1. 2089, 2092, 2095, 2096, 2098, 2100, 2101, 2102, 2106
Pecke, Thomas, 1. 1337
Peckham, Sir George, 1. 2151
Peckham, Harry, 2. 1422, 1427
Pecock, Reginald, 1. 665–6, 805
Pecuniae obediunt omnia, 2. 340
Peden, Alexander, 2. 2036
Pedersen, Christiern, 1. 921
Pedler's prophecie, 1. 1410
Peek, Francis, 3. 1850
Peeke, Richard, 1. 2080

Peele, George, 1. 1431–4, 881, 1133, 2056
Peend, Thomas, 1. 1133
Peep at the Continent, A, 3. 1679
Peep into Paris, A, 2. 1429
Peeper, 2. 1288
peerage, year-books, nineteenth century, 3. 1879
Peerage (and baronetage) of the British Empire, 3. 1879
Peeris, William, 1. 1133
Peerson, Martin, 1. 1356
Peg's companion, 4. 1365
Peg's paper, 4. 1363
Pegasus, with news, 2. 1342
Pegge, Samuel, the elder, 2. 1796
Peirse, Thomas, 1. 1998, 2339
'Pelham, M.', (Dorothy Kilner), 2. 1024
Pelican, 3. 1815
Pelican Press, 4. 98
Pelican record, 3. 1869; 4. 1396
Pellham, Edward, 1. 2080, 2128
Pellisson-Fontanier, Paul, 2. 67
Pellow, Thomas, 2. 1449
Pelopidarum secunda, 1. 1760
Peltier, Jean Gabriel, 2. 1338
Pem, 3. 1867; 4. 1393
Pemberton, Sir Max, 3. 1826, 1851
Pemble, William, 1. 2120
Pembroke, its library, 2. 308
Pembroke, Henry Herbert, 10th Earl of, 2. 1554
Pembroke, Mary Herbert, Countess of, 1. 1115–16, 1468–9, 1906
Pen! 4. 1384
Pen and pencil, 3. 1816
Pendred, W., 1. 2101
Penguin film review, 4. 58
Penguin new writing, 4. 1375
Penguin parade, 4. 1373
Penhallow, Samuel, 2. 1461
Penhouet, A. B. L. Maudet de, 2. 1407
Penington, Isaac, 2. 1647–8
Penington, Mary, 2. 1651
Penitent hermit, 2. 979
Penitent's prayer (OE); see *Resignation*, 1. 296
penitential texts, Old English, 1. 328
Peniworþ of witte, A, 1. 457
Penkethman's jests, 2. 354
Penn, John, 2. 1472
Penn, Richard, 3. 1688
Penn, Sir William (1621–70), admiral, 1. 2129–30, 2160
Penn, William (1644–1718), quaker, 2. 1644–7, 114–15, 1413, 1455
Pennant, Thomas, 2. 1403, 1420, 1486
Pennecuik, Alexander, MD (1652–1722), 2. 1965–6

Pennecuik, Alexander (d. 1730), merchant and poet, 2. 1977–8
Pennell, Harry Cholmondeley, 3. 1689–90
Pennington, Thomas, 2. 1431
Penny-farthing, 4. 1369
Penny illustrated paper, 3. 1816; 4. 1401
Penny i[ntelligencer?] 2. 1328
Penny London morning advertiser (January 1744), 2. 1331
Penny London morning advertiser (August 1744), 2. 1331
Penny London post (1725), 2. 1326
Penny London post (1744), 2. 1331
Penny magazine (1832), 3. 1813
Penny magazine (1903), 4. 1355
Penny medley, 2. 1299, 1332
Penny newsman and Sunday morning mail, 3. 1812
Penny pictorial news, 3. 1817
Penny pictorial weekly, 3. 1817
Penny-post (1715). 2. 1323
Penny post (1717), 2. 1324
Penny satirist, 3. 1813
Penny story-teller, 4. 1361
Penny Sunday times, 3. 1811
Penny weekly journal, 2. 1325
Penrith observer, 4. 1401
Penrose, Bernard, 2. 1469
Penrose, Elizabeth, 3. 1089
Penrose, Ethel Charlotte, 3. 1105
Penrose, Francis, 2. 1908
Penrose annual, 4. 81
Penrose's annual, 4. 81
Penrose's pictorial annual, 3. 62; 4. 81
Penry, J., 1. 1959
Pentelow, J. N., 3. 1698
People, 3. 1812; 4. 1403
People's and Howitt's journal, 3. 1814
People's conservative and trades union gazette, 3. 1818
People's journal, 3. 1814
People's paper (1852), 3. 1819
People's paper (1906), 4. 1381
People's press, 3. 1820
Pepler, Douglas, 4. 1363
Peppa, 2. 982
Pepper, W., 2. 1564
Pepperell, Sir William, 2. 1463
Pepys, Samuel, 2. 1582–4, 110, 310–11, 1446
Perceval, romance of, 1. 410–11
Perceval, Arthur Philip, 3. 1633
Percy, Elizabeth, Duchess of Northumberland, 2. 1423
Percy, Henry, 9th Earl of Northumberland, 1. 1002
Percy, R., 4. 824, 1358

Percy, Thomas, 2. 242–5, 43, 134, 167, 205, 236, 312
Percy, William, 1. 1133–4
Peregrinations of Jeremiah Grant, 2. 1000
Pérez, Alonso, 1. 912
Pérez de Montalvan, Juan, 1. 916, 2063
Perez de Pineda, Juan, 1. 909
Pérez Galdós, Benito, 3. 142–3
Perfect account of the daily intelligence, A, 1. 2107
Perfect and impartial intelligence, 1. 2109
Perfect and more particular relation, A, 1. 2106
Perfect collection of all the songs now in mode, A, 2. 332
Perfect collection of the several songs now in mode, A, 2. 332
Perfect declaration, A, 1. 2101
Perfect description of Virginia, A, 1. 2164
Perfect diary of passages of the Kings army, A, 1. 2104
Perfect diurnall, A (1642–54), 1. 2095–6, 2098, 2105, 2106, 2109
Perfect diurnal(l), A (1660), 2. 1315
Perfect narrative of the . . . tryal of the King, A, 1. 2104
Perfect occurrences (1644–54), 1. 2100, 2108
Perfect occurrences (1659?), 2. 1315
Perfect occurrences (1660), 2. 1315
Perfect particulars of every daies intelligence, 1. 2107
Perfect passages of each dayes proceedings, 1. 2101
Perfect passages of every daies intelligence, 1. 2106
Perfect proceedings of state affaires, 1. 2106
Perfect relation or summarie, A, 1. 2097
Perfect summary of an exact diarye, A, 1. 2104
Perfect summary of chiefe passages, A, 1. 2102, 2103, 2104
Perfect summary of exact passages, A, 1. 2104
Perfect tiurnall, A, 1. 2100
Perfect weekly account, 1. 2099, 2103, 2106
Perfidious P —, 2. 985
Perfidus Hetruscus, 1. 1778
Performer, 4. 825, 859, 866
Performer annual, 4. 825, 859, 866
Performer handbook, 4. 866
Performing Right (bulletin), 4. 874
Performing right gazette, 4. 874
Performing Right Society (emergency) bulletin, 4. 874
Performritings, 4. 874
Periegetes, Dionysius, 1. 2119
Periodical, 4. 1397
periodical essays, Restoration and eighteenth century
    Irish, 2. 1377–80
    London, 2. 1269–90
    provinces, 2. 1347–50

periodical essays (*cont.*)
  Scottish, 2. 1369–72
  see also magazines, newspapers, periodicals
Periodical essays, 2. 1286
periodicals
  Renaissance to Restoration, 1. 2067–110
  Restoration and eighteenth century, 2. 1255–
    1390
    general, 2. 1257–66
    annuals, 2. 1313–14
    Channel Isles, 2. 1389–90
    French, 2. 86–90
    Irish, 2. 1377–90; bibliography, 2. 1377–8;
      magazines, 2. 1379–80; newspapers, 2.
      1381–90; periodical essays, 2. 1377–
      80
    London, magazines, 2. 1291–1312; news-
      letters, 2. 1339–40; newspapers, 2. 1313–
      40; periodical essays, 2. 1269–90; serials,
      2. 1339–46
    printing, 2. 1265–70
    provinces, 2. 1345–70; bibliography, 2.
      1345–8; magazines, 2. 1349–52; news-
      papers, 2. 1353–70; periodical essays, 2.
      1347–50
    Scottish, 2, 1369–78; bibliography, 2. 1369–
      70; magazines, 2. 1371–4; newspapers, 2.
      1373–8; periodical essays, 2. 1369–72
    Welsh, 2. 1389–90
  nineteenth century
    advertising, 3. 1758
    angling, 3. 1687
    archery, 3. 1691
    athletics, 3. 1691
    billiards, 3. 1692
    book trade, 3. 85
    boxing, 3. 1692
    chess, 3. 1694
    children's, 3. 1109–10
    cricket, 3. 1695
    football, 3. 1701
    golf, 3. 1702
    hunting, 3. 1703
    journalism, 3. 1762
    mountaineering, 3. 1708–9
    newspapers and magazines, annuals, 3. 1873–
      84; daily and weekly press, 3. 1789–1838;
      journalism, 3. 1761–88; magazines and
      reviews, 3. 1839–66; school and university
      journalism, 3. 1865–74; technical develop-
      ment, 3. 1755–62
    newspaper management, 3. 1758–60
    printing trade, 3. 59–62, 81–4
    racing, 3. 1703
    rowing, 3. 1711

    shooting, 3. 1712
    tennis, 3. 1715
    theatre, 3. 1123–4
    yachting, 3. 1716
  twentieth century
    advertising, 4. 1342–4
    authorship, 4. 71–4
    children's books, 4. 819–20
    current books, 4. 117–20
    book collecting, 4. 110
    book plates and stamps, 4. 108
    bookselling, 4. 106–8
    broadcasting, 4. 60
    film, 4. 56–8
    gramophone, 4. 54
    journalism, 4. 1340
    librarianship, 4. 116–18
    newspapers and magazines; history, 4. 1329–
      38; individual newspapers and magazines,
      4. 1349–1408; journalism, 4. 1337–44; lists,
      4. 1347–50; studies, 4. 1343–8
    newspaper and magazine publishing, 4.
      1343–4
    paper, 4. 77–8
    printing trade, 4. 81–4
    publishing, 4. 100
    song-writing, 4. 74
    theatre, 4. 823–8, 848–52, 854, 858–62, 866–
      8, 873–4, 877–8, 879–80
    see also magazines, newspapers, periodical
      essays
Periodicals and books, 4. 119
Perjur'd citizen: or female revenge, 2. 993
Perkins, Sue Chesnutwood, 3. 1104
Perkins, William, 1. 1931–2, 878, 910, 2331
Perlès, Alfred, 4. 1372
Pernety, Antoine Joseph, 2. 1468
Perondinus, Petrus, 1. 850
Perrault, Charles, 2. 1525, 116, 142, 992, 1031
Perronet, Edward, 2. 675
Perronet, Vincent, 2. 1865
Perry Charles, 2. 1438
Perry, James, 2. 1306, 1334, 1337; 3. 1789, 1792,
  1840
Perry, John, 2. 1416
Perry, Sampson, 3. 1792
Persepolis illustrata, 2. 1438
Persius, 1. 2174; 2. 1499, 35
Person, David, 1. 2049
Personal landscape, 4. 1375
Personal letter, 4. 1407
Personality, 4. 74
'Perspective, John', 2. 1327
*Persuasion, advertising, public relations and
  propaganda*, 4. 1344

Perth, printing, 2. 272
Perth magazine, 2. 1374
Pertwee, Roland, 4. 975
Pervigilium Veneris, 1. 2174; 2. 1500
Pery, Edmund Sexton, Viscount, 2. 999
Pestalozzi, Mrs Conrad, 3. 1680
Pestalozzi, John Henry, 3. 1719
Pestel, Thomas, 1. 1316
Peter of Blois, 1. 764
Peter, Hugh, 1. 1998
Peter Hoey's publick journal, 2. 1386
Peter Idley's instructions, 1. 504
Peter Parley's annual, 3. 1878
Peter Parley's magazine, 3. 1847
Peterborough Abbey library, 1. 995
Peterhouse magazine, 3. 1867
Peters, Hugh, 1. 1998
Peters, J. G., 3. 1704
Peterson, Arthur E., 4. 860, 880
Peterson, Robert, 1. 2120
Pétis de la Croix, François, 2. 1519, 986, 987
Petowe, Henry, 1. 1134, 2073
Petrarch, Francesco, 1. 2191, 850, 855, 890;
    2. 1548, 192
Petrarchism, in Renaissance Europe, 1. 890–93
Petrić, Francesco, 1. 850, 889
Petrie, Sir Charles Alexander, 4. 1202–3
Petrie, George, 3. 1889
Petronius, 1. 2174; 2. 1500, 983
Pett, Peter, 1. 1134
Pett, Phineas, 1. 2247
Petter, George William, 3. 1816
Pettie, George, 1. 2052
Pettigrew, J. J., 3. 1693
Petty, Sir William, 2. 1848–9, 1908
Petyt, William, 2. 1696
Pevsner, Sir Nikolaus, 4. 1101–2
Peyron, Jean-François, 2. 1425
Pfeiffer, Emily Jane, 3. 546, 1748
Pfeil, J., 2. 1540
Phaer, Thomas, 1. 1135
Phanatick intelligencer, 2. 1315
'Phantom, Felix' (R. Heron), 2. 1372
Pharaoh, J., 2. 1351
Pharaoh, 1. 293
Pharos, 2. 1287
Phelan, Charlotte Elizabeth, 3. 1846, 1876
Phelps, Thomas, 2. 1446
Phenix (1707), 2. 1344
Phenix (1789), 2. 1387
Pheon, 4. 1393
Phil May's illustrated annual, 4. 1353
Philadelphian magazine, 2. 1308
Philadelphian Society, 2. 1658
Philalethes, Mercurius, 1. 2034

'Philander', 1. 1316
Philanthropic gazette, 3. 1812
Philanthropist, 2. 1289
'Philanthropos', 2. 1306
'Philaretes', 1. 2037
Philibert de Vienne, 1. 2191, 864
'Philidor' (F. A. Danican), 2. 1567
Philip, Alexander John, 4. 106
Philip, George, 3. 80
Philip, John, 1. 2071
Philipot, Thomas, 1. 1316
Philipott, John, 1. 2136
Philipps, Fabian, 1. 2040
Philips, Ambrose, 2. 562–3, 1276
Philips, Erasmus, 2. 1277
Philips, George, 2. 1446
Philips, John (1676–1709), 2. 563
Philips, John (fl. 1744), 2. 1478
Philips, John Burton, 3. 1677
Philips, Katherine, 2. 480
Philips, Samuel, 2. 1293, 1321
Philips, William, 2. 797
Phillip, Arthur, 2. 1482
Phillip, John, 1. 1135, 1417
Phillipps-Wolley, Sir Clive, 3. 1713
Phillips, Edward (1630–96?), 1. 2032
Phillips, Edward (fl. 1730–9), 2. 797, 1800
Phillips, Ernest, 3. 1774
Phillips, J. S. Ragland, 3. 1795
Phillips, John (fl. 1566–94), 1. 1135, 1417
Phillips, John (1631–1706), 2. 480–2, 1291; 1.
    2028–9
Phillips, Sir Richard (1767–1840), publisher, 3.
    80, 1774, 1792, 1841
Phillips, Richard (1778–1851), chemist, 3. 1841,
    1842, 1843
Phillips, S., 3. 83
Phillips, S. C., 3. 32
Phillips, Samuel, 3. 958, 1809
Phillips, Stephen, 3. 1194–6; 4. 1359
Phillips, Thomas, 2. 1448
Phillips, Watts, 3. 1154
Phillpotts, Eden, 4. 699–704; 3. 1098
Phillpotts, Henry, 3. 1723
Philomel, 2. 370
Philosopher (1762), 2. 1283
Philosopher (1776), 2. 1286
Philosopher (1777), 2. 1286
Philosophical collections, 2. 1291
Philosophical magazine, 3. 1841–2; 2. 1311
Philosophical observator, 2. 1269
Philosophical Quixote, 2. 1006
Philosophical Society of Edinburgh, *essays*, 2.
    1371
Philosophical transactions (Royal Society), 2. 1291

philosophy
  Middle English, 1. 750–2
  Renaissance to Restoration
    English, 1. 2321–42
    French, 1. 862–5
    humanism, 1. 1781–826
    Italian, 1. 886–90
    Latin, 1. 843–54
    Spanish, 1. 907–8
  Restoration and eighteenth century
    English, 2. 1833–900
    French, 2. 90–113
    German, 2. 156–60
    Italian, 2. 188
    Royal Society, 2. 1899–902
    Spanish, 2. 198–9
  nineteenth century, 3. 169–71, 1509–600
  twentieth century, 4. 1241–310
Philotus, 1. 2429
Philp, Robert Kemp, 3. 1814
Philpot, Charles, 2. 1789
Philpot, Stephen, 2. 1566
Philpott, A. R., 4. 880
'Philroye, Humphrey' (R. Steele), 2. 1276
Phineas, 4. 1396
Phipps, Constantine Henry, 1st Marquis of Normanby, 3. 756
Phipps, Constantine John, 2nd Baron Mulgrave, 2. 1485
Phoenix (OE poem), 1. 294
Phoenix (OE prose), 1. 327
Phoenix (1792), 2. 1374
Phoenix (1817), 3. 1817
Phoenix (1860), 3. 1870
Phoenix (1874), 3. 1870
Phoenix (Eastbourne 1938), 4. 1373
Phoenix (Woodstock, N.Y. 1938), 4. 1373
Phoenix: a magazine for young writers (Ayton 1939), 4. 73, 1374, 1387
Phoenix (Manchester and Lewes 1943), 4. 1376
Phoenix nest, 1. 1009
Phoenix of Europe, 1. 2101
Phoenix quarterly, 4. 1378
Phonetic record, 4. 1382
phonology, general, 1. 59–112
  Old English, 1. 59–76
  Middle English, 1. 75–90
  Modern English, 1. 89–112
Photo playwright, 4. 57
Photographic news, 3. 1828
Photographic news almanac, 3. 1878
phrasebooks, Renaissance to Restoration, 1. 2402
Phreas, John, 1. 804
Physical and mathematical memoirs, 2. 1292
Physician of the heart, 2. 1285

Physick, Edward Harold, 4. 799
Physiogno-magnetic mirror, 2. 1288
Physiologus, 1. 294–5
'Physiologus, Philotheos' (Thomas Tryon), 2. 1553
physiology, Renaissance to Restoration, 1. 2369–74
Pi, 4. 1396
Pianoforte magazine, 2. 1311
Pibrac, Guy du Faur de, 1. 870
picaresque novel, 2. 870
Piccolomini, Enea Silvio, Pope Pius II, 1. 2191, 850, 857, 2064; 2. 1548
Pichon, Thomas, 2. 1466
Pick, John Barclay, 4. 1376
Pick, Samuel, 1. 1316
Pick of Punch, 4. 1373
Picken, Andrew, 3. 756
Pickering, John, 1. 1423
Pickering, Percival A., 3. 1870
Pickering, Wilhelmina, 3. 1105
Pickering, Sir William (1516–75), book collector, 1. 1003
Pickering, William (fl. 1556–71), bookseller, 1. 963
Pickering, William (d. 1854), 3. 80, 1875
Pickersgill, Richard, 2. 1483
Pico, Giovanni Francesco, 1. 856
Pico della Mirandola, Giovanni, 1. 850, 889
'Picolomini, Don Diego', 2. 1274
Picton, James Allanson, 3. 1577
Pictorial album, 3. 1875
Pictorial news, 3. 1817
Pictorial times, 3. 1816
Pictorial world, 3. 1817
Picture, 2. 1285
Picture magazine, 2. 1030
Picture of the times, A, 2. 1289
Picture post, 4. 1408, 1347
Picture show, 4. 57, 1364
Picture times, 3. 1816
Picturegoer, 4. 56
Pictureland, 4. 57
Pictures, 4. 56
Pictures and pleasures, 4. 56
Pictures and the picturegoer, 4. 56
Pidou de Saint Olon, François, 2. 1446
Pieces of ancient popular poetry, 2. 415
Pieces on the subjects of love and marriage, 2. 424
Pieces selected from the Italian poets, 2. 399
Pierce, James, 2. 1674
Pierce, Thomas, 1. 1998, 2339
Pierce Egan's life in London, 3. 1683, 1810
Pierce Egan's weekly courier, 3. 1810
Pierce the ploughman's crede, 1. 544–5

Pierrepoint, Mary, 2. 1584–5
Pierreville, G. 2. 1412
Pietas academiae cantabrigiensis in funere principis Wilhelminae Carolinae, 2. 367
Pietas academiae oxoniensis in obitum reginae Carolinae, 2. 367
Pietas et gratulatio . . . apud Novanglos, 2. 382
Pietas universitatis oxoniensis in obitum Georgii I, 2. 357
Pietas universitatis oxoniensis in obitum Georgii II, 2. 382
Pig's meat, 2. 1310
Pigafetta, Filippo, 1. 887, 2143
Pigafetta, Marc-Antonio, 1. 2122
Piggot, L. 2. 1350
Pigott, Edward F. S., 3. 1814
Pigott, Harriet, 2. 1008
Pigott, Montague H. M. T., 3. 1868
Pike, J. C., 3. 1842
Pike, Samuel, 2. 1908
Pilborough's Colchester journal, 2. 1356
Pilgrim, 2. 1274
Pilgrim's tale, 1. 1135
Pilgrimage to Parnassus, 1. 1778
Pilgrimage to the grand jubilee at Rome, A, 2. 1414
Pilkington, Francis, 1. 1352
Pilkington, James, 1. 2071
Pilkington, Mary Hopkins, 2. 1014, 1028
Pilkington, Matthew, 2. 563
Pill to purge state-melancholy, A, 2. 349
Pillans, James, 3. 1721, 1731
Pillans and Wilson (printers), 3. 59
Pills to expel spleen, 2. 376
Pills to purge melancholy, 2. 401
Pilon, Frederick, 2. 856–7, 179
Pilot (1807), 3. 1792
Pilot (1900), 4. 1404
Pilot papers, 4. 1408
Pinchard, Mrs — (fl. 1791–1816), 2. 1027
Pinckard, George, 4. 1351
Pindar, 2. 1493
'Pindar, Peter' (John Wolcot), 2. 695–7
Pinero, Sir Arthur Wing, 3. 1166–9
Pink'un holiday annual, 4. 1351
Pinkerton, John, 2. 1766–8, 237, 246, 1394, 1397, 1739; 1. 2113
Pinks, W. J., 3. 1684
Pinnell, Richard, 2. 1441
Pinney, John, 2. 1674
Pinto, Isaac de, 2. 1567
Pinto, Vivian de Sola, 4. 1102
Piozzi, Hester, 2. 1596–7
Pipe, 4. 1396
Pirie-Gordon, Clinton, 4. 1396
Pisan, Christine de, 1. 874

'Pisano', 2. 1288
'Piscator' (Thomas Pike Lathy), 3. 1687
'Piscator' (fl. 1871), 3. 1715
Pistill of Susan, 1. 480
Pistoríus, Johann, 1. 850
Pitcairne, Archibald, 2. 2059–60
Pitcher, Charles, 3. 1811
Pitman, Henry (fl. 1689), 2. 1456
Pitman, Henry (fl. 1865), 3. 1820
Pitman, Sir Isaac, 3. 80
Pits, John, 1. 1904
Pitt, Christopher, 2. 563–4
Pitt, George Dibdin, 3. 1154–5
Pitt, James, 2. 1324
Pitt, Moses, 2. 280, 1411
Pitter, Ruth, 4. 327–8
Pittis, William, 2. 1292, 1324, 1343, 1344
Pittman, Philip, 2. 1468
Pitton de Tournefort, Joseph, 2. 1437
Pitts, John, 1. 1904
Pitts, Joseph, 2. 1436, 1447
Pius II, Pope (Aneas Silvius), 1. 2191, 850, 857, 2064; 2. 1548
Pix, Mary, 2. 797–8, 983
Place, Francis, 3. 1300, 1722, 1745, 1817
Plagiarist, 2. 1286
Plain dealer (1712), 2. 1274
Plain dealer (1717), 2. 1324
Plain dealer (1724), 2. 359, 1277
Plain dealer (1728), 2. 1378, 1384
Plain dealer (1763), 2. 1283
Plain dealer (1775), 2. 1286
Plain dealer (East Grinstead 1929), 4. 1368
Plain dealer's intelligencer, 2. 1378
Plain English, 4. 1351
Plaindealer (1933), 4. 108
Plaintiff, 2. 1290
Plaisted, Bartholomew, 2. 1439
Planché, James Robinson, 3. 1135–6, 1108
Planché, Matilda Anne, 3. 1093
Planet (1837), 3. 1811
Planet (1907), 4. 825
Plant, George, 3. 1815
Plantagenet, Beauchamp, 1. 2164
Plantin, Arabella, 2. 991
Plarr, Victor Gustave, 3. 644, 1879
Plastique, 4. 1372
Platen, 4. 84
Plato, 1. 2174; 2. 1493, 34–5, 65
Platt, David, 4. 1369
Platt, H., 1. 2278
Platte, T., 1. 2074
Plautus, 1. 2174; 2. 1500
Play: an illustrated monthly, 4. 824, 859
Play of Robin Hood, A (ME), 1. 742

Play pictorial (1902), 4. 824
Play pictorial (1905), 4. 824, 859
Play-house journal, 2. 1379
Playbox, 4. 820
Playboy, 4. 1363
Players tragedy: or fatal love, 2. 983
Playfair, Lyon, 3. 1728
Playfair, P., 3. 1694
Playfere, Thomas, 1. 1944
Playford, Henry, 2. 1293, 1344
Playford, John, 1. 1358, 963
Playgoer (1901), 4. 824
Playgoer (Playhouse, Liverpool 1924), 4. 850
Playgoer (1949), 4. 1357
Playgoer and Millgate, 4. 824, 1357
Playgoer and society illustrated, 4. 825
Playgoers' Club journal, 4. 849
Playhouse, 4. 824
Playhouse news, 4. 851
Playlet and monologue magazine, 4. 859
Plays, 4. 1388
Plays and players (1904), 4. 848, 866
Plays and players (1929), 4. 826, 867
Pleasant intrigues. . .of an English nobleman, 2. 985
Pleasant musical companion (1709), 2. 346
Pleasant musical companion (1715), 2. 349
Pleasing companion (1798), 2. 425
Pleasing companion (1799?), 2. 426
Pleasing jester, 2. 417
Pleasing melancholy, 2. 418
Pleasing reflections on life and manners, 2. 408
Pleasing songster, 2. 408
Pleasing variety, 2. 420
Pleasure, 4. 1387
Pleasure for a minute, 2. 355
Pleasures of coition, 2. 354
Plebian, 2. 1276
Pledge of friendship, 3. 1873
Plenipotentiary, 2. 1288, 1307
Plescheef, F., 2. 1429
Pliny the elder, 1. 2174
Pliny the younger, 1. 2175; 2. 1500
Plomer, William Charles Franklyn, 4. 704–5
Plotinus, 2. 1493, 65
Plough, 4. 1373
Plow, 4. 1376
Plowman, Max, 4. 1366
Plowman's tale, 1. 545, 1136
Ploy, 4. 1377
Pluche, Antoine ('Noël'), 2. 1526, 96
Pluck, 4. 819
Plumb, Charles, 4. 1397
'Plummericus', 2. 1287
Plumpton correspondence, 1. 684

Plumptre, Anne, 2. 166
Plumptre, Edward Hayes, 3. 547
Plumptre, James, 2. 1790
Plunket, Frederica, 3. 1681
Plunket, Louisa Lilias, 3. 1103
Plunkett, Edward John Moreton Drax, 18th Baron Dunsany, 3. 1945–8
Plunkett, Joseph, 4. 1360
Plutarch, 1. 2175, 2064; 2. 1494
Plyeschchyeev, Sergyei, 2. 1429
Plymouth and Exeter gazette, 2. 1364
Plymouth chronicle, 2. 1364
Plymouth gazette, 2. 1364
Plymouth magazine (1758), 2. 1352
Plymouth magazine (1772), 2. 1352
Plymouth weekly-journal, 2. 1364
Pocket album, 3. 1875
Pocket book for the German flute, A, 2. 399
Pocket book for the guitar, 2. 399
Pocket companion and history of Free-Masons, 2. 377
Pocket companion for Free-Masons, A, 2. 364
Pocket companion for gentlemen and ladies, 2. 355
Pocket companion for the guittar, 2. 378
Pocket magazine (1794), 2. 1310
Pocket magazine (1818), 3. 1844
Pocket magazine (1922), 4. 1365
Pocket vade-mecum through Monmouthshire, A, 2. 1405
Pocock, Edward, 2. 1831–2; 1. 2149–50
Pocock, Isaac, 3. 1136
Pocock, Robert, 3. 59
Pocock's everlasting songster, 2. 429
Pococke, Edward, the elder (1604–91), 2. 1831–2; 1. 2149–50
Pococke, Edward, the younger (1648–1727), 2. 1832
Pococke, Richard, 2. 1401, 1438, 1449
Poellnitz, Karl Ludwig von, 2. 1540, 994, 1400, 1417–18
Poema morale, 1. 509
Poemata partim reddita, partim scripta, 2. 405
Poematia, 2. 363
Poems [by Coleridge] (1797), 2. 424
Poems: a chosen collection (1736?), 2. 365
Poems and epistles on several occasions, 2. 346
Poems and translations by several hands, 2. 348
Poems by a literary society, 2. 405
Poems by eminent ladies, 2. 378
Poems by Roscommon and Dorset (1731), 2. 360
Poems by Roscommon and Dorset (1739), 2. 367
Poems by several gentlemen of Oxford, 2. 379
Poems by several hands and on several occasions, 2. 335
Poems by the Earl of Roscommon, 2. 351

Poetical miscellanies (1729), 2. 358
Poetical miscellany (1754), 2. 377
Poetical miscellany (1762), 2. 383
Poetical monitor, 2. 423
Poetical museum, 2. 405
Poetical observator, 2. 1293, 1343
Poetical observator revived, 2. 1293, 1343
Poetical pieces by several hands, 2. 376
Poetical preceptor, 2. 398
Poetical prolusions, 2. 426
Poetical recreations, 2. 336
Poetical reflexions, 2. 345
Poetical register, 3. 1873
Poetical remains, 2. 340
Poetical rhapsody, A, 1. 1009
Poetical tell-tale, 2. 385
Poetical works [of Sedley], 2. 344
Poetical works of Philip, late Duke of Wharton, 2. 360
Poetical works of Rochester, Roscommon, Dorset . . ., 2. 367
poetry
  general anthologies, 1. 29–32
  general histories, 1. 25–7
  Old English, 1. 225–312
  Middle English
    ballads, 1. 711–20
    Bible renderings, 1. 477–82
    Chaucer, 1. 557–628
    Chaucerians, 1. 639–52
    chronicles, 1. 459–68
    fifteenth century, 1. 679–98
    fourteenth century and earlier, 1. 455–556: Gower, 1. 553–6; Langland, 1. 533–48; Pearl poet, 1. 547–54; prophecies, 1. 473–8; religious and devotional, 1. 477–90, 495–517; saints' legends, 1. 523–34; tales, 1. 455–60
    romances, 1. 383–454
    Scottish poets, 1. 651–64
    songs, 1. 697–712
  Renaissance to Restoration, 1. 1007–360
    emblem books, 1. 1327–34
    epigrams and satire, 1. 1333–8
    Jacobean and Caroline, 1. 1161–326
    Milton, 1. 1237–96
    Scottish, 1. 2421–36
    song books and miscellanies, 1. 1007–16, 1337–60
    sonnet, Elizabethan, 1. 1073–8
    Tudor, 1. 1015–162
  Restoration and eighteenth century, 2. 313–700, 1959–2032
    miscellanies, collections and anthologies, 2. 327–436

    periods: 1660–1700, 2. 435–90; 1700–50, 2. 489–578; 1750–1800, 2. 577–700
    Scottish, 2. 1959–2032
  nineteenth century, 3. 159–656; Anglo-Irish, 3. 1899–938
    poetic forms, 3. 167–70
    scope and range, 3. 169–74
    see chronological conspectus, 3. vii–ix
  twentieth century, 4. 131–380
  see also literary history and literary relations
Poetry (1917), 4. 826, 1363
Poetry (Liverpool 1949), 4. 1380
Poetry and drama, 4. 825, 1361
Poetry and the people, 4. 1373
Poetry and the play, 4. 826, 1363
Poetry awards, 4. 1380
Poetry commonwealth, 4. 1379
Poetry folio, 4. 1378
Poetry folios, 4. 1375
Poetry in Nottingham, 4. 1378
Poetry Ireland, 4. 1379
Poetry journal, 4. 1373
Poetry London, 4. 1373, 1347
Poetry made familiar and easy, 2. 373
Poetry Manchester, 4. 1380
Poetry of the Anti-Jacobin, 2. 426
Poetry of the world, 2. 410
Poetry of to-day, 4. 1364
Poetry of various glees, 2. 425
Poetry, original and selected, 2. 429
Poetry: past and present, 4. 1368
Poetry quarterly (1933), 4. 827, 1370
Poetry quarterly (Dawlish 1939), 4. 1374
Poetry review, 4. 1359, 1347
Poetry-Scotland, 4. 1376
Poetry studies, 4. 1370
Poets in brief, 4. 1370
Poets now in the services, 4. 1375
Poets of tomorrow, 4. 1374
Poets on the poets, 4. 1368
Poets' Guild quarterly, 4. 1385
Pogmoor olmenack, 'T, 4. 1353
Points, 4. 1380
Poiret, Jean Louis Marie, 2. 1451
Polanyi, Michael, 4. 1280
Pole, Thomas, 3. 1720, 1745
Polemic, 4. 1376
Polezhayev, Aleksandr Ivanovich, 3. 153
Police, 2. 1348
Polidori, John William, 3. 756–7
Polish literature and Shakespeare, 1. 1633
Polite academy, 2. 1021
Polite companion (1749), 2. 373
Polite companion (1760), 2. 381
Polite correspondence, 2. 359

Polite gamester, 2. 1567
Polite jester, 2. 423
Polite miscellany, 2. 385
Polite preceptor, 2. 394
Polite singer, 2. 402
Polite songster (1758), 2. 380
Polite songster (1800), 2. 429
Polite traveller, 2. 1396
Politeuphia, 1. 1009
Political cabinet, 2. 1298
Political controversy, 2. 1283, 1303, 1353
Political courier, 2. 1323
Political herald and review, 2. 1307
Political letter and pamphlets, 3. 1818
Political magazine, 2. 1306
Political manager, 2. 1385
Political mercury, 2. 1294
Political merriment, 2. 349
Political miscellanies, 2. 408–9
Political prophecy by the dice, A, 1. 478
Political register, 2. 1304
Political review of Edinburgh periodical publi-
    cations, 2. 1373
Political state of Europe (1697), 2. 1292
Political state of Europe (1792), 2. 1309
Political state of Great Britain, 2. 1294
Political tatler, 2. 1276
Politician, 2. 1338
Politick spy, 2. 1343
Politicks in miniature, 2. 369
Politicks of Europe, 2. 1291
politics
    Renaissance to Restoration, 1. 2275
    twentieth century, 4. 71–2, 1135–1242
    see also economics, essays, history, prose
Politics and letters, 4. 1378
Politics for the people (1793), 2. 1310
Politics for the people (1848), 3. 1819
Politique informer, 1. 2108
Politique post, 1. 2108
Pollard, Albert Frederick, 4. 1203
Pollard, Alfred William, 4. 1103–4
Pollen, John Hungerford, 3. 1633
Pollexfen, John, 2. 1899
Pollock, Edith Caroline, 3. 1095
Pollock, Sir Frederick, 3. 644, 1858
Pollock, Walter Herries, 3. 1814, 1865, 1870
Pollok, Robert, 3. 395–6
polo, 3. 1711
Polo, Marco, 1. 2191, 889, 2142–3
Polwhele, Richard, 2. 675–7, 240
Polybius, 1. 2175, 2137; 2. 1494
'Polycephalus, Hydra' (W. D. Whittington), 3.
    1865
Polyhymnia (1769), 2. 390

Polyhymnia (1799), 2. 427, 1374
'Pomerano, Castalion', 1. 2058
Pomfret, John, 2. 564
Pompadour, Jeanne Antoinette Poisson Lenor-
    mand d'Etioles, Marquise de, 2. 1526
Pomponius Mela, 1. 2172
Poncet, Charles Jacques, 2. 1447
Pond, John, 2. 1313
Ponet, John, 1. 1822
Ponsonby, Caroline, Lady Lamb, 3. 740
Pont, Robert, 1. 1903
Pont, Timothy, 1. 2135
Pontet, F., 4. 1382
Pontier, Gédéon, 2. 1412
Pontis, Louis de, 2. 1457
Pontoppidan, Erik, 2. 1419
Pontoppidan, Henrik, 3. 148
Pontoux, Claude de, 1. 870
Poole, John (1786–1872) dramatist, 3. 1137, 1876
Poole, John (fl. 1812), educationalist, 3. 1719
Poole, Joshua, 1. 2320
Poole, Matthew, 1. 2295
Poole, Reginald Lane, 3. 1858
Poole, Robert, 2. 1418, 1464
Poor Gillian, 2. 1339
Poor man's advocate, 3. 1818
Poor man's guardian, 3. 1818
Poor Robins collection of antient prophecyes, 2. 331
Poor Robin's intelligence (1676), 2. 1339
Poor Robin's intelligence (1691), 2. 1342
Poor Robin's intelligence newly revived, 2. 1339
Poor Robin's intelligence revived, 2. 1339
Poor Robin's memoirs, 2. 1339
Poor Robin's publick. . .occurances, 2. 1341
Pope, Alexander, 2. 500–27, 43, 110–11, 117–18,
    127, 134–5, 167, 170, 172, 189, 194, 199, 200,
    212, 218, 1773–4
Pope, Charles, 3. 1882
Pope, Walter, 2. 482, 1908
Pope, William Burt, 3. 1857
Pope's Bath chronicle, 2. 1353
Pope's miscellany, 2. 351
Popery and tyranny, 2. 1411
Popham, Sir Home Riggs, 2. 1444
Popish mass display'd, 2. 1341
Popper, Sir Karl Raimund, 4. 1204
Popple, William, 2. 798
Popular ballads preserved in memory, 2. 421
Popular writing, 4. 72
Porcupine, 2. 1339–40; 3. 1789
Pordage, John, 1. 2338
Pordage, Samuel, 2. 482
pornography, twentieth century, 4. 101–2
Porson, Richard, 2. 1822–4
Porta, Giovanni Battista della, 1. 850, 895

Porter, Alan, 4. 328, 1391, 1397
Porter, Anna Maria, 3. 757
Porter, George Richardson, 3. 1724
Porter, Henry, 1. 1468
Porter, Sir James, 2. 1421
Porter, Jane, 3. 758, 1099
Porter, John (fl. 1781), 2. 1441
Porter, John (1838–1922), 3. 1707
Porter, Josias Leslie, 3. 1675
Porter, Sir Robert Ker, 3. 1673, 1677
Porter, Thomas (1636–80), dramatist, 2. 770–1
Porter, Thomas (fl. 1659), geographer, 1. 2122, 2135
Porter, Walter, 1. 1357
Portfolio, 3. 1851; 4. 1351
Portfolio of 450 advertising illustrations, 4. 1344
Portico, 4. 1394
Porticus etonensis, 3. 1870
'Portland' (James Hogg), 3. 1693
Portlock, Nathaniel, 2. 1481
Portraits of the children of the nobility, 3. 1875
Portraits of the female aristocracy, 3. 1876
Portsmouth and Gosport gazette, 2. 1364
Portsmouth gazette, 2. 1364
Portsmouth telegraph, 2. 1364
Portu, Mauritius a (O'Fihely), 1. 805
Portuguese, literary relations with
   Renaissance to Restoration, Shakespeare, 1. 1633
   Restoration and eighteenth century, 2. 195–206
   nineteenth century, 3. 141–4
Portwine, Edward J., 3. 81
Pory, John, 1. 2156
Positivist review, 3. 1854
Post-angel, 2. 1293
Post boy (1695), 2. 1319–20
Post boy (1709), 2. 1322
Post boy (Dublin 1712?), 2. 1382
Post-boy (Dublin 1718), 2. 1383
Post-boy (Dublin 1724), 2. 1383
Post-man (1695), 2. 1320
Post-man (Dublin 1703), 2. 1381
Post-man (Dublin 1707), 2. 1381
Post man (Dublin 1708), 2. 1381
Post man (Dublin 1712), 2. 1382
Post-man (Dublin 1716), 2. 1383
Post-man (Dublin 1727), 2. 1382
Post-master (Exeter 1717), 2. 1358, 1348
Post Office guide 3. 1881
Post-Office intelligence, 2. 365
Post Office London directory, 3. 1881
postcards, 4. 126
Poster, 4. 1342
Posters and publicity, 4. 1343
Postgate, Raymond William, 4. 1204–5

Posthumous works in prose and verse [*Samuel Butler*], 2. 349
Posthumous works of Boileau, 2. 348
Postlethwayt, Malachy, 2. 1899
Postmaster (1720), 2. 1325
Postscript, 4. 1383
Postscript to Image, 4. 83
Postscript to the evening packet, 2. 1323
Postscript to the post-boy, 2. 1319
Pote, Benjamin Edward, 3. 1856, 1873
Potent ally, 2. 369
'Potocki, Geoffrey Wladislas', Count, 4. 1372
Pott Shrigley, early library of, 1. 995
Potter, Frederick Scarlett, 3. 1104
Potter, George (1832–93), 3. 1820
Potter, George (fl. 1890), 3. 1853
Potter, Helen Beatrix, 3. 1098–9
Potter, John (1674?–1747), 2. 1828
Potter, John (fl. 1754–1804), 2. 1002, 1284
Potter, Stephen Meredith, 4. 1104–5
Potts, James, 3. 1805
Potts, John, 3. 1805
Potts, Joseph Trumperant, 3. 1805
Potts, Thomas, 1. 2074
Pouilly, Louis Jean Levesque de, 2. 1520, 67
Poulain de la Barre, François, 2. 1526, 96
Poulter, M. R., 4. 880
Poultney, Alfred H., 3. 1795
Pound, Ezra, 4. 1362, 1367
Pound, William, 3. 1727
Povey, Charles, 2. 1272, 1321
Powell, A. J. C., 3. 60
Powell, Anthony Dymoke, 4. 705–6
Powell, Baden, 3. 1609, 1724
Powell, David, 1. 2211
Powell, Frederick York, 3. 1494–5
Powell, George, 2. 771
Powell, L. C., 4. 1373
Powell, Thomas, 1. 1136, 2026
Powell, William, 3. 1881
Power, Eileen Edna, 4. 1205–6
Power, Henry, 2. 1908
Power, Marguerite, Countess of Blessington (1789–1849), 3. 710–11, 1874
Power, Marguerite A. (c. 1815–67), 3. 1874
Power, Rhoda Dolores le Poer, 4. 802
Powicke, Sir Frederick Maurice, 4. 1206–7
Powis Castle, 2. 1008
Pownall, Thomas, 2. 1427, 1470
Powney, Richard, 2. 1558
Powys, John Cowper, 4. 706–10
Powys, Llewelyn, 4. 1105–7
Powys, Theodore Francis, 4. 710–12
Poynet, John, 1. 1822
Poyntz, John, 2. 1456

Poyntz, Sydenham (Sydnam), 1. 2247, 2128
Practical advertising, 4. 1342
Practical handbook to the principal schools of England, 3. 1881
Praed, Winthrop Mackworth, 3. 411–12, 1870
Praga, Anthony, 4. 1365
Pranceriana, 2. 396
Prater, 2. 1282
Pratt, Daniel, 3. 1820
Pratt, Josiah, 3. 1842
Pratt, Peter, 3. 1694
Pratt, Samuel Jackson, 2. 677–8, 1005, 1006, 1029, 1407, 1424; 3. 1681
'Prattle, Goody', 2. 1023
Prattler, 2. 1331
Prayer, A. (OE), 1. 295
Prayer to the Sacrament (ME), 1. 515
prayers and prayer-books
 Old English
  general, 1. 328
  Latin, 1. 350
 Renaissance to Restoration, 1. 1887–96
Prayers and charms (ME), 1. 515
Prayers of the Byble (1535), 1. 1935
Praz, Mario, 4. 1380
Preceptive, moral and sentimental pieces, 2. 424
Precepts, 1. 295
Préchac, Jean de, 2. 1526, 979, 980, 992
Precipitate choice, 2. 1003
'Preedy, George R.' (Gabrielle M. V. Campbell), 4. 535–8
Premier, 4. 1391
Premier magazine, 4. 1362
Prendergast, Harris, 3. 1814
pre-Raphaelitism, 3. 173–6
Presbyterianism
 general bibliography, 1. 22
 Restoration and eighteenth century, 2. 1666, 1671–4
Prescott, Henrietta, Lady Lushington, 3. 1103
Prescott's Manchester journal, 2. 1361
Present age, 4. 1372
Present Etonian, 3. 1870
Present for a young lady, A, 2. 370
Present for children, A, 2. 1021
Present peerage of the United Kingdom, 3. 1879
Present state of Europe (1690), 2. 1291–2, 1371
Present state of Europe (1692), 2. 1292
Present state of Europe (1705), 2. 1415
Present state of Germany, 2. 1412
Present state of his Majesty's dominions in Germany, 2. 1416
Present state of Holland, 2. 1419
Present state of Hungary, 2. 1412
Present state of Jamaica, 2. 1456

Present state of Louisiana, 2. 1463
Present state of the German and Turkish empires, 2. 1412
Present state of the republick of letters, 2. 1294
Present state of the sugar plantations, 2. 1460
Present state of the West Indies, 2. 1470
Preservation of Henry VII, 1. 1115
President's guide, 2. 427
press
 Restoration and eighteenth century, 2. 273–8, 1257–70
 nineteenth century, 3. 1777–84, 1829–30, 1833, 1833–4
 twentieth century, 4. 1329–32
 see also magazines, newspapers, periodicals, printing
Press (1797), 2. 1387
Press (1853), 3. 1814, 1835
Press (1950), 4. 74
Press, amateur journal (Southport 1950), 4. 1388
Press advertising and trade, 4. 1344
Press and the people, 4. 1344
Press, film and radio in the world, 4. 1344
Press world, 4. 1343
Pressly, David L., 3. 1805
Preston, Edward Hayter, 4. 1361
Preston, John, 1. 1999
Preston chronicle, 3. 1832
Preston journal, 2. 1365
Preston review and county advertiser, 2. 1365
Preston songster, 2. 411
Preston weekly journal, 2. 1365
Prestwich, Edmund, 1. 1316, 1753
Prevost, Francis, 3. 1873
Prévost d'Exiles, Antoine François, 2. 1526, 142–3, 993, 994, 995, 998, 1400
Price, D., 1. 2276
Price, Elizabeth Lees, 3. 1670
Price, Ellen, 3. 971–2
Price, Henry Habberley, 4. 1280
Price, James, 4. 1397
Price, John, 1. 2305
Price, Jonathan, 4. 1397
Price, Laurence, 1. 2058
Price, Richard, 2. 1890
Price, T., 3. 1842
Prices of merchandise in London, 2. 1316
Prichard, Harold Arthur, 4. 1281
Pricke of conscience, 1. 503
Pricket, Robert, 1. 1136
Pride of life, 1. 1404
Prideaux, Humphrey, 2. 1705
Priestley, John Boynton, 4. 712–17
Priestley, Joseph, 2. 1890–1, 1309, 1349, 1908
Primaleon, 1. 2191

Psalm 50 (OE), 1. 296
psalms and psalters
  Old English
    fragments, 1. 280
    general, 1. 73–4
    psalm 50, 1. 296
    Paris psalter, 1. 293
  Middle English
    commentary, 1. 90–1, 479
    Brampton's 1. 480
    Maydestone's penitential, 1. 480
    Midland, 1. 479
    Surtees, 1. 479–80
  Renaissance to Restoration, 1. 1895–1914
Psyche et filii ejus, 1. 1778
psychology, 4. 1241–1310
Public advertiser (1752), 2. 1328
Public advertiser (Sheffield 1760), 2. 1365
Public advertiser (Dublin 1774), 2. 1386
Public characters of 1798–1810, 3. 1878
Public gazetteer, 2. 1386
Public ledger, 3. 1789; 2. 1282, 1333
Public ledger evening report, 3. 1789
Public magazine, 2. 1302
Public monitor, 2. 1386
Public occurrences truely stated, 2. 1374
Public opinion, 3. 1814; 4. 1401
Public prompter and Irish journal, 2. 1386
Public register, 2. 1386; 3. 1805
Public schools calendar, 3. 1881
Public schools magazine, 3. 1868
Publicity world, 4. 1342
Publick advertisements, 2. 1316
Publick adviser, 1. 2109
Publick intelligence, 2. 1316
Publick intelligencer (1655), 1. 2109; 2. 1313
Publick intelligencer (1660), 2. 1315
Publick journal, 2. 1386
Publick occurrences truely stated, 2. 1318
Publick register, 2. 1298, 1331
Publilius Syrus, 1. 2175
Publisher, 2. 371, 1298
Publisher and bookseller (1905), 4. 100
Publisher and bookseller (1928), 3. 81; 4. 100, 106
Publisher's miscellany, 4. 100
Publishers' circular, 3. 81; 4. 100
Publishers' mail, 4. 100
Publishers' trade announcements, 4. 100
Publishers' weekly, 4. 1347
publishing
  nineteenth century, 3. 75–82
  twentieth century, 4. 69–72, 89–102
  see also book production and distribution
Publishing world, 4. 100
Puccini, Vincenzo, 2. 1548

Puck, 4. 819
Pudney, John, 4. 1376
Pue's occurrences, 2. 1381
Puente, Luis de la, 1. 909
Pufendorf, Samuel, 2. 77
Pugh, Edward, 3. 1682
Pugh, Edwin William, 4. 717–18
Pughe, William Owen, 2. 248, 238
Pugin, Augustus Welby Northmore, 3. 1398
Pulci, Luigi, 3. 138
Pullein-Thompson, Christine, 4. 814–15
Pullein-Thompson, Dennis, 4. 920–1
Pullein-Thompson, Joanna Maxwell, 4. 804
Pullen, Robert, Cardinal, 1. 758
Pullin, A. W., 3. 1698
Pulling, Frederick S., 3. 1868
Pullus, Robert, Cardinal, 1. 758
Pulman, G. P. R., 3. 1689
pulp novels, twentieth century, 4. 127
Pulteney, Richard, 2. 1807
Punch: or the London Charivari, 3. 1825, 1838; 4. 1349–50, 1347–8, 1400
Punch anthology, A., 4. 1370
Punch in Cambridge, 3. 1865
Punch library of humour, 4. 1358
Punchard, H., 2. 1017
Punchbowle, 4. 1385
Puppet master, 4. 860, 880
Puppet post, 4. 880
Puppet year book, 4. 880
Purbeck, Elizabeth, 2. 1010
Purbeck, Jane, 2. 1010
Purcell, Sir John Samuel, 3. 1881
Purchas, Samuel, 1. 2111–12, 2120, 2277
Purdom, Charles Benjamin, 4. 1361, 1370
Puritaine, 1. 1761
Puritan attack on the stage, 1. 1395–1402
Purity, 1. 553–4
Purney, Thomas, 2. 564
Purpose, 4. 1368
Pusey, Edward Bouverie, 3. 1633–4
Pushkin, Aleksandr Sergeevich, 3. 153–4
Puttenham, George, 1. 2312
'Puzzlebrains, Peregrine', 2. 1030
'Puzzlewell, Peter', 2. 1027
Puzzling cap, 2. 1022
Pycroft, James, 3. 1696, 1714, 1724
Pye, Henry James, 2. 678–9, 184, 1012, 1561
Pye, Virginia, 4. 807
Pyers, William, 1. 1133
Pylgrymage of Sir Richarde Guylforde, 1. 2121
Pym, Barbara Mary Crampton, 4. 718
Pynson, Richard, 1. 963
Pyrrye, Charles, 1. 1137, 2032
Pyttes, John, 1. 1904

'Q' (Sir Arthur Quiller-Couch), 3. 1071–3, 1098
Quad, 3. 1868; 4. 1396
Quadratum musicum, 2. 336
Quain, Richard, 3. 1728
Quaint quarterly, 4. 1368
Quakers, Restoration and eighteenth century, 2. 1639–52
Quakers art of courtship, 2. 337
Quakers Dublin weekly oracle, 2. 1383
Quaritch, Bernard, 3. 86
Quarles, Francis, 1. 1199–1201, 2049; 2. 33, 167
Quarles, John, 1. 1317, 2040
Quarterly journal of education, 3. 1856
Quarterly journal of science, 3. 1858
Quarterly journal of the New Fabian research bureau, 4. 1407
Quarterly magazine, 3. 1855
Quarterly musical magazine and review, 3. 1855
Quarterly review, 3. 1855, 1864; 4. 1349
Quarto, 3. 1858
Quatrefoil of love, 1. 507
Quaver, 3. 1851
Queen 3. 1816; 4. 1401
Queen Anne's weekly, 2. 1297, 1328
Queen Jane, the chronicle of, 1. 2206
Queen's College miscellany, A, 4. 1397
Queen's messenger, 3. 1815, 1835
Queens' courier, 4. 1393
Queer stories from Truth, 4. 1357
Quelch, H., 3. 1820
Quennell, Peter Courtney, 4. 1107–8, 1351, 1397
Querry, W. Edmund, 4. 826
Query, A. 4. 1384
Query magazine, 4. 1393
Quesnay, François, 2. 96
Quevedo Villegas, Francisco de, 1. 916, 2064; 2. 204, 977, 983–4
'Quick, Jeremy' (J. Oldmixon), 2. 1275
Quick, Robert Hibert, 3. 1728
Quiet hour (Birmingham 1937), 4. 1372
Quiet hour (Nov. 1937), amateur journal, 4. 1386
Quill (1902), 4. 1340
Quill (1919), 4. 1384
Quiller-Couch, Sir Arthur Thomas, 3. 1071–3, 1098
Quillinan, Edward, 3. 397–8
Quilter, Harry, 3. 1853
Quin, Edward, 3. 1792
Quin, Michael Joseph, 3. 1822, 1839, 1856
Quin, Windham Thomas Wyndham, Earl of Dunraven, 3. 1673
Quin's jests, 2. 387
Quinault, Philippe, 1. 868; 2. 1526
Quincey, Thomas, 2. 1403
Quincy, John, 2. 1908

Quincy, Josiah, 2. 1404
Quintana, Francisco de, 1. 916, 2063; 2. 204, 988
Quintessence of English poetry, 2. 368
Quintilian, 2. 1500, 65
Quintus Curtius, 1. 2168; 2. 1497
Quinze joyes de mariage, 1. 2192
'Quis', 3. 1704
Quittenton, Richard M. H., 3. 1103
Quiver, 3. 1850
Quixley, J., 1. 687
Quiz, 2. 1290
'Quiz, Rolland' (R. M. H. Quittenton), 3. 1103
Quizzical gazette and merry companion, 3. 1825
Quorum, 4. 1364
quotations, collections of, Renaissance to Restoration, 1. 2029–32
Quotidian occurrences, 1. 2096

R., B. (fl. 1593), 1. 2034
R., C. (fl. 1569), 1. 2071
R. Cruttwell's Bath and Bristol chronicle, 2. 1353
R. Dickson's Dublin post-man, 2. 1382
R. Dickson's White-hall gazette, 2. 1384
R. Douglas Cox's theatrical. . .directory, 4. 859
R., E. (fl. 1678), 2. 1553
R., H. (fl. 1594), 1. 2124
R., H. (fl. 1616), 1. 2125
R., N. (fl. 1659), 1. 2032
Raabe, Wilhelm, 3. 127
Rabelais, François, 1. 2192, 872; 2. 1527, 37, 143
Rabener, Gottlieb Wilhelm, 2. 171
Rabutin-Chantal, Marie de, Marquise de Sévigné, 2. 1533, 136
Race at Sheriff-Muir, A, 2. 350
Racine, Jean, 2. 1527, 37, 123–4, 861–2
racing, nineteenth century, 3. 1703–8
Racing calendar, 2. 1314, 1370; 3. 1703, 1882
Racing illustrated, 3. 1684
Racing times, 3. 1703, 1824
Racing world, 3. 1703, 1825
Rackham, Arthur, 3. 67
Raconteur, 4. 1385, 1387
Rada news, 4. 880
Radcliffe, Alexander, 2. 482
Radcliffe, Ann, 3. 758–60; 2. 148–9, 184, 1009, 1010, 1011, 1013, 1407, 1430
Radcliffe, Frederick P. D., 3. 1704
Radcliffe, William, 3. 1808
Radcliffe, 3. 1868
Radcliffe-Brown, Alfred Reginald, 4. 1207
Radford, Ernest, 3. 645
Radical, 3. 1820
radio
    drama, 4. 861–4
    writing for, 4. 68

Radio digest, 4. 60, 864
Radio fun, 4. 820
Radio times, 4. 60, 864
Radio trade directory, 4. 60
Radishchev, Aleksandr Nikolayevich, 2. 216
Radnor, W. Pleydell-Bouverie, 3rd Earl of, 3. 1731
Rae, Gwynedd, 4. 800
Raffles, Thomas, 3. 1677
Rag, 3. 1867
Raigne of King Edward the Third, 1. 1471
Railway director, 3. 1793
Railway gazette, 3. 1827
Railway magazine, 3. 1854
Railway news, 3. 1827
Railway review, 3. 1820
Railway times, 3. 1827
Raimbach, Abraham, 3. 67
Rainbow, 4. 819
Raine, Kathleen Jessie, 4. 329
Rainolde, Richard, 1. 2308
Rainolds, John, 1. 1932, 2298, 2305, 2309
Rainolds, William, 1. 2299
Raithby, John, 2. 1010
Rajan, B., 4. 1377, 1394
Rake's progress poem (ME), 1. 514
Ralegh, Sir Walter, 1. 2214–19, 876, 2049, 2077, 2123, 2152–3
Raleigh, Sir Walter Alexander, 3. 1449–50
Ralph de Diceto, 1. 776
Ralph de Hengham, 1. 794
Ralph of Coggeshall, 1. 776
Ralph, James, 2. 798–9, 1279, 1281, 1326, 1332, 1565
Ralph, John R. K., 3. 1794, 1797
Ram, N. Sri, 4. 1352
Ram, 4. 1395
Ramazzini, Bernardino, 2. 1548
Ramberti, Benedetto, 1. 2136
'Ramble, Humphrey', 2. 1287
'Ramble, Reuben', 3. 1683
Ramble round the world, A, 2. 1341
Ramble through Holland, France and Italy, A, 2. 1429
Rambler (1712), 2. 1274
Rambler (1750), 2. 1279–80, 1371
Rambler (1848), 3. 1848, 1862
Rambler (Eton 1883), 3. 1870
Rambler (1901), 4. 1356
Rambler's magazine, 2. 1307
Rameau, Pierre, 2. 1565
Ramsay, Allan, 2. 1965–73, 241–2
Ramsay, Allan, the younger (d. 1784), 2. 1283
Ramsay, Allen Beville, 3. 1871
Ramsay, Andrew, 1. 2436, 2464

Ramsay, Andrew Michael, 2. 1527, 1908
Ramsay, Sir William Mitchell, 3. 1614
Ramsay's Waterford chronicle, 2. 1390
Ramsey, John, 3. 1714
Ramsey, Laurence, 1. 1137
Ramus, Petrus, 1. 851; 2. 37
Ramusio, Giovanni Battista, 1. 2112
Randall, John, 3. 1706, 1715
Randall, Maria, 2. 1474
Randall, Vernon, 4. 1349
Randolph, — (fl. 1784), 2. 1426
Randolph, Bernard, 2. 1412
Randolph, Edward John, 3. 1727
Randolph, Thomas, 1. 1773, 1336
'Random, Roderic', 2. 1347
Rands, William Brighty, 3. 548, 1092
Ranelaugh concert, 2. 396
Ranger, 2. 1347
Ranger's magazine, 2. 1311
Ranger's report of travels, A, 2. 1462
Ranjitsinhji, K. S., 3. 1698
Rankin, James R. L., 3. 1870
Rankins, William, 1. 1137, 1334, 2024
Rann, Joseph, 2. 1784
Rann, 4. 1379
Ransome, Arthur Michell, 4. 718–19, 797; 3. 1774
Ranulf de Glanville, 1. 764–5
Raoul de Diceto, 1. 776
Rape of the faro bank, 2. 1568
Rape of the smock, 2. 351
Rapin, René, 2. 1527–8, 37, 67, 116, 129
Rapin de Thoyras, Paul de, 2. 1706, 96
Rarities of Richmond, 2. 365
Rashdall, Hastings, 4. 1208; 3. 1614
Raspe, Rudolf Eric, 2. 1007, 1423
Rastell, John, 1. 1405, 1412, 963
Rastell, William, 1. 963
Ratazzi, Peter, 4. 1361, 1377, 1378
Ratcliffe, Bertram, 4. 1369
Ratcliffe, Dorothy Una, 4. 1362
'Ratcliffe, Sir Isaac' (J. Henley), 2. 1278
Rational amusement, 2. 377
Rationalist review, 4. 1352
Rattigan, Sir Terence Mervyn, 4. 976–7
Rattle, 3. 1868
Rattle for grown children, A, 2. 387
Rattler (1917), 4. 1397
Rattler (1950), 4. 1398
Ratts rhimed to death, 1. 1011; 2. 328
Rauwolff, Leonhart, 2. 1434
Raven (1910), 4. 1382
Raven (May 1922), 4. 1393
Raven, Charles Earle, 4. 1281–2
Raven-Hill, Leonard, 3. 1853; 4. 1353

Raveneau de Lussan, —, 2. 1458
Ravenscroft, Edward, 2. 771, 179, 1908
Ravenscroft, Thomas, 1. 1353-4, 1901
Ravisius Textor, Joannes, 1. 854
Rawlet, John, 2. 483
Rawlins, Edward, 2. 1340
Rawlins, John, 1. 2127
Rawlins, Thomas (c. 1618-70), 1. 1753
Rawlins, Thomas, the younger (fl. 1677), 2. 771
Rawlinson, Christopher, 2. 241, 1795
Rawlinson, Richard, 2. 1701-2, 311
Rawlinson, Thomas, 2. 311
Rawlinson NT strophic passages, 1. 481
Rawnsley, Hardwick Drummond, 3. 645
Raworth, Benjamin C., 3. 1880
Rawstorne, Lawrence, 3. 1712
Ray, James, 2. 1401
Ray, John, 2. 1391, 1410-11, 1556, 1908
Raymond, John, 1. 2129
Raymond, Richard John, 3. 1137
Raynal, Guillaume Thomas François, 2. 1528, 96, 1454
Rayner's (London) morning advertiser, 2. 1328
Reach, Angus Bethune, 3. 1398-9
Read, Carveth, 3. 1578
Read, Sir Herbert Edward, 4. 1108-13
Read, Sylvia, 4. 1375
Read, Walter William, 3. 1698
Read, William, 3. 1693
Read's weekly journal, 2. 1322-3
Reade, Charles, 3. 878-82
Reade, Henry James, 4. 1356
Reade, William Winwood, 3. 1399, 1671
Reader (1714), 2. 1275
Reader (1762), 2. 1283
Reader (1863), 3. 1821
Reader's digest, 4. 1366
Reader's forum, 4. 1364
Readers' review, 4. 117, 1358
reading, analysis of, twentieth century, 4. 119-30
Reading, John, 1. 2040
Reading journal, 2. 1365
Reading lamp, 4. 1340, 1377
Reading mercury, 2. 1365; 3. 1832
Reading post, 2. 1365
Reading University College review, 4. 1398
Real John Bull, 3. 1809
Realist, 4. 1368
Realm, 4. 1357
Reasoner (March 1773), 2. 1285
Reasoner (November 1773), 2. 1285
Reasoner (1784), 2. 1287
Reasoner and herald of progress (1846), 3. 1819
Reasoner and secular world (1865), 3. 1819
Rebellion of Naples, 1. 1761

Recalled to life, 4. 1363
Reck, P. G. F., Baron von, 2. 1462
Reckitt, William, 2. 1470
Recluse, 2. 1348
Reconciler, 2. 1275
Record (1828), 3. 1808, 1822
Record (1914), 4. 1383
Record (Glasgow 1954), 3. 1805; 4. 1404
Recorder (1909), 4. 1381
Recorder (1911), 4. 1382
Records of love, 2. 1293
Recreation, 3. 1878
Recreations in agriculture, 2. 1312
Recreative reading, 4. 1356
Recuyell of the histories of Troye, 1. 428
Red blooded stories, 4. 1389
Red magazine (1908), 4. 1359
Red magazine (1908-39), 4. 1359
Red republican, 3. 1819
Red rose magazine, 4. 1358
Red rose novels, 4. 1358
Red stage, 4. 867, 874
Red-white-blue, 4. 1383
Redbrick, 4. 1392
Redde racionem, 1. 490
Redding, Cyrus, 3. 1774, 1791, 1843
Rede, Leman Thomas, 2. 1799
Rede, William Leman, 3. 1155
Redford, John, 1. 1405-6
Redgrave, Michael, 4. 1368, 1394
Redlich, Monica, 4. 810
Redman, Robert, 1. 963
Redpath, Robert, 3. 1796
'Redway, Ralph' (C. H. St J. Hamilton), 4. 792
Reece, Richard, 3. 1881
Reece, Robert, 3. 1196
Reed, Daniel, 3. 1806
Reed, Sir Edward James, 3. 1827
Reed, Henry, 4. 330
Reed, Isaac, 2. 1761-2
Reed, Joseph, 2. 857
Reed, L. M., 3. 1828
Reed, Langford, 4. 807
Reed, Talbot Baines, 3. 1097
Reed, W., 3. 1828
Rees, Josiah, 2. 1389
Rees, Richard, 4. 1366
Reeve, Clara, 2. 149, 184, 1004, 1005, 1007, 1008, 1010, 1014
Reeve, Henry, 3. 1774, 1855
Reeve, J. S., 3. 1708
Reeve, Lovell A., 3. 1821
Reeves, Helen Buckingham, 3. 1068
'Reeves, James' (John Morris Reeves), 4. 330-1, 810

Reeves, John, 2. 1554
Reeves, John Morris, 4. 330–1, 810
Reeves, William, 3. 1891
Referee, 3. 1812; 4. 1402
reference works, bibliography of, 1. 5–8
Reflections, 4. 1388
Reflections, moral, comical, satyrical, 2. 344
Reflector (1797), 2. 1290
Reflector (1811), 3. 1855
Reflector (Cambridge, 1888), 3. 1866
Reflector (1911), 4. 1382
Reformer (1748), 2. 1378
Reformer (1756), 2. 1333
Reformer (1776), 2. 1347
Reformer (1780), 2. 1286
Reformist's register, 3. 1817
Regent magazine, 4. 1389
Reginald of Canterbury, 1. 758
Register book of shipping, 2. 1346
Register of the times, 2. 1310
Register of the trade of the port of London, A, 2. 1346
Regnard, Jean François, 2. 1528, 124
Regnault, G. L., 1. 868
Regularis concordia, 1. 327
Rehearsal (of observator), 2. 1344
Rehearsal rehears'd, 2. 1344
Rehearsal reviv'd, 2. 1322
Reid, Alexander, 2. 2036
Reid, Andrew, 2. 1294
Reid, Forrest, 4. 719–20
Reid, Hugh Gilzean, 3. 1798
Reid, Peter, 2. 1286
Reid, Sir T. Wemyss, 3. 1774, 1796, 1815
Reid, Thomas, 2. 1892, 43, 111
Reid, Thomas Mayne, 3. 958–60, 1793, 1826
Reid, Walter, 3. 1796
Reilly's weekly oracle, 2. 1384
Reiner, Charles, 3. 1722
Rejected mss., 4. 1371
Rejection, 4. 1370
Rejoinder of Jack Upland, 1. 546
Relation of a brave and resolute sea-fight, A, 1. 2127
Relation of a short survey of 26 counties, A, 1. 2128
Relation of a wonderfull voiage made by. . . Schouten, 1. 2156
Relation of Maryland, A, 1. 2159
Relation of the new mission to the Moxos Indians, A, 2. 1460
Relation of the revolution in Siam, A, 2. 1434
Relatyon of the discovery of our river, A, 1. 2153
religion
  general bibliography, 1. 19–22
  Old English prose, 1. 323–8

Middle English
  Bible, 1. 477–82
  liturgical drama, 1. 721–6
  miscellaneous, 1. 495–524
  prophecies, 1. 473–8
  saints' legends, 1. 523–34
  sermons, 1. 481–90
  Wyclif and Wycliffites, 1. 491–6
Renaissance to Restoration, 1. 1781–2006
  Bible, 1. 1825–88; commentaries, 1. 1853–88; scholarship, 1. 2295–6; studies, 1. 1845–54; versions, 1. 1829–46
  devotional writings, 1. 1915–48
  Caroline divines, 1. 1963–2006
  Early Fathers and Schoolmen, 1. 2295–8
  education, 1. 2395–6
  Hooker, 1. 1949–58
  humanists and reformers, 1. 1781–1826
  Marprelate controversy, 1. 1957–64
  prayer book, 1. 1887–96
  psalms, 1. 1895–1914
  Scottish controversies, 1. 2453–66
  sermons, 1. 1915–48
  theology, 1. 2297–300
Restoration and eighteenth century, 2. 1599–1676
  baptists, 2. 1665–6, 1668–72
  book catalogues, 2. 297–8
  congregationalists, 2. 1664–5, 1667–70
  dissenting academies, 2. 1933–4
  divines, 2. 1599–1640
  mystics, 2. 1651–62
  presbyterians, 2. 1666, 1671–4
  quakers, 2. 1639–52
  Scottish, 2. 2031–46
  unitarians, 2. 1666, 1673–6
nineteenth century, 3. 1599–1636
  dissenters, 3. 1732–3
  evangelicals, 3. 1615–22
  journalism, 3. 1822–23, 1837, 1880
  liberal theology, 3. 1599–1616
  Oxford movement, 3. 1621–36
  poetry, relationship with, 3. 169–71
twentieth century, 4. 1241–1310
see also philosophy, prose, theology
Religious magazine, 2. 1371
Reliques of ancient English poetry, 2. 385
Reliquiae Wottonianae, 2. 331
Relph, Josiah, 2. 564–5
Remains concerning Britain, 2. 332
Remains of John, Earl of Rochester, 2. 352
Remarkable occurrences from . . . Parliament, 1. 2095
Remarkable passage, or a perfect diurnall, 1. 2096, 2099

Richardson, Gabriel, 1. 2140
Richardson, John, 2. 1402
Richardson, Jonathan, the elder (1665–1745), 2. 1769, 1416
Richardson, Jonathan, the younger (1694–1771), 2. 1769, 1416
Richardson, Joseph, 2. 679
Richardson, Joseph Hall, 3. 1774
Richardson, Philip J. S., 4. 826, 860
Richardson, R. J., 4. 1356
Richardson, Richard, 2. 1908
Richardson, Robert, 1. 2452
Richardson, Samuel, 2. 917–25, 149, 184–5, 195–6, 205–6, 208, 212, 218, 266
Richardson, W. (fl. 1789), 2. 1393
Richardson, William, 2. 1426, 1468
Richer, Adrien, 2. 1031
Richmond, printing, 2. 269
Richmond, Bruce, 4. 1405
Richmond, Legh, 3. 1617, 1102
Richson, Charles, 3. 1725
Richter, Johann Paul Friedrich, 3. 127
Rickets, J. 1. 1773
Ricketts, Charles, 3. 68
Rickinghall fragment (M.E. play), 1. 738
Rickman, E. S., 3. 1679
Rickman, John, 2. 1480
Rickword, Edgell, 4. 1366, 1371, 1375
Rid, Samuel, 1. 2035
Riddell, Mrs J. H., 3. 1073–4, 1850
Riddell, Maria, 2. 1474
riddles
    Old English, 1. 296–9, 288
    Renaissance to Restoration, 1. 2031–2
Rideout, W. J., 3. 1789
Rider, William (fl. 1655), 1. 1754
Rider, William (1723–85), 2. 1802
Ridewell, John, 1. 789
Ridge, Antonia Florence, 4. 813
Ridge, Lola, 4. 1365
Ridge, William Pett, 4. 722–3
Ridgway, Alfred, 4. 1378
Ridgwell, B., 4. 1385
riding, nineteenth century, 3. 1703–8
Riding, Laura, 4. 1371
Ridler, Anne Barbara, 4. 331–2
Ridley, Annie E., 3. 1748
Ridley, James, 2. 1001, 1283
Ridley, Nicholas, 1. 1819–20
Ridpath, George (d. 1726), 2. 2060, 1320
Ridpath, George (1717?–72), 2. 2055
Riedesel, Johann Hermann, Baron von 2. 1423
Rieu, Émile Victor, 4. 799
Rigaud, Stephen Peter, 2. 1908
Rigby, Edward, 2. 1428

Rigby, Elizabeth, Lady Eastlake, 3. 1378–9
Rigg, G. H., 3. 1728
Rigg, James Harrison, 3. 1857
Rigg, John Clulow, 3. 1822
Riggs, Anne, Lady Miller, 2. 675, 1423
Right review, 4. 1372
Rights of Irishmen, 2. 1386
Riley, W. Harrison, 3. 1820
Riming poem, 1. 299
Rinaldi, Orazio, 1. 889
Rintoul, Robert Stephen, 3. 1774, 1804, 1810, 1813
Riou, Edward, 2. 1451
Ripa, Cesare, 2. 1548
Ripault, Louis Madeleine, 2. 1452
Ripley, George, 1. 649, 692
Ripperda, Jan Willem, Duke van, 2. 1418
Rippon, John. 2. 1314
Riquetti, Honoré Gabriel de, Comte de Mirabeau, 2. 1521–2, 1405
Risbeck, Johann Caspar, 2. 1427
Rispin, Thomas, 2. 1469
Ritchie, David George, 3. 1578
Ritchie, James Ewing, 3. 1816
Ritchie, John, 3. 1804
Ritchie, Leitch, 3. 961, 1679, 1683, 1813, 1873, 1875
Ritchie, William, 3. 1804
Ritson, Joseph, 2. 1763–6, 237, 246–7, 1025
Rival beauties: a poetical contest, 2. 393
Rivers, David, 2. 1803
Rivers, George, 1. 2057
Rivers, Jean, 4. 1371
Rivers, John, 1. 1295
Rivers, Marcellus, 1. 2160
Rivers, William Halse Rivers, 4. 1282
Rivington, Alexander, 3. 1680
Rivington, Francis, 3. 1855
Rivington and Co, 2. 281; 3. 80
Roach, Richard, 2. 1658
Roach's beauties of the poets, 2. 420
Road to Hymen, 2. 413
Roads of Italy, 2. 1423
Robb, G., 3. 1702
Robbins, Lionel Charles, Baron, 4. 1208–9
Robe, James, 2. 1371
Roberd of Cisyle, 1. 452
Robert of Bridlington, 1. 766
Robert of Cricklade, 1. 766
Robert of Gloucester, 1. 463–4
Robert of Melun, 1. 766
Robert of Reading, 1. 796
Robert and Adela, 2. 1011
Robert Arthur theatres illustrated journal programme, 4. 825

Robert Owen's journal, 3. 1819
Robert Owen's weekly letter, 3. 1819
Robert the devil, 1. 1138
Roberts, — (fl. 1699), 2. 1414
Roberts, Cecil Edric Mornington, 4. 723–4
Roberts, Denys Kilham, 4. 874, 1371, 1373, 1377
Roberts, Francis, 1. 1912–13
Roberts, George, 2. 1395, 1448
Roberts, Henry (fl. 1585–1606), 1. 1138, 2053, 2078, 2079, 2152
Roberts, Henry (fl. 1760), 2. 1554
Roberts, James, 2. 1554
Roberts, John (1623?–84), 2. 1651–2
Roberts, John (1823–93), 3. 1692
Roberts, Lewes, 1. 2120, 2278
'Roberts, Michael' (William Edward Roberts), 4. 332–3
Roberts, Sir Randal Howland, 3. 1690, 1707
Roberts, Richard Ellis, 4. 1368
Roberts, Robert D., 3. 1746
Roberts, Thomas, 3. 1691
Roberts, William (fl. 1763), 2. 1467
Roberts, William (1767–1849), 2. 1289, 1349; 3. 1843
Roberts, William Edward, 4. 332–3
Roberts, William Hayward, 2. 679–80
Robertson, Bartholomew, 1. 2031
Robertson, C. G., 3. 1868
Robertson, David, 2. 1406
Robertson, Eric, 3. 1852
Robertson, Frederick William, 3. 1609
Robertson, George Croom, 3. 1578, 1858
Robertson, James, 2. 680
Robertson, James Logie, 3. 646
Robertson, John, 2. 1908
Robertson, John Mackinnon, 3. 1450–1, 1854
Robertson, Joseph, 3. 1804, 1823
Robertson, Joseph Clinton, 3. 1827
Robertson, Robert, 2. 1396, 1450, 1470
Robertson, Thomas William, 3. 1141–4, 1793, 1827
Robertson, William (1721–93), 2. 1719–21, 111, 199, 1454
Robertson, William (fl. 1865), 3. 1713
Robie, James, 3. 1803
Robin (1749), 2. 374
Robin (1774?), 2. 394
Robin Conscience, 1. 1138
Robin Goodfellow, 2. 1021
Robin Hood, legend of, 1. 742, 1138–9, 1418
Robin Hood: a collection, 2. 421
Robin Hood and the sheriff of Nottingham (ME), 1. 742
Robin Hoods garland (1663), 2. 329
Robin Hood's garland (1787), 2. 409

Robin's last shift, 2. 1323
Robin's panegyrick, 2. 358
Robins, Benjamin, 2. 1478, 1909
Robins, P., 4. 1380
Robins, Robert, 1. 2036
Robins's London and Dublin magazine, 3. 1845
Robinson, Agnes Mary Frances, 3. 646–7
Robinson, Bartholomew, 1. 2031
Robinson, Charles Edmund, 3. 1716
Robinson, Clement, 1. 1139
Robinson, Elizabeth, 2. 1597–8
Robinson, Emma, 3. 961–2
Robinson, Francis, 2. 1316
Robinson, Heath, 4. 791
Robinson, Henry Crabb, 3. 1301–2, 133, 1774, 1789
Robinson, J. (fl. 1860?), Dublin journalist, 3. 1805
Robinson, Joan Violet, 4. 1209
Robinson, John (d. 1625), essayist, 1. 2049
Robinson, John (fl. 1641–57), author of *Endoxa*, 1. 854
Robinson, John (1650–1723), traveller in Sweden, 2. 1413
Robinson, John (fl. 1774), in Nova Scotia, 2. 1469
Robinson, John (fl. 1794), novelist, 2. 1011
Robinson, Sir John Richard, 3. 1775, 1790, 1793
Robinson, Lennox, 3. 1943–4
Robinson, Mary, 2. 680–1, 1010, 1013
Robinson, Mary Elizabeth, 2. 1011
Robinson, Philip, 3. 1810
Robinson, Richard, of Alton (fl. 1569–89), 1. 1139, 1905
Robinson, Richard, of London (fl. 1576–1600), 1. 1139
Robinson, Robert (fl. 1594), 1. 963
Robinson, Robert (1735–90), 2. 1670–1
Robinson, Thomas (fl. 1609), musician, 1. 1353
Robinson, Thomas (fl. 1620), poet, 1. 1317
Robinson, Thomas (1701?–61), 2. 1828
Robinson, William, 3. 1678
Robinson, William Heath, 4. 791
Robinson Crusoe's daily London evening post, 2. 1331
Robinson Crusoe's London daily evening post, 2. 1331
Robinson's merchant's weekly remembrancer, 2. 1316
Robison, John, 2. 1909
Robson, Charles, 1. 2080, 2127
Robson, Horatio, 2. 1287
Robson, Joseph, 2. 1464, 1484
Robson, Mary, 3. 1089
Robson, Simon, 1. 2030
Roby, H. J., 3. 1728, 1732

Roch, Jeremy, 2. 1393
Roch, John, 2. 1472
Rochdale observer, 3. 1832
Roche, Eugenius, 3. 1775, 1789, 1790, 1792, 1809
Roche, Regina Maria, 3. 760; 2. 1012, 1013
Roche, Robert, 1. 1140
Rocheford, Jorevin de, 2. 1397
Rochefort, Charles César de, 2. 1454
Rochester, manuscripts from, 1. 995
Rochester, George Ernest, 4. 809
Rochester, John Wilmot, 2nd Earl of, 2. 464–6, 167
Rochon, Alexis, 2. 1452
Rocket (Eton 1890), 3. 1870
Rocket (1935), 4. 1371
Rocques de Montgaillard, J. G. M., 2. 1429
Rodd, James Rennell, 1st Baron Rennell, 3. 647
Rodd, Thomas, 3. 86
Roderick, Richard, 2. 1776
Rodger, Alexander, 3. 399
Rodgers, William Robert, 4. 333
Rodney, George Brydges, 1st Baron, 2. 1467
Rodrigues Cirão, João, 1. 889
Rodriguez, Alonso, 1. 909
Rodwell, George Herbert Buonaparte, 3. 1155–6
Roe, — (fl. 1646), 1. 2249
Roe, Sir Thomas, 1. 2146; 2. 1418, 1436
Roger of Hoveden (Howden), 1. 781
Roger of Wendover, 1. 781
Roger, James Cruickshank, 3. 1684
Roger, Robert, 2. 1321
Rogers, E., 4. 1386, 1387
Rogers, Francis, 2. 1395
Rogers, Henry, 3. 1621
Rogers, John, 1. 1833–4, 2023, 2036
Rogers, Richard, 1. 1945
Rogers, Robert, 2. 1467
Rogers, Samuel, 3. 181–2
Rogers, Thomas, of Bryanston (d. 1609?), 1. 1140
Rogers, Thomas (d. 1616), 1. 1945, 1905
Rogers, Woodes, 2. 1478
Rojas Zorrilla, Francisco de, 2. 201
Rolamb, Nicholas, 2. 1417
Roland, George, 3. 1701
Roland, Joseph, 3. 1701
Roland, Marie Jeanne, 2. 86
Roland and Vernagu, 1. 419
Roland de la Platière, Jeanne Marie, 2. 1408
Rolf, John, 1. 2156
Rolfe, Frederick W. S. A. L. M., 4. 724–5
Rolland, John, 1. 2429
Rolland, William, 2. 1375
Rolle, Richard, 1. 517–20, 795
Rolleston, Thomas William Hazen, 3. 1909
Rolliad, 2. 699–700, 1287

Rollin, Charles, 2. 1529, 67
Rollington, Ralph, 3. 1825
Rollock, Robert, 1. 1945
Rolt, Richard, 2. 1804, 1465
Romaine, William, 2. 1627
Roman postboy, 2. 1341
Romance (1923), 4. 1389
Romance (1934), 4. 1390
Romance—illustrated (1897), 4. 1389
Romance journal, 4. 1405
romances
    Middle English, 1. 383–454
        'ancestral', 1. 447–50
        antiquity, 1. 421–8
        Arthurian, 1. 389–416
        Breton lays, 1. 435–42
        Charlemagne, 1. 415–22
        courtly, 1. 445–8
        Godfrey of Bouillon, 1. 427–30
        legends, 1. 441–4; didactic, 1. 449–52;
        'Matter of England, 1. 429–36
    Restoration and eighteenth century genre, 2. 869
    twentieth century fiction, 4. 127–8, 1389–92
Romances, 4. 1392
Romances album, 4. 1391
Romanes, George John, 3. 1578
Romans, Bernard, 2. 1469–70
romantic novel writing, manuals on, 4. 66
Romantic stories, 4. 1386
Romanticism, 2. 11–14; 3. 159–62, 163–8
Romany, 4. 1387
Romauns of Partenay (Lusignan), 1. 449
Rome rhym'd to death, 2. 334
Romei, Annibale, 1. 2192, 889
Romeus et Julietta 1. 1778
Romilly, Esmond, 4. 1371
Romilly, Samuel, 3. 1302
Ronalds, Alfred, 3. 1688
Ronksley, William, 2. 1017
Ronsard, Pierre de, 1. 870–1
Rook, Alan, 4. 1374, 1398
Rooke, Sir George, 2. 1415
Rooke, Henry, 2. 1442, 1450
Roome, E., 2. 1278
Rooper, George, 3. 1689
Rooper, Thomas G., 3. 1730
Roos, Sir Richard, 1. 652
Roosmale, R., 4. 1383
Roosmale-Cocq, R. D., 4. 1382, 1383, 1384
Root and branch, 4. 1361
Roper, Abel, 2. 1319
Roper, William, 1. 2205
Rosalind, 2. 999
Roscoe, Edward Stanley, 3. 1690

Roscoe, Thomas, 3. 1302–3, 1679, 1682, 1874, 1875, 1877
Roscoe, William, 3. 1087; 2. 1348
Roscoe, William Caldwell, 3. 548
Roscoe, William Stanley, 3. 399
Roscommon, Wentworth Dillon, 4th Earl of, 2. 483
Roscrea southern star, 2. 1389
Rose, H. E., 4. 1388
Rose, Hugh, 2. 1457
Rose, Hugh James, 3. 1634
Rose, Robert Traill, 3. 68
Rose, Stewart, 3. 1678
Rose, William Stewart, 3. 400
Rose's breakfast, 3. 1088
Rosebery, Archibald Philip Primrose, 5th Earl of, 3. 1809, 1815
Rosemary, 4. 1382
Rosenbaum, M., 4. 1408
Rosenberg, Isaac, 4. 333–4
Rosenblum, J. M., 4. 1390
Rosier, James, 1. 2153
'Roslyn, Guy' (Joshua Hatton), 3. 1852
Ross, Miss —, 3. 1821
Ross, Alan, 4. 334–5
Ross, Alexander (1591–1654), 1. 1317–18, 2121, 2318, 2337
Ross, Alexander (1699–1784), 2. 1978
Ross, Charles, 3. 1825
'Ross, Diana' (Diana Denney), 4. 810–11
Ross, Sir James Clark, 3. 1672
Ross, James Coulman, 3. 1865
Ross, Sir John, 3. 1671
'Ross, Martin' (Violet Martin), 4. 739–40; 3. 1707
Ross, Robert Baldwin, 3. 1866
Ross, Thomas, 2. 483
Ross, Sir William David, 4. 1282–3
Rossall herald, 3. 1871
Rossall news, 3. 1871
Rossallian, 3. 1871
Rosse, John, 1. 1140
Rosseter, Philip, 1. 1350–1
Rossetti, Christina Georgina, 3. 496–500, 1091–2
Rossetti, Dante Gabriel, 3. 490–6, 68, 133, 140
Rossetti, William Michael, 3. 1399–1400, 1848
Rossi, Giacomo, 2. 1548
Roswall and Lillian, 1. 448
Roth, Matthias D., 3. 1725
Roth, Queenie Dorothy, 4. 1073
Roth, Samuel, 4. 1367
Rothwell, John, 1. 963
Rotterdam's courant, 2. 1317
Roughton, Roger, 4. 1372
Round, F. S., 4. 1377

Round robin, 4. 1397
Roundelay or the new syren, 2. 402
Rous, Francis, the elder, 1. 1140, 1911, 2048, 2140
Rous, Henry John, 3. 1705
Rouse, William Henry Denham, 4. 789
Rousseau, Jean-Baptiste, 2. 37
Rousseau, Jean-Jacques, 2. 1529–30, 37, 96–8, 124, 131, 136, 143–4, 1000; 3. 106
Routh, Martin Joseph, 3. 1634
Routledge and Co, 3. 80
Rover (1714), 2. 987
Rover (1785), 2. 1287
Rover (1922), 4. 820
Row, John (d. 1646), 1. 2468
Row, John, the younger (d. 1672?), 1. 2474
Row, Walter, 2. 1311; 3. 1841
Rowe, Andrew, 1. 963
Rowe, Bryan, 1. 1003
Rowe, Elizabeth, 2. 565, 170–1, 992
Rowe, Nicholas, 2. 780–1, 127, 179, 1771
Rowe-Mores, Edward, 2. 1797
rowing, nineteenth century, 3. 1711–12
Rowing almanack and oarsman's companion, 3. 1711
Rowlands (Verstegan), Richard, 1. 1140, 921, 1907, 2137
Rowlands, Samuel, 1. 2013–14, 1140, 1335, 2029
Rowlandson, Mary, 2. 1455–6
Rowlandson, Thomas, 3. 68; 2. 1406
Rowley, Samuel, 1. 1468
Rowley, William, 1. 1719–21, 2025
Rowntree, Benjamin Seebohm, 4. 1209–10
Roworth, C., 2. 1564
Rows, John, 1. 682
Rowse, Alfred Leslie, 4. 1210–11
Rowson, Susanna, 2. 1008, 1009, 1012
Roxburghe Club, 3. 55
Roxby, Robert, 3. 1689
Royal chronicle and the British evening post, 2. 1334
Royal College of Physicians, its library, 2. 304
Royal College of Surgeons, its library, 2. 304
Royal blue book, 3. 1879
royal entries, speeches at (M.E.), 1. 741–2
Royal female magazine, 2. 1302
Royal game of the ombre, 2. 1566
Royal garland of love, 2. 332
Royal gazette, 2. 1334
Royal informer, 2. 1315
Royal jester, 2. 417
Royal Library, 1. 1003
Royal magazine (1750), 2. 1300
Royal magazine (1759), 2. 1302
Royal magazine (1788), 2. 1308

Royal magazine (1898), 3. 1854; 4. 1355
Royal Navy List, 3. 1880
Royal pictorial, 3. 1854; 4. 1355
Royal screen pictorial, 3. 1854; 4. 1355
Royal sermons (M.E.), 1. 487
Royal Society, foundation and history, 2. 1899–1902, library, 2. 304
Royal Society of Edinburgh, *transactions*, 2. 1372
Royal Society of London, *Philosophical transactions*, 2. 1291
Royal sportsman's delight, 2. 1559
Royal tatler, 4. 850
Royal toastmaster, 2. 415
Royal valour: a poem, 2. 1562
Royal Westminster journal, 2. 1331
Royall diurnall, 1. 2104, 2106
Royalty songster, 2. 410
Royde-Smith, Naomi Gwladys, 4. 725–6
Rubinstein, Harold Frederick, 4. 977–8
Ruby, 4. 1382
Rudbeck, Olof, 2. 1415
Ruddiman, Thomas, 2. 1771–2, 2068
Ruddiman, Walter, 2. 1371, 1372, 1375
Ruddiman's weekly mercury, 2. 1375
Ruddock, — 3. 1795
Ruddock, Margot, 4. 335
Rudierd, Sir Benjamin, 1. 2075
Ruff, William, 3. 1882
Ruff's guide to the turf, 3. 1882
Ruffhead, Owen, 2. 1282
Ruffini, Giovanni Domenico, 3. 962
'Ruffini, John' (Giovanni Domenico Ruffini), 3. 962
Rufus, Richard, 1. 777
Rugbaean, 3. 1871
Rugby magazine, 3. 1871, 1874
Rugby miscellany, 3. 1871
Ruggle, George, 1. 1773–4
Ruin, 1. 299–300
Rule, Gilbert, 2. 2037
Rule, William H., 3. 1840
Rule of Chrodegang, 1. 328
Rule of St Benedict, 1. 498
rules, Old English, religious, 1. 327–8
Rules for casino, 2. 1568
Rules for quadrille, 2. 1568
Rules of reversis, 2. 1568
Rumanian, literary relations with
  Renaissance to Restoration, Shakespeare, 1. 1634
  Restoration and eighteenth century, 2. 219–20
  nineteenth century, 3. 158
Rumford, Sir Benjamin Thompson, Count, 2. 1909
Rump, 1. 1011; 2. 328

Runciman, James, 3. 1775
Runciman, Sir James Cochran Stevenson, 4. 1211–12
Rundle, Elizabeth, 3. 514–15
Rune poem, 1. 300
runes, 1. 220–6
'Runt, Harry', 1. 2024
Rural songster, 2. 430
Ruscelli, Girolamo, 1. 2179
Rush-light, 2. 1378
Rushton, W. L., 3. 1691
Rushworth, John, 1. 2092, 2099, 2100, 2101, 2106
Ruskin, John, 3. 1340–64, 114, 156, 1091, 1747
Ruskin Collegian, 4. 1397
Russel, Alexander, 3. 1775, 1804
Russel, John, 1. 789
Russel, Richard, 2. 1278, 1327
Russell, Alexander, 2. 1439
Russell, Bertrand Arthur William, 3rd Earl, 4. 1283–91
Russell, C. F., 2. 1310
Russell, C. J., 4. 1373
Russell, C. W., 4. 1385, 1386, 1387
Russell, Charles, 3. 1791, 1804
Russell, Charles William, 3. 1856
Russell, Sir Edward Richard, 3. 1775, 1795
Russell, Fox, 3. 1707
Russell, Francis, 2nd Earl of Bedford, 1. 1003
Russell, Francis, 5th Duke of Bedford, 2. 1426
Russell, George William, 3. 1912–16; 4. 1354
Russell, James 2. 1419
Russell, John (d. 1494), 1. 1003
Russell, John (fl. 1634), 1. 1318
Russell, Lord John Russell, 1st Earl, 3. 1138, 1723, 1733
Russell, Leonard, 4. 1375
Russell, Matthew, 3. 1851
Russell, Percy, 3. 1852
Russell, Peter, 4. 1380
Russell, Richard, 2. 1909
Russell, Robert, 2. 1018
Russell, Thomas, 2. 681
Russell, William (fl. 1607), 1. 2078
Russell, William (1741–93), 2. 1739
Russell, William Clark, 3. 1074–5
Russell, William Howard, 3. 1775, 1826
Russen, David, 2. 985
Russian, literary relations with
  Renaissance to Restoration, 1. 921–4
    Shakespeare, 1. 1634
  Restoration and eighteenth century, 2. 213–18
  nineteenth century, 3. 151–6
Rust, George, 2. 1849
'Rustick, Reuben', 2. 1285
Rutherford, John, 1. 2452

'Rutherford, Mark' (William Hale White) 3. 1075–7, 1729
Rutherford, Samuel, 1. 2464–5, 2297
Ruthwell cross, 1. 222–3, 300–1
Rutland, John Henry Manners, 5th Duke of, 3. 1682
Rutledge, Jean Jacques, 2. 1531
Rutter, Frank, 4. 1363
Rutter, Joseph, 1. 1754
Ryall, M. Q., 3. 1819
Ryan, Frederick, 4. 1357, 1394
Ryan, John, 4. 1380
Rycaut, Sir Paul, 2. 1689, 1410
Rye, Peter, 2. 1452
Ryland, John Collett, 2. 1671
Ryland, Jonathan Edwards, 3. 1842
Ryle, Edward Herbert, 3. 1870
Ryle, Gilbert, 4. 1291
Ryleyev, Kondratiy Fyodorovich, 3. 154
Rymer, James, 2. 1470
Rymer, Thomas, 2. 1703–5, 44, 1767–8
Rymington, William, 1. 802
Ryves, Bruno, 1. 2098
Ryves, Elizabeth, 2. 1009

S., A., gent. (fl. 1697), writer on horses, 2. 1553
S., A., gent (fl. 1697), writer on farming, 2. 1557
S., C. (fl. 1704), 2. 1415
S., D. (fl. 1573), 1. 2071
S., E. (fl. 1656), 1. 2036
S. Farley's Bristol journal, 2. 1354
S., H. (fl. 1791), 2. 1027
S., I. (fl. 1655), 1. 2160
S., J. (fl. 1639), 1. 2057
S., J. (fl. 1692), Description of France, 2. 1413
S., J., gent. (fl. 1696), angler, 2. 1557
S., J., gent. (fl. 1697), writer on fowling, 2. 1557
S., J. (fl. 1741), 2. 1559
S., M. (fl. 1581), 1. 2072
SONA, 4. 74
S., P. (fl. 1591), 1. 1330
S.P.C.K., 3. 80
S., R. (fl. 1595), 1. 1141
S., R. (fl. 1683), 2. 980
S., S. (fl. 1653), 1. 2028, 2050
'S., S.' (Mary Ann Kilner), 2. 1024
'S., S.' (fl. 1919), 4. 1397
S., T. (fl. 1682), 2. 980
Sabie, Francis, 1. 1141
Sacchi de Platina, Bartholomaeus, 2. 1548
Sacheverell, William, 2. 1399
Sachs, Hans, 1. 877
Sackville, Charles, 6th Earl of Dorset, 2. 472
Sackville, John, 1. 775

Sackville, Thomas, 1st Earl of Dorset, 1. 1141–2, 1772, 1423
Sackville-West, Edward Charles, 4. 726
Sackville-West, Victoria Mary, 4. 335–7
Sacrae scripturae locorum quorundam versio metrica, 2. 365
Sacred miscellaneis, 2. 348
Sacred offering, 3. 1874
Sacred oratorios, as set by Handel, 2. 427
Sacred poems, 2. 376
Sad news from the seas, 1. 2129
Sadleir, Sir Edward, 2. 1446
Sadleir (Sadler), Michael, 4. 1116–18, 1360, 1361, 1363
Sadler, — (fl. 1791), 2. 1010
Sadler, John, 1. 1774; 2. 975
Sadler, Michael Ernest, 3. 1746
Sadler, Michael Thomas Harvey, 4. 1116–18, 1360, 1361, 1363
Safegard of sailers, 1. 2137
Sage, John, 2. 2037
Sage, Robert, 4. 1367
'Sagebaro, Solomon', 2. 1287
St Alban's Abbey library, 1. 995
Saint-Amant, Marc Antoine de Gérard de, 1. 871; 2. 131
St Andrews
   general library catalogues, 1. 8
   Renaissance to Restoration
      libraries, 1. 995
      printing and bookselling, 1. 970
   Restoration and eighteenth century
      printing, 2. 272
      library, 2. 308
   nineteenth century, 3. 1869, 1874
   twentieth century, 4. 1398
St Andrews University magazine, 3. 1869
St Andrews University news sheet, 3. 1869
St Catharine's College, Cambridge, library, 2. 306
St Catharine's College magazine, 4. 1393
St Catharine's Society magazine, 4. 1394
St Cecilia, 2. 399–400
St Cuthbert's magazine, 4. 1395
St David's College and School gazette, 4. 1395
Saint Dominic's Press, 4. 98
St Edmund's Hall magazine, 4. 1397
Saint-Étienne, Jean Paul Rabaut de, 2. 1526
Saint Evremond, Charles de Marguetel de Saint-Denis, Seigneur de, 2. 1531, 44, 67, 98, 116
Saint-Gelais, Mellin de, 1. 871
Saint George (Ruskin Society), 4. 1354
St George plays, 1. 741–2
Saint Hyacinthe, Hyacinthe Cordonnier, 'Chevalier de Thémiseul', 2. 991, 994

Salzmann, Christian Gotthilf, 2. 1032
Sam Farley's Bristol news-paper, 2. 1354
Sam Farley's Bristol post man 2. 1354
Sam Farley's Exeter post-man, 2. 1357
Samber, Robert, 2. 1411
Samhain, 4. 824, 854, 1356
Sammes, Aylett, 2. 1795
Samples, 4. 1388
Sampson, Henry, 3. 1812, 1815, 1816, 1825
Sampson, William, 1. 1754–5
Samuel, E., 3. 1792, 1877
Samuel, Sydney M., 3. 1822
Samuel, William, 1. 1143, 1904
Samuelson, James, 3. 1858
Samwell, David, 2. 1480
San Pedro, Diego de, 1. 2187, 916
Sancroft, William, 1. 1983
'Sand, George' (Aurore Dupin), 3. 106–7
Sanday, William, 3. 1614
Sandbach, Samuel, 3. 1870
Sandby, Paul, 2. 1424
Sandeman, Fraser, 3. 1690
Sander(s), Nicholas, 1. 1945, 854, 2211, 2276
Sanderson, George P., 3. 1713
Sanderson, John, 1. 2330, 2124
Sanderson, Robert, 1. 1983–4, 2331
Sanderson, Sir William, 1. 2246
Sandford, A. W., 4. 1397
Sandford, Robert, 2. 1455
Sandham, Elizabeth, 2. 1030, 1008
Sandwich, Edward Montagu, 1st Earl of, 2. 1409
Sandwich, John Montagu, 4th Earl of, 2. 1418, 1431
Sandys, Edwin (1516?–88), 1. 1946
Sandys, Sir Edwin (1561–1629), 1. 867, 1908, 2138
Sandys, Frederick, 3. 68
Sandys, George, 1. 1186–7, 1911, 2125
Sanforde, James, 1. 2026
Sangs of the Lowlands, 2. 427
Sankey, John, 4. 1380
Sannazaro, Giacomo, 1. 902
Sansom, J., 3. 1677
Sansom, William, 4. 728–9
Sanson, Nicolas, 2. 1434
Sansovino, Francesco, 1. 2192, 889
Santa Cruz, Mechier de, 1. 908
Santa Maria, Juan de, 1. 909
Santos, Francisco de los, 2. 1410
Sapientia Salomonis, 1. 1778
'Sapper' (Herman Cyril McNeile), 4. 729–30
Sappho, 2. 1494
Sappho, 2. 377
Sapte, W., 3. 1697
Sarah Farley's Bristol journal, 2. 1354

Sardou, Victorien, 3. 107
Sare, Richard, 2. 281
Sargeaunt, W. C., 3. 1880
Saris, Edward, 1. 2146
Saris, John, 1. 2145
Sarmun, A (M.E.), 1. 489
Sarolea, Charles, 4. 1360, 1405
Saroyan, William, 4. 1372
Sarpi, Pietro (Paolo Servita), 1. 2192, 890; 2. 1548–9
Sarratt, J. H., 3. 1694
Sassoon, Siegfried Loraine, 4. 337–40
Sastres, Francesco, 2. 1308
Satellite, 2. 1349
satire
    Renaissance to Restoration
        formal, 1. 1333–8
        French, 1. 871–2
        German, 1. 879–80
        Italian, 1. 890
        Latin, 1. 857–8
        social, 1. 2023–6
        women and marriage, 1. 2031–4
    Restoration and eighteenth century
        German, 2. 171–2
        studies of, 2. 8–9, 59–60, 317–18
Satire, 4. 1406
Satire and burlesque, 4. 1371
Satires of Decimus Junius Juvenalis, 2. 338
Satirist (1807), 3. 1843
Satirist (1831), 3. 1810
Saturday analyst and leader, 3. 1814
Saturday book, 4. 1375
Saturday review, 3. 1814, 1835; 4. 1351, 1401
Saturday Westminster gazette, 4. 1404
Saturday's evening-post, 2. 1329
Saturday's post, 2. 1323
Satyrical, humourous and familiar pieces, 2. 421
Satyrical reflections, 2. 344
Satyrical works of Titus Petronius Arbiter, 2. 345
Saugnier, — (fl. 1791), 2. 1452
Saulnier, Gilbert, Sieur du Verdier, 1. 874, 2064
Saumaise, Claude de, 1. 851
Saunders, Howard, 3. 1857
Saunders, James, 2. 1558
Saunders, John, 3. 1814, 1849
Saunders, R. Crombie, 4. 1376, 1377
Saunders, Thomas, 1. 2123
Saunders, William, 3. 1791, 1796, 1797, 1803
Saunders's Irish daily news, 3. 1805
Saunders' news-letter (1755), 2. 1385–6
Saunders's news-letter (1777), 3. 1805
Saunier, Gaspar de, 2. 1554
Saunterer, 2. 1286
Saurin, Jacques, 2. 1531–2

Saussure, César de, 2. 1400

Saussure, Horace Bénédict de, 2. 1532

Savage, John, 2. 1415

Savage, Marmion W., 3. 964, 1809

Savage, Richard, 2. 565–6

Savary, Claude Etienne, 2. 1427, 1450

Savery, Thomas, 2. 1909

Savile, George, 1st Marquis of Halifax, 2. 1040–1

Savile, Sir Henry (1549–1622), scholar, 1. 1003, 2297, 2299

Savile, Henry, of Banke (1568–1617), book collector, 1. 1003

Savile, Henry (fl. 1596), voyager, 1. 2152

Savile, Sir Thomas, 1. 1003

Saville, Leonard Malcolm, 4. 807

Savona, Lorenzo Traversagni da, 1. 805–6

Savory, Gerald, 4. 978

Savoy, 3. 1854, 1863

Sawles warde, 1. 524–5

Saxey, Samuel, 1. 2072

Saxo Grammaticus, 1. 922

Saxton, Christopher, 1. 2131

Say, Charles, 3. 1812

Say, William, 1. 1003

Sayer, George, 4. 1372

Sayers, Dorothy Leigh, 4. 730–1, 1397

Sayers, Frank, 2. 681

Sayers, Tom, 3. 1692

Sayings of St Bernard, 1. 509

Scales, Catherine, 4. 811

Scaliger, Julius Caesar, 1. 851

Scallop-shell, 4. 849, 1360

Scamozzi, Vincenzo, 2. 1549

Scan, 4. 60, 864

Scandinavia, literary relations with
  loan-words, 1. 168–9
  Renaissance to Restoration, 1. 919–22
    Shakespeare, 1. 1634–5
  Restoration and eighteenth century, 2. 209–14
  nineteenth century, 3. 143–50
  twentieth century, 4. 27

Scarborough daily post, 3. 1800

Scarborough evening news, 3. 1801

Scarborough mercury, 3. 1832

Scarborough miscellany, 2. 362

Scarborough post, 3. 1800

Scarborough weekly post, 3. 1800

Scargill, William Pitt, 3. 760–1

Scarlatti, Alessandro, 2. 1549, 191

Scarron, Paul, 1. 874; 2. 1532, 124, 130–1, 144, 977

Scarron incens'd, 2. 983

'Scelter, Helter van' (J. Ridley), 2. 1283

Scenario, 4. 57

Scenic annual for 1838, 3. 1875

Schaw, Janet, 2. 1470

Schede, Paul, 1. 856

Scheffer, John, 2. 1411

Schelandre, Jean de, 1. 871

Schemer, 2. 1283

Schiff, Sydney, 4. 606–7

Schiller, Ferdinand Canning Scott, 4. 1291–2

Schiller, Johann Christoph Friedrich von, 2. 1540, 175, 39, 68, 181, 863, 1012; 3. 127–8

Schimanski, Stefan K., 4. 1374, 1376, 1398

Schlegel, August Wilhelm von, 3. 128

Schlegel, Friedrich von, 3. 128

Schmid, Christoph von, 3. 1110

Schnitzler, Arthur, 3. 128

Schofield's Middlewich journal, 2. 1362

Scholae edinensis in Caroli II reditum, 2. 328

scholarship
  general
    bibliographies, 1–22
    histories and anthologies, 1. 21–32
    language, 1. 53–186
    prosody and prose rhythm, 1. 33–52
  Old English translations, 1. 313–18, 323–4
  Middle English Bibles, 1. 477–82
  Renaissance to Restoration, 1. 2285–306
    Bible, 1. 1829–46, 1853–88, 2295–6
    literary criticism, 1. 2307–22
    dictionaries, 1. 2291–4
    disputation, 1. 2297–8
    Early Fathers and schoolmen, 1. 2295–8
    ecclesiastical, 1. 2297–300
    Greek, 1. 2303–6
    history and biography, 1. 2201–54, 2267–74
    Latin, 1. 2299–304
    prayer book, 1. 1887–96
    psalms, 1. 1895–1914
    Scottish, 1. 2465–70
    translations, 1. 2059–68, 2165–200
  Restoration and eighteenth century, 2. 1741–1820
    aesthetic theory, 2. 45–54
    biographical dictionaries, 2. 1797–1808
    classical and oriental, 2. 1819–32
    Collier controversy, 2. 721–4
    criticism, 2. 61–4
    dictionaries and glossaries, 2. 1807–16
    dramatic theory, 2. 715–22
    grammars, 2. 1815–20
    history, 2. 1675–1742
    literary forms, 2. 53–64
    medievalists, 2. 231–50, 1789–98
    Scottish, 2. 2047–58
    translations, 2. 63–8, 1029–34, 1485–1550
  nineteenth century, 3. 1635–68
    Gaelic, 3. 1887–94
    history, 3. 1457–1510

Seeley, Sir John Robert, 3. 1495–6, 1579, 1610, 1727, 1732, 1867
Seeley, Robert Benton, 3. 1621
Segar (Seager), Francis, 1. 1144, 1902
Segar, William, 1. 2047
Sege of Melayne, 1. 420
Segrais, Jean Regnauld de, 2. 990
Seinte Marherete, 1. 525–6
Seinte resureccion, 1. 726–7
Seizin Press, 4. 98
Selby, Charles, 3. 1156
Selden, John, 1. 2331, 1003, 2275, 2284, 2306
Seldom, 4. 1393
Select and remarkable epitaphs, 2. 379
Select ayres and dialogues, 2. 330
Select beauties of ancient English poetry, 2. 409
Select collection of English songs, A, 2. 404
Select collection of epigrams, A, 2. 423
Select collection of epitaphs, A, 2. 380
Select collection of favourite Scotish ballads, A, 2. 414
Select collection of favourite Scots songs, 2. 414
Select collection of modern poems, A (1713), 2. 348
Select collection of modern poems, A (1744), 2. 370
Select collection of new, favourite and popular songs, A, 2. 423
Select collection of new songs, A, 2. 401
Select collection of original love letters, A, 2. 378
Select collection of original Scottish airs, A, 2. 418
Select collection of poems, A, 2. 401
Select collection of poems from admired authors, A, 2. 414
Select collection of poems from the most approved authors, A, 2. 389
Select collection of Scots poems, A, 2. 398
Select collection of the most admired songs, A, 2. 400
Select collection of the psalms of David, A, 2. 379
Select collection of vocal music, A, 2. 391
Select epigrams, 2. 424
Select epigrams of Martial, 2. 378
Select epitaphs, 2. 378
Select essays from the Batchelor, 2. 393
Select essays relating to...Shakespeare, 2. 1286
Select fables, 2. 405
Select lessons in prose and verse, 2. 386
Select letters between the late Duchess of Somerset, Shenstone and others, 2. 399
Select musicall ayres and dialogues, 1. 1357
Select pieces of poetry intended to promote piety, 2. 421
Select poems (Glasgow 1783), 2. 404
Select poems (1795), 2. 421
Select poems and ballads (Glasgow 1777), 2. 398
Select poems from a larger collection, 2. 396

Select poems from Ireland, 2. 359
*Select poems of Akenside, Gray...*2. 383
Select tales and fables, 2. 1020
Select views in Italy, 2. 1430
Selected poetical works of the Earls of Rochester, Roscommon and Dorset, 2. 379
Selected writing, 4. 1375
Selection of fables, A, 2. 425
Selection of favourite catches, A, 2. 424
Selection of Masonic songs, A, 2. 386
Selection of recent books (National Book Council), 4. 118
Selection of Scots songs, A, 2. 420
Selection of the most favourite Scots-songs, A, 2. 414
Selections, 4. 1386
Selections from the most celebrated foreign literary journals, 2. 1312
Selector (1776), 2. 1306
Selector (1783), 2. 1348
Selector (1795), 2. 1338; 3. 1808
Selector (1797), 2. 424, 1028
Selig, Richard, 4. 1397
Selimus, 1. 1470
Selkirk, Alexander, 2. 1460
Selkirk, G. H., 3. 1697
Selkirk, Thomas Douglas, 5th Earl of, 3. 1671
Sell, 4. 1393
Seller, Abednego, 2. 1434
Sellman, Edward, 1. 2150
Sellyng, William, 1. 805
Selous, F. C., 3. 1713
Selwyn, Mrs — (fl. 1824), 3. 1682
Selwyn, Edward Carus, 3. 1870
Selwyn, George Augustus, 3. 1870
Selwyn, T. K., 3. 1711
Selwyn, William, 3. 1732
Semmedo, Alvaro, 1. 2150
Sempill, Robert, 1. 2429–31
Semple, Sir James, 1. 2431
Senat, Conrad, 4. 1377
Senator (1728), 2. 1278
Senator (1790), 2. 1337
Senatus of Worcester, 1. 766
Seneca, 1. 2176, 1421–2; 2. 1500–1
'Seneca', 2. 1290
Senefelder, Alois, 3. 68
'Senex', 2. 1348
Senilis Amor, 1. 1778
Senior, Nassau William, 3. 1303–4, 1726, 1856
Senior, William, 3. 1690, 1816
Sentences and maxims, 2. 347
Sentimental and masonic magazine, 2. 1379
Sentimental connoisseur, 2. 391
Sentimental magazine, 2. 1305

Sentimental philosopher, 2. 1285
Sentimental spouter, 2. 394
sentimentalism, Restoration and eighteenth century, 2. 13–14
Sentinel (1843), 3. 1813
Sentinel (1913), amateur journal, 4. 1383
Sepp, Anthony, 2. 1459
Septem miracula, 1. 504
September annual, 4. 1386
Sepulchrorum inscriptiones, 2. 357
Sequin's Hibernian magazine, 2. 1379
Seres, William, 1. 2071
Sergeant, Howard, 4. 1376
Sergeant, John, 2. 1849, 983
Serial magazine, 4. 1359
Series of letters on English grammar, A, 2. 1348
Serio-jocular medley, 2. 1388
Serious and comical essays, 2. 346
Serious thoughts, 2. 1272
Serle, Thomas James, 3. 1138, 1808
Serlio, Sebastiano, 1. 890
Serlo of Wilton, 1. 766
Sermo in festo Corporis Christi, 1. 489
Sermon against miracle plays, A, 1. 490
sermons
    Middle English, 1. 481–90
        fifteenth century, 1. 693
        Latin, 1. 752
    Renaissance to Restoration, 1. 1915–48
    Restoration and eighteenth century, 2. 9, 61
Serraillier, Ian, 4. 812
Serres, Jean de, 1. 2193, 862
Servant's magazine, 3. 1846
Servants' magazine, 3. 1846
Service in life and work, 4. 1370
Servita, Paolo (Pietro Sarpi), 1. 2192, 890; 2. 1548–9
Session of the critics, 2. 359
Sessions, William, 3. 59; 4. 81
Seth, Andrew, later Pringle-Pattison, 3. 1579–80, 1614
Seton, Ernest Thompson, 3. 1098
Seton, Walter John, 3. 1870
Settle, Dionyse, 1. 2149
Settle, Elkanah, 2. 772–3, 982, 983, 1318
Settle, John, 1. 865, 876
Seven, 4. 1373
Seven gifts of the Holy Ghost, 1. 514
Seven Portuguese letters, 2. 979
Seven poyntes of trewe loue, 1. 517
Seven sages of Rome, 1. 453–4
Several copies of verses on the death of Cowley, 2. 330
Several letters from Scotland, 1. 2107

Several proceedings of state affaires, 1. 2106
Several years' travels through Portugal. . .and the United Provinces, 2. 1415
Severall proceedings in Parliament, 1. 2106
Severall proceedings of Parliament, 1. 2106, 2108
Severall proceedings of state affaires, 1. 2106
'Severn, David' (David Storr Unwin), 4. 814
Sévigné, Marie de Rabutin-Chantal, Marquise de, 2. 1533, 136
Seward, Anna, 2. 682–3
Seward, William, 2. 1462
Sewell, Anna, 3. 1092, 1706
Sewell, Elizabeth Missing, 3. 964, 1102, 1680, 1727, 1747
Sewell, George, 2. 566–7, 1772
Sewell, William, 3. 1634, 1721, 1731, 1732
Sex, 3. 1867; 4. 1393
Sexton, A. H., 3. 1746
Seymour, Lady Anne, 1. 856–7
Seymour, Beatrice Kean, 4. 732
Seymour, Richard, 2. 1566–7
Shaack, Peter van, 2. 1404
Shadgett's weekly review of Cobbett, 3. 1818
'Shadow, Samuel', 2. 1286
Shadwell, A. T. W., 3. 1711
Shadwell, Charles, 2. 799
Shadwell, Thomas, 2. 744–6, 128, 1909
Shaffer, Anthony, 4. 1394
Shaftesbury, Anthony Ashley Cooper, 3rd Earl of, 2. 1865–7, 44, 111, 159, 189
Shaftesbury, Anthony Ashley Cooper, 7th Earl of, 3. 1728
Shairp, Alexander Mordaunt, 4. 978
Shairp, John Campbell, 3. 1400–1
Shakelton, Francis, 1. 2072
Shakespear's garland, 2. 390
Shakespeare, William, 1. 1473–1636, 881–2, 920, 1144; 2. 221–32
Shakespeare journal, 4. 825
Shakespeare League journal 4. 825
Shakespeare Memorial Theatre, 4. 847
Shakespeare Memorial Theatre: a photographic record, 4. 852
Shakhovskoy, Prince Aleksandr Aleksandrovich, 3. 154
Shamroc, 2. 1387
Shamrock (1772), 2. 393
Shamrock (1800?), 2. 430
Shanachie, 4. 1358
Shand, Alexander I., 3. 1775
Shanks, Edward Buxton, 4. 341
Shannon, Charles, 3. 68
Sharp, Abraham, 2. 1909
Sharp, Bartholomew, 2. 1456

Smetoun, Thomas, 1. 2452
Smibert, Thomas, 3. 1813
Smiles, Samuel, 3. 1091
Smith, — 4. 1383
Smith, Adam, 2. 1880–2, 44, 111, 159–60, 207, 1909; 3. 134
Smith, Albert Richard, 3. 966–7, 1675, 1680, 1709, 1846
Smith, Alexander (fl. 1714–26), 2. 987, 991
Smith, Alexander (1760?–1829), 2. 1481
Smith, Alexander (1829–67), 3. 550–1
Smith, Sir Andrew, 3. 1670
Smith, Arthur, 3. 1689
Smith, Baker Peter, 3. 1682
Smith, Charles Lesingham, 3. 1682
Smith, Charles Manby, 3. 59–60, 1775
Smith, Charlotte, 2. 683–4, 1008, 1009, 1010, 1012, 1027–8
Smith, David Nichol, 4. 1119
Smith, Dodie, 4. 980–1
Smith, Dorothy Gladys, 4. 980–1
Smith, E. A., 4. 1361
Smith, Edmund, 2. 800
Smith, Edward Augustin Wyke, 4. 791
Smith, Edward Tyrrell, 3. 1810
Smith, Egerton, 3. 1795
Smith, Ernest, 3. 1775
Smith, Ernest Bramah, 4. 538–9
Smith, F. E., 3. 1869
Smith, Francis, 2. 275
Smith, Francis Sladen, 4. 981
Smith, G., 4. 1387
Smith, Mrs G. Castle, 3. 1104
Smith, George (fl. 1643), 1. 2092, 2099
Smith, George (fl. 1754), 2. 1559
Smith, George (1815–71) writer on China, 3. 1674
Smith, George (1824–1901), publisher, 3. 80, 1775–6, 1790, 1793, 1804, 1849
Smith, George Henry, 3. 1809
Smith, Goldwin, 3. 1496–7, 1733
Smith, Goodsir, 4. 351–2
Smith, Henry (1550–91), 1. 1932–3, 2276
Smith, Henry Stooks, 3. 1879
Smith, Herbert Greenough, 3. 1853
Smith, Horatio (Horace), 3. 400, 767–8, 1776
Smith, Hubert Llewellyn, 3. 1730
Smith, J. E. (fl. 1710), 2. 1399
Smith, J. Murray (fl. 1880), 3. 1804
Smith, James (1605–67), 1. 1318
Smith, James (1775–1839), 3. 400, 767–8
Smith, James (fl. 1837), 3. 1856
Smith, Sir James Edward, 2. 1429
Smith, James Elimalet (Elishama), 3. 1621, 1776, 1818

Smith, James Moore, 2. 1326
Smith, Captain John (1580–1631), 1. 2078, 2154, 2277
Smith, John (1618–52), Platonist, 1. 2340
Smith, John (fl. 1657), writer on rhetoric, 1. 2320
Smith, John (1659–1715), editor of Bede, 2. 1795
Smith, John (fl. 1684), angler, 2. 1557
Smith, John (fl. 1713), poet, 2. 568
Smith, John (1747–1807), Scottish antiquary, 2. 236
Smith, John (1749–1831), artist and traveller, 2. 1429
Smith, John (fl. 1950), 4. 1359
Smith, John Pye, 3. 1604
Smith, Kemp, 4. 1294
Smith, Logan Pearsall, 4. 1119–20
Smith, Lucy Toulmin, 3. 1663
Smith, M., 2. 1321, 1344
Smith, Miles, 1. 2296
Smith, Norman Kemp, 4. 1294
Smith, Pamela Colman, 4. 1356, 1357
Smith, Reginald John, 3. 1849; 4. 1351
Smith, Richard, seventeenth century printer, 1. 964
Smith, Richard (1590–1675), 1. 1003; 2. 309
Smith, Richard (fl. 1769), 2. 1468
Smith, Robert (1689–1768), 2. 1909
Smith, Robert (fl. 1768), rat-catcher, 2. 1559
Smith, Robert Percy, 3. 1870
Smith, Ronald Gregor, 4. 1378
Smith, S. W., 4. 1366
Smith, Samuel, 2. 281–2
Smith, Sarah, 3. 1094
Smith, Sydney, 3. 1304–6, 1604, 1718, 1745, 1776, 1854
Smith, Sydney Fenn, 3. 1850; 4. 1351
Smith, Sydney Goodsir, 4. 351–2
Smith, T. (fl. 1670), merchant, 2. 1445
Smith, T. (fl. 1714), 2. 1275
Smith, T. (fl. 1859), writer on cricket, 3. 1696
Smith, T. (fl. 1878–87), journalist, 3. 1758; 4. 1342
Smith, Terence, 4. 1377
Smith, Sir Thomas (1513–77), 1. 2211, 1145, 1898, 2132, 2275
Smith, Thomas (fl. 1549), 1. 2039
Smith, Thomas (1638–1710), 2. 1832, 1411, 1432–3
Smith, Thomas (fl. 1707), 2. 1806
Smith, Thomas (fl. 1770), 2. 1560
Smith, Thomas (c. 1775–1830), 2. 1030
Smith, Thomas (fl. 1838–43), sportsman, 3. 1704
Smith, Mrs Toulmin, 3. 1097
Smith, W. (fl. 1601–15) 1. 1756
Smith, W. C. (fl. 1796), 2. 1380

Somervile, William, 2. 568, 1558
Somerville, Edith Œnone, 4. 739–40; 3. 1707
Somerville, Elizabeth, 2. 1029; 3. 1099
Somerville, Mary, 3. 1748
Somerville, Thomas, 2. 1740
Somme-times, 4. 1362
Somner, William, 1. 2254, 2134; 2. 1794
'Son of the Marshes, A' (Denham Jordan), 3. 1439–40
Song book for 1798, 2. 425
Song of Roland, 1. 420
Song on the famous fox-chase, A, 2. 1561
Song Writers' Guild, its *bulletin*, 4. 74
Songes and sonettes (Tottel's miscellany), 1. 1007–8
songs
    Middle English, 1. 697–720
    Renaissance to Restoration, 1. 1337–60
    Restoration and eighteenth century, 2. 327–430
    twentieth century, 4. 127
    see also anthologies, ballads, lyrics, miscellanies, poetry
Songs and chorusses in the Tempest, 2. 398
Songs and poems of love and drollery, 1. 1010
Songs by Pietro Reggio, 2. 338
Songs, chorusses . . . in the new entertainment, 2. 390
Songs compleat, pleasant and divertive, 2. 353
Songs, descriptive, moral and pastoral, 2. 423
Songs, duets, choruses, 2. 419
Songs: elegiac, sea, 2. 423
Songs for little folks, 3. 1108
Songs for 1, 2 and 3 voyces (1677), 2. 333
Songs for one, two and three voices (1692?), 2. 338
Songs for sixpence, 4. 1368, 1394
Songs from the dramatists, 4. 1369
Songs from the ship and castle, 4. 1369
Songs, hymns and psalms, 2. 404
Songs of love in a village, 2. 411
Songs of the chace, 3. 1704
Songs of the Edinburgh Angling Club, 3. 1689
Songs, political, satyrical and convivial, 2. 420
Songs set by signior Pietro Reggio, 2. 334
Songs sung in the several lodges, 2. 377
Songs, trios, choruses, 2. 419
Songs, trios, glees, 2. 424
Songster for the year 1800, 2. 430
Songster's companion (1787), 2. 409
Songster's companion (1800?), 2. 430
Songster's delight, 2. 385
Songster's favourite (1780), 2. 401
Songster's favourite (1785?), 2. 407
Songster's favourite companion, 2. 430

Songster's miscellany, 2. 414
Songster's pocket book, 2. 392
Songster's polite tutor, 2. 396
Songster's repository, 2. 419
Songwriter, 4. 74
sonnet
    Renaissance to Restoration
        Elizabethan, 1. 1073–8
        Shakespearean, 1. 1560–4
    Restoration and eighteenth century, 2. 316
    nineteenth century, 3. 167–8
Sonnini de Manancourt, C. N. S., 2. 1452
Soowthern, John, 1. 1146
Sophocles, 1. 2177; 2. 1494
Soranzo, Lazzaro, 1. 2138
Sorbière, Samuel de, 2. 1397
Sorel, Charles, 1. 874, 2064; 2. 975
Sorley, Charles Hamilton, 4. 353
Sorley, William Ritchie, 3. 1583
Sotheby, William, 3. 400–1, 2. 240
Sotheran and Co, 3. 86
Soto, Andrés de, 1. 909
Soul and body I and II (OE), 1. 304
Soulby, John, 3. 60
Soulsby, L. H. M., 3. 1732
Sound, 4. 54
Sound and vision, 4. 54
Sound wave, 4. 54
Soutar, William, 4. 353–4
South, Robert, 2. 1614–15, 1416
South eastern amateur, 4. 1383
South Eastern texts, Middle English, 1. 86
South London observer (*Camberwell and Peckham times*), 3. 1808
South London press, 3. 1808
South-sea pills, 2. 354
South Wales argus, 3. 1802
South Wales daily news, 3. 1799
South Wales daily post, 3. 1803; 4. 1404
South Wales daily star, 3. 1800
South Wales daily telegram, 3. 1798
South Wales daily telegraph, 3. 1800
South Wales daily times, 3. 1800
South Wales echo, 3. 1802; 4. 1403
South Wales evening express, 4. 1403
South Wales evening post, 3. 1803; 4. 1404
South Wales evening telegram, 3. 1798
South Wales evening telegraph, 3. 1798
South Wales news, 3. 1799
South Western texts, Middle English, 1. 86–8
South westerner, 4. 1395
Southampton, Henry Wriothesley, 3rd Earl of, 1. 1006
Southampton repertory magazine, 4. 851
Southern, Henry, 3. 1844, 1855

Southern Cross, 4. 1383
Southern daily echo, 3. 1802
Southern daily mail, 3. 1801
Southern echo (and Bournemouth telegraph), 3. 1802
Southern evening echo, 3. 1802
Southern legend collection (ME), 1. 529–31
Southern reporter, 3. 1805
Southerne, Thomas, 2. 773–4, 128, 179
Southesk, James Carnegie, 9th Earl of, 3. 1673
Southey, Caroline Anne, 3. 368–9
Southey, R. K., 4. 1385, 1386, 1387
Southey, Robert, 3. 254–61, 144, 1107, 1677, 1682, 1719, 1776, 1873, 1877; 2. 1289, 1349, 1430
Southport daily news, 3. 1799
Southport Dramatic Club magazine, 4. 877
Southport independent, 3. 1799
Southport playbill, 4. 852
Southwell, Charles, 3. 1819
Southwell, Robert, 1. 1059–61, 1933–4
Southwold, Stephen, 4. 523–4
Southworth, Mary, 2. 478
Sovereign magazine, 4. 1364
Soviet literature, 4. 1369
Sowdone of Babylone, 1. 418
Sowerby, Katherine Githa, 4. 982
Sowler, John, 3. 1796
Sowler, Robert S., 3. 1796
Sowler, Sir Thomas, 3. 1796, 1799
Spagnuoli, Baptista, 1. 856, 2191, 2193; 2. 1549
Spalding, Augustine, 1. 2148
Spalding, John, 1. 2469
Spalding, William, 3. 1401
Spallanzani, Lazzaro, 2. 1549, 1430
Spanish, literary relations with
  Renaissance to Restoration, 1. 903–18
    dictionaries, 1. 905–6
    drama, 1. 910–11; Shakespeare, 1. 1635
    mystical writings, 1. 908–10
    Palmerin cycle, 1. 913–17
    philosophy, 1. 907–8
    prose fiction, 1. 912–13
    translations, 1. 2179–94
    travel, 1. 907
  Restoration and eighteenth century, 2. 195–206
    criticism, 2. 68
    drama, 2. 201–2
    literary theory, 2. 39
    philosophy, 2. 198–9
    poetry, 2. 199–201
    prose fiction, 2. 202–6
  nineteenth century, 3. 141–4

Spanish libertines, 2. 985
Spanish spy, 2. 1298
Spare, Austin O., 4. 1363, 1365
Spare moments (1912), 4. 1361
Spare moments (1939), 4. 1387
Spark, Muriel, 4. 1359, 1379
Sparke, Michael, 1. 964
Sparrman, André, 2. 1450, 1480
Sparrowe, Thomas, 1. 1774
Spateman, Thomas, 2. 1019
Speaker (1774), 2. 394
Speaker (1890), 3. 1815; 4. 1352
Speaking of poetry, 4. 1368
Spear, 4. 1355
Spearman, Charles Edward, 4. 1295
Spears, Robert, 3. 1776
Speciall passages and certain informations, 1. 2096
Speciall passages continued, 1. 2098
Specimen of a book . . . of godly and spiritual sangs, A, 2. 386
Specimens of the early English poets, 2. 414
spectacles, Middle English, 1. 739–42
Spectakle of luf, 1. 2452
Spectator (1711), 2. 1272–4
Spectator (1715), 2. 1275
Spectator (1716), 2. 1276
Spectator (1753), 2. 1281
Spectator (Edinburgh 1776), 2. 1375
Spectator (1828), 3. 1813, 1834–5; 4. 1349, 1348, 1400
Speculatist (1725), 2. 1277
Speculatist (1773), 2. 1285
Speculatist (1774), 2. 1285
Speculator (1774), 2. 1285
Speculator (1780), 2. 1286
Speculator (1790), 2. 1288
Speculum Christiani (ME), 1. 490
Speculum Gy de Warewyke, 1. 489
Speculum misericordie (fifteenth century), 1. 688
Speculum sacerdotale (ME), 1. 488
Spedding, James, 3. 1401–2
Speech made by a member of the convention . . . in Scotland, 2. 1319
Speech news, 4. 1368
Speeches by the Nine Worthies, 1. 741
Speed, Frederick Maurice, 4. 58
Speed, H. F., 3. 1716
Speed, John, 1. 2238, 2120, 2133
Speed, Robert, 1. 2035
Speed, Samuel, 2. 484
Speirs, H. W., 4. 1383
Speke, John Hanning, 3. 1671
Spelman, Sir Henry (1564?–1641), lawyer, 1. 2251–3, 921, 1003, 2135
Spelman, Henry (fl. 1609), 1. 2155

Spelman, Sir John, 1. 1912
Spelman, William, 1. 2124
Spence, Joseph, 2. 1748–9, 1828
Spencer, Charles Bernard, 4. 354, 1375, 1397
Spencer, Herbert, 3. 1583–92, 1726, 1824
Spencer, John, 1. 2032
Spencer, Nicholas, 2. 1302
Spencer, Terence J. B., 4. 1369
Spencer, Thomas, 3. 1847
Spencer, Walter T., 3. 86
Spencer, William, 1. 2297–8
Spencer, William Robert, 3. 401
Spender, Edward, 3. 1796
Spender, John Alfred, 4. 1212, 1404; 3. 1776, 1794, 1797
Spender, Stephen Harold, 4. 355–7, 1397
Spendthrift, 2. 1284
Spens, — (fl. 1757), 2. 1333
Spenser, Edmund, 1. 1029–47, 1905, 2134, 2275, 2310; 2. 33; 3. 1887
Sphere, 3. 1817; 4. 1404
Sphinx (Liverpool University 1893), 4. 1395
Sphinx (1921), amateur journal, 4. 1384
Sphynx (1827), 3. 1810
Spider, 4. 1381
Spie, 1. 2100
Spielmann, Marion Harry, 3. 1852
Spiess, Christian Heinrich, 2. 1541, 181
Spilling, J., 3. 1798
Spilman, James, 2. 1438
Spindrift, 4. 1383
Spinnet, 2. 375
Spinoza, Benedictus de, 2. 39, 77, 207
Spinster, 2. 1346
Spirit lamp, 3. 1868
Spirit of the age, 3. 1819
Spirit of the public journals, 2. 1314; 3. 1873
Spirit of the times (1790), 2. 1288
Spirit of the times (1849), 3. 1819
Spiritual magazine, 2. 1303
Spiv's gazette, 4. 1408
Splenetick pills, or mirth alamode, 2. 375
Splinters, 4. 1386
Spokesman, 4. 1393
Spon, Isaac, 2. 1412
Spon, Jacob, 2. 1412
sport
    Restoration and eighteenth century, 2. 1549–70
      boxing, 2. 1562
      cards, 2. 1566–8
      chess, 2. 1566–8
      cricket, 2. 1564–5
      dancing, 2. 1565–6
      duelling, 2. 1562
      fencing, 2. 1562

      hunting, hawking etc., 2. 1555–61
      horsemanship, 2. 1551–5
    nineteenth century, 3. 1683–1716
      general periodicals, 3. 1683–4
      angling, 3. 1687–91
      boxing, 3. 1692–3
      cards, 3. 1693
      chess, 3. 1693–5
      cricket, 3. 1695–9
      fencing, 3. 1701
      football, 3. 1701–2
      golf, 3. 1702–3
      hunting, 3. 1703–8
      journalism, 3. 1824–5, 1837, 1882–3
      mountaineering, 3. 1708–11
      racing, 3. 1703–8
      riding, 3. 1703–8
      rowing, 3. 1711–2
      shooting, 3. 1712–14
      tennis, 3. 1715
      yachting, 3. 1716
    twentieth century, 4. 1311–28
Sport and country, 3. 1817; 4. 823, 1402
Sport and fiction, 4. 1366
Sporting almanack, 3. 1683
Sporting calendar (1751), 2. 1313
Sporting calendar (1769), 2. 1314
Sporting chronicle, 3. 1798
Sporting clipper, 3. 1824
Sporting gazette, 3. 1684, 1824; 4. 1362
Sporting life, 3. 1684, 1791
Sporting magazine, 2. 1309; 3. 1683, 1840, 1860
Sporting oracle, 3. 1683
Sporting review, 3. 1683
Sporting telegraph, 3. 1791
Sporting times, 3. 1684, 1824, 1837; 4. 823, 858, 1351
Sportive wit, 1. 1010
Sports of the Muses, 2. 376
Sportsman (1834), 3. 1683, 1846
Sportsman (1865), 3. 1684, 1791
Sportsmans and breeders vade mecum, 2. 1352
Sportsman's annual, 3. 1875
Sportsman's delight, 2. 1561
Sportsman's evening brush, 2. 415, 1561
Sportsman's garland, 2. 1560
Sportsman's weekly guide to the turf, 3. 1825
'*Spotlight*' *(casting directory)* (1927), 4. 826, 860, 866
Spotlight (International edition 1949), 4. 861, 868, 874
Spotlight (Hall Green Little Theatre), 4. 828
Spotlight (Swindon and District Theatre Guild), 4. 852
Spotlight-contacts, 4. 868, 874

'*Spotlight*' *year book*, 4. 860, 867, 874
Spottiswoode, Andrew, 3. 1816
Spottiswoode, John, 1. 2241
Spottiswoode and Co, 3. 60; 4. 81
Spouter's companion, 2. 392
Spouter's new guide, 2. 423
Sprat, Thomas, 2. 485
Sprenger, Jacob, 1. 851
Sprigg, Christopher St John, 4. 1016–17
Sprigg, William, 1. 2047, 2050
Sprigge, Joshua, 1. 2244
Sprigge, Sylvia, 4. 1374
Sprightly Muse, 2. 392
Spring, Howard, 4. 741, 799
Spring annual, 4. 1386
Spring-garden journal, 2. 1332
Spring pie, 4. 1376
Springer, Balthazar, 1. 2142–2
Sproat, G. M., 3. 1728
Spur, 4. 1406
Spurgeon, Arthur, 4. 1358
Spurgeon, Caroline Frances Eleanor, 4. 1121
Spurgeon, Charles Haddon, 3. 1622, 1843
Spurstow, William, 1. 2001
Spy (1720), 2. 1325
Spy (1790), 2. 1288
Spy (1795), 2. 1366
Spyri, Johanna, 3. 1110
Squib annual, 3. 1875
'Squint, Sam', 2. 1290
Squire, Sir John Collings, 4. 357–9, 1362, 1364
'*Squire Randal's excursion round London*, 2. 1005
Squirt, 4. 1397
Squyr of Lowe Degre, 1. 446
Stables, William Gordon, 3. 1095
Stacey, E., 2. 1322
Stack, James West, 3. 1678
Stackhouse, Thomas, 2. 164
Staël-Holstein, Anne Louise Germaine Necker, Baronne de, 3. 107–8; 2. 1533, 116
Stafford(shire)
  general bibliography, 1. 18
  Renaissance to Restoration printing, 1. 968
  Restoration and eighteenth century
    newspapers, 2. 1367
    printing and bookselling, 2. 270
  nineteenth century newspaper, 3. 1832
Stafford, Anthony, 1. 2048
Stafford, Henry, 1st Baron, 1. 1003
Stafford, R., 1. 1776
Stafford, Sir Thomas, 1. 2241, 2134; 3. 1887
Stafford, W., 1. 2024
Stafforde, Robert, 1. 2120
Staffordshire advertiser, 2. 1367; 3. 1832
Staffordshire (*daily*) *sentinel*, 3. 1799

Stage, 3. 1124, 1826; 4. 823, 859, 866
Stage and field, 4. 848
Stage and screen (*miscellany*), 4. 828, 860
Stage and sport, 4. 825
Stage and variety artistes guide, 4. 862, 868, 874
Stage directory, 3. 1124, 1826; 4. 823, 859, 866
Stage guide, 4. 825, 859, 866
Stage props, 4. 866
Stage Society annual report, 4. 823, 873
Stage Society news, 4. 824
Stage souvenir, 4. 859
Stage staff journal, 4. 873
Stage stars of today, 4. 867
Stage year book, 4. 825, 849, 859, 866
Stageland, 4. 849
Stahl, Wilhelm, 2. 1443
Stählin [-Storcksburg], Jacob von 2. 1485
Stair, Sir James Dalrymple, 1st Viscount, 2. 2057–8
Stalker, A., 2. 1376
Stamford mercury (1713), 2. 1367
Stamford mercury (1736), 2. 1367
Stamford-post, 2. 1367
Stamma, Philip, 2. 1567
Stamp, Sir Laurence Dudley, 4. 1213
Stamper, C., 4. 1386, 1388
Stamper, E., 4. 1386
Stanbury, W., 4. 1388
Standard, 3. 1790, 1793, 1828; 4. 1400
Standard of freedom, 3. 1819
Standard stories, 4. 1367
'Standfast, A.' (E. Roome?), 2. 1278
'Standfast, J.', 2. 1276
Standing, P. C., 3. 1697–8
Stanfield, James Field, 2. 1451
Stanford, Charles S., 3. 1846
Stanford, Derek, 4. 1378
Stanford, Edward, 3. 80
Stanhope, Charles, 2. 1307
Stanhope, Louisa Sidney, 3. 768
Stanhope, Philip Dormer, 4th Earl of Chesterfield, 2. 1585–8, 85, 136, 1279
Stanhope, Philip Henry, 5th Earl; 3. 1498, 1679
Stanley, Arthur Penrhyn, 3. 1610
Stanley, Edward (fl. 1786), 2. 1450
Stanley, Edward (fl. 1827), 3. 1704
Stanley, Edward George Geoffrey Smith, 14th Earl of Derby, 3. 551
Stanley, Edward Lyulph, 4th Baron, 3. 1729
Stanley, H., 4. 851
Stanley, Sir Henry Morton, 3. 1671
Stanley, Thomas (d. 1570), 1. 1146
Stanley, Thomas (1625–78), 1. 1319, 2306, 2338; 2. 193, 200
Stansby, William, 1. 964

Stephens, William, 2. 1462
Stephensen, Percy Reginald, 4. 1368
Stephenson, Albert Frederick, 3. 1776
Stephenson, Elizabeth, 3. 1103
Stepney, George, 2. 485
stereotyping
    Restoration and eighteenth century, 2. 255–8
    nineteenth century, 3. 34–6
Sterling, Edward, 3. 1777
Sterling, John, 3. 1306, 1610, 1777, 1821
Sterling, Joseph, 2. 236, 240
Stern, Gladys Bertha, 4. 742–3
Stern, Seymour, 4. 1369
Sterne, Laurence, 2. 948–62, 112, 150–1, 166, 185–6, 196, 206, 209, 212–13, 218
Sternhold, Thomas, 1. 1146–7, 1899–1900
Sterry, Ashby, 3. 1810
Sterry, Peter, 1. 2001
Steuart, Sir James, 2. 1892
Stevens, B. F., 3. 86
Stevens, Catherine, 3. 928
Stevens, Charles, 3. 1825
Stevens, George Alexander, 2. 569, 1000
Stevens, H. I., 3. 1876
Stevens, Henry, 3. 86
Stevens, John, 2. 1391, 1398
Stevens, Lee, 3. 1789
Stevens, Phineas, 2. 1464
Stevens, Sacheverell, 2. 1419
Stevens, W., 3. 1876
Stevens, William, 3. 1848
Stevens, William Bagshaw, 2. 239
Stevenson, Elizabeth Cleghorn, 3. 873–8
Stevenson, George, 3. 1792
Stevenson, James, 3. 1795
Stevenson, James Cochrane, 3. 1795
Stevenson, James Hamilton, 3. 1672
Stevenson, John Hall, 2. 685, 1421
Stevenson, Mrs M. I., 3. 1678
Stevenson, Matthew, 1. 1319; 2. 1556
Stevenson, R. W., 3. 1842
Stevenson, Robert Alan Mowbray, 3. 1454
Stevenson, Robert Louis, 3. 1004–14, 115, 156, 1096, 1681, 1869
Stevenson, Seth William, 3. 1678
Stevenson, W. R., 3. 1842
Stevenson, William (fl. 1553), 1. 1417, 1774
Stevenson, William (1730?–83), 2. 685
Stevenson's daily express, 3. 1795
Steward, Charles, 3. 1704
Steward, Richard, 1. 2001
Stewart, Miss — (fl. 1885), 3. 1817
Stewart, Dugald, 2. 1893, 44
Stewart, J. L., 3. 1703
Stewart, Sir James (d. 1713), 2. 2038–9

Stewart, James (fl. 1792), 2. 1474
Stewart, James (1831–1905), 3. 1671
Stewart, John (c. 1540–c. 1600), 1. 2432
Stewart, John (1749–1822), 2. 1396
Stewart, John Innes Mackintosh, 4. 617–18
Stewart, Mary Louisa, 3. 1094–5, 1110
Stewart, W. C., 3. 1689
Stewart, William James, 3. 1816
Stewart's Dublin weekly journal, 2. 1386
Stickney, Sarah, 3. 928–9
Stiff, George, 3. 1789, 1808, 1811, 1814
Stifter, Adalbert, 3. 128–9
Stiles, Ezra, 2. 1465
Still, Alexander W., 3. 1797
Stillingfleet, Edward, 2. 1615
Stillman, William J., 3. 1777
Stirling, Mrs A. M. W., 3. 1105
Stirling, Edward, 3. 1157
Stirling, James Hutchinson, 3. 1593
Stirling, William Alexander, Earl of, 1. 1080–2, 2317
Stirling observer, 3. 1833
Stirling-Maxwell, Caroline, Lady, 3. 544
Stobart, M. A., 3. 1703
Stock Exchange year book, 3. 1882
Stockdale, Percival, 2. 686–7, 1299, 1784–5; 3. 1839
Stockport echo, 3. 1801
Stockton bee, 2. 1352
Stocqueler, Joachim H., 3. 1810
Stodart, Robert, 1. 2146
Stoddart, Isabella, 3. 1101
Stoddart, James Hastie, 3. 1804
Stoddart, Sir John, 3. 1789, 1790
Stoddart, Thomas Tod, 3. 552
Stoicus Vapulans, 1. 1778
Stokes, Adrian Durham, 4. 1121–2
Stokes, Francis Griffin, 3. 1868
Stokes, G. W., 4. 1382, 1383
Stokes, Whitley, 3. 1892
Stolberg, Friedrich Leopold, Graf zu, 2. 167, 1430
Stone, Cyril, 4. 1378
Stone, Marcus, 3. 68
'Stonecastle, Henry' (Henry Baker), 2. 1278
'Stonehenge' (John Henry Walsh), 3. 1695, 1713
Stoner, B. G., 4. 1384
Stonhill, W. J., 3. 32, 61
Stonor letters, 1. 684
Stonyhurst pageants, 1. 739–40
Stoppard, John, 3. 1677
Storer, Anthony, 2. 312
Storer, Nathaniel, 2. 1323
Storer, Thomas, 1. 1147
Storey, H. V., 4. 1396

Storey, Samuel, 3. 1799, 1800
Stories: a magazine, 4. 1366, 1384
Stories for all, 4. 1360
Stork, William, 2. 1467
'Storm, Lesley' (Mabel Margaret Clark), 4. 982
Storm, Nigel, 4. 1376
Storm, Theodor, 3. 129
Storm (1798), 2. 1387
Storm (1933), 4. 1371
Stormy petrel, 4. 1358
Storr, Francis, 3. 1728
Storrs, Sir Ronald Henry Amherst, 4. 1214
Story, Douglas, 3. 1854
Story, George, 3. 1840
Story, John, 2. 1418
Story, Robert, 3. 401–2
Story, Thomas, 2. 1652, 1401, 1463
Story, 4. 1378
Story journal, 4. 1359
Story of King Daryus, 1. 1410
Story-teller (1784), 2. 1287
Story-teller (1907), 4. 1358
Storyteller (1946), 4. 1378
Stothard, Anna Eliza, 3. 711–12
Stothard, Thomas, 3. 68
Stoughton, John, 3. 1840
Stoup, George, 3. 1820
Stout, Benjamin, 2. 1452
Stout, George Frederick, 3. 1593–5, 1858
Stovin, Aistroppe, 2. 1555
Stow, David, 3. 1721
Stow, John, 1. 2209–10, 2133
Stowell, William Hendry, 3. 1842
Strabane, printing, 2. 274
Strabane journal, 2. 1390
Strabane magazine, 2. 1380
Strabane news-letter, 2. 1390
Strachan, Andrew, 1. 2466
Strachey, Evelyn John Saint Loe, 4. 1214–15
Strachey, John St Loe, 3. 1777, 1813, 1849; 4. 1218
Strachey, Lytton, 4. 1215–18
Strachey, Mary Amabel Nassau, 4. 801
Strachey, Richard Philip Farquhar, 4. 807
Strachey, William, 1. 2156, 2277
Strada, Famiano, 1. 856; 2. 1549
Stradling, Sir John, 1. 1319
Strahan, Alexander, 3. 80, 1777, 1823, 1849, 1850, 1851
Strahan, William, 2. 266
Strahlenberg, Philip Johann von, 2. 1417, 1438
Straight, Sir Douglas, 3. 1793, 1854
Strains of the British Muses, 2. 400
Straker Bros., 3. 60; 4. 81
Strand magazine, 3. 1853, 1863; 4. 1353, 1348

'Strang, Herbert' (George Herbert Ely), 4. 794
Strang, John, 3. 1803
Strang, William, 3. 68
Strange, James, 2. 1481
Strange and merveilous news [from China], 1. 2147
Strange detective mysteries, 4. 1391
Strange histories of kings (1600), 1. 1009
Straparola, Giovanni Francesco, 1. 902–3
Stratford, Shipston and Aulcester journal, 2. 1367
Stratford-upon-Avon
  Renaissance to Restoration printing, 1. 968
  Restoration and eighteenth century
    newspapers, 2. 1367
    printing and bookselling, 2. 270
  twentieth century, Shakespeare Memorial
    Theatre, 4. 847
Stratford-upon-Avon herald, 4. 1402
Strauss, David Friedrich, 3. 129
Strauss, Gustave L. M., 3. 1777, 1828
Strauss, Jans J., 2. 1394–5
Strawberry Hill Press, 2. 264
Stray thoughts, 4. 1384
Streater, John, 1. 2092, 2109
Streatfeild, Marion Catherine, 4. 796
Streatfeild, Noel, 4. 803–4
Strecche, John, 1. 805
Street, Arthur George, 4. 1326
Street, George Edmund, 3. 1680
Street, Peter, 3. 1792
Street and Smith's western story magazine, 4. 1390
Streeter, Burnett Hillman, 4. 1296
*Strenae natalitiae academiae oxoniensis in celsis-
  simum principem*, 2. 336
Strephon's revenge, 2. 353
Stretser, Thomas, 2. 980
'Stretton, Hesba' (Sarah Smith), 3. 1094
Strickland, Agnes, 3. 1090, 1877
Strickland, Jane, 3. 1877
Stride, W. K., 3. 1868
Strindberg, August, 3. 148
Stringer, Arthur, 2. 1558
strip cartoons, 4. 123–5
Strode, Warren Chetham, 4. 982–3
Strode, William, 1. 1320, 1774, 2002
Stroller, 4. 877
Strong, Charles, 3. 402
Strong, James, 1. 2033
Strong, Leonard Alfred George, 4. 744–6, 803, 1370
Strousberg, Bethel Henry, 3. 1848
Struther, William, 1. 2466
Strutt, Elizabeth, 3. 1679
Strutt, Joseph, 2. 1740, 1798, 1808
Strutt, William, 3. 1678
Strutton, Richard, 2. 1412

Sunday London gazette, 2. 1287
Sunday magazine, 3. 1823
Sunday mail, 3. 1812; 4. 1404
Sunday Mercury, 3. 1812
Sunday mirror, 4. 1405
Sunday monitor, 3. 1807
Sunday news, 3. 1811; 4. 1400
Sunday pictorial, 4. 1406
Sunday referee, 3. 1812; 4. 1402
Sunday reformer, 2. 1338; 3. 1807
Sunday review, 2. 1337; 3. 1807
Sunday special, 3. 1812
Sunday story journal, 4. 1359
Sunday sun (1891), 3. 1812; 4. 1403
Sunday sun (1919), 4. 1406
Sunday times, 3. 1810, 1834; 4. 1400
Sunday worker, 4. 1406
Sunday world, 3. 1820
Sunderland daily echo, 3. 1799
Sunderland daily post, 3. 1800
Sunderland daily shipping news, 3. 1797
Sunderland daily times, 3. 1800
Sunderland echo, 3. 1799
Sunderland morning mail, 3. 1803
Sunny mag, 4. 1367
Sunny stories for little folks, 4. 820
Sunrise, 4. 1356
Superman, 4. 1362
Supplement [to Post boy] (1708), 2. 1321
Supplement by way of postscript to the weekly
    journal, 2. 1322
Supplement to Boletarium, 2. 409
Supplement to Dr Swift's works, A, 2. 400
Supplement to Swift's and Pope's works, A, 2. 367
Supplement to Swift's works, A, 2. 397
Supplement to the antiquities of St Peter's, A, 2. 348
Supplement to the asylum for fugitive pieces, A, 2.
    405
Supplement to the Athenian mercury, 2. 1292
Supplement to the Athenian oracle, A, 2. 346
Supplement to the collection of miscellany poems
    against Popery, A, 2. 337
Supplement to the Dublin Gazette. A, 2. 1384
Supplement to the Dublin impartial news letter, A,
    2. 1384
Supplement to the Dublin mercury, A, 2. 1383
Supplement to the Muses farewel to Popery, A, 2.
    338
Supplement to the second book of the pleasant
    musical companion, A, 2. 342
Supplement to the weekly journal, 2. 1322
Supplement to the works of the most celebrated
    minor poets, A, 2. 375
Supplementary journal to the advice from the
    scandal club, A, 2. 1344

Suppose pig walk, 4. 1388
surgery, Renaissance to Restoration, 1. 2369–74
Surprize, 2. 1274
Surr, Thomas Skinner, 3. 768; 2. 1014
Surrey, Henry Howard, Earl of, 1. 1023–4, 1899
Surrey amateur, 4. 1381
Surtees, Robert Smith, 3. 967–8
Surtees psalter, 1. 479–80
Survey, 4. 1370
Susanna: or traits of a modern miss (1795), 2. 1011
Susannah (ME), 1. 480
Susenbrotus comoedia, 1. 1778
Sussex
    general bibliography, 1. 19
    printing to 1850, 2. 270
Sussex agricultural express, 4. 1400
Sussex county herald, 4. 1400
Sussex daily news, 3. 1798
Sussex evening times, 3. 1801
Sussex weekly advertiser, 2. 1360
Sutcliffe, Matthew, 1. 1962, 2298
Sutherland, David, 2. 1428
Sutherland, James (d. 1791), 2. 1450
Sutherland, James (fl. 1878), 3. 1815
Sutherland, James Runcieman, 4. 1124
Sutherland, Robert Garioch, 4. 278
Sutro, Alfred, 4. 983–4
Suttner, Bertha von, 3. 129
Sutton, Christopher, 1. 1947
Sutton, Henry Septimus, 3. 553, 1857
Sutton, Peter, 1. 794
Sutton, T. R., 3. 1824
Swadlin, Thomas, 1. 2101, 2103
Swain, Charles, 3. 553
Swaine, Charles, 2. 1484
Swaine, Stephen A., 3. 1843
Swallow, Norman, 4. 1376
Swansea daily shipping register, 3. 1800
Swansea gazette, 3. 1800
Swansea journal, 4. 1401
Swedenborg, Emanuel, 2. 77–8, 214
Sweet, Henry, 3. 1663–4
Sweet Robin, 2. 420
Swetnam the woman-hater, 1. 1761
Swift, Jonathan, 2. 1054–91, 112, 151, 172, 196,
    199, 206, 209–10, 213, 214, 218, 233, 1313,
    1377, 1909
Swift, Theophilus, 2. 1568
swimming, 3. 1714–15
Swimming and swimmers, 3. 1715
Swinburne, Algernon Charles, 3. 571–9, 115–16,
    134, 140
Swinburne, Henry, 2. 1425
Swindrage, Theodore, 2. 1468
Swineshead, Richard, 1. 795

Swingler, Randall Carline, 4. 362, 1371, 1375, 1379, 1380
Swinhoe, Gilbert, 1. 1756
Swinnerton, Frank Arthur, 4. 746–7
Swinney's Birmingham and Stafford chronicle, 2. 1353
Swinney's Birmingham chronicle, 2. 1353–4
Swinton, Andrew, 2. 1429
Swiss, literary relations with
  Renaissance to Restoration, Shakespeare, 1. 1635–6
  Restoration and eighteenth century, 2. 220–2
sword dances, 1. 741–2
Sydenham, Thomas, 2. 1909
Sydserf, Sir Thomas, 2. 772
Sylph (1779), 2. 1005–6
Sylph (1795), 2. 1289, 1347
Sylphid, 2. 1290
Sylvae, 2. 335
Sylvaine, Vernon, 4. 984–5
'Sylvan, Agricola', 2. 1305
Sylvanus, 1. 1778
Sylvester, Joshua, 1. 1147–8, 1320, 2038
Sylvia's (home) journal, 3. 1850
Symes, Michael, 2. 1444; 3. 1673
Symes, R. 3. 1704
Symington, A. B., 3. 1853
Symmons, Edward, 1. 2040
Symonds, B., 2. 1560
Symonds, John Addington, 3. 1501–3, 140
Symonds, William, 1. 2276
Symons, Alphonse James Albert, 4. 1219, 110
Symons, Arthur, 3. 649–51, 116, 1854, 4. 1367
Symons, Julian Gustave, 4. 362–3, 1372
Symons, W. T., 4. 1368
Symson, Archibald, 1. 2465–6, 2299
'Symson, William', 2. 987, 1437
Synge, Edmund John Millington, 3. 1934–8
Synopsis, 4. 1373
Synopsis musicae, 2. 338
Synopsis of vocal musick, 2. 334
syntax, general, 1. 111–42
  Old English, 1. 117–22
  Middle English, 1. 121–6
  Modern English, 1. 127–42
Syon Monastery, Isleworth, library of, 1. 991
Syre Gawane and the Carle of Carelyle, 1. 406
Syren (1735), 2. 364
Syren (1765?), 2. 386
Syren (1789?), 2. 412
Syren (1797?), 2. 424

T., B. A. (fl. 1807), 3. 1107
T.B. no 31 telegraph, 4. 1384
T., C. (fl. 1615), 1. 2038

T., F. (fl. 1570), 1. 1148
T., G. (fl. 1642), 1. 2046
T., J. (fl. 1592), 1. 1148
TMA monthly report, 4. 874
T.P.'s (and Cassell's) weekly, 4. 1356, 1366, 1405
T., T. W. (fl. 1568), 1. 2032
Taafe, Francis, Count, 2. 1412
Taaffee's national shamroc, 2. 1387
'Tabby, A.', 3. 1088
Table book, 3. 1874, 1877
Tablet, 3. 1822; 4. 1400
Tabloid, 4. 1388
Tabor, Elizabeth, 3. 1103
Tachard, Guy, 2. 1434
Tachmas, Prince of Persia, 2. 978
Tacitus, 1. 2177, 2138; 2. 1501
'Tagg, Tommy' (John Newbery?), 2. 1019
Taill of Rauf Coilyear, 1. 420–1
Tailo(u)r, Robert, 1. 1355, 1756
Taine, Hippolyte, 3. 108–9
Tait, William, 3. 1845
Tait's Edinburgh magazine, 3. 1845
Taitt, David, 2. 1469
Talaeus, Audomerus, 1. 852
Talbot, Catherine, 2. 1598
Talbot, Sir Gilbert, 1. 1756
Talbot, Robert (d. 1558), 1. 2131
Talbot, Sir Robert (fl. 1771), 2. 1422
Tale of Beryn, 1. 652
tales, Middle English, 1. 455–60
Tales and novels in verse from La Fontaine, 2. 364
Tales from town topics, 4. 1353
Tales of danger and daring, 4. 1389
Tales to kill time, 2. 379
Tales well told, 4. 1360
Talfourd, Sir Thomas Noon, 3. 1140–1, 1777
Talisman (1829), 3. 1874
Talisman (1831), 3. 1875
Talking bird, 3. 1106
Talkyng of þe loue of God, A, 1. 516
Tallis, John, 3. 1816
Talon, Omer, 1. 852
Tambimuttu, —, 4. 1373
Tambour, 4. 1368
Taming of a shrew (1594), 1. 1470
Tannahill, Robert, 3. 402
Tanner, Thomas, 2. 1801
Tansillo, Luigi, 1. 894; 2. 1549
Taplin, William, 2. 1555, 1560
Tarbat, George Mackenzie, Viscount, 2. 1689–90
Tarleton, Sir Banastre, 2. 1472
Tarlton, Richard, 1. 2056, 2071
Tarn, Sir William Woodthorpe, 4. 791
Tartaglia, Niccoló, 1. 2193
Tasker, William, 2. 240

Tasso, Ercole, 1. 890
Tasso, Torquato, 1. 2193, 890, 895, 897–8; 2. 1549–50, 192–3
Tassoni, Alessandro, 2. 194
Taste and critical observations of J.H., 2. 1285
Tate, Nahum, 2. 774–6
Tate, Thomas, 3. 1725
Tatham, John, 1. 1756–7
Tatham, M. T., 3. 1870
'Tatler, Duncan', 2. 1370
Tatler (1709), 2. 1269–71, 1321
Tatler (Dublin 1710), 2. 1377
Tatler (Edinburgh 1710), 2. 1369
Tatler (Edinburgh 1711), 2. 1369
Tatler (1753), 2. 1281
Tatler (1830), 3. 1790
Tatler (1901), 4. 824, 1404
Tatler in Cambridge, 3. 1866
Tatler reviv'd (1727), 2. 1278
Tatler reviv'd (1750), 2. 1279, 1332
Tatling harlot, 2. 1345
'Tattle, Timothy', 2. 1328
Tattler, 3. 1815
Tattoo, 4. 1378
Tatwine, 1. 345
Tauchnitz, Bernard, 3. 80
Taunton, T. H., 3. 1707
Taunton herald, 2. 1367
Taunton-journal, 2. 1367
Taurus, 4. 1388
Tautphoeus, Jemima, Baroness, 3. 968
Taverner, Richard, 1. 1834, 2029
Taverner, William, 2. 800
Tavernier, Jean Baptiste, Baron d'Aubonne, 2. 1433
Tawney, Richard Henry, 4. 1219–20
Tayler, Charles Benjamin 3. 1876
Tayler, John James, 3. 1856
Taylor, Alan John Percivale, 4. 1220–1
Taylor, Alfred Edward, 4. 1297–8
Taylor, Allan N., 4. 1370
Taylor, Ann (1757–1830), 3. 1087
Taylor, Ann (1782–1866), 3. 1087, 1088; 2. 1029
Taylor, C. 4. 110
Taylor, C. L., 3. 1827
Taylor, Charles, 3. 1813
Taylor, Daniel, 2. 1312
Taylor, Doreen, 4. 1380
Taylor, Edward, 1. 1321–3
Taylor, Edward Samuel, 3. 1693
Taylor, Emily, 3. 1101
Taylor, Frances, 3. 1850
Taylor, G., 2. 1468
Taylor, George, 4. 878
Taylor, Sir Henry, 3. 553

Taylor, Isaac (1759–1829) of Ongar, writer for children, 3. 1087
Taylor, Isaac the younger (1787–1865), 3. 1595, 1087, 1604, 1722
Taylor, James, 3. 1714
Taylor, Jane, 3. 1087
Taylor, Jefferys, 3. 1087
Taylor, Jeremy, 1. 1984–7
Taylor, Jesse Paul, 3. 1690
Taylor, John (1580–1653), 1. 2014–20, 1336, 2028, 2035, 2040, 2041, 2075, 2080, 2089, 2092, 2102, 2104, 2105, 2125–7, 2134, 2146, 2163
Taylor, John (fl. 1709), in America, 2. 1459
Taylor, John (1694–1761), divine, 2. 164–5
Taylor, John (1703–72), itinerant oculist, 2. 1420
Taylor, John (1704–66), classical scholar, 2. 1828
Taylor, John (1757–1832), miscellaneous writer, 2. 1338; 3. 1777, 1792
Taylor, John (1781–1864), publisher, 3. 80, 1844
Taylor, John (d. 1808), writer on India, 2. 1444
Taylor, John Edward (1791–1844), 3. 1777, 1795
Taylor, John Edward (1830–1905), 3. 1795
Taylor, Joseph (fl. 1705), 2. 1399
Taylor, Joseph (fl. 1804–15), 3. 1099
Taylor, Peter Alfred, 3. 1809
Taylor, Philip Meadows, 3. 969
Taylor, R. S., 3. 1795
Taylor, Rachel Annand, 4. 363
Taylor, Richard, 3. 1841, 1842
Taylor, S. A., 3. 1695
Taylor, Samuel, 2. 1561; 3. 1687
Taylor, Simon Watson, 4. 1377
Taylor, T. D., 3. 1797
Taylor, Thomas (1576–1633), 1. 2002
Taylor, Thomas (fl. 1704), 2. 1850
Taylor, Thomas (1758–1835), philosopher, 3. 1595
Taylor, Tom (1817–80), dramatist, 3. 1157–8, 1825
Taylor, William (1765–1836), 3. 1306–7
Taylor, William F., 3. 1802
Tea phytologist, 4. 1394
Tea table (1715), 2. 1276
Tea-table (1724), 2. 1277
Tea-table miscellany, 2. 355
Tea-table tatler, 2. 1276
'Teachem, Toby', 2. 1023
'Teachwell, Mrs' (Lady Fenn), 2. 1024–5
Teasdale-Buckell, G. T., 3. 1714
technical and educational writing, twentieth century, 4. 67
Techo, Nicholas de, 2. 1459
Tegg, Thomas, 3. 80–1
Tegg's magazine of knowledge and amusement, 3. 1847

Teixeira, José, 1. 2064, 2078
Teixeira, Pedro, 2. 1437
Telegraph (1794), 2. 1338
Telegraph and argus (and Yorkshire observer), 3. 1797; 4. 1402
Telegraph and independent, 3. 1794; 4. 1401
Telegraph and star, 3. 1802; 4. 1403
'Telescope, Tom' (John Newbery?), 2. 1020
Telescope, 3. 1810
television
    drama, 4. 861–4
    writing for, 4. 68
Television (and short wave world) (1928), 4. 60
Television (1946), 4. 60, 864
Television and the viewers, 4. 60, 864
Television news, 4. 60, 864
Television pictorial, 4. 60
Tell tale (1734), 2. 1328
Tell-tale (1823), 3. 1108
Tell-tale: or the invisible witness (1711), 2. 986
Tell-truth remembrancer, 2. 1343
Telles, Balthasar, 2. 1448
Téllez, Gabriel, 1. 910
Telltale, 1. 1761
'Telltruth, Stentor', 2. 1333
Temperance and humility, 1. 1408
Temperley, Sir Harold William Vazeille, 4. 1221–2
Tempest, 4. 1375
Templar (1773), 2. 1285
Templar (1788), 2. 1308
Temple, Alfred George, 4. 1357
Temple, Frederick, 3. 1606, 1725–6
Temple, Henry, 2nd Viscount Palmerston, 2. 1428
Temple, Henry John, 3rd Viscount Palmerston, 3. 1298–9
Temple, Joan, 4. 985
Temple, Sir Richard, 2. 1850
Temple, Sir William (d. 1627), 1. 2311, 2330
Temple, Sir William (1628–99), 2. 1038–40, 112, 233, 1411
Temple, William (fl. 1758), 2. 1899
Temple, William (1881–1944), 4. 1298–9
Temple Bar, 3. 1849, 1862; 4. 1351
Temple magazine, 3. 1854; 4. 1354
Temple of Apollo, 2. 372
Temple of Comus, 2. 386
Temple of death, 2. 339
Temple of love, 2. 365
Temple of mirth, 2. 405
Temple of the fairies, 3. 1107
Temple-oge intelligence, 2. 1378, 1384
Temple Press, 3. 81
Ten minutes advice to every gentleman going to purchase a horse, 2. 1554

Tench, Watkin, 2. 1430, 1481
Tencin, Claudine A. G. de, 2. 995
Tende, Gaspard de, 2. 1414
Tenison, Thomas, 2. 1616; 1. 2341
Tennant, Charles, 3. 1678
Tennant, Frederick Robert, 4. 1299–1300
Tennant, William, 3. 403
Tenniel, Sir John, 3. 68
tennis, nineteenth century, 3. 1715
Tennyson, Alfred, 1st Baron, 3. 412–35, 116, 134
Tennyson, Charles, 3. 554
Tennyson, Frederick, 3. 555
Ten Rhyne, William, 2. 1447
Teonge, Henry, 2. 1411
Terence, 1. 2177; 2. 1501–2
Terence in English, 1. 1148, 1420
Terence White's verse-reel, 4. 1374
Teresa, St, 1. 909–10
Terilo, William, 1. 2027
'Termagant, Priscilla' (B. Thornton), 2. 1332
'Termagant, Roxana' (B. Thornton), 2. 1332
Termagant, 2. 1287
Terrae filius (1721), 2. 1277
Terrae-filius (1763), 2. 1284
Terrae-filius (1764), 2. 1284
Terrae filius extraordinary, 2. 1284
Terrasson, Jean, 2. 1533, 68, 993
Terrible sea-fight [at Goa], A, 1. 2147
Terry, Edward, 1. 2147
Tessimond, Arthur Seymour John, 4. 364
Tessin, Carl Gustaf, 2. 214
Test, 2. 1282
Test-paper, 2. 1341, 1373
Testament of love, 1. 506–7
Tetlow, R., 4. 1382
Teugels, Olive, 4. 1385, 1388
Texas rangers, 4. 1391
textbooks, educational
    Renaissance to Restoration, 1. 2395–406
    Restoration and eighteenth century, 2. 1943–50
Thacker, Thomas, 3. 1695
Thackeray, Anne Isabella, Lady Ritchie, 3. 1079–80
Thackeray, William Makepeace, 3. 855–64, 116, 134, 156, 1091, 1777, 1849, 1865
Thalia, 4. 1386
Thalia diary, 4. 825, 859
Thalia diary...for music halls, 4. 860
Thatcher, Anthony, 1. 2159
Theater of mortality, An, 2. 343
Theater of music, 2. 335
theatre
    Renaissance to Restoration, 1. 1379–96
        actors, 1. 1387–91

theatre (*cont.*)

    censorship, 1. 1383–4

    drama, 1. 1361–1762; general, 1. 1361–
    80; comedies, early, 1. 1411–20; Eliza-
    bethan, 1. 1423–74; Jacobean and
    Caroline, 1. 1637–1762; moralities, 1.
    1401–12; Shakespeare, 1. 1473–1636;
    tragedies, early, 1. 1421–4; university,
    1. 1761–80

    history, 1. 1381–2

    management, 1. 1393–6

    production, 1. 1387–94

    public and private, 1. 1383–8

    Puritan attack, 1. 1395–1402

  Restoration and eighteenth century, 2. 723–40

    actors, 2. 733–40

    drama, 2. 701–864; general, 2. 701–24;
    eighteenth century, 2. 777–862; Restora-
    tion, 2. 741–78; translations, 2. 861–4

    London, 2. 725–8

    production, 2. 731–4

    provinces, 2. 727–32

  nineteenth century, 3. 1111–24

    actors, 3, 1117–22

    design, 3. 1121–2

    drama, 3. 1111–96

    history, 3. 1111–16

    Irish, 3. 1939–48

    periodicals, 3. 1123–4

  twentieth century, 4. 821–80

    amateur, 4. 875–80

    censorship, 4. 875–6

    economics, 4. 871–4

    history, 4. 829–46

    individual dramatists, 4. 879–992

    Irish, 4. 853–4

    London, 4. 845–52

    music-hall, 4. 853–62

    periodicals, 4. 823–8, 848–52, 854, 858–62,
    866–8, 873–4, 877–80

    production, 4. 867–8

    stage design, 4. 869–72

  see also drama

Theatre (January 1720), 2. 1277

Theatre (April 1720), 2. 1277

Theatre (1757), 2. 1282

Theatre (1877), 3. 1124, 1852

Theatre (1904), 4. 824

Theatre (1909), 4. 825

Theatre (1937), 4. 827

Theatre (Bradford 1945), 4. 851

Theatre (1952), 4. 828

Theatre and film illustrated, 4. 860

Theatre-craft (1919), 4. 826, 1364

Theatre de luxe gazette, 4. 849

Theatre digest, 4. 828

Theatre forum, 4. 851

Theatre guild review, 4. 828

Theatre illustrated quarterly, 4. 827

Theatre in education, 4. 880

Theatre industry (*journal*), 4. 874

Theatre managers journal, 4. 874

Theatre mirror, 4. 868

Theatre, music hall and cinema (*companies'*) *blue
  book*, 4. 826, 860, 873

Theatre news, 4. 851

Theatre newsletter, 4. 828

Theatre notebook, 4. 827

Theatre of compliments, 2. 337

Theatre of ingenuity, 2. 343

Theatre of mirth, 2. 401

Theatre of the earth, 1. 2119

Theatre of the present war, 2. 1418

Theatre of wit, 2. 372

Theatre Royal, 4. 851

Theatre today, 4. 828

Theatre world, 4. 826, 860, 866

Theatre world annual, 4. 862, 868

Theatrecraft (1938), 4. 827

Theatreland, 4. 825

Theatrical artistes road book, 4. 874

Theatrical bouquet, 2. 401

Theatrical employees journal, 4. 873

Theatrical guardian, 2. 1337

Theatrical magazine, 2. 1306

Theatrical manager, 4. 866–7, 874

Theatrical monitor, 2. 1284, 1334

Theatrical museum, 2. 397

Theatrical news, 4. 850

Theatrical observer (1821), 3. 1123

Theatrical observer (1926), 4. 850

Theatrical register, 2. 1370

Theatrical review (1758), 2. 1313

Theatrical review (1763), 2. 1303

Theatrical review (1767), 2. 1347

Theatrical review (1771), 2. 1284

Thebes, romances of, 1. 428

Thelwall, John, 3. 403–4, 1809; 2. 1308

Theobald, Lewis, 2. 800–2, 234–5, 988, 1275,
  1745–6

Theocritus, 1. 2177, 1148; 2. 1494, 35

Theological and political comet, 3. 1818

Theological comet or free thinking Englishman, 3.
  1818

Theological magazine, 2. 1300

Theological miscellany, 2. 1307

Theological repository, 2. 1349

Theological review 3. 1858

theology

  Old English, prose, 1. 323–8

theology (*cont.*)

  Middle English

    Bible, 1. 477–82

    Latin, 1. 750–2

    miscellaneous, 1. 495–524

    prophecies, 1. 473–8

    saints' legends, 1. 523–34

    sermons, 1. 481–90

    Wyclif and Wycliffites, 1. 491–6

  Renaissance to Restoration

    English, 1. 1781–2006; Bible, 1. 825–88, 2295–6; Caroline divines, 1. 1963–2006; Early fathers and schoolmen 1. 2295–8; ecclesiastical learning, 1. 2297–300; Hooker, 1. 1949–58; humanists, 1. 1781–1826; Marprelate controversy, 1. 1957–64; prayer book, 1. 1887–96; psalms, 1. 1895–1914; sermons, 1. 1915–48

    French, 1. 865–7

    German, 1. 877–8

    Scottish, 1. 2453–66

  Restoration and eighteenth century

    English, 2. 1599–1676; baptists, 2. 1665–6, 1669–72; congregationalists, 2. 1664–5, 1667–70; mystics, 2. 1651–62; presbyterians, 2. 1666, 1671–4; quakers, 2. 1639–52; unitarians, 2. 1666, 1673–6

    French, 2. 114–15

    German, 2. 160–5

    Scottish, 2. 2031–46

  nineteenth century, 3. 1599–1636

    Evangelicals, 3. 1615–22

    liberal, 3. 1599–1616

    Oxford movement, 3. 1621–36

  twentieth century, 4. 1241–1310

Theophrastus, 1. 2177; 2. 1494–5

Theosophical review, 3. 1853; 4. 1352

Theosophical transactions of the Philadelphian Society, 2. 1293

Theosophist, 4. 1352

Thersytes, 1. 1418, 1420

Thesaurus aenigmaticus, 2. 356

Thesaurus dramaticus, 2. 355

Thesaurus musicus (1693), 2. 338

Thesaurus musicus (1743), 2. 370

Thespian magazine, 2. 1309

Thespian telegraph, 2. 1311

Thevenot, Jean, 2. 1434

Thévenot, Melchisedech, 2. 1569

Thevet, André, 1. 2149

Thibault, — 2. 990

Thicknesse, Philip, 2. 1421

Third and last volume of [Butler's] posthumous works, 2. 351

Third collection of poems against Popery, A, 2. 337

Third part of the collection of poems on affairs of state, 2. 337

Third part of the works of Cowley, 2. 337

Thirkell, Angela Margaret, 4. 747–8

Thirlwall, Connop, 3. 1503–4, 1610, 1732

Thirty Scots songs, 2. 379

This day arrived a packet from north-Britain, 2. 1382

This quarter, 4. 1367

This unrest, 4. 1398

This week, 4. 1374

Thistle, 2. 1375

Thistlethwaite, James, 2. 1005

Thom, Adam Bisset, 3. 1879

Thom, John Hamilton, 3. 1610, 1856

Thom, William, 3. 404

Thomas de Hibernia, 1. 782

Thomas of Buckingham, 1. 797

Thomas of Claxton, 1. 805

Thomas of Eccleston, 1. 782

Thomas of Ersseldoune, 1. 475–6

Thomas of Sutton, 1. 797–8

Thomas of York, 1. 782–3

Thomas, Antoine Léonard, 2. 1533

'Thomas, B.' (Thomas Burgeland Johnson), 3. 1712

Thomas, David, 3. 1814

Thomas, Dylan Marlais, 4. 220–30, 1372

Thomas, E., 2. 1319

Thomas, Edward, 4. 364–7, 793

Thomas, Ernest Chester, 3. 90

Thomas, Gilbert, 4. 1364

Thomas, H. P., 3. 1697

Thomas, Nathaniel, 2. 1333

Thomas, Philip Edward, 4. 364–7, 793

Thomas, Ronald Stuart, 4. 368

Thomas, S. E., 3. 1852, 1879

Thomas, Timothy, 2. 1770

Thomas, William, 1. 2136

Thomas, Sir William Beach, 3. 1777

Thomas, William Luson, 3. 1777, 1791, 1817

Thomas, William Moy, 3. 1816

Thomas, William Thomas, 3. 1134–5

Thomas Humes the Dublin courant, 2. 1383

Thomas Humes the Dublin intelligence, 2. 1383

Thomas of Woodstock, 1. 1472–4

Thomason, George, 1. 964, 1004; 2. 309

Thompson, Alexander, 2. 1568

Thompson, Alice, 3. 638–9

Thompson, Sir Benjamin, Count Rumford (d. 1814), scientist, 2. 1909

Thompson, Benjamin (d. 1816), dramatist, 3. 1141

Thompson, Bonar, 4. 1369

Thompson, Charles, 2. 1395, 1418, 1439, 1554

Thompson, D. C., 4. 1397
Thompson, D'Arcy Wentworth (1829–1902), 3.
 1103, 1727
Thompson, Sir D'Arcy Wentworth (1860–1948),
 4. 1300
Thompson, David, 3. 1671
Thompson, Denys, 4. 1370
Thompson, Edward (1738?–86), 2. 687, 1396,
 1785
Thompson, Edward (d. 1860), 3. 1856
Thompson, Flora, 4. 1326–7
Thompson, Francis, 3. 597–601, 1699
Thompson, George (fl. 1648–79), 2. 1901
Thompson, George (fl. 1798), 2. 1408
Thompson, Harry, 4. 1353
Thompson, Henry Yates, 3. 1793
Thompson, P. Gilchrist, 4. 1370
Thompson, Thomas, 2. 1395, 1450, 1465
Thompson, Thomas Perronet, 3. 1855
Thompson, William, 2. 569–70
Thompson, William Marcus, 3. 1811
Thompson's pocket companion, 2. 399
Thoms, William John, 3. 1664–5, 1108, 1821
'Thomson, Mrs', (Harriet Pigott), 2. 1008
Thomson, Alexander, 2. 1396
Thomson, Andrew, 3. 1843
Thomson, Anthony Francis, 3. 1727
Thomson, D. C., 4. 110
Thomson, George (fl. 1594–1612), 1. 2452
Thomson, George (fl. 1648–79), 2. 1901
Thomson, George Derwent, 4. 1124–5
Thomson, Hugh, 3. 68
Thomson, Isaac, 2. 570
Thomson, J., 2. 1373
Thomson, J. E., 3. 1703
Thomson, James (1700–48), 2. 527–31, 128, 135,
 171, 179, 193, 207, 214, 218
Thomson, James (1834–82), 3. 579–81
Thomson, John, 3. 1703
Thomson, John Anstruther, 3. 1707
Thomson, Joseph, 3. 1672
Thomson, Robert Dundas, 3. 1877
Thomson, Thomas, 3. 1843
Thomson, William (fl. 1739), 2. 1449
Thomson, William (1746–1817), miscellaneous
 writer, 2. 1007, 1307
Thomson, William (1819–90) philosopher, 3.
 1596
Thomson, William, Baron Kelvin (1824–1907),
 scientist, 3. 1842
Thomson, William (fl. 1835), traveller, 3. 1679
'Thomsonby' (H. P. Thomas), 3. 1697
Thoresby, Ralph, 2. 1714–15, 1398, 1909
Thorild, Thomas, 2. 214
Thorius, Raphael, 1. 2038

'Thormanby' (W. Willmott Dixon), 3. 1693,
 1707, 1767
'Thorn, Ismay' (Edith Caroline Pollock), 3. 1095
Thorn, Walter, 3. 1691
Thorn and Sons, C. P., 3. 60
Thornborough, F. C., 4. 1382
Thornbury, George Walter, 3. 555, 1684
Thorndike, Herbert, 1. 2002
Thorne, James, 3. 1683
Thorneley, George, 1. 2306
Thornes, Edward, 1. 2134
Thornhill, R. B., 3. 1712
Thornley, A. J. F., 4. 1386
Thornley, George, 1. 2306
Thornley, Lubbock, 2. 1286
Thornton, A. G., 4. 748
Thornton, Bonnell, 2. 687–8, 1280, 1281, 1332,
 1351
Thornton, Henry (1760–1815), 3. 1618
Thornton, Henry (1818–1905), 3. 1149
Thornton, L., 3. 1840
Thornton, Thomas, 2. 1405; 3. 1677, 1681
Thornton, William Thomas, 3. 1403
Thorny-Abbey, 1. 1761
Thoroton, Robert, 2. 1696–7
Thorowgood, G., 1. 2034
Thorowgood, Thomas, 1. 2164
Thorp, Joseph, 4. 1363
Thorpe, Benjamin, 3. 1665
Thorpe, Thomas, 1. 964
Thou, Jacques Auguste de, 2. 78
Thoughts moral and divine, 2. 380
Thoughts on a future state, 2. 423
Thoughts on the present laws for . . . game, 2.
 1559
Thracian wonder, 1. 1761
Thrale, Hester Lynch, 2. 1596–7, 1403–4, 1423
Three elegies on . . . Prince Henrie, 1. 1009
Three great and bloody fights (1655), 1. 2160
Three kings of Cologne, 1. 728
Three kings' sons, 1. 453
Three new poems, 2. 354
Three poems (1720), 2. 353
Three poems upon the death of Oliver Cromwel, 1.
 1011; 2. 334
Three songs in English and Latin, 2. 375
*Threni cantabrigiensis in exequiis Henriettae
 Mariae*, 2. 330
Thriller, 4. 1389
'thrillers', 4. 129–30, 1389–92
Thrilling detective, 4. 1391
Thrilling ranch stories, 4. 1391
Thrilling western, 4. 1391
Thrilling wonder stories, 4. 1392
Thring, Edward, 3. 1727

Throkmorton, Job, 1. 1962
Thrush (1749), 2. 374
Thrush (1901), 4. 1355
Thrush (1909), 4. 1360
Thrush and the nightingale, 1. 511
Thuanus (J. A. de Thou), 2. 78
Thucydides, 1. 2177–8; 2. 1495
Thunberg, Carl Pehr, 2. 1396, 1444, 1452
Thureth, 1. 305
Thurloe, John, 1. 2106, 2109
Thurlow, Edward, 2nd Baron, 3. 404
Thursday's journal, 2. 1324
Thursfield, James Richard, 4. 1405
Thurston, Joseph, 2. 570, 1567
Thwaite, Anthony, 4. 1397
Thwaites, — (fl. 1843), 3. 1789
Thwaites, Edward, 2. 1792
Thyer, Robert, 2. 1778
Thynne, Francis, 1. 1148, 1335, 2314
Thynne, William, 1. 1004
Tibbits, Charles J., 3. 1808
Tibullus, 2. 1502
Tickell, Richard, 2. 688, 1560
Tickell, Thomas, 2. 570–1, 1558
'Ticklepitcher, Toby', 2. 1022
Tickler (1748), 2. 1378
Tickler (1770), 2. 1284
Tickler (1818), 3. 1844
Tieck, Ludwig, 3. 129
Tierney, Mark Aloysius, 3. 1856
Tiger, 4. 1356
Tiger Tim's tales, 4. 819
Tiger Tim's weekly, 4. 819
Tighe, Mary, 3. 405
Tigrid, Pavel, 4. 1375
Till Eulenspiegel, 1. 2193–4; 2. 1537
Tiller, Terence, 4. 368
Tilley, Arthur A., 3. 1870
Tilley, John A. C., 3. 1870
Tilloch, Alexander, 2. 1311, 1337; 3. 1792, 1841
Tillotson, Geoffrey, 4. 1125
Tillotson, John (d. 1694), 2. 1616–17, 165
Tillotson, John (d. 1871), 3. 1850
Tillotson, William Frederic, 3. 1777, 1797
Tillotsons (printers), 3. 60
Tillyard, Eustace Mandeville Wetenhall, 4. 1125–6
Tilney, Edmund, 1. 2051
Tilney, Emery, 1. 1149
Tilt, Charles, 3. 1875
Timberlake, Henry (d. 1626), 1. 2124
Timberlake, Henry (fl. 1765), 2. 1467
Timbs, John, 3. 1816, 1877
Time, 3. 1852, 1863
Time's triumph, 1. 1761

Time and tide, 4. 1406
Times, 2. 1336; 3. 1789, 1827; 4. 1399, 1345
Times educational supplement, 4. 1405
Times literary supplement, 4. 790, 1348, 1405
Timon, 1. 1778–9
Tindal, Matthew, 2. 1867–8, 112, 165
Tindale, William, 1. 1809–11, 1829–32
Tindall, Joseph, 3. 1670
Tinling, Charles, 3. 1797
Tinsley, William, 3. 81, 1777
Tinsley's magazine, 3. 1851
Tiny tots, 4. 820
Tip top, 4. 820
Tip-top semi-monthly, 4. 1362
Tip top stories, 4. 1389
Tipper, J. (fl. 1749), 2. 1313
Tipper, John, 2. 1294
Tiptoft, John, Earl of Worcester, 1. 1004, 2130
Tissot, Victor, 3. 1681
Tit-bits, 3. 1815; 4. 1352, 1403
Titan, a monthly magazine, 3. 1847
Titchell, W., 4. 1385
Titchfield Abbey library, 1. 996
Titt for tatt, 2. 1271
Titterton, William Richard, 4. 1354
Titus, Edward W., 4. 1367
Titus (17th century play), 1. 1761
Titus and Vespasian (poem), 1. 453
Titus and Vespasian (prose), 1. 453
'Tityrus' (J. A. H. Cotton), 3. 1702
Tlysau yr hen oesoedd, 2. 1390
Toase, C. A., 4. 1388
Toasts of the Patriots Club, 2. 363
Toasts of the Rump-Steak Club, 2. 363
tobacco, pamphlets on, 1. 2037–8
Tobago: or a geographical description, 2. 1464
Tobin, John, 3. 1141–2
tobogganing, nineteenth century, 3. 1714
Toby in Cambridge, 3. 1865
Tocqueville, Alexis de, 3. 109
To-day (1893), 3. 1815; 4. 1404
Today (1916), 4. 1353
To-day (1938), 4. 1408
Today and tomorrow, 4. 1407
Today in Eastbourne, 4. 849
To-day's London guide, 4. 824
Todd, Barbara Euphan, 4. 802
Todd, Henry John, 2. 1789; 3. 1665–6
Todd, James Henthorn, 3. 1890
Todd, Ruthven, 4. 368–9
Todhunter, Isaac, 3. 1729
Todhunter, John, 3. 1906
Toeman, Edward, 4. 1377
Tofte, Robert, 1. 1149, 1335, 2033
Toland, John, 2. 1868–9, 112, 165, 235, 1416

Toldervy, William, 2. 999
Tolkien, John Ronald Reuel, 4. 748–9, 800
Tollet, Elizabeth, 2. 571
Tolmie, A. W., 4. 825, 859
Tolstoy, Count Lev Nikolayevich, 3. 154–5
Tom Brown's complete jester, 2. 380
Tom Gay's comical jester, 2. 399
Tom Gaylove's compleat jester, 2. 382
Tom Smart's new comical jester, 2. 430
Tom Spring's life in London and sporting chronicle, 3. 1811
Tom Tit's song book, 2. 1027
Tom Tyler and his wife, 1. 1418
Tomahawk (1795), 2. 1338
Tomahawk (1867), 3. 1825
Tomahawk (St Andrews 1874), 3. 1869
Tombes, John, 1. 2002
Tomkin, C., 2. 165
Tomkins, Charles, 2. 1407
Tomkins, Thomas, 1. 1356
Tomkis, Thomas, 1. 1775
Tomlins, Frederick G., 3. 1811
Tomlinson, Charles, 3. 1694
Tomlinson, Henry Major, 4. 749–50
Tomlinson, Kellom, 2. 1566
Tommy Trip's Valentine gift, 2. 1027
To-morrow (1896), 3. 1854
To-morrow (Dublin 1924), 4. 1366
Toms, Frederick, 3. 1816
Tongue, Cornelius, 3. 1705
Tonna, Charlotte Elizabeth, 3. 1846, 1876
Tonson, Jacob, 2. 282
Tonti, Henri de, 2. 1457
Tooke, Andrew, 2. 1829
Tooke, John Horne, 2. 1893, 1829
Tooke, William, 2. 1003, 1431
Top, Alexander, 1. 1909
Top book of all, 2. 1021
Top of the news, 4. 790
Topaz of Ethiopia, 4. 1397
Toper's delight, 2. 370
Topham, Edward, 2. 1336, 1404
Topics of the day, 2. 1334
Topix, 4. 1388
Toplady, Augustus Montague, 2. 1629, 1305
Topographer, 2. 1309
Topographical miscellanies, 2. 1309
Torbuck, John, 2. 1400
Torch (1796), 2. 1378
Torch (1798), 2. 1387
Torch (Dublin 1926?), amateur journal, 4. 1385
Torch (Hull University 1928), 4. 1395
Torch (1933) Birmingham School of Printing, 4. 83
Torch (1945), Amateur Printing Association, 4. 84

Torquemada, Antonio de, 1. 2194, 916
Torr, John Berry, 3. 1813
Torrens, Robert, 3. 1792
Torrens, William M., 3. 1809
Törring-Cronsfeld, Joseph August, 2. 175
Torrington, George Byng, 1st Viscount, 2. 1418
Torrington, John Byng, 5th Viscount, 2. 312, 1404
Torsellino, Orazio, 1. 852
Tory pill, A, 2. 349
Tory pills, 2. 350
Tory tatler, 2. 1272, 1322
Tott, Francis, Baron de, 2. 1426
Tottel, Richard, 1. 964
Tottel's miscellany, 1. 1007–8
'Touchit, Thomas', 2. 1331
'Touchstone, Timothy' (J. H. Allen), 2. 1308
Touchstone, 2. 1287
Toulmin, John, 3. 1802
Toup, Jonathan, 2. 1829
Tour from London to the lakes in 1791, A, 2. 1406
Tour in England and Scotland in 1784, A, 2. 1405
Tour of health and pleasure, A, 2. 1408
Tour of the river Wye, A, 2. 1408
Tour sentimental and descriptive, A, 2. 1427
Tour through Germany, A, 2. 1429
Tour through Ireland, A (1746), 2. 1401
Tour through Ireland, A (1748), 2. 1401
Tour through the theatre of war, A, 2. 1429
Tour to Ermenonville, A, 2. 1426
Tour to Great St Bernard, A, 3. 1678
Tournament of Tottenham, 1. 687
Tourneur, Cyril, 1. 1694–7, 1149, 1335
Tourtechot de Granger, —, 2. 1450
Tourtel, Mary, 4. 792
Tout, Thomas Frederick, 4. 1222–3
Tovey, Sir Donald Francis, 4. 1126–7
Tovey, Duncan Crookes, 3. 1666
Tovey, J., 4. 1385
Towers, John, 3. 1820
'Town, Mr' (Colman and Thornton), 2. 1281
Town (1762), 2. 1283
Town (1788), 2. 1386
Town (1832), 3. 1810
Town (1837), 3. 1813
Town and country jester, 2. 382
Town and country magazine (1769), 2. 1304
Town and country magazine and Irish miscellany (1784), 2. 1379
Town and country song-book, 2. 414
Town and country songster, 2. 409
Town and country songster's companion, 2. 426
Town and country tales, 3. 1108
Town and country weekly magazine, 2. 1379
Town mistress: or street-walker, 2. 356

Town spy, 2. 1344
Town talk (1715), 2. 1275
Town talk (1858), 3. 1814
Town-talker, 2. 1287
Towneley plays (ME), 1. 734
Townley, C., 4. 859
Townley, James, 2. 859
Townley, Richard, 2. 1406
Townsend, Aurelian, 1. 1323, 1757
Townsend, Elizabeth, 3. 1099
Townsend, Francis, 3. 1680
Townsend, George Henry, 3. 1814, 1879
Townsend, J., 3. 1819
Townsend, Jack, 4. 813
Townsend, Joseph, 2. 1893, 1428
Townsend, Meredith White, 3. 1777, 1813
Townshend, Aurelian, 1. 1323, 1757
Townshend, Chauncey Hare, 3. 1683
Townshend, Henry, 1. 2252
Townshend, Petrie, 4. 1368
Townsman, 4. 1373
Townson, Robert, 2. 1430
Townson, Thomas, 2. 165
Toynbee, Arnold Joseph, 4. 1223–6
Toynbee, Theodore Philip, 4. 750–1
Tozer, Katharine, 4. 809
tracts, Renaissance to Restoration
    anthologies, 1. 2023–4
    education, 1. 2387–96
    moral and political, 1. 2037–42
    women and marriage, 1. 2031–8
    see also pamphlets, periodicals
Tracy, Louis, 3. 1794
'Tradam, Lampada', 4. 1359
Trade unionist, 3. 1820
Trader's magazine, 2. 1305
Trafford, Margaret, 4. 1383
tragedy, Renaissance to Restoration
    early, 1. 1421–4
    Shakespearean, 1. 1609–11
    studies, 1. 1369–70
    see also drama
Traherne, Thomas, 1. 1235–8
Traill, Henry Duff, 3. 1454–5, 1807, 1822; 4.
    1354
Train, 3. 1849
Traiteur, 2. 1286
Tramp, 4. 1360
*Transactions and proceedings of the...Library
    Association*, 3. 90
Transactions of the Theosophical Art-Circle, 4.
    1358
Transactions of the universe, 2. 1363
Transatlantic, 3. 1851
Transatlantic review, 4. 1366, 1348

Transatlantic tales, 4. 1353
Transformation, 4. 1376
transition, 4. 1367, 1348
Translation, 4. 1377
translations
    Old English
        Alfred's reign, 1. 313–18
        Bible, 1. 323–4
    Renaissance to Restoration
        Bible, 1. 1848, 1851–2
        classics, Greek and Latin, 1. 2165–80
        criticism, 1. 2193–200
        medieval and contemporaneous writers, 1.
            2179–94
        prayer book, 1. 1892–3
        prose fiction, 1. 2059–68
        Shakespeare, 1. 1622–3, 1629–30
    Restoration and eighteenth century, 2. 1485–
        1550
        children's books, 2. 1029–34
        European drama, 2. 861–4
        French, 2. 1501–38
        German, 2. 1537–42
        Greek, 2. 1487–96
        Italian, 2. 1541–50
        Latin, classical, 2. 1495–1502
        literary criticism, 2. 63–8
        medieval, 2. 241–8
    nineteenth century, 3. 1109–10
    twentieth century, 4. 69–70
    see also literary relations
Trapaud, Elisha, 2. 1443
Trapham, Thomas, 2. 1455
Trapp, Joseph, 2. 571
'Trapwit, Tommy' (John Newbery?), 2. 1019
travel
    Middle English, 1. 467–74
    Renaissance to Restoration, 1. 840–2, 2109–66
        Africa, 1. 2141–50
        America, 1. 2149–66
        Asia, 1. 2141–50
        Dutch, 1. 918–19
        Europe, 1. 2121–42
        French, 1. 861
        German, 1. 876
        Italian, 1. 885–6
        Scandinavian, 1. 921
        Spanish, 1. 907
    Restoration and eighteenth century, 2. 1389–
        1486
        Africa, 2. 1445–54
        America, 2. 1453–76
        Arctic, 2. 1483–6
        Asia, 2. 1431–46
        Australasia, 2. 1475–84

travel (*cont.*)
    British Isles, 2. 1395–1410
    Europe, 2. 1409–32
    French, 2. 84–5
  nineteenth century, 3. 1669–84
    Africa, 3. 1669–72
    America, 3. 1671–4
    Asia, 3. 1673–6
    Australasia, 3. 1675–8
    Europe, 3. 1677–84
  twentieth century, 4. 1311–28
Traveller (1764), 2. 1284
Traveller (1783), 2. 1287
Traveller (1785), 2. 1287
Traveller (1801), 3. 1792
Traveller (1871), 3. 1851
Traveller's companion and guide, 2. 1419
Travellers magazine, 2. 1299
Traveller's vade mecum, 2. 1426
Travels and adventures of Mademoiselle de Richelieu, 2. 995
Travels and adventures of William Bingfield, 2. 997
Travels in Egypt, Turkey, Syria and the Holy-Land, 2. 1439
Travels in Switzerland, 3. 1680
Travels into France and Italy, 2. 1422
Travels of an English gentleman from London to Rome on foot, 2. 1415
Travels of Hildebrand Bowman, 2. 1005
Travels of several learned missioners, 2. 1391
Travels through Denmark and some parts of Germany, 2. 1414
Travers, Ben (b. 1886), 4. 985–6
Travers, Benjamin (1783–1858), 3. 1681
Travers, H., 2. 571
Travers, Pamela Lyndon, 4. 809
Travers, Walter, 1. 1960, 854
travesties, Restoration and eighteenth century, 2. 489–90
Trawl, 4. 1356, 1380
Treadgold, Mary, 4. 811
Trease, Robert Geoffrey, 4. 810
Treasure of knowledge, 3. 1874
Treasuries of modern prose, 4. 1369
Treasury, 4. 1356
Treasury of divine raptures, A, 2. 330
Treasury of musick, 2. 330
Treasury of wit, 2. 410
Treatise of love, 1. 693
Treatise of oxen, A., 2. 1557
Treatise of perfection of the sons of God (fifteenth century), 1. 517
Treatise on boxing, A, 3. 1692
Treatise on the nature of man (M.E.), 1. 515

Treaty traverst, 1. 2104
Trediakovsky, Vasily Kirillovich, 2. 216
Tree and xii frutes of the Holy Ghost, 1. 516
Treece, Henry, 4. 369–70, 1374, 1376, 1398
Tregellas, J. T. 3. 1695
Trelawny, Edward John, 3. 1307
Tremayne, Sydney D., 4. 1373
Trench, Frederic Herbert, 3. 1911
Trench, Richard Chenevix, 3. 556
Trenchard, John, 2. 1277, 1325
Trenck, Friedrich, Baron von der, 2. 1541, 166
Trendell, Arthur, 3. 1852
Trentalle Sancti Gregorii, 1. 458–9
T[ren]t[ha]m and V[an]d[epu]t: a collection, 2. 374
Tressan, Maurice Elisabeth de Lavergne de, 2. 1533
'Tressell, Robert' (Robert Noonan), 4. 751
Tresswell, Robert, 1. 2125
Tretyse of love, 1. 1935
Trevecca, printing, 2. 271
Trevelyan, — (fl. 1685), 2. 1412
Trevelyan, George Macaulay, 4. 1226–7
Trevelyan, Sir George Otto, 3. 1504–5, 1865
Trevelyan, Robert Calverley, 4. 370–1
Trevet, Nicolas, 1. 793–4
Trevisa, John, 1. 467–8, 806, 2130
Trevor-Roper, Hugh Redwald, 4. 1227–8
Trevytham, Richard, 1. 806
Trew-Hay, J., 3. 1698
Trewin, John C., 4. 828, 1378
Trewman's Exeter evening (flying) post, 2. 1358
Treyssac de Vergy, Pierre Henri, 2. 1003, 1004
Triad, 4. 1378
Triall of treasure, 1. 1411–12
Tribune (Dublin 1729), 2. 1378
Tribune (1795), 2. 1310
Tribune (1900), 4. 1404
Tribune (1904), 4. 1404
Tribune (1906), 4. 1405
Tribune (1937), 4. 1407
Tribute to liberty, A, 2. 419
Tricks of state, 1. 2103
Tricks of the town laid open, 2. 1569
Trident (1889), 3. 1867
Trident (1911), 4. 1382
Trifle (1748?), 2. 1020
Trifle (1911), 4. 1360
Trifle (1915), 4. 1362
Trifler (1722), 2. 1277
Trifler (1760), 2. 1282
Trifler (1765), 2. 1284
Trifler (1786), 2. 1287
Trifler (York 1786), 2. 1350
Trifler (1788), 2. 1308
Trifler (1789), 2. 1288

Trifler (1795), 2. 1372

Trilling, Ossia, 4. 828

Trimmer, Sarah, 2. 1023, 1288, 1308; 3. 1717

'Tring, A. Stephen' (Laurence Meynell), 4. 806

Trinity homilies (ME), 1. 484–5

Trinity magazine, 4. 1393

Trio, 4. 1398

Trip to Spain, A, 2. 1416

Trip to the jubilee, A, 2. 1419

Tripod, 4. 1393

Trissino, Giovanni Giorgio, 1. 895, 898

Tristram, romances of, 1. 414–16

Tristram, Henry Baker, 3. 1671, 1675

Tristram, William Outram, 3. 1700

Triumph, 4. 820

Triumph of truth, 2. 976

Triumph of wit, 2. 337

Triumphs of Bacchus, 2. 358

Triumphs of female wit, 2. 334

Triumphs of goodnature, 2. 1030

Triumvirate (Harrow School 1860), 3. 1871

Triumvirate (1912?), 4. 1383

Trivet, Nicolas, 1. 793–4

'Triviator', 3. 1706

Trogus Pompeius, 1. 2178

Troil, Uno von, 2. 1425

Trollope, Anthony, 3. 882–9, 1672, 1674, 1697, 1705, 1778, 1851

Trollope, Frances, 3. 769–70

Trollope, Thomas Adolphus, 3. 969–70

Trotter, Catharine, 2. 802, 983, 1860

Trotter, Wilfred Batten Lewis, 4. 1228

Troubador, 4. 1404

Troublesome raigne of King John, 1. 1469–70

Troughton, John, 1. 2152

Troughton, Thomas, 2. 1449

Troup, George, 3. 1778, 1803, 1845

Trowbridge and Wiltshire advertiser, 3. 1833

Troy, romances of, 1. 425–8

Trublet, Nicolas Charles Joseph, 2. 68

Trubner, Nicholas, 3. 81

Trubner and Co, 3. 1855

True and faithful relation of the forces...against the French, A, 2. 1456

True and impartial account of the remarkable accidents, A, 2. 1318

True and impartial collection of pieces . . . published during the Westminster election, A, 2. 374

True and large discourse of the voyage...to the East Indies, A, 1. 2144

True and perfect diurnall, 1. 2096

True and perfect diurnall of...Lancashire, 1. 2096

True and perfect Dutch diurnall, 1. 2108

True and perfect informer, 1. 2108

True and perfect journall of the warres, A, 1. 2100

True and perfect relation of the newes sent from Amsterdam, A, 1. 2144

True and sincere declaration [about Virginia], A, 1. 2155

True anti-Pamela, 2. 995

True British courant, 2. 1365

True Briton (1723), 2. 1277

True Briton (1751), 2. 1280, 1300, 1332

True Briton (1793), 2. 1338; 3. 1789

True Briton (Boston 1819), 3. 1818

True Briton (1820), 3. 1792

True character of Mercurius urbanicus and rusticus, 2. 1316

True chronicle historie of...Thomas Cromwell, 1. 1472

True-Coventry plays (ME), 1. 733

True declaration of the arrival of Cornelius Haga, A, 1. 2125

True declaration of the estate...in Virginia, A, 1. 2155

True description and direction of...Italy, 1. 2139

True description of Jamaica, A, 1. 2164

True detective, 4. 1392

True discourse of the late voyage made by . . . Sherley, A, 1. 2124

True diurnal occurrences, 1. 2095

True diurnall, A, 1. 2094, 2095

True diurnall occurrences, 1. 2094

True diurnall of the last weeks passages in Parliament, A, 1. 2094

True domestick intelligence, 2. 1316

True gangster stories, 4. 1390

True history of a little old woman, A, 3. 1105

True informer, 1. 2099, 2101, 2104, 2107, 2108

True intelligence from the head quarters, 1. 2107

True love stories, 4. 1389

True loyalist, 2. 400

True narrative of the late success of the fleet, A, 1. 2160

True news: or mercurius anglicus, 2. 1317

True patriot, 2. 1279, 1331

True post boy, 2. 1322

True Protestant domestick intelligence, 2. 1317

True Protestant mercury (1680), 2. 1317

True Protestant mercury (1681), 2. 1317

True Protestant mercury (1689), 2. 1319

True relation of a brave English stratagem, A, 1. 2127

True relation of certaine speciall . . . passages, A, 1. 2096

True relation of...his Majestys forces (1644), 1. 2470

True relation of that which lately hapned to the great Spanish fleet, A, 1. 2157

True relation of that worthy sea fight . . . in the Persian Gulph, 1. 2146

True relation of the fleete . . . under . . . Le Hermite, 1. 2157

True relation of the vanquishing of . . . Olinda, A, 1. 2158

True relation without all exception of . . . the Kingdome of the great Magor, A, 1. 2146

True report and description of the taking of . . . St Maries, A, 1. 2124

True report of a great fight at sea, A, 1. 2124

True report of Sir Anthony Shierlies journey, A, 1. 2144

True report of the gainefull . . . voiage to Java, A, 1. 2143–4

True romances, 4. 1390

True story magazine, 4. 1366

True strange stories, 4. 1389

True sun, 3. 1793, 1829

True tablet, 3. 1822

True tragedie of Richard Duke of Yorke, 1. 1471

True tragedie of Richard the Third, 1. 1470

True tragi-comedie formarly acted at Court (1654), 1. 1761

'Truepenny, Timothy', 2. 1298, 1330

Trusler, John, 2. 1310

Trussel, John, 1. 1150

Trussell, John, 1. 2242

Truth, 3. 1815, 1835; 4. 1351

Truth about writing, 4. 73, 1386

Truth and honesty, 2. 1343

Tryall of chevalry, 1. 1761

Tryon, Thomas, 2. 1658, 1553

Tryout, 4. 1383

Trysorfa gwybodaeth, 2. 1389

Trysorfa ysprydol, 2. 1390

Tryvytlam, Richard, 1. 806

Tschinck, Cajetan, 2. 1541, 181

Tuam gazette, 2. 1390

Tubbe, Henry, 1. 1323, 2050

Tucker, Abraham, 2. 1893–4

Tucker, Charlotte Maria, 3. 1093

Tucker, Edward, 3. 81

Tucker, Josiah, 2. 1899–1900

Tucker, Marwood, 3. 1792

Tucker, Thomas, 1. 2135

Tuckett, Elizabeth, 3. 1103

Tuer, Andrew White, 3. 32, 60, 61, 1730

Tuesdaies journall, 1. 2105

Tuke, Sir Samuel, 2. 776

Tuke, Thomas, 1. 2048

Tulip, 4. 1355

Tull, Jethro, 2. 1909

Tulloch, John, 3. 1596, 1845

Tunbridge and Bath miscellany, 2. 349

Tunbridge-Miscellany, 2. 347

Tunbrigalia, 2. 353

Tuner, 2. 1284

Tunstall, Cuthbert, 1. 1947

Tupper, J. L., 3. 1728

Tupper, Martin Farquhar, 3. 557

Turbervile, George, 1. 1150–1, 1333, 2122

Turgenev, Ivan Sergeyevich, 3. 155

Turgot, Anne Robert Jacques, 2. 1533, 98

Turke and Gowin, 1. 406

Turle, Henry F., 3. 1821

Turlerus, Hieronymus, 1. 2137

Turnbull, George, 2. 165

Turnell, Martin, 4. 1372

Turner, Alfred, 3. 1802

Turner, Catherine Ann, 3. 1087

Turner, Charles, 3. 68

Turner, Elizabeth, 3. 1088

Turner, Godfrey W., 3. 1809

Turner, Joseph Mallord William, 3. 68

Turner, Robert, 1. 854

Turner, Samuel, 2. 1444

Turner, Sharon, 2. 238

Turner, T., 2. 1352

Turner, Thomas, 3. 1682

Turner, Walter James Redfern, 4. 371–2

Turner's annual tour, 3. 1875

Turnor, Philip, 2. 1474

Turrell, — (fl. 1846), 3. 1814

Turton, Thomas, 3. 1732

Tusser, Thomas, 1. 1151, 2033, 2277

Tutchin, John, 2. 486, 1343

Tuting, William, 2. 1314

Tuvill, Daniel, 1. 2048

Twamley, Louisa Anne, 3. 1876

'Twas right to marry him, 2. 1004

'Twas wrong to marry him, 2. 1004

Tweddell, John, 2. 688

Tweedie, Mrs Alec, 3. 1778

Tweedsmuir, John Buchan, 1st Baron, 4. 540–4; 3. 1100, 1690

Twelve arietts or ballads, 2. 364

Twelve new songs (1699), 2. 341

Twelve news songs (1727?), 2. 357

Twelve pages, 4. 1384

Twentieth century (1901), 4. 1355

Twentieth century (1931), 4. 1369

Twentieth century (1951), 3. 1852; 4. 1351–2

Twentieth-century advertising 4. 1342

Twentieth-century amateur magazine, 4. 1385

twentieth century literature
    general, 4. 3–34
    autobiography, 4. 1135–1242

'Tytler, Sarah' (Henrietta Keddie), 3. 1103
Tytler, William, 2. 1741, 1779

UCL union magazine, 3. 1867; 4. 1395
Ubaldino, Petruccio, 1. 2123
Udall, John, 1. 1947, 1959
Udall, Nicholas, 1. 1414–16, 1151, 1420, 2029
Uffenbach, Zacharias Conrad von, 2. 1399
Uhthred of Bolton, 1. 798
Ulloa, Antonio de, 2. 1465
Ulster echo, 3. 1806
Ulster examiner (and northern star), 3. 1806
Ulster miscellany, 2. 377, 1380
Ulster parade, 4. 1375
Ulster voices, 4. 1375
Ulverston, printing, 2. 270
Umfreville, Edward, 2. 1471
Umpire, 3. 1812; 4. 1403
Unamuno, Miguel de, 3. 143
'Uncle Adam' (George Mogridge), 3. 1089
'Uncle Newbury' (George Mogridge), 3. 1089
Under cover, 4. 1384
Underdowne, Thomas, 1. 1152
Undergrad, 4. 1398
Undergraduate (1819), 3. 1867
Undergraduate (1888), 3. 1868
Undergraduate (London 1913), 4. 1395
Undergraduate papers, 3. 1868
Undergraduate review, 4. 1397
Underhill, Evelyn, 4. 1301–2
Underhill, George Frederick, 3. 1707
Underhill, John, 1. 2163
Underneath the arches, 4. 1386
Undertaker, 2. 1288
Undertaker redivivus, 4. 1398
Underwood, James, 2. 1563
Underwood, W., 3. 1842
Unemployed drama news, 4. 867, 874
Unfortunate Dutchess, 2. 994
Unhappy lovers (1694), 2. 983
Unhappy lovers (1732), 2. 362
Unicorn, 4. 1395
Union, 2. 377
Union chronicle, 3. 1820
Union Jack, 3. 1825
Union journal, 2. 1358
Union song book (1759), 2. 380
Union song-book (1781), 2. 402
Union star, 2. 1387
Unit, 4. 1384
unitarianism, Restoration and eighteenth century, 2. 1666, 1673–6
United Kingdom, 3. 1810
United Methodist Free Churches' magazine, 3. 1846

United service journal, 3. 1845
United service magazine, 3. 1845
United services (and Empire) review, 3. 1826
United services gazette, 3. 1826
Universal advertiser (1731), 2. 1384
Universal advertiser (1753), 2. 1379, 1385
Universal and Ludgate magazine, 4. 1355
Universal catalogue for the year, 2. 1346
Universal chronicle, 2. 1282, 1333
Universal corn reporter, 3. 1823
Universal harmony, 2. 370
Universal historical bibliotheque, 2. 1291
Universal intelligence (1681), 2. 1318
Universal intelligence (1688), 2. 1318
Universal jester, 2. 377
Universal journal (1723), 2. 1325
Universal journal (1747), 2. 1385
Universal journalist, 2. 1386
Universal librarian, 2. 1300
Universal London morning advertiser, 2. 1331
Universal London price-courant, 2. 1336
Universal magazine (1798), 2. 1380
Universal magazine and review (1789), 2. 1379
Universal magazine of knowledge and pleasure (1747), 2. 1299; 3. 1839
Universal magazine (1900), 4. 1355
Universal melody, 2. 387
Universal mercury, 2. 1294
Universal monitor, 2. 1289
Universal monthly intelligencer, 2. 1373
Universal museum (1762), 2. 1303
Universal museum (1764), 2. 1350
Universal musical and dramatic directory, 4. 860
Universal musician, 2. 366
Universal politician, 2. 1311
Universal review (1760), 2. 1303
Universal review (1888), 3. 1853
Universal Scots songster, 2. 402
Universal songster (1782?), 2. 403
Universal songster (1793?), 2. 419
Universal spectator, 2. 1278, 1326
Universal spy (March 1732), 2. 1327
Universal spy (April 1732), 2. 1327
Universal spy (1739), 2. 1298, 1330
Universal visiter, 2. 1300–1
Universal weekly journal, 2. 1330
Universalists' miscellany, 2. 1311
Universe, 3. 1823, 1837; 4. 1401
universities
    general bibliography, 1. 15–20
    Middle English, 1. 632, 635–7
    Renaissance to Restoration
        drama, 1. 1761–80
        education, 1. 2406, 2409–10, 2414–15
    Restoration and eighteenth century, 2. 1927–34

universities (*cont.*)
  nineteenth century
    education, 3. 1731–40
    journalism, 3. 1865–74
  twentieth century
    journalism, 4. 1335–6, 1391–8
    libraries, 4. 112
    publishing, 4. 95
  see also education
Universities quarterly, 4. 1391
University, 4. 1391
University College gazette, 3. 1867; 4. 1395
University College London gazette, 3. 1867, 1872
University College magazine, 3. 1867, 1872; 4. 1395
University digest, 4. 1395
University gazette, 4. 1392
University maga, 3. 1869
University magazine (Cambridge 1795), 2. 1349
University magazine (Dublin 1878), 3. 1845–6, 1869
University magazine and free review, 3. 1854; 4. 1391
University miscellany, 2. 348
University news, 4. 1398
University of Bristol gazette, 4. 1392
University of Bristol studies, 4. 1392
University pulpit, 4. 1392
University review, 4. 1391
University squib, 3. 1869
Unnatural mother and ungrateful wife, 2. 992
Unsuspected observer, 2. 1337
Unwin, David Storr, 4. 814
Unwin Brothers (printers), 3. 60
Unzer, Johann Christoph, 2. 1541, 175
Up-to-date, 4. 1366
Up-to-date boys, 3. 1825
Upper ten thousand, 3. 1879
Upton, Bertha, 3. 1100
Upton, Florence, 3. 1100
Upton, James, 2. 1771
Upton, John, 2. 1750
Upton, W., 3. 1101
Upward, Edward Falaise, 4. 751–2
'Urban, Sylvanus' (E. Cave), 2. 1295
Ureisun of God almihti, On, 1. 516
Ureisun of oure Louerde, On, 1. 516
Urfé, Honoré d', 1. 2194, 874; 2. 145
Uring, Nathaniel, 2. 1395
Urquhart, David, 3. 1778, 1849
Urquhart, John, 3. 1853
Urquhart, Sir Thomas, 1. 2236, 1336
Urry, John, 2. 1770
Ursula, St, 1. 1152
Us: Mass-Observation weekly, 4. 1408

Use and abuse of Free-Masonry, 2. 404
Use and abuses of money, 2. 1900
Useful intelligencer for promoting of trade and commerce, 2. 1322
Useful transactions in philosophy, 2. 1293
Ushas, 4. 1388
Ushaw magazine, 4. 1395
Usher, 4. 1397
Usk, Thomas, 1. 506–7
Ussher, James, 1. 1987–8, 1004, 2140, 2298, 2300, 2306; 3. 1887
Ustinov, Peter Alexander, 4. 986
Ustonson, Onesimus, 2. 1561
usury, Renaissance to Restoration, 1. 2276
Uttley, Alison, 4. 797–8

'V., B.' (James Thomson), 3. 579–81
VE-time drama, 4. 827
VJ-time drama, 4. 827
Vachell, Horace Annesley, 4. 752–4
Vacuum, 4. 1396
Vaenius, Otho, 1. 1330
Vagarist, 2. 1289
Vainglory (OE), 1. 305
Vairasse d'Allais, Denis, 2. 1533, 978
Valdés, Francisco de, 1. 2194, 908
Valdes, Juan de, 1. 910
Valdin, Monsieur —, 2. 1562
Valdory, Guillaume de, 2. 993
Vale Press, 3. 56; 4. 98
Valentine, Isaac, 3. 1822
Valentine and Orson, 1. 448
Valera, Cipriano de, 1. 910
Valhalla, 4. 1385
Valiant Scot, 1. 1762
Valiant Welshman, 1. 1762
Vallancey, Charles, 3. 1888
Vallans, William, 1. 1152
Vallenger, Stephen, 1. 1004
Valpy, — (fl. 1822), 3. 1810
Valvasone, Erasmo da, 1. 894
Vanbrugh, Sir John, 2. 749–50, 128, 179
Vancouver, George, 2. 1483
Vancouver, John, 2. 1483
Vanderlint, Jacob, 2. 1900
Vandervell, H. E., 3. 1714
Van Druten, John William, 4. 986–8
'Vandyke' (H. Walpole), 2. 1281
Vane, Vane Hunt Sutton, 4. 988
'Vangrin, Peter Nicholas', 2. 1343
Vanitas, 3. 1870
Vanity Fair (1868), 3. 1815; 4. 1402
Vanity fair (1917), 4. 1383
Vanity of human wishes, 2. 1002
Van Oven, Lionel, 3. 1822

Vanneschi, Francesco, 2. 1550, 191
Vansittart, Henry, 2. 1440
Vansleb, John Michael, 2. 1446
Vanson, Frederic, 4. 1379
Varchi, Benedetto, 1. 890
Varenius, Bernard, 2. 1433
Variete, 4. 1387
Variety, cabaret, film news, 4. 860
Variety fare, 4. 860
Variety, music, stage and film news, 4. 860
Variety stage illustrated, 4. 859
Variety theatre, 4. 859
Variety theatre annual, 4. 825, 859
Variety time table, 4. 859
Varley, G., 4. 1382
Varlo, Charles, 2. 1472
Varnhagen von Ense, Karl August, 3. 129
Varsity (Oxford 1901), 4. 1396
Varsity (Cambridge 1931), 4. 1394
Varsity (Cambridge 1939), 4. 1394
Varsity (Cambridge 1947), 4. 1394
Vasari, Giorgio, 2. 1550
Vaughan, Charles James, 3. 1726
Vaughan, Henry, 1. 1230–4, 1913
Vaughan, Herbert, Cardinal, 3. 1822, 1856
Vaughan, Rice, 2. 1900
Vaughan, Robert (fl. 1542), 1. 1152, 2032
Vaughan, Robert (1795–1868), 3. 1778, 1857
Vaughan, Robert Alfred, 3. 1404, 1610
Vaughan, Thomas (1622–66), 2. 1909
Vaughan, Thomas (fl. 1761–1820), 2. 859
Vaughan, Walter, 2. 1437
Vaughan, Sir William, 1. 1152–3, 1906, 2162, 2314
Vaumorière, Pierre d'Ortigue, Sieur de, 2. 1533, 975
Vauquelin de la Fresnaye, Jean, 1. 871
Vautor, Thomas, 1. 1355
Vautrollier, Thomas, 1. 964
Vaux, Frances Bowyer, 3. 1101
Vaux, Thomas, 2nd Baron, 1. 1153
Vauxhall songs for the year 1795, 2. 422
Veal, George, 2. 1403
Veen, Otto van, 1. 1330
Veer, Gerrit de, 1. 2125
Vega, Lope de, 1. 910, 916–17, 2065; 2. 201, 994
Vegetius, 1. 688, 2178
Vegius, Mapheus, 1. 856
Veitch, John, 3. 1596
Velvet coffee-woman, 2. 992
Venables, George Stovin, 3. 1778
Venables, Robert, 1. 2160; 2. 1556
Venegas, Miguel, 2. 1466
Venn, Henry, 2. 1629
Venn, John, 3. 1596–7

Vennar(d), Richard, 1. 1153
Venner, Tobias, 1. 2038
Ventum, Harriet, 3. 1099–1100
Ventura, E. M., 4. 1382
Ventura, J. O., 4. 1385
Venture (1731), 2. 360
Venture (1903), 4. 1357
Venture (Bristol 1912), 4. 1361
Venture (1912), amateur journal, 4. 1383
Venture (Cambridge 1928), 4. 1368, 1394
Venturer, 4. 1364
Venus looking-glass, 2. 341
Venuti, Rudolfini, 2. 1420
'Veramund, Ernest' (F. Hotman), 1. 2076
Verbiest, Ferdinand, 2. 1433
Vercelli book, 1. 230
Vercelli homilies, 1. 324–6
Vere, Sir Francis, 1. 2214
Verelst, Harry, 2. 1441
Vergil, Polydore, 1. 2203–5, 852, 2131
Verist, 4. 1378
Veritas, 4. 1384
Verity, Arthur Wilson, 3. 1666
Verlaine, Paul, 3. 109
Vermigli, Pietro Martire, 1. 852
Verne, Jules Gabriel, 3. 109, 1110
Verney, Sir Francis, 1. 1775
Vernon, John, 2. 1017
Vernon collection, smaller (ME), 1. 531
Vernon miracles of Mary, 1. 459–60
Vernon's glory, 2. 368
Verri, Alessandro, 2. 1550
Versailles illustrated, 2. 1416
Versatile ingenium, 2. 333
Verse, 4. 1378
Verse and song, 4. 74, 1368
Verse lover, 4. 1379
Verses against thieves (ME), 1. 514
Verses by the university of Oxford on. . . Grenvill, 2. 335
Verses for little children, 3. 1107
Verses of prayse and joye (1586), 1. 1009
Verses on the coronation of George II, 2. 383
Verses on the death of. . .Grenvil, 1. 1010
Verses on the death of Queen Caroline, 2. 367
*Verses on the peace by the scholars. . .*2. 348
Verstegan (Rowlands), Richard, 1. 1140, 921, 1907, 2137
Verulam, Francis Bacon, Baron, 1. 2324–5, 852, 862, 865, 876, 890, 1909, 1962, 2028, 2047, 2050, 2056, 2073, 2275, 2276, 2313; 2. 31, 75, 103–4, 214
Verulam, James Grimston, Earl of, 2. 1402
Verve, 4. 1372
Very full and particular relation, A, 1. 2106

Veryard, Ellis, 2. 1415, 1435
'Veteran, Valentine', 2. 1281
Vial de Saint Bel, Charles, 2. 1555
Vicars, John, 1. 1910
Vicars, Thomas, 1. 2316
Vices and virtues (ME), 1. 501–2
Vickridge, Alberta, 4. 1368
Vico, Giambattista, 2. 38, 188
Victor, Benjamin, 2. 998
Victoria annual, 3. 1876
Victoria magazine, 3. 1850
Victoria Press, 3. 60
Vida, Marcus Hieronymus, 1. 852, 856; 2. 1550, 65, 78
Vidler, William, 2. 1311
Vidocq, François Eugène, 3. 109
'Vieille Moustache' (R. Henderson), 3. 1706
View of Paris and places adjoining, A, 2. 1415
View of the beau monde, A, 2. 360, 992
View of the coasts . . . within the limits of the South-Sea Company, A, 2. 1460
View of the state of the trade to Africa, A, 2. 1447
View of the town, A, 2. 360
Viewpoint, 4. 1371
Vigilance gazette, 3. 61
Vigny, Alfred de, 3. 109–10
Villare anglicum, 1. 2135
Villaut, Nicolas, Sieur de Bellefond, 2. 1445
Villegas, Antonio de, 1. 912
Villiers, Claude Deschamps, Sieur de, 2. 977
Villiers, Frederick, 3. 1778
Villiers, George, 2nd Duke of Buckingham, 2. 758–9
Villiers, Henry, 3. 1821
Villiers, John Charles, 3rd Earl of Clarendon, 2. 1428
Villiers-Chapman, Charles, 4. 1358
Vince, Samuel, 2. 1909
Vincent, Charles W., 3. 1877
Vincent, James Edmund, 3. 1701
Vincent, John, 3. 1712
Vincent, Louis, 4. 1362
Vincent, Philip, 1. 2163
Vincent, Sir R., 2. 1347
Vincent, Thomas, 1. 1775
Vincent, William, 2. 1829–30, 1444
Vincula, 4. 1395
Vinculum societatis, 2. 336
Vine, J. R. S., 3. 1882
Vine, 4. 1363
'Vinegar, Capt. Hercules' (Fielding and Ralph), 2. 1279, 1330
Vines, Sherard, 4. 1397
Viney, Josiah, 3. 1840

Vineyard, 4. 1360
Viniard of devotion, 1. 1935
Vinogradoff, Sir Paul Gavrilovich, 4. 1228–9
Vinovia, 4. 1384
Vint, Mary, 3. 1812
Violet, Thomas, 1. 2278
Violet magazine, 4. 1365
Violet novels, 4. 1364
'Vipont, Elfrida' (Elfrida Vipont Foulds), 4. 808
'Virakam, Soror', 4. 1359
Viret, Pierre, 1. 2194, 866
Virgil, 1. 2178–80; 2. 1502, 35
Virgin Muse, 2. 351
Virtue and vice, 2. 1023
Virtue in a cottage, 2. 1026
Virtue rewarded, 2. 983
Virtue's friend, 2. 1352
'Visiak, E. H.' (Edward Harold Physick), 4. 799
Vision (1919), 4. 1364
Vision (1923), 4. 1366
Vision of St Paul, 1. 532–3
Vision of Tundale, 1. 534
Visionary, 2. 1284
Visions of Sir Heister Ryley, 2. 1272
Visitant, 2. 1288
Visiter (1723), 2. 1277
Visiter (1746), 2. 1279
Visits to the aviary, 2. 1030
Vistas, 4. 1378
Vitell, Christopher, 1. 1130
Vivès, Juan Luis, 1. 852, 2194, 2277
Vizard, John, 3. 1681
Vizetelly, Henry, 3. 82, 1778, 1816
vocabulary, general, 1. 141–70
    Old English, 1. 143–54
    Middle English, 1. 153–6
    Modern English, 1. 157–64
Vocal companion (1757?), 2. 380
Vocal companion (1759), 2. 380
Vocal enchanter, 2. 415
Vocal enchantress, 2. 404
Vocal magazine (1778), 2. 1306
Vocal magazine (1781), 2. 1306
Vocal magazine (1782), 2. 403
Vocal magazine (1784), 2. 1307
Vocal magazine (1797), 2. 424, 1373
Vocal medley, 2. 374
Vocal melody, 2. 376
Vocal miscellany (1733), 2. 363
Vocal miscellany (1784), 2. 405
Vocal miscellany of Great Britain, 2. 424
Vocal music, 2. 392
Vocal musical mask, 2. 369

Voice and verse, 4. 1367
Voice of Scotland, 4. 1373
Voice of the world, 4. 60
Voices (1919), 4. 1364
Voices (1943), 4. 1376
Voisin, A. C., 4. 1385
Voiture, Vincent de, 1. 2194, 867; 2. 1534, 131, 136, 978
Volder, Willem de, 1. 854
Volney, Constantin François, Comte de, 2. 1442; 3. 110
Volontés, 4. 1373
Voltaire, François Marie Arouet de, 2. 1534–8, 37–8, 68, 98–103, 116, 124, 131, 136, 145, 861–2, 999, 1002, 1400
Volunteer, 2. 1284
Volunteer evening post, 2. 1386
Volunteer journal, 2. 1388
Volunteer's journal, 2. 1386
Voluptuary, 2. 1289
Vondel, Joost van den, 1. 920; 2. 208
Vosper, Frank, 4. 988
Vossius, Isaac, 2. 1909
Vota oxoniensa pro Guilhelmo rege et Maria regina nuncupata, 2. 337
Votes of both Houses, 2. 1315
Votes of the House of Commons (1680), 2. 1317
Votes of the House of Commons at Oxford (1681), 2. 1317
Votes of the House of Commons (1690), 2. 1319
Votes of the House of Commons in Ireland (1692), 2. 1319, 1381
Votes of the House of Commons (1696), 2. 1320
Votes of the House of Commons (Dublin 1707), 2. 1381
Votes of the House of Commons (Dublin 1713), 2. 1382
Votes of the House of Commons (Dublin 1715), 2. 1382
Votes of the House of Commons (1718), 2. 1324
Votes of the new parliament of women, 2. 1322
Votivum Carolo, 2. 328
Voules, Horace, 3. 1791, 1793, 1815
Vox and the wolf, 1. 456
Vox populi vox dei, 1. 1154
Voyage of Nicholas Downton, 1. 2145
Voyage of the Barbara to Brazil, 1. 2149
Voyage round the world in the years 1764–6, 2. 1479
Voyage to Shetland, A, 2. 1401
Voyage to the East Indies, A, 2. 1439
Voyage to the island of Ceylon, A, 2. 1439
Voyage to the new island Fonseca, A, 2. 985
Voyage to the South Seas by Commodore Anson, A, 2. 1478

Voyager (Bristol 1924), 4. 1366
Voyager (Manchester 1946), 4. 1388
Voyages and travels of Columbus...2. 1477
Voyages and travels of Fletcher Christian, 2. 1481
Voyages of Governor Phillip, 2. 1481
Voynich, Ethel Lilian, 3. 1080
Vulpius, Christian August, 2. 1541, 175, 181
Vyllagon, Nicholas, 1. 2075
Vyner, Robert Thomas, 3. 1705

W., D., archdeacon (fl. 1580), 1. 1154
W., F. (fl. 1673), 2. 1411
W., G. (fl. 1600), 1. 2073
W. H. Smith & Son trade circular, 4. 108
W., J. (fl. 1682), 2. 1456
W. K. magazine, 4. 1360
W., M. (fl. 1699), 2. 1462
W., R. (fl. 1570), 1. 1155
W., R., gent (fl. 1688), 2. 1557
W., S. (fl. 1805), 3. 1105
W., T. (fl. 1593–1603), poet, 1. 1155
W., T. (fl. 1606), pamphleteer, 1. 2074
W., T. (fl. 1672), 2. 1410
W., T. (fl. 1712), 2. 1017
W., W. (fl. 1544), 1. 2026
W., W. (fl. 1582), 1. 2072
Wace, 1. 393–6.
Wace, Henry, 3. 1622
Wace, Mrs M. A., 4. 807
Wächter, Leonhard, 2. 1541–2, 181–2
Waddell, Helen Jane, 4. 1127–8, 799
Waddell, Samuel, 3. 1941
Waddington, Conrad Hal, 4. 1302–3
Wade, John, 3. 1817
Wade, Thomas, 3. 558, 1808, 1847
Wade's London review, 3. 1847
Wagner, (Wilhelm) Richard, 3. 129
Wadham College gazette, 3. 1869; 4. 1396
Wadsworth, Benjamin, 2. 1457
Wadsworth, James, 1. 2127–8
Waerferth of Worcester, 1. 315
Wafer, Lionel, 2. 1458
'Wagbucket, Walter', 2. 1333
Wagenaer, Lucas Jansen, 1. 2137
Wager, Lewis, 1. 1408
Wager, William, 1. 1409
'Wagstaffe, Jeoffrey' (J. Courtenay), 2. 1284
Wagstaffe, William, 2. 1274
Waifs and strays, 3. 1868
Wail, 4. 1398
Wain, John, 4. 1376
Wainewright, Thomas Griffiths, 3. 1778
Waite, Arthur Edward, 3. 651–2; 4. 1357
Wake, William, 2. 1850

Wakefield
  Middle English drama, 1. 734–6
  nineteenth century newspapers, 3. 1833
Wakefield, Daniel, 2. 1900
Wakefield, Gilbert, 2. 1830
Wakefield, Priscilla, 2. 1027
Wakefield evening herald, 3. 1799
Wakefield express, 3. 1833
'Wakefield Master's' plays (ME), 1. 734–6
Wakefield plays (ME), 1. 734
Wakley, James, 3. 1826
Wakley, Thomas, 3. 1778, 1826
Wakley, Thomas Henry, 3. 1826
Walcot, James, 2. 1463
Waldegrave, Powle, 1. 2149
Waldegrave, Samuel, 3. 1621
Waldere, 1. 305–6
Waldie, Jane, 3. 1677
Waldron, Francis Godolphin, 2. 859–60, 1785–6, 1290
Waldron, George, 2. 1482
Wales
  library catalogues, 1. 8, 11
  manuscript studies, 1. 214
  medieval drama, 1. 727–8
  monastic libraries, 1. 996
  Renaissance printing and bookselling, 1. 969–70
  Restoration and eighteenth century
    periodicals, 2. 1389–90
    printing and bookselling, 2. 270–2
    theatre, 2. 727–9
  nineteenth century education, 3. 1740, 1747–50
  twentieth century
    theatre, 4. 847
    university journalism, 4. 1398
Wales, printing 2. 270–2
Wales, William, 2. 1479–80
Wales (1937), 4. 1372–3, 1348
Waley, Arthur David, 4. 372–4
Waleys, Thomas, 1. 798
Walford, Edward, 3. 1778, 1814, 1821, 1839, 1850, 1879
Walker, Adam, 2. 1406, 1428
Walker, B., 2. 1314
Walker, Charles, 2. 990
Walker, Sir Edward, 1. 2245
Walker, George (d. 1651), 1. 2040
Walker, George, Commodore (d. 1777), 2. 1395–6
Walker, George (1772–1847), novelist, 3. 770–1; 2. 1012, 1014
Walker, George (1803–79), chess-player, 3. 1694
Walker, Gilbert, 1. 2024, 2034
Walker, Henry, 1. 2092–3, 2099, 2100, 2101, 2102, 2103, 2104, 2105, 2106, 2107, 2108; 2. 1315

Walker, Sir Hovenden, 2. 1460
Walker, John (fl. 1582), 1. 2143
Walker, John (1674–1747), ecclesiastical historian, 2. 1804
Walker, John (1692?–1741), classical scholar, 2. 1830
Walker, John (fl. 1792), journalist, 2. 1309
Walker, John (1770–1831), antiquary, 3. 1881
'Walker, Johnny' (J. Badman), 3. 1692
Walker, Joseph, 3. 1889
Walker, Joseph Cooper, 2. 237
Walker, Kenneth Macfarlane, 4. 796
Walker, Lady Mary, 2. 1005
Walker, Obadiah, 2. 1795
Walker, Patrick, 2. 2045
Walker, Ray, 4. 828
Walker, Richard Johnson, 4. 1361, 1391
Walker, Thomas, 3. 1790
Walker, William Sidney, 3. 1666
Walker's half-penny London spy, 2. 1329
Walker's half-penny post, 2. 1328
Walker's Hibernian magazine, 2. 1379; 3. 1840
Walker-Smith, Derek, 4. 1359
Walking amusements, 2. 396
Walkington, Thomas, 1. 2048
Walkley, Arthur Bingham, 3. 1455
Walkley, Thomas, 1. 964
Wall, Bernard, 4. 1371
Wall, E. J., 3. 1878
Wall, Richard, 2. 1554
Wallace, — (fl. 1835), 3. 1856
Wallace, Alfred Russel, 3. 1674, 1678
Wallace, Edgar, 4. 754–8
Wallace, J. Bruce, 3. 1820
Wallace, Richard Horatio Edgar, 4. 754–8
Wallace, Robert (d. 1771), 2. 1370, 1900
Wallace, Robert (1831–99), 3. 1804
'Wallace, Sir William', 2. 1375
Wallace, William, 3. 1597
Wallas, Graham, 4. 1229–30
Waller, Edmund, 1. 1211–13; 2. 33
Waller, John, 4. 1374, 1398
Waller, John Francis, 3. 1846
Waller, Richard, 2. 1910
Walley, Henry, 1. 964
Wallington, Nehemiah, 1. 2245
Wallis, — (fl. 1794), 2. 1407
'Wallis, A. S. C.' (Adèle Opzoomer), 3. 94
Wallis, John, 1. 2003, 2306, 2336–7; 2. 1899, 1910
Wallis, Samuel, 2. 1479
Wallis, Thomas, 2. 1554
Walmsley, Joshua, 3. 1790
Walmsley, Leo, 4. 800
Walpole, Horace, 2. 1588–94, 86, 136, 151, 186, 312, 1281, 1418, 1802, 1807

Walpole, Sir Hugh Seymour, 4. 758–61, 798
Walpole, Sir Robert, 2. 987
Walpole, Sir Spencer, 3. 1505
Walpoole, George Augustus, 2. 1405
Walrond, Henry, 3. 1882
Walrus, 4. 1396
Walsh, Edward, M.D. (1756–1832), traveller in Holland, 2. 1431
Walsh, Edward (1805–50), Irish poet, 3. 1901
Walsh, Ernest, 4. 1367
Walsh, Frances Eliza, 3. 1098
Walsh, John Henry, 3. 1695, 1713, 1816
Walsh, William, 2. 486–7
Walsh's Dublin post-boy, 2. 1384
Walsh's (Dublin weekly) impartial news-letter, 2. 1383
Walshe, Edward, 1. 2131
Walsingham, Edward, 1. 2249
'Walsingham, Francis' (W. Arnall), 2. 1278
Walsingham, Thomas, 1. 806
Walter of Chatton, 1. 799
Walter of Evesham, 1. 799
Walter of Wimborne, 1. 767
Walter the Englishman, 1. 767
Walter, Arthur Fraser, 3. 1789
Walter, J., 3. 1727
Walter, J. C., 3. 1689
Walter, John, the first (1739–1812), 2. 266; 3. 1789
Walter, John, the second (1776–1847), 3. 1789
Walter, John, the third (1818–94), 3. 1789
Walter, Richard, 2. 1478
Walter, Weever, 3. 1678
Walter, William, 1. 1155, 2031
Walter and Hubert, 3. 1107
Walters, John (1721–97), 2. 236
Walters, John, the younger (1759–89), 2. 246, 1789
Walton, Brian, 1. 2003, 2295
Walton, Catherine Augusta, 3. 1104
Walton, Izaak, 1. 2222–3
Walton, John, 1. 688
Walton, William, 2. 1471
Walwayn, John, 1. 789
'Wanderer' (E. H. D'Avigdor), 3. 1706
Wanderer (OE), 1. 306–8
Wanderer (1717), 2. 1276
Wanderer (1783), 2. 1287
Wanderer (1798), 2. 1290
Wanderer (Dublin 1798), 2. 1380
Wanderer (Larling 1933), 4. 1370
Wanderer (Hayes 1935), 4. 1386
Wandering spy, 2. 1269
Wandering whore, 2. 1339
Wanley, Humfrey, 2. 1792–3, 311

Wanley, Nathaniel, 2. 487
Wanostrocht, Nicholas, 3. 1696
Wansey, Henry, 2. 1475
Wanton widow, 2. 1002
Wapull, George, 1. 1409
War cry and official gazette of the Salvation Army, 3. 1823
War express and daily advertiser, 3. 1794
war stories, twentieth century, 4. 129–30
War stories, 4. 1390
War telegraph (Edinburgh 1854), 3. 1803
War telegraph (Manchester 1855), 3. 1794
War thriller, 4. 1389
War-time drama, 4. 827, 878
Warbler, 2. 393
Warbler's delight, 2. 388
Warbling muses, 2. 374
Warbling Philomell, 2. 392
Warburton, Bartholomew Eliot George, 3. 1404
Warburton, William, 2. 1869–71, 44, 112, 165, 235, 1775–6
Ward, Sir Adolphus William, 3. 1666–7
Ward, Ann, 3. 758–60
Ward, Arnold S., 3. 1871
Ward, Atkinson, 4. 1380
Ward, C. W., 3. 62
Ward, Edward, 2. 1091–5, 984, 1293, 1342, 1344, 1399, 1414, 1457–8, 1557, 1565
Ward, Frederick William Orde, 3. 652
Ward, H. Snowden, 3. 62
Ward, Sir Henry George, 3. 1811
Ward, Mrs Humphry (Mary Augusta), 3. 1081–2, 1616
Ward, James, 3. 1597–8, 1616
Ward, John (d. 1638), 1. 1355
Ward, John (1679?–1758), 2. 806, 1818, 1832
Ward, Mary Augusta, 3. 1081–2, 1616
Ward, Robert (fl. 1623–42), 1. 1775
Ward, Robert, later Plumer Ward (1765–1846), 3. 771–2
Ward, Samuel, 1. 1947–8
Ward, Seth, 1. 2003, 2338
Ward, Thomas Humphry, 3. 1455–6, 1868, 1879
Ward, Valentine, 3. 1721
Ward, Veronica, 4. 1372
Ward, William, 2. 1554
Ward, William George, 3. 1598–9, 1634, 1856
Ward, Lock and Co, 3. 82, 1771
Warder, Ann, 2. 1472
Wardlaw, Elizabeth, Lady, 2. 1978, 242
Ware, Fabian, 3. 1732
Ware, Sir James 1. 1004, 2135; 2. 1805; 3. 1887–8
Waring, Anna Laetitia, 3. 558
Waring, Thomas, 3. 1691

Warkworth, Henry A. G. Percy, Baron, 3. 1870
Warkworth, John, 1. 682
Warman, Erik, 4. 1370
Warne and Co, Frederick, 3. 82
Warner, Ferdinando, 2. 1777
Warner, Sir Pelham Francis, 3. 1699
Warner, Rex, 4. 761–2, 809
Warner, Richard (1713–75), 2. 1779
Warner, Richard (1763–1857), 2. 1406, 1408
Warner, Sylvia Townsend, 4. 762–3
Warner, William, 1. 1155–6, 2053, 2124
Warner's world-wide writers' weekly, 4. 73, 1387
Warning for faire women, A, 1. 1471
Warr, John, 4. 866
Warren, Mrs — 3. 1849
Warren, Arthur, 1. 1156
Warren, Charles Edmund, 3. 1880
Warren, F., 4. 1384
Warren, George, 2. 1455
Warren, John Byrne Leicester, 3rd Baron de Tabley, 3. 652–3
Warren, Samuel, 3. 970
Warren, Sir Thomas Herbert, 3. 653
Warren, William, 1. 1156
Warres of Cyrus (sixteenth century), 1. 1470–1
Warrington, printing, 2. 270
Warrington, A. P., 4. 1352
Warrington daily guardian, 3. 1802
Warrington evening post, 3. 1800
Warriston, Archibald Johnston, Lord, 1. 2463
Wars of Alexander (ME), 1. 423
Warton, Joseph, 2. 689–90, 44, 1781–2
Warton, Thomas, the elder (1688?–1745), 2. 571
Warton, Thomas, the younger (1728–90), 2. 690–2, 44, 1754–5
Warwick, St Mary's library, 1. 996
Warwick, Arthur, 1. 2049
Warwick, Frances Evelyn, Countess of, 3. 1748
Warwick and Staffordshire journal, 2. 1329, 1353
Warwickshire
  general bibliography, 1. 19
  Restoration and eighteenth century printing, 2. 270
Warwickshire (weekly) journal, 2. 1353
Wase, Christopher, 1. 1757, 2306; 2. 241
Washbourne, Thomas, 1. 1323–4
Washington, George, 2. 1465
Wasp (17th century play), 1. 1762
Wasp (Cambridge 1891), 3. 1866
Wasp (Lampeter College 1935), 4. 1395
Wasse, Joseph, 2. 1830
Watchman (1796), 2. 1347
Watchman (1835), 3. 1822
Water poetry, 2. 396
Waterford chronicle, 2. 1390

Waterford daily mail, 3. 1806
Waterford flying post, 2. 1390
Waterford herald, 2. 1390
Waterford journal, 2. 1390
Waterford mail, 3. 1806
Waterford news-letter, 2. 1390
Waterhouse, Edward, 1. 2162
Waterland, Daniel, 2. 1630
Waterlow Brothers and Layton, 3. 60; 4. 81
Waters, — (fl. 1921), 4. 1384
Waterton, Charles, 3. 1674
Watkins, — (fl. 1820), 3. 1843
Watkins, Harry F. G., 3. 1871
Watkins, John, 2. 1800, 1288
Watkins, T., 3. 1800
Watkins, Thomas, 2. 1429
Watkins, Vernon Phillips, 4. 374–5
Watkins-Pitchford, Denys James, 4. 808
Watkinson, John, 2. 1404
Watkinson, William L., 3. 1857
Watkyns, Rowland, 1. 1324
Watson, Aaron, 3. 1778, 1793, 1795, 1802
Watson, Alfred Edward Thomas, 3. 1706, 1883
Watson, David, 2. 1830
Watson, Edmund Henry Lacon, 4. 1357
Watson, Elkanah, 2. 1405
Watson, George Lennox, 3. 1716
Watson, Henry, 1. 693, 2065
Watson, James, 3. 1778
Watson, John, 3. 1690, 1713–14
Watson, Richard, 2. 1894, 165, 1910
Watson, Robert, 2. 1741
Watson, T., 2. 1554
Watson, Thomas, Bishop of Lincoln (1513–84), 1. 1948
Watson, Thomas (1557?–92), poet, 1. 1156–7, 857, 893, 1346
Watson, Sir William (1715–87), 2. 1910
Watson, Sir William (1858–1935), 3. 653–4
Watson, Mrs William John, 4. 1357
Watson's Limerick chronicle, 2. 1389
Watt, Donald, 4. 1397
Watt, P. B., 3. 61
Watt, William, 3. 405, 1712
Watts, Alaric Alexander, 3. 405, 1778, 1793, 1796, 1826, 1843, 1873, 1879
Watts, Ernest A., 4. 1358
Watts, Isaac, 2. 572–3, 165, 1017–18, 1668–70, 1910
Watts, John (fl. 1672), 2. 1446
Watts, John (1818–87), 3. 1724
Watts, Zillah, 3. 1874, 1875, 1877
Watts's literary guide, 4. 1352
Watts-Dunton, Theodore, 3. 1456
Waugh, Alexander Raban (Alec), 4. 763–4

Waugh, Arthur, 3. 1700
Waugh, Benjamin, 3. 1823
Waugh, Edwin, 3. 558
Waugh, Evelyn Arthur St John, 4. 764–8
Waverley, 4. 1384
Waverley Book Store, 3. 86
Way, Gregory Lewis, 2. 1005
Way, William, 1. 693, 806
Wayfarer (Birmingham 1935), 4. 1372
Wayfarer (1935) amateur journal, 4. 1386
Wayland, John, 1. 964
Wayside words, 3. 1850; 4. 1351
Wayte, S. C., 3. 1705
Wayth, C., 3. 1689
Weakest goeth to the wall, 1. 1472
Weale, John, 1. 2129
Weamys, Anna, 1. 2058
Weatherby, Charles, 3. 1882
Weatherby, Edward, 3. 1882
Weatherby, James, the elder, 2. 1314; 3. 1882
Weatherby, James, the younger, 3. 1882
Weatherby, John Philip, 3. 1882
Weatherly, Frederic Edward, 3. 1868
Weatherly, George, 3. 1825
Weaver, Harriet, 4. 1361
Weaver, John, 2. 1565
Weaver, 2. 1346
Webb, Beatrice, Baroness Passfield, 4. 1230–4; 3. 1678
Webb, Clifford, 4. 802
Webb, Cornelius, 3. 405–6
Webb, Daniel, 2. 44
Webb, Daniel Carless, 3. 1682
Webb, Gladys Mary, 4. 768–9
Webb, Mrs J. B., 3. 1101
Webb, Marion St John, 4. 794
Webb, Mary, 4. 768–9
Webb, Matthew, 3. 1715
Webb, R., 4. 1385
Webb, Sidney James, Baron Passfield, 4. 1231–4; 3. 1678
Webbe, Edward, 1. 2123
Webbe, William, 1. 2311
Webber, Alexander, 3. 1712
Webber, Byron, 3. 1706
Weber, Friedrich Christian, 2. 1416
Weber, Henry William, 3. 1667
'Weber, Veit' (L. Wächter), 2. 1541–2, 181–2
Webster, Benjamin Nottingham, 3. 1142, 1816
Webster, Sir Charles Kingsley, 4. 1234
Webster, H., 4. 1380
Webster, James, 2. 2039–40
Webster, John (d. 1625), dramatist, 1. 1697–1703, 869, 2316
Webster, John (1610–82), scientist, 2. 1899, 1910

Webster, Pelatiah, 2. 1467
Webster, William, 2. 1278, 1327
Webster's royal red book, 3. 1879
Weckherlin, Georg Rudolf, 1. 880
Wedd, Nathaniel, 3. 1866
Weddell, A. J., 3. 1702
Wedderburn, David, 1. 2475–6
Wedderburn, John, 1. 2432, 1898
Weddynge of Sir Gawen and Dame Ragnell, 1. 408
Wedgwood, Cicely Veronica, 4. 1234–5
Wedlake, George, 3. 1812
Wedmore, Sir Frederick, 3. 1456–7
Wednesday packet, 2. 1376
Wednesday's journal, 2. 1324
Wednesday's Mercury, 1. 2098
Wee nipper, 4. 1382
Week (1878), 3. 1815
Week (1933), 4. 1407, 1348
Week-end novels, 4. 1364
Week-end review, 4. 826, 1369
Weekely post-master, 1. 2101
Weekley, Ernest, 4. 1128
Weekly abstract, 1. 2109
Weekly accompt, A, 1. 2098
Weekly account, 1. 2099, 2110
Weekly advertisements of things lost and stollen, 2. 1339
Weekly amusement (1734), 2. 1278, 1297, 1328
Weekly amusement (1735), 2. 1379
Weekly amusement (1763), 2. 1303–4
Weekly amusement (1784), 2. 1307
Weekly bill of mortality, 2. 1313
Weekly character: being the character of a Pope, 2. 1340
Weekly chronicle (1836), 3. 1811
Weekly chronicle (Newcastle 1946), 4. 1399
Weekly comedy (1699), 2. 1343
Weekly comedy (1707), 2. 1344
Weekly companion, 4. 1362
Weekly courant (Nottingham), 2. 1363
Weekly critical review, 4. 1405
Weekly discoverer strip'd naked, 2. 1340
Weekly discovery of the mystery of iniquity, 2. 1340
Weekly dispatch (1801), 3. 1808, 1834
Weekly dispatch (1816), 3. 1809
Weekly entertainer, 2. 1352
Weekly entertainment, 2. 1269, 1343
Weekly essay, 2. 1279, 1329
Weekly friend, 4. 1362
Weekly friend and family stories, 4. 1360
Weekly general post, 2. 1323
Weekly globe, 3. 1810
Weekly herald, 3. 1818
Weekly history, 2. 1330–1
Weekly illustrated (1907), 3. 1817; 4. 1404

Weekly illustrated (1934), 4. 1407
Weekly information, 1. 2109
Weekly intelligence (1642), 1. 2097
Weekly intelligence (1679), 2. 1317
Weekly intelligence (1816), 3. 1809
Weekly intelligencer and British luminary, 3. 1809
Weekly intelligencer of the commonwealth (1650), 1. 2107
Weekly intelligencer of the commonwealth (May 1659), 1. 2110; 2. 1314
Weekly intelligencer of the commonwealth (July 1659), 1. 2110; 2. 1314
Weekly journal (1714), 2. 1322
Weekly journal, A (1714), 2. 1322
Weekly journal (1715), 2. 1275, 1322
Weekly-journal (May 1716), 2. 1323
Weekly journal (Dec 1716), 2. 1276, 1323–4
Weekly journal (1720), 2. 1325
Weekly journal from London, 2. 1373
Weekly kinema guide, 4. 57
Weekly lampoon, 2. 1342
Weekly liar, 4. 1366
Weekly magazine (Dublin 1733), 2. 1379
Weekly magazine (1759), 2. 1302
Weekly magazine (1763), 2. 1303
Weekly magazine (Edinburgh 1768), 2. 1371–2
Weekly magazine and historical register (1793), 2. 1379
Weekly magazine and literary review (1758), 2. 1302
Weekly magazine and literary review (1779), 2. 1379
Weekly magazine and memoirs of modern literature (1760), 2. 1302
Weekly magazine of instruction, 2. 1374
Weekly mail (Cardiff 1870), 4. 1402
Weekly mail and record (Glasgow 1915), 4. 1401
Weekly medley (1718), 2. 1276, 1324
Weekly medley (1729), 2. 1326
Weekly memorial, 2. 1342
Weekly memorials (1689), 2. 1291
Weekly memorials for the ingenious (Jan 1682), 2. 1291
Weekly memorials for the ingenious (March 1682), 2. 1291
Weekly mercury, 2. 1363
Weekly mirror, 2. 1371
Weekly miscellany (1701), 2. 1343
Weekly miscellany (1732), 2. 1278, 1327
Weekly miscellany (Dublin 1734), 2. 1384
Weekly miscellany (Sherborne 1773), 2. 1352
Weekly miscellany for the improvement of husbandry, 2. 1294
Weekly news (1730), 2. 1327
Weekly news (Llandudno 1907), 4. 1381

Weekly news and chronicle (1851), 3. 1811
Weekly news and financial economist (1850), 3. 1814
Weekly news from forraigne parts, 1. 2100
Weekly news-letter, 2. 1320
Weekly Newspaper and Periodical Proprietors' Association authorised list, 4. 1343–4
Weekly observator (1692), 2. 1341
Weekly observator (1716), 2. 1276, 1345
Weekly oracle (1734), 2. 1278, 1328
Weekly oracle (1735), 2. 1384
Weekly packet (1712), 2. 1322
Weekly packet (1718), 2. 1324
Weekly packet (1741), 2. 1331
Weekly packet of advice from Ireland, 2. 1319
Weekly pacquet (1678), 2. 1339
Weekly pacquet (Dublin 1720), 2. 1383
Weekly pacquet of advice from Geneva (1681), 2. 1341
Weekly pacquet of advice from Geneva (1683), 2. 1341
Weekly pacquet of advice from Germany, 2. 1339
Weekly pacquet of advice from Rome restored, 2. 1339
Weekly playgoer, 4. 825
Weekly political and literary record, 3. 1817
Weekly post (1654), 1. 2108
Weekly post (1659), 1. 2110; 2. 1314
Weekly post (1711), 2. 1322
Weekly post (1729), 2. 1384
Weekly press, 3. 1813
Weekly record, 4. 1401
Weekly register (1730), 2. 1278, 1327
Weekly register (1798), 2. 1338
Weekly register (1823), 3. 1809
Weekly register (1855), 3. 1823
Weekly remarks and political reflections (1715), 2. 1323
Weekly remarks and political reflections (1716), 2. 1323
Weekly remarks on the transactions abroad, 2. 1342
Weekly remembrancer, 2. 1343
Weekly report, 4. 1382
Weekly repository, 2. 1380
Weekly repository of letters, 2. 1309
Weekly review (1717), 2. 1324
Weekly review (1780), 2. 1375
Weekly review (1799), 2. 1312
Weekly review (1938), 4. 1406
Weekly review of the affairs of France, A, 2. 1343–4
Weekly spectator and English theatre, 2. 1328–9
Weekly sporting review, 4. 827
Weekly sun, 3. 1812, 1834; 4. 1403
Weekly survey of the world, 2. 1342

Whimsies of Senor Hidalgo, 1. 1762
Whincup, Thomas, 2. 1801
Whipping-post, 2. 1344
Whishaw, Frederick J., 3. 1106
Whisperer (1709), 2. 1271
Whisperer (1770), 2. 1284
Whisperer (1795), 2. 1289
Whistler, Alan Charles Laurence, 4. 376
Whistler, James Abbott McNeill, 3. 68
Whistler, Laurence, 4. 376
Whiston, James, 2. 1316, 1318
Whiston, William, 2. 1638, 1871–2, 1910
Whiston's merchant's weekly remembrancer, 2. 1316
Whitaker, — (fl. 1783), 2. 1307
Whitaker, Alexander, 1. 2156, 2277
Whitaker, Evelyn, 3. 1104–5
Whitaker, John, 2. 1741–2
Whitaker, Joseph, 3. 81, 82, 1878
Whitaker, Richard, 1. 964
Whitaker's almanack, 3. 1878
Whitbourne, Richard, 1. 2156–7
Whitby, printing, 2. 270
Whitby, the monk of (c. 710), 1. 345
Whitby spy, 2. 1367
White, Andrew, 1. 2158–9
White, E. (fl. 1807), billiard player, 3. 1692
White, E. (fl. 1823), children's writer, 3. 1101
White, Gilbert, 2. 1594, 1910
White, Henry, 3. 1809, 1810
White, Henry Kirke, 3. 406–7
White, J. D., 3. 1803
White, James (d. 1799), novelist, 2. 1009
White, James (1794–1861), sportsman, 3. 1705, 1713
White, James (fl. 1801–17), veterinary surgeon, 2. 1555
White, John (1574–1648), 1. 1913, 2163
White, John (fl. 1790), 2. 1482
White, Joseph Blanco, 3. 1604, 1856
White, Joseph Gleeson, 3. 1853
White, Percy, 3. 1794, 1814
White, Terence Hanbury, 4. 771–2, 809
White, Thomas (1593–1676), philosopher, 1. 2337; 2. 1900
White, Thomas (d.c. 1672), writer for children 2. 1017
White, W. (fl. 1895), educationalist, 3. 1746
White, Walter, 3. 1680
White, William, 2. 1444, 1452
White, William Hale, 3. 1075–7
White dwarf, 3. 1817
White Ethiopian, 1. 1762
White hat, 3. 1818
White heather, 4. 1385
White magazine, 4. 1360

White rose of York, 3. 1875
White rosebud, 4. 1381
Whitefield, George, 2. 1638–40, 1462
Whitefoot, Thomas, 3. 1791
Whitehall, John, 1. 2342; 2. 488
Whitehall, Robert, 2. 488
Whitehall (1704), 2. 1381
Whitehall (1706), 2. 1381
Whitehall-courant, 2. 1323
Whitehall evening post (1718), 2. 1324
Whitehall evening post (1746), 2. 1332
White-hall gazette, 2. 1384
Whitehall journal, 2. 1325
Whitehall review, 3. 1815; 4. 1402
Whitehaven weekly courant, 2. 1367
Whitehead, Alfred North, 4. 1303–6
Whitehead, Charles, 3. 560
Whitehead, George, 2. 1652
Whitehead, Paul, 2. 575, 1562
Whitehead, William, 2. 860–2, 179
Whitehorn, William, 3. 1820
Whitehurst, Frederick Feild, 3. 1706, 1713
Whitehurst, John, 2. 1910
Whiteing, Richard, 3. 1778
Whitelaw, M., 3. 1714
Whitelock, Bulstrode, 1. 2228, 2129; 2. 1416, 1422
Whitelock, Mary, 4. 1387
Whitelock, S., 4. 1387
Whitelocke, Bulstrode, 1. 2228, 2129; 2. 1416, 1422
Whiter, Walter, 2. 1789
Whitforde, Richard, 1. 1948
Whitgift, John, 1. 1934
Whiting, Nathaniel, 1. 1324
Whiting, Thomas, 2. 1311
Whitlock, Pamela, 4. 814
Whitlock, Richard, 1. 2050
Whitney, Geoffrey, 1. 1159, 1330
Whitney, Isabella, 1. 1159
Whitney, John, 2. 1557
Whittaker, Meredith J., 3. 1801
Whittaker, T. P., 3. 1791
Whittemore, Jonathan, 3. 1823
Whittie, John, 2. 1412
Whittingham, William, 1. 1159, 1899, 2076
Whittingham and Co, C., 3. 60
Whittington, W. D., 3. 1865
Whitty, Edward Michael, 3. 1806
Whitty, Michael James, 3. 1795, 1845
Whitworth, Charles, Baron (d. 1725), 2. 1420
Whitworth, Sir Charles (d. 1778), 2. 1346
Whitworth's Manchester advertiser, 2. 1361
Whitworth's Manchester magazine, 2. 1361, 1348
Who's who, 3. 1879

Who's who in amateur journalism, 4. 1385
Who's who in British advertising, 4. 1342
Who's who in broadcasting, 4. 60, 864
Who's who in dancing, 4. 826, 860
Who's who in filmland, 4. 57
Who's who in press, publicity, printing, 4. 83
Who's who in the press, 4. 1343, 1344
Who's who in the theatre, 4. 824–5, 859
Who's who on the stage, 4. 824, 859
Who's who on the wireless, 4. 60, 864
Whole art and mystery of modern gaming, 2. 1567
Whole life...of bold Robin Hood, 2. 366
Whole of the chapters...during the late election for Hull, 2. 423
Whole proceedings of the sessions of the peace, 2. 1313
Whole proceedings on the King's commission, 2. 1335
Whole prophecies of Scotland, 2. 352
Whole volume of Mercurius musicus, 2. 341
Whybrow, George, 4. 1370
Whymper, Edward, 3. 1674, 1680, 1709
Whyte, J. H., 4. 1369
Whyte, James Christie, 3. 1704
Whyte, Samuel, 2. 692–3
Whyte-Melville, George John, 3. 971
Whytford, Richard, 1. 1948
Whythorne, Thomas, 1. 1159–60, 1345
Wibourne, Nathaniel, 1. 1776
Wickens, John, 3. 1870
'Wickham, Anna' (E. A. M. Hepburn), 4. 377
Wickins, Nathan, 1. 2035
Wicks, Frederick, 3. 1804
Wicksteed, Charles, 3. 1856
Wicksteed, Philip Henry, 4. 1236–8
Wiclif, John, 1. 491–6, 789–93, 487
Widders, Robert, 2. 1456
Wide world magazine, 3. 1854; 4. 1354
Wideawake magazine, 4. 1369
Widsith, 1. 308–10
Wieland, Christoph Martin, 2. 39, 168, 171, 182, 1004, 1542
Wife: a poem, 2. 346
Wife lapped in morel's skin, A, 1. 1160
Wife's lament, 1. 310–11
Wiffen, F. S., 4. 1385
Wiffen, Jeremiah Holmes, 3. 407
Wigan, Alfred Sydney, 3. 1158
Wigglesworth, Michael, 1. 1324–5
Wight, C. H. H., 3. 1850
Wight, Thomas, 1. 964
Wightman and Co, 3. 60
Wigstead, Henry, 2. 1406
Wilberforce, Henry William, 3. 1634–5, 1823
Wilberforce, Robert Isaac, 3. 1635

Wilberforce, Samuel, 3. 1102
Wilberforce, William, 3. 1618
Wilbert magazine, 4. 1383
Wilbye, John, 1. 1349
Wilcocks, J. C., 3. 1689
Wilcox, C. B., 3. 1865
Wilcox, Thomas, 1. 2024
Wild, Robert, 2. 488–9, 1568
Wild west weekly, 4. 1390
Wilde, George, 1. 1776
Wilde, Jane Francesca, Lady, 3. 1905
Wilde, Oscar Fingall O'Flahertie Wills, 3. 1182–8, 134, 156, 1097, 1852
Wilde, Sir William, 3. 1891
Wilder, F., 3. 1679
Wilderspin, Samuel, 3. 1720
'Wildfowler' (Lewis Clements), 3. 1713
Wildfowler's illustrated shooting times, 3. 1712
Wilenski, Reginald Howard, 4. 1128–9
Wilford, John, 2. 1804
Wilkes, John, 2. 1283, 1303
Wilkes, Thomas, 2. 1783
Wilkes, Wetenhall, 2. 1559
Wilkes's jest book, 2. 392
Wilkie, William, 2. 693
Wilkin, Simon, 3. 1668
Wilkins, A., 3. 1732
Wilkins, David, 2. 1796
Wilkins, George, 1. 1757–8, 2056
Wilkins, John, 1. 2003–4, 2318; 2. 165, 1900, 1910
Wilkins, William Henry, 3. 1853
Wilkins, William Vaughan, 4. 799
Wilkinson, Edward (fl. 1600), 1. 1160
Wilkinson, Edward (fl. 1774), 2. 1568
Wilkinson, Henry Spenser, 3. 1778
Wilkinson, J., 3. 1725
Wilkinson, Sir John Gardner, 3. 1680
Wilkinson, Joshua Lucock, 2. 1422, 1430
Wilkinson, Louis Umfreville, 4. 659
Wilkinson, Thomas, 3. 1682, 1709
Wilkinson, William, 2. 1446
Wilkley, E., 3. 1679
Wilks, Matthew, 2. 1310; 3. 1840
Wilks, Samuel Charles, 3. 1842
Wilks, Thomas Egerton, 3. 1158–9
Will A. Bradley's pantomime annual, 4. 859
Will o'the wisp, 4. 1384
Willan, Leonard, 1. 1758
Willcock, H. D., 4. 1371
Willes, Richard, 1. 2309
Willet, Andrew, 1. 1160, 1330
Willet, Rowland, 1. 2028, 2066
Willett, W. M., 3. 1792
Willey, Basil, 4. 1129

William de Pagula, 1. 802
William de Walcote, 1. 1004
William of Alnwick, 1. 799
William of Conches, 1. 767–8
William of La Mare, 1. 783–4
William of Macclesfield, 1. 799–800
William of Malmesbury, 1. 758–60
William of Nassyngton, 1. 520
William of Newburgh, 1. 784
William of Nottingham, 1. 800
William of Ockham, 1. 800–2
William of Palerne, 1. 435–6
William of St Carilef, 1. 1003
William of Sherwood (Shyreswood), 1. 784
William of Shoreham, 1. 710
William of Ware, 1. 784
William of Wykeham, 1. 1006
Williams, Anna, 2. 575
Williams, Charles, 3. 1793, 1794, 1809, 1815
Williams, Sir Charles Hanbury, 2. 575–6
Williams, Charles Walter Stansby, 4. 772–4
Williams, Daniel, 2. 1618
Williams, David, 2. 165
Williams, Dawson, 3. 1827
Williams, E. G. Harcourt, 4. 793
Williams, E. M. Abdy, 3. 1852
Williams, Edward (fl. 1650). 1. 2164
Williams, Edward (1746–1826), Welsh poet, 2. 248
Williams, Edward (1750–1813), of *Evangelical magazine*, 3. 1840
Williams, Emlyn, 4. 989
Williams, F. C., 3. 1778
Williams, George Emlyn, 4. 989
Williams, Griffith, 2. 1467
Williams, Helen Maria, 2. 693–4, 1428
Williams, Hugh William, 3. 1678
Williams, Isaac, 3. 560
Williams, J., 4. 1386
Williams, John (1582–1650), 1. 2004, 1004
Williams, John (1761–1818), 2. 694–5, 1568
Williams, John, M. D. (fl. 1777), traveller, 2. 1424
Williams, Sir John Fischer, 3. 1868
Williams, Margery Winifred, 4. 793–4
Williams, Miles Vaughan, 4. 1374, 1398
Williams, O. E., 3. 1844
Williams, Oliver, 1. 2109, 2110; 2. 1314, 1315
Williams, P., 4. 828, 862
Williams, Peggy Eileen Arabella, 4. 567
Williams, Raymond, 4. 1378
Williams, Robert, 3. 1809
Williams, Roger, 1. 2163–4
Williams, T. (fl. 1805), 3. 1842
Williams, Thomas, 2. 1310
Williams, Ursula Moray, 4. 812

Williams, W. Phillpotts, 3. 1707
Williams's Library, Dr, 2. 304
Williams-Ellis, Mary Amabel Nassau, 4. 801, 1371
Williamson, Benjamin, 3. 1870
Williamson, David, 3. 1854
Williamson, Henry, 4. 774–6
Williamson, Hugh Ross, 4. 990
Williamson, J., 3. 1722
Williamson, John, 2. 1559
Williamson, Peter, 2. 1371, 1375, 1465, 1468
Williamson, Ross, 4. 990
Williamson, Thomas, 3. 1687, 1712
Williamson's Liverpool advertiser, 2. 1360
Willich, Anthony F. M., 2. 1312
Willis, Browne, 2. 1717
Willis, D. A., 4. 1371
Willis, George Anthony Armstrong, 4. 906–8
Willis, H. Norton, 2. 1808
Willis, John, 1. 854
Willis, R. L., 2. 1406
Willis, Richard, 2. 1293
Willis, Thomas, 2. 1910
Willison, John, 2. 2045–6
Willm, J., 3. 1724
Willmer, Charles, 3. 1794, 1796
Willmer's Liverpool morning news, 3. 1796
Willmott, H. J., 4. 1380
Willmott, Robert Eldridge Aris, 3. 1404
Willoby, Henry, 1. 1160–1
Will(o)ughby, Francis, 2. 1411, 1556, 1910
Willox, John A., 3. 1797
wills (O.E.), 1. 332
Wills, Alfred, 3. 1680, 1709
Wills, Charles James, 3. 1675
Wills, Freeman, 3. 1852
Wills, James, 3. 1846
Wills, Noel H., 4. 1360
Wills, William Gorman, 3. 1159–60
Wills, William Henry, 3. 1813
Willughby, Francis, 2. 1411, 1556, 1910
Willyams, Cooper, 2. 1475
Wilmot, Barbarina, Baroness Dacre, 3. 370–1
Wilmot, John, 2nd Earl of Rochester, 2. 464–6, 167
Wilmot, Robert, 1. 1776
Wilson, Alexander (1766–1813), 2. 2030–1
Wilson, Alexander (d. 1852), 3. 561
Wilson, Angus Frank Johnstone, 4. 776–7
Wilson, Anthony Eldred Clifford, 4. 813–14
Wilson, Arthur, 1. 1758, 2241
Wilson, Benjamin, 2. 1906
Wilson, Caroline, 3. 1618
Wilson, Daniel, 3. 1618
Wilson, Effingham, 3. 82

Wilson, Elias, 2. 1411
Wilson, Florence Roma Muir, 4. 777
Wilson, Sir Frederick William, 3. 1792, 1797
Wilson, George Louis Rosa, 4. 1372
Wilson, Henry Schütz, 3. 1709
Wilson, James (d. 1787), 2. 2032
Wilson, James (1805–60), 3. 1824
Wilson, James Maurice, 3. 1727, 1728
Wilson, John (1595–1674), lutenist, 1. 1359–60
Wilson, John (1627?–96), dramatist, 2. 776–8
Wilson, John (1720–89), 2. 2032
Wilson, John ('Christopher North' 1785–1854),
  3. 1308–10, 1873
Wilson, John Cook, 4. 1306–7
Wilson, John Dover, 4. 1129–31
Wilson, John Gideon, 4. 1359
Wilson, Margaret Oliphant, 3. 954–6
Wilson, Norman, 4. 1370
Wilson, Robert, 1. 1409
'Wilson, Romer' (Florence R. M. Wilson), 4.
  777
Wilson, Samuel, 2. 1456
Wilson, Thomas (1524?–81), 1. 1824, 2276, 2308,
  2329
Wilson, Thomas (1663–1755), 2. 1640
Wilson, W. (fl. 1873–83), 3. 1715
Wilson, William (fl. 1799), editor of travel book,
  2. 1483
Wilson, William (fl. 1825), educationalist, 3. 1720
Wilson's musical miscellany, 2. 400
Wilton, Richard, 3. 561
'Wily' (Thomas Smith), 3. 1704
Wily beguilde, 1. 1779–80
Wimbledon, Edward Cecil, Viscount, 1. 2127
Wimbledon, Thomas, 1. 490
Wimpffen, Alexandre Stanislas de, 2. 1475
Winch, W. H., 3. 1732
Winchester
  Renaissance to Restoration
    printing and bookselling, 1. 968
    school library, 1. 996
  Restoration and eighteenth century
    magazines, 2. 1352
    newspapers, 2. 1367–8
    printing and bookselling, 2. 270
    school library, 2. 308
  nineteenth century school magazines, 3. 1871
Winchester College, library, 1. 996; 2. 308,
  magazines, 3. 1871
Winchester journal, 2. 1367
Winchester review, 3. 1871
Winchilsea, Anne Finch, Countess of 2. 576–7
Winchilsea, Heneage Finch, 2nd Earl of, 2. 1410
Winckelmann Johann Joachim, 2. 157
Wind and the rain, 4. 1375

Windham, William, 2. 1401, 1418
Windhus, John, 2. 1448
Windmill (1898), 4. 1355
Windmill (1944), 4. 1376
Window (1930), 4. 1369
Window (1950), 4. 1380
Windsor and Eton express, 3. 1833
Windsor and Eton journal, 2. 1357
Windsor drollery, 2. 331
Windsor forest, with the French translation, 2. 427
Windsor magazine, 3. 1854; 4. 1354
Windsor medley, 2. 360
Windsor projects and Westminster practices, 1.
  2103
Windus, John, 2. 1448
Wine, beere and ale (seventeenth century inter-
  lude), 1. 1762
Wingate, David, 3. 562
Wingfield, Anthony, 1. 2123, 876
Wingfield, Edward-Maria, 1. 2154
Wingfield, Lewis Strange, 3. 1671, 1676
Wingfield, Sheila Claude, 4. 377
Wingfield, W. C., 3. 1715
Winks, Joseph F., 3. 1745
Winkworth, Catherine, 3. 562
'Winlove, Solomon', 2. 1021
Winne, Edward, 1. 2157
Winne, Peter, 1. 2154–5
Winocour, Jack, 4. 1398
Winskill, B., 4. 1382, 1383, 1385
Winskill, Lottie, 4. 1382
Winslow, Edward (fl. 1606–11), printer, 1. 964
Winslow, Edward (1595–1655) of New England,
  1. 2080, 2157
Winslow, Lyttleton S. F., 3. 1882
Winstanley, — (fl. 1775), 2. 1305
Winstanley, Gerrard, 1. 2039
Winstanley, William, 2. 1797, 984, 1339, 1800,
  1803
Winter, John Keith, 4. 990–1
Winter, Thomas, 1. 1161
Winter-Evenings companion, 2. 381
Winter evenings tales, 2. 992
Winter medley, 2. 395
Winter's wreath, 3. 1874
Winter-Wood, E. J., 3. 1694
Winterbone, H. J., 4. 1381, 1383
Winterbotham, William, 2. 1442, 1444, 1454,
  1474–5
Winterton, Ralph, 1. 2306
Winthrop, John, 1. 2159
Wintringham, Thomas Henry, 4. 1371
Winzet, Ninian, 1. 2453–4
Wipers times, 4. 1362
Wireker, Nigel, 1. 763–4

Wisden's cricketer's almanack, 3. 1695, 1882

Wisdom, Arthur John Terence Dibben, 4. 1307

Wisdom, who is Christ (Tudor morality), 1. 1403–4

Wisdome of Doctor Dodypoll, 1. 1472

Wise, Thomas James, 4. 1131–4

Wiseman, Nicholas Patrick Stephen, Cardinal, 3. 1636, 1856

Wishart, George, 1. 2470

Wit: modern mirth and mystery (1947), 4. 1392

Wit: the magazine of humour (Dublin 1947), 4. 1378

Wit à-la-mode (1775), 2. 396

Wit a-la-mode (1778), 2. 399

Wit and drollery, 1. 1010; 2. 328

Wit and loyalty reviv'd, 2. 334

Wit and mirth (1682), 2. 334

Wit and mirth (1699), 2. 341

Wit at a venture, 2. 332

Wit for the ton! 2. 398

Wit musically embellish'd, 2. 360

Wit of a woman, 1. 1762

Wit of the day, 2. 405

Wit restor'd in severall select poems, 1. 1011

Wit, women and wine, 2. 385

Wit's cabinet, 2. 347

Wit's magazine, 2. 1307

Wit's miscellany, 2. 395

Wit's triumvirate, 1. 1762

witchcraft, Renaissance to Restoration, 1. 2377–80

Witchell, George, 2. 1303

Witcop, Rose, 4. 1406

Witham, T. M., 3. 1714

Wither, George, 1. 1191–4, 1330, 1336, 1908, 2035, 2089, 2099, 2316

Witherby and Co, 4. 81

Withers, John James, 3. 1866

Witherspoon, John, 2. 2046

Withington, J. S., 3. 1846

Withington, Nicholas, 1. 2145

Witness, 3. 1822

Wits: or sport upon sport, 2. 329

Wits academy, 2. 333

Wits cabinet, 2. 335

Wits interpreter, 1. 1010; 2. 329

Wits museum, 2. 401

Wits recreations, 1. 1010; 2. 329

Wits secretary, 2. 341

Witt's recreations refined, 2. 329

Wittgenstein, Ludwig Josef Johann, 4. 1307–10

Witticisms and strokes of humour, 2. 389

Witting's chronicle, 2. 1284

Wodehouse, Pelham Grenville, 4. 778–81, 795–6

Wodrow, Robert, 2. 2056–8

Wohunge of ure Lauerde, 1. 516

Wolcot, John, 2. 695–7

Wolf, Johann Christoph, 2. 1442

Wolf, John, 2. 1421

Wolfe, Charles, 3. 408

Wolfe, Humbert, 4. 377–9, 798

Wolfe, John, 1. 964–5

Wolfe, Reyner, 1. 965

Wolfreston, Frances, 1. 1004

Wollaston, Francis John Hyde, 2. 1910

Wollaston, George, 2. 997

Wollaston, William, 2. 1872, 112

Wolley, Charles, 2. 1458

Wolley, Hannah, 2. 1556

Wolley, R., 2. 1413

Wollstonecraft, Mary (Mrs William Godwin), 2. 1254–6, 112, 183, 1008, 1013, 1026, 1430

Wollton, John, 1. 1948

Wolstenholme, E. C., 3. 1747

Wolverhampton, printing, 2. 270

Wolverhampton chronicle, 2. 1368

Woman (1890), 3. 1828

Woman (1898), 4. 1355

Woman (1912), 4. 1405

Woman (1919), 4. 1406

Woman (1924), 4. 1366

Woman (1937), 4. 1408

Woman and beauty, 4. 1407

Woman and home, 4. 1406

Woman journalist, 4. 1340

Woman's companion, 4. 1406

Woman's daily newspaper, 4. 1408

Woman's home magazine, 4. 1362

Woman's hour, 4. 1371

Woman's journal, 4. 1406

Woman's life, 4. 1404

Woman's malice, 2. 984

Woman's mirror, 4. 1407

Woman's national newspaper, 4. 1408

Woman's newspaper, 4. 1408

Woman's own (1913), 4. 1406

Woman's own (1932), 4. 1407

Woman's pictorial, 4. 1406

Woman's realm, 4. 1358

Woman's sphere, 4. 1372

Woman's stories, 4. 1361

Woman's weekly, 4. 1405

Woman's wit, 2. 401

Woman's world (1887), 3. 1852, 1863

Woman's world (1903), 4. 1405

Woman's world library, 4. 1361

Women of Samaria (ME), 1. 480

Women's home stories, 4. 1360

Women's stories, 4. 1360

Women's suffrage journal, 3. 1851

Writers of tomorrow, 4. 1377
Writers parade, 4. 73
Writers' and artists' year book, 4. 71
Writers' and photographers' reference guide, 4. 74
Writers' medley (1933), 4. 1386
Writers' medley (1939), 4. 73
Writers' year book, 4. 71
Writing news, 4. 73
Writing today, 4. 1376
writs (OE), 1. 332
Wroth, Mary, Lady, 1. 1326, 2056
Wroth, Sir Thomas, 1. 1336
Wulf and Eadwacer, 1. 311–12
Wulfstan of Winchester (fl. 965), 1. 352
Wulfstan (d. 1023) homilist, 1. 321–4
Wyatt, —, Captain (fl. 1594), 1. 2152
Wyatt, Susan, 4. 1375
Wyatt, Sir Thomas, 1. 1020–3, 1898
Wyatt, Woodrow, 4. 1375
Wycherley, William, 2. 742–4, 128–9, 179–80, 202
Wyclif, John, 1. 491–6, 789–93, 487
Wycliffite writings, 1. 491–6
Wyer, Robert, 1. 966
Wykehamist, 3. 1871
Wyld, Henry Cecil Kennedy, 4. 1134
Wylde, Zachary, 2. 1562
Wylie, William H., 3. 1804
Wyman, C. W. H., 3. 61
Wyman and Sons, C. H., 3. 60; 4. 81
Wyndham, Francis, 4. 1378
Wyndham, Henry Penruddocke, 2. 1404
Wynfrith, 1. 349
Wynne, C. G., 3. 1870
Wynne, George, 3. 1795
Wynne, John, 2. 1850
Wynne, John Huddlestone, 2. 1022–3, 1304
Wynne, Peter, 1. 2154–5
Wynne, Sir Richard, 1. 2127
Wynnere and Wastoure, 1. 548
Wynter, Andrew, 3. 1826
Wynyard, Noel, 4. 1378
Wyrley, William, 1. 1162
Wyse, Sir Thomas, 3. 1722
Wyss, Johann David, 3. 129, 1110
Wyss, Johann Rudolf, 3. 129, 1110
Wyvill, Sir Christopher, 1. 1326

X: an unknown quantity, 3. 1868; 4. 1355, 1396
XX songes, 1. 1343
Xamolxis and Perindo 1. 1762
'Xantippe, Mrs', 2. 1287
Xenophon, 1. 2180, 2146; 2. 1495–6

'Y., Y.' (Robert Wilson Lynd), 4. 1083–4
Y creal, 2. 1350

Y Dioddefaint, 1. 728
Y drysorfa ysprydol, 2. 1350
Y geirgrawn, 2. 1389, 1350
Y llwyfan, 4. 877
Y tri brenin o Gwlen, 1. 728
Y wawr, 4. 1398
yachting, nineteenth century, 3. 1716
Yachting racing calendar and review, 3. 1883
Yachting sailing and motor-boating, 3. 1716
Yachting world, 3. 1716
Yachtsman, 3. 1716
Yalden, Thomas, 2. 578
Yaldren, W., 4. 1383
Yarington, Robert, 1. 1469
Yarmouth, printing, 2. 270
Yarmouth gazette, 2. 1368
Yarmouth gazette extraordinary, 2. 1368
Yarmouth post, 2. 1368
Yarranton, Andrew, 2. 1900
Yates, Mrs Ashton, 3. 1679
'Yates, Dornford' (Cecil William Mercer), 4. 781
Yates, Edmund Hodgson, 3. 1083–4, 1778, 1814, 1815, 1849, 1850, 1851, 1852
Yates, James, 1. 1162
Yates, Peter, 4. 992
Ye Pepys journal, 4. 1364
Ye roonde table, 3. 1868
Ye Sette of Odd Volumes, 4. 98
Ye tea-potte, 3. 1868
Ye true blue, 3. 1866
Year book (NODA), 4. 877
Year book of daily recreation, 3. 1875
Year-book of facts in science and art, 3. 1877
Year-book of photography, 3. 1878
Year-book of the scientific and learned societies, 3. 1881
Year book of women's work, 3. 1878
year books, nineteenth century, 3. 1877–84
   general, 3. 1877–8
   biography, 3. 1878–9
   commerce, 3. 1881–2
   education, 3. 1880–1
   official, 3. 1879–80
   peerage, 3. 1879
   professions, 3. 1881
   religion, 3. 1880
   sport, 3. 1882–3
   see also annuals, magazines, newspapers, periodicals
Year's art, 3. 1878
Year's poetry, 4. 1371
Year's sport: a review, 3. 1883
Year's work in literature, 4. 1380
Year's work in the theatre, 4. 828
Yeardley, Francis, 1. 2160

Young misses magazine (1800), 2. 1374
Young Oxford, 4. 1396
Young Roscius, 3. 1107
Young Welshman, 4. 1382
Younge, Robert, 1. 2040
Younger, John, 3. 1689
Younger brother, 2. 1003
Younghusband, Sir Francis Edward, 3. 1710
Younghusband, Sir George John, 3. 1676
Your own magazine, 4. 1387
Yours, 4. 1388
Youth (16th century morality), 1. 1408
Youth (1882), 3. 1825
Youth (St John's College 1920), 4. 1393
Youth: the authors' magazine (1922), 4. 72, 1365
Youth library group news, 4. 790
Youth's advertiser, 4. 1381
Youth's entertaining and instructive calendar, 2. 1020
Youth's instructive and entertaining story-teller, 2. 1023
Youths lookinglass, 2. 1017
Youth's treasury, 2. 337
Youthful recreations, 2. 1026
Ypotis, 1. 513
Yr einion, 4. 1398
Yugoslavian, literary relations with
   Renaissance to Restoration, Shakespeare, 1. 1. 1636
   Restoration and eighteenth century, 2. 222

Yule, Henry, 3. 1675
Yver, Jacques, 1. 874
Ywain and Gawain, 1. 408–9

Zachariä, Just Friedrich Wilhelm, 2. 171
Zagoskin, Mikhail Nikolayevich, 3. 155
Zangwill, Israel, 3. 1084
Zappi, Giovanni Battista Felice, 2. 1550
Zarate, Augustin de, 1. 2150
Zayas y Sotomayor, Maria de, 1. 917
Zedlitz, Joseph Christian, Freiherr von, 3. 129
Zelotypus, 1. 1780
Zenith, 4. 1375
Zepheria, 1. 1162
Zhukovsky, Vasiliy Andreyevich, 3. 155
Ziegenbalg, Bartholomew, 2. 1435
Zimmerman, Heinrich, 2. 1480
Zimmermann, Johann Georg von, 2. 1542, 157–8
Zimmern, Alice, 3. 1748
Zinzendorf, Nikolaus Ludwig, Graf von, 2. 161
Zion's trumpet, 2. 1349
Zoccola, Alexander R., 4. 1370
Zola, Emile, 3. 110
Zoological keepsake, 3. 1874
zoology, Renaissance to Restoration, 1. 2375–8
Zouch, Henry, 2. 1560
Zouch, Thomas, 2. 1785
Zouche, Richard, 1. 1776, 2120, 2286
Zschokke, Heinrich, 2. 182; 3. 129
Zwingli, Ulrich, 1. 2194, 852, 878